SIXTH EDITION

Business Decision Making
TEXT and CASES

Elizabeth Grasby

Mary Crossan

Ann Frost

John Haywood-Farmer

Michael Pearce

Lyn Purdy

Richard Ivey School of Business
The University of Western Ontario

Nelson
Thomson Learning™

Australia • Canada • Denmark • Japan • Mexico • New Zealand • Philippines
Puerto Rico • Singapore • South Africa • Spain • United Kingdom • United States

1120 Birchmount Road
Scarborough, Ontario M1K 5G4
www.nelson.com
www.thomson.com

Canadian Cataloguing in Publication Data

Main entry under title:

Business Decision Making : text and cases

6th ed.
First ed. by M.R. Pearce, D.G. Burgoyne and J.A. Humphry
ISBN 0-17-616737-4

1. Industrial management — Canada — Case studies. I. Grasby, Elizabeth, 1955– .

HF5351.P42 2000   658.4'03   C00-930365-0

Editorial Director	Evelyn Veitch
Executive Editor	Tim Sellers
Marketing Manager	Anthony Rezeck
Project Editor	Mike Thompson
Production Editor	Tracy Bordian
Copy Editor	Marcia Miron
Proofreaders	Dawn Hunter, Marg Bukta
Art Director	Angela Cluer
Cover Design	Ken Phipps
Cover Image	First Light
Senior Composition Analyst	Alicja Jamorski
Production Coordinator	Hedy Later
Printer	Best Book

1   2   3   4   03   02   01   00

Printed in Canada

To

Al, Sarah, and Matthew
Larry, Corey, and Matthew
Tony, Zoë, and Eden
Mary, Anne, and Jennifer
Kathy
Brad, Cameron, and Margaret

CONTENTS

4   An Introduction to Managing People in Organizations 203

5   AN INTRODUCTION TO MARKETING MANAGEMENT   323

6 AN INTRODUCTION TO OPERATIONS MANAGEMENT 465

7 | AN INTRODUCTION TO GENERAL MANAGEMENT **587**

CASES FOR PART 7

PREFACE

A number of cases from the fifth edition have been replaced by newer and more relevant cases in this edition of *Business Decision Making: Text and Cases.* This edition has 26 new cases and retains 31 cases from the fifth edition, many of which have been revised or updated. Most of the introductory material to the Parts of this edition have been extensively revised. These changes reflect a large investment of time and money by a great number of people over the past few years in case writing activities at the Richard Ivey School of Business. The authors would like to thank the instructors who have been teaching at the School over the past few years, without whom this edition would not exist. Their enthusiasm, dedication to students and teaching, and the energy they have brought to the task have been outstanding. In particular, we would like to thank the following past and current faculty members who have used the fifth edition at both Western and its affiliated colleges:

Carlie Bell	*Niels Billou*
Jannalee Anderson	*Ewa Borzecka*
Ken Bowlby	*Elizabeth Gray*
Andrew Fletcher	*Lorrie Kope*
Sonya Head	*Chuck Lemmon*
Kristina Krupka	*Jacqueline Murphy*
Cara Maura	*John Siambanopoulos*
Timothy Silk	*Vicki Sweeney*
Timothy Tattersall	*Sarah Tremblay*
Talmage Woolley	*Krista Wylie*

A number of current and past members at the Richard Ivey School of Business have co-authored earlier editions of this book. The sixth edition owes a great deal to David Burgoyne, James Erskine, John Graham, Richard Mimick, and Michael Pearce who, along with Marilyn Campbell, Elizabeth Grasby, John Haywood-Farmer, Sonya Head, and John Humphrey were responsible for the first five editions of the book. We thank them for their support and encouragement and for letting us build on the firm foundation they established. Several Ivey colleagues gave us significant assistance with textual material in this and previous editions.

We would also like to acknowledge the ongoing support of Renata Djurfeldt and Carol Fuller, area group coordinators. In addition to typing many of the new case and text material, Renata and Carol happily undertook many of the support tasks that enabled us to complete this edition. Denise Ritchie and Dorothy Zavitz also assisted.

In addition, we would like to thank Lawrence Tapp, Dean of the Richard Ivey School of Business, and Paul Beamish, Associate Dean—Research, for their support of this project. Financial assistance for case writing was provided through the Plan for Excellence.

One of the joys of being involved in the Business 020 course at Ivey is the opportunity to work with young people, both students who take the course and the instructors who deliver it. They keep all of us challenged and stimulated. We hope that our future students will find this new edition one that actively involves them in the exciting task of decision making.

Elizabeth Grasby
Mary Crossan
Ann Frost
John S. Haywood-Farmer
Michael Pearce
Lyn Purdy
Richard Ivey School of Business
The University of Western Ontario

PART

An Introduction to the Case Method

What Is a Case?

In this text, we use the term *case* to refer to a written description of a situation actually faced by a manager.[1] Cases commonly involve a decision to be made, a problem to be solved, or an issue to be settled. Although in some cases the authors might have disguised names, places, and other facts at the request of the organizations involved, the cases in this book are real situations that real people have faced. The objective of each case is to leave you at a point much like the one that the individual in the case actually confronted — you must make a decision.

In each case situation, the decision maker is expected to determine what problems and opportunities existed, to analyze the situation, to generate and evaluate alternative courses of action, and to recommend and implement a plan of action. Except for the fact that you will not have the actual opportunity to implement the plan of action and see the results, we expect that you will go through this same process.

As they grapple with problems, decision makers encounter a number of common frustrations: a shortage of good information on which to base decisions, a shortage of time in which to make decisions, uncertainty about how plans will work out, and a lack of opportunity to reduce this uncertainty at a reasonable cost. You will experience these same frustrations because the cases try to give you the same information about time pressures and so on that the decision maker had.

In short, you will simulate the experience of decision making. However, cases do simplify the task somewhat: someone has already collected and sorted all the available data for you and presented it in a reasonably neat package. In real life the decision maker also faces the task of collecting the data that might be relevant for making a decision.

THE CASE METHOD

The case method is not a single approach, but rather several variations. The general theme, however, is to learn by doing, rather than by listening. Class sessions are not lectures but discussions that emphasize the development of skills in problem solving and decision making. In a typical case discussion everyone in the room works toward a solution to the particular problem being addressed. Consequently, students will interact with one another as well as with the instructor. The student's role, then, is one of participation — active listening and talking with others in the class. The instructor's role is not to lecture the group but to guide the discussion by probing, questioning, and adding some input.

Cases can be used in several ways. You will probably be asked to deal with them in some or all of the following ways:

1. a. Individual preparation for a class discussion, followed by
   b. Small group discussion in preparation for a class discussion, followed by
   c. Class discussion
2. A written report or in-class presentation of a case
3. A written examination of your ability to handle a case

Each of these methods is somewhat different and will require some variation in your approach. Also, your instructor will undoubtedly have his or her own comments to add to the following general remarks about approaches to cases.

INDIVIDUAL PREPARATION FOR CLASS

Cases can be complicated and controversial. In reality, they are unstructured problems. Watch out — the process of case preparation can be deceiving! Some students think they are on top of the situation without really having done much work. They read over cases casually once or twice, jot down a few ideas, go to class, and listen to the discussion. As points come up they think, "I touched on that," or "I would have reached the same conclusion if I had pushed the data a little further." However, when exam, report, or presentation time arrives and they must do a case thoroughly on their own, they find themselves in serious difficulty. These students spend all their time in the exam trying to learn how to deal with a case, rather than tackling the case issues on which they are being tested. Because this is the first case these students have really tried to do from beginning to end, this situation is not surprising. Their position is similar to that of someone who trained by watching others practise for a number of months and then entered a 100-metre race at an official track meet.

To help provide you with some structure, your instructor might assign specific questions to be addressed as you work on a case. You should consider such assignment questions as a means to assist you in getting started on the case and *not* as the limit of your preparation. When your instructor assigns no questions, it is up to you to develop the structure. In class, your instructor will still expect you to be ready to give a supported decision concerning what you would do as the decision maker in the case. Accordingly, you should regard each case as a challenge to your ability to:

1. Define a problem;
2. Sort relevant from irrelevant information;
3. Separate fact from opinion;
4. Interpret and analyze information;
5. Come to a reasoned decision and course of action; and
6. Communicate your thoughts clearly and persuasively to others during class discussions.

Cases also serve to communicate a good deal of descriptive information about a wide variety of institutions and business practices. Many cases are sufficiently complex to absorb all the preparation time you have — and then some! Therefore, it is extremely important that you develop skill in using your preparation time efficiently.

Much of your preparation time should be spent analyzing and interpreting information. In effect, the case presents facts and opinions. Your job is to become acquainted with those facts and opinions and to know how they relate to the decision.

We offer the following steps to help you in your individual case preparation:

1. Read the case once quickly to get an overview.
2. Skim any exhibits in the case just to see what information is available.
3. Find out — frequently from the few paragraphs at the beginning and end of the case — who the decision maker is (this will be your role); what his or her immediate concern, problem, or issue appears to be; why this concern has arisen; and when the decision must be made.
4. Read the case again, more carefully. This time highlight key information, make notes to yourself in the margin, and write down ideas as they occur to you. At this stage you are trying to familiarize yourself as thoroughly as possible with the case information. Having done so, you are ready to begin your analysis.

5. Try to answer at least the following questions:
    a. What business is the organization in? What are its objectives? What are its strengths and weaknesses? What opportunities and threats exist? Who are its customers? What does it have to do well to satisfy customers? How do you know?
    b. What is the decision to be made, problem to be solved, or issue to be resolved? How do you know — what is your evidence? (Let the case data guide you — most cases will have sufficient data for you to "solve" the problems and are unlikely to contain vast amounts of completely irrelevant data.)
    c. What facts are relevant and key to a solution? Are they symptoms? Causes? What is your quantitative and qualitative evaluation of the organization's strengths and weaknesses?
    d. What do the facts mean for the problem? Here, learn to analyze — ask and answer lots of questions.
    e. What are the decision criteria?
    f. What are the alternatives? Are they relevant to the problem at hand? Although it is usually unwise to ignore the obvious solutions, most instructors appreciate creative solutions, provided they are sensible and supported by reasonable data.
    g. What is your evaluation of the alternatives in view of the decision criteria? What are the pros and cons of each?
    h. Which alternative or combination of alternatives would you choose? Why?
    i. What is your plan of action? Outline your plan by answering the questions who, when, what, where, why, and how.
    j. What results do you expect? Why?

SMALL GROUP PREPARATION FOR CLASS

If possible, prior to class you should informally discuss your preparation of each case with some of your classmates. Many students find such study group sessions to be the most rewarding part of case method learning. A good group session is a sharing experience in which you discover ideas you might have missed or to which you did not give enough weight. Your colleagues will also benefit from your input.

The effectiveness of a small group case discussion can be increased substantially if you and the other members of the group adhere to the following guidelines:

1. Each student must come to the group meeting with a thorough knowledge of any assigned readings and analysis of the case. The small group session is not the place to start case preparation.

2. Each group member is expected to participate actively in the discussion — it is an excellent place to check your analysis before going into class.

3. It is not necessary to have a group leader. All members of the group are responsible for making their own decisions based on what is said plus their own case analysis.

4. It is also not necessary to have a recording secretary. Participants are responsible for their own notes. It is important to be able to recognize a good idea when you hear one.

5. Consensus is normally not necessary. No one has to agree with anyone else.

6. If it is important to you, work at clarifying individual disagreements after the small group discussion, especially if only one or two people are involved.

7. Set a time limit for discussion and stick to it. Effective small group case discussions can take less than 30 minutes and, because of your workload, 30 minutes will have to be adequate for most cases.

Remember, a group can be as small as two people. If you cannot get together in one place, spend some time on the phone with a classmate reviewing your respective case analyses. You will be more confident, feel better about your own preparation, and probably contribute more to the class discussion.

CLASS DISCUSSION

Cases are complex and there are never any completely right or wrong answers. Consequently, groups of managers who address the kinds of issues represented by this book's cases nearly always express different views on how to interpret the data and what action could and should be taken. They see the world differently, and this diversity is one reason management is worth studying. You should expect something similar: during discussion of a case, your classmates will express several different views. The essence of the case method is the process of putting forward different points of view, defending your position, and listening actively to others in order to understand and constructively criticize others' points of view. Only rarely will you leave the classroom with your position or perspective unchanged after discussing a case; indeed, if you do so, it was a waste of your time to go to class.

However, despite the common interest of all class members in resolving the case issues, and regardless of guidance from the instructor, class discussions sometimes will seem repetitious and unorganized. This is unavoidable and natural, especially during the early stages of a course. Over time, as a group develops its group decision-making ability, case discussions will become more orderly, effective, efficient, rich, and satisfying to all.

The need to be a skillful communicator arises repeatedly in management. The case method presents an ideal opportunity to practise communication skills — both talking and listening. Some people, because they find talking in a group difficult and threatening, avoid talking in class even though they might realize that by being silent they are not getting full value out of the experience. If you are one of these individuals, the only way to overcome this problem is to jump in and begin. Make a habit of participating regularly in class. Do not wait until you have a major presentation to make in which you will hold the floor for a lengthy period. You can add a key piece of information or question something in just a few sentences, and this might be the best way for you to begin active involvement. Your instructor and your classmates will support your efforts. Remember, the classroom is a place where we can learn from one another's mistakes as much as, and often more than, from one another's solutions. The cost of making a mistake in class is very small compared to making it in an actual situation. Other people have poorly developed listening skills. Some individuals do not listen: they simply wait for their turn to talk. The case method depends on the willing two-way interaction of the students. Without that essential ingredient, the cases become interesting stories rather than opportunities to develop the ability to make and argue for and against management decisions.

Not surprisingly, students are interested in finding out what actually happened in a case or what the instructor would do. Only rarely will you be provided with this information. Learning comes from the process and habit of making decisions, not from reviewing what others decided to do.

AFTER CLASS

After class take a few minutes to assess your preparation by comparing it with what happened in class. Were you in the ball park or completely off base? Did you spend enough time preparing on your own? Was your small group session effective? What can you do better next time? What general lessons did you learn? For example, although you might not be interested in remembering how the market for athletic shoes can be segmented, you should want to remember how to segment a market.

EVALUATING PERFORMANCE

In a typical class discussion of a case, exactly what gets done depends not only on the work done by the students — what preparation they did, who actively participated in the discussion, how well people related their comments to previous discussion — but also on the instructor's pedagogical objectives and performance as a moderator and discussion leader. Instructors view case courses as sequences of problems that gradually foster the development of decision-making skills. With this longer time horizon, instructors often find it advisable to emphasize a specific analytical technique on one occasion, stress problem identification on another, and so on. Thus, it is possible that many class sessions will seem to be incomplete, unbalanced developments of a case analysis and plan of action. Although this might frustrate you, have faith that your instructor is trying to develop your skills over one or more terms.

How do instructors assess performance? The answer, of course, varies from one instructor to another. However, we suggest that there are some common factors. Above all, instructors develop your ability to demonstrate that you can think logically and consistently by being able to:

1. Identify, prioritize, and deal with issues and problems;
2. Judge the quality and relevance of information — fact, opinion, hearsay, lies, and so on;
3. Make and assess necessary assumptions;
4. Relate the information to the issues, problems, and decisions in the case;
5. Resolve conflicting information;
6. Analyze by asking and answering the right questions and correctly using appropriate analytical tools;
7. Determine and rank appropriate criteria for making decisions;
8. Generate and evaluate alternative courses of action;
9. Make a decision (take a stand) and defend it with persuasive, well-ordered, convincing argument;
10. Develop a reasonably detailed action plan showing an awareness of what might happen;
11. Build on other students' arguments to advance the discussion toward a coherent conclusion rather than making unrelated points or repeating ones already made; and
12. Generalize: in traditional lectures instructors expect students to take the general lessons from the lecture and apply them to specific problems; case method instructors expect students to go from the specific lessons in a case to more general lessons.

In addition to assessing performance in class on a daily basis, most instructors will provide some opportunities for more complete, balanced treatment of cases. Sometimes instructors allow extra preparation time and ask for an oral presentation of a case by an individual or group. Sometimes instructors require students to prepare a written report on how they would handle a particular situation and why. Frequently, case method courses have cases as examinations: students are given a case and asked to do whatever analysis and make whatever recommendations they deem appropriate.

In reports, presentations, and examinations, instructors expect a more complete, balanced argument for a particular course of action. Such exercises are not usually intended to result in a diary of how a student or group looked at a case or in a rewritten version of the case. A report, presentation, or examination is supposed to be a concise, coherent exposition of what to do and why — it usually starts where most students leave off in their regular individual preparation for a case class. Think of a report, a presentation, or an examination as an organized, more fully developed (and perhaps rewritten) version of your regular class preparation notes.

You will find that your audience — instructor, business executive, or whoever — has particular ideas about how a report, presentation, or examination should be organized. We urge you to find out as much as you can about format expectations before embarking on your task. We suggest that students use the following general outline:

1. Executive summary (written last but appearing first);
2. Statement of problem, opportunity, and objectives;
3. Analysis of the situation;
4. Identification and evaluation of alternatives; and
5. Decision, course of action, and implementation.

CONCLUDING REMARKS

We are less interested in the relatively straightforward problems typically found at the ends of chapters in most texts than in the unstructured problems more typical of real situations and exemplified in this text by cases. The key to dealing with unstructured problems is to learn what questions to ask. Ironically, answering the questions is usually easier than asking them because the questions focus thinking. It is like trying to find your way in the wilderness. Almost anyone can follow a trail; the key skill is knowing which trail to follow.

We believe that you will find case study a very rewarding way to learn. Good luck with it!

NOTE

1. For a more detailed account of the process of learning with cases see L.A. Mauffette-Leenders, J.A. Erskine, and M.R. Leenders, *Learning with Cases* (London, Ont.: Richard Ivey School of Business, 1997).

PART

AN INTRODUCTION TO
FINANCIAL STATEMENTS

The purpose of this chapter is to introduce and explain financial statements, which give a picture of a company's operating results and its financial condition. The topics that will be discussed are:

- The income statement
- The balance sheet
- The statement of retained earnings
- The auditor's report and footnotes

The income statement, the balance sheet, and the statement of retained earnings provide the basic information a company employee, investor, lender, competitor, or shareholder needs to gauge the financial well-being of a company. Part 2 concentrates on the definition of the three financial statements.

Proper use of financial tools aids financial decision making. However, before analytical concepts can be used for decision making, an understanding of the basic financial vocabulary, the relationships among the different financial statements, and the terms used in these statements is necessary. Once this understanding is complete, financial tools useful in analyzing these statements will be discussed in Part 3, "An Introduction to Financial Management."

THE INCOME STATEMENT

The income statement, also referred to as a statement of earnings or a (consolidated) statement of operations, shows how profitable the corporation was *during* a particular period of time. Often, this statement is of greater interest to investors than the balance sheet because the income statement shows a record of the company's activities for an operating cycle, normally a year, whereas the balance sheet shows a company's financial position at a given date.

EXHIBIT 1

XYZ Retail Co. Ltd.
Income Statement
for the Year Ending December 31, 1999

Gross sales		$2,100,000
Less: Sales returns and allowances	$ 50,000	
Sales discounts	34,000	84,000
Net sales		$2,016,000
Cost of goods sold:		
Inventory, December 31, 1998	$ 200,000	
Plus: Net purchases	1,316,000	
Cost of goods available for sale	$1,516,000	
Less: Inventory, December 31, 1999	192,000	
Cost of goods sold		1,324,000
Gross income		$ 692,000
Operating expenses:		
General and administrative expenses	$ 120,000	
Selling expenses	185,000	
Depreciation expense	65,000	
Total operating expenses		370,000
Operating income		$ 322,000
Plus: Other income		16,000
Less: Other expenses, interest		80,000
Net income before tax		$ 258,000
Estimated income tax expense (44%)		113,520
Net income after tax		$ 144,480

An income statement matches the revenue generated from selling goods or services against the related expenses incurred to generate these revenues *during the same period*. The difference between the revenues generated and the related expenses incurred results in a net income or net loss for the period. Emphasis must be placed on the phrase "during the same period." For example, if the period ended December 31 and a sale was made on December 30, it would be recorded as revenue for the period even if the customer did not pay for the product until January. Similarly, expenses incurred in December but not yet paid by December 31, such as employees' wages or bank loan interest, are recorded as expenses for the period. Thus, the income statement does not reflect the actual cash receipts and cash payments made; rather, it records the revenues and expenses generated in the specified period.

XYZ Retail Co. Ltd. owns a retail business that sells its manufactured products. The components and format of the retail company's income statement are shown in Exhibit 1.

NET SALES

Net sales for XYZ Retail Co. Ltd. (from here on referred to as XYZ) represent revenue earned by the company from its customers for goods sold or services rendered. When a company sells services rather than goods (e.g., a railway, theatre, or dry cleaners), its net sales are usually called "operating revenues." The net sales figure reflects the revenue earned after taking into consideration the value of returned goods and the amount of cash discounts taken for quick payment by credit customers.

Remember, net sales refers to sales made during the period, not cash collected during the period.

Gross sales		$2,100,000
Less: Sales returns and allowances	$50,000	
Sales discounts	34,000	84,000
Net sales		$2,016,000

COST OF GOODS SOLD

In the income statement (Exhibit 1), two steps are needed to calculate the cost of goods sold figure. The first step is to determine the cost of goods available for sale: this is the sum of the finished goods left over on December 31, 1998 (this year's opening balance of finished goods available for sale) and the cost of net purchases in 1999. The second step in determining the cost of goods sold is to subtract the finished goods inventory on hand on December 31, 1999, from the total cost of goods available for sale. *Only those costs associated with the goods during the period in which these same goods generate sales revenue are expensed.*

Cost of goods sold	$1,324,000

Nonmanufacturer or Merchandiser

In merchandising or nonmanufacturing enterprises, such as distributors and retailers, the economic function of the merchandiser is to bring the goods to a convenient location for resale. Therefore, the merchandising company's cost of goods sold includes the purchase and related delivery costs (often referred to as "freight-in") of the product to be used for resale. XYZ's cost of goods sold section is shown in Exhibit 2.

This cost of goods sold section is similar to that reported in Exhibit 1 but with more detail on how net purchases are calculated. Since the company does not transform or change the goods it sells, there is only one type of inventory: finished goods. Consequently, nonmanufacturing companies will often include the full details of all the activities associated with cost of goods sold within the cost of goods sold section of the income statement.

To calculate the cost of goods sold in this case, four steps are required:

1. Determine the delivered cost of purchases made during the period. This is the cost of purchasing the product plus delivery costs (freight-in) related to the purchases.

2. From the delivered cost of purchases, deduct purchase returns and allowances, as well as purchase discounts (reductions for quick payment).

3. Add "net purchases" to the finished goods inventory on hand at the beginning of this period for the "cost of goods available for sale."

4. Not all of the goods available for sale are sold each period; consequently, the remaining goods on hand must be subtracted from the cost of goods available for sale to determine "cost of goods sold."

EXHIBIT 2

XYZ Retail Company Ltd.
Statement of Cost of Goods Sold
for the Year Ending December 31, 1999

Inventory, December 31, 1998			$ 200,000
Purchases		$1,320,000	
Freight-in		48,000	
Delivered cost of purchases		$1,368,000	
Less: Purchase discounts	$12,000		
Purchase returns and allowance	40,000	52,000	
Net purchases			1,316,000
Cost of goods available for sale			$1,516,000
Less: Inventory, December 31, 1999			192,000
Cost of goods sold			$1,324,000

Manufacturer

The components and format for XYZ's cost of goods sold section must reflect all costs associated with the transformation of unprocessed raw materials into finished goods available for sale. The accounting for costs and for the different types of inventory for a manufacturer is complex. See Appendix A for further explanation of how the financial statements for XYZ reflect the flow of costs in a manufacturing setting.

Service Organizations

XYZ owns another subsidiary, which is a service organization. This company provides repair services for selected products. Because this organization's activity is based on service and not on the manufacture or distribution of goods, it will have no cost of goods sold or gross income on its income statement. Instead, the direct expenses of generating service revenue, and then selling and general and administrative expenses, will be deducted from sales or revenues to determine operating income.

GROSS INCOME

Gross income (or gross margin or gross profit) is determined by subtracting the "cost of goods sold" from "net sales." It represents the markup, or margin, the company charges or earns on its product costs.[1]

Gross income	$692,000

OPERATING EXPENSES

Operating expenses are often categorized as "general and administrative" or "selling" expenses. The categories are usually listed separately, but this is not always necessary. Executive salaries, office payroll, office expenses, rent, electricity, and the like are the usual items included as general and administrative expenses. Selling expenses include salespeople's salaries and commissions, as well as advertising, promotion, and travel costs.

Operating expenses	
General and administrative	$120,000
Selling	$185,000

DEPRECIATION EXPENSE

Eventually, plant and equipment will become useless through wear or obsolescence. In order to allow for this loss of use, the asset is "written down" or depreciated based on the *expected useful life* of the asset and its estimated residual or salvage value.[2] Therefore, *depreciation is the allocation of the cost of an asset over its useful life.* This depreciation expense is then recorded as a cost associated with obtaining revenue on the income statement for that period. (It should be noted that depreciation applied to production-related fixed assets is recorded under manufacturing or factory overhead, whereas depreciation on all other fixed assets, such as office furniture, company cars, and so on, is recorded under operating expenses.)

The initial capital expenditures (such as those made to acquire production equipment or trucks to deliver goods) are not charged against revenues earned in the year of purchase, since the asset has several years of use and this method would result in understating incomes in the first year and overstating incomes in subsequent years. The issue of understating or overstating is handled by spreading the purchase cost of the asset over several operating statement periods.

For XYZ, the following depreciation expense is listed:

Depreciation expense	$65,000

The next line on the income statement totals all the operating expenses listed earlier:

Operating expenses	$370,000

OPERATING INCOME

Operating income (or operating profit) represents the net gain from the company's normal operating activities. From a management point of view, the operating income figure can be useful information when it comes to making business decisions. These decisions can range from evaluating manager performance, to making financial projections, to providing direction on future business decisions. Operating income is calculated by subtracting "operating expenses" from "gross income."

Operating income	$322,000

OTHER INCOME AND OTHER EXPENSES

The company may have revenues not directly related to its primary business (such as interest earned on investments and sale of land or equipment). To include these revenues under net sales would distort that figure and make comparison of performance from year to year unrealistic and inappropriate. Additionally, these items are often uncontrollable by operational managers and must be viewed separately when making business decisions affecting company operations.

Other income	$16,000

Other expenses record the unusual or infrequent activities that occur but are not deemed part of the company's routine operations. Interest the company must pay on money it has borrowed is often included here, since it is viewed as a financing activity and is not related to the operational activity of the business. Other income and other expenses are usually reported after operating income has been calculated.

Other expenses, interest $80,000

Net Income Before Tax

Net income (or net profit) before tax represents the company's determination of its net income before estimation of its tax liability.

Net income before tax $258,000

Estimated Income Tax Expense

Corporations earning income must pay income tax. This tax is calculated by applying a predetermined tax rate to the net income before tax. If the net income before tax is $258,000 and the tax rate is 44 percent, the estimated income tax would be $113,520.

Estimated income tax expense (44 percent) $113,520

Net Income After Tax

After all revenues have been added and all expenses subtracted, the residual is net income (or net earnings or net profit) after tax for the period. If revenues exceed expenses, the residual is a net income. If expenses exceed revenues, the residual is a net loss.

Net income after tax $144,480

Facts to Remember about the Income Statement

1. The income statement reports on activities during a specific time period.
2. The company name, the name of the statement, and the date must appear in the title.
3. The sales (revenues) generated and the expenses incurred to generate these sales during a specific period are recorded on the income statement.
4. The income statement does not necessarily reflect the actual cash collected or paid out in this period, since the timing of these receipts and payments may vary.
5. The formal structure of an income statement is sales first, then expenses, ending with net earnings (or loss).

6.   Above all, an income statement matches expenses incurred to revenues earned for a specified period of time.

THE BALANCE SHEET

The balance sheet presents the financial position of an enterprise as of a particular day, such as December 31, 1999. Whereas the income statement shows the profitability of a company during a specific time period, the balance sheet takes a "snapshot" of a firm's financial condition *at a particular point in time.*

The purpose of a balance sheet is to reflect what a company owns, what it owes, and the owner's investment in the business. Assets represent economic benefits available for future use. The assets — what a company owns — are listed on the left side of the statement and the liabilities — what a company owes — are listed on the right side. The net worth, which is known as shareholders' equity for incorporated companies, represents the difference between what a company owns and what it owes, and it is also listed on the right side of the statement. Both sides of the balance sheet are always in balance.

The balance sheet can be presented in account form, in which case the assets are on the left side of the statement and the liabilities and owner's equity on the right, or in report form, whereby the liabilities and owner's equity sections are listed below the assets section. The income statement in Exhibit 1 is in report form. Both formats are used widely.

Assets represent all the physical goods and items of value "owned" by the company, including finished and unfinished inventory, land, building, equipment, cash, and money owed to the company from credit sales or money lent to others. All assets provide future benefits to the company's operations.

Liabilities consist of all debts or claims "owed" by the company, such as loans from the bank and unpaid accounts due to suppliers. The company has an obligation to repay these liabilities in the future.

Shareholders' equity (net worth) represents the interest, stake, or claim the owners have in the company. It is the owners' original investment plus (or minus) the accumulation of all incomes (or losses) that have been retained in the firm since the company's inception.

Individuals can develop personal balance sheets. Before studying a business balance sheet, try to develop your own personal balance sheet. As a suggestion, first list your assets or items of value. Then, after adding them up, list the credit claims against those assets. Such claims may be government loans to further your education or loans to purchase some of the assets you have listed previously. Subtract the total of the liabilities from your assets. The residual is your net worth or equity. This net worth figure represents your claim as owner against the assets.

A balance sheet is presented for XYZ as at December 31, 1999 (Exhibit 3). Each of the XYZ accounts will be discussed in turn.

Exhibit 3

XYZ Retail Co. Ltd.
Balance Sheet
As at December 31, 1999

ASSETS

Current assets:

Cash			$ 24,000
Marketable securities at cost (market value $230,000)			225,000
Accounts receivable		$400,000	
Less: Allowance for doubtful accounts		20,000	
Net accounts receivable			380,000
Finished goods inventory			192,000
Prepayments			21,000
Total current assets			$ 842,000
Investment in subsidiaries			170,000
Other investments (market value $60,000)			80,000

Property, plant, and equipment:

Land		$120,000	
Plant	$770,000		
Less: Accumulated depreciation	370,000		
Net plant		400,000	
Machinery	$300,000		
Less: Accumulated depreciation	190,000		
Net machinery		110,000	
Office equipment	$ 52,000		
Less: Accumulated depreciation	18,000		
Net office equipment		34,000	
Total property, plant, and equipment (net)			664,000

Intangibles:

Goodwill (net)		$ 40,000	
Organization expenses (net)		30,000	
Total intangibles (net)			70,000
TOTAL ASSETS			$1,826,000

EXHIBIT 3
(cont.)

LIABILITIES AND SHAREHOLDERS' EQUITY

LIABILITIES

Current liabilities:

Notes payable (demand note)	$250,000	
Accounts payable	210,000	
Accrued expenses payable	70,000	
Taxes payable	23,000	
Current portion of long-term debt (1st mortgage bonds)	50,000	
Total current liabilities		$603,000

Long-term liabilities:

First mortgage bonds (7% interest, due 2004)	$200,000	
Debentures (9% interest, due 2009)	460,000	
Deferred taxes	50,000	
Total long-term liabilities		710,000

TOTAL LIABILITIES $1,313,000

SHAREHOLDERS' EQUITY

Capital stock:

Preferred shares, $4 cumulative, authorized, issued, and outstanding 1,400 shares	$ 90,000	
Common shares, authorized, issued, and outstanding 140,000 shares	140,000	$ 230,000
Retained earnings		283,000
TOTAL SHAREHOLDERS' EQUITY		$ 513,000

TOTAL LIABILITIES AND SHAREHOLDERS' EQUITY $1,826,000

ASSETS

The size of the company is often measured in terms of its assets. Two major categories of assets are current assets and property, plant, and equipment (or fixed assets).

Current Assets

Current assets include cash and items that in the normal course of business will be converted into cash within an operating cycle, usually a year from the date of the balance sheet. Each current asset item should be listed in order of liquidity (ease of conversion to cash). This order signals to the reader the likelihood of the company meeting its short-term debt obligations by identifying those assets that would be easiest to convert into cash if necessary. Current assets generally consist of cash, marketable securities, accounts receivable, inventory, and prepayments (prepaid expenses).

Cash

Cash is the money on hand and the money on deposit in the bank.

Cash $24,000

Marketable Securities

This asset represents the investment of temporary cash surpluses in some form of short-term, interest-earning instrument. Because these funds may be needed on short notice, it is usually considered wise to make investments that are readily convertible to cash and subject to minimum price fluctuations (such as certificates of deposit, commercial paper, and short-term government notes). It is general practice to show marketable securities at the lower of their cost or their market value (thus ensuring a conservative value for the assets on the balance sheet). If market value differs from lower of cost or market, it is also shown, either in parentheses or as a note to the financial statements.

Marketable securities at cost
(market value, $230,000) $225,000

Accounts Receivable

Accounts receivable are amounts owed to the company by its customers who have purchased on credit and usually have 30, 60, or 90 days in which to pay. The total amount due from customers as shown in the balance sheet is $400,000. However, some customers fail to pay their bills. Therefore, a provision for doubtful accounts is estimated (based on previous industry data or company experience), so that the net accounts receivable amount will represent the actual cash from credit sales that is expected to be collected. The balance of $380,000 is thus shown as the net accounts receivable on the balance sheet.

Accounts receivable	$400,000	
Less: allowance for doubtful accounts	20,000	
Net accounts receivable		$380,000

Inventory

Nonmanufacturer or Merchandiser

Retailers' and wholesalers' inventories consist of the goods they have for sale to their customers. The functions these companies perform are to store, promote, sell, and distribute goods. The goods themselves are not changed in any major way from the time they are received to the time they are sold. In other words, a merchandising business does not add any value to the goods it holds in inventory and, therefore, accumulates only the "out-of-pocket" costs associated with purchasing its inventories and transporting them to the point of sale. The inventory is valued at its original cost or its present market value, whichever is lower.

Manufacturer

Accounting for the operations of a manufacturing business is more complex than in other types of businesses. Since manufacturing businesses engage in several activities that merchandising and service businesses do not perform, the accounting system for a manufacturing firm must be modified and expanded in order to efficiently capture and record these additional activities. This accounting system for XYZ is illustrated in Appendix A.

Prepayments (Prepaid Expenses)

At times, it is necessary or convenient to pay for items in advance. Prepayments or prepaid expenses are often items intended to be used up in the short term, such as property or equipment rental and fire insurance.

Although the payment is made at one time, the contract (in the case of rent) or the anticipated benefit or reward (in the case of insurance) is expected to last over a span of time. As the "value" is not fully received when the payment is made, the "unused" portion, or the benefit to come, is considered an asset of the company. For example, if two years of insurance are still unused on a five-year policy that originally cost $3,000, then $1,200 will be shown on the balance sheet as prepaid expense.

Prepayments	$21,000

To summarize, current assets include cash, marketable securities, accounts receivable, inventories, and prepaid expenses.

Cash		$ 24,000
Marketable securities at cost (market value $230,000)		225,000
Accounts receivable	$400,000	
Less: Allowance for doubtful accounts	20,000	

Net accounts receivable	380,000
Finished good inventory	192,000
Prepayments	<u>21,000</u>
Total current assets	$842,000

Investment in Subsidiaries

XYZ owns a small business that provides repair services for selected products. Investment in the subsidiary represents a controlling interest (allowing input into how the subsidiary is managed), more than 50 percent of the common stock. Common stock is not a tangible asset, and therefore it is not included with property, plant, and equipment. As well, XYZ has no intention of selling its investment. Consequently, the investment is listed in this separate category after current assets.

Investment in subsidiaries $170,000

Other Investments

XYZ has invested in other business operations and processes. None of these investments represents a controlling interest in the project; consequently, they are listed separately on the balance sheet. Also, XYZ has no intention of selling the investments. Therefore, the other investments are listed in this separate category, setting it apart from investment in subsidiaries; marketable securities in current assets; and property, plant, and equipment. Other investments are listed at cost, *not* lower of cost or market, unless there is a loss in value of an investment that is other than a temporary decline.

Other investments (market value $60,000) $80,000

Property, Plant, and Equipment

Property, plant, and equipment (or fixed assets) are physical assets that are expected to last more than one operating period. These assets, such as land, buildings, machinery, equipment, furniture, automobiles, and trucks, are intended for use in the operation of the company and are not intended for resale. All fixed assets, with the exception of land, are shown at their original cost, less accumulated depreciation. Only land is recorded at its original cost and is never depreciated because the economic benefits provided by the land do not diminish over time. The presentation of these assets may be conservative: the original cost may well be lower than either present market value or replacement cost. For example, land that appears on the books as $120,000 may actually be worth $250,000. Although the order can vary, fixed assets are usually stated in order of "permanence," with land generally considered the most permanent.

Accumulated Depreciation

The accumulated depreciation amount reflects the portion of the original cost of the asset which has been depreciated to date (charged through the years as an expense) by the company. Thus, the net asset balance after accumulated depreciation (the net book value) is not intended to reflect the current or market value of the asset as of the balance sheet date, but rather the original cost less the accumulated depreciation to date.

For example, suppose a machine is bought for $100,000 on January 1, 1998, has an estimated life of five years, and is depreciated on a straight-line basis, assuming no money would be received upon its disposal.[3] The company's fiscal year-end is December 31. The machine's cost will be allocated at the rate of $20,000 each year, and each year this amount will be shown as depreciation expense on the income statement. As shown in Table 1, by the end of the sixth year, the entire original cost of the machine will have been depreciated.

Table 1 illustrates how depreciation expense and accumulated depreciation are calculated on the purchase of this asset. The accumulated depreciation would be $20,000 at the end of the first year; $40,000 at the end of the second year; $60,000 at the end of the third year, and so on. By the end of the fifth year, the net book value of the machine would be zero.

Table 1: Depreciation Expense and Accumulated Depreciation on $100,000 Machine

For the month ending:	December 31, 1998	December 31, 1999	December 31, 2000	December 31, 2001	December 31, 2002	Amount recorded in
Depreciation expense	$20,000	$20,000	$20,000	$20,000	$20,000	Income Statement
Machine, original cost	$100,000	$100,000	$100,000	$100,000	$100,000	Balance Sheet
Less: Accumulated depreciation	$20,000	$40,000	$60,000	$80,000	$100,000	
Machine, net book value	$80,000	$60,000	$40,000	$20,000	$0	

The accumulated depreciation for each fixed asset is best shown separately so that the asset's original cost figure on the balance sheet is preserved, though often only one accumulated depreciation total is shown for all the fixed assets.

In summary, fixed assets are the investments in property, plant, and equipment. As explained, they are generally expressed in terms of their cost, diminished by the depreciation accumulated as of the date of the financial statement.[4]

Land		$120,000
Plant	$770,000	
Less: accumulated depreciation	370,000	
Net plant		400,000
Machinery	$ 300,000	
Less: Accumulated depreciation	190,000	
Machinery (net)		110,000
Office equipment	$ 52,000	
Less: Accumulated depreciation	18,000	
Net office equipment		34,000
Total property, plant, and equipment (net)		$664,000

Sometimes, this section of the balance sheet is condensed, in which case it would look like this:

Land		$120,000
Plant and equipment	$1,122,000	
Less: Accumulated depreciation	578,000	
Plant and equipment (net)		544,000
Total property, plant, and equipment (net)		$664,000

Intangibles

Most of the company's assets can be seen and touched. There are, however, some items of value, such as patents, franchise rights, developmental costs, organization costs, and goodwill, that are not tangible yet are customarily recorded as assets.

For example, patents and franchise rights are recorded at the actual amounts paid for these items. Many companies expense their research and development costs as incurred. Others, such as XYZ, choose to record their development costs as assets, often referred to as *capitalizing* the expenses. Certain development costs may be capitalized only if they meet specific criteria addressing the potential certainty of benefit and the company's commitment to following through on these benefits.

Organization costs are related to the legal formation of the company. In setting up a corporation, there are fees that are owed to the jurisdiction that grants the incorporation, plus legal fees associated with preparing the documentation for incorporation.

Another intangible, "goodwill," is encountered only when companies change hands. When a company is purchased, establishing a price for it is difficult. Often a purchaser will pay more for a company than its fair market value of the net assets (ignoring the balance sheet's "book value" since many assets may be drastically undervalued). Purchasers may do this if they believe that the loyalty of existing customers or the company's reputation is worth a premium over the tangible net assets value. The purchaser's balance sheet for the company after it is purchased will include an intangible account called goodwill, which reflects the amount of the premium paid.

For example, a large U.S. document company acquired a photocopying/fax division spun off from its Canadian manufacturer. Much of the division's assets had little value; however, the U.S. firm paid $1.5 million more than the division's tangible net worth. The document company was willing to pay this premium because the division's existing customers gave the U.S. company an immediate captive market base to which it could sell its other products in Canada.

All intangible assets are amortized, or written down, and are usually presented on the balance sheet net of the accumulated amortization amount. Intangible assets can be amortized over various lengths of time; however, CICA (Canadian Institute of Chartered Accountants) regulations apply maximum periods of time allowable for these write-downs in a manner similar to depreciation on a tangible fixed asset. One might expect to find listed under intangibles the value of trained, competent personnel, but the human resources of a company are typically not valued and reported on the balance sheet, primarily because there is no agreement on how to arrive at an appropriate value.

Intangibles:		
Goodwill (net)	$40,000	
Organization intangibles	30,000	
Total intangibles (net)		$ 70,000
All the assets are added together:		
TOTAL ASSETS		$1,826,000

LIABILITIES

Now that we have identified what a company owns, we need to understand how it acquired these assets. The company can finance these assets through debt (liabilities) or through its own investment (equity) in the business.

Liabilities refer to all the debts a company owes. They are categorized into current liabilities and long-term liabilities. Terms and conditions of liabilities are often identified in the notes to the financial statements. These terms and conditions include the listing of certain assets pledged as security and other specifics (due dates, interest rates, payments required, etc.).

Current Liabilities

Current liabilities reflect the amount of money the company owes and must pay within the coming year. Some of these debts include debt due within a year; amounts owed to material and service suppliers; unpaid wages; and outstanding bond interest, legal fees, pension payments, and taxes payable. In addition, it is common practice to include in current liabilities the portion of long-term debts due within the next year. Current liabilities are usually listed in order of liquidity by maturity date; however, companies may list them in other ways.[5]

Notes Payable

Companies often need additional cash to operate. Thus, they borrow money from banks or other lenders, such as suppliers, who usually demand formal recognition of amounts owed them. On receipt of cash, the borrower gives the lender a written promissory note, stating that borrowed funds will be returned within a specified period on a specific due date and usually detailing accrued interest (plus any other agreed-upon arrangements). The term "demand note" means the lender may demand repayment at any time.

Notes payable (demand note)	$250,000

Accounts Payable

Funds owed by the company for goods and services provided on credit by its suppliers are accounts payable. The company usually has 30, 60, or 90 days in which to pay. Sometimes, suppliers offer a cash discount of, say, 2 percent, as an inducement for its buyers to pay promptly.

Accounts payable	$210,000

Accrued Expenses Payable (Accruals)

In addition to its debt to suppliers and lenders, a company may owe for various goods not yet delivered in full or for services not yet fully performed or billed. These accruals must be recorded as expenses for the period, along with the matching liability. For example, salaries and wages earned prior to the employees' payday accumulate daily, yet the payment to these employees is usually recorded only when they are paid (on payday). Other examples include interest and fees to lawyers, architects, and so on, for partially completed undertakings. Thus, accrued expenses are expenses that have been incurred, but because there has been no transaction to date, they have not been recorded.

Accrued expenses payable	$70,000

Taxes Payable

For most companies, tax payments must be made monthly and may be based either on the estimate of the current year's taxes owed or on the previous year's taxes. The general practice is for corporations to choose the lower of the two bases to determine their monthly payment. In most cases, the final payment for the estimated taxes owed is due within two months after the end of the fiscal year.[6] As a consequence, the taxes payable account will have a balance in it as long as there is a difference between the base used for payment and the estimated tax liability that is determined when the company draws up its financial statements at the end of its fiscal year.

Taxes payable $23,000

Current Portion of Long-Term Debt

Long-term debt contracts specify repayment terms. Of XYZ's long-term debts, the first mortgage bonds have a principal repayment of $50,000 due within one year. This portion of the long-term debt is added to current liabilities, or debts due within one year. The 9 percent debentures have no principal payments until 2004.

Current portion of long-term debt $50,000

To review, total current liabilities is the sum of all the debts that the company will have to pay within one year from the balance sheet date.

Notes payable (demand note)	$250,000	
Accounts payable	210,000	
Accrued expenses payable	70,000	
Taxes payable	23,000	
Current portion of long-term debt		
(1st mortgage bonds)	50,000	
Total current liabilities		$603,000

Long-Term Liabilities

Current liabilities were defined as debts due within one year. Long-term liabilities are debts due after one year from the date of the balance sheet. Long-term liabilities are usually listed in terms of due dates. The principal portions of mortgages, bonds, and some loans are examples. The interest on these items may be payable monthly, quarterly, semiannually, or annually. This year's or any previous year's interest, if not yet paid, would therefore be shown as an accrued expense payable, a current liability. Interest is charged against only those periods that have already passed. The interest that will be payable for the future may be known, but it is not considered a debt until it has been incurred (but not paid). Therefore, future interest does not appear as a liability on the balance sheet.

First Mortgage Bonds

In the sample balance sheet, one long-term liability is the 7 percent first mortgage bonds due in 2004. The money was received by the company as a loan from the bondholders, who in turn were given a certificate called a bond as evidence of the loan. The bond is a formal promissory note issued by the company, which states that the company agrees to repay the debt at maturity in 2004 plus interest at the rate of 7 percent per year. The term *first mortgage* is a safeguard initiated by the lenders. This means that if the company is unable to pay off the bonds in cash when they are due, the bondholders have a claim, or lien, before other creditors on the mortgaged assets. The mortgaged assets may be sold and the proceeds used to satisfy the debt.

First mortgage bonds (7% interest, due 2004) $200,000

Debentures

The debentures (or bonds) are a certificate of debt. The security of the debenture is the general credit standing of the company. In other words, the debenture holders rank equally with the other general creditors, such as the trade creditors and nonsecured creditors.

Debentures 9%, due 2009 $460,000

Deferred Taxes

Often, CICA's accounting principles for the determination of net earnings and the government's legal determination of taxable income are in conflict. As a consequence, the taxpayer, in establishing financial statements, may estimate one level of income tax payable, and when filing taxable income according to government regulations, set a different level of tax liability. The difference between the two amounts is put in this account. See Appendix B for an illustration of how this discrepancy arises.

Deferred taxes $ 50,000

To review, total long term liabilities is the sum of all the debts that the company will have to pay after one year from the date of the balance sheet.

First mortgage bonds (7% interest, due 2004) $ 200,000
Debentures (9% interest, due 2009)   460,000
Deferred taxes   50,000
Total long-term liabilities $ 710,000

Finally, all liabilities, current and long-term, are added and listed under the heading of total liabilities.

TOTAL LIABILITIES $1,313,000

Shareholders' Equity

The total equity interest that all shareholders (owners of the company) have in a corporation is called shareholders' equity or net worth. It is what is left after subtracting total liabilities from total assets. For corporations, equity is separated into two categories, capital stock and retained earnings; the capital structure for proprietors and partnerships is somewhat different.

Capital Stock

In a public or private company, the shares of ownership are called capital stock. The capital stock account reflects the owners' initial equity investment in the company. This account is treated differently depending on the company's form of ownership. (Forms of ownership will be discussed in more detail in Part 3.) In a sole proprietorship, capital stock will appear as a single account, which includes both invested capital and retained income; for example:

Scott Meddick, capital	$50,000

In a partnership, the capital stock accounts will show the respective amounts of the partners' shares of the ownership equity, which also includes both invested capital and retained profits; for example:

Scott Meddick, capital	$50,000	
Bill West, capital	30,000	
Total capital		$80,000

A public company often issues more than one kind of stock in order to appeal to as many investors as possible. Anyone can purchase capital stock shares in a public firm, whereas the sale of a private company's shares is restricted. Shares are represented by stock certificates issued by the company to its shareholders.

The number of shares and type (common or preferred) of capital stock that a company is authorized to issue and the par value,[7] if any, of these shares are specified in the articles of incorporation.[8] *Issued* means the number of shares sold, while outstanding shares represent the shares that are still in the hands of shareholders.

Preferred Shares

Dividends to preferred shareholders are normally limited to a stated percentage of share value and are not related to the level of profit. Since there are many different kinds of preferred shares, the terms are specified on the balance sheet. If the company should be liquidated, preferred shareholders have first claim on remaining assets, after its creditors (those to whom the company owes money, as shown in the liabilities section) have been repaid.

In the XYZ example, the preferred shares have a 4 percent cumulative feature; this means that each share is entitled to $4 in dividends a year when declared by the board of directors. The preferred shares are cumulative, which means that if in any year the dividend is not paid, it accumulates in favour of the preferred shareholders and must be paid to them before any dividends are distributed to common stock shareholders. In general, preferred shareholders do not have voting rights in the company, unless dividends are in arrears (i.e., have not been paid).

Preferred shares, $4 cumulative

  authorized, issued, and outstanding 1,400 shares $90,000

Common Shares

Common shareholders control the company because these shareholders vote for a board of directors and vote on other management issues at shareholders' meetings. Common shares can be either par value or no par value. Dividends are not preset or guaranteed. Normally, dividends are not declared on common shares until preferred shareholders have received their full dividend. When company earnings are high, dividends may be high; when earnings drop, so may dividends.

Common shares,

  authorized, issued, and outstanding 140,000 shares $140,000

The preferred shares and common shares accounts are then added for a total capital stock amount.

Preferred shares, $4 cumulative,

  authorized, issued, and outstanding 1,400 shares $ 90,000

Common shares,

  authorized, issued, and outstanding, 140,000 shares   140,000

Total capital stock $230,000

Retained Earnings

The second component of equity is retained earnings. This represents the accumulated total of after-tax profits and losses from operations over the life of the corporation that have been retained in the company, in other words not paid out in dividends. Any dividends declared by the company are also subtracted from cumulative earnings in the statement of retained earnings, which is discussed in Section Three. Profits add to retained earnings, whereas losses reduce it. If a corporation has had more losses than profits, the amount in retained earnings will be negative (usually shown in brackets) and labelled "Retained deficit." XYZ, since it started, has retained a net total of $283,000 from its operations.

Retained earnings $ 283,000

The shareholders' equity accounts are then totalled.

Total shareholders' equity $ 513,000

All liabilities and shareholders' equity items are added together. This amount balances with the total assets.

TOTAL LIABILITIES AND SHAREHOLDERS' EQUITY $1,826,000

Facts to Remember about the Balance Sheet

1. The balance sheet shows the financial picture at a specific point in time.
2. The company name, the name of the statement, and the date must appear in the title.
3. Assets are listed on the left, liabilities and shareholders' equity are listed on the right. (Sometimes they are listed below one another on a page.)
4. Current assets are shown first, followed by fixed assets.
5. Current assets are listed in order of liquidity, from most liquid to least liquid.
6. Fixed assets are listed in order of permanence, from most permanent to least permanent.
7. Current liabilities are listed first, followed by long-term liabilities.
8. Liabilities are listed chronologically in terms of due dates.
9. Shareholders' equity has two components: capital stock and retained earnings.
10. A balance sheet must *always* balance: Assets = Liabilities + Equity.

Section

Three

The Statement of Retained Earnings

Before preparing the balance sheet for XYZ, retained earnings must be calculated. The retained earnings account is the connection between the balance sheet and the income statement, as shown in Figure 1.

As mentioned earlier, the retained earnings are the period's earnings remaining after dividends on preferred and common stock have been paid — that is, the earnings retained in the company. When an enterprise starts in business, it has no retained earnings. As soon as it has any profits or losses, however, the retained earnings account is affected. (If losses are greater than earnings, the account is listed as "Retained deficit.")

A separate statement of retained earnings for XYZ is presented in Exhibit 4.[9]

The statement of retained earnings is straightforward. To the initial opening balance of retained earnings ($144,120 as of December 31, 1998) is added the net earnings for the year as determined from the statement of earnings ($144,480 for 1999). The resulting subtotal is $288,600. From this subtotal the total of dividends paid during 1999 — $5,600 on the preferred shares (1,400 shares × $4 per share) — is subtracted, yielding the retained earnings as of December 31, 1999: $283,000.

FIGURE 1

Relationship Between the Income Statement and Balance Sheet

XYZ Retail Co. Ltd. Income Statement December 31, 1999	XYZ Retail Co. Ltd. Statement of Retained Earnings: December 31, 1999	XYZ Retail Co. Ltd. Balance Sheet December 31, 1999

XYZ Retail Co. Ltd.
Income Statement
December 31, 1999

XYZ Retail Co. Ltd.
Statement of Retained
Earnings:
December 31, 1999

XYZ Retail Co. Ltd.
Balance Sheet
December 31, 1999

ASSETS   **LIABILITIES**

Retained earnings, December 31,
1998 $144,120

Plus net income, 1999   144,489

Less: Dividends   5,600   **EQUITY**

Retained earnings: December 31,
1999 $283,000

Net income after tax $144,480   Retained earnings $283,000

EXHIBIT 4

XYZ Retail Co. Ltd.
Statement of Retained Earnings
for the Year Ended December 31, 1999

Retained earnings: December 31, 1998	$144,120
Net earnings for the year, 1999	144,480
	$288,600
Less: Preferred dividends	$ 5,600
Retained earnings: December 31, 1999	$283,000

SECTION

FOUR

THE AUDITOR'S REPORT AND FOOTNOTES

All incorporated companies are obliged by law to provide annual financial statements to their shareholders. This information is usually presented in a firm's annual report. In addition to financial statements, these reports often contain a message from the president describing the corporation's past and planned activities, including new product developments, plant expansion, and assessment of changes in market conditions.

Management, shareholders, creditors, and potential investors rely on the financial statements of a company. Shareholders and creditors place more credibility on statements prepared by independent auditors. Also, statutory regulations require an independent auditor for public corporations and for some private companies. Auditors report to the shareholders, not to the management, stating whether, in their opinion, the statements present fairly the financial position of the firm in accordance with generally accepted accounting principles and in a manner consistent with the previous year's report.

Financial reports are condensed and formalized. Notes to the financial statements are used where explanation is necessary and where additional relevant information is required, such as stock options, details of long-term debt, and details of unconsolidated subsidiaries. It is essential to read these notes in addition to the numbers in the financial statements in order to appreciate fully the implications of the financial statements.

NOTES

1. For a manufacturing company, product costs are those incurred to manufacture inventory. See Appendix A.
2. There are a number of ways to calculate depreciation. The simplest method is the straight-line method, whereby the cost of the fixed asset is allocated evenly over its useful life.
3. Often referred to as "zero salvage value" or "no salvage value."
4. If known, the market value of these assets is required to be disclosed in the notes to the financial statements.
5. Examples of other ways of listing current liabilities include listing by magnitude (the largest obligations first) or based on historical customs.
6. Companies are required to file a tax return for the previous year's income tax within six months of their fiscal year-end.
7. Par value is an amount selected by the company stating a specific value per share. This amount is stated in the corporate charter.
8. The company usually requests authorization of a larger number of shares than it will issue immediately. Therefore, if more capital is needed in future years, the company will not have to change its charter by increasing the number of authorized shares.
9. The content of the retained earnings statement may be included in the balance sheet, eliminating the necessity for a separate retained earnings statement.

⋮ EXERCISES IN INCOME STATEMENT CONSTRUCTION

Exercise 1
Buckner Department Store Ltd.
(in 000s of dollars)

Selling expenses	$1,104
Net operating income	483
Cost of goods sold	6,670
Other income	46
Gross income (profit)	1,840
Net sales	8,510
Administrative expenses	253
Other expenses	69

Assignment

Different income statement items for Buckner Department Store Ltd. are listed above in random order. All refer to the year ending January 31, 2000, and are in thousands of dollars. The tax rate is 40 percent. Prepare an income statement for the period ending January 31, 2000, for Buckner Department Store Ltd.

Exercise 2

J. Crawford Retail Sales Inc.
(in 000s of dollars)

Gross income	$ 543
Net income before tax	240
Selling expenses	160
Ending Inventory	475
Net sales	2,125
Beginning inventory	393
General and administrative expenses	143

Assignment

Different income statement items of J. Crawford Retail Sales Inc. are listed above in random order for the three-month period ending March 31, 2000. Prepare an income statement for the period ending March 31, 2000, for J. Crawford Retail Sales Inc. Assume the income tax rate is 50 percent. **Note**: To complete this exercise the following will have to be calculated: (a) cost of goods sold, (b) purchases, and (c) net income after tax.

Exercise 3
Young Textile Mills Inc.
(in 000s of dollars)

Direct labour	$ 753
Goods in process, January 15, 2000	384
Sales discounts	27
Manufacturing overhead	579
Other income	75
Goods in process, January 15, 1999	390
Other expense, interest	84
Raw materials, January 15, 2000	489
Administrative expenses	294
Finished goods, January 15, 1999	222
Selling expenses	147
Sales returns and allowances	33
Raw materials, January 15, 1999	498
Finished goods, January 15, 2000	219
Sales	5,490
General expenses	255
Indirect labour	99
Other expense, royalty	18
Material purchases	2,958

Assignment

Income statement items are listed above in random order. All are period accounts for the year ending January 15, 2000, except where noted by date. Assuming a tax rate of 40 percent, prepare a statement of cost of goods manufactured and an income statement for Young Textile Mills Inc. for the year ending January 15, 2000.

Exercise 4
Durham Lumber Ltd.
(in 000s of dollars)

Selling expenses	$ 504
Direct labour	1,980
Finished goods, February 15, 1999	604
Other revenue	284
Depreciation, manufacturing equipment	848
Indirect labour	1,320
Sales returns and allowances	44
Depreciation, office equipment	96
Sales discounts	60
Administrative expenses	940
Raw materials used	8,360
Other manufacturing overhead	324
Net sales	15,356
Goods in process, February 15, 1999	292
Gross income	2,520
Estimated income tax expense	68
Raw materials, February 15, 2000	2,160
Cost of goods manufactured	12,848
General expenses	628
Net earnings	116
Other expenses, interest	452
Raw materials, February 15, 1999	2,146
Net operating income	352

Assignment

Income statement items for Durham Lumber Ltd. are listed above in random order. All represent activity for the year ending February 15, 2000, except where noted by date. Prepare a statement of cost of goods manufactured and an income statement for Durham Lumber Ltd. To complete the assignment, sales, material purchases, ending goods in process, and finished goods inventories and cost of goods sold will have to be calculated.

⠿ *EXERCISES IN BALANCE SHEET CONSTRUCTION*

Exercise 1
Paul Webster Retail Florist

Capital, P. Webster	$27,900
Accumulated depreciation, store fixtures	12,000
Accounts payable	12,300
Goodwill	6,000
Store fixtures, cost	22,500
Inventory	7,500
Bank loan (90-day note)	6,600
Cash	11,100
Accrued expenses payable	900
Accounts receivable	12,600

Assignment

Different accounts are listed above, in random order, for the florist business of Paul Webster. The accounts are as at March 1, 2000.

1. Determine whether the account is a current asset, fixed asset, intangible asset, current liability, long-term liability, or net worth account.

2. Prepare a balance sheet as at March 1, 2000.

Exercise 2
Thomas Hardware Store Ltd.

Land	$ 19,500
Prepaid expenses	12,800
Accrued expenses payable	10,500
Notes payable, due in 90 days	34,800
Long-term debt	54,000
Accumulated depreciation, building and equipment	57,200
Marketable securities	18,000
Accounts payable	73,700
Accounts receivable	60,000
Common stock (authorized 2,500 shares; issued 2,052)	51,300
Organization expenses	2,500
Building and equipment, cost	119,000
Retained earnings	131,500
Taxes payable	5,200
Cash	4,400
Inventory	182,000

Assignment

Different accounts as at January 31, 2000, are listed above in random order for Thomas Hardware Store Ltd.

1. Determine whether the account is a current asset, fixed asset, intangible asset, current liability, long-term liability, or equity item.

2. Prepare a balance sheet as at January 31, 2000, for Thomas Hardware Store Ltd.

Exercise 3
Smith Furniture Manufacturer Inc.

Accumulated depreciation, buildings	$59,800
Patents	7,900
Building, cost	170,100
Accumulated depreciation, equipment	137,700
Bank loan, short term	153,300
Common stock (authorized and issued 20,000 shares)	58,500
Equipment, cost	230,600
Inventory	299,200
Accrued expenses payable	16,300
Long-term debt, due within one year	8,800
Cash	?
Investment in subsidiary[1]	52,600
Prepaid expenses	9,000
Taxes payable	19,400
Marketable securities	60,000
Land	23,100
Mortgage, due in 2013	100,500
Goodwill	16,100
Organization expenses	3,300
Accounts receivable	296,300
Preferred stock (authorized 2,000 shares, issued 521 shares)	52,100
Retained earnings	348,500
Accounts payable	178,900
Debentures, due 2006	44,000

1. Represents a 50 percent ownership in a major hardwood supplier.

Assignment

The above accounts are taken from the records of Smith Furniture Manufacturer Inc. as at March 15, 2000. Prepare a balance sheet for the company and determine the cash position. *Hint: a balance sheet must balance!*

EXERCISES ON THE INCOME STATEMENT AND BALANCE SHEET RELATIONSHIP

Exercise 1
Bargain Stores Incorporated
(in 000s of dollars)

Inventory, June 30, 2000	$ 758
Gross income (profit)	857
Long-term notes payable	31
Store fixtures, net	144
Selling expenses	341
Accounts payable	288
Income tax expense	12
Retained earnings, June 30, 1999	540
Cash	48
General and administrative expenses	432
Accrued expenses payable	96
Accounts receivable	324
Dividends	12
Notes payable	252
Inventory, June 30, 1999	684
Common stock	36
Sales	3,398
Depreciation expense	36
Income tax payable	7
Store fixtures, cost	180

Assignment

Different balance sheet and income statement accounts are listed above in random order. The balance sheet accounts are as at June 30, 2000, except where noted. The income statement amounts are for the year July 1, 1999, to June 30, 2000, in thousands of dollars.

1. Determine whether each account is a balance sheet or income statement item.

2. Prepare an income statement for Bargain Stores Incorporated for the year ending June 30, 2000.

3. Prepare a statement of retained earnings for the year ended June 30, 2000.

4. Prepare a balance sheet as at June 30, 2000, for Bargain Stores Incorporated.

Exercise 2
Oliver Wholesalers — Proprietorship
(in 000s of dollars)

Capital — Oliver, May 31, 1999	$ 600
Cash	44
Net sales	4,326
Accounts receivable	413
Gross income (profit)	1,024
Accumulated depreciation, May 31, 1999	416
Net earnings	90
Notes payable — bank	520
Purchases	3,502
Long-term bank loan	26
Prepaid expenses	29
Depreciation expense	52
Inventory, May 31, 1999	822
Accrued expenses payable	34
Drawings — Oliver	56
Selling expenses	437
Equipment, cost	520
Inventory, May 31, 2000	1,022
Capital — Oliver, May 31, 2000	634
Cost of goods sold	3,302
Accounts payable	346
General and administrative expenses	445

Assignment

Different balance sheet and income statement accounts are listed above in random order, in thousands of dollars. The balance sheet accounts are as at May 31, 2000, except where noted. The income statement amounts are for the year ending May 31, 2000.

1. Determine whether each account is a balance sheet or income statement item.

2. Prepare an income statement for Oliver Wholesalers — Proprietorship for the year ending May 31, 2000.

3. Prepare a statement of retained earnings for the year ended May 31, 2000.

4. Prepare a balance sheet as at May 31, 2000.

Exercise 3
Wilson Commercial Printers Limited
(in 000s of dollars)

Equipment, cost	$ 490
Goodwill	37
Goods-in-process inventory, April 15, 1999	53
Accounts receivable, net	318
Gross profit	451
Accounts payable	166
Raw materials used	611
Accumulated depreciation, building	98
Net income before tax	154
Accumulated depreciation, equipment	223
Preferred stock	16
Investment in subsidiary (more than 50 percent ownership)	154
Estimated income tax expense	48
Selling expense	88
Prepayments	10
Finished goods inventory, April 15, 1999	46
Bank loan, due in 90 days	104
Raw materials inventory, April 15, 1999	61
Marketable securities	38
Long-term debt due within one year	10
General and administrative expenses (includes depreciation expense)	239
Land	12
Material purchases	625
Taxes payable	25
Other income	53
Direct labour	336
Common stock	114
Building, cost	109
Other expenses, interest	23
Net long-term debt	226
Cost of goods manufactured	1,046
Net sales	1,482
Cash	?
Retained earnings	328
Accrued expenses payable	49
Factory overhead (includes depreciation expenses)	98
Retained earnings, April 15, 1999	222

Assignment

Listed in random order are balance sheet and income statement accounts as at April 15, 2000, except where otherwise noted by date, for Wilson Commercial Printers Limited (WCPL).

1. Prepare an income statement, a statement of cost of goods manufactured, and a statement of retained earnings for WCPL for the year ending April 15, 2000.

2. Prepare a balance sheet as at April 15, 2000, using cash to balance assets against liabilities and shareholders' equity.

Exercise 4
Allison Boat Makers Inc.
(in 000s of dollars)

Long-term bank loan	$ 100
Goods-in-process inventory, April 30, 1999	110
Insurance expense — factory equipment	22
Net sales	4,603
Net income after tax	278
Factory heat, light, and power	58
Other expenses, interest	85
Cost of goods available for sale	3,420
Accounts receivable	448
Wages payable	228
Direct labour	1,350
Sales returns and discounts	243
Raw materials inventory, April 30, 1999	78
Goodwill	238
Prepaid expenses	43
Total manufacturing costs	3,173
Accumulated depreciation, factory building and equipment, April 30, 1999	1028
Factory supervision	280
Cost of goods sold	3,223
Total cost of goods in process, 2000	3,283
Organization expenses	10
Selling expenses	238
Total current liabilities	610
Retained earnings, April 30, 2000	835
Raw material used	1,363
Bonds payable, 2006	493
Factory building and equipment depreciation expense	100
Marketable securities	85
Common stock	433
General and administrative expenses	377
Accounts payable	148
Cost of goods manufactured	3,193
Taxes payable	83
Office space rental	275
Dividends paid on common stock, 2000	23
Raw material purchases	1,355
Factory building and equipment, cost	2,348
Net operating income	490

Investment in subsidiary	388
Other income	23
Accrued expenses payable	18
Preferred shares	358
Estimated income tax	150
Dividends paid on preferred shares, 2000	28
Cash	40
Bank loan, due March 2001	?

Assignment

Listed above in random order are balance sheet and income statement accounts for the year ending, or as at April 30, 2000, except where otherwise noted by date for Allison Boat Makers Inc. (ABMI).

1. Prepare a statement of cost of goods manufactured, an income statement, and a statement of retained earnings for the year ending April 30, 2000.

2. Prepare a balance sheet as of April 30, 2000, using "Bank loan due March 2001" as the balancing figure.

APPENDIX A

XYZ Manufacturing Co. Ltd.
Cost of Goods Manufactured

In most firms, one of the major expenses associated with generating sales revenue is the company's cost to make or buy the product. For a manufacturer like XYZ Manufacturing Co. Ltd., the cost of goods manufactured includes all costs associated with the transformation or production process; thus, because the company transforms raw materials into finished goods available for sale, the cost of goods manufactured within the cost of goods sold section is more complex. In the statement of cost of goods manufactured, the manufacturing costs included are raw materials costs, direct labour, and factory overhead items associated with the actual manufacturing process during the period.

A manufacturing firm transforms unprocessed raw materials into the desired final products, referred to as finished goods, which are then available for sale. The manufacturing process involves the acquisition of raw materials (the product of another manufacturer) and the processing of these raw materials into the desired product through an effective combination of labour and machinery. In processing the goods, many costs are incurred, such as wages for assembly-line workers and plant supervisors, the cost of power used by the factory, and the cost of operating production machinery. Figure A-1 illustrates this physical flow of manufactured goods.

FIGURE A-1
The Manufacturing Process

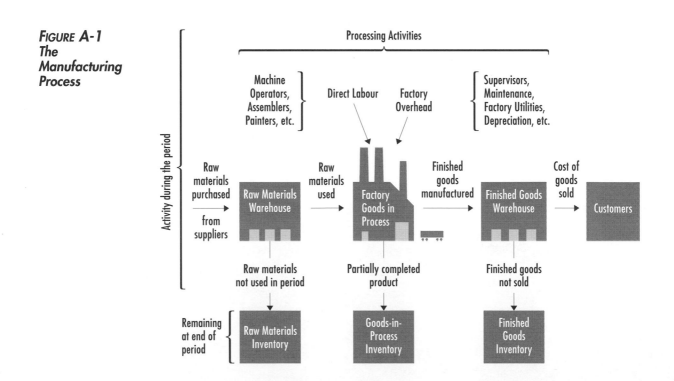

In summary:

1. Raw materials are purchased and placed in inventory, awaiting processing.
2. Raw materials are taken out of inventory and placed into production.
3. Raw materials are processed.
4. Finished goods are completed and placed into inventory, awaiting sale.
5. Finished goods are sold and are removed from inventory.

This physical flow of goods through the production process is also reflected in the company's statement of cost of goods manufactured (Exhibit A-1).

EXHIBIT A-1

XYZ Manufacturing Co. Ltd.
Statement of Cost of Goods Manufactured
for the Year Ending December 31, 1999

Work-in-process inventory, December 31, 1998			$ 316,000
Raw materials used:			
Raw material inventory, December 31, 1998	$ 580,000		
Raw material purchases	2,900,000		
Raw materials available	$3,480,000		
Less: Raw material inventory, December 31, 1999	520,000		
Raw materials used		$2,960,000	
Direct labour		530,000	
Factory overhead:			
Supervision	$ 130,000		
Indirect factory labour	370,000		
Power	110,000		
Heat and light	40,000		
Depreciation	120,000		
Other	150,000		
Total factory overhead		920,000	
Total manufacturing costs			4,410,000
Total cost of goods in process, 1999			$4,726,000
Less: Goods-in-process inventory, December 31, 1999			326,000
Cost of goods manufactured			$4,400,000

Determining the cost of goods manufactured is a five-step process:

1. The raw materials used figure is made up of the beginning raw materials inventory and raw material purchases during 1999, less the raw materials inventory remaining at the end of the period — December 31, 1999.
2. Add direct labour costs, $530,000, representing the factory labour that is directly involved in the production of the goods.

3. Add the last component of the manufacturing process, factory overhead. Included under this heading are the costs of supervision (the salaries paid to supervisors and plant managers), indirect factory labour (the cost of maintenance and clean-up crews), power (the electricity used to run the machines), heat and light (only costs associated with the factory facility), depreciation (the write-down of the useful life of the plant and equipment used directly in the production process), and other expenses (the cost of supplies for maintenance, incidental materials used in the manufacturing process too minor to be costed as raw materials, insurance on the plant and equipment, and so on). The sum of the factory overhead items included in the statement of cost of goods manufactured is $920,000. This means XYZ incurred total manufacturing costs in 1999 of $4,410,000.

4. Determine the total cost of work in process for 1999. This is the addition of the total manufacturing costs and the partially completed goods-in-process inventory at the beginning of the period (last period's ending balance as at December 31, 1998).

5. At the end of the period, there are usually products that have not completed the production process and are, therefore, not finished. These partially completed units make up the period's ending goods-in-process inventory. Thus, to determine the cost of goods manufactured, the goods-in-process inventory (as at December 31, 1999) of $326,000 must be subtracted from the total cost of goods in process for 1999.

Accounting for inventories in a manufacturing business centres on the physical state of the goods. In a manufacturing operation many costs are incurred in converting the inventory to a finished state. The costs associated with the conversion are attached to the inventory so that all production costs are included in the cost of the finished products. Consequently, as the inventory changes physically by being processed, the cost of that inventory increases to reflect the value added by processing the goods. Thus, partially finished products and finished products are given a higher unit cost than raw materials, since many costs have been added to the original raw materials cost. The goods may be completely processed, partially processed, or completely unprocessed. The accounting system, therefore, uses three separate inventory accounts based on the degree of processing: raw materials (completely unprocessed goods); goods in process (subassemblies and partially completed goods); and finished products (completely processed goods) that are manufactured but not yet sold. These three inventory accounts provide the foundation for the accounting system used to record for manufacturing activities.

Sometimes, where specific costs belong on the financial statements is unclear. Figure A-2 expands on Figure A-1 by identifying the placement (balance sheet, income statement) of these costs in financial statements. This accounting system reflects the physical flow of the goods from unprocessed raw materials to completed goods in the hands of the consumer.

XYZ's income statement (Exhibit A-2) is similar to that reported in Exhibit 1 of Part 2. As illustrated earlier, the cost of goods manufactured figure for the period and the beginning balance in finished goods inventory figure determine the cost of goods available for sale. Those finished goods not yet sold at the end of the accounting period become part of the company's finished goods ending inventory balance. Once the finished goods ending inventory figure is subtracted from the cost of goods available for sale, the cost of goods sold figure can be calculated.

FIGURE A-2
Identifying
Manufacturing
Costs

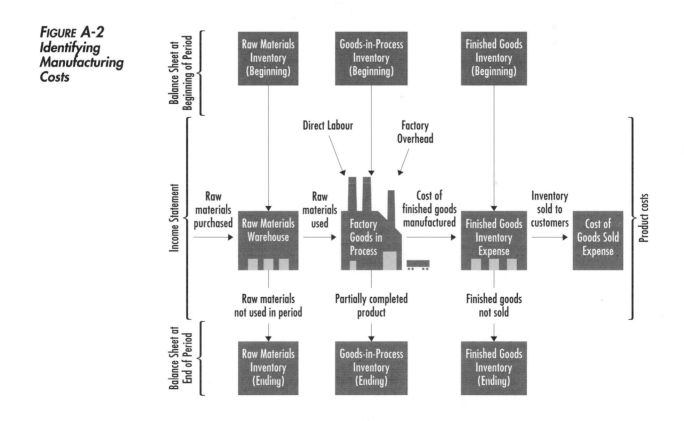

EXHIBIT A-2

XYZ Manufacturing Co. Ltd.
Income Statement
for the Year Ending December 31, 1999

Gross sales		$6,000,000
Less: Sales returns and allowances	$ 120,000	
Sales discounts	80,000	200,000
Net sales		$5,800,000
Cost of goods sold:		
Finished goods inventory, December 31, 1998	$ 494,000	
Cost of goods manufactured (Exhibit A-1)	4,400,000	
Cost of goods available for sale	$4,894,000	
Less: Finished goods inventory, December 31, 1999	570,000	
Cost of goods sold		4,324,000
Gross income		$1,476,000
Operating expenses:		
General and administrative expenses	$ 290,000	
Selling expenses	450,000	
Depreciation expense	160,000	
Total operating expenses		900,000
Operating income		$ 576,000
Plus: Other income		40,000
Less: Other expenses, interest		200,000
Net income before tax		$ 416,000
Estimated income tax expense (44%)		183,040
Net income after tax		$ 232,960

On XYZ's balance sheet, the three types of inventory would be represented as follows:

Raw materials inventory	$ 520,000
Goods-in-process inventory	326,000
Finished inventory	570,000
Total inventories	$1,416,000

SOURCES

Griffith, Scott P., "Accounting for Manufacturing Activities." Lecture, 6 October 1993, Ivey Business School.

Heisz, Mark A., and Richard H. Mimick, "Accounting for Manufacturing Activities," No. 9A83K032. Published by Ivey Management Services.

APPENDIX B

Deferred Taxes

Most cases with deferred tax credits arise because of the different rules for depreciation. For example, XYZ may have purchased new machinery in 1998 worth $20,000. XYZ's normal accounting practice is to depreciate the $20,000 over its useful life of 10 years, assuming a $0 salvage value. As a consequence (as illustrated in Table B-1), it would deduct from its earnings depreciation expense of $2,000 per year. However, the government regulations allow 40 percent depreciation on the declining balance of the asset, or $8,000 in 1998 and $4,800 in 1999 $(0.20 \times [\$20,000 - \$8,000])$.

This means that in 1998 (related to this asset alone), the taxable income as reported on XYZ's tax form would be less than it reports on its financial statements. The difference would be $6,000 ($8,000 − $2,000). Assuming a 44 percent tax rate, the difference in income tax expense for 1998 is $2,640 ($0.44 \times $6,000). The reduction in income tax expense is added to the deferred taxes account. In later years, when the net book value of the asset for tax regulations is below $5,000, the situation will be reversed.

Table B-1: XYZ's Depreciation Method Government Allowance for Tax Purposes

	XYZ's Depreciation Method	Government Allowance for Tax Purposes
Cost of asset, purchased January 1, 1998	$20,000	$20,000
Estimated life	10 years	10 years
1998 depreciation expense	$ 2,000	$ 8,000
1999 depreciation expense	$ 2,000	$ 4,800
Total accumulated depreciation, December 31, 1999	$ 4,000	$12,800

PART

AN INTRODUCTION TO
FINANCIAL MANAGEMENT

Part 3 introduces basic financial tools and techniques used by financial managers and analysts to assess and project the financial performance and position of a business. An understanding of the basic financial statements discussed in Part 2 is essential to comprehension of this part. Financial analysis and management are more than "doing the numbers"; judgment must be exercised in deciding which numbers to look at and how to interpret them. Often, a "qualitative factor," something not expressed in numbers, is just as or more important to the solution of a problem than all the numbers involved.

The topics that will be discussed are:

- Forms of ownership
- Cash sources and uses statement
- Financial ratio analysis
- Projected financial statements
- Sensitivity analysis
- Credit
- Sources and types of financing
- Bankruptcy

SECTION

ONE

FORMS OF OWNERSHIP

There are three primary legal forms of ownership: the sole proprietorship, the partnership, and the limited company. It is important to note which form of ownership is operating within a company because each has different financial implications.

Sole Proprietorship

A sole proprietorship is a business owned and usually operated by a single individual. Its major characteristic is that the owner and the business are one and the same. The proprietor takes ownership of the company's profitability and assets but also assumes full responsibility for the company's losses and debts. A sole proprietorship is also referred to as the proprietorship, single proprietorship, individual proprietorship, and individual enterprise.

A sole proprietorship is the oldest and most common form of ownership. Some examples of this form of ownership include small retail stores, doctors' and lawyers' practices, and restaurants.

Business Implications

A sole proprietorship is easily formed with minimal legal requirements and, often, minimal capital requirements. It can also be dissolved as easily as it was established. Because of its limited life, a proprietorship can terminate should the owner become disabled, die, or file for bankruptcy. Retirement or the whim of the owner can also end the proprietorship.

A sole proprietorship offers the owner freedom and flexibility in making decisions easily and quickly. Major policies can be changed according to the owner's wishes because the firm does not operate under a rigid charter. Because there are no others to consult, the owner has absolute control over the use of the company's resources. The owner need only strive to meet personal goals, without concern for the best interests of shareholders. Although this is a benefit to the proprietor, some creditors may view this characteristic with some apprehension. A sole proprietorship may experience difficulties in obtaining capital because lenders are leery of lending money to only one person who is pledged to repay. As a result, the sole proprietor may frequently have to rely on friends, relatives, and government agencies for funds or loan guarantees.

As mentioned earlier, the financial condition of the firm is the same as the financial condition of the owner. This makes the proprietor personally liable for any debts incurred by the company, which can make it difficult to attract suppliers of credit. A proprietorship, depending on its size and provision for succession, may also experience difficulties in attracting new employees because there are often few opportunities for advancement, minimal fringe benefits, and little employment security.

When assessing the financial attractiveness of a sole proprietorship, the risks must be considered along with the company's size, the provisions that have been made for succession, the length of its existence, and any historical relationship with creditors.

Partnership

A partnership is an unincorporated enterprise owned by two or more individuals. There are three types of partnerships: general partnerships, limited partnerships, and joint ventures. A partnership agreement expresses the rights and obligations of each partner. For example, one partner may have the financial resources to start the business, whereas the other partner possesses the management skills to operate the business.

Business Implications

Partnerships, like sole proprietorships, are easy to start up. Registration details vary by province but usually entail obtaining a licence and registering the company name. Partners' interests can be protected by formulating an "agreement of partnership." This agreement specifies all the details of the partnership. Because partnerships usually benefit from the complementary management skills of two or more people, they are often a stronger entity. As a result, they can attract new employees and creditors more readily than can a sole proprietorship. A stronger entity also makes it easier for partnerships to raise additional capital. Lenders are often more willing to advance money to partnerships than to proprietorships because all general partners are subject to unlimited financial liability. In a partnership, the unlimited liability is both joint and personal, meaning that if a partner cannot meet his or her share of the debts, the other partner must pay all debts. Partners are also legally responsible for actions of other partners.

Partnerships are not as easy to dissolve as sole proprietorships. Termination can occur on the death of any one partner or when one partner breaks the partnership agreement or gives notice to leave. It is frequently difficult for firms to find new partners to buy an interest. As a result, partners often take out term insurance on the lives of other partners to purchase the interest of a deceased partner, with preset sale prices.

CORPORATIONS

Corporations, unlike proprietorships or partnerships, are created by law and are separate from the people who own and manage them. Corporations are also referred to as limited companies. In corporations, ownership is represented by shares of stock. The owners, at an annual meeting, elect a board of directors, which appoints company officers and sets the company's objectives.

Business Implications

Corporations are the least risky from an owner's point of view. Shareholders of corporations can lose only the amount of money they have invested in company stock. If an incorporated business goes bankrupt, owners do not have to meet the liabilities with their personal holdings unless they, as individuals, have guaranteed the debts of the corporation. However, banks, before granting loans to smaller companies, usually ask for personal guarantees from the shareholders/managers. Corporations are taxed at lower rates than individuals, which permits a corporation that retains earnings to build its equity base faster than unincorporated enterprises. As well, corporations may be able to raise larger amounts of capital than proprietorships or partnerships through the addition of new investors or through better borrowing power.

Limited companies do not end with the death of owners. A limited company can terminate only by bankruptcy, expiry of its charter, or a majority vote of its shareholders. With this continued life and greater growth possibilities, limited companies usually can attract more diversified managerial talent.

It is marginally more expensive and complicated to establish corporations than proprietorships or partnerships. A charter, which requires the services of a lawyer, must be obtained through the provincial or federal government. In addition to legal costs, a firm is charged incorporation fees for its charter by the authorizing government.

Dividends to shareholders from limited companies are taxed twice — the company pays tax on the profits earned and the shareholder pays tax on the dividends received from the profits. In proprietorships and partnerships, earnings are taxed only once — as the personal income of the individuals involved. Furthermore, if the enterprise suffers a loss, the shareholders of a corporation cannot use the loss to reduce other taxable income.

With diverse ownership, corporations do not enjoy the secrecy that proprietorships and partnerships have. A company must send each shareholder an annual report detailing the financial condition of the firm.

AN ILLUSTRATION: LMN RETAIL CO. LTD.

Financial analysis and projections are used to assess the achievement of financial goals. The financial statements of LMN Retail Co. Ltd. will form the basis on which to illustrate the development of the cash sources and uses statement, financial ratios, and projected financial statements. Exhibit 1 presents the income statements of LMN for 1998, 1999, and 2000; Exhibit 2 shows the balance sheets as at January 31, 1998, 1999, and 2000.

EXHIBIT 1

LMN Retail Company Ltd.
Income Statement
for the Years Ending January 31
(in 000s of dollars)

	1998	1999	2000
Net sales	$2,188	$2,123	$2,715
Cost of goods sold:			
Beginning inventory	$ 380	$ 383	$ 388
Purchases	1,695	1,672	2,167
Cost of goods available for sale	$2,075	$2,055	$2,555
Less: Ending inventory	383	388	450
Cost of goods sold	$1,692	$1,667	$2,105
Gross income	$ 496	$ 456	$ 610
Operating expenses:			
General and administrative	$ 188	$ 203	$ 238
Selling	193	210	282
Depreciation — office equipment	37	37	35
Total operating expenses	$ 418	$ 450	$ 555
Net operating income	$ 78	$ 6	$ 55
Other expenses — interest	8	6	8
Net income before tax	$ 70	$ 0	$ 47
Estimated income tax	18	0	12
Net earnings	$ 52	$ 0	$ 35

Exhibit 2

LMN Retail Company Ltd.
Balance Sheet
as at January 31
(in 000s of dollars)

	1998	1999	2000
ASSETS			
Current assets:			
Cash	$ 5	$ 12	$ 15
Net accounts receivable	200	180	200
Inventory	383	388	450
Total current assets	$588	$580	$665
Fixed assets, net	122	85	80
TOTAL ASSETS	$710	$665	$745
LIABILITIES			
Current liabilities:			
Accounts payable	$170	$160	$178
Notes payable — bank	70	58	108
Taxes payable	15	0	12
Accrued expenses	13	30	20
Total current liabilities	$268	$248	$318
Long-term liabilities	75	50	25
Total liabilities	$343	$298	$343
EQUITY			
Common stock	$ 37	$ 37	$ 37
Retained earnings	330	330	365
Total equity	$367	$367	$402
TOTAL LIABILITIES AND EQUITY	$710	$665	$745

Cash Sources and Uses Statement

There are a number of ways to analyze a set of balance sheets; one is to use the cash sources and uses statement. The purpose of this statement is to trace the past financial activities of a company. The movement of cash is analyzed, and the depreciation account and retained earnings account are also included, because the statement outlines the *overall* financial activity of a company. By evaluating the differences between the accounts on two balance sheets, this statement summarizes where a company has received its cash (sources) and where the company spent its cash between the two periods of time.

STEPS TO CREATE A CASH SOURCES AND USES STATEMENT

1. Focus on the time period involved by identifying the first and last balance sheet to use. Remember, the first balance sheet should be compared with the last balance sheet. To understand where LMN Retail Company Ltd. received and paid cash during fiscal 1999, the 1998 and 1999 balance sheets will be used.

2. Calculate the changes in the balance sheet accounts by subtracting the previous year's figure from this year's figure. Table 1 shows these changes from 1998 to 1999. Table 1 shows what has happened in each account, but it does not give much insight into how these changes were related and resulted in $45,000 fewer assets (or $45,000 fewer total liabilities and equity) at the end of fiscal 1999.

Table 1: Changes in Balance Sheet Accounts

ACCOUNT	1998 ($000s)	1999 ($000s)	INCREASE DECREASE	AMOUNT ($000s)
ASSETS				
Cash	$ 5	$ 12	an increase of	$ 7
Net accounts receivable	200	180	a decrease of	20
Inventory	383	388	an increase of	5
Fixed assets	122	85	a decrease of	37
LIABILITIES				
Accounts payable	$170	$160	a decrease of	$10
Notes payable — bank	70	58	a decrease of	12
Taxes payable	15	0	a decrease of	15
Accrued expenses	13	30	an increase of	17
Long-term liabilities	75	50	a decrease of	25
EQUITY				
Common stock	$ 37	$ 37	no change	–
Retained earnings	330	330	no change	–

3. Record the changes for each account as a source or use of cash. To do this, it is important to understand the nature of the account. It might be useful to take the viewpoint of an owner of a small enterprise at the cash register. The collection of a sale immediately increases the cash. If customers pay their bills by credit card rather than cash, the retailer receives no cash immediately but the accounts receivable account increases — effectively, customers are taking

longer to pay their debts to the company, and the company waits longer to receive the money owed. Thus, the company's "financing" of its customers' accounts results in a use of the retailer's cash. If a supplier demands immediate payment upon the delivery of goods, the owner must reach into the cash register to make payment. However, if the supplier does not wish payment immediately, the owner can preserve the cash until the supplier requires payment. (The company has use of that additional cash during this period.) Therefore, the supplier's "financing" of the retailer's debt results in an incremental source of cash for the retailer. For example, the $17,000 increase of accrued expenses is a source of cash for LMN. Subsequently, when the account payable is paid, it will be a use of LMN's cash.

Figure 1 helps to classify whether an account is a source or use.

FIGURE 1
Sources and Uses

	Sources	Uses
Assets	↓	↑
Liabilities	↑	↓
Equity	↑	↓

As illustrated, a general rule can be followed. If an asset increases, it is a use of cash, and if it decreases, it is a source of cash. Increases and decreases in liabilities and equity work in the reverse order.

For LMN, some of the account changes in Table 1 represent cash coming into the company. For example, the reduction of net accounts receivable increases the owner's cash position and represents an incremental cash collection of $20,000. In other words, the reduction through collection of accounts receivable is a source of cash to LMN. Similarly, the reduction of net fixed assets ($37,000) has generated a source of cash.

Inspection of the income statements in Exhibit 1 reveals that in the 1999 fiscal year, net income was $0. This, however, does not reflect the cash flow from operations for 1999 because depreciation expense of $37,000 — the noncash allocation of a previously paid-for asset — was one of the expenses deducted from revenues to determine the net income for 1999. Since the cash was used to purchase the fixed asset originally, the allocation of the original expenditure through depreciation expense is a noncash item. Thus, if LMN operated on a cash basis (that is, all sales were paid for with cash and all expenses paid as incurred), the impact on operations in the 1999 fiscal year would have been to generate $37,000 cash ($0 net income plus $37,000 depreciation expense, noncash allocation).

Total sources of cash for the year ending January 31, 1999, for the LMN Retail Company Ltd. were:

Sources	(in 000s of dollars)
Net accounts receivable	$20
Fixed assets, net	37
Accrued expenses	17
Total sources	$74

Some of LMN's account changes represent cash outflows or uses of cash. The inventory level increased $5,000 over last year. This amount represents a use of cash by LMN to purchase additional inventory. Similarly, a reduction in a creditor's claim represents the use of cash, since the company would be repaying its debt to the creditor. The decrease of accounts payable by $10,000; notes payable — bank by $12,000; taxes payable by $15,000; and long-term liabilities by $25,000 are all uses of cash.

Total uses of cash for the year ending January 31, 1999 by LMN Retail Company Ltd. were:

Uses	(in 000s of dollars)
Inventory	$ 5
Accounts payable	10
Notes payable — bank	12
Taxes payable	15
Long-term liabilities	25
Total uses	$67

4. Compile the classified accounts into a sources and uses statement. As with other financial statements, the heading will include the name of the company, the name of the statement, and the period covered by the statement. Sources are listed first, followed by uses.

   For the 1999 fiscal year, the sources of cash for LMN were $7,000 greater than its uses of cash. In other words, the firm had a net cash inflow of $7,000 in the cash account from one year to the next. Added to this figure is the original cash balance from the first balance sheet (in this case, the cash figure on the 1998 balance sheet). Note that the total of the net cash increase plus the original cash balance matches the cash figure on the 1999 balance sheet.

   Exhibit 3 presents the cash sources and uses statement of LMN Retail Company Ltd. for the year ending January 31, 1999.[1]

Exhibit 3

LMN Retail Company Ltd.
Cash Sources and Uses Statement
for the Year Ending January 31, 1999
(in 000s of dollars)

Sources of cash:

Net accounts receivable	$20
Fixed assets, net	37
Accrued expenses	17
Total sources	**$74**

Uses of cash:

Inventory	$ 5
Accounts payable	10
Notes payable — bank	12
Taxes payable	15
Long-term liabilities	25
Total uses	**$67**

Net cash increase	$ 7
Cash, January 31, 1998	5
Cash, January 31, 1999	$12

As an analytical tool, cash sources and uses statements can be prepared for any period the analyst desires, providing balance sheets are available. For example, a cash sources and uses statement could be completed based on LMN's first balance sheet (January 31, 1998) and its last balance sheet (January 31, 2000). By comparing the first balance sheet with the last, all the years in between are taken into account. This method also saves time because only one statement is needed instead of two to compare 1998 with 1999 and then 1999 with 2000. Exhibit 4 presents the cash sources and uses statement for the LMN Retail Company Ltd. for a two-year period ending January 31, 2000.

EXHIBIT 4

LMN Retail Company Ltd.
Cash Sources and Uses Statement
for Two Years Ending January 31, 2000
(in 000s of dollars)

Sources of cash:

Fixed assets, net	$ 42
Accounts payable	8
Notes payable — bank	38
Accrued expenses	7
Retained earnings	35

Total sources $130

Uses of cash:

Inventory	$ 67
Taxes payable	3
Long-term liabilities	50

Total uses $120

Net cash increase	$ 10
Cash, January 31, 1998	5
Cash, January 31, 2000	$ 15

INTERPRETING THE CASH SOURCES AND USES STATEMENT

Completing the cash sources and uses statement is only part of the analysis. The next step is to analyze the results and draw some concrete conclusions from the statement. This statement not only helps people understand the previous activities of a company but also creates a solid base from which to project future company activities. The following points outline what to look for in the sources and uses statement.

Analyzing Major Sources and Uses

There are a number of things to look for when interpreting the sources and uses statement. The first step is to identify and interpret those items that have the most impact on the statement — the *major* sources and *major* uses. Exhibit 4 revealed that LMN's major sources and major uses of cash were:

Sources	(in 000s of dollars)
Fixed assets decrease	$42
Notes payable — bank	38
Retained earnings (profits)	35
Uses	**(in 000s of dollars)**
Inventory increase	$67
Payment of long-term liabilities	50

The analyst cannot tell whether the profits were used to increase inventory or whether the bank loan was used to pay off the long-term debt; instead, a general flow of cash can be observed. Also, without more information, the decrease in fixed assets may be a result of either depreciation expense or the sale of fixed assets. On this point, income statement records show total depreciation expense for 1999 and 2000 of $72,000 ($37,000 + $35,000). Thus, if the only change in fixed assets had been an increase in accumulated depreciation on the balance sheet, the decrease in fixed assets would have been $72,000, not $42,000. This is not the case, so LMN must have bought $30,000 worth of fixed assets. In other words, the changes in financial position may be more accurately reported as a $72,000 source (increase in accumulated depreciation) and a $30,000 use (increase in cost of fixed assets):

Source of cash:	
Depreciation expense	$72
Use of cash:	
Fixed assets purchases	$30

The second step in analysis is to interpret the desirability of these major changes. Essentially, LMN management used most of its cash generated from operations (net income plus depreciation) to (a) invest in inventory, (b) buy more fixed assets, and (c) pay off some of the company's long-term debt. Because cash from operations was insufficient for this purpose, it appears that LMN management substituted short-term debt (notes payable — bank) for long-term debt (the $50,000 paid off). Were all of these moves appropriate? It depends. For example, it appears that LMN's sales are now beginning to grow (see Exhibit 1). It is possible that the inventory increase was made in anticipation of growth; alternatively, offering a larger variety or quantity of goods available for sale may have precipitated the growth. The amount of inventory relative to company operations will be examined in Section Three of this chapter ("Financial Ratio Analysis"). Because the terms of the long-term debt are not known, it is impossible to comment on the appropriateness of retiring some of this debt. Ordinarily, more information would be available about the company's financial structure and its corporate objectives to make better judgments about the desirability of these changes.

The Matching Principle

Sound financial practice requires the financing of current assets with an appropriate combination of short- and long-term sources, and of long-term assets with long-term financing sources. One principle used to evaluate sound financial practice is the matching principle. This principle addresses the need to match revenues and expenses within the accounting periods in which they occur. For example, if the purchase of a $35,000 car is made on an American Express credit card, the debt has to be paid off in the short term. If the credit card company does not allow the debt to continue on the card, it will demand the $35,000. If there is not enough cash on hand to pay the debt, the car will have to be sold. This situation could have been avoided if longer-term financing had been secured for an asset that was expected to last several years.

This matching principle can be applied once the cash sources and uses statement has been completed. Identifying the sources and uses as short term (aspects of the operations) and long term (investing or financing activities) provides the necessary information to compare short-term sources with short-term uses and long-term sources with long-term uses. Sometimes there can be large discrepancies between long-term sources and long-term uses. For example, if long-term sources exceeded long-term uses, the balance of the long-term sources must be financing short-term uses (i.e., inventory). Keep in mind that current long-term sources of cash will eventually become long-term uses of cash as they are paid off!

The cash sources and uses statement is just one tool to help uncover the past financial activities of a company,[2] and it clearly has limitations. For example, the analyst is unable to determine in the LMN example whether the increase in inventory was excessive or related to the increase in sales for LMN. To fully understand the past financial history of a company, a ratio analysis is required to complement the cash sources and uses statement. Combined, these two tools can be used to further explain the variances among specific sources and uses of cash.

FINANCIAL RATIO ANALYSIS

As changes occur in the size of a company's various accounts, it is difficult to analyze what is happening by casually inspecting income statements and balance sheets. If only one or two accounts changed, identifying and interpreting such developments would be relatively straightforward. However, many items fluctuate simultaneously, making the reasons for the fluctuations hard to determine.

Financial ratio analysis is a useful financial management tool developed to assist in identifying, interpreting, and evaluating changes in the financial performance and condition of a business over a period of time. Its purpose is to provide information about the business entity for decision making by both external and internal users. For example, creditors use ratio analysis in making lending decisions, and potential shareholders may use this information to make investment decisions. Financial ratio analysis also provides the firm's managers with the information required to make a variety of operating and financing decisions.

A ratio is simply a fraction: it has two parts, a numerator (the top) and a denominator (the bottom). Using the LMN example, endless possible ratios could be calculated by taking various numbers on the income statements and balance sheets and deriving fractions. Most of the calculations would be meaningless; however, financial analysts have agreed on a common set of 15 to 20 ratios that they deem useful in assessing financial performance and financial position. Exhibit 5 presents several ratios for the LMN Retail Company Ltd.

EXHIBIT 5

LMN Retail Company Ltd.
Ratio Analysis
for the Years Ending January 31

	1998 %	1999 %	2000 %
Profitability			
Vertical analysis:[1]			
Sales	100.0	100.0	100.0
Cost of goods sold	77.3	78.5	77.5
Gross income	22.7	21.5	22.5
Operating expenses:			
General and administrative	8.6	9.6	8.8
Selling	8.8	9.9	10.4
Depreciation — office equipment	1.7	1.7	1.3
Subtotal operating expenses	19.1	21.2	20.5
Net operating income	3.6	0.3	2.0
Other expenses — interest	0.4	0.3	0.3
Net income before tax	3.2	0.0	1.7
Estimated income tax	0.8	0.0	0.4
Net earnings	2.4	0.0	1.3
Return on Equity[2]	15.2	0.0	9.1
Efficiency/Investment Utilization:			
Age of accounts receivable[3]	33.4 days	30.9 days	26.9 days
Age of inventory in days[3] (based on cost of goods sold)	82.6 days	85.0 days	78.0 days
Age of payables[3] (based on days purchases)	36.6 days	34.9 days	30.0 days
Inventory turnover	4.4x	4.3x	4.7x
Fixed asset turnover	17.9x[4]	20.5x	32.9x
Total asset turnover	3.1x[4]	3.1x	3.8x
Liquidity:			
Current ratio	2.2/1	2.3/1	2.1/1
Acid test	0.8/1	0.8/1	0.7/1
Working capital ($000s)	320	332	347
Stability:			
Net worth to total assets	51.7	55.2	54.0
Debt to total assets	48.3	44.8	46.0
Debt to equity	.93:1	.81:1	.85:1
Interest coverage (times)	9.8x	1.0x	6.9x
Growth (%):[5]			
Sales		(3.0)	27.9
Profit		(100.0)	–
Assets		(6.3)	12.0

1. Detail may not add to totals because of rounding.
2. Assumes 1997 retained earnings equal 1998 retained earnings less 1998 net earnings, i.e., $330,000 – $52,000 = $278,000.
3. A 365-day year is used.
4. For 1998, only the year-end figure is used (1997 data not given).
5. Parentheses indicate negative amounts.

Some observations of Exhibit 5 follow:

1. The ratios are grouped according to the five basic financial goals: profitability, efficiency, liquidity, stability, and growth. To survive, every business must meet each of these goals to some extent, though financial managers must determine the relative emphasis to place on each of the various corporate financial goals. This emphasis is shaped by the principal objectives of an organization and the environment in which it operates.

   - *Profitability* refers to the generation of revenues in excess of the expenses associated with obtaining the revenues during a given period. The net income listed at the end of the income statement is the "bottom-line" test of how successful the firm's management has been.

   - *Liquidity* is a business's ability to meet its short-term obligations. For example, if a company has tied up all its cash in inventory and equipment, leaving it unable to pay its employees or creditors on time, that company can be forced into bankruptcy.

   - *Efficiency* in business means the efficient use of assets. Efficient use of assets has an impact on profitability, stability, liquidity, and the ability of the enterprise to grow.

   - *Stability* refers to a business's overall financial structure. For example, an owner may wish to invest as little personal money as possible in the firm and finance the operation primarily through loans. If the debt–equity mix is too far out of balance, the firm could go bankrupt should some of the creditors want their money back at an inconvenient time. Many of the spectacular financial disasters reported in the news result from neglecting the goal of stability.

   - *Growth* refers to increasing operations in size or acquiring more assets. Firms will assess financial performance by calculating, for example, how much sales or assets have increased this year over last year. Although there are many widely held concerns about growth in general (for example, the zero population growth movement), business managers and investors remain very interested in prudent financial growth.

   There are no clear-cut guidelines on how much or how little financial performance is adequate or on how to trade off performance on one financial goal in favour of another. For example, a 10 percent sales growth may be poor for a firm in one industry but excellent for a firm in another. Similarly, a high level of liquidity may be preferable to growth for a firm at one time and detrimental for the same firm at another time. Historical financial analysis can be used to assess the company's progress and its achievement of each of these financial goals.

2. The ratios do not look like fractions! Each fraction has been simplified as much as possible.

3. Some ratios are expressed as percentages; others are expressed in days[3]; others are in the form of proportions, and so on. The differences are the result of the varying combinations of numbers used in the fractions.

4. Where possible, each ratio has been calculated over three years. This allows direct comparison of the ratio from year to year and helps to identify changes

in the ratios. A single ratio does not provide much insight into the direction in which a firm is heading.

FINANCIAL GOALS

Financial ratio analysis evaluates the financial performance and condition of a business unit by measuring its progress toward financial goals. The primary goal of a business is to earn a satisfactory return on investment while maintaining a sound financial position. Growth over time may also be a goal in certain businesses, though it is not a prerequisite for achieving acceptable financial performance and position. These broad objectives provide the basis for a financial analyst's evaluation.

Financial analysts assess a firm's progress toward a satisfactory return on investment and sound financial position by focusing on the components of these objectives. Profitability and efficiency/investment utilization are associated with return on investment, whereas liquidity and stability are the key elements of financial position.

Financial position is a financial analyst's term that describes the quality of the balance sheet. A sound financial position is indicated when the balance sheet shows that the business can pay its current debts as they fall due. In addition, the balance sheet should show that the business has used an acceptable level of debt in financing its investments. A sound financial position is important because a business may be forced into bankruptcy if it cannot pay its debts as they become due. A firm that is unable to meet its current obligations is said to be insolvent. The level of debt used by a business is an important consideration, since the fixed payment obligations imposed by debt financing increase the risk of insolvency if a downturn in business activity occurs. As well, a company crippled with debt will likely be unable to raise additional outside funds, so any future decisions will need to include financing plans.

Figure 2 presents an overview of the relationships among these objectives.

FIGURE 2
Financial Goals:
An Overview

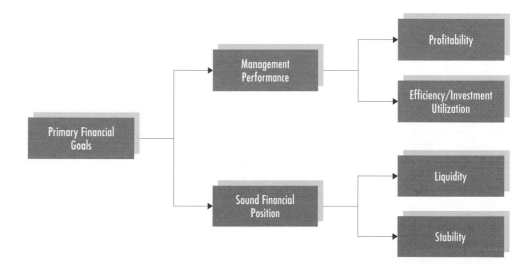

INTERPRETATION OF RATIOS

Ratios are indicators of change and simplify relationships. The ratio does not tell us if the change was good or bad or even why it occurred. Clearly, a ratio changes if the numerator changes, the denominator changes, or both change. In order to understand changes in ratios, the *cause* of that change must be found. In short, a close look at the components of the ratio is required, which will then lead the analyst to investigate the reasons for the change.

CALCULATION OF RATIOS

The mathematics required to calculate the ratios are quite straightforward. In contrast, interpreting the ratios is a complex task. Evaluating ratios is difficult because in many cases there are no precise guidelines as to whether a ratio is favourable or unfavourable. For example, a favourable relationship for one company may be totally unacceptable for a business operating under a different set of conditions. Similarly, a certain relationship for a business may be favourable at one point in time but unacceptable for the same firm at another point in time. Therefore, the financial analyst attempts to find some standard of comparison to determine whether the relationships found are favourable or unfavourable. The two most common standards of comparison are the past performance of the company and the performance of other similar companies operating in the same industry. There are many sources of data for these comparisons. A well-known source of industry norms and key business ratios is Dun & Bradstreet (available at most business libraries). Some of the cases for Part 3 include related industry information for comparison.

MANAGEMENT PERFORMANCE[4]

Profitability

Financial analysts view profitability in two ways: first, as a return obtained from sales activities, and second, as a return generated on capital invested in the business. The first definition of profitability refers to the generation of revenue in excess of the expenses associated with obtaining it. This is a "bottom-line" test of how successful a firm's operations have been, as shown at the bottom of its income statement. Since profits (or incomes) are generated by the use of resources controlled by a business, it is also useful to relate them to the level of capital invested in the firm. This second view of profitability is often a better measure of a firm's operating and financial success, since it relates outputs (income) to inputs (capital).

Financial analysts perform a vertical analysis to measure operating efficiency. Vertical analysis is the restatement of the income statement in percentages, using net sales for the year as the base — that is, 100 percent. The term *vertical* arises from the fact that percentages are calculated on a vertical axis within one year, in contrast to growth ratios, such as sales growth, which make a *horizontal* comparison across several years of statements. The purpose of vertical analysis is to examine the relationship between the level of each item and the firm's sales level.

For example:

$$\text{Cost of goods sold to sales} = \frac{\$ \text{ Cost goods sold}}{\$ \text{ Net sales}} \times 100 = ?\%$$

This ratio indicates the cost of providing the product sold; its complement is the company's "margin":

$$\text{Gross profit or (gross income) to sales} = \frac{\$ \text{ Gross profit}}{\$ \text{ Net sales}} \times 100 = ?\%$$

This ratio measures the percentage of each sales dollar left to pay operating expenses and contribute to profits after paying for cost of goods sold. An increasing gross profit to sales ratio trend may be the result of a reduction in cost of goods sold (through better cost control in a manufacturing firm, more astute buying in a retailing firm, etc.) or the result of an increase in selling prices or both. The opposite is true of a declining trend in gross profit to sales. Because cost of goods sold is usually the major expense associated with obtaining sales revenue, financial managers pay close attention to changes in this ratio. For manufacturing concerns, percentages should be calculated for each component of the cost of goods sold.

The next area of study is the level of operating expenses:

$$\text{Operating expenses to sales} = \frac{\$ \text{ Operating expenses}}{\$ \text{ Net sales}} \times 100 = ?\%$$

This ratio shows the percentage of each sales dollar spent on operating costs. Percentages are usually calculated for individual expense items in order to explain more precisely any changes that have occurred. Once again, movements in these ratios can be explained by one or more factors, including an absolute increase or decrease in the level of the cost incurred, changes in selling price levels, and shifts in the volume of activities undertaken by the firm. Analysts must pay particular attention to this last factor; the ratio of a fixed-cost item (one that does not change with production volume) to net sales will, automatically, decline as volume rises and increase as volume shrinks.

The residual after deducting total operating expenses from gross income is:

$$\frac{\text{Earnings before interest \& taxes (\$)}}{\text{Net sales (\$)}} \times 100 = ?\%$$

This ratio indicates what percentage of each sales dollar is left to cover financing costs, taxes, and profits after meeting all product and operating expenses.

It is preferable to ignore interest in the calculation of the operating expenses to net sales ratio and in the calculation of earnings before interest and taxes to net sales ratio because interest expense is a cost related to the company's financial policy rather than to its operating efficiency. Interest and taxes can then be separately expressed in ratios as a percentage of net sales.

The remaining amount is the company's income (or profit) for the period. Net operating income to net sales, or profit margin, is calculated as follows:

$$\text{Net operating income (profit margin) to net sales} = \frac{\$ \text{ Net operating income}}{\text{Net sales}} \times 100 = ?\%$$

This ratio indicates what percentage of each sales dollar is left after meeting all expenses. The objective is to gain an indication of the change in profit relative to the change in sales. For LMN Retail Company Ltd., two numbers from the income statement are used: net earnings and net sales.

From LMN's income statements (Exhibit 1) earnings declined from $52,000 (in 1998) to $0 (in 1999) and then rose to $35,000 (in 2000). Because sales declined from 1998 to 1999, some decrease in profits could be expected. Did profits decline more or less than sales? That is a hard question to answer without preparing the net earnings to net sales ratio. If both profits and sales had declined simultaneously to the same extent, the relationship between them would have remained the same — that is, the ratio of net earnings to net sales would be constant. From the ratios in Exhibit 5, the analyst can see that the relationship has changed: in 1998, net earnings were 2.4 percent of sales; in 1999, they are 0 percent of sales. In short, earnings declined more than net sales.

On further review of the operating expenses ratios and cost of goods ratios, the factor creating the downward trend is the operating expenses ratios. Despite the decrease in the operating expenses ratios between 1999 and 2000, the analyst may wish to investigate the substantial increase in selling expenses ratios for this same period. A possible explanation is that LMN management, after suffering a decline in sales in 1999, decided to expand sales volume through increased promotion expenses. Additionally, from 1999 to 2000, sales increased, as did the ratio of net earnings to net sales. Seemingly, this increase in the profitability ratio is good; however, this conclusion might be premature. For one thing, other firms in LMN's industry might have performed better. It would be useful to look at a set of industry ratios to check this possibility. For another, maybe LMN was intentionally trading off profitability for some other financial goal, such as growth, in which case the return to profitability at a level below 1998 might be an expected consequence. To verify whether the latter is the case, other ratios must be inspected and the goals of management must be investigated.

Return on Equity

Return on equity (ROE), is the ratio of earnings to shareholders' total investment. (A company's equity section includes the original investment by shareholders and net earnings [after dividends] retained in the company.)

$$\text{Return on equity} = \frac{\$ \text{ Net profit, usually after tax, before dividends}}{\$ \text{ Average year's equity}} \times 100 = ?\%$$

$$\text{Average year's equity} = \frac{\text{Last year's ending equity*} + \text{This year's ending equity}}{2}$$

*The previous year's equity is found on the previous year's balance sheet.

Because there are several ways to calculate return on equity, care should be exercised in using this ratio. Other methods of calculating these components are equally good. It is important to use one method consistently and to identify which method was used. The ratio provides a broad view of management's effectiveness in handling the company's business resources. A satisfactory return on investment compensates investors for the use of their capital and for the riskiness of their investment. To assess ROE, look both at the trend (it is downward for LMN) and at alternative investment returns shareholders might make. For example, if a shareholder is comparing LMN with government bonds, he or she would have to assess the relative returns (returns have been higher for LMN) with the relative risks (risk is much lower with government bonds). If the ROE is the same or less for LMN stock versus government bonds over time, prudent shareholders will invest in the lower-risk bonds. Earning a satisfactory return on investment is fundamental to the existence and survival of every firm, because all businesses must compete against alternative investments for scarce capital resources.

For the LMN shareholders, ROE has been declining from 15.2 percent in 1998 to 9.1 percent in 1999.

Efficiency/Investment Utilization Ratios

A business must invest capital in various resources in order to support its activities. In general, the greater the amount of activity a business undertakes, the greater the required support or investment. For example, consider a business that is operating near capacity and expanding its sales. The sales growth must be supported by a higher level of investment in accounts receivable, inventories, and plant capacity (machinery and equipment). Too little investment in these areas will result in lost opportunities, whereas too much investment means that the excess will be unproductive, providing a very low rate of return. Therefore, a proper balance should exist between sales and the various asset accounts.

Investment utilization ratios measure how well a firm is using its resources. These ratios are derived from both income statement and balance sheet accounts. The intent in each case is to relate the level of an asset to the undertaking of an operating activity. For example, since accounts receivable are generated by credit sales, the level of investment in this asset is viewed in relation to sales activity.

Age of Accounts Receivable
The average age of accounts receivable is calculated in two steps:

1. Calculate the average daily sales:

$$\text{Average daily sales} = \frac{\text{Total period net sales (\$)}}{\text{Number of days in period}} = ? \, \$/\text{day}$$

2. Calculate the number of days of net sales represented by the level of accounts receivable currently outstanding:

$$\text{Age of accounts receivable} = \frac{\text{Accounts receivable (\$)}}{\text{Average daily sales (\$/day)}} = ? \, \text{days}$$

The average daily sales figure (the denominator of the age of accounts receivable ratio) is calculated by dividing total sales for the period by the number of days in the period. For example, the average daily sales for LMN Retail Company Ltd. in 1998 is:

$$\frac{\$2,188,000}{365 \text{ days}} = \$5,995/\text{day}$$

The age of accounts receivable ratio, expressed in days, shows the average number of days' sales that remain uncollected. In other words, on January 31, 1998, LMN averaged 33.4 days' worth of sales for which it had not yet received money. In 1999 and 2000, the sales and accounts receivable amounts changed for LMN. The amount of money LMN had invested in accounts receivable, relative to the period's sales level, declined from about 33 days to 31 days to 27 days. Without applying this ratio analysis, an inspection of the balance sheet (Exhibit 2) may not have revealed the extent of this improvement in the receivables position.

Another way to view the age of accounts receivable ratio is in terms of the average length of time a company must wait after making a credit sale to collect its money. If LMN had credit terms of "due in 10 days," an age of accounts receivable ratio of 30 days indicates poor credit management. The opposite would be true if its terms were "due in 60 days." The greater the age of accounts receivable ratio in days, the more money the firm will need to operate because the company's customers have the extended use of the company's money between the time goods are delivered and the time they are paid for. Conversely, credit terms and collection procedures that are too stringent may drive customers away.

Sometimes, the "average" nature of the age of accounts receivable ratio is misleading because some accounts may be due in the very short term, whereas others are long overdue. One approach to analyzing this problem is to prepare an "aging schedule," which groups the various accounts according to the number of days they have been outstanding. For example, an aging schedule may look like this:

Age	Percentage of Accounts Receivable
0–30 days	60%
31–60 days	30%
Over 60 days	10%

Such a breakdown would give more insight into the reasons for changes in the level or quality of the firm's accounts receivable.

Age of Inventory

The calculation of the average inventory period is a two-step procedure, similar to the process used to calculate average age of accounts receivable:

1. Calculate the average daily cost of goods sold:

$$\text{Average daily cost of goods sold } = \frac{\text{Total period cost of goods sold (\$)}}{\text{Number of days in period}} = \$?/\text{day}$$

2. Calculate the number of days of goods sold represented by the inventory currently on hand:

$$\text{Age of inventory} = \frac{\text{Ending inventory (\$)}}{\text{Average daily cost of goods sold (\$/day)}} = ? \text{ days}$$

Because inventory is valued at cost, the cost of goods sold (the number of units sold times the cost per unit figure, not the sales figure) is used for the calculation. This ratio, expressed in days, measures how quickly merchandise moves through the business — from the date received to the date sold. For example, even though LMN substantially increased its investment in inventory between 1999 and 2000, the flow of inventory to sales improved (85 days to 78 days).

A trend of increasing age of inventory may indicate that the company is carrying excessive inventory for its sales level or that its inventory is becoming obsolete. Higher inventory levels tie up larger amounts of the company's money. Reducing inventory levels will not only release cash that may be used more productively elsewhere, but usually it will also cut down on storage costs, obsolescence, and so on. On the other hand, firms can lose business by not having adequate inventory (known as "stock-outs") available to their customers. Thus, companies try to balance the costs of running out of inventory with the costs of keeping larger inventory levels.

Average Age of Accounts Payable

The average age of accounts payable is also calculated in two steps:

1. Calculate the average daily purchases:

$$\text{Average daily purchases} = \frac{\text{Total period purchases (\$)}}{\text{Number of days in period}} = \$?/\text{day}$$

2. Calculate the number of days of purchases represented by the accounts payable currently owing:

$$\text{Age of accounts payable} = \frac{\text{Accounts payable (\$)}}{\text{Average daily purchases (\$/day)}} = ? \text{ days}$$

The age of accounts payable ratio, expressed in days, shows how long the company is currently taking to pay for what it buys on credit. Compared with industry figures and the terms of credit offered by the company's suppliers, this ratio can indicate whether the company is depending too much on its trade credit. If the age of accounts payable is excessive, creditors may demand repayment immediately (causing acute cash problems for the company), stop supplying the company until it pays for its previous purchases, or place the company on COD (cash on delivery).

Even though stretching the age of accounts payable generates funds for a firm, a bad credit reputation may develop and cost the company dearly in the longer term. In contrast, if the age of payables is very low in comparison with industry practice, it may indicate the company is forgoing a potential source of cash that could be better utilized elsewhere in its operations. LMN has shown a decline in its accounts payable days each year; thus, it appears to be using cash to decrease this liability (perhaps as a direct result of purchase discounts taken by LMN).

Since the purchases figure is often unavailable in condensed financial statements, cost of goods sold or cost of finished goods manufactured may be substituted for the purchases figure. Although doing so will not provide a days figure that is comparable to the firm's credit terms, it does provide a reasonable basis for computing the ratio, since the relationship between cost of sales or cost of finished goods manufactured and purchases would likely be fairly stable in most situations. The variations of the ratio using these substitutions should, therefore, provide the analyst with at least a sense of the direction of accounts payable within the firm.

Good management of accounts payable can save a company money. Many suppliers offer credit terms such as "1/10, net 30," which means that a 1 percent discount will be given if the total invoice is paid within 10 days, and the total bill must be paid within 30 days. The savings made possible by paying 1 percent less within 10 days works out to an annual interest rate of approximately 18 percent.[5] Since bank loan rates are normally less than 18 percent, borrowing to take advantage of such discounts can increase company profits.

Inventory Turnover

An important ratio for examining inventory movement is the inventory turnover ratio. This ratio measures the number of times inventory "turned over," that is, was sold in that operating period. This ratio is calculated by dividing the cost of goods sold for the period by the average level of inventory.

$$\text{Inventory turnover} = \frac{\text{Cost of goods sold (\$)}}{\text{Average inventory (\$)}^*} = \text{? times}$$

*Average inventory = (Beginning inventory + Ending inventory) ÷ 2

The faster goods move through the business, the higher the turnover ratio will be. Although a high inventory turnover is desirable, a rate that is too high may indicate that the firm risks losing sales by not carrying enough inventory to service its customers properly.

Fixed Asset Turnover

The fixed asset turnover ratio measures the amount of investment the firm has tied up in fixed net assets in order to sustain a given level of sales:

$$\text{Fixed asset turnover} = \frac{\text{Net sales (\$)}}{\text{Average net fixed assets (\$)}^*} = \text{? times}$$

* Average net fixed assets = (Beginning net fixed assets + Ending net fixed assets) ÷ 2

This ratio attempts to gauge how efficiently and intensively the firm's net fixed assets are being used. It should be noted, however, that this ratio is strongly influenced by depreciation policies, age of the assets, and whether the firm leases rather than buys certain fixed assets (e.g., vehicles, building). As a result, comparisons between companies, even within the same industry, are difficult. LMN has made increasingly efficient use of fixed assets given the increase in the ratio from 17.9 times to 32.9 times.

Total Asset Turnover

The total asset turnover ratio relates sales to the total assets owned by the firm:

$$\text{Total asset turnover} = \frac{\text{Net sales (\$)}}{\text{Average total assets (\$)}^*} = ? \text{ times}$$

* Average total assets = (Beginning total assets + Eending total assets) ÷ 2

This ratio indicates how well the firm's overall investment is managed relative to the sales volume it supports. LMN's total turnover ratio has improved from 3.1 times in 1998 to 3.6 times in 2000.

Turnover ratios should be interpreted very carefully, since the level of investment in plant and equipment is affected by a firm's depreciation and inventory policies, financing decisions (i.e., lease versus buy, type of financing used), and the purchase date of a company's assets. The inconsistencies make comparisons of different firms' ratios difficult. However, increasing or decreasing trends over time within a particular firm can provide clues to the efficiency with which its assets are being used.

A high total asset turnover ratio is regarded as a good sign. The ratio suggests that for a given sales volume a lower amount of investment will give a better ratio. Too much investment in any asset is undesirable because there is a cost associated with using capital. In addition, a business may be forgoing other better opportunities by having excessive funds tied up in an asset.

Liquidity Ratios

Liquidity refers to a firm's ability to meet its short-term obligations and to the level of rapidly available resources that could be marshalled to meet unexpected needs. Businesses must be able to pay their current liabilities as they become due; otherwise, they could face bankruptcy. There are a number of ways to assess liquidity for a company. Ratio analysis is used to decipher whether liquidity problems appear to exist and whether more complex analysis is warranted.

Current Ratio

The simplest and most common ratio relates all outstanding current assets to current liabilities:

$$\text{Current ratio} = \frac{\text{Total current assets}}{\text{Total current liabilities}} = ?/1$$

The current ratio is a measure of a company's short-term liquidity. It reflects the relative balance between short-term assets and short-term liabilities. In the LMN example, the 1998 current ratio is 2.2/1 (also expressed as 2.2:1), which can be interpreted as $2.20 in current assets for every $1 in current liabilities. The rationale for using this ratio is that a company must meet its short-term obligations with short-term assets. As long as the company has more current assets than current liabilities, there is a margin of safety, which is necessary in case the company must quickly pay off some of its current liabilities.

Every industry has found a different level of current ratio to be appropriate. There are no firm guidelines as to the "right" current ratio for a company. In fact, in some industries, a current ratio of less than 1:1 is desired. Analysts look at a number of factors in determining the adequacy of the ratio. First, they may take into consideration the nature of the company's business. In general, firms with predictable cash flows can afford to have a smaller margin of safety than others. Analysts also look at the composition of the individual current assets and the turnover of the various assets.

The current ratio can be too high as well as too low. If too much money is kept in cash or marketable securities, for example, perhaps it was not used in the business as effectively as it could have been. Enterprises usually earn more from reinvestment in improvements to the business than from the interest earned from a marketable securities investment.

Acid Test Ratio

A second liquidity ratio, the acid test ratio or "quick" ratio, is a more rigorous measure of immediate liquidity. It is calculated as follows:

$$\text{Acid test (quick) ratio} = \frac{\text{Cash + Marketable securities + Accounts receivable (\$)}}{\text{Current liabilities (\$)}} = ?/1$$

The difference between the current and acid test ratios is usually the amount of money invested in inventory. Because inventory is often the least liquid current asset (the most difficult to convert into cash quickly), its inclusion in a liquidity ratio may overstate a company's immediate liquidity. There is no standard to help decide what is an appropriate acid test ratio; for example, an acid test ratio of less than 1:1 ($1 of "quick" assets for every $1 of current liabilities) may still be acceptable, depending on the nature of the industry and the stability of the firm's cash flow.

Working Capital

Another way to assess liquidity is to calculate the total dollar amount of working capital on hand:

$$\text{Working capital = Current assets (\$) – Current liabilities (\$) = \$?}$$

The rationale is that after the firm has enough current assets available to cover its current liabilities, the funds (working capital) left over are available to "work with." With this ratio, too, there are no standards — the amount may vary with the company's size and the nature of its operations. Many managers believe "more is better" since it improves the firm's solvency; however, having more working capital than is needed for operations has a cost (capital is being used, thus there is an interest cost), so many firms will consider optimizing models that maximize the firm's profits and minimize the cost of carrying working capital.[6]

Stability Ratios

Stability refers to a firm's overall financial structure, or the relative amounts of debt and equity on the right-hand side of the balance sheet. Since debt must be repaid, the use of debt capital increases the risk of bankruptcy. Why do firms use debt capital if it increases risk? First, debt financing is typically less expensive than equity capital. Second, the return on ownership capital can be increased if money can be borrowed from others at an interest rate that is lower than the firm's rate of return on assets. This is known as *leverage*. Third, existing owners may want to retain control of a business by limiting ownership investment. As a result, companies attempt to find an optimal financial structure, or balance, between debt and equity financing which is suitable for their objectives and the conditions of the industry in which they are operating.

Stability ratios measure the amount of debt in the firm's financial structure and the company's ability to meet the payment schedules associated with long-term debt. The purpose of these ratios is to help the financial analyst assess the financial risk of the firm (the risks that result from using debt) and the protection afforded to creditors in the event of unprofitable operations.

Net Worth to Total Assets Ratio

The net worth to total asset ratio indicates the proportion of the assets that have been financed by the owners:

$$\text{Net worth to total assets} = \frac{\text{Total shareholders' equity (\$)}}{\text{Total assets (\$)}} \times 100 = ? \%$$

In general, the higher the ratio, the more interested prospective lenders will be in advancing funds. An unfavourable ratio or trend may cause difficulty in raising additional capital, should it be required. Additionally, if the ratio is too low, there is a danger of encouraging irresponsibility by the owners and of leaving inadequate protection for the company's creditors. In general, firms that operate in industries in which the risk of fluctuations in earnings (and hence operating cash flow) is high (e.g., resource industries, high-technology industries) should target higher ratios than firms in industries that exhibit stable earnings patterns (e.g., utilities, grocery stores). For example, the earnings potential of the steel industry is highly dependent on general economic conditions. In an economic recession, steel companies suffer sharp declines in profitability, while an economic boom has the opposite effect on their earnings. Since these firms must cover their fixed payments associated with debt in both good and bad years, they cannot afford to carry too much debt. As a general rule, it is important to look for trends and to seek comparative industry data to assess the appropriateness of this ratio.

Debt to Total Assets Ratio

The total debt to total assets ratio is another way of expressing similar information. Given the fundamental accounting equation (Assets = Liabilities + Equity), this ratio will always be the complement of the net worth calculation just discussed:

$$\text{Total debt to total assets} = \frac{\text{Total liabilities (\$)}}{\text{Total assets (\$)}} \times 100 = ?\%$$

In 1998, LMN's net worth to total assets ratio was 51.7 percent, and its debt to total assets ratio was 48.3 percent. These results may or may not create difficulties for the company if it needs to raise additional debt financing — this will be highly dependent on many factors, such as how the results compare with other companies in the industry. In the future, the company may want to consider increasing the equity position in the company so that it may benefit from further leveraging through debt.

Debt to Equity Ratio

Another ratio often used is the total debt to equity ratio. This ratio measures the extent to which a company's assets are debt financed, relative to investor (owner) financed. In other words, this ratio points to how a company is leveraged (the amount of debt financing of assets relative to equity financing of assets). The higher this ratio, the more highly leveraged the company is, making it less attractive from a creditor's viewpoint, since increased debt relative to equity reduces the creditor's potential claim on the company's assets.

$$\text{Total debt to equity ratio} = \frac{\text{Total debt}}{\text{Equity}}$$

In manageable amounts debt is good, as long as the firm continues to be able to invest funds in assets that yield returns higher than the cost of debt financing. Debt financing allows ownership to be retained and is often less expensive than equity; however, too much debt increases the risk of insolvency.

Interest Coverage Ratio

The interest coverage calculation measures how many times the company's profit (or income) could pay the interest on the debt it owes. This ratio reflects the margin of safety that creditors have in the event of a decline in earnings. The ratio is calculated as follows:

$$\text{Interest coverage} = \frac{\text{Earnings before interest and taxes (\$)}}{\text{Interest expenses (\$)}} = ?\text{ times}$$

To calculate the earnings before interest and taxes, to the net earnings after taxes and interest figure *add back* the income tax expense and the interest expense amounts listed on the company's income statement. The net income before interest and taxes is used because income taxes are calculated after deducting interest expenses. Thus, the ability to pay interest expenses is not affected by income taxes.

A high interest coverage ratio indicates minimal risk for lenders and potential capacity for increasing present loans. If a company cannot cover the interest payments from its operational income, it will need to delve into its cash position and/or liquidate other assets to meet its debt obligations. Failure to meet these debt obligations can cause bankruptcy. An unfavourable trend or a weak comparison with the industry average also may give the company a poor credit rating, impairing its ability to obtain additional debt.[7] For LMN, the interest coverage ratio in 1999 dropped to 1.0 times, just enough to cover the (reduced) interest expense for the same period. This is clearly the result of the poor net income that year.

Growth Ratios

Growth refers to increasing in size or to acquiring more of something. Growth ratios show the percentage increase or decrease in any financial statement item. Growth can be calculated over any period of time, one week or one decade. A businessperson may assess the firm's financial performance by calculating how much sales or assets have increased from one period to the next. This measure of a firm's growth, however, should not be viewed as absolute when assessing a firm's operating and financial success. For example, a business that experiences growth in assets and sales without a corresponding increase in profits would, normally, not be considered a successful enterprise. Moreover, many static but healthy companies exist, which illustrates that growth is not a necessity for every business.

In calculating growth ratios, special care has to be taken in two instances. First, the year 1 position will always be zero, thereby generating a growth ratio of infinity. Second, one or both of the years may have negative figures. The best practice is to treat such situations as undefined and not to report any number. For example, a review of the profit growth ratio from Exhibit 5 for the fiscal year 2000 shows that net earnings grew from zero in 1999 to $35,000 in 2000. The profit growth ratio calculation would require the analyst to divide by zero, yielding a meaningless number. The ratios for LMN in Exhibit 5 are for one-year periods. Growth is expressed as a percentage change from one point in time to another point in time, with the first point in time used as the base.

Sales Growth

Sales growth summarizes the overall activity level of the firm from year to year:

$$\text{Sales growth} = \frac{\text{Year 2 sales (\$)} - \text{Year 1 sales (\$)}}{\text{Year 1 sales (\$)}} \times 100 = \text{?\%}$$

To evaluate the quality of this ratio, the analyst compares the sales growth percentage with related company price increases and the rate of inflation, in order to assess whether a company has truly experienced real growth in volume. In addition, the analyst looks at both the trend over time and the industry growth rates, where available. A well-established firm selling a mature product will demonstrate slower growth than a small, young enterprise introducing new products or entering new markets.

Profit Growth

Profit (income) growth[8] is of great concern to the owners and managers of a business, since it describes the overall efficiency of operations relative to previous periods:

$$\text{Profit growth} = \frac{\text{Year 2 profit (\$)} - \text{Year 1 profit (\$)}}{\text{Year 1 profit (\$)}} \times 100 = ?\%$$

Profit growth may also be assessed with comparisons to the rate of inflation and industry growth rates. As mentioned earlier, profit growth rates may be compared to sales growth rates.

Asset Growth

Asset growth summarizes the change in the level of all resources owned by the firm over the course of the period:

$$\text{Asset growth} = \frac{\text{Year 2 total assets (\$)} - \text{Year 1 total assets (\$)}}{\text{Year 1 total assets (\$)}} \times 100 = ?\%$$

Asset growth normally goes hand in hand with sales growth. If assets are growing significantly and sales are not, it is a sign that something may be wrong. Conversely, substantial sales growth without corresponding asset growth is often a signal that existing resources are becoming more fully utilized and that expansions (e.g., new factory capacity, increased inventories) may have to be undertaken to support continued growth.

In addition to these measures of a firm's performance, potential investors also may wish to evaluate the performance of the company's common stock in the marketplace. Data such as the price earnings multiple, the relationship of the share price to book value per common share, dividend yields, and share price trends may be useful in this context.

The ratios presented in this chapter need not all be calculated to a company's financial statements; instead, they should be viewed as several working tools available to the analyst to paint a picture of the firm's financial strength to date and historical management performance. This thorough understanding of these aspects of the firm will provide the analyst with the necessary foundation on which effective future business decision making can be based.

LMN Retail — Summary

The financial ratio analysis of LMN reveals a basically healthy company despite a decline in both sales and profitability in 1999. The firm's return on investment (ROI) has been erratic throughout the three years, primarily owing to sales fluctuations. A closer examination of the vertical analysis points to an increasing trend in selling expenses, with all other items remaining relatively constant throughout the three-year period. The investment utilization ratios are improving each year. The liquidity ratios indicate that the company's position is sound (given that this is a retail operation, the acid test of less than 1:1 is of little concern, assuming the inventory is resaleable). The stability ratios show that credits are fairly well protected and, as of January 31, 2000, the company can readily meet its interest payment obligations. The growth ratios reflect a period of decline from 1998 to 1999; however, from 1999 to 2000, growth resumed.

LIMITATIONS OF FINANCIAL RATIO ANALYSIS

Financial analysis can be an extremely powerful tool. It does, however, have a number of limitations.

1. Financial ratio analysis deals primarily with the assessment of quantitative data. The analyst should keep in mind that financial analysis, like other decision-making tools, involves the assessment of both *qualitative* and *quantitative* data.

2. The standards of comparison used by the financial analyst are imperfect. For example, a comparison between past and present performance may tell the analyst whether the company's position is better or worse, or whether the trend in the relationship is upward or downward. However, it provides no true indication of what an acceptable ratio actually would be, nor does it necessarily follow that any trends will continue into the future. The analyst must use common sense, experience, and other information to draw conclusions from the patterns suggested by the numbers.

3. Comparisons involving external standards may be invalid if the situations being compared are different. One common problem is that few companies, even within the same industry, are similar enough to facilitate good comparisons. Attributes such as sizes, product lines, customers, and suppliers, to name but a few, can represent significant differences. As well, it would be difficult to draw precise conclusions from a comparative analysis of companies using different accounting practices, since the accounting methods used have an effect on the ratios. Similarly, a comparison of ratios between companies may be misleading because of differences in fiscal year-end (especially in seasonal industries) or differences in the acquisition dates of long-lived assets. As a result, analysts must attempt, whenever possible, to make at least crude adjustments for significant differences before making comparisons.

4. Many common ratios have a number of different definitions or methods of calculation, creating the potential for confusion. By labelling ratios clearly, the financial analyst can attempt to reduce any possible ambiguity that may arise.

5. Comparisons of past and present performance can be misleading, since conventional financial accounting records are not adjusted for price level changes. For example, consider a firm that is raising prices to keep pace with inflation but that is not experiencing any real growth in sales. Other things being equal, the company's fixed asset turnover ratio will tract upward, giving the analyst a false signal of improvement.

6. Financial ratios may be biased if a firm is experiencing rapid growth or is in a state of decline. For example, the average age of receivables ratio will be overstated for growing firms. To understand this distortion, consider the method used to derive average daily sales (the denominator of the average age of receivables ratio). Average daily sales are based on sales experience over the entire period under consideration. As a result, in a situation of extremely rapid growth the average will be understated relative to present sales experience (i.e., the most recent weeks or months). If the denominator of the ratio is understated, it follows that the ratio itself will be overstated. Financial analysts must make allowances for this type of discrepancy.

7. Most important, since financial ratios are based on historical information, they reflect past relationships only. These patterns may or may not continue into the future. As a result, the financial analyst must make predictions about future relationships carefully. Good financial analysts view a past relationship merely as one possible guideline for making projections.

Although financial ratio analysis has several inherent limitations, the technique can provide a great deal of information for decision makers. The quality of the information provided is directly related to the thoughtfulness exercised when performing the analysis.

SUMMARY

When undertaking a financial investigation, the first task of the financial analyst is to identify the types of financial ratio analysis that would be useful for a particular type of investigation. Different types of investigations require different forms of financial analysis. For example, a banker investigating the possibility of extending a line of credit to a business would be concerned primarily with the firm's short-run, debt-paying ability. A financial analysis focusing on the liquidity of the business would be relevant for this investigation. In contrast, a potential investor may be interested in the long-run performance of a business. In this case, an analysis concentrating on profitability and growth may be of most interest.

The second task is to broadly size up the company and the industry in which the firm operates. This overview should include factors such as the size of the industry, nature of product groupings and market segments, competitors, seasonality, stage in the product life cycle, susceptibility to general economic conditions, production strategy, and technological factors. Such an overview will provide much of the perspective necessary to make sense of the ratios being generated. As well, the notes to the financial statements should be scanned and significant accounting policies should be observed.

After identifying the relevant areas of analysis, the analyst can perform the quantitative aspects of the analysis. This third step of "number crunching" in financial analysis rarely provides answers. Rather, it suggests questions that need to be answered. As a result, the analyst's investigation is never complete until a fourth stage has been undertaken. Using the ratio data plus other qualitative information about the industry, the analyst attempts to draw conclusions and implications that will aid in making better decisions.

PROJECTED FINANCIAL STATEMENTS

Every financial statement reviewed so far reflects past performance or position, but in order to plan future operations, anticipation of future performance or position is required. Statements prepared in anticipation of the future are called *projected* or *pro forma* statements. There are three basic reasons for preparing projected statements:

1. To forecast financial performance or position (e.g., what will profit likely be next year?);
2. To examine the interrelationship of financial policies with changes in marketing and production policies (e.g., if sales double, how much more money will be required in inventory investment?); and
3. To forecast cash needs, debt needs, capacity to expand operations, and others (e.g., how large will the bank loan have to be six months from now?).

Projections can be made if enough information is available to prepare meaningful estimates of future performance and position. However, *a projected statement is only as good as the estimates, assumptions, and judgments that went into its preparation.* Three sources of information can be used to prepare projected statements:

1. Managers' estimates (e.g., a sales forecast);
2. Past financial relationships (e.g., financial ratios of previous years); and
3. Assumptions as to what might occur.

It is important to explain the source of every number on a projected statement, usually with footnotes that outline the basis of the calculations. For example, a footnote for an inventory estimate may be as follows:

> Inventory calculated on the basis of 35 days average daily cost of goods sold. The age of inventory during the previous 5 years ranged between 30 and 40 days.

There are two basic types of projected statements. One is a projection based on the assumption that management will continue to follow past financial policies. The objective of this approach is to show what would happen if this were so. The other type of projection is based on a suggested set of changes. The objective of this approach is to show the likely impact on future performance and position if these changes were followed. These two approaches are often mixed in practice.

PROJECTED INCOME STATEMENT

Always begin a set of projected statements with the income statement, followed by the statement of retained earnings and then the balance sheet. This order is important because certain balance sheet accounts, such as inventory, accounts receivable, and accounts payable, are based on the projected income statement and statement of retained earnings figures. Also, it is pointless to estimate the change in retained earnings on the balance sheet before attempting to project net income on the income statement.

The following guidelines may be useful when projecting the income statement:

1. Estimating a new sales volume is the first and most important step. Use managers' estimates and/or past growth trends as guidelines.

2. Use the profitability ratio analysis to estimate cost of goods sold, gross profit, and operating expenses. Modify these estimates for new information or for a developing trend.

3. Choose the extent of detail in the operating expenses section according to the quality of the information available and the objectives of preparing the projected income statement.

4. Prepare more than one projected income statement when appropriate. For example, if sales volume estimates vary significantly, statements based on a high, reasonable, or low projected sales volume may prove useful.

Exhibit 6 outlines a projected income statement for fiscal 2001 for LMN Retail Company Ltd. Included in the exhibit is the basis of the estimate. Note that the first step is estimating sales. The general manager of LMN, given his promotion plans, the economic potential in his region, and inflation rates, expected a 20 percent growth rate in sales over the previous fiscal year. In reviewing the cost of goods sold from his ratio analysis, the general manager believed that he could maintain the previous fiscal year's performance; that is, cost of goods sold would be 77.5 percent of sales. The complement, gross profit, would be 22.5 percent of sales. In reviewing his control of expenditures in the past year, the general manager felt that he could maintain general and administrative expenses at 8.8 percent of sales, and he intended to spend a fraction less on promotion, making a total of 10 percent of sales on selling expenses. Because there would be no purchases or dispositions of the equipment and store fixtures, the general manager expected no change in the depreciation charges in fiscal 2001. With regard to other expenses, such as interest, he was not certain how much to set aside, but he decided to allow 0.3 percent of sales, which was in line with past trends. The tax rate was given to him by his accountant.

Exhibit 6

LMN Retail Company Ltd.
Projected Income Statement
for the Year Ending January 31, 2001
(in 000s of dollars)

Item	Basis of Estimate	Amount
Sales	20% growth from 2000[1]	$3,258
Cost of goods sold	77.5% of sales[2]	2,525
Gross profit	Sales – Cost of goods sold	$ 733
Operating expenses:		
General and administrative	8.7% of sales[1]	$ 283
Selling	10% of sales[1]	326
Depreciation	same as 2000[1]	35
Subtotal		644
Net operating income		$ 89
Other expenses	0.3% of sales[1]	10
Net income, before tax		$ 79
Taxes	25% of net profit before tax[3]	20
Net earnings		$ 59

1. Manager's estimate.
2. Last year's best estimate.
3. Supplied by accountant.

The determination of the income statement, after the assumptions have been made, is nothing more than an exercise in arithmetic. The key judgment is whether the analyst agrees with the assumptions and their implications. No two projected statements are likely to be identical: individuals tend to use different assumptions about the future and, consequently, to have different balancing figures. At this point, it may be helpful to review the assumptions outlined in Exhibit 6 with the financial ratios provided in Exhibit 5 and reach your own conclusions as to the reasonableness of the projected income statement.

PROJECTED BALANCE SHEET

Preparing a projected balance sheet is usually more difficult than preparing a projected income statement. The main reason for this is that there is no one key account, such as sales on the income statement, that helps determine many others on the balance sheet. Generally, each balance sheet account must be calculated separately. Here are a few guidelines:

1. Begin by deciding what the balancing account will be (usually cash or bank loan payable).
2. Fill in all the accounts that will probably remain the same (e.g., land will be the same if none is to be bought or sold).
3. Fill in the accounts already calculated. For example, retained earnings will change in accordance with the estimated income from the projected income statement and in accordance with any plans for dividend payments to shareholders. The inventory account and accumulated depreciation accounts can also be adjusted once the projected income statement is complete.
4. Calculate the remaining accounts. Usually, a good way to begin is by using averages or trends of previous years' ratios and then adjusting these as needed. For example, assume the estimated sales for next year were $3,258,000 and, based on an average of the historical trends, the age of accounts receivable was expected to be 30 days. All but one component of the formula used to calculate age of accounts receivable, accounts receivable total dollar amount, is known. Solve the formula to determine an estimate of this missing number.

$$\text{Age of accounts receivable} = \frac{\text{Accounts receivable (\$)}}{\frac{\text{Sales (\$)}}{365}}$$

$$\text{Therefore, 30 days} = \frac{\text{Accounts receivable (\$)}}{\frac{\$3,258,000}{365 \text{ days}}}$$

$$\begin{aligned}\text{Accounts receivable} &= 30 \text{ days} \times \$8,926 \text{ per day} \\ &= \$267,780\end{aligned}$$

Therefore, estimated accounts receivable is $268,000. A similar process using the appropriate formula and estimates can be used to estimate ending inventory and accounts payable balances.

5. Calculate the balancing figure — the number that makes the balance sheet balance. A balancing figure is needed for any projected balance sheet. Seldom can each account on each statement be projected in such a way as to make the statement balance. As mentioned earlier, it is common when projecting a balance sheet to leave either "cash" or "bank loan payable" until the end and then to insert a number that makes the balance sheet balance.

Exhibit 7 presents a projected balance sheet as of January 31, 2001, based on stated assumptions, for LMN Retail Company Ltd. In this projection, the general manager decided to maintain a minimum cash balance of $15,000 and to "plug" the balancing loan figure for notes payable — bank. The manager reviewed the ratio analysis and determined the assumptions as set out. With regard to fixed assets, the general manager planned to invest $35,000 in new equipment during the year, and after considering depreciation expense of $35,000 for the period, there would be no net change in the fixed asset account. Initially, the manager planned to pay off the long-term debt. Again, *note the key role that judgment plays in the development of an appropriate assumption*. The determination of the remaining amounts for the accompanying balance sheet accounts is a matter of arithmetic calculation. The reader should verify the calculations, noting that the calculations have been rounded to the closest $1,000. The balance sheet equation (Assets = Liabilities + Equity) must be used to determine the bank loan, that is, the plug figure. Before calculating the plug figure, the assets total $916,000, and equity totals $461,000. This means that the total liabilities must equal $455,000. There are no long-term liabilities to be deducted, meaning total current liabilities must equal $455,000. From this total of $455,000, $248,000 in current liabilities, which include accounts payable, taxes payable, and accrued expenses, are already projected. This means that the only other current liability available, notes payable — bank, must provide the residual amount of $207,000 in order for the balance sheet to balance.

In this case, the interpretation of the balancing figure was fairly straightforward. However, if it was assumed that the cash was used as the balancing figure and the bank loan was set at $70,000, what would the resulting balance showing in the cash account be? In this case, the sum of all (current and long-term) liabilities and equity would need to be calculated. The current liabilities are accounts payable, $216,000; bank loan, $70,000; taxes payable, $12,000; and accrued expenses, $20,000; yielding a total of $318,000. To this total, add long-term liabilities of zero and the total equity of $461,000, giving a total of $779,000. This, then, would be the figure for total assets needed to balance the balance sheet. Since net fixed assets total $80,000, the total current assets should be $699,000. However, the current asset section already includes assets worth $821,000, the sum of net accounts receivable and inventory. To balance, cash would have to equal *negative* $122,000. Negative cash is a bank overdraft, indicating an additional loan in the amount of $122,000 is needed and must be added to the $70,000 note payable — bank.

Sometimes, you may find that if you use a bank loan as a plug, it is negative. How do you interpret this? Since this is the only way to balance the two sides of the balance sheet, it means that the company has no need for a bank loan; in fact, the company has an additional $30,000 in cash for use.

EXHIBIT 7

	LMN Retail Company Ltd. Projected Balance Sheet as at January 31, 2001 (in 000s of dollars)	
Item	Basis of Estimate	Amount
ASSETS		
Current assets:		
Cash	Minimum equal to 2000 level[1]	$ 15
Net accounts receivable	30 days sales[2]	268
Inventory	80 days cost of goods sold[2]	553
Total current assets		$836
Fixed assets, net	No change[3]	80
TOTAL ASSETS		$916
LIABILITIES		
Current liabilities:		
Accounts payable	30 day purchases[4]	$216
Notes payable — bank	Plug or balancing figure	207
Taxes payable	No change[3]	12
Accrued expenses	No change[3]	20
Total current liabilities		$455
Long-term liabilities	Paid off[3]	0
Total liabilities		$455
EQUITY		
Common stock	No change[1]	$ 37
Retained earnings	2000 plus 2001 net earnings	424
Total equity		$461
TOTAL LIABILITIES AND EQUITY		$916

1. Manager's estimate.
2. Manager's estimate from ratios.
3. Last year's level, best estimate.
4. Projected purchases equal cost of goods sold plus increased inventory
   ($2,525 000 + [$553,000 − $450,000]) = $2,628,000).

SUMMARY

In the preceding example, the general manager should review the projected statements to see whether they make sense and to draw conclusions. One obvious observation is that if he is successful in gaining the $207,000 loan, the provision he has made in his projected income statement for interest expense of $10,000 will be insufficient. A second concern would be that his plans call for a 92 percent increase of the current bank loan. Finally, while the return on equity is 13 percent, a substantial increase from the fiscal 2000 levels can be accomplished only with the bank's commitment to an increase in the business and may not compensate for the risk involved.

One thing to remember is that no projected statement is "right." The analysis can, and often should, continue to try new possibilities to see "what would happen if…." This is often referred to as a sensitivity analysis which is discussed in the next section.

■
SECTION
■
FIVE
■

SENSITIVITY ANALYSIS

The accuracy of projected statements hinges on the assumptions that go into their development. Sensitivity analysis illustrates how different sets of assumptions made about specific revenues, expenses, assets, and liabilities may have an impact on the "base case" projected statements. Performing this analysis allows business decision makers to account for uncertainty and to make more fully informed decisions.

PERFORMING SENSITIVITY ANALYSIS

The following guidelines can be used to perform sensitivity analysis:

1. Choose the assumption(s) you plan to vary. These may be internal factors that the company controls or external factors which the company does not control.
2. Revise your assumption(s), making other reasonable assumption(s).
3. Recalculate the appropriate accounts for the projected statements.
4. Reconstruct the projected statements with the new assumption(s) and determine the effect on key accounts (required financing, net income).
5. Use this additional information to supplement your original conclusions.

Consider the following example in Table 2.

Table 2: Company X Historical Ratio Analysis

	1996	1997	1998	1999	Industry Average
Accounts receivable days	60	65	68	70	65
Accounts payable days	72	70	72	71	67
Inventory days	95	94	95	96	96

The manager of Company X would like to begin paying her suppliers within 65 days, and she believes that this can be financed by tightening her company's credit policies and demanding that customers pay their accounts within 60 days. These goals would dictate the assumptions used when projecting financial statements for fiscal 2000.

After projecting statements using this base case scenario, sensitivity analysis examines the possibility that the manager's goals do not materialize. What if she finds that by tightening credit policies, she begins to lose customers to the competition? If this were to occur, credit policies would need to return to industry levels, and, as a result, the decrease in accounts payable days could not be financed. Because this possibility is likely, the manager should perform sensitivity analysis to view the effect on the need for external financing with accounts receivable days at 65, the industry average, and also at 68, reflecting past company trends. Accounts payable days should also be altered to 70 and 72, given past trends. If there is no reason to believe that an account will change, there is no need to perform sensitivity analysis on the account: such is the case with inventory.

After deciding which accounts may vary and to what degree, the changes to financing can be easily calculated. Given a sales level of $1,000,000 and a purchases level of $220,000, the changes to the original required financing amount of $150,000 are shown in Table 3.

When accounts receivable days are increased, customers are taking longer to pay the company; as a result, the need for financing increases. This financing can be generated in a number of ways, two of which include generating monies internally by taking a longer time to pay suppliers or by seeking external financing from the bank. In this example, only the effect of an increase in accounts receivable days on external financing has been tested, and we see that it rises dramati-

Table 3: Accounts Receivable

Assumption Age of Accounts Receivable	Required Accounts Receivable Amount	Change in required Financing (Plug)[1]	Required Financing (Plug)
60 days	$164,384[2]	0	$150,000
65 days	$178,082[3]	$13,698	$163,698
68 days	$186,301	$21,917	$171,917

1. Change in required financing = Change in asset assumption from original estimate
= New estimate − Original estimate
2. Value from projected balance sheet using original estimate of 60 days accounts receivable.
3. Accounts receivable = Days accounts receivable × Average daily sales
= 65 days × ($1,000,000 / 365 days)

cally. A further analysis of what would happen to the need for external financing if the days of accounts payable are increased is shown in Table 4.

Table 4: Accounts Payable

Assumption Age of Accounts Payable	Required Accounts Payable Amount	Change in Required Financing (Plug)	Required Financing (Plug)
65 days	$39,178[1]	0	$150,000
70 days	$42,192[2]	– $3,014	$146,986
72 days	$43,397	– $4,219	$145,781

1. Value from projected balance sheet using original estimate of 65 days accounts payable.
2. Accounts payable = Days accounts payable × Average daily purchases
   = 70 days × ($220,000 / 365 days)

When accounts payable days are increased, the company is taking a longer time to pay its suppliers, and money is retained for a longer period of time, which decreases the need for external financing.

Why, with a similar degree in variance, have we seen a much smaller change in the need for financing in the second example? This has occurred because the dollar amount for purchases is much less than the dollar amount for sales, creating a less dramatic shift in its corresponding required financing (plug) balance sheet account.

If the manager believes that the change in the two accounts will occur simultaneously, the two changes in required financing should be combined to view the cumulative effect. In this instance, if the company was forced to keep its accounts receivable days at 1997 levels to retain customers and, as a result, increased its accounts payable days to 70 days, the combined effect would be an $18,903 increase over the original estimate of external financing needed.[9]

Upon reviewing this data, a bank manager would have to decide whether to grant the increased funds in the event that the situation illustrated with sensitivity analysis occurs. Sensitivity analysis also aids in establishing convenants on the loan. For example, in this case, if the company extended its accounts receivable days any further, it would require a larger loan. If the bank manager is not comfortable financing this, a condition that the company's accounts receivable must be kept to a level below 68 days may be stipulated.

DECIDING WHICH ASSUMPTIONS TO TEST

The accounts most often critical to sensitivity analysis are accounts receivable, inventory, and accounts payable.[10] These are important accounts to test for sensitivity for two reasons: the management of a company has a great degree of control over these accounts, and these accounts often represent the majority of the company's working capital funds.

There are no set rules or standards for other assumptions to test. It is not necessary to test all of the aforementioned accounts for sensitivity in every case. As a guide, only those assumptions that are apt to vary and that have a significant impact on key accounts in the statements need to be tested. In summary, testing sensitivity is important if an account has fluctuated significantly in the past and if the initial assumption represents some uncertainty as to what will actually happen.

INTERPRETING SENSITIVITY ANALYSIS

The numbers generated in the sensitivity analysis provide "what if" scenarios and sometimes help an analyst ensure that the best assumptions have been made. If the amount requested by the company is very different from the required financing generated by the analyst's original set of projected statements, one possible explanation is that the assumptions the analyst used did not accurately reflect what the company expected to happen. In this case, the analyst should consider the validity of the other set of assumptions rather than the original set. However, if it is apparent from the discrepancy between the analyst's projected financing needs and the company's projected financing needs that the company is being unrealistic about its expectations, then it is up to the lender to convince the company's management to use more realistic assumptions.

In many cases, financial analysts use these numbers to provide financial advice to companies. For example, a loans officer[11] may recommend that a company decrease its accounts payable to take advantage of discounts offered for early payment, even though this action will mean that the company requires more financing than initially requested. In other instances, a bank may recommend that a company control its inventory levels better to reduce the financing needed from the bank, or that a company consider introducing strict collection policies to reduce the days of accounts receivable in order to decrease the amount of required financing.

In some cases, a bank may put restrictions on the loan based on the sensitivity analysis. For example, a company has a days of inventory figure that has been volatile in the past but that is currently at 50 days, resulting in required financing of $100,000 from the bank. If the bank does not want to lend the company any more than $100,000, it may lend the company money on the condition that the days of inventory not exceed 50. To ensure these conditions are met, the bank will likely request and monitor quarterly statements from the company.

SECTION

SIX

CREDIT

When customers can purchase goods or services without paying cash immediately, they are buying "on credit." Credit is commonplace in today's business environment for both the seller and the buyer. Consumers use credit cards; firms purchase from suppliers on credit; banks lend short-term money to help companies or individuals. Attractive credit terms can increase a firm's sales by keeping present customers and attracting new ones.

Credit is riskier and more expensive than cash operations. The decision to offer credit means the credit-granting company must also be ready to accept the risk that some customers will fail to pay their debts. Credit management attempts to differentiate good-risk customers from poor-risk ones. Credit managers[12] evaluate a loan request by examining the company's ability to pay back the loan. This evaluation includes an analysis based on business conditions, character, the capacity to repay, and the company's past and projected future performance. These characteristics are often referred to as the "four Cs of Credit": business conditions, character, capacity to repay, and collateral. The principles of credit analysis apply to bank loans, supplier credit, applications for charge accounts, and numerous other instances where credit is involved.

BUSINESS CONDITIONS

There are many external factors beyond a company's control that will affect the company's operations. These business conditions include current or pending legislation (which could drastically affect the operation of a firm), economic conditions (such as current interest rates, seasonal and cyclical sales patterns, growth and profit potential, and competitive conditions), social trends (such as changes in market and in customer buying behaviour), and technological changes (such as innovations) — all of which are important indicators of a firm's likely success within an industry. Credit officers and bankers often assess what any firm operating within the context of its industry must do to succeed and whether a specific firm will be able to meet these requirements.

CHARACTER

An important consideration is the character of the borrower. Past credit records are good indicators of a firm's (or an individual's) chances and inclinations for paying liabilities. The marketing, production, and financial expertise of the management are critical to the success of a corporation. "Character," therefore, involves not only the trustworthiness of the borrower, but also the capacity to achieve operating goals.

CAPACITY TO REPAY

We have learned that ratio analysis provides insight into the firm's past financial performance and that projected statements highlight the firm's future financial position. In analyzing a company's ability to repay the needed financing, calculating ratios based on projections is necessary. There are three ratios best suited to do this: the interest coverage, current, and acid test ratios. Often there are other considerations, as well:

- Where multiple years of projections have been completed, it may be useful to see if the loan is increasing or decreasing in the second year of projections. If it is increasing, the payback outlook is unfavourable, and it is necessary to examine why this increase is occurring and whether it is likely to change in the future.
- If you know the firm's credit history, it may be helpful to review how the company has repaid its debt in the past.
- If repayment seems doubtful in the near term, the analyst will review the projected stability and return on equity ratios to ascertain whether the company can gain longer-term debt or equity financing.

After this comprehensive review, a comfort level with the company's capacity to repay can be factored into the decision. Depending on the risk the lender is willing to accept, the ratios and projections may indicate the need for securing a loan against the possibility of default or bankruptcy. Restrictions on future borrowing or further capital investment also may be necessary. These methods of protection help ensure the lender of a higher likelihood of repayment.

COLLATERAL

There is always the possibility that a company will default on its loan (meaning the credit loan is not repaid in full or in the time specified). For this reason, banks seek protection in the event of a default in the form of collateral, which refers to assets pledged against the loan. Collateral is the lender's last resort of collection and is used only when there is no hope of loan repayment to the lender through normal business operations.

Collateral analysis determines how much of the outstanding loan issued could be retrieved through the liquidation of assets if the borrower were to declare bankruptcy[13] and become unable to pay the lender some or all of its outstanding debt. To determine this value, the lender assesses the borrower's current assets and any assets that would be purchased with the loan, and forecasts an actual amount of money the lender would likely receive in the event of bankruptcy.

Many terms, such as *secured, assigned,* and *mortgaged* also refer to assets that are pledged against money owing. *Mortgage* is the term applied to an assignment of immovable property, while *chattel mortgage* is a pledge against moveable property. For most secured business loans, a *floating charge* is applied. A floating charge is a charge against all assets in a category, whether owned currently or in the future.

Creditors who are secured recognize that they rank ahead of all claimants to the company's assets. However, the creditor's willingness to accept certain assets as collateral varies according to the lender and the loan situation. The realizable value of collateral varies with the selling and collecting skills of the lender, the state of the economy, and the saleability of the asset. Although lenders take collateral, their main protection against default is the capability of the borrower's management. As a firm sinks into bankruptcy, the value of the borrower's assets deteriorates significantly. The best security against loan default is, of course, a well-run company in a prosperous industry. However, when the borrower declares bankruptcy, it a clear indication that there is little possibility of loan repayment, and the borrower's collateral becomes the bank's only hope of collection for the outstanding loan amount.

It is important to note that although collateral analysis is an important tool in assessing the attractiveness of a potential customer, it is only one of a collection of tools used to determine whether credit will be granted.

Assessing Collateral Availability

Most lenders use an in-house computer software program designed to perform a collateral analysis. The contents of these programs mirror the chart shown in Exhibit 8 and have similar specific headings listing the asset, its value, the identified liquidation factor expressed as a percentage, and the resulting asset's realizable value.

Exhibit 8

Collateral Analysis Worksheet			
Asset	Value	Factor %	Realizable Value

Total Realizable Value:

Value of New Loan:
Previous Loans Outstanding with Our Bank:
Total Amount Owed to Our Bank:

Excess Collateral Available:

The following are the steps a bank would typically perform in the collateral process:

1. Set up (or access) a chart with the specific headings.
2. Refer to the most recent balance sheet provided by the borrower. Projected statements would be used only if there is going to be a drastic change in the

balance sheet; for example, if there will be a change of ownership, considering the projected balance sheet may be more beneficial.

3. Identify those assets not available as collateral to the lender because they are already secured by another creditor (these cannot be secured again).

4. Assume there will be no cash left over in the company if the borrower has declared bankruptcy; however, marketable securities may be available to secure as collateral.

5. List all remaining assets in the "asset column" of the collateral chart. If the borrower is requesting the loan in order to buy a new asset, such as a building or a specific piece of equipment, that asset will also be listed under the "asset column" (at its purchase value).

6. List the value of each of the assets in the "value column" of the chart. These data are collected directly from the borrower's balance sheet. Fixed assets will be listed at their net value — historical cost less the accumulated depreciation to date. If the depreciation amount is unknown, the bank will use the asset's original purchase price but with a lower factor value when calculating the asset's realizable value.

7. Set a "factor value" for each asset. When multiplied by the value of the asset, a factor value will determine the realizable value of that asset — that is, the amount of money the bank can reasonably expect to collect once that asset has been liquidated in a bankruptcy situation. The following is a list of suggested factor values for common assets. The creditor will always exercise judgment when assigning factor values, and the list below should be used only as a general guide.

Assets

	Factor Value
Marketable Securities	0%–100%

The evaluation of marketable securities will vary considerably with the type of investment. A high-risk stock, for example, will be assigned a low factor value, whereas a secure investment, such as government Treasury bills, will be assigned a factor value of 100 percent.

	Factor Value
Accounts Receivable	60%–90%

The assessment of accounts receivable depends on both the nature of the customers who owe the money and the age (how long the debt has been outstanding) of the account. For example, the factor value may be higher if the borrower's accounts receivable is made up of customers, such as banks or governments, where payment history is reliable and the likelihood of fully collecting monies is high.

	Factor Value
Inventory	25%–60%

The amount of cash that will be recovered from inventory is highly dependent on the goods themselves. If the inventory has strong marketability — that is, the asset can be easily sold — then a higher factor value will be assigned. For example, an inventory consisting of hula hoops will be assigned a much lower factor value than an inventory consisting of raw steel because raw steel has much greater marketability.

Work-in-process inventory (raw materials only partially transformed into finished saleable form) frequently receives a 0 percent factor value, since it is considered virtually unsaleable.

	Factor Value
Machinery, Equipment, Furniture	25%–50%

Again, the marketability is considered when evaluating these assets. For instance, a standard pick-up truck would be easier to sell than one which has been customized to suit the specific needs of a particular company.

	Factor Value
Land and Building	Varies

Land and building must always be secured as a package because a mortgage is a lien against real property, which is defined as land and everything permanently attached to that land. When determining a factor value, the creditor must evaluate each case separately and consider many factors. Poor economic times and high vacancy rates can dictate a low factor value for commercial property. In some cases, the property value of the land may have increased drastically since the date of purchase; therefore, the purchase price on the balance sheet may be significantly lower than what it could sell for today, resulting in the lender's estimating this asset at more than 100 percent of its book value.

8. The lender will then multiply the asset's deemed value by the factor value to calculate the realizable value of each asset.

9. Once the total realizable value of the company's assets is calculated, the lender will compare this value to the total amount of money being requested. The total amount of money being requested should include the amount currently being requested plus any outstanding loan amounts to the same lending institution.

10. In the case of small businesses or start-ups, banks will also consider securing personal assets of the owner(s) as collateral.

ANALYZING THE COLLATERAL SITUATION

Banks next compare the total realizable value of the assets with the total loan amount requested. If the total realizable value is more than the amount requested, it appears the borrower has sufficient assets available for collateral if bankruptcy occurs. It is also important to look at the individual assets available for collateral, since a lender usually attempts to match the collateral secured with the term of the loan: accounts receivable and inventory assignments will be used as collateral for short-term loans, and fixed assets (mortgages) for medium- and long-term loans.

If the assets available to secure as collateral do not cover the amount being requested, the lender will want to review the previous collateral analysis, evaluate the likelihood of the borrower's bankruptcy and how it will affect repayment of the loan, and possibly deny the loan request. Alternatively, the lender may secure as much collateral as possible and leave the balance of the loaned funds unsecured. In this situation, the lender assumes a greater risk of not collecting the loan amounts if bankruptcy occurs.

Lenders may choose not to secure collateral if there appears to be little risk in providing the loan. However, if lenders decide to secure assets as collateral, they must determine the specific assets they will secure. Banks are always aware of the need to balance the risk of lending a customer money with the provision of good service to that customer. For instance, if the lender wants to secure too many assets as collateral, a customer may seek a better arrangement with another lending institution. Astute lenders understand that customers are reluctant to pledge more assets as collateral than absolutely necessary, since a borrower who has pledged most assets as collateral to one lending institution will have trouble securing loans with other institutions in the future.

SOURCES AND TYPES OF FINANCING

There are several sources of financing. The costs, availability, and conditions must be analyzed for each source in order to obtain the right "fit" for the firm. Financing sources can be categorized into three maturities: short term, medium term, and long term. The cost of financing varies directly with the investor's perception of the risk of financing.

SHORT-TERM FINANCING

Enterprises can obtain short-term financing from trade creditors, chartered banks, factor companies, and the short-term money market. Short-term financing is usually for a period of less than one year.

Trade credit refers to purchasing goods or services from suppliers on credit. It appears on the balance sheet as accounts payable. The buyer is allowed a period of time, usually 30 or 60 days, in which to pay for the goods or services received. To encourage prompt payments of credit sales, sellers often offer a discount from the invoiced amount if total payment is made within 10 days of billing. If the purchaser cannot pay the account within the given period, the creditor often will charge an interest penalty.

The Canadian chartered banks are another important source of short-term financing. Demand loans with a "line of credit" are the most common type of credit given by banks. A line of credit means the bank can arrange for an individual or a company to borrow up to an agreed sum over a certain period of time. This helps companies with seasonal products that may experience cash shortages in the off-season. The borrower is charged a rate of interest for demand notes and a fee for the unused portion of the line of credit. However, a bank can demand repayment of these demand loans at any time. Most lines of credit work under the assumption that the borrower will "clear" the line of credit at least once during the company's operating period. Figure 3 shows a hypothetical example of a line of credit being reduced to zero.

FIGURE 3
Line of Credit
Behaviour

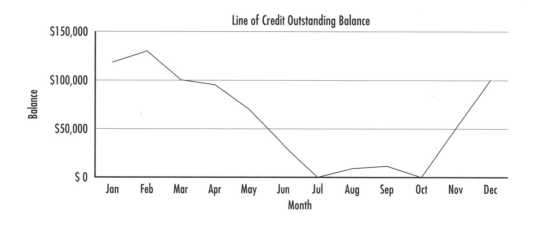

Another method of short-term financing is factoring. Instead of pledging accounts receivable for a bank loan, a borrowing company will sell the accounts receivable to a factoring company. Thus, except for paying the factoring company a fee, the firm does not have to concern itself with collecting the accounts or risking a bad debt. Customers' payments go to the factoring company rather than the seller.

MEDIUM-TERM FINANCING

Medium-term financing is for a period of over one year but not longer than ten years. Firms often require medium-term financing for growth, either for additional working capital or for new assets such as plant expansion, equipment, or machinery. Medium-term financing in the form of term loans can be obtained from chartered banks, life insurance companies, or pension funds.

The most common source of this type of financing is the chartered or commercial banks. Banks usually permit loans of this nature to remain unpaid for reasonable periods of time provided the company has pledged the required collateral, the interest payments are made on time, and the amount of the loan is reduced in an orderly fashion.

Mortgage companies, life insurance companies, and trust companies are other sources for medium-term financing. As with banks, collateral usually is required. If financing is required for equipment purchases, the equipment supplier often will provide financing.

LONG-TERM FINANCING

Long-term financing takes place over a period of 10 years or longer and is most often used to finance the acquisition of fixed assets. The major sources of long-term financing are from equity and long-term debt financing. Equity financing refers to the original money invested by common and preferred shareholders plus new issues of stock and all profits (after dividend payments) retained in the business. This money is seldom repaid. Individuals, investment companies, and pension plans are the major purchasers (owners) of preferred and common stocks.

Long-term debt financing refers to bonds or debentures issued by the lender. Insurance companies, trust companies, mortgage loan companies, and pension plans are the major purchasers of long-term debt issues. Fixed interest rates are levied and must be paid with repayments of principal at specified times.

Leasing is used increasingly in Canada. As a financial source, leasing is a surrogate for medium-term and long-term debt. A financial lease is an arrangement whereby the lessee acquires the use of an asset over its useful life. In return, the lessee promises to pay specified amounts, which are sufficient to cover the principal and interest objectives of the lessor. Normally, the lessor looks solely to the contract with the lessee to meet his financial objectives.

Generally, long-term interest rates are higher than medium- and short-term rates, though market conditions will influence this relationship. Because of the premium demanded for forgoing liquidity, plus the increased instability of long-term security prices, interest rates increase with the length of loans. See Exhibit 9 for more detail on annualized returns for selected investments and lending rates.

EXHIBIT 9

Annualized Returns as of December 31
for Selected Investments and Lending Rates
(in percentages)

Year	3-Month Government of Canada Treasury Bill[1]	Government of Canada Bond Yield Average, 10 Years and Over[1]	Chartered 90-day Deposit Receipts[1]	Chartered Prime Business Loan Rate[1]	Toronto Stock Exchange Index[2]
1990	11.47	10.51	11.58	12.75	(14.1)
1991	7.42	9.00	7.48	8.00	12.0
1992	7.01	8.36	7.08	7.25	(1.4)
1993	3.87	7.28	3.91	5.50	32.6
1994	7.14	9.13	7.29	8.00	(0.2)
1995	5.54	7.63	3.63	7.50	14.5
1996	2.85	7.09	3.11	4.75	28.3
1997	3.99	5.95	4.79	6.00	15.0
1998	4.66	5.23	5.00	6.75	(1.6)

1. Source: Bank of Canada
2. Source: Toronto Stock Exchange
   $$\text{Return} = \frac{\text{Dividends} + (\text{TSE }[t] - \text{TSE }[t-1])}{\text{TSE } t-1}$$
   t = any year

Note: Parentheses denote losses.

SUMMARY

The financial analysis and management of an enterprise are complex tasks. This chapter has presented only an elementary framework. Using judgment, not just calculations, is required to successfully apply the framework in the following exercises and cases.

The overall objective of the financial manager is to determine the expected return on investment while evaluating the risk incurred to earn the return. Projected results are required to determine the expected return. Quantitative analysis (cash sources and uses statement, ratio analysis, projections, and collateral appraisal) plus evaluation of qualitative factors (character and business conditions) are employed to assess the risk.

NOTES

1. This is only one method of many by which to record and follow the flow of funds through a company. Another method does not segregate the cash account and actually includes it as either a source or a use. In this method, there are no cash balances at the end of the statement, and total sources equals total uses.
2. This statement is also useful in predicting the impact on cash flow when considering future assumptions/scenarios.
3. For those ratios expressed in days, either a 360- or 365-day year can be used.
4. It is suggested that in the following examples the reader insert the data from the financial statements (Exhibits 1 and 2) of LMN Retail Company Ltd. to verify the calculations in Exhibit 5.
5. There are approximately eighteen 20-day periods in a year.
6. Harold Blerman, Jr., and Seymour Smidt, *Financial Management for Decision Making* (New York: Macmillan, 1986)
7. By taking into account any additional fixed charges or payment obligations the company may incur, this ratio can be made more inclusive and therefore more indicative of potential problems in meeting all contractual obligations.
8. Profit (or net earnings) growth may be calculated before or after tax. In either case, the approach used should be acknowledged.
9. Calculated by subtracting the decrease in the need for financing using accounts payable days 70 from the increase in the need for financing using accounts receivable days of 68: $21,917 – $3,014 = $18,903 (net increase in the need for financing).
10. Although sensitivity analysis can be done manually on certain accounts with relative ease, computer spreadsheet applications make it easy to test sensitivity on any one or more of the accounts in the projected financial statements — automatically calculating the impact on the other accounts.
11. Since many smaller companies do not have the resources for financial experts on staff, the banker will often be the only financial advisor available to them.
12. The terms *bank, lender,* and *creditor* will be used to identify all institutions or individuals who loan money.
13. See Appendix C at the end of Part 3 for more about bankruptcy.

Exercise 1
ABC Distribution Company Ltd.
(Cash Sources and Uses Statement)

Balance Sheets
as at November 30
(in 000s of dollars)

	1997	1998	1999
ASSETS			
Current assets:			
Cash	$ 12	$ 40	$ 16
Accounts receivable	3,820	4,532	6,440
Inventories	4,720	5,048	9,460
Total current assets	$ 8,552	$ 9,620	$15,916
Other investments	600	552	712
Net fixed assets	1,772	2,160	5,176
Other assets	368	336	940
TOTAL ASSETS	$11,292	$12,668	$22,744
LIABILITIES			
Current liabilities:			
Working capital loan	$2,688	$ 1,512	$ 4,252
Accounts payable	912	1,752	3,856
Taxes payable	328	952	736
Other current liabilities	312	56	252
Total current liabilities	$ 4,240	$ 4,672	$ 9,096
Term bank loan			4,200
Mortgages payable	752	564	468
Total liabilities	$ 4,992	$ 5,236	$13,764
SHAREHOLDERS' EQUITY			
Common stock	$ 4,384	$ 4,384	$ 4,384
Retained earnings	1,916	3,048	4,596
Total shareholders' equity	$ 6,300	$ 7,432	$ 8,980
TOTAL LIABILITIES AND SHAREHOLDERS' EQUITY	$11,292	$12,668	$22,744

Assignment

From the balance sheets of ABC Distribution Company Ltd., prepare a cash sources and uses statement:

1. For one year ending November 30, 1998;

2. For one year ending November 30, 1999; and

3. For two years ending November 30, 1999.

Exercise 2
ABC Distribution Company Ltd.
Calculation of Ratios

Income Statements
for the Years Ending November 30
(in 000s of dollars)

	1997	1998	1999
Net sales	$19,436	$23,544	$32,624
Cost of sales	14,284	16,492	22,520
Gross income	$ 5,152	$ 7,052	$10,104
Operating expenses:			
Bad debt expense	$ 264	$ 20	$ 108
General and administrative expense	736	828	1,012
Salaries	2,776	3,280	4,420
Selling expense	752	888	1,320
Depreciation	264	264	416
Total operating expenses	$ 4,792	$ 5,280	$ 7,276
Operating income	$ 360	$ 1,772	$ 2,828
Plus: Other income	396	552	444
Less: Interest expense	248	220	412
Income before tax	$ 508	$ 2,104	$ 2,860
Income taxes	248	972	1,312
Net earnings	$ 260	$ 1,132	$ 1,548

ABC Distribution Company Ltd.
Ratio Sheet
for Selected Dates and Periods
(365-day year)

	1997	**1998**	**1999**
PROFITABILITY:			
Vertical analysis			
Sales	100.0%	–	–
Cost of goods sold	–	70.0%	–
Gross profit	–	–	31.0%
Operating expenses:			
Bad debt expense	1.4%	–	–
General and administrative	–	3.5%	–
Salaries	14.3%	–	–
Selling	–	3.8%	–
Depreciation	–	–	1.3%
Operating income	1.9%	–	–
Other income	–	2.3%	–
Interest expense	–	–	1.3%
Income before tax	–	–	8.8%
Return on average equity	–	16.5%	–
EFFICIENCY:			
Age of receivables in days	71.7 days	–	–
Age of inventory in days (based on COGS)	–	111.7 days	–
Age of payables in days (based on purchases)	–	–	52.3days
Fixed assets/sales (%)	9.1%	–	–
LIQUIDITY:			
Current ratio	2.02:1	–	–
Acid test	–	0.98:1	–
Working capital ($000)	–	–	6, 820
STABILITY:			
Net worth to total assets	55.8%	–	–
Interest coverage (times)	–	10.6X	–
Debt to equity	.79:1	.70:1	1.53:1

	1997–98	**1998–99**
GROWTH:		
Sales	21.1%	–
Net earnings	–	36.7%
Assets	12.2%	–
Equity	–	20.8%

Assignment

Pages 104–105 contain the income statements of the ABC Distribution Company Ltd. and a ratio sheet. Calculate the missing ratios and evaluate the company's performance.

Exercise 3
DEF Company Ltd.
Projected Statements

1. Sales projection	$750,000
2. Gross profit	20% of sales
3. Last year's ending inventory	$150,000
4. This year's age of ending inventory	90 days
	Cost of goods sold
5. Other operating expenses	8% of sales
6. Income tax	25% of net earnings before tax
7. Accounts payable	40 days purchases
8. Accounts receivable	10 days sales
9. Taxes payable	30% of year's taxes
10. Land — at cost	$30,000
11. Buildings and fixtures — at cost	$90,000
12. Accumulated depreciation — building and fixtures at end of last year	$21,000
13. Depreciation expense for the year	$6,000
14. Common stock	$100,000
15. Retained earnings at the end of last year	$75,000
16. Salary expense	$42,000
17. Dividends	25% of net earnings after tax
18. Cash or bank loan	Plug

Assignment

The above data have been supplied to you by the owner of DEF Company Ltd., a retailing firm.

1. Prepare a projected income statement for the next year.

2. Prepare a projected balance sheet as at the end of the next year.

3. The sales manager disagrees with the owner's sales projections. She believes sales will be $1,000,000. Do another set of projections using the sales manager's estimates.

APPENDIX C

Bankruptcy

Bankruptcy has been mentioned a number of times in this chapter, but what is it? How does it happen? What occurs when you are bankrupt? What are the implications of bankruptcy?

Bankruptcy proceedings are a court-administered process that supervises the disposition of property of an individual or a corporation that is unable to pay its obligations. The process may start with either a voluntary petition to the court by the debtor or an involuntary petition by a creditor. For an involuntary petition to be granted, the creditor must prove that the debtor committed an act of bankruptcy, which includes handing over assets to a trustee for benefit of the creditors, a fraudulent transfer of property, a failure to meet obligations when due, or an admission of insolvency. In these cases, the petition to the court is a request for the appointment of a trustee to oversee the debtor's property, with the ultimate goal of eliminating the outstanding debt through orderly payment, or discharge by the court.

In granting a petition, the court will establish a trustee. The trustee will take dominion over the debtor's property. The property will be disposed of and the proceeds will be distributed in a prescribed order. Lenders will receive their money in the following order, regulated by the Bankruptcy (Declaration) Act:

1. Secured creditors: Anyone who has specific assets pledged as collateral.
2. Priority creditors: Anyone to whom unpaid rent, salaries, or wages and municipal taxes are owed. Outstanding payroll deductions such as employment insurance, provincial sales taxes (PST), and goods and services taxes (GST), and severance pay or workers' compensation are also included as priority creditors.
3. Unsecured creditors: Anyone to whom money is owed who does not fall into the first two categories. Any other outstanding debts to the government are also included.
4. Shareholders: Preferred shareholders are paid any dividends owing before common shareholders are paid.

Since this order is mandatory, the ranking is important: secured and priority creditors must be satisfied from the proceeds from the property before any proceeds from assets given as collateral can be used to satisfy the claims of the next strata of creditors — unsecured creditors. Given this order of distribution, deemed trusts and secured creditors fare much better than lower-ranked creditors. Usually, the bankrupt's property is insufficient to make even nominal payments to unsecured creditors. Any lender who has not secured collateral on a loan is classified as an unsecured creditor and will not be paid until the first two groups of creditors (stated above) have been paid. It is for this reason that the lender must complete a collateral analysis to determine the value of assets that are available to be secured as collateral.

Once the court has approved the trustee's disposition of the bankrupt's property, all amounts still outstanding are forgiven or discharged. If the bankrupt is an enterprise, the enterprise ceases to exist. If the bankrupt is an individual, the individual is free to restart unencumbered with debt and possessing minimal, if any, assets.

Sources

Mimick, Richard H., "Financial Ratio Analysis," No. 9A85K031. Published by Ivey Management Services.

Paul, Tracey L., and John F. Graham, "Note on Sources and Uses Statement," No. 9A92J003. published by Ivey Management Services.

Wylie, Krista, and Elizabeth M.A. Grasby, "Collateral Analysis Note," No. 9A97J004. Published by Ivey Management Services.

———. "Sensitivity Analysis Note," No. 9A97J003. Published by Ivey Management Services.

■ ■ ■ CASES FOR PART 3 ■ ■ ■

CASE 3.1 Dawson Lumber Company Limited

■

CASE 3.2 Ellington Industrial Supply Inc.

■

CASE 3.3 Gardiner Wholesalers Incorporated (A)

■

CASE 3.4 Gardiner Wholesalers Incorporated (B)

■

CASE 3.5 GE Capital Canada

■

CASE 3.6 Lawsons

■

CASE 3.7 Maple Leaf Hardware Ltd

■

CASE 3.8 Materiaux Boisvert Ltée

■

CASE 3.9 Plumb Parts Supply Ltd.

■

CASE 3.10 Sandalias Finas de Cuernavaca, S.A.

■

CASE 3.11 Studio Tessier Ltée

■

CASE 3.12 Talich Fabricating Inc.

C A S E 3.1   DAWSON LUMBER COMPANY LIMITED

By J.A. Humphrey and J.K. Pliniussen

In March 1999, Sheila Spence, the new vice-president of the Eastern Ontario Region of the National Bank of Canada, was reviewing the file of the Dawson Lumber Company, one of the region's biggest borrowers. The following day, Doug Dawson and John Manning, the president and controller, respectively, of the Dawson Lumber Company, would present their request to the bank's loan committee for a line of credit of up to $10 million. The line of credit was in addition to the current term bank loan. The loan committee, consisting of Spence, the central credit manager, and the assistant central credit manager, would then make a recommendation to the bank's board of directors. This recommendation would be the basis of the bank's decision on Dawson Lumber's request.

PRE-1996

The Dawson Lumber Company was founded in the 1870s by the Dawson family to market the lumber on their land. After the original lumber stands near Cornwall, Ontario, had been depleted, the wholesale lumber business was continued and slowly expanded. In 1950, Dawson Lumber owned four small lumberyards in the Cornwall area, each operating as a separate company.

In 1965, J.H. Dawson became president and amalgamated the four companies into the Dawson Lumber Company. The company acquired seven more lumberyards north and west of Cornwall, Ontario, but further growth was limited by J.H. Dawson's belief that growth should be financed only by internally generated funds. For over one hundred years, Dawson Lumber had been dealing with the Cornwall branch of the Eastern Bank and, in 1993, borrowed approximately $1.5 million to finance an inventory build-up needed to meet seasonal sales. From April to November, 77 percent of the sales occurred evenly, while 23 percent were evenly distributed from December to March. The company's sales were between $10 and $15 million in the late 1980s, with 90 percent being wholesale sales to local residential contractors. Exhibit 1 presents profit before tax from 1988 to 1998.

In 1994, J.H. Dawson realized that, because of his health, he would not be able to continue managing the company. His son, Doug Dawson, agreed to take over as president. Doug Dawson had taken over the business initially in the summer of 1992 when his father became ill. After his father returned, Doug Dawson assumed the advertising and budgeting responsibilities for the company.

1996 AND 1997

Doug Dawson had a postgraduate degree in business administration and several years' teaching experience. When he became president of the company, Dawson Lumber had been primarily a wholesale business, subject to the volatility of the demand for housing. Exhibit 2 outlines selected ratios for the wholesale lumber industry. The new president felt that, with minimal changes in inventory and yard operations, the company could take advantage of the growing retail market for building products and thereby stabilize its operations.

He approached the company's banker, the Cornwall branch manager of the Eastern Bank, with a request for a loan to finance these changes in the company. However, the Eastern Bank branch manager would support only a seasonal loan to finance inventory and refused to pass the loan application on to his superiors.

Consequently, Doug Dawson approached the National Bank of Canada with his plans and needs. The National Bank of Canada, in 1996, granted an initial operating line of credit of $3 million, to be used for working capital. The National Bank took accounts receivable and inventory as collateral, and, as a condition of the loan, Dawson Lumber undertook to provide quarterly financial statements and monthly reports of inventory, sales, and receivables.

Doug Dawson reorganized the company's 11 branches into three regions. The Northern Region served an urban market and consisted of three yards just outside the city of Ottawa. Four lumberyards in the Cornwall area made up the Eastern Region, and five lumberyards near Kingston formed the Western Region. The Eastern Region was a rural market, while the Western Region was partially a resort and partially an urban area. In an attempt to minimize inventory levels, one branch in each region operated as a depot. A fleet of trucks kept frequent and regular schedules between the lumberyards and the depot to provide rapid delivery to the customer.

Each region was made the responsibility of an area supervisor who had worked for many years in the company's lumberyards. A management committee — consisting of the president, controller, and area supervisors — met monthly to discuss operational strategy. The committee set budgets for each branch every four months. Exhibits 3, 4, and 5 outline the company's financial statements and ratios from 1996 to 1998.

1998 PROJECTIONS

Exhibit 6 outlines the projected capital expenditures for 1998 and 1999. The projected 1998 capital expenditures of $1.8 million were primarily for improvements in the company's showrooms and display areas. Depreciation and profit were expected to cover these capital expenditures. A sales increase of $6.4 million was anticipated for 1998, based on the opinions of contractors, yard managers, and business publications on the outlook for the economy and the housing market. Operating profit was expected to be $2.92 million, assuming a gross margin of 30 percent and expenses of $6.08 million. To finance an increase of $2.52 million in receivables and inventory, a total operating line of credit of $3.6 million for working capital was requested and granted by the National Bank.

1998 ACTUAL

After spending six months studying the potential of the Ottawa market and discussing the revised capital budget with the bank, Dawson Lumber opened a discount home centre in September 1998. To finance the new outlet, the bank granted a term loan of $4.2 million.

The discount home centre was aimed at the retail market. Exhibit 7 presents selected ratios for the retail building materials and hardware industry. The concept enabled the consumer to purchase in one store all types of building and household products such as tiles, wallpaper, carpet, lumber, plumbing supplies, and lighting fixtures. Each item in the store had two prices clearly marked so that the customer paid only for the services received. The regular price was the price at which the item could be charged and delivered. The discount price applied if the customer wished to pay cash and take the goods away. A third price was also charged if the customer wished to pay cash and have the purchase delivered. The new store's sales in its first two months of operations were $2.28 million.

Sales in 1998 were $2,680,000 greater than projected, and capital expenditures were $3,600,000 over budget. In addition to granting the term loan, the National Bank increased the company's operating line of credit to $5 million.

1999 PROJECTIONS

For 1999, Doug Dawson projected a 65 percent increase in sales to $54 million and an operating profit of 8 percent of sales. To finance inventory and receivables of up to $24 million in June and July, an operating line of credit of $10.8 million was requested.

THE NATIONAL BANK

As she reviewed the file, Spence looked for anything suggesting that the bank should take steps to increase its protection of the loan. She particularly noted the increase in profits since 1994 and her predecessor's confidence in Dawson's management. However, she closely examined the 1999 projections, questioning their accuracy. It was obvious that because 65 percent of Dawson Lumber's sales were to contractors, the company was still dependent on the housing market. Total housing starts in Canada were 138,000 in 1998 versus 148,000 in 1997. New housing construction had slowed slightly in January and February of 1999, being about 97 percent of the starts in the same period of 1998.[1] Five-year mortgage interest rates had increased slightly to 6.9 percent in February 1999 from 6.85 percent in 1998, although she noted an overall downward trend throughout the 1990s.[2] As she examined this information, Spence wondered whether she should recommend an increase in Dawson Lumber's operating line of credit, and, if so, by how much and under what terms as to collateral and management growth plans.

NOTES

1. Statistics Canada, *Canadian Economic Observer,* January 1999, 40.
2. Statistics Canada, *Canadian Economic Observer,* May 1999, 52.

EXHIBIT **1**

INCOME BEFORE TAX ($000s)	
1988	$ 40
1989	12
1990	(144)
1991	440
1992	512
1993	536
1994	644
1995	1,020
1996	508
1997	2,104
1998	2,860

EXHIBIT **2**

Dun & Bradstreet Canadian Industry Norms and Key Business Ratios Industry: Wholesale — Lumber		
	1996	**1997**
PROFITABILITY		
Vertical analysis		
Gross profit	7.4%	8.4%
Net profit after tax	2.2%	2.5%
Return on investment	29.1%	31.4%
LIQUIDITY		
Current ratio	1.4:1	1.5:1
Acid test	0.8:1	0.8:1
Working capital	$1,085,780	$1,154,636
EFFICIENCY		
Age of Receivables	36.1 days	41.2 days
Age of Inventory	29.1 days	27.5 days
Age of Payables	21.2 days	23.5 days
STABILITY		
Net worth: total assets	35.8%	37.0%
GROWTH	**1996–97**	
Sales	5.6%	
Net profit	20.3%	
Equity	5.1%	
Assets	1.7%	

Exhibit 3

	Income Statements for the Years Ending November 30 ($000s)		
	1996	**1997**	**1998**
Net sales	$19,436	$23,544	$32,624
Cost of sales	14,284	16,492	22,520
Gross profit	$ 5,152	$ 7,052	$10,104
Operating expenses:			
Bad debt expense	$ 264	$ 20	$ 108
General and administrative expense	736	828	1,012
Interest expense	248	220	412
Salaries	2,776	3,280	4,420
Selling expense	752	888	1,320
Depreciation	264	264	416
Total operating expenses	5,040	5,500	7,688
Operating income	$ 112	$ 1,552	$ 2,416
Other income	396	552	444
Income before tax	$ 508	$ 2,104	$ 2,860
Income taxes	248	972	1,312
Net earnings	$ 260	$ 1,132	$ 1,548

EXHIBIT **4**

	Balance Sheets as at November 30 ($000s)		
	1996	**1997**	**1998**
ASSETS			
Current assets:			
Cash	$ 12	$ 40	$ 16
Accounts receivable	3,820	4,532	6,440
Inventories	4,720	5,048	9,460
Total current assets	$ 8,552	$ 9,620	$15,916
Other investments	600	552	712
Net fixed assets	1,772	2,160	5,176
Other assets	368	336	940
TOTAL ASSETS	$11,292	$12,668	$22,744
LIABILITIES AND SHAREHOLDERS' EQUITY			
Liabilities			
Current liabilities:			
Working capital loan	$ 2,688	$ 1,512	$ 4,252
Accounts payable	912	1,752	3,856
Taxes payable	328	952	736
Other current liabilities	312	456	252
Total current liabilities	$ 4,240	$ 4,672	$ 9,096
Term bank loan			4,200
Mortgages payable	752	564	468
Total liabilities	$ 4,992	$ 5,236	$13,764
Shareholders' equity			
Common stock	$ 4,384	$ 4,384	$ 4,384
Retained earnings	1,916	3,048	4,596
Total shareholders' equity	$ 6,300	$ 7,432	$ 8,980
TOTAL LIABILITIES AND SHAREHOLDERS' EQUITY	$11,292	$12,668	$22,744

Exhibit 5

Ratio Analysis			
	1996	**1997**	**1998**
PROFITABILITY			
Sales	100.0%	100.0%	100.0%
Cost of sales	73.5%	70.0%	69.0%
Gross margin	26.5%	30.0%	31.0%
Operating expenses:			
Bad debt expense	1.4%	0.08%	0.3%
General and administrative expense	3.8%	3.5%	3.1%
Interest expense	1.3%	0.9%	1.3%
Salaries	14.3%	13.9%	13.5%
Selling expense	3.9%	3.8%	4.0%
Depreciation	1.4%	1.1%	1.3%
Total operating expenses	25.9%	23.3%	23.6%
Operating income	0.6%	6.6%	7.4%
Other income	2.0%	2.3%	1.4%
Income before tax	2.6%	8.9%	8.8%
Income taxes	1.3%	4.1%	4.0%
Net earnings	1.3%	4.8%	4.8%
Return on average equity	n/a	16.5%	18.9%
STABILITY			
Net worth to total assets	55.8%	58.7%	39.5%
Interest coverage (times)	3.0X	10.6X	7.9X
LIQUIDITY			
Current ratio	2.02:1	2.06:1	1.75:1
Acid test ratio	0.90:1	0.98:1	0.71:1
Working capital	$4,312,000	$4,948,000	$6,820,000
EFFICIENCY			
Age of receivables	71.7 days	70.3 days	72.1 days
Age of inventory	120.6 days	111.7 days	153.3 days
Age of payables	n/a	39.6 days	77.7 days
Fixed assets/sales	$ 0.09	$ 0.09	$ 0.16

GROWTH	**1996–97**	**1997–98**
Sales	21.1%	38.6%
Net profit	335.4%	36.7%
Assets	12.2%	79.5%
Equity	18.0%	20.8%

EXHIBIT 6

Capital Expenditures 1998 and 1999 ($000s)			
	1998		**1999**
	Projected	Actual	Projected
Showroom renovations	$ 140	$ 320	$ 160
Showroom expansion for two lumberyards	320	280	–
New showrooms for two lumberyards	1,040	1,700	400
Land for new yard in Northern Region	100	100	–
Land for new yard in Western Region	–	–	60
New vehicles	200	1,400	480
New retail outlet in Ottawa	–	1,600	–
Total	$1,800	$5,400	$1,100

EXHIBIT 7

Dun & Bradstreet Canadian Industry Norms and Key Business Ratios Industry: Retail — Hardware, Home Improvement		
	1996	**1997**
PROFITABILITY		
Vertical analysis		
Gross profit	26.3%	25.3%
Net profit after tax	2.2%	2.6%
Return on investment	10.7%	12.5%
LIQUIDITY		
Current ratio	1.6:1	1.6:1
Acid test	0.6:1	0.6:1
Working capital	$554,686	$555,271
EFFICIENCY		
Age of receivables	44.5 days	47.2 days
Age of inventory	104.9 days	99.1 days
Age of payables	46.3 days	51.9 days
STABILITY		
Net worth: total assets	42.2%	40.7%
GROWTH	**1996–97**	
Sales	6.2%	
Net profit	25.9%	
Equity	1.7%	
Assets	6.0%	

C A S E **3.2** ELLINGTON INDUSTRIAL SUPPLY INC.

By O. Richardson, D.G. Burgoyne, and J.A. Humphrey

In June 1995, Jake Ellington was working out the financial details of a tentative plan to build an extension onto his warehouse. He was concerned about what source of funds he should use in order to raise the $100,000 required for construction costs.

THE COMPANY

Ellington Industrial Supply Inc. (EISI) was a distributor of machine tools, maintenance parts, and related equipment in Lakeside. One hundred kilometres north of a metropolitan area and situated on a large lake, Lakeside was the largest and fastest-growing industrial centre in its region, with a population of 55,000. In addition, it served the surrounding farming communities and summer cottage trade. The customers of EISI were mostly industrial maintenance departments, but there was also some high-margin retail business, principally from farmers in the surrounding area.

Ellington purchased the business from its previous owner, Mr. Hodges, in February 1992. As part of the purchase agreement, Hodges took a note payable from EISI. By 1992, Ellington had already gained wide experience in a series of jobs. He had worked for a variety of different companies, including one of his current metropolitan-based competitors. During those years, however, he was dominated by a persistent ambition to operate his own business. His first personal venture was a retail hardware store in Riverton, which he sold when he acquired EISI.

Ellington felt pleased with the progress his company had made in the three years since he had purchased it. He had enjoyed considerable success in building up sales. His confidence was such that, in August 1994, EISI purchased its rented facilities, when the landlord offered the property to EISI at what Ellington regarded as "a very attractive price." By June 1995, monthly sales volume averaged more than $100,000. (Exhibits 1 to 3 present the past three years' financial data and selected company and industry financial ratios.)

Ellington was also proud of the company's reputation for dependability and integrity. He believed his success was due largely to the personalized service and engineering advice he offered his customers. He also realized that an important factor in attracting new customers and building lasting customer relationships

[VEY O. Richardson, D.G. Burgoyne, and J.A. Humphrey prepared this case solely to provide material for class discussion. The authors do not intend to illustrate either effective or ineffective handling of a managerial situation. The authors may have disguised certain names and other identifying information to protect confidentiality. Ivey Management Services prohibits any form of reproduction, storage or transmittal without its written permission. This material is not covered under authorization from CanCopy or any reproduction rights organization. Copyright © 1999, Ivey Management Services.

was his success in obtaining exclusive rights to handle the products of some of the better manufacturers. Maintaining good supplier relations with those manufacturers who granted him exclusivity was a key element to future success.

COMPETITION

Until late 1994, EISI had been the only distributor of machine tools and parts in Lakeside. Competition had come from salespeople operating from out-of-town warehouses. In the fall of 1994, another distributor started up an operation in Lakeside. Ellington believed, however, that the new competitor would not conflict directly with more than a small part of his business because of the exclusive distribution rights EISI held and its specialized products. This new distributor also did not as yet have the reputation for dependable service that EISI had earned.

THE FUTURE

Although market information was limited, Ellington thought that EISI had about 35 percent of the machine tool and equipment market in Lakeside and the surrounding region. Given the existing market potential, he believed sales could not increase beyond $2,000,000 without expanding EISI's geographical market area. For the next two years he projected probable sales at $1,400,000 for the year ending January 31, 1996, and $1,600,000 for the year ending January 31, 1997. However, he felt sales could fall as low as $1,300,000 and $1,500,000 for fiscal years 1996 and 1997, respectively, or go as high as $1,600,000 and $1,800,000.

THE PROBLEM

In June 1995, one of Ellington's major concerns was the cramped space in EISI's warehouse. He felt EISI could not handle any significant increases in inventory on hand with its present facilities. In order to maintain the high standard of service and delivery, he wanted to add a warehouse extension as soon as possible. At the same time, one of his top priorities was to reduce the age of EISI's accounts payable to 60 days before the end of the fiscal year. If he failed to do so, he feared that he would put some of EISI's exclusive distribution agreements in jeopardy.

Ellington wanted to first determine the amount of money EISI needed to carry out these plans, and then to decide on the appropriate source of funds. EISI's existing long-term debt-servicing schedule is provided in Exhibit 4. Several options were available. His preference was to borrow either from the bank or from a private lender. He did, however, have another alternative, namely selling shares in EISI to a local investor. At the time of his decision, Ellington was hesitant to use equity financing. He felt he would not get as much now for a share in the company as he could expect in a year when his hard work had paid off through increased profits. He was also wondering about the company's capability of generating its own funds.

Exhibit 1

	Income Statements for the Years Ending January 31		
	1993	**1994**	**1995**
Net sales	$465,055	$799,960	$1,033,410
Cost of sales:			
Opening inventory	$113,255	$154,490	$171,040
Purchases	363,330	602,430	804,695
Cost of goods available for sale	$476,585	$756,920	$975,735
Less: closing inventory	154,490	171,040	237,315
Cost of sales	322,095	585,880	738,420
Gross margin	$142,960	$214,080	$294,990
Expenses:			
Wages and commissions	$ 91,810	$126,955	$153,085
Rent[1]	9,715	11,100	5,550
Interest expense	13,615	14,610	16,875
Provision for doubtful accounts	3,355	–	–
General selling expenses	14,550	13,780	11,930
General administrative expense	38,215	52,360	66,425
Depreciation	–	5,150	12,180
Total expenses	$171,260	$223,955	$266,045
Net profit (loss)	$ (28,300)	$ (9,875)	$ 28,945

1. With the purchase of the land and building in August 1994, rent expense had now been eliminated.

EXHIBIT 2

	Balance Sheets as at January 31		
	1993	**1994**	**1995**
ASSETS			
Current assets:			
Cash	$ 43,030	$ 8,755	$ 710
Accounts receivable, net	64,250	100,835	169,345
Inventory	154,490	171,040	237,315
Prepaid interest	1,510	1,510	870
Total current assets	$263,280	$281,140	$408,240
Fixed assets:			
Automobiles	$ 17,175	$ 17,175	$23,925
Land			30,440
Building			61,470
Equipment			1,995
Subtotal	$ 17,175	$ 17,175	$117,830
Less: accumulated depreciation		5,150	17,330
Total fixed assets	$ 17,175	$ 12,025	$100,500
Other assets:			
Goodwill	15,000	15,000	15,000
Deferred charges	3,285	1,925	1,375
TOTAL ASSETS	$298,740	$311,090	$525,115

EXHIBIT 2 (cont.)

	Balance Sheets as at January 31		
	1993	1994	1995
LIABILITIES AND EQUITY			
Liabilities			
Current liabilities:			
Accounts payable	$ 92,320	$145,370	$251,250
Other current liabilities	7,895	5,925	17,925
Total current liabilities	$100,215	$151,295	$269,175
Long-term liabilities:			
Bank loan[1]	$ 63,450	$ 50,850	$38,250
GMAC payable[2]	15,120	8,865	2,605
Hodges payable[3]	98,255	88,255	88,255
Mortgage payable[4]			86,060
Total long-term liabilities	$176,825	$147,970	$215,170
Total liabilities	$277,040	$299,265	$484,345
Equity			
Common stock[5]	$ 50,000	$ 50,000	$ 50,000
Retained earnings	(28,300)	(38,175)	(9,230)
Total equity	$ 21,700	$ 11,825	$ 40,770
TOTAL LIABILITIES AND EQUITY	$298,740	$311,090	$525,115

1. In 1992, $75,000 was borrowed. Principal payments: $1,050 per month, interest: 0.75 percent per month.
2. Balance owing on a truck bought in 1992. It was totally repaid in April 1995.
3. Loan from previous owner of the business, secured by inventory, incurred in February 1992 as part of the purchase agreement. Principal payments of $5,000 due in January 1993 and 1994, with payment of $10,000 due every succeeding January. Interest of 10 percent to be paid half-yearly on the balance of principal owing in January and June.
4. Mortgage loan made in August 1994 when EISI purchased the property and building. Five-year mortgage for $87,500 at 9 percent. Combined interest and principal payments of $880 were due each month.
5. Ellington originally invested $50,000.

EXHIBIT 3

		Ratio Analysis		
		EISI Ratio Analysis		**Selected Industry Ratios**
	1993	**1994**	**1995**	**1995**
PROFITABILITY				
Sales	100.0%	100.0%	100.0%	
Cost of sales	69.3%	73.2%	71.5%	
Gross margin	30.7%	26.8%	28.5%	
Expenses:				
Wages and commissions	19.7%	15.9%	14.8%	
Rent	2.1%	1.4%	0.5%	
Interest expense	2.9%	1.8%	1.6%	
Provision for doubtful accounts	0.7%	–	–	
General selling expense	3.1%	1.7%	1.2%	
General administrative expense	8.2%	6.5%	6.4%	
Depreciation	0.0%	0.6%	1.2%	
Total expenses	36.8%	28.0%	25.7%	
Net profit	n/a	n/a	2.8%	3.0%
Return on average equity	n/a	n/a	110.1%	24.0%
STABILITY				
Net worth to total assets	7.3%	3.8%	7.8%	30.7%
Interest coverage (times)	n/a	n/a	2.7X	
LIQUIDITY				
Current ratio	2.63:1	1.86:1	1.52:1	1.6:1
Acid test ratio	1.07:1	0.72:1	0.63:1	1.0:1
Working capital	$163,065	$ 129,845	$ 139,065	$165,856
EFFICIENCY				
Age of receivables	50.4 days	46 days	59.8 days	60.6 days
Age of inventory	175.1 days	106.6 days	117.3 days	
Age of payables	92.7 days	88.1 days	114.0 days	
Fixed assets/sales (%)	3.7%	1.5%	9.7%	5.0%

GROWTH	**1993–94**	**1994–95**
Sales	72%	29.2%
Net profit	n/a	n/a
Assets	4.1%	68.8%
	(45.5%)	244.8%

Exhibit 4

**Long-Term Debt Principal and Interest Payments
for Selected Fiscal Years Ending January 31**

Fiscal Year	Opening Balance	Interest Payment	Principal Payment	Ending Balance
1. Bank loan				
January 31, 1996	$38,250	$2,875	$ 12,600	$25,650
January 31, 1997	25,650	1,740	12,600	13,050
January 31, 1998	13,050	590	13,050	0
2. GMAC payable				
January 31, 1996	$ 2,605	$ 100	$ 2,605	0
3. Hodges payable				
January 31, 1997	$88,255	$8,826	$ 20,000[1]	$68,255
January 31, 1998	68,255	$6,826	10,000	58,255
4. 9% mortgage payable				
January 31, 1996	$86,060	$7,481	$ 3,079	82,981
January 31, 1997	82,981	$7,198	3,362	79,619
January 31, 1998	79,619	$6,889	3,671	75,948

1. The $10,000 principal payment due January 31, 1996, could not be paid and would have to be added to the January 31, 1997, payment.

C A S E 3.3   GARDINER WHOLESALERS INCORPORATED (A)

By F. Mastrandrea and R.H. Mimick

In early February 1999, Kathy Wilson, assistant credit manager of Gardiner Wholesalers Incorporated, sat at her desk reviewing the financial information she had gathered on two of her company's accounts — S.D. Taylor Jewellers Ltd. and Elegance Jewellers Inc. Gardiner Wholesalers Incorporated, a jewellery wholesaler located in southwestern Ontario, had for many years followed a policy of thoroughly assessing the credit standing of each of its accounts about one month after Christmas. The assessment, which would be used to determine if changes in credit policy were necessary, had to be submitted to both the credit manager and the sales manager in one week. Wilson wondered what comments and recommendations concerning the two accounts should be put in her report.

The retail jewellery trade was largely composed of national chain stores such as Birks, Peoples, and Mappins, plus smaller independent jewellers like S.D. Taylor Jewellers Ltd. and Elegance Jewellers Inc. Most retail jewellers carried both jewellery lines, such as gold and diamond rings, and giftware items, such as silverplated items and crystal. Most jewellery chains purchased jewellery pieces from jewellery manufacturers and mounted the finished products in-house. Independent jewellers were supplied by wholesalers, like Gardiner Wholesalers Incorporated, who received the jewellery and giftware from such manufacturers as Jolyn Jewellery Products, the French Jewellery Co. of Canada Ltd., the Royal Doulton Company, and Belfleur Crystal. The wholesalers distributed products to regional department stores, small regional jewellery chains, and independent jewellery stores. An independent jeweller would be supplied by at least five jewellery wholesalers.

Jewellery store sales were lowest during the summer months and peaked during the Christmas season. The smaller, often family-owned, independent jewellers were much more affected by the seasonal pattern of jewellery sales than were the national chain-store operations. As a result, the independent jewellers relied heavily on their suppliers for financial support in the form of extended credit, in order to remain competitive with national chain stores. The competition among suppliers for the retail jewellery trade made credit terms and retailer financing necessary wholesale features. Factors that influenced the consumer purchase decision were style, selection, quality, and customer credit. In 1998, layaway sales accounted for 25 percent of all retail jewellery store sales. Layaway sales were necessary in the jewellery business because people often balked at making large cash expenditures for luxury items. The layaway sales technique was also a powerful tool in influencing customers to purchase more expensive items.

S.D. Taylor Jewellers Ltd., located in London, Ontario, had been purchasing jewellery products from Gardiner Wholesalers for the last 25 years. The store handled a complete line of jewellery and giftware items. Peak periods of sales were traditionally Christmas, Valentine's Day, Mother's Day, and graduation time. Seventy percent of S.D. Taylor's sales were cash, and 30 percent were on 90-day installment plans. Installment terms called for a 10 percent deposit, and there were no interest charges or carrying costs on the remainder of payments made within 90 days.

S.D. Taylor Jewellers Ltd. had been established in 1969 as a sole proprietorship and was incorporated in 1974. The couple who owned and operated the business were noted for their friendliness and were well respected in the local business community. Taylor was a member of the Southwestern Ontario Jewellers' Association and had attended numerous courses offered by the Gemological Institute of America. On reviewing the company's file, Wilson found that payments on account had, for the most part, been prompt.

Elegance Jewellers Inc. was a comparatively new customer of Gardiner Wholesalers Incorporated, having switched suppliers in early 1997. No reason for the change was given in the files. Elegance Jewellers Inc. was owned by a small group of businessmen who had interests in four other unrelated businesses. The company owned and operated two small-sized jewellery stores, both located in Sarnia, Ontario. The Elegance jewellery stores carried mostly jewellery lines and very little giftware. Most of Elegance Jewellers' sales were for cash. Installment plans were available and called for a 20 percent deposit plus a 1 percent per month carrying charge on the outstanding balance. Comments in the file indicated that Elegance Jewellers' account had been satisfactory through 1998.

Both accounts were sold on standard terms of 1/10, net 30, and the terms were extended to net 90 during the fall. The sales manager felt that the extension of a fairly liberal credit policy to Gardiner Wholesalers' customers was necessary to remain competitive in a tough market.

Prior to starting her report, Wilson investigated some pieces of economic information. She was aware that the Canadian economy was doing well and that consumer spending was up in 1998, accounting for 3 percent of GDP. It was expected to slow somewhat in 1999 to 2.25 percent of GDP. The Statistics Canada report on retail jewellery store sales confirmed her belief that they were on the rise (see Exhibit 1). Wilson also had some 1997 financial information on the jewellery industry published by Dun & Bradstreet. She found that, on average, the age of receivables was 9.2 days; the current ratio was 2.4:1; and net worth was 40 percent of total assets. With this information in mind, Wilson leafed through the available company files (Exhibits 2 through 8) and prepared to write her report.

EXHIBIT 1
Annual Sales
Growth of
Jewellery Stores
in Canada

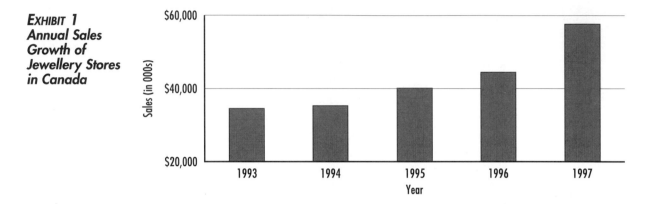

Source: Statistics Canada, CANSIM, Matrix 34.

Exhibit **2**

	Elegance Jewellers Inc. Income Statements for Years Ending June 30 ($000s)	
	1997	**1998**
Sales	$1,721.5	$ 1,982.8
Cost of sales	774.0	945.6
Gross income	$ 947.5	$ 1,037.2
Operating expenses:		
Selling and administrative	$ 584.1	$ 714.2
Depreciation	44.6	53.8
Total operating expenses	$ 628.7	$ 767.9
Operating income	$ 318.8	$ 269.3
Unusual income (loss)	(10.5)	(11.7)
Subtotal	$ 308.3	$ 257.6
Less: interest expense	34.8	152.1
Net income before tax	$ 273.5	$ 105.5
Income taxes	68.4	26.4
Net earnings[1]	$ 205.1	$ 79.1

1. Dividends paid were $35,000 for 1997 and $50,000 for 1998.

Exhibit 3

	1997	1998
Elegance Jewellers Inc. **Balance Sheets** **as at June 30** **($000s)**		
ASSETS		
Current assets:		
Cash	$ 1.2	$ 1.3
Accounts receivable	9.2	43.2
Inventory	1,148.2	1,155.4
Prepaid expenses	5.3	6.0
Total current assets	$1,163.9	$1,205.9
Loans to employees	$ 26.4	$ 25.7
Investment in subsidiary	–	686.2
Other investments	17.6	17.8
Fixed assets:		
Land	$ 25.5	$ 25.5
Buildings	374.0	441.1
Furniture and fixtures	61.9	108.5
Fixed assets, cost	$ 461.4	$ 575.1
Less: accumulated depreciation	167.3	221.0
Total fixed assets (net)	$ 294.1	$ 354.1
TOTAL ASSETS	$1,502.0	$2,289.7
LIABILITIES AND EQUITY		
Liabilities		
Current liabilities:		
Working capital loan	$ 133.0	$ 10.4
Accounts payable	379.8	223.7
Income taxes payable	123.7	2.5
Long-term debt due within one year	9.9	–
Total current liabilities	$ 646.4	$ 236.6
Bank loan (due December 31, 1999)	$ –	$ 418.4
Long-term notes payable	152.8	902.8
Total liabilities	$ 799.2	$1,557.8
Equity		
Common stock	$ 110.0	$ 110.0
Retained earnings	592.8	621.9
Total equity	$ 702.8	$ 731.9
TOTAL LIABILITIES AND EQUITY	$1,502.0	$2,289.7

EXHIBIT **4**

	S.D. Taylor Jewellers Ltd. Income Statements for Years Ending June 30 ($000s)	
	1997	**1998**
Sales	$2,059.5	$2,325.0
Cost of sales	968.5	1,133.8
Gross income	$1,091.0	$1,191.2
Operating expenses:		
Salaries and benefits	$ 370.3	$ 430.7
Overheads	123.4	147.0
Advertising	74.0	92.6
Supplies	70.0	83.5
Depreciation	35.1	39.4
Bad debt	4.1	6.9
Other miscellaneous	80.5	93.4
Total operating expenses	$ 757.3	$ 893.6
Operating income	$ 333.6	$ 297.6
Plus: other income	32.8	37.4
Subtotal	$ 366.5	$ 335.0
Less: interest expense	37.0	53.7
Net income before tax	$ 329.5	$ 281.3
Income taxes	82.4	70.3
Net earnings[1]	$ 247.1	$ 211.0

1. Dividends paid were $99,000 for 1997 and $84,000 for 1998.

Exhibit 5

	1997	1998
S.D. Taylor Jewellers Ltd. Balance Sheets as at June 30 ($000)		

	1997	1998
ASSETS		
Current assets:		
Cash	$ 9.7	$ 10.1
Accounts receivable	105.3	126.5
Inventories	885.5	1,076.7
Prepaid expenses	16.6	23.3
Total current assets	$1,017.1	$1,236.6
Loans to employees	$ 28.3	$ 28.3
Investment in subsidiary	120.7	79.2
Other investments	17.4	18.2
Fixed assets:		
Land	$ 29.8	$ 29.8
Buildings and fixtures	442.0	512.6
Less: accumulated depreciation	280.2	319.6
Total fixed assets (net)	$ 191.6	$ 222.8
TOTAL ASSETS	$1,375.1	$1,585.1
LIABILITIES		
Liabilities		
Current liabilities:		
Working capital loan	$ 30.2	$ 69.5
Notes payable (bank)	212.3	328.9
Accounts payable	183.0	184.9
Income taxes payable	84.1	21.4
Total current liabilities	$ 509.7	$ 604.7
Long-term debt	24.4	12.2
Total liabilities	$534.1	$ 616.9
Equity		
Capital stock	$ 40.7	$ 40.7
Retained earnings	800.3	927.5
Total equity	$ 841.0	$ 968.2
TOTAL LIABILITIES AND EQUITY	$1,375.1	$1,585.1

Exhibit 6

S.D. Taylor Jewellers Ltd.			
Sources and Uses Statement			
for the Year ended June 30, 1998			
(000s)			

SOURCES:	SHORT TERM	LONG TERM	
Investment in subsidiary		$ 41.5	
Working capital loan	$ 39.3		
Notes payable (bank)	116.6		
Accounts payable	1.9		
Retained earnings	–	127.1	
Subtotal	$157.8	$168.6	
Total sources			$326.4

USES:	SHORT TERM	LONG TERM	
Accounts receivable	$ 21.2		
Inventory	191.2		
Prepaid expenses	6.7		
Other investments		$0.8	
Buildings and fixtures (net)		31.2	
Income taxes payable	62.7		
Long-term debt		12.2	
Subtotal	$281.8	$ 44.2	
Total uses			$326.0
Net cash increase			$ 0.4
Cash, June 30, 1997			9.7
Cash, June 30, 1998			$ 10.1

Exhibit **7**

	S.D. Taylor Jewellers Ltd. Ratio Analysis for the Years Ended June 30, 1997 and 1998	
	1997	**1998**
PROFITABILITY		
Sales	100.0%	100.0%
Cost of goods sold	47.0%	48.8%
Gross income53.0%	51.2%	
Operating expenses	36.8%	38.4%
Operating income	16.2%	12.8%
Other income	1.6%	1.6%
Interest expense	1.8%	2.3%
Net earnings	12.0%	9.1%
Return on average equity	32.2%[1]	23.3%
LIQUIDITY		
Current ratio	2.00:1	2.05:1
Acid test	0.23:1	0.23:1
Working capital	$ 507,400	$ 631,800
EFFICIENCY		
Age of receivables	18.7 days	19.9 days
Age of inventory	333.8 days	346.6 days
Age of payables[2]	69.0 days	59.5 days
Net fixed assets/sales	$ 0.093	$ 0.096
STABILITY		
Net worth/total assets	61.2%	61.1%
Interest coverage	9.9 X	6.2 X
GROWTH	**1997–98**	
Sales	12.9%	
Profit/income	(14.6%)	
Assets	15.3%	
Equity	15.1%	

1. Last year's equity = $692.9 ($841.0 + $99 – $247.1).
2. Calculation assumes purchases = cost of goods sold.

Exhibit **8**

	Gardiner Wholesalers Incorporated Aging of Accounts Receivable as at December 31, 1998					
Due From	**Prior**	**Sept.**	**Oct.**	**Nov.**	**Dec.**	**Total**
S.D. Taylor Jewellers Ltd.	–	$30,846	$4,852	$18,732	$5,464	$59,894
Elegance Jewellers Inc.	$2,640	$33,832	$7,108	$30,146	$63,202	$136,928

C A S E 3.4 GARDINER WHOLESALERS INCORPORATED (B)

By F. Mastrandrea and R.H. Mimick

Two days had passed since Kathy Wilson, assistant credit manager for Gardiner Wholesalers Incorporated, had begun her report[1] on two of the company's accounts — S.D. Taylor Jewellers Ltd. and Elegance Jewellers Inc. Her analysis of the past financial performance of the two companies was complete, and Wilson felt she was ready to make some recommendations; however, lunch with Jim Ferraro changed her mind. Ferraro was the assistant manager in charge of loans at a downtown bank and a personal friend of Wilson. He suggested that a credit appraisal report should include projected statements so that the future financing needs of the two jewellery retailers could be estimated. This additional information would then help Wilson to determine if these accounts would need to extend their payables in order to finance operations.

The next day, Wilson proceeded to have a meeting with Laurine Breen and Bert Haase, the managers of the two Elegance jewellery stores. Haase discussed operations for the past few months, describing them as "a little slow." He mentioned that because of the slowdown in sales volume, Elegance Jewellers had reduced prices on some items, which "squeezed our margins a little more." Breen added that the company was dropping its 1 percent per month carrying charge on layaway sales, "in order to stimulate sales." Haase thought that the overall sales growth for the fiscal year would be between 5 and 10 percent and that even though operating expenses had increased substantially last year, this year they would increase at about the same rate as sales. Haase also thought that inventory would be reduced because of closer scrutiny of inventory levels in the past few months and that capital expenditures for renovations to the building were expected to equal depreciation expenses. Breen concluded the meeting with a remark that she hoped Wilson would acknowledge in her report: "I hope you noticed that we've been paying our accounts more quickly than last year!"

In a meeting with Stan Taylor, manager and owner of S.D. Taylor Jewellers Ltd., Wilson again discussed recent retail performance. Taylor said that he experienced a "negligible" reduction in margins. He felt the expected sales growth for the coming year would be between 5 and 10 percent with operating expenses expected to increase at the same rate. Taylor had no plans for changes in the credit policy of his company. Taylor noted that S.D. Taylor Jewellers Ltd. had been paying its accounts at comparatively the same rate as last year and that he had been watching inventory levels more carefully. Taylor also told Wilson that the increase in buildings and fixtures was expected to equal depreciation, so the net book value would remain the same.

With this additional information from the two retailers in mind, Wilson set out to complete her report.

Note

1. For details on the nature of this report see "Gardiner Wholesalers Incorporated (A)."

CASE 3.5 GE CAPITAL CANADA: COMMERCIAL EQUIPMENT FINANCING DIVISION

By Elizabeth Grasby and Tim Silk

It was early morning on April 15, 1998, when Steve Rendl, assistant account manager for the Commercial Equipment Financing Division of GE Capital Canada in Toronto, finished reading the morning copy of the *Financial Post* and began reviewing a loan request for $270,000 submitted by an existing client — Clark Carriers Ltd. Clark Carriers, a trucking company, requested the $270,000 loan to purchase two new 1998 Freightliner transport trucks, four new 53-foot trailers, and four new mobile satellite systems, which would be used to track the location of the transport trucks. Rendl had to make a decision on the loan request and forward his report to the senior account manager for approval that afternoon.

GE CAPITAL

GE Capital comprised 27 diversified businesses, including operations in North America, Latin America, Europe, and the Asia-Pacific region. Its head office was located in Stamford, Connecticut. General Electric, GE Capital's parent company, was a publicly traded corporation with net earnings of over US$8 billion. GE Capital was a major competitor in every industry it competed in, achieving record net earnings of US$3.3 billion in 1997. It expected each of its divisions to generate a 20 percent after-tax profit, and if divisions fell below the goal of 20 percent, they would have to justify why profit targets had not been met.

COMMERCIAL EQUIPMENT FINANCING

Commercial Equipment Financing (CEF) was one of GE Capital's 27 divisions. The majority of CEF's business was loans to medium- and large-sized transportation and construction companies. Loans from $30,000 to $1 million were provided to purchase assets such as transport trucks, trailers, paving equipment, and heavy machinery.

CEF was under tremendous pressure to generate profits. The selling strategy at CEF was "Find, Win, Keep" — find new business, win new business, and keep new and existing clients. As of April 1, 1998, less than 1 percent of CEF's portfolio of over 2,000 accounts had been lost to bad debt. Account managers for the

IVEY Tim Silk prepared this case under the supervision of Elizabeth Grasby solely to provide material for class discussion. The authors do not intend to illustrate either effective or ineffective handling of a managerial situation. The authors may have disguised certain names and other identifying information to protect confidentiality. Ivey Management Services prohibits any form of reproduction, storage or transmittal without its written permission. This material is not covered under authorization from CanCopy or any reproduction rights organization. Copyright © 1999, Ivey Management Services.

Southern Ontario Region were expected to generate $12 million in new loans each year, without exposing GE Capital to unreasonable levels of risk.

Several minimum requirements had to be met before CEF would approve a loan. First, CEF did not deal with any company that had been in business for less than three years. Second, the company applying for the loan had to generate enough cash flow to cover the monthly interest payments of the new loan. Third, the company's debt to equity ratio could not be greater than 4:1 when including the new loan. Fourth, CEF would not finance more than 90 percent of the value of any asset, thereby requiring the company to have enough cash to pay for at least 10 percent of the value of the assets it wanted to purchase. Lastly, CEF considered the character of the business owners, general economic conditions, and any company assets that could be pledged as collateral as additional factors in the loan request.

THE TRANSPORTATION INDUSTRY IN SOUTHERN ONTARIO

The trucking industry had been very profitable from 1985 to 1988 until a massive recession in 1989. During the recession, there was less manufacturing, resulting in fewer goods being shipped by trucking companies. Many trucking companies went bankrupt, and those that survived the recession had to lower prices to stay competitive. The industry recovered during a manufacturing boom in the mid-1990s, and the amount of freight shipped between Windsor and Toronto was at its highest level ever; however, the transportation industry in southern Ontario was very competitive, with thousands of trucking companies competing for business. By 1998, the transportation industry had experienced strong growth, but prices and profits remained low, with trucking companies typically generating after-tax net incomes of less than 8 percent of revenues.

With prices low, trucking companies relied on higher volumes of business to generate profits. One way to increase sales volume was to purchase more trucks and trailers and hire additional drivers. For every truck and trailer, a trucking company would typically generate $150,000 to $200,000 in annual sales. However, the high cost of purchasing new trucks and equipment required large loans to finance the purchase of new assets. Because so many trucking companies borrowed money to expand, it was important to maximize the amount of time a truck spent on the road generating sales, to cover not only operating expenses but also the loan payments.

NEW LEGISLATION

It was mandatory that all vehicles (trucks and trailers) used by a trucking company meet the safety standards set by the Ministry of Transportation of Ontario (MTO). These standards were enforced on major highways at weigh scale stations, where all trucks were required to stop for inspections. Effective February 2, 1998, new legislation gave the MTO the right to impound any vehicle (truck or trailer) deemed to have a critical defect.[1] If a critical defect was found during an inspection, the MTO impounded the vehicle for 15 days, and the vehicle could not be operated until the equipment had been repaired to meet safety standards. If the same or additional critical defects were found during any subsequent inspection, the MTO impounded the vehicle for 30 days. In addition to impounding vehicles, the MTO also charged fines ranging from $2,000 to $20,000 for equipment that did not pass inspection. Despite the risk of impoundment, thousands of trucks failed safety inspections annually, and the MTO impounded an average of 30 trucks per month.[2]

CLARK CARRIERS LTD.

Background

Doug and Annette Clark had founded Clark Carriers Ltd. (CCL) in Oakville, Ontario, in 1987. The company began as a one-truck operation hauling freight for a larger trucking company that contracted work to independent truck drivers. Doug was the driver and mechanic, while Annette managed the accounting records. The Clarks survived the economic recession between 1989 and 1993 and continued to operate their business as a one-truck company until the spring of 1996, when they began searching for exclusive hauling contracts.

In March 1996, CCL signed a two-year contract, effective April 1, 1996, making it the exclusive carrier for a small manufacturer of auto parts that supplied the Ford Motor Co. assembly plant in Oakville. Ford required its suppliers to make deliveries according to just-in-time inventory schedules, which meant that CCL would haul multiple trailer loads several days a week.

To accommodate the new contract, CCL borrowed $336,000 from Newcourt Credit on April 1, 1996, to finance the purchase of three new transport trucks and three new trailers. The company hired three drivers to drive the new trucks. As of December 31, 1997, CCL still owed $189,000 on the loan from Newcourt Credit. CCL paid $7,000 of this loan each month.

The trucking volume generated by the contract continued to increase. In October 1997, CCL sought financing to purchase two new trailers. A loan for $38,400 was arranged through GE Capital on October 1, 1997. As of December 31, 1997, the current balance still owing on the GE Capital loan was $36,000. CCL paid $800 of this loan each month. The trucking company's financial statements and ratios are shown in Exhibits 1, 2, and 3.

The New Contract

In March 1998, the auto parts manufacturer signed a new supplier contract, effective May 1, 1998, with Ford. The new contract reflected a 60 percent increase in trucking volume. CCL's two-year contract with the auto parts manufacturer had expired on March 31, 1998, and had not yet been renewed. In an effort to reduce its own costs, and because the trucking volume would increase by 60 percent, the auto parts manufacturer was allowing several trucking companies (including CCL) to bid for the new trucking contract. If CCL hoped to win the new trucking contract, it would need to expand its fleet to accommodate the higher trucking volume and to outbid competing trucking companies.

Projected Requirements for the New Contract

To expand its fleet, CCL required approximately $300,000. Since CCL was required to pay at least 10 percent of the cost in cash ($30,000), it requested a $270,000 loan to purchase two new 1998 Freightliner transport trucks, four new 53-foot trailers, and four new mobile satellite systems. In projecting its income statements for 1998, CCL estimated revenues to be 30 to 60 percent higher than in 1997. Salaries and wages were expected to increase by $60,000 to hire two new drivers, and general and administration expenses were expected to increase by $13,000 owing to the larger fleet. Additionally, bank charges and interest expense on the new loan would be $17,300. Depreciation expenses on the new assets would be $30,000. Legal and accounting fees and rent and utilities were expected to remain unchanged from 1997 amounts. The other operating expenses for 1998 were expected to remain at the same proportion of sales as they had been in 1997. No other purchases of new assets were expected for 1998. The company's income tax rate was approximately 45 percent.

In projecting its balance sheets, CCL estimated the value of the new loan to be $270,000, less the monthly payments to be made between May 1998 and December 1998.[3] CCL anticipated no changes to the age of receivables or the age of payables. The company also had a bank line of credit of up to $50,000 that it had never used. It planned to use $30,000 from this line of credit to make the cash payment required by GE Capital (10 percent of the new assets). The Clarks had used $50,000 in personal assets to secure the bank line of credit. None of the assets on CCL's current balance sheet were pledged as collateral. The main question for Rendl was whether CCL would show a cash surplus on its projected balance sheet. A cash surplus would indicate that CCL would be capable of making the required loan payments, whereas a cash deficit would indicate that CCL would be incapable of paying back the loan.

Since profits remained low across the industry, the Clarks believed that continued growth would ensure their profitability. If CCL lost this contract, the Clarks knew it would be difficult to find enough work to keep their fleet working at 100 percent capacity. Doug and Annette had worked hard to grow their business and had never been late with a loan payment, despite having trailers impounded on two occasions. Annette commented: "We've been through good times and bad and we've expanded before. I feel that this is the right thing to do. We can't afford to stay small!"

RENDL'S DECISION

The new loan request would bring the total of CCL's loans with GE Capital to $306,000. Rendl's report would have to be reviewed by his senior manager, since the total loan amount exceeded his account manager's credit limit of $200,000. Rendl had been with the company for eight months, and it was important he make a well thought-out decision that followed CEF's minimum lending requirements. His report was due in a few hours.

NOTES

1. Examples of critical defects included loose or broken lug nuts, cracked wheels, cracked brake rotors, broken steering components, broken suspension components, and tires with less than 25 percent of the tread remaining across any part of the tire.
2. Ministry of Transportation, Enforcement and Vehicle Inspection, August 1998.
3. The monthly principal payment on the new loan would be $5,625.

EXHIBIT 1

Income Statement (Unaudited) and Ratios
for the Years Ended December 31, 1995, 1996, and 1997

	1995	% sales	1996	% sales	1997	% sales
Revenue	$202,232	100.0%	$645,118	100.0%	$835,295	100.0%
Cost of sales[1]	147,239	72.8%	407,432	63.2%	518,805	62.1%
Gross margin	$ 54,993	27.2%	$237,686	36.8%	$316,490	37.9%
Operating expenses:						
Salaries and wages	$ 26,362	13.0%	$116,757	18.1%	$120,259	14.4%
General and administration	2,058	1.0%	15,556	2.4%	18,512	2.2%
Telephone and fax	1,091	0.5%	6,858	1.1%	8,924	1.1%
Legal and accounting	800	0.4%	1,500	0.2%	1,491	0.2%
Travel and auto	–	0.0%	6,734	1.0%	9,430	1.1%
Rent and utilities	7,140	3.5%	8,142	1.3%	10,075	1.2%
Bank charges and interest	3,227	1.6%	17,127	2.7%	18,505	2.2%
Bad debts	–	0.0%	2,841	0.4%	1,302	0.2%
Depreciation expense	14,348	7.1%	48,565	7.5%	42,795	5.1%
Advertising and promotion	–	0.0%	1,330	0.2%	1,235	0.1%
Meals and entertainment	–	0.0%	867	0.1%	1,042	0.1%
Total operating expenses	$ 55,026	27.1%	$226,277	35.0%	$233,570	27.9%
Net income before taxes	(33)	27.2%	11,409	35.1%	82,920	28.0%
Provision for income taxes	–	0.0%	3,084	1.8%	34,246	9.9%
Net income after taxes	$ (33)	0.0%	$ 8,325	1.3%	$ 48,674	5.8%

1. Cost of sales includes the costs of operating the trucking fleet. These costs include fuel, licences, trip permits, toll payments, fine payments, and maintenance of the trucking fleet.

Statement of Retained Earnings (Unaudited)
for the Years Ended December 31, 1995, 1996, and 1997

	1995	1996	1997
Beginning retained earnings	$(121)	$ (154)	$ 8,171
Add: net income after taxes	(33)	8,325	48,674
Ending retained earnings	$(154)	$8,171	$56,845

Source: GE Capital Equipment Financing Division.

Exhibit 2

	Balance Sheets (Unaudited) as at December 31, 1995, 1996, and 1997		
	1995	1996	1997
ASSETS			
Current assets:			
Cash [STS]	$ 8,107	$ 2,605	$ 4,230 (3877)
Accounts receivable [STU]	21,912	28,230	42,004 20042
Other receivables [STS]	482	478	429 53
Prepaid expenses [STS]	16,237	12,820	15,065 1172
Total current assets	$ 46,738	$ 44,133	$ 61,728
Fixed assets:			
Trucks and trailers (cost) [LTU]	95,000	426,500	463,800 368800
Fixtures (cost)	5,480	5,480	5,480
Company vehicle (cost)	21,500	21,500	21,500
Computer (cost) [LTU]	–	3,200	3,200 (3200)
Less accumulated depreciation [LTU]	95,196	143,761	186,556 91340
Total fixed assets (net)	$ 26,784	$312,919	$307,424
TOTAL ASSETS	$ 73,522	$357,052	$369,152
LIABILITIES			
Current liabilities:			
Accounts payable [STS]	$ 13,676	$ 15,881	$ 27,307 13631
Bank line of credit ($50,000 limit)	–	–	–
Total current liabilities	$ 13,676	$ 15,881	$ 27,307
Long-term liabilities:			
Loan (Newcourt Credit) [LTS]	–	273,000	189,000 84000
Loan GE Capital [LTS]	–	–	36,000 36000
Total long-term liabilities	–	$273,000	$225,000
Total liabilities	$ 13,676	$288,881	$252,307
Owner's equity:			
Share capital	60,000	60,000	60,000
Retained earnings [LTS]	(154)	8,171	56,845 56691
Total owner's equity	$ 59,846	$ 68,171	$116,845
TOTAL LIABILITIES AND OWNER'S EQUITY	$ 73,522	$357,052	$369,152

Source: GE Capital Equipment Financing Division.

EXHIBIT **3**

Financial Ratios
for the Years Ended December 31, 1995, 1996, and 1997

	Industry Average	1995	1996	1997
PROFITABILITY				
Return on average equity	24.5%	0.0%	13.0%	52.6%
STABILITY				
Debt/equity	2.9:1	.23:1	4.2:1	2.2:1
Interest coverage	4.0X	1.0X	1.7X	5.5X
LIQUIDITY				
Current ratio	2.1:1	3.4:1	2.8:1	2.3:1
Acid test ratio	1.9:1	2.2:1	1.9:1	1.7:1
Working capital	n/a	$33,062	$28,252	$34,421
EFFICIENCY				
Age of receivables[1]	30 days	40 days	16 days	18 days
Age of payables[2]	28 days	34 days	14 days	19 days
GROWTH				
Sales growth	21.0%	–	219.0%	29.5%
Profit growth	22.7%	–	253.3%	484.7%
Asset growth	19.4%	–	385.6%	3.4%
Equity growth	14.2%	–	13.9%	71.4%

1. Age of receivables is based on average daily sales and 365 days per year.
2. Age of payables is based on average daily cost of sales and 365 days per year.

Source: GE Capital Equipment Financing Division.

C A S E 3.6   LAWSONS

By Peter Farrell and Richard H. Mimick

"I think I have all the information needed for your request Mr. Mackay. Give me a couple of days to come up with a decision and I'll contact you one way or another — good day!" So said Jackie Patrick, a newly appointed loans officer for the Commercial Bank of Ontario. She was addressing Paul Mackay, sole proprietor of Lawsons, a general merchandise retailer in Riverdale, Ontario. He had just requested a $194,000 bank loan to reduce his trade debt, as well as a $26,000 line of credit to service his tight months of cash shortage. Jackie felt she was fully prepared to scrutinize all relevant information in order to make an appropriate decision. Her appointment as loans officer, effective today, February 18, 1998, was an exciting opportunity for her, as she had been preparing for this position for some time.

LAWSONS

Lawsons had been operating in Riverdale for nearly five years. Mackay felt that his store stressed value at competitive prices, targeting low- to middle-income families. The store offered a wide range of products in various categories, including:

- Infants', children's, and youths' wear;
- Ladies' wear;
- Men's wear;
- Accessories (footwear, pantyhose, jewellery, etc.);
- Home needs (domestics, housewares, notions, yarn, stationery);
- Toys;
- Health and beauty aids; and
- Seasonal items (Christmas giftwrap and candy).

To help finance the start-up of the business in 1982, Mackay secured a $50,000 long-term loan from the Commercial Bank of Ontario at the prime lending rate plus 1.5 percent. As Mackay's personal assets were insufficient for security, the bank loan had been secured by a pledge against all company assets and by a guarantee from Lawsons' major supplier, Forsyth Wholesale Ltd. (FWL).

Mackay's store, with the exception of its first partial year, had always generated net income. However, after withdrawals, Mackay's equity in the firm decreased each year to its present level of $18,914. Exhibits 1, 2, and 3 present Lawsons' income statements, balance sheets, and selected financial ratios. Exhibit 4 presents selected industry ratios.

PURCHASING PROCEDURES

Mackay purchased most of his inventory from FWL, a wholesaler who dealt in the product categories and merchandise that Mackay stocked in his store. Other stock, not supplied through FWL, was purchased directly from local suppliers. Through an arrangement with FWL, Mackay made his merchandising decisions at two annual trade shows in May and October. At the May show, Mackay decided on back-to-school supplies, Christmas merchandise, and fall and winter clothing. Spring and summer merchandise was decided upon at the October show. FWL's purchasing agents accumulated all of the orders from the various retailers it dealt with and, as a large buying group, executed the orders and negotiated prices with the manufacturers. The merchandise was sent to FWL from the individual manufacturers and then was distributed to respective retail outlets, such as Lawsons. FWL required partial payment for this merchandise before the start of the particular selling season. The remainder was due in scheduled repayments throughout the selling season. Mackay was pleased with this arrangement that he had secured with FWL. He was convinced that his product costs were lower as a result.

PAUL MACKAY

Paul Mackay was 40 years old. He had immigrated to Canada in 1982 from his native England, where he had been employed by an insurance company as an accountant. Educationally, Mackay had completed a business economics degree at a military academy. When Mackay came to Canada, he admitted that he was unsure about what recognition he would receive for his previous labour, both corporate and educational. Consequently, Mackay embarked upon an entrepreneurial career. Candidly, Mackay expressed, "I knew I wouldn't be satisfied in some corporate hierarchy — I knew I needed to be in business for myself." In May 1982, a retail vacancy became available in Riverdale. Mackay seized this opportunity to turn his dream of independence into a reality, and he opened Lawsons with the financial backing of FWL.

Mackay was an active resident of Riverdale, often involving himself in community activities. He worked long hours at his store, performing both managerial and clerical duties. Frequently, Mackay could be seen in his store with price gun in hand, pricing and stocking goods or bagging merchandise at the cash register.

THE PROBLEM

Low earnings and necessary owner withdrawals had contributed to Mackay's increasing trade debt. Past due amounts on trade debt were charged a penalty of 13.5 percent interest. Mackay indicated that of the present $217,236 in trade debt, he was paying penalty interest on $193,668. All of the overdue trade debt was owed to FWL. It was this overdue debt that had prompted his loan request. Mackay knew that if he could transfer this trade debt to some other form of debt with lower interest charges, profitability could be increased. Mackay indicated that the current portion of the trade debt would be an acceptable amount to carry for this time of year.

The total trade debt had increased to its present level in fiscal 1998 when Mackay decided that additional retail space would increase sales volume. Mackay felt that his store was too small to effectively display product lines and, therefore, decided that the expansion was a necessary step in the store's turn-around. Additional furniture, fixtures, and leasehold improvements totalled $36,000, which was financed by FWL and added to Mackay's trade debt. Mackay explained that FWL financed the improvements at Lawsons because it was interested in Mackay's improving to the point where he could start paying off the trade debt owed to FWL. At the time of the expansion, FWL's financial director stated, "If this expansion is a means toward debt repayment, and I believe it is, FWL is committed to financing the expansion." To go along with this capital expenditure, a greater investment in inventory was needed. Sales results in 1998 indicated to Mackay that the expansion was helping to improve sales volume.

Mackay believed that with his purchasing arrangements with FWL, a seasonal line of credit was necessary, so that he could manage the months with tight cash positions. February through June were months of cash outflows, with the total cumulative cash outflows peaking at about 4 percent of sales. Exhibit 5 presents monthly sales percentages as well as the cash flows, whether cumulative net inflows or outflows.

PROJECTIONS

Mackay did not anticipate any additional capital expenditures for some time, given the just-completed expansion. Sales growth of 10 percent in each of the next two years was projected. With respect to interest charges, Mackay calculated that if less expensive debt could be found, Lawson's interest expense for all debt, including the proposed line of credit, would be $27,500 and $26,920 for 1999 and 2000, respectively. Store salaries were to remain constant as a dollar amount because of improved employee productivity. Mackay realized that he had a great deal of money tied up in inventory, but he hoped that, as he gained greater experience in handling the added sales volume, inventory could be reduced to pre-1998 levels. With respect to withdrawals, Mackay explained that owing to his depleted savings, future withdrawals from the firm would be at the 1998 level.

JACKIE PATRICK

Patrick had hoped that her first loan request in her new position would be straightforward. However, a closer look indicated that this request would certainly require careful attention and scrutiny. She suspected her superiors would be reviewing her first series of recommendations carefully, given her newness in the position.

Exhibit 1

| | **Income Statements** **for the Years Ending January 31** | | | |
	1995	**1996**	**1997**	**1998**
Sales	$425,398	$507,778	$526,332	$650,210
Cost of goods sold	305,748	386,356	383,948	467,510
Gross profit	$119,650	$139,422	$142,384	$182,700
Operating expenses:				
Store salaries	$ 29,818	$ 38,154	$ 41,234	$ 44,578
Heat and utilities	7,324	7,022	8,524	8,888
Building maintenance and repairs	338	406	508	362
Rent and property tax	28,364	28,364	24,710	23,992
Insurance and taxes	5,934	4,708	3,454	6,922
Depreciation:				
Furniture and fixtures	6,374	3,570	2,952	7,828
Leaseholds	–	160	484	3,176
Interest:				
Long-term debt	11,418	11,332	9,280	8,418
Trade debt	4,724	5,954	11,476	29,570
Other operating expenses	14,016	23,840	26,112	27,692
Total operating expenses	$108,310	$123,510	$128,734	$161,426
Net income	$ 11,340	$ 15,912	$ 13,650	$ 21,274

EXHIBIT 2

	Balance Sheets as at January 31			
	1995	1996	1997	1998
ASSETS				
Current assets:				
Cash	$ 2,596	$ 2,798	$ 3,960	$ 9,664
Accounts receivable	2,278	2,344	4,824	12,028
Inventory	121,218	140,792	153,628	199,700
Prepaids	2,786	3,162	3,002	3,760
Total current assets	$128,878	$149,096	$165,414	$225,152
Fixed assets:				
Furniture and fixtures, cost	$ 32,164	$ 32,164	$ 34,792	$ 61,200
Less: accumulated depreciation	14,314	17,884	20,836	28,662
Net furniture and fixtures	$ 17,850	$ 14,280	$ 13,956	$ 32,538
Leaseholds, cost	$ –	$ 1,200	$ 6,798	$ 16,174
Less: accumulated depreciation	–	160	644	3,820
Net Leaseholds	$ –	$ 1,040	$ 6,154	$ 12,354
Total fixed assets	$ 17,850	$ 15,320	$ 20,110	$ 44,892
Intangibles	84	–	–	–
TOTAL ASSETS	$146,812	$164,416	$185,524	$270,044
LIABILITIES AND PROPRIETOR'S CAPITAL				
Liabilities				
Current liabilities:				
Accounts payable	$ 43,392	$ 71,286	$106,494	$217,236
Other current liabilities	–	934	270	2,450
Total current liabilities	$ 43,392	$ 72,220	$106,764	$219,686
Long-term bank loan	89,836	$ 83,464	76,168	68,872
Total liabilities	$133,228	$155,684	$182,932	$288,558
Proprietor's capital				
Balance, beginning of year	$ 21,152	$ 13,584	$ 8,732	$ 2,592
Add: net income	11,340	15,912	13,650	21,274
Subtotal	$ 32,492	$ 29,496	$ 22,382	$ 23,866
Less: drawings	18,908	20,764	19,790	42,380
Balance, end of year	$ 13,584	$ 8,732	$ 2,592	$ (18,514)
TOTAL LIABILITIES AND PROPRIETOR'S CAPITAL	$146,812	$164,416	$185,524	$270,044

EXHIBIT 3

Ratio Analysis				
	1995	**1996**	**1997**	**1998**
PROFITABILITY				
Vertical analysis:				
Sales	100.0%	100.0%	100.0%	100.0%
Cost of goods sold	71.9%	72.5%	72.9%	71.9%
Gross profit	28.1%	27.5%	27.1%	28.1%
Operating expenses:				
Store salaries	7.0%	7.5%	7.8%	6.9%
Heat and utilities	1.7%	1.4%	1.6%	1.4%
Building maintenance and repairs	0.1%	0.1%	0.1%	0.1%
Rent and property tax	6.7%	5.6%	4.7%	3.7%
Insurance and taxes	1.4%	0.9%	0.7%	1.1%
Depreciation:				
Furniture and fixtures	1.5%	0.7%	0.6%	1.2%
Leaseholds		0.1%	0.5%	
Interest:				
Long-term debt	2.7%	2.2%	1.8%	1.3%
Trade debt	1.1%	1.2%	2.2%	4.6%
Other operating expenses	3.3%	4.7%	5.0%	4.3%
Total operating expenses	25.5%	24.3%	24.6%	25.1%
Net income	2.6%	3.2%	2.6%	3.3%
Return on investment	65.3%	142.6%	241.1%	n/a
LIQUIDITY				
Current ratio	2.97:1	2.06:1	1.55:1	1.02:1
Acid test ratio	0.11:1	0.07:1	0.08:1	0.10:1
Working capital	$85,486	$76,876	$58,650	$ 5,466
EFFICIENCY (Based on 365-day year)				
Age of receivables	2 days	2 days	3 days	7 days
Age of inventory	145 days	140 days	146 days	156 days
Age of payables[1]	55 days	67 days	98 days	154 days
Net fixed assets/sales	$0.04	$ 0.03	$ 0.04	$0.07
STABILITY				
Net worth/total assets	9.3%	5.3%	1.4%	n/a
Interest coverage	1.7X	1.9X	1.7X	1.6X

GROWTH	**1995–96**	**1996–97**	**1997–98**
Sales	9.4%	3.7%	23.5%
Net profit	40.3%	(14.2%)	55.9%
Total assets	12.0%	12.8%	45.6%
Net worth	(35.7%)	(70.3%)	n/a

1. Aging is based on purchases, which are equal to cost of goods sold plus ending inventory less beginning inventory.

Exhibit **4**

Dun & Bradstreet Canadian Norms and Key Business Ratios Industry: Retail — Miscellaneous General			
	1995	1996	1997
PROFITABILITY			
Vertical analysis			
Gross profit	25.1%	26.9%	24.2%
Net income	4.0%	4.0%	2.3%
Return on investment	15.3%	15.4%	8.4%
LIQUIDITY			
Current ratio	2.3:1	2.8:1	2.4:1
Acid test	1.1:1	0.9:1	0.8:1
Working capital	$ 203,704	$216,484	$189,334
EFFICIENCY			
Age of receivables	17.8 days	17.3 days	15.5 days
Age of inventory	101.8 days	93.4 days	93.9 days
Age of payables	n/a	23.2 days	24.0 days
Net fixed assets/sales	$ 0.08	$ 0.09	$ 0.10
STABILITY			
Net worth: total assets	56.9%	60.5%	54.5%
GROWTH			
Sales		6.1%	(7.8%)
Net income		4.2%	(47.6%)
Asset		0.7%	(4.2%)
Net worth		6.9%	(13.7%)

Exhibit **5**

Sales and Cumulative Net Cash Outflow by Month		
Month	**% of Sales**	**Cumulative Net Cash Outflow**
February	3.5	Yes
March	5.4	Yes
April	7.5	Yes
May	8.3	Yes
June	11.1	Yes
July	12.9	No
August	12.4	No
September	9.3	No
October	5.8	No
November	6.2	No
December	13.6	No
January	4.0	No

C A S E 3.7   MAPLE LEAF HARDWARE LTD.

By S. Foerster and R.H. Mimick

On May 29, 1999, Stuart Foreman, assistant manager of the London, Ontario, branch of the Central Canadian Bank, was reviewing information he had received from Robert Patrick, president and manager of Maple Leaf Hardware Ltd., who had requested an increase in his line of credit with the bank to cover seasonal working capital needs. Foreman, who had just received a transfer and promotion to the London branch, realized that he would have to evaluate this request carefully.

COMPANY BACKGROUND

Patrick was 32 years of age. His father had established his own hardware business in Nova Scotia in 1969. Robert had worked in his father's store since the age of 16, gaining valuable sales and management experience. In 1991, Patrick accepted a job offer from a large department store chain. Two years later he was transferred to London, Ontario, and eventually became manager of one of the branch stores. In 1996, he decided to leave the department store chain in order to become his own boss. He opened his own retail hardware store with a personal investment of $120,000 and $80,000 from a close friend, Les Harrison, and incorporated the company on September 1, 1996. Patrick was able to arrange a long-term loan of $240,000 and a line of credit of $60,000 with the Central Canadian Bank through Terry Woods (Foreman's predecessor, who had recently left the bank). After a detailed analysis, Patrick decided to locate his business on Maple Leaf Street in a growing area of the city. He was able to rent a recently vacated building with 600 square metres of space and adequate parking facilities. The nearest store was located several kilometres away. Initially, only two full-time and three part-time employees were hired to assist Patrick. As the business grew, additional part-time employees were hired. Sales increased steadily during the first few years, and in 1998, Maple Leaf Hardware Ltd. realized its first profit.

THE INDUSTRY

During the 1950s, home and garden supplies, or hardware, were distributed primarily through small, independently owned stores. The major alternative distributor was the hardware department of major department stores. Since that decade, many large-scale retailers had begun to sell hardware. "Big box" retailing, a 1990s phenomenon, had emerged throughout North America. In the hardware and home improvement sector, Home Depot, a big box retailer, was considered to be the "category killer."[1] Home Depot operated warehouse retail outlets catering to the "do-it-yourselfer." With over 700 stores in the United States and over 40 in Canada, Home Depot was a major competitive force in the industry. Home Depot achieved worldwide sales of over $8 billion with profit margins of 5.5 percent in 1998. There were two locations in London, one in the south end of the city and one in the northeast end. The increased competition resulted in much consolidation within the industry. There were cooperative groups, such as Pro Hardware and Home Hardware. These large organizations bought on a central basis.

In addition to Home Depot, there were over 20 stores in London in the retail hardware business, including independently owned, chain, and department stores. These stores offered a wide variety of goods, including tools, plumbing and electrical supplies, appliances, cookware, lawn and garden equipment, and in some cases, sporting goods and toys. The major determinant of a hardware store's success was its location, as it was important to have a large area from which to draw customers. This was especially true for independent stores.

Hardware sales were traditionally highest around Christmas. January to April were slow months, whereas sales were much stronger from May to August. Because of this seasonality, and since a company had to order inventory well in advance, a hardware store's greatest need for working capital financing usually occurred in February or March. The strongest cash position was in December. In February or March, a hardware store the size of Maple Leaf Hardware Ltd. would require from $80,000 to $120,000 more working capital than in December.

In difficult economic times, with increasing inflation and interest rates, many industries were hit hard financially; however, this was not the case with the hardware industry. During economic recessions, consumers' emphasis shifted from purchasing new goods to repairing and rebuilding old goods. Statistics Canada reported the value of new residential construction to be $45,068,000 in 1997 and $44,905,000 in 1998.

PRESENT SITUATION

Patrick presented his proposal for an increase in the short-term line of credit from $100,000 (the line of credit that had been granted last year) to $160,000. Patrick included in his report specific information that Foreman had requested, including financial statements for the years the company had been in operation (see Exhibits 1 and 2). Exhibit 3 provides financial ratios for the company and also includes available industry information. Patrick stated that sales for the year ending December 31, 1999, were expected to be close to $1,700,000. A further increase in sales of 10 to 20 percent was anticipated in 2000. There were no anticipated purchases of fixed assets in the next few years. Patrick planned to pay a common stock dividend of $20,000 each year starting on December 31, 1999. The rent was expected to increase by $2,400 per month over the current level of $10,000 per month, commencing in September with the signing of a new two-year lease. Patrick was planning to introduce a new inventory control system, which he hoped would eventually reduce the age of inventory to the industry average of the past few years; however, he was not sure if he would be able to accomplish this within the next year.

Foreman set out to decide whether to increase the size of the line of credit for Maple Leaf Hardware Ltd. He noted in his file that on one occasion in the past the company had been slow in sending financial data the bank had requested, but when Foreman mentioned the incident, Patrick dismissed it as a misunderstanding with Woods. In further conversation, Foreman learned that Patrick and Harrison (who owned 40 percent of the common shares) had recently had some disagreements about how Patrick should be running the business. Patrick commented:

> Les and I go way back. We've had our differences throughout the years, but things always get straightened out. I'm the major shareholder in this business, and I know how to run a hardware store profitably. I think sometimes Les forgets that.

Since this was Foreman's first evaluation of a loan request in his new position, he wanted to proceed cautiously and perform a thorough analysis. He realized he would have to present his decision within the week.

NOTE

1. Category killers specialize in and offer a wide variety of one type of good (e.g., Toys "R" Us).

Exhibit **1**

	Income Statements for Selected Periods ($000s)		
	4 Months to Dec. 31, 1996	Year Ended Dec. 31, 1997	Year Ended Dec. 31, 1998
Sales	$400	$1,218	$1,418
Cost of goods sold	270	812	936
Gross profit	$130	$ 406	$ 482
Operating expenses:			
Wages[1]	$ 56	$ 182	$ 192
Rent	36	114	120
Property tax	6	20	24
Utilities	4	14	16
Depreciation	6	18	18
Advertising	6	22	24
Other	30	30	18
Interest	8	26	22
Total operating expenses	$152	$ 426	$ 434
Net income before tax	$(22)	$ (20)	$ 48
Income tax[2]	–	–	2
Net income after tax	$(22)	$ (20)	$ 46

1. Includes manager's salary of $24,000 in 1997 and $39,000 in 1998.
2. Tax laws allow the company to offset the $48,000 profit of 1998 with the combined $42,000 loss of the previous two years. Thus, in 1998, the company pays tax only on the $6,000 difference at the rate of 25 percent ($1,500 but rounded up to 2,000 for reporting purposes).

Exhibit 2

	Balance Sheets as at December 31 ($000s)		
	1996	1997	1998
ASSETS			
Current assets:			
Cash	$ 34	$ 12	$ 10
Accounts receivable	20	30	32
Inventory	294	320	416
Total current assets	$348	$362	$458
Fixed assets			
Leasehold improvements (net)	$ 78	$ 72	$ 66
Fixtures (net)	96	84	72
Total fixed assets	$174	$156	$138
TOTAL ASSETS	$522	$518	$596
LIABILITIES AND EQUITY			
Liabilities			
Current liabilities:			
Accounts payable	$110	$124	$170
Working capital loan	–	18	20
Current portion of long-term debt	16	16	16
Total current liabilities	$126	$158	$206
Long-term debt[1]	$218	$202	$186
Total liabilities	$344	$360	$392
Equity			
Common stock			
R. Patrick	$120	$120	$120
L. Harrison	80	80	80
Retained earnings	(22)	(42)	4
Total equity	$178	$158	$204
TOTAL LIABILITIES AND EQUITY	$522	$518	$596

1. The loan was secured by personal assets of the owners.

Exhibit **3**

Financial Ratios and Selected Industry Ratios					
	Maple Leaf Hardware Ltd. Ratios			Canadian Hardware Stores Industry Ratios[1]	
	1996	1997	1998	1996	1997
PROFITABILITY					
Vertical analysis					
Sales	100.0%	100.0%	100.0%	100.0%	100.0%
Cost of goods sold	67.5%	66.7%	66.0%	73.7%	74.7%
Gross profit	32.5%	33.3%	34.0%	26.3%	25.3%
Expenses:					
Wages	14.0%	14.9%	13.5%		
Rent	9.0%	9.4%	8.5%		
Property tax	1.5%	1.6%	1.7%		
Utilities	1.0%	1.1%	1.1%		
Depreciation	1.5%	1.5%	1.3%		
Advertising	1.5%	1.8%	1.7%		
Other	7.5%	2.5%	1.3%		
Interest	2.0%	2.1%	1.6%		
Total expenses	38.0%	35.0%	30.6%		
Net income before tax	(5.5%)	(1.6%)	3.4%		
Income tax	0.0%	0.0%	0.1%		
Net income after tax	(5.5%)	(1.6%)	3.2%	2.2%	2.6%
Return on investment	n/a	n/a	20.5%	10.7%	12.5%
LIQUIDITY					
Current ratio	2.76:1	2.29:1	2.22:1	1.6:1	1.6:1
Acid test	0.43:1	0.27:1	0.20:1	0.6:1	0.6:1
Working capital ($000s)	222	204	252	555	555
EFFICIENCY (Based on 365 days, except 1996 which is based on ⅓ of a year)					
Age of accounts receivable in days sales	6	9	8	44.5	47.2
Inventory in days cost of goods sold	132.5	143.8	162.2	104.9	99.1
Age of accounts payable in days cost of goods sold	49.3	55.7	66.3	46.3	51.9
STABILITY					
Net worth/total assets	34.1%	30.5%	34.2%	42.2%	40.7%
Interest coverage	n/a	0.23X	3.2X		

GROWTH (percentages)	1996–97	1997–98
Sales	6.2%	16.4%
Net income	25.9%	–
Total assets	6.0%	15.1%
Equity	1.7%	29.1%

1. Compiled from Dun & Bradstreet Industry Norms and Key Business Ratios.

CASE 3.8   MATERIAUX BOISVERT LTEÉ

By Elizabeth Grasby and Leena Malik

In January 1992, Yvan Martinault, commercial account manager at the main branch of the Crown Bank of Canada in Chicoutimi, Quebec, stared at his computer, wondering how to approach his most recent loan request. François Lachapelle, new owner and president of Materiaux Boisvert Ltée, had just requested an increase in the company's line of credit from $1.6 million to $2.2 million. Although Yvan was expecting a request for additional funds to cover working capital needs, previous financial forecasts had indicated a need of only $1.8 million. Yvan was somewhat surprised by the amount requested, but he knew the application had to be processed quickly for head office approval in Montreal.

COMPANY BACKGROUND

Materiaux Boisvert sold hardware and building materials to retail customers as well as industrial contractors. The business was founded in 1982 in Chicoutimi by five partners who established a loyal customer base through reliable customer service and the establishment of a family-oriented atmosphere. The company operated two retail and distribution outlets in Chicoutimi. A large hardware store and lumberyard were located near the centre of the city, while a smaller outlet was situated in the suburbs. The business was very successful, with sales reaching an all-time high of $20 million in 1985, which resulted in profits of $500,000 for the same year.

In 1986, the firm was purchased by Produits Forestier Saguenay (PFS), a large company whose core business was the manufacture of hardwood materials for export. The owners of PFS wished to invest extra money in a cash-producing business and thus purchased Materiaux Boisvert for its cash potential. Although Materiaux Boisvert became a separate operating division of PFS, management goals focused solely on the desire to make money. This new style of management created constant friction between managers and employees, which resulted in the unionization of employees in 1987. Management neglect and employee tensions began to affect many aspects of business operations, especially the company's reputation for customer service. By late 1989, the economic climate also began to deteriorate. A deepening recession worsened the firm's sales and receivables position, and the company suffered three consecutive years of losses before being purchased by the Lachapelle family in September 1991. The firm's financial statements and financial ratios are provided in Exhibits 1 to 4.

At the time of the purchase, the Lachapelles had owned a major hardware and building supply outlet in Chicoutimi and were looking to penetrate further into the market. Thus, they took advantage of the opportunity to buy out their competitors. The rights to the company name as well as the physical assets of Materiaux Boisvert were purchased, with the exception of the land and buildings, which were rented for $200,000 per year with an option to purchase them within five years.

Mr. Lachapelle, François's father, was a well-respected client of the Crown Bank of Canada, which was financing a line of credit for his first company. Since Mr. Lachapelle wanted his son to take over the family business eventually, he placed François in charge of Materiaux Boisvert's operations. François Lachapelle was 27 years of age and was in the process of completing a master's degree in business administration in Toronto. François was very familiar with all aspects of the hardware industry, having worked in the family business in various positions for many years. For François, the opportunity to run his own business was a personal goal. He had many ideas for turning Materiaux Boisvert into a thriving business and was eager to devote all his attention to the firm's operations.

THE HARDWARE AND BUILDING MATERIALS INDUSTRY

The majority of hardware and building materials firms in Chicoutimi serviced both the retail and industrial markets. Hardware products consisted of tools, plumbing, paint, and electrical and garden supplies, while building materials included all supplies required for external and internal home or building construction. Building materials products were numerous and ranged from lumber and drywall to shower moulds, windows, and doors.

The retail and industrial markets for hardware and building supplies were highly seasonal. Retail sales were slowest during the winter months, particularly in January and February. Peak periods occurred in May and June, with highest sales in May. Retail sales were not adversely affected by economic swings, since customers delayed the purchase of new goods by repairing existing goods during difficult economic times. Although industrial sales also peaked in May and June, the industrial market remained strong during the period of May to November. Unlike the retail market, the industrial market's close ties with the construction industry had a greater impact on sales during difficult economic periods. See Exhibit 5 for industry ratios for the retail (building materials and hardware) market.

THE COMPETITION

The Chicoutimi market was served by two types of competitors: pure hardware and building supply outlets (the independents) and mass merchandisers (the chain stores). Canadian Tire was the only mass merchandiser in Chicoutimi with two locations in the area. Canadian Tire was a national chain that competed mainly in the retail hardware market, with a product mix that ranged from traditional hardware goods sold in most hardware stores to sporting goods and electrical appliances. Canadian Tire promoted its products using an aggressive advertising and promotion strategy; however, once in the store, customers received minimal service.

Independent hardware and building supply outlets sold a wide range of products necessary for the complete construction of homes or buildings. Advertising was more localized and achieved mainly through the use of pamphlets, flyers, newspapers, or radio. Customer service was an extremely important differentiating factor for most independents, and many stores catered to their own loyal clientele.

Hardware and building materials companies in Chicoutimi faced intense competition due to the numerous competitors in the area. Seven local hardware and building supply companies competed through intense price wars, especially on most traditional materials and big ticket items.

MATERIAUX BOISVERT

Materiaux Boisvert operated in both the retail and industrial markets, with the majority of sales (70 percent) in the industrial contract market. The company's retail margins traditionally ranged from 26 to 29 percent, while contract margins ranged from 18 to 20 percent, compared with margins of approximately 32 and 23 percent for the industry. As margins were higher for retail sales, François hoped eventually to penetrate further into this market.

Materiaux Boisvert offered a 3 percent discount to its best customers for accounts paid before the 15th of the following month, with the remaining balance due in 60 days. Other customers were offered net 60 days for debt payments, while less stable customers were offered payment terms of net 30 days. François would have preferred to reduce all receivables to net 30 days; however, industry standards of 60 days restricted tight credit control.

The company relied on several hardware suppliers for the purchase of its hardware and building materials. Building materials prices, with the exception of lumber, were negotiated by a buying group consisting of 15 buyers from different geographic regions. Materials were then purchased by Materiaux Boisvert separately, based on the negotiated price. Although many of the company's competitors also purchased materials from the same suppliers, none participated in the buying group process. The volatility of the lumber industry demanded good insight into the lumber market and required sharp purchasing skills. Materiaux Boisvert had its own purchaser who bought wood and lumber materials based on market dynamics and prices.

Industry terms for the majority of supplies were traditionally 2 percent in 10 days, net 30 days. François hoped to take advantage of the 2 percent discount as much as possible. The company's working capital needs were traditionally highest in June, and François estimated that he would need approximately $150,000 more in June than in September.

EVENTS LEADING UP TO THE LINE OF CREDIT REQUEST

Before the purchase, Materiaux Boisvert was given a liberal maximum line of credit of $3.2 million because of the size and equity position of Produits Forestier

Saguenay. Unfortunately, the Lachapelles did not have similar equity to place in the business and the loan was subsequently renegotiated to $1.6 million. The loan was guaranteed by the company's accounts receivable and inventories as well as $250,000 of the Lachapelles's personal assets.

Both the Lachapelles and the bank realized that the new line of credit would likely be insufficient for peak period operations. Therefore, Yvan agreed to reexamine the company's loan requirements after several months of operations under new management. Yvan estimated that the new loan requirements would likely be close to $1.8 million; however, François requested $2.2 million.

PRESENT SITUATION

The purchase of Materiaux Boisvert caused significant changes to the financial position of the company under new management. First, the company's fiscal year automatically changed from ending May 31 to ending September 30, since the firm was purchased in September. Second, Materiaux Boisvert was no longer a division of PFS, and, therefore, investments and interdivisional accounts related to PFS would no longer be relevant. Third, the purchase of Materiaux Boisvert resulted in the creation of a new business entity for the Lachapelles. Therefore, 1992 opening retained earnings would have a zero balance.

Finally, François's plans for turning the business around required a different set of operating assumptions than under previous management. François provided Yvan with three sales scenarios for the new fiscal year: most likely, optimistic, and least likely. Under the most likely scenario, 1992 sales were estimated to be close to 1991 sales, with a 5 percent increase for 1993.

François planned to reduce wages and salaries to 10.2 percent of sales, while better account management would reduce bad debts to no more than 0.5 percent of sales. Accounting and lawyer's fees would return to pre-1991 levels of approximately $40,000 per year. François also estimated that tight control of travelling expenses, advertising, office supplies, and vehicle rentals would result in yearly expenditures of $24,000, $53,000, $60,000, and $5,000, respectively. Maintenance and repairs would likely remain the same in dollars as in 1991. Materiaux Boisvert also rented a small portion of a nearby parking lot. The parking lot lease had expired and would not be renewed in the future.

The Lachapelles purchased the company for $1.1 million, of which $600,000 was paid in cash, resulting in an inflow of owner's capital for 1992. The remaining $500,000 would be owed to PFS as long-term debt of the company; previous long-term debt owed to the bank by PFS would not be assumed by the Lachapelles. Changes in the company's debt position would reduce interest expenses to approximately $300,000 per year.

THE MEETING

A meeting was scheduled between the Lachapelles and Yvan to discuss the new request. As Yvan began to arrange for the meeting, he reflected that although the Lachapelles were long-standing customers of the bank, he had never dealt with François before. He knew he would have to perform a more thorough analysis of Materiaux Boisvert's operations and statements to prepare for the session.

can't pay interest payment debt high

EXHIBIT 1

	1989	1990	1991
Income Statement for the Years Ending May 31 ($000s)			
Net sales	$16,222	$ 15,093	$13,807
Cost of goods sold:			
Beginning inventory	3,765	3,553	3,369
Purchases[1]	12,766	11,915	9,882
Cost of goods available for sale	$ 16,531	$ 15,468	$13,251
Ending inventory	3,553	3,369	2,538
Cost of goods sold	$ 12,978	$ 12,099	$10,713
Gross profit	$ 3,244	$ 2,994	$ 3,094
Operating expenses:			
Wages and salaries	1,655	1,521	1,488
Insurance	32	36	15
Utilities	81	70	76
Maintenance and repairs	260	262	199
Office equipment rental and maintenance	16	20	20
Travelling expenses	32	31	31
Vehicle rental	41	46	9
Parking lot rental	8	8	9
Advertising	49	58	72
Property tax	49	44	47
Office supplies	65	68	77
Bad debt expense	97	104	316
Accounting and lawyer's fees	65	52	124
Corporate expenses paid to PFS	32	35	88
Depreciation: buildings	49	42	46
Depreciation: other fixed assets	227	206	225
Other operating expenses	32	3	32
Total operating expenses	$ 2,790	$ 2,634	$ 2,874
Operating profit	$ 454	$ 360	$ 220
Other expenses:			
Interest	443	441	442
Other	13	308	19
Total other expenses	$ 456	$ 749	$ 461
Net profit before tax	$ (2)	$ (389)	$ (241)
Income tax expenses (credit)[2]	0	33	0
Net profit after tax	$ (2)	$ (356)	$ (241)

1. Purchases include any purchase discounts taken.
2. Tax laws allow the company an income tax credit of $33,000 to offset previous losses. The company's tax rate is 15 percent on income of $200,000 and 45 percent on all income above $200,000. Therefore, if profit were $500,000, tax would be calculated at 15 percent of $200,000 and 45 percent of $300,000.

EXHIBIT **2**

	Statement of Retained Earnings for the Years Ending May 31 ($000s)		
	1989	**1990**	**1991**
Retained earnings at beginning of the year	$3,574	$3,572	$3,216
Net profit	(2)	(356)	(241)
Retained earnings at end of the year	$3,572	$3,216	$2,975

Exhibit **3**

	Balance Sheet as at May 31 ($000s)		
	1989	**1990**	**1991**
ASSETS			
Current assets:			
Cash	$ 0	$ 0	$ 29
Accounts receivable	2,727	2,678	2,124
Due from Produits Forestier	9	741	228
Inventory	3,553	3,369	2,538
Prepaid expenses	71	61	49
Other current assets	125	34	0
Total current assets	$ 6,485	$ 6,883	$4,968
Investments	665	676	914
Fixed assets:			
Land	527	527	527
Buildings (net)	1,299	1,257	1,252
Other fixed assets (net)	1,329	1,123	898
Total fixed assets	$ 3,155	$ 2,907	$2,677
TOTAL ASSETS	$10,305	$10,466	$8,559
LIABILITIES			
Current liabilities:			
Working capital loan	$ 2,660	$ 2,811	$1,354
Accounts payable	2,195	2,576	2,513
Owed to Produits Forestier	46	18	65
Current portion of long-term debt	193	212	253
Total current liabilities	$ 5,094	$ 5,617	$4,185
Long-term debt	1,634	1,422	1,188
Total liabilities	$ 6,728	$ 7,039	$5,373
OWNER'S EQUITY			
Common stock	5	5	5
Contributed capital	0	206	206
Retained earnings	3,572	3,216	2,975
TOTAL LIABILITIES AND EQUITY	$10,305	$10,466	$8,559

Exhibit **4**

Financial Ratios			
	1989	**1990**	**1991**
PROFITABILITY			
(A) Vertical analysis			
Net sales	100.0%	100.0%	100.0%
Cost of goods sold	80.0%	80.2%	77.6%
Gross profit	20.0%	19.8%	22.4%
Operating expenses:			
Wages and salaries	10.2%	10.1%	10.8%
Insurance	0.2%	0.2%	0.1%
Utilities	0.5%	0.5%	0.6%
Maintenance and repairs	1.6%	1.7%	1.4%
Office equipment rental and maintenance	0.1%	0.1%	0.1%
Travelling expenses	0.2%	0.2%	0.2%
Vehicle rental	0.3%	0.3%	0.1%
Parking lot rental	0.0%	0.1%	0.1%
Advertising	0.3%	0.4%	0.5%
Property tax	0.3%	0.3%	0.3%
Office supplies	0.4%	0.5%	0.6%
Bad debt expense	0.6%	0.7%	2.3%
Accounting and lawyer's fees	0.4%	0.3%	0.9%
Corporate expenses paid to PFS	0.2%	0.2%	0.6%
Depreciation: buildings	0.3%	0.3%	0.3%
Depreciation: other fixed assets	1.4%	1.4%	1.6%
Other operating expenses	0.2%	0.2%	0.2%
Total operating expenses	17.2%	17.5%	20.8%
Operating profit	2.8%	2.4%	1.6%
Other expenses:			
Interest	2.7%	2.9%	3.2%
Other	0.1%	2.0%	0.1%
Total other expenses	2.8%	5.0%	3.3%
Net profit before tax	0.0%	–2.6%	–1.7%
Income tax expense (credit)	0.0%	0.2%	0.0%
Net profit after tax	0.0%	–2.4%	–1.7%

Exhibit 4 (cont.)

Financial Ratios			
	1989	**1990**	**1991**
(B) Return on investment	–0.1%	–10.2%	–7.3%
LIQUIDITY			
Current ratio	1.27:1	1.23:1	1.19:1
Acid test	0.54:1	0.48:1	0.51:1
Working capital ($000s)	1391	1266	783
EFFICIENCY			
Age of receivables	61 days	65 days	56 days
Age of inventory	100 days	102 days	86 days
Age of payables	63 days	79 days	93 days
STABILITY			
Net worth/total assets	34.7%	32.7%	37.2%
Interest coverage	1.0X	0.1X	0.5X

	1989–90	**1990–91**
GROWTH		
Sales	–7.0%	–8.5%
Net profit	–	–
Total assets	1.6%	–18.2%
Equity	–4.2%	–7.0%

EXHIBIT 5

Dun & Bradstreet Canadian Industry Norms and Key Business Ratios Industry: Retail — Building Materials, Hardware			
	1989	**1990**	**1991**
PROFITABILITY			
(A) Vertical analysis			
Gross profit	23.9%	26.2%	27.4%
Net profit after tax	2.7%	2.6%	2.5%
(B) Return on investment	16.6%	14.2%	11.8%
LIQUIDITY			
Current ratio	1.6:1	1.6:1	1.6:1
Acid test	0.6:1	0.6:1	0.6:1
Working capital	$487,484	$460,208	$445,999
EFFICIENCY			
Age of receivables	38.7 days	37.8 days	38.8 days
Age of inventory	96.6 days	97.1 days	102 days
Age of payables	n/a	40 days	47.7 days
STABILITY			
Net worth: total assets	34%	40%	41.1%
GROWTH		**1989–90**	**1990–91**
Sales		−2.7%	−9.3%
Net profit		−8.1%	−10%
Equity		15.2%	3.3%
Assets		−2.3%	0.6%

C A S E 3.9   PLUMB PARTS SUPPLY LTD.

By Elizabeth Grasby and Krista K. Wylie

It was October 1992 when Murray Cowan, the loans manager at the Dorchester, Ontario, branch of the Canadian Commercial Bank, reviewed the loan request for $60,000 that he had received from Sean Taggart of Plumb Part Supplies Ltd. (PPS), a distributor of construction products. James Taggart, Sean's father, was the founder and owner of PPS and wanted to sell most of the business to Sean. Although the loan would be a personal loan to Sean, Mr. Cowan had to carefully review the business entity of PPS because his decision would need to be based on the past and future success of the company. Since Sean's only source of income was from PPS, the company must generate sufficient funds to service both company debts and Sean's personal debts. Mr. Cowan also wanted to ensure that PPS's current $75,000 line of credit was sufficient for the upcoming years before deciding whether to grant the loan to Sean.

COMPANY BACKGROUND

Incorporated in 1975, PPS was first located in Embro, Ontario, before moving to a 130-square-metre building in Dorchester, Ontario. After two years in this location, PPS moved to a 260-square-metre space in an industrial mall. PPS stayed in the industrial mall for 11 years before building its current 750-square-metre location in 1988.

PPS was primarily a distributor of construction products ranging from sandpaper and staples to larger items such as drain cleaners and pumps. James Taggart felt strongly about filling all the needs of his customers. Therefore, if PPS could not fill a customer's request for a product or find a company that could provide the product, PPS would attempt to develop that product for the customer. Consequently, PPS also assembled certain construction products.

The products assembled by PPS over the years contributed significantly to the company's success, particularly early on when James knew that the only way for the company to become successful was to be able to supply the specific products needed by his customers. Mr. Taggart's first venture into assembling was in

1975, after a friend in the industry complained about not being able to buy a tool tester that was easy to use. Recognizing a need in the marketplace, James developed such a product.

Tool testers were used frequently in the construction business to ensure that equipment was safe. The tool tester that PPS invented was much easier to use than any others on the market and sold extremely well. In these early days of PPS, James also saw that there was a market for 15- and 30-metre heavy duty extension cords. Hence, he began to buy 300-metre rolls of electrical cord, which could easily be cut and manufactured into CSA (Canadian Standards Association) approved extension cords. These extension cords have remained extremely popular since their inception.

The company has always used a catalogue as its primary source of advertising. The catalogue expanded from one page of seven products in 1975 to 52 pages of 4,700 products in 1993. In 1987, the catalogue was sent coast to coast, allowing the company to achieve nationwide distribution. In addition to the catalogue, trade shows provided excellent exposure for PPS.

INDUSTRY

The economic conditions since 1990 had not been favourable for companies involved in the construction industry. Many companies experienced decreases in sales of up to 50 percent. Since there had not been any growth in the industry as a whole, any sales increases experienced by individual companies were at the expense of their competitors. Therefore, in order for companies to be successful in this environment, they had to have a unique advantage over their competition. As well, with increased sales each year becoming more difficult to attain, many companies started to focus instead on increasing their profitability. Measures such as increasing prices, tightening credit policies and purchasing more cost effectively were being taken by companies in the industry. As he looked over the financial statements, Mr. Cowan noted that PPS had been able to maintain and even strengthen its position within the industry during the tough economic and competitive conditions of the past three years. See Exhibit 4 for wholesalers-hardware industry ratios.

THE FUTURE

When Mr. Cowan had discussed the future of PPS with Sean Taggart, the young man had been confident that the company would continue to be successful in the upcoming years. He expected sales growth to slow somewhat to approximately 10 percent in both 1993 and 1994 and hoped to maintain the cost of sales at 1992 levels. Furthermore, Sean intended to focus on controlling the age of receivables, with the goal of bringing it below 60 days while maintaining PPS's current age of payables. PPS currently had good relations with its suppliers and Sean did not wish to jeopardize this relationship. Finally, Sean wanted to pay off the company's long-term debt within the next two years and noted that the company would likely pay 45 percent in taxes in each of the next two years.

SEAN TAGGART   Sean joined the company in October 1984. Since that time, Sean had worked in almost all facets of the business. He started out in the manufacturing side of the business, assembling some of the products that PPS made, and from there he moved to the financial side of the business, keeping the company books. He then became involved in sales and was successful in opening up the Quebec territory for PPS in 1987.

In 1988, James Taggart foresaw that he would not be able to run PPS forever and that Sean would eventually take over the business. Therefore, James started to transfer partial ownership to his son in each of the subsequent five years until 1992, at which time James decided Sean should buy out most of the business from him. In September 1992, James approached an accountant to determine a fair selling price. James had two other children and did not want them to feel as though he was being overly generous to their brother, nor did he want to charge his son a price that was too high. A price was decided upon, $60,000 of which was to be paid immediately to James as a down payment and part of the remainder of which would be paid to James in the form of a $20,000 salary in each of the next five years. According to the agreement drawn up, James could choose to have nothing to do with the business and still draw his salary each year.

THE CURRENT SITUATION   Mr. Cowan knew he had to evaluate PPS's financial prospects carefully before deciding to extend the $60,000 personal loan to Sean. The business must be able to generate sufficient profits in the future to cover the $8,600 loan repayment expense each year while providing Sean with at least $25,000 personally. If this was not possible, Mr. Cowan knew he would have difficulty justifying the loan, even though the Taggart family had been excellent customers of the bank for many years.

Exhibit 1

	1990	1991	1992
Income Statements for the Years Ended July 31 ($000s)			
Sales	$1,611	$1,184	$1,422
Cost of sales:			
Beginning inventory	252	336	274
Purchases	1,105	714	969
Cost of goods available for sale	$1,357	$1,050	$1,243
Ending inventory	336	274	286
Cost of sales	$1,021	$ 776	$ 957
Gross income	$ 590	$ 408	$ 465
Operating expenses:			
General and administrative	$ 374	$ 335	$ 332
Salary to Sean	30	30	30
Salary to James	30	30	30
Depreciation	16	11	11
Total operating expenses	$ 450	$ 406	$ 403
Operating income	$ 140	$ 2	$ 62
Plus: other income	3	3	5
Less: interest expense	11	5	8
Net income (loss) before taxes	$ 132	$ 0	$ 59
Provision for income taxes	29	0	13
Net income (loss) for the year	$ 103	$ 0	$ 46

Note: In 1991, $14,000 was paid out to shareholders.

Exhibit 2

	1990	1991	1992
Balance Sheets as at July 31 (000's)			
ASSETS			
Current assets:			
Accounts receivable	$222	$200	$279
Income taxes recoverable	0	33	0
Inventory	336	274	286
Total current assets	$558	$507	$565
Fixed assets:			
Equipment and vehicles, cost	$ 42	$ 73	$ 73
Less: accumulated depreciation	22	33	44
Fixed assets, net	$ 20	$ 40	$ 29
Other:			
Cash surrender value of life insurance	25	23	0
TOTAL ASSETS	$603	$570	$594
LIABILITIES AND SHAREHOLDERS' EQUITY			
Current liabilities:			
Bank overdraft	$ 66	$ 21	$ 45
Accounts payable and accrued expenses	77	141	136
Bonus payable	100	35	15
Income taxes payable	6	0	11
Total current liabilities	$249	$197	$207
Long-term debt	$ 21	$ 54	$ 22
Shareholders' equity:			
Share capital	$ 30	$ 30	$ 30
Retained earnings	303	289	335
Total shareholder's equity	$333	$319	$365
TOTAL LIABILITIES AND SHAREHOLDERS' EQUITY	$603	$570	$594

EXHIBIT **3**

	Plumb Parts Supply Ltd. Ratio Sheet		
	1990	**1991**	**1992**
PROFITABILITY			
Sales	100.0%	100.0%	100.0%
Cost of sales	63.4%	65.5%	67.3%
Gross profit	36.6%	34.5%	32.7%
Operating expenses:			
Salaries	3.7%	5.1%	4.2%
General and administration	23.2%	28.3%	23.3%
Depreciation	1.0%	0.9%	0.8%
Total	27.9%	34.3%	28.3%
Operating profit	8.7%	0.2%	4.4%
Other income	0.2%	0.3%	0.4%
Interest	0.7%	0.4%	0.6%
Net profit before taxes	8.2%	0.0%	4.2%
Provision for taxes	1.8%	0.0%	0.9%
Net income	6.4%	0.0%	3.3%
ROI	32.5%	0.0%	13.3%
LIQUIDITY			
Current ratio	2.2	2.6	2.7
Acid test	0.9	1.0	1.4
Working capital	$309,000	$310,000	$358,000
EFFICIENCY			
Age of receivables (days)	50.3	61.7	71.6
Age of inventory (days)	120.1	128.9	109.1
Age of payables (days)	25.4	72.1	51.2
STABILITY			
Net worth: total assets	55.2%	56.0%	61.4%
Interest coverage	13.0X	1.0X	8.4X
GROWTH			
Sales		(26.5%)	20.1%
Net profit		n/a	n/a
Equity		(4.2%)	14.4%
Assets		(5.5%)	4.2%

Exhibit **4**

Dun & Bradstreet Canadian Industry Norms and Key Business Ratios Industry: Wholesalers — Hardware		
	1990	**1991**
PROFITABILITY		
Net income	2.9%	3.6%
ROI	13%	20%
LIQUIDITY		
Current ratio	2.0	1.5
Acid test	0.8	0.7
Working capital	$218,632	$128,370
EFFICIENCY		
Age of receivable (days)	51.4	43.5
STABILITY		
Net worth: total assets	45.5%	38.7%
GROWTH		
Sales	10.9%	
Net profit	35.2%	
Equity	(28.6%)	
Assets	(16.2%)	

C A S E 3.10 SANDALIAS FINAS DE CUERNAVACA, S.A. – EXPORT DECISION

By Elizabeth Grasby and Niels Billou

"Now that the sale is confirmed, all we need is the financing to ship our first export order." It was mid-November 1996, and John Kortright, president of Sandalias Finas de Cuernavaca (SFC), a casual shoe manufacturing company, sat in his office in Cuernavaca, Mexico, and wondered how he would convince the bank to give him the US$80,000[1] he needed to fulfill the order. Time was of the essence because the order would need to be completed for the spring season.

600,000 peso

THE MEXICAN FOOTWEAR INDUSTRY

The Mexican footwear industry[2] was primarily composed of family-run, small-scale producers, with many of these operations passed down from generation to generation (see Exhibit 1 for Mexican footwear industry data). For decades, Mexican shoe manufacturers were protected by high tariffs that kept imports out, thus guaranteeing a captive market. As a result, product quality and productivity levels were much lower than those found outside Mexico.

When Mexico became a member of the General Agreement on Tariffs and Trade (GATT) in 1986 and the North American Free Trade Agreement (NAFTA) in 1992, tariffs on foreign-manufactured footwear were reduced from 100 percent to 20 percent, and imported footwear began arriving in Mexico to a receptive consumer market. With lower prices and a perception of better quality, foreign producers' sales grew quickly, capturing a third of all Mexican footwear industry sales by 1994.

Increased foreign competition and the peso devaluation crisis of December 1994 shut down many of the smaller operations and forced inefficient domestic manufacturers to compete at home and abroad or go out of business. By 1996, Mexico, and in particular the footwear industry, were still recovering from the devaluation-induced recession. As a result, companies were increasingly looking to export markets where sales prospects looked brighter.

SANADALIAS FINAS DE CUERNAVACA

Sandalias Finas de Cuernavaca was located in Cuernavaca, a city of approximately one million people, about 90 kilometres south of Mexico City (a map of Mexico is given in Exhibit 2). SFC was originally run by a Mexican family as more of an artisan shop than a factory. Kortright bought 50 percent of the firm in 1975 and a year later purchased the remaining 50 percent from his partner. The company currently employed over 70 employees and was projecting sales of approximately 6.6 million pesos for fiscal 1996 (see Exhibit 3 for SFC's financial statements).

The company designed and manufactured dressy sandals for women 40 to 50 years of age, who wanted a comfortable sandal that was dressy yet casual enough to wear every day. The company had produced over 50 styles of sandals and carried two product lines every year to correspond with the two annual shoe fashion seasons: spring/summer and fall/winter. Production peaked for the two months prior to Christmas and fell off sharply from early December through to mid-January.

The company sold its products to upscale department stores and high-end independent shoe stores in Mexico City and throughout the country. Orders were received at trade shows and fairs as well as through meetings with store buyers. Orders ranged anywhere from 50 pairs of sandals (a small order) to over 2,000 pairs (a large order). The company had several major, long-time customers such as Sears (positioned as an upscale store in Mexico and a customer for 19 years) and El Puerto de Liverpool (an upscale department store and a customer for 10 years).

SFC offered credit terms to its customers of 30 days, although major customers often took up to 75 days to pay. Discounts of 5 percent were given to those customers who paid in 15 days, with a further discount of 10 percent to customers whose orders exceeded 10,000 shoes per year. The discounts taken by customers approximated 3 percent of total annual sales. SFC's suppliers offered terms of 15 to 30 days, although due to the current economic situation, some suppliers were accepting payments of 45 days. Many others had resorted to placing slow-paying customers on cash-on-delivery (COD).

Running the operations of the company was a family affair, with Kortright and his wife responsible for sales, marketing, and administration, and their eldest son responsible for design and operations.

JOHN KORTRIGHT

John Kortright grew up in Toronto and had completed an undergraduate degree in modern history and a master's degree in international affairs at Carleton University in Ottawa. After his undergraduate degree, Kortright spent some time studying Spanish in Mexico, where he met and married his wife, Martha, who was born and raised in Cuernavaca.

In 1975, the Kortrights returned to Mexico and settled in Cuernavaca. Kortright, looking for the challenge of running his own operation, purchased a 50 percent share in a small sandal factory using funds he had inherited from a relative. He then bought the remaining 50 percent ownership a year later. Kortright reflected on his experiences:

I knew nothing about the shoe business; but I learned pretty quickly — I had to! There have been a lot of ups and downs, but I think we're finally at the stage where we're efficient in our operations and have the skills and expertise to go to the next level.

After spending 20 years learning about business through trial and error, Kortright used his 1996 visit to Canada to fine-tune his business skills by taking an executive education course at the Richard Ivey Business School in London, Ontario.

THE ORDER

In October 1996, at a shoe fair in Guadalajara, Kortright met a U.S.-based distributor who wanted to order 5,000 pairs of women's sandals to be sent to Russia. Kortright commented on the order:

We were coming up to our slow period between winter and spring, and this order would nicely fill up a month where we basically had no work. At the same time, I was looking at the future of exporting. With the current machinery, it would be easy to double our production capacity with minimal addition to our fixed costs. The distributor I spoke with was excited about our designs, and if this order works out, it could mean an additional 5,000 pairs per month.

It was now mid-November and Kortright was meeting with his banker next week. Although he had a 20-year history with the bank and had built a close relationship that was common in the Mexican business culture, Kortright knew that banks were cautious about lending in the current economic climate. Many were requesting personal guarantees and twice as much collateral as the loan amount. Kortright knew that the bank could ask for his house, estimated at US$100,000 as collateral; however, both he and Martha were very reluctant to pledge it as collateral. Kortright had asked for and repaid loans in the past; however, this was the first time he had asked for an export loan, and he was anxious to present a convincing proposal. Kortright knew that, at the very least, the bank would want to see detailed projected financial statements.

As a starting point, Kortright felt he could double sales in 1997, with 50 percent of total sales coming from exports, and 1998 sales would increase by a further 15 percent. He expected his cost of goods manufactured would increase slightly in 1997, since new lines had been introduced for the export market, but that 1998's cost of goods manufactured would revert to the 1996 level. Purchases would be 65 percent of cost of goods manufactured. Selling expenses would rise from current levels as Kortright planned more trips abroad to develop export markets — but he did not know how much more. Administrative expenses would remain at the same percentage of sales. Interest of 12 percent per year was charged on export loans.[3]

SFC would have to invest in new lasts, dies, and moulds for the new export lines. These would cost 13,000 to 33,000 pesos per line, and four new lines would have to be added each year. A new truck would also have to be purchased, at a cost of 150,000 pesos, in the next two years.

Kortright planned to keep his accounts receivable for his domestic sales at 30 days. Export sales were done on a letter of credit[4] basis and, therefore, were considered to be cash sales. Kortright was hoping to pay his suppliers more quickly, in order not to be put on COD.

As he settled in his chair for a long night ahead of him, Kortright said to himself:

> There's no easy way to do this. I'm going to have to put a proposal together that will be approved quickly if we're going to meet the order deadline.

Notes

1. In November 1996, one U.S. dollar = 7.5 pesos.
2. Information in this section is based on "Strategic Planning '95 — The Mexican Marketplace: Analysis and Forecast," American Chamber of Commerce of Mexico, A.C., August 1994.
3. Interest on domestic loans was charged at 24 to 30 percent per year. Interest on export loans was lower because the loan was given in U.S. dollars and had to be repaid in U.S. dollars. Interest rates in the rest of North America averaged 5 to 6 percent per year at the time.
4. A letter of credit is a document issued by a bank guaranteeing the payment of a customer's purchases up to a stated amount for a specified period. It substitutes the bank's credit for the buyer and eliminates the seller's risk.

Exhibit **1**

Mexican Footwear Industry Data		
Percent of Industry	**Category**	**Pairs of Shoes per Day**
75	Micro manufacturers	Less than 50
21	Small manufacturers	50 to 500
3	Medium manufacturers	500 to 2,000
1	Large manufacturers	More than 2,000

Exhibit **2**   **Map of Mexico**

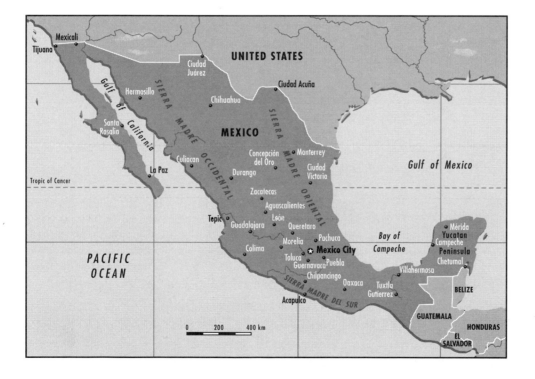

Exhibit 3

	Financial Statements **Income Statement** **for the Period Ending December 31** **New Pesos (N$)**	
	1995	**1996 (Projected)**
Gross sales	N$ 4,689,100	N$ 6,698,744
Less: discounts	134,008	155,245
Less: returns	136,162	94,181
Net sales	N$ 4,418,930	N$ 6,449,318
Cost of goods manufactured[1]	3,431,655	5,106,131
Gross profit	N$ 987,275	N$ 1,343,187
Operating expenses:		
Administrative expenses:	N$ 455,085	N$ 569,868
Selling expenses	235,251	323,982
Interest and factoring charges[2]	286,022	348,815
Total operating expenses	N$ 976,358	N$ 1,242,665
Net operating profit	N$ 10,917	N$ 100,522
Add: other income	2,680	3,080
Net income before taxes	N$ 13,597	N$ 103,602
Income tax[3]	N$ –	4,623
Profit sharing[4]	N$ –	N$ 1,360
Net income after tax and profit sharing	N$ 13,597	N$ 97,619

1. Cost of goods manufactured includes raw materials and work-in-progress and finished goods inventories, as well as direct labour, purchases, and depreciation on production equipment. Purchases of materials were: 1996: N$3,339,404; 1995: N$1,784,318
2. Factoring refers to a financial service whereby the manufacturer sells its accounts receivable to a factoring company, which then becomes responsible for collection. The factor used is determined by an interest rate based on daily balances, in this case 2.5 percent a month.
3. Mexican taxes are calculated at 34 percent of the previous year's income.
4. Profit sharing is calculated at 10 percent of the previous year's income.

Exhibit 3 (cont.)

	Balance Sheet as at December 31 New Pesos (N$)	
	1995	**1996 (projected)**
ASSETS		
Current assets:		
Cash	N$ 51,056	N$ 39,435
Accounts receivable	581,950	540,365
Inventory	525,001	1,146,893
Employee loans	55,860	64,325
Total current assets	N$1,213,867	N$1,791,018
Fixed assets:		
Plant equipment	N$ 191,490	N$ 231,490
Vehicles	75,322	75,322
Lasts, dies, and moulds	184,048	236,533
Furniture and fixtures	63,398	63,398
Subtotal	514,258	606,743
Less: accumulated depreciation	232,354	288,386
TOTAL FIXED ASSETS	N$ 281,904	N$ 318,357
TOTAL ASSETS	N$1,495,771	N$2,109,375
LIABILITIES		
Current liabilities:		
Accounts payable	N$ 465,970	N$ 955,654
Total current liabilities	N$ 465,970	N$ 955,654
Long-term liabilities[1]	225,000	251,301
Total liabilities	N$ 690,970	N$1,206,955
Shareholders' equity		
Common stock	N$ 5,000	N$5,000
Retained earnings	799,801	897,420
Total equity	N$ 804,801	N$ 902,420
TOTAL LIABILITIES AND SHAREHOLDERS' EQUITY	N$1,495,771	N$2,109,375

1. Payment of 50,000 pesos per year to start in 1997.

Exhibit 4

Ratio Analysis		
	1995	**1996**
PROFITABILITY		
i) Vertical analysis		
Gross sales	100.0%	100.0%
Less: discount	2.9%	1.4%
Less: returns	1.9%	1.4%
Net sales	94.2%	96.3%
Cost of goods manufactured	73.2%	76.2%
Gross profit	21.1%	20.1%
Operating expenses		
Administrative expenses	9.7%	8.5%
Selling expenses	5.0%	4.8%
Interest	6.1%	5.2%
Total operating expenses	20.8%	18.6%
Net operating profit	0.2%	1.5%
Add: other income	0.1%	0.0%
Net income	0.3%	1.5%
ii) Return on equity	2.0%	11.0%
STABILITY		
Net worth/total assets	54.0%	43.0%
Interest coverage	1.05X	1.3X
LIQUIDITY		
Current ratio	2.61	1.87
Acid test	1.48	0.67
EFFICIENCY		
Age of receivables	48.0	30.6
Age of inventory	55.8	82.0
Age of payables	95.3	102.6

GROWTH	**1995–96**
Sales	43%
Net profit	723%
Total assets	41%
Equity	12%

CASE 3.11   STUDIO TESSIER LTÉE

By R.H. Mimick and Fraser MacDonald

On the morning of August 8, 1992, Monique Lavoie took another sip of coffee as she leafed through the loan request on her desk. As manager of the Quebec City branch of the Atlantic Bank of Canada, Monique had to make a decision concerning an extension on a working capital loan. The clients, Paul and Nicole Tessier, owned and managed Studio Tessier Ltée., a women's clothing shop and an interior design studio. Armed with their most recent financial statements (see Exhibits 1 to 3), company and industry financial ratios (see Exhibits 4 to 6), and a detailed set of floor plans, the Tessiers had requested a $37,000 increase in their working capital loan, in order to finance an expansion of the design business. Monique knew she would have to respond as soon as possible because Paul and Nicole were anxious to complete the expansion for the Christmas season.

The Tessiers had been clients of the bank since their business began in 1986. They were an energetic couple who felt that the opportunity for creativity and the chance to pursue their interests in a career context outweighed the difficulties of running a small business. Paul was well known in the community and served on the boards of several community service organizations. He was currently the president of the Quebec City Executives Club and served on the board of directors for the city's Business Improvement Association. Nicole coordinated several major fashion shows a year to raise funds for local charities such as the hospital and art gallery. The couple were also very involved in their church and worked on many parish projects.

STUDIO TESSIER

Studio Tessier was located on the outskirts of Quebec City, in an 18th-century home that once belonged to Nicole's grandmother. The main floor of the house was home to Salon Tessier, an upscale women's clothing boutique. The interior design business operated out of the second floor, which consisted of two showrooms of furnishings and artwork, Paul's office, and a second smaller office that Nicole shared with the office manager of the two businesses. Nicole managed the boutique and Paul ran the interior design business. Their small support staff included a full-time seamstress, a shipper, an office manager who handled the accounts for both businesses, and an assistant who alternated between the sales floor and the design studio.

Paul and Nicole had been in business together for approximately seven years, and their management styles were as different as their personalities. Nicole kept detailed records of her business. A perpetual inventory count was kept, and with each sale, client files and sales records were adjusted. Nicole also kept a close watch on her payables and receivables.

In contrast, Paul's approach was more tactical, and he was less committed to record keeping. Paul enjoyed the people-interaction of the business, the thrill of a sale, and the details of negotiating a contract. He did not keep up-to-date inventory records and was somewhat lax in recording sales and collections. At one point in the year, the office manager approached Paul with a severe cash flow problem. After making several phone calls, Paul calmly collected $44,000 in billings he had not yet recorded. Recently, Paul had been very flexible with customer deposits, usually required as down payment before work began. Despite Paul's relaxed approach to paperwork, much of the growth for Studio Tessier over the past few years had come from the design business.

SALON TESSIER

Nicole's boutique carried lines by designers such as Albert Nipon, Alfred Sung, Ellen Tracey, and Louis Guy Giroux, as well as a selection of fine jewellery and leather goods. Over the years, Salon Tessier had developed a reputation as a fashion boutique that provided excellent service and offered exclusive lines in the Quebec City area. Two main aspects of Nicole's marketing plan were her client files and fashions shows. Detailed records on each customer were kept to enhance the personalized service the boutique provided. Fashion shows also helped reinforce the high-fashion image Nicole wanted to project. In-store shows were held once a month and major shows occurred 10 times a year.

Nicole did all the buying for the boutique and made frequent trips to Montreal, Toronto, and New York. Because orders were placed six to eight months before each season, there was little flexibility in the fashion business. Overall, Nicole aimed for margins of 40 percent of selling price.

PAUL TESSIER, INTERIOR DESIGN

Paul ran the design business with the help of an assistant who sold in the boutique during slow periods. Paul worked on both residential and institutional projects. The latter category was very price-sensitive, and contracts were awarded through a bidding process. While he aimed for gross margins of 30 percent overall, competition in the institutional market made this goal difficult to achieve. Residential clients were more attractive because jobs were personal in nature and cost was not the principal concern with each decorating decision. As a result, margins were closer to his 30 percent target with this segment. Over the past year, Paul had handled many institutional projects, but he wanted to increase his efforts with the residential sector in the future.

HISTORY

The Tessiers opened Salon Tessier in April 1986. Nicole worked full time in the boutique, while Paul continued working with a local manufacturing firm and accepted design projects on a part-time basis. During the first two years, Salon Tessier experienced strong sales growth and solid profits.

In 1988, based on the advice of a management consultant, the Tessiers decided to expand the clothing business. The second storey of the house was redecorated and the boutique's sales area was doubled, along with inventories. At this time, Paul left his job to commit full time to the interior design business. But by Christmas 1988, it was apparent that the boutique's expansion was premature. Sales did not materialize to the degree anticipated, and merchandise had to be discounted drastically. The sales area was reduced to its original size by the spring of 1989, and a loss of $30,823 was incurred that year.

A new accounting/consulting firm was contracted for 1990. During this year, Studio Tessier incorporated, and the land and building were transferred to the Tessiers's personal holdings. In 1990, a profit was once again realized.

A mild recession in 1991 caused layoffs with local manufacturers and affected sales at Studio Tessier, resulting in a net loss. Yet 1992 was a record year, with a net income of $40,483. Selected industry ratios are presented in Exhibits 5 and 6.

Over the last two years, sales in the boutique appeared to have levelled off owing to increased competition in the area. Much of the growth anticipated for fiscal 1993 would come from the decorating business. Sales for Paul Tessier, Interior Design would constitute approximately 65 percent of total sales for Studio Tessier in the coming year. Income tax expense was projected at 25 percent of profit for 1993.

INVENTORIES

The inventories of Studio Tessier could be divided into three main categories: (1) garments and jewellery, (2) wallpaper, draperies, and carpeting, and (3) furnishings and artwork. Given the five distinct seasons in the women's clothing business (summer, fall, winter, "holiday," and spring), each approximately two to four months in length, turnover of inventory was very important. Despite the seasonality, working capital requirements stayed relatively consistent throughout the year. Unpopular items were discounted in order to move them and make room for the next season's line. Accounts with clothing suppliers were payable every 30 days or 60 days. For wallpaper and carpeting, orders were placed and inventory was held a very short period of time before installation. Manufacturers gave 30 to 45 days to pay and were not especially strict. Furnishings and artwork caused more of a cash shortage, and pieces were carried an average of one year. Suppliers expected payment in 30 days. A large inventory for furniture and artwork was essential in the design business.

EXPANSION PROPOSAL

"If the expansion is completed by November 1992, I believe sales should reach $925,000 in fiscal 1993. At the very least, I anticipate 10 percent growth over current sales levels," Paul had said to Monique.

The expansion proposal consisted of adding three boutiques to the existing house. The idea was to create an exclusive shopping area, increasing the benefits of travelling the distance to Studio Tessier. The Tessiers already had clients who were interested in renting space, among them, a shoe store, a beauty salon, and a jewellery shop. The second floor of the expansion would provide floor space needed to expand Paul's business and give Nicole a better office. The rental income from the three outlets would cover the mortgage payments on the addition. In this way, Paul could increase the floor space for his business without major additions to fixed costs. However, Paul felt that $5,000 in fixtures would be required in the new showroom and office.

The Tessiers planned to keep the ownership of the building in their name and would finance the addition with a mortgage. A working capital loan of $100,000 was requested to finance the inventories and accounts receivable. At present, the Tessiers had a working capital loan of $63,000, which was secured by inventories, and other personal assets with a realizable value of $12,500.

THE DECISION   Monique Lavoie recalled the excitement in Paul Tessier's voice as he described the expansion and presented the blueprints. She knew she would have to work fast, as her clients were anxious to know her decision.

Exhibit 1

	Consolidated Income Statements for the Years Ending July 31		
	1990	**1991**	**1992**
Net sales	$660,155	$561,540	$720,106
Cost of goods sold	348,320	388,750	473,763
Gross profit	$311,835	$172,790	$246,343
Operating expenses:			
Subcontracting[1]	$ 97,825	$ —	$ —
Executive salaries	51,500	58,213	68,813
Wages	47,356	49,743	37,033
Auto travel	14,420	8,145	18,767
Rent	9,426	9,845	9,680
Local accounting	7,026	5,691	5,229
Advertising and promotion	17,676	18,320	20,370
Telephone	3,399	3,623	4,078
Insurance	3,168	4,103	4,560
Bank interest and charges	8,595	7,686	7,346
Employee benefits, etc.	1,259	1,343	3,788
Utilities	2,393	3,255	2,833
Supplies, office, and store	8,948	4,196	4,660
Miscellaneous expenses	5,499	4,068	4,663
Credit card charges	3,960	2,953	2,939
Depreciation	1,811	1,449	1,601
Total expenses	$284,261	$182,633	$196,360
Net income before tax	$ 27,574	$ (9,843)	$ 49,983
Income tax	2,500	—	9,500
Net profit after tax	$ 25,074	$ (9,843)	$ 40,483

1. In 1990, the accountant recorded subcontracting as a separate expense. In the following years, subcontracting expense was included in cost of goods sold.

Exhibit 2

	Statement of Retained Earnings for the Years Ending July 31		
	1990	**1991**	**1992**
Retained earnings, beginning of year	$ –	$23,824	$11,618
Net income after tax	25,074	(9,843)	40,483
Subtotal	$25,074	$13,981	$52,101
Less: dividends	1,250	2,363	2,500
Retained earnings, end of year	$23,824	$11,618	$49,601

EXHIBIT **3**

	Balance Sheets as at July 31		
	1990	1991	1992
ASSETS			
Current assets:			
Cash	$ 1,562	$ –	$ – s
Accounts receivable	12,273	6,154	28,706 u 16433
Notes receivable	24,473	–	– s
Inventory	90,705	108,473	149,044 u 58379
Income tax recoverable	–	1,388	–
Prepaid expenses	2,393	2,524	3,087 u 694
Total current assets	$131,406	$118,539	$180,838
Fixed assets:			
Furniture and fixtures, cost	$ 9,054	$ 9,054	$ 13,479 u 3425
Less: accumulated depreciation	1,811	3,260	4,861 u 3050
Total fixed assets (net)	$ 7,243	$ 5,794	$ 8,618
Goodwill	3	3	3
TOTAL ASSETS	$138,652	$124,335	$189,458
LIABILITIES AND SHAREHOLDERS' EQUITY			
Liabilities			
Current liabilities:			
Accounts payable	$ 32,281	$ 43,306	$ 46,731 s 14450
Bank loan	47,500	53,064	62,905 s 15405
Loan payable	12,500	–	– u
Customer deposits	13,253	13,625	110 u 13143
Taxes payable	8,435	2,578	17,238 s 8803
Bonus payable	–	–	10,625 s
Due to shareholders	854	139	2,243 s 1389
Total current liabilities	$114,823	$112,712	$139,852
Shareholders' equity			
Common stock			
authorized 5 million shares,			
issued 5	$ 5	$ 5	$ 5
Retained earnings	23, 824	11,618	49,601 s 25777
TOTAL LIABILITIES AND			
SHAREHOLDERS' EQUITY	$138,652	$124,335	$184,458

Exhibit 4

Ratio Analysis			
	1990	1991	1992
PROFITABILITY			
Vertical analysis:			
Sales	100.0%	100.0%	100.0%
Cost of goods sold[1]	52.8%	69.2%	65.8%
Gross profit	47.2%	30.8%	34.2%
Operating expenses:			
Subcontracting	14.8%	–	–
Executive salaries	7.8%	10.4%	9.6%
Wages	7.2%	8.9%	5.1%
Auto travel	2.2%	1.5%	2.6%
Rent	1.4%	1.8%	1.3%
Local accounting	1.1%	1.0%	0.7%
Advertising and promotion	2.7%	3.3%	2.8%
Telephone	0.5%	0.6%	0.6%
Insurance	0.5%	0.7%	0.6%
Bank interest and charges	1.3%	1.4%	1.0%
Employee benefits	0.2%	0.2%	0.5%
Utilities	0.4%	0.6%	0.4%
Supplies	1.4%	0.7%	0.6%
Miscellaneous	0.8%	0.7%	0.6%
Credit card charges	0.6%	0.5%	0.4%
Depreciation	0.3%	0.3%	0.2%
Total operating expenses	43.1%	32.5%	27.3%
Net income	4.2%	(1.8%)	6.9%
Return on equity	210.4%	(55.5%)	132.2%
STABILITY			
Net worth/total assets	17.2%	9.3%	26.2%
Interest coverage	4.2X	nil	7.8X
LIQUIDITY			
Current ratio	1.14:1	1.05:1	1.29:1
Acid test ratio	0.33:1	0.07:1	0.21:1
Working capital	$16,583	$5,826	$40,989
EFFICIENCY (Based on 365-day year)			
Age of receivables	7 days	4 days	15 days
Age of inventory	95 days	102 days	115 days
Age of payables	34 days	41 days	36 days
Fixed assets/sales	.01	.01	.01

GROWTH	1990–91	1991–92
Sales	(15.0%)	28.0%
Net profit	(139.0%)	n/a
Total assets	(10.3%)	52.4%
Equity	(51.0%)	327.0%

1. For 1991 and 1992 included cost of subcontracting.

Exhibit 5

Dun & Bradstreet Industry Norms and Key Business Ratios Industry — Women's Ready-to-Wear Stores		
PROFITABILITY	**1990**	**1991**
Gross profit	35.3%	31.9%
Net income	0.2%	2.4%
Return on equity	1.2%	15.7%
STABILITY		
Net worth/total assets	33.4%	34.5%
LIQUIDITY		
Current ratio	1.6:1	1.6:1
Acid test ratio	0.2:1	0.2:1
Working capital	$ 36,072	$ 38,603
EFFICIENCY (Based on 365-day year)		
Age of receivables	12.0 days	9.3 days
Age of inventory	145.1 days	140.7 days
Age of payables	57.6 days	53.6 days
Fixed assets/sales	.09	.08
GROWTH		
Sales	(1.2%)	
Net profit	1289.7%	
Total assets	(0.9%)	
Equity	2.4%	

Exhibit 6

**Dun & Bradstreet Industry Norms and Key Business Ratios
Industry — Special Trade Contractors**

PROFITABILITY	**1989**	**1990**
Net income	7.3%	3.1%
(B) Return on equity	45.4%	17.3%
STABILITY		
Net worth/total assets	49.3%	46.0%
LIQUIDITY		
Current ratio	1.6:1	1.9:1
Acid test ratio	1.4:1	1.6:1
Working capital	$ 38,525	$ 48,380
EFFICIENCY (Based on 365-day year)		
Age of receivables	46.6 days	59.1 days
Fixed assets/sales	.09	.12
GROWTH	**1989–90**	
Sales	(6.7%)	
Net income	(60.6%)	
Total assets	14.1%	
Equity	6.5%	

C A S E 3.12   TALICH FABRICATING INC.

By D.G. Burgoyne, J.A. Humphrey, and R.A. Lefebvre

Ted Heath, manager of the downtown branch of the Dominion of Canada Bank in London, Ontario, had to make a decision regarding a loan proposal in time for a meeting Monday morning. It was now late Friday afternoon. Mr. Talich, president of Talich Fabricating Inc. (TFI) and a long-standing customer of the bank, had visited Mr. Heath the previous week with a plan for an expansion of TFI's facilities. Mr. Talich needed money for working capital and for the construction of the plant addition. He had gone to the mortgage division of a life insurance company, which had agreed to lend him the money needed for the plant addition. He was asking Mr. Heath to increase TFI's line of credit to cover his increasing need for working capital. Mr. Heath knew as he reviewed the TFI file that he would have to evaluate the proposal as objectively as possible, especially in view of a recent memo received from the bank's head office (Exhibit 1).

COMPANY HISTORY

Mr. Talich was 52 years of age. He and his wife had immigrated to Canada from Europe in 1980. For several months he worked in Toronto as a labourer, then he moved to London in response to an advertisement for trained machinists. Since Mr. Talich had both excellent qualifications and experience, he was given a position in a newly formed division of a large Canadian metal-fabricating company. The division produced metal furniture, metal partitions, and lockers for educational institutions, hospitals, and other customers.

The division grew rapidly. Mr. Talich advanced within the company on the basis of his own skill and determined nature. Eventually, he was made plant superintendent of the division, and his responsibilities included meeting production requirements, maintaining plant efficiency through a system of standards, and supervising a staff of over 100 workers, most of whom were highly trained. Mr. Talich was expected to select, train, and supervise foremen. As well, he participated in the industrial relations procedures in the plant. As plant superintendent he earned a reputation for his product knowledge, his ability to solve problems, and the exacting standards he set for himself. These attributes resulted in Mr. Talich's increasing participation in the design of new products and the capital budgeting for the plant.

Late in 1985, Mr. Talich's company merged with another large company, and he learned that the new management had decided to phase out the metal furniture division. He wanted to remain in the metal furniture industry, and the company's decision prompted him to enter into business for himself.

In 1986, Mr. Talich started TFI. The company's financing was provided primarily by Mr. Talich's own savings and a bank loan secured by his personal assets. The first years were extremely difficult ones. Mr. Talich worked long hours with little help and with limited facilities. During this period he withdrew only $15,000 to $25,000 a year from the company for the support of his family. Gradually, however, the company began to grow, producing a quality product at a price that made TFI highly competitive. Mr. Talich maintained that high product quality and guaranteed service combined with a fair price would be a successful combination for the metal furniture market.

Producing metal furniture, partitions, and lockers exclusively for educational institutions in the years 1986 to 1990 created certain problems for TFI. Most of TFI's orders were gained by tendering a bid. Skillful bidding is required as contracts missed owing to noncompetitive bids could not easily be replaced. Nor could contract estimates be adjusted to offset rising costs. In addition, government-funded agencies, who were TFI's principal clients, were traditionally slow in settling their accounts. In most instances these customers took from 60 to 120 days after delivery to complete payment.

In 1993, Mr. Talich purchased the Pioneer Co. Ltd. in order to help offset the government business. Pioneer was a small, specialized operation that produced a high quality line of metal office furniture. A drafting table that Pioneer had manufactured and marketed as a licensee was redesigned by Mr. Talich and became a very profitable product for TFI.

In 1994, TFI moved from its rented quarters in an old building to a more modern plant in an industrial area of the city. At that time, Mr. Talich's lawyer and accountant advised him that, for estate and tax management purposes, TFI should not purchase the new building. They advised Mr. Talich to form a property company called Talich Property Inc. (TPI), which would buy the plant and then rent it to TFI. Acting on behalf of TPI, Mr. Talich convinced the mortgage division of a life insurance company to loan TPI $1 million to finance the building. The loan was secured by a mortgage on the property. TFI paid a monthly rental for the use of the facility. The rent had been established by an appraiser at fair market value.

INDUSTRY SITUATION

At the start of the 1990s, government-financed institutions faced continued pressure to reduce costs in view of rising government deficits. Pressure was felt among the suppliers as competition for contracts increased. Some metal furniture manufacturers, particularly those with other related product lines or those that were divisions of large established companies, began to cut prices. Industry participants viewed this as a move to force small and inefficient operators out of the industry. The price-cutting policy intensified through 1992, 1993, and 1994. TFI was able to compete in these years because of its low overhead, company reputation, and contacts already developed by Mr. Talich through his years in the industry. In early 1995, with the sharp increase in material costs and continued price competition, the outlook looked bleak for industry participants. From the half dozen or more Ontario manufacturers who had been in the industry in 1985, only four major competitors remained. Midway through 1995, a year that promised to be difficult for TFI, two major manufacturers announced their withdrawal from the market. Each of these Ontario-based operations was a division of a large company, and each cited inadequate returns as the major reason for quitting the metal furniture industry.

EXPANSION PROPOSAL

Mr. Talich assessed this turn of events in 1994 as an opportunity for the makers of metal furniture to pass increased raw material costs, previously absorbed by the manufacturers, on to customers. There was also the chance for enterprising companies to increase their market share significantly.

In order to compete during the lean years of the early 1990s, TFI had been forced to restrict capital expansion. Lack of plant facilities now posed a severe impediment to any expansion plans. Even at present levels of production, raw materials and finished goods were stacked in aisles on the production floor. The blocked aisles restricted the workers' ability to perform their jobs, limited productive capacity, and increased costs.

In early 1995, Mr. Talich purchased from Trans World Manufacturers the manufacturing rights to a new line of metal shelving for institutional and commercial use. This product's earnings potential, based on market response to date, was limited by the lack of plant capacity. Mr. Talich wished to build a 651-square-metre addition to the present plant, which would increase the plant area by approximately one-third and provide ample storage for finished goods and raw materials. Mr. Talich, acting on behalf of TPI, had asked TPI's mortgagee to finance the addition to the plant. The mortgagee agreed to provide the $750,000 needed to finance the plant extension. The cost of the addition would be reflected in increased rent charged to TFI by TPI.

In presenting his request for the bank to extend TFI's current line of credit of $1.9 million to handle the expected increase in working capital needs, Mr. Talich had indicated that, effective immediately, prices on existing products would be raised by 5 percent. The price increase would reflect the high cost of materials and labour and would be passed directly on to the consumer. Most customers to whom he had spoken did not object to price increases reflecting increased costs. These individuals had indicated that they were more concerned that quality and service remain the same. Mr. Talich felt that the price increase would do much to improve his profitability (Exhibits 2, 3, 4, and 5). As a result of this increase, the cost of goods sold as a percentage of sales was projected to decrease to 78 percent.

In addition to the price increase, Mr. Talich projected TFI's future total sales volume to increase by 25 percent in 1996 and by a further 20 percent in 1997 if the expansion could be financed. Purchases were expected to be 75 percent of cost of goods sold. He also felt that working capital requirements would increase in direct proportion to sales increases but that expenses would remain constant as a percentage of the new dollar sales figure. Income taxes were expected to rise to a 42 percent rate. With regard to capacity, Mr. Talich projected that current equipment would be adequate to handle the proposed increases in sales and that any further capital expansion could be put off until late 1997.

EXHIBIT 1

Bank Memo

MEMO: DOMINION BANK OF CANADA
DATE: August 16, 1995
TO: Branch Managers
FROM: Vice-President, Commercial Services

In view of the recent forecasts by our economists on the movement of interest rates, the shortage of raw materials, the tightening of the money supply, and the general business outlook for the upcoming quarter, I would like to remind all managers that in periods of economic uncertainty our standards for quality and risk factor should be weighed even more heavily in investigating alternative commercial placements.

The growth of loans outstanding at the branch level should not exceed 2 percent. Similarly, as loans are repaid, every effort should be made to place available funds with the proposals offering the highest return and least risk.

EXHIBIT 2

	Income Statements for the Years Ending September 30 (in 000s of Dollars)			
	1992	**1993**	**1994**	**1995**
Sales[1]	$9,230	$7,913	$7,728	$11,420
Cost of goods sold[2]	7,075	6,305	6,163	9,332
Gross profit	$2,155	$1,608	$1,565	$ 2,088
Operating expenses:				
Selling expenses	$ 323	$ 294	$ 298	$ 419
Administrative expenses	280	293	324	487
General expenses	405	374	359	518
Management bonus	725	184		
Depreciation	47	93	70	174
Total	1,780	1,238	1,051	1,598
Net operating profit	$ 375	$ 370	$ 514	$ 490
Interest	27	21	47	101
Less: extraordinary expenses[3]	–	–	119	–
Net profit before tax	$ 348	$ 349	$ 348	$ 389
Income tax	146	147	146	164
Net earnings	$ 202	$ 202	$ 202	$ 225
Initial retained earnings	381	583	785	987
Ending retained earnings	$ 583	$ 785	$ 987	$ 1,212

1. Sales and profit ($000s) for the years 1989 through 1991 were as follows:

	1989	**1990**	**1991**
Sales	$2,336	$5,014	$6,252
Net earnings	15	140	211

2. Cost of goods included raw materials, rent, direct labour, indirect labour, depreciation, and plant overhead. Purchases of materials for the years 1992 to 1995, respectively, were:

	1992	**1993**	**1994**	**1995**
Purchases	$5,329	$3,126	$5,605	$7,152

3. In 1994, TFI experienced nonrecurring expenses as part of its relocation to a new plant site.

Exhibit 3

	Balance Sheet as at September 30 ($000s)			
ASSETS	**1992**	**1993**	**1994**	**1995**
Current assets:				
Cash	$ 13	$ 8	$ 3	$ 3
Accounts receivable	2,179	1,804	1,760	2,173
Inventory	456	794	834	1,547
Prepaid expenses	17	19	31	28
Total current assets	$2,665	$2,625	$2,628	$3,751
Due from Talich Properties			367	174
Fixed assets:				
Plant equipment	$ 381	$ 489	$ 867	$1,140
Vehicles	168	168	274	303
Tooling[1]	–	–	–	295
Subtotal	$ 549	$ 657	$1,141	$1,738
Less: accumulated depreciation	249	341	411	585
Total fixed assets	$ 300	$ 316	$ 730	$1,153
Other assets:				
Goodwill	104	104	104	104
TOTAL ASSETS	$3,069	$3,045	$3,829	$5,182

1. In previous years tooling had been expensed in the year purchased. TFI's accountant recommended that tooling be capitalized and depreciated. Mr. Talich felt that the purchase of tooling would be sufficient to maintain the 1995 level for the next two years. Mr. Talich intended to depreciate all tooling at the rate of one-third per year.

Exhibit 3 (cont.)

	Balance Sheet as at September 30 (in 000s of Dollars)			
LIABILITIES	**1992**	**1993**	**1994**	**1995**
Current liabilities:				
Bank loan	$ 440	$ 752	$ 993	$1,815
Accounts payable	853	542	1,061	1,237
Other payables	957	404	313	276
Total current liabilities	$2,250	$1,698	$2,367	$3,328
Long-term liabilities:				
Lien notes payable[1]	$ –	$ 69	$ 172	$ 127
Due to shareholders[2]	135	306	170	124
Notes payable Pioneer	$ –	86	17	–
Notes payable Trans World	–		–	269
Deferred income tax	–	–	15	21
Total long-term liabilities	$ 135	$ 461	$ 374	$ 541
Total liabilities	$2,385	$2,159	$2,741	$3,869
SHAREHOLDERS' EQUITY				
Authorized:				
10,000 common, no par value				
Issued:				
Common	$ 101	$ 101	$ 101	$ 101
Retained earnings	583	785	987	1,212
Total equity	$ 684	$ 886	$1,088	$1,313
TOTAL LIABILITIES AND SHAREHOLDERS' EQUITY	$3,069	$3,045	$3,829	$5,182

1. Purchases of tooling and equipment were financed through suppliers and finance companies using lien instruments. Mr. Talich felt that the lien notes would remain relatively constant over the next two years.

2. For tax purposes this money was considered to be distributed to the shareholders (principally Mr. Talich). However, to accommodate TFI's working capital requirements, the account was set up as a liability.

EXHIBIT 4

	Sales and Manufacturing Cost Breakdown by Product Line in 1995 (in 000s of Dollars and Percentages)			
	TFI	**Pioneer**	**Trans World**	**Total**
Sales	$9,011	$1,299	$1,110	$11,240
Manufacturing costs:				
Material	$5,135	$ 533	$ 467	$ 6,135
Labour	986	234	241	1,460
Overhead	1,117	285	336	1,737
Total	$7,237	$1,051	$1,044	$ 9,332
Gross profit	$1,774	$ 248	$ 66	$ 2,088
Sales	100.0%	100.0%	100.0%	100.0%
Manufacturing costs:				
Material	57.0%	41.0%	42.1%	53.7%
Labour	10.9%	18.0%	21.7%	12.8%
Overhead	12.4%	21.9%	30.3%	15.2%
Total	80.3%	80.9%	94.1%	81.7%
Gross profit	9.7%	19.1%	5.9%	18.3%

EXHIBIT 5

	Ratio Analysis			
	1992	**1993**	**1994**	**1995**
PROFITABILITY ANALYSIS				
Vertical analysis				
Sales	100%	100%	100%	100%
Cost of goods sold	<u>76.7</u>	<u>79.7</u>	<u>79.7</u>	<u>81.7</u>
Gross margin	23.3	20.3	20.3	18.3
Expenses:				
Selling expenses	3.5	03.7	3.9	3.7
Administrative expenses	3.0	3.7	4.2	4.3
General expenses	4.4	4.7	4.6	4.5
Management bonus	7.9	2.3		
Depreciation	0.5	1.2	0.9	1.5
Interest	<u>0.3</u>	<u>0.3</u>	<u>0.6</u>	<u>0.9</u>
Net operating profit	3.8	4.4	6.0	3.4
Extraordinary expense	<u>1.5</u>			
Net profit before taxes	3.8	4.4	4.5	3.4
Income taxes	<u>1.6</u>	<u>1.9</u>	<u>1.9</u>	<u>1.4</u>
Net earnings	<u>2.2</u>	<u>2.6</u>	<u>2.6</u>	<u>2.0</u>
Return on investment	34.6%	25.7%	20.5%	18.7%
STABILITY				
Interest coverage (times)	13.9	17.6	10.9	4.8
Net worth to total assets	22.3%	29.1%	28.8%	25.7%
LIQUIDITY				
Current ratio	1.18	1.55	1.11	1.13
Acid test ratio	0.97	1.07	0.74	0.65
Working capital ($000)	414	927	261	423
EFFICIENCY (Based on 365 days)				
Age of receivables (days)	86.2	83.2	83.1	69.5
Inventory interval (days)	23.5	46.	49.4	60.5
Payment period (days purchases)	58.4	63.3	69.1	63.1
Fixed assets/sales	0.033	0.040	0.094	0.101
GROWTH				
Sales		(14.3)%	(2.3)%	47.8%
Net earnings		0%	0%	11.4%
Assets		(0.8)%	25.7%	35.3%
Equity		29.5%	22.8%	20.7%

PART

AN INTRODUCTION TO
MANAGING PEOPLE IN ORGANIZATIONS

The work of organizations is done through people. Elaborate structures, systems, rules, and reporting relationships do little more than provide guidance for such behaviour — they do not produce it. Eliciting the needed behaviour is the job of managers. Increasingly, firms are also dependent on more than mere compliance to the dictates of management. Rather, a firm's competitive success rests on its ability to respond quickly and flexibly, to innovate, and to continually improve. To achieve success, the organization requires the commitment of its members. Today's managers face the daunting task of converting their subordinates' compliance into the commitment required to meet the organization's strategic objectives.

Clearly then, the work of a manager goes beyond organizing, assigning, and deploying resources. Perhaps the most critical management skill is managing people — not only subordinates, but also superiors and peers. Your performance as a manager will be evaluated on the basis of how well you are able to do these things. Yet to do it well is a difficult task.

We often think good management skills can be reduced to effective interpersonal skills. Good interpersonal skills, however, are not enough. Being nice to people may result in higher levels of job satisfaction or at least satisfaction with the manager in question, but satisfaction is, at best, only tenuously related to performance. More critical than good interpersonal skills is the ability to understand people's interests (based on their personal characteristics as well as their place in the organization), motivations, and abilities, so that a manager can lead people to accomplish the organization's goals. Without an understanding of people and the mechanisms by which they operate, a manager is left virtually powerless to be effective in his or her role.

This chapter introduces the topic of managing people in organizations. As a survey chapter, it is by no means exhaustive or highly detailed. Rather, we have attempted to introduce you to the critical areas that apply most directly to the job of a manager and to some of the research that has produced what we know in this area. Where appropriate, we have provided citations to original sources that you may want to refer to on your own for more detail.

ORGANIZATIONAL STRUCTURE AND DESIGN

A rapidly globalizing economy, ongoing technological change, and deregulation have all contributed to intensifying competition over the past two decades. Old sources of competitive advantage are drying up as technology is now easily copied, monopoly positions give way in the wake of deregulation, and barriers to entry fall. Organizational capabilities are one of the few remaining sources of sustainable competitive advantage. These capabilities come from the way an organization structures its work and motivates its people to achieve its strategic objectives.

This section looks at the fundamental components of organizational structure, outlines some basic organizational forms, discusses the costs and benefits associated with each of them, and highlights the conditions for which particular forms are best suited.

THE PURPOSE OF ORGANIZATIONAL STRUCTURE

Organizational structure has two specific purposes: to divide work into various distinct tasks to be performed and to coordinate these tasks to accomplish the overall objectives of the organization. Breaking activities into smaller parts, referred to here as differentiation, makes the work easier or more efficient to do but, ultimately, results in the need to put these smaller parts back together again to complete the activity. We refer to this putting back together again as integration.

Differentiation

Differentiation occurs at two levels within the organization. Decision makers must first decide on the extent of horizontal and vertical specialization of an individual job — the breadth of the job in terms of how many separate tasks will be assigned to the job, as well as the depth of the job in terms of how much planning, conception, execution, and administrative activities are included. Decision makers must also determine the groupings of jobs that make the most sense for the organization based on the goods and services it produces; the geographic or client markets it serves; and the skills, knowledge, and expertise the organization needs to produce its product. Extreme differentiation or specialization creates greater expertise, builds economies of scale, and focuses attention. However, it tends to produce monotonous work, narrow interests, and the need for higher levels of integration to bring the specialized parts back together again to form a whole.

Integration

Differentiation provides the organization with efficiency through the division of labour and aligns group goals within specific areas. However, to make the organization as a whole effective, various tasks, departments, and subunits must be integrated. The greater the degree of differentiation and the greater the interdependence, the greater is the need for integration. Various mechanisms can be used to accomplish this objective. The right one will depend on the amount of integration needed.

As the need for interaction, information flow, and coordination increases, the integration process will be more resource intensive. At very low levels, rules and procedures will suffice to coordinate activities. Similarly, planning and hierarchy serve well at fairly low levels. As the need for integration rises, liaison roles, task forces, and teams become necessary to deal with more nonstandard integration needs. Finally, at the most extreme level, whole integrating departments may become necessary to oversee the coordination of activities between groups.

ORGANIZATIONAL STRUCTURE — BASIC FORMS

There are three basic organizational forms: the functional, the divisional, and the matrix.[1] Each is designed to deal with different challenges — size of organization, complexity of environment, multiplicity of markets served, and so on. An organization rarely appears in the pure form of any of the following three types; however, most organizations basically conform to one of them. Knowing the basic characteristics of these forms can provide a manager with considerable insight.

The Functional Form

When organizations are grouped by function, positions are grouped based on particular skills or processes. For example, all accountants would be grouped together, all engineers would be grouped together, and all marketing personnel would be grouped together. With this approach, the work of the organization is divided so that a single group handles each part (or function). Each function or department becomes differentiated and adopts similar values, goals, and orientation, encouraging collaboration, innovation, and quality within the department. This differentiation may, however, make coordination with other departments more difficult.

The activities of all these groups must be put together in order to accomplish the overall goal of the organization. This integration necessitates a good deal of information processing among the different functional groups. Procedures need to be developed to coordinate work in order to produce the organization's final product. In a stable environment, coordination may be relatively easy, but in a rapidly changing environment, it becomes increasingly difficult.

The advantages of grouping by function are:

1. Resources are used efficiently (there is no duplication of equipment or efforts).
2. Professional development is promoted (group members can learn from one another and career paths are obvious).
3. There is a comfortable setting for socialization and evaluation (there is an ease of interaction between people of similar interests and backgrounds, and evaluations are conducted by someone knowledgeable in the area).

In grouping by function several disadvantages also emerge. There is typically poor intergroup coordination; the goals of the organization often become secondary to the goals of the functional group; there is diffuse accountability for the final product or service of the organization; and the organization tends to be more formalized and less flexible, as work is strictly divided between functions. Overall, this form is best suited for small to medium-size organizations that produce a single or closely related set of products and services.

The Divisional Form

The divisional structure is organized by the outputs the organization produces. Each division is responsible for different products, geographic markets, or clients. Regardless of the basis on which it is organized, the division is a self-contained unit that contains all the functional areas necessary to serve its specified market. For example, General Motors, a divisional organization based on product market groups, has separate divisions for cars and trucks in which each group has all the necessary marketing, sales, production, accounting, engineering, and distribution personnel it requires to produce and sell its set of products.

The divisional structure is excellent when the predominant goal of the organization is to respond effectively to satisfy clients in a particular market segment. Because each division has the necessary complement of skills, it can respond quickly to the changing needs of its market. Moreover, corporate control can be more effectively exerted because each division can be held accountable for its own performance.

The advantages of the divisional form are:

1. There is good coordination of activities — everyone who is responsible for a single product is grouped together and the groups are relatively small.
2. Attention is more directed at the organizational goal and less directed at the individual functional group goals.

3. There is increased flexibility (organizations can respond to changes in their markets by adding or deleting divisions as required with little negative impact on other parts of the organization).

The divisional form also has drawbacks. There is often duplication of resources across the organization; professional development is not as clear in terms of career paths and in terms of developing specialized talents; and the setting for socialization and evaluation is less comfortable (evaluations may become particularly problematic because individuals may be evaluated by someone with little expertise in their area). The divisional form works best in medium- or large-size organizations that operate in heterogeneous environments and produce multiple products, serve different customers, and/or sell products in different geographic regions.

The Matrix Form

Matrix structures combine both functional and divisional forms. In some instances organizations want the benefits of both forms: the deep technological expertise within functions, as well as coordination across functions. In a matrix structure, all organizational members maintain a homebase in a functional group while working on projects for specific products, regions, or clients. Individuals can be involved with several projects and with tasks for the functional group. As they complete projects, individuals return, either physically or time-wise, to their functional base for reassignment. The intention of the matrix structure is to reap the advantages of the divisional form and the functional form and to avoid the pitfalls of either one. The advantages of the matrix structure are:

1. It adapts easily to a changing workload (projects are added and deleted as required).
2. Resources are used efficiently (there is no need to duplicate specialists across projects).
3. It provides a homebase for specialists (expertise can be pooled).
4. There is flexibility for workers and variety in their task assignments.
5. It promotes innovation (people with diverse backgrounds are drawn together on projects).

The matrix structure does, however, have its own set of drawbacks, including the following:

1. There is a high degree of dependency on teamwork, which may not be the preferred situation for all individuals.
2. There is conflict for the individual (should one listen to the project manager or the functional manager if priorities conflict?), and there is often uncertainty with regard to evaluation (will the functional manager or the project managers do the evaluation?).

3.   Power struggles often arise between project groups and between project and functional groups in determining personnel assignments to tasks.

4.   There is a lack of stability in the work environment for individuals (owing to the constant change of projects and considerable variation in time demands).

5.   There is a relatively high cost to administering these structures (tracking of individuals, constant renegotiation for project assignments, etc.).

The matrix structure is the ideal structure under the following conditions. First, a matrix structure is appropriate when the organization faces environmental pressures from two sources, such as function and product or function and region. In cases such as this, the dual authority structure is needed to balance these pressures. Second, it is well suited when the firm is in an uncertain and complex task environment. In such instances, the matrix provides the organization with the requisite responsiveness. Finally, the matrix form is well suited to situations in which the firm requires economies of scale in the use of internal resources.

IMPLICATIONS OF ORGANIZATIONAL STRUCTURE FOR MANAGERS

Organizational structure is a key component in creating the unique and difficult to imitate capabilities that organizations now require for sustainable competitive advantage.[2] Organizational structure is important, too, at a more micro level. For individual managers, the redesign or restructuring of their own areas of responsibility has the potential to fundamentally change patterns of performance. Organizational design decisions define where an organization channels its resources, how it defines jobs, shapes work processes, motivates performance, and moulds informal interactions between people over time. A manager will be judged on the basis of how well his or her area performs. An understanding of organizational design helps a manager in doing his or her job effectively.

SECTION

TWO

ORGANIZATIONAL CULTURE

Organizational culture is a central and important feature of organizations. Its effects are pervasive and operate unconsciously, moulding the way employees see and respond to their environment. Although its abstract nature makes it difficult to understand and to study, it greatly affects the way in which an organization's members behave. This section considers culture, its manifestations, and its impact on organizational performance.

DEFINING ORGANIZATIONAL CULTURE

Definitions of culture are difficult to agree on because of the phenomenon's inherently fuzzy nature. Culture can be broadly defined as a basic pattern of assumptions developed by a group as it learns to cope with the problems of surviving in its environment and functioning as a unit.[3] The assumptions that have been found to work well enough in accomplishing these ends and are thus considered valid are then taught to new members as the correct way to perceive, think, and feel in relation to those problems. In short, culture can be thought of as the set of shared assumptions, values, beliefs, and norms that guide organizational members' behaviour.

Any definable group with a shared history can have a culture, creating the possibility for the existence of multiple subcultures within a given organization. The tendency is for these cultures to be consistent, but it is also possible for them to be independent or even inconsistent. For example, the culture within the R&D function of a large company would likely value innovativeness and the importance of new discovery. In contrast, the manufacturing function within the same organization may value cost effectiveness and high levels of efficiency.

Culture originates from the unique history of the firm. The roles and actions of leaders (especially founders) are particularly important. There are four primary mechanisms by which an organizational culture becomes embedded:

1. What leaders pay attention to, measure, and control;
2. How leaders react to organizational crises or critical incidents;
3. The deliberate role modelling and coaching of behaviour; and
4. The criteria used for recruitment, selection, promotion, retirement, and excommunication.

MANIFESTATIONS OF ORGANIZATIONAL CULTURE

Culture manifests itself in many different ways: from the layout of company facilities, to jargon used by members, to stories told, to the rules of the game for getting along or ahead in the organization. One gets a sense of two very different corporate cultures simply by looking at the environment the organization has designed for itself. The large, green playing fields surrounding Microsoft's Redmond, Washington, "campus" contrast markedly with the enormous skyscraper in the heart of New York City that houses GE's corporate head office. Similarly, an unabashed culture of individual recognition is manifested throughout the Mary Kay organization by the singing of songs ("I've Got That Mary Kay Enthusiasm," sung to the tune of "I've Got That Old Time Religion") and the presentation of beauty queen sashes, tiaras, and pink Cadillacs to top performers at lavish, boisterous conventions.[4] As well, stories told in an organization convey considerable cultural meaning. For example, stories are told of Herb Kelleher, the highly visible, slightly over-the-top CEO of Southwest Airlines, regularly showing up armed with a box of doughnuts at maintenance facilities in the early morning, and proceeding to put on a pair of coveralls to go out to clean planes.[5] Such stories only reinforce norms of egalitarianism, cooperation, and pitching in to help one another out. Such values and norms have succeeded in making Southwest Airlines the only major U.S. airline to earn a profit throughout the 1990s and to win the industry's "triple crown."[6]

SOCIALIZATION PROCESSES

Organizations must provide mechanisms by which new members can become familiar with the culture of the organization. Socialization processes are designed to do that.[7] Almost all organizations with strong cultures enact socialization processes by (1) using rigorous, multistep selection and orientation processes that develop the individual's commitment to the organization through participation in the selection process, (2) signalling that certain goals, attitudes, and behaviours are important, and (3) developing reward systems that reinforce appropriate attitudes and behaviours and provide continuous recognition. Socialization can occur in groups (as in boot camp) or individually (as in professional offices). New recruits may be taken through a formal orientation program consisting of video, written material, and lectures, or socialization may be handled more informally through on-the-job training or apprenticeship programs.[8] Regardless of the means, the individual may decide to adopt the assumptions and conform to the norms of the organization; adopt a number of core assumptions and norms, but be innovative in how he or she actually behaves in the organization; or rebel, rejecting all the assumptions of the organization. Clearly, the last option is the least desired by the organization. The organization most desires members who adopt the values, attitudes, behaviours, and norms of the organization. People are then more likely to fulfill the goals of the organization without the use of formal controls and to form a sense of commitment to the organization's goals. Employees will also benefit from "fitting in." It is more likely that people who "fit" will be recognized, rewarded, and ultimately promoted within the organization.

MAINTENANCE OF ORGANIZATIONAL CULTURE

Organizational culture is maintained over time by a number of reinforcing mechanisms. Organizational design and structures, as well as organizational systems and procedures, guide behaviour and reinforce organizational values. For example, a formal and distant culture is maintained by steep hierarchies and bureaucratic systems for gaining project approval. The design of physical space and buildings also reinforces particular cultural features.

What is rewarded also sends out powerful signals of what is valued in a particular organization. The recognition of the Four Seasons Hotel bellhop who used his own money to fly out to return a guest's forgotten suitcase sent a powerful message about the value placed on excellent and unsurpassed levels of customer service.[9]

Processes of recruitment and selection also emphasize the core values of the organization. Southwest Airlines, known for its lighthearted, fun-loving, and caring culture puts up with no egos or with people who have no sense of humour.

As an example, in interviewing eight potential pilot recruits, the men were teased about their formal business attire and were invited to exchange their suit pants for the standard Southwest Bermuda shorts for the duration of the day of interviews. The six who accepted the offer and continued their day in suit jackets, ties, dark socks, dress shoes, and Bermuda shorts were hired.[10] Organizational rites and ceremonies are important, as well, for reinforcing an organizational culture. Weekly beer bashes and barbecues were a fundamental part of maintaining the close-knit culture of Hewlett-Packard. Company Christmas parties, gifts of Christmas turkeys, family picnics, and other social gatherings also reinforce cohesive cultures.[11]

THE IMPACT OF CULTURE ON ORGANIZATIONAL PERFORMANCE

So what does culture mean for the bottom line? Quite a lot it seems. Harvard Business School's John Kotter and James Heskett found that firms with cultures that emphasized all key stakeholders (customers, employees, and shareholders) and leadership from managers at all levels (not just the top) overwhelmingly outperformed firms that did not. Over an 11-year period, the former companies increased revenues by 682 percent, expanded their work forces by 282 percent, increased their share price by 901 percent, and improved their net incomes by 756 percent.[12] In contrast, the other firms increased revenues by 166 percent, expanded their work forces by 36 percent, increased their share price by 74 percent, and improved their net incomes by only 1 percent.

It is important to note, however, that it is not a strong culture but rather a strategically appropriate one that is critical to performance. In particular, the ability of the culture to adapt as the competitive environment shifts seems especially important. However, studies have shown repeatedly that culture is extremely difficult to change. Often, it is changed only through indirect means and over an often considerable period of time. Managers need to be conscious of what kind of culture they are seeking to establish or maintain through their actions and policies because of the profound effects it can have on organizational members' behaviour.

SECTION

THREE

LEADERSHIP

Effective leadership is critical to all organizations. Because organizational tasks are divided into separate activities assigned to various individuals, an effective leader must be able to influence those individuals to work toward achieving the organization's goals. The question, What makes someone an effective leader? has been asked for many years. In trying to answer this question, researchers have attempted to identify universal traits of leaders, to explain effective leadership by the behaviours that the leader displays, and to describe which leadership approaches are effective in various situations.

LEADER TRAITS

Researchers have tried to identify universal traits of leaders under the premise that if a set of traits could be identified, then the organization could select the "right" person to be the leader. The basic belief was that great leaders possessed traits (e.g., ability, personality, or physical characteristics) that distinguished them from the people who followed them and that would be effective in any situation. After more than 60 years of research that has tried to identify the traits of effective leaders, many researchers have concluded that "possession of particular traits increases the likelihood that a leader will be effective, but they do not guarantee effectiveness, and the relative importance of different traits is dependent on the nature of the leadership situation."[13] In other words, although some traits are consistently associated with effective leadership (e.g., decisiveness, initiative, self-confidence, adaptability to situation[14]), the specific situation — the followers, the task, and the organization — will determine which particular traits are essential for effective leadership. Thus, traits alone are insufficient to define effective leaders.

LEADER BEHAVIOURS

A second stream of research has sought to determine whether effective leaders behave in distinctive ways. It was assumed that if critical behaviour patterns of effective leadership could be identified, then potential leaders could be trained in those behaviours. Over the past 45 years, a number of studies have been conducted to examine leaders' behaviours and their impact on the satisfaction and performance of their followers. Typically, leader behaviours have been grouped into two broad categories: task-oriented behaviours and relationship-oriented behaviours.[15] Task-oriented leaders emphasize the technical aspects of the job and the completion of group goals by, for example, establishing goals and work standards, assigning people to tasks, giving instructions, and checking performance. Relationship-oriented leaders emphasize interpersonal relationships by, for example, taking interest in followers' personal needs, accepting individual differences, and being friendly and approachable. For the most part, leaders who display both behaviours simultaneously are most effective.

Nonetheless, the specific situational context must be considered in terms of the requirements and constraints it places on the leader's behaviour. For example, in cases where the task is already highly structured, a leader who focuses mainly on task-oriented aspects of the job is often disliked. The requirements of the task are quite clear-cut, and further structuring of the task is annoying; in these cases, leaders who focus mainly on the relationship-oriented aspects of the job are more appreciated. However, leaders who demonstrate little relationship orientation do not always have dissatisfied subordinates. For example, if the task is highly unstructured, leaders high in task orientation are often appreciated despite their lack of relationship-oriented behaviours.

Figure 1 and Table 1 present a taxonomy of managerial behaviours.[16] The taxonomy was developed to categorize and describe more specific behaviours that are part of all leadership roles in varying degrees. These practices include behaviours that are concerned with both tasks and relationships. Some of the behaviours are clearly more task-oriented, such as monitoring and planning. Appropriate use of specific task-oriented or relationship-oriented behaviours is critical to leadership effectiveness; leaders must consider which form of the behaviour is appropriate to the particular situation and subordinate.

FIGURE 1
Integrating Taxonomy of Managerial Behaviour

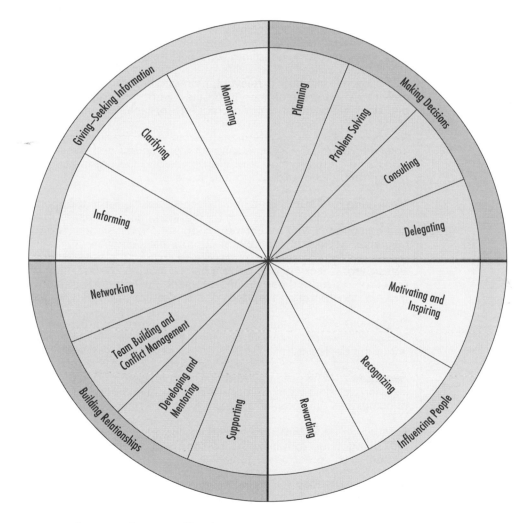

Table 1: Definition of the Managerial Practices

Planning and Organizing: Determining long-term objectives and strategies, allocating resources according to priorities, determining how to use personnel and resources to accomplish a task efficiently, and determining how to improve coordination, productivity, and the effectiveness of the organizational unit.

Problem Solving: Identifying work-related problems, analyzing problems in a timely but systematic manner to identify causes and find solutions, and acting decisively to implement solutions to resolve important problems or crises.

Clarifying Roles and Objectives: Assigning tasks, providing direction in how to do the work, and communicating a clear understanding of job responsibilities, task objectives, deadlines, and performance expectations.

Informing: Disseminating relevant information about decisions, plans, and activities to people that need to do their work, providing written materials and documents, and answering requests for technical information.

Monitoring: Gathering information about work activities and external conditions affecting the work, checking on the progress and quality of the work, evaluating the performance of individuals and the organizational unit, analyzing trends, and forecasting external events.

Motivating and Inspiring: Using influence techniques that appeal to emotion or logic to generate enthusiasm for the work, commitment to task objectives, and compliance with requests for cooperation, assistance, support, or resources; setting an example of appropriate behavior.

Consulting: Checking with people before making changes that affect them, encouraging suggestions for improvement, inviting participation in decision making, incorporating the ideas and suggestions of others in decisions.

Delegating: Allowing subordinates to have substantial responsibility and discretion in carrying out work activities, handling problems, and making important decisions.

Supporting: Acting friendly and considerate, being patient and helpful, showing sympathy and support when someone is upset or anxious, listening to complaints and problems, looking out for someone's interests.

Developing and Mentoring: Providing coaching and helpful career advice, and doing things to facilitate a person's skill acquisition, professional development, and career advancement.

Managing Conflict and Team Building: Facilitating the constructive resolution of conflict, and encouraging cooperation, teamwork, and identification with the work unit.

Table 1: Definition of the Managerial Practices (cont.)

Networking: Socializing informally, developing contacts with people who are a source of information and support, and maintaining contacts through periodic interaction, including visits, telephone calls, correspondence, and attendance at meetings and social events.

Recognizing: Providing praise and recognition for effective performance, significant achievements, and special contributions; expressing appreciation for someone's contributions and special efforts.

Rewarding: Providing or recommending tangible rewards such as a pay increase or promotion for effective performance, significant achievements, and demonstrated competence.

Source: *Leadership in Organizations* 4/E by Yukl, Gary, © 1981. Reprinted by permission of Prentice-Hall, Inc., Upper Saddle River, NJ.

SITUATIONAL LEADERSHIP

A number of factors are important to understanding which leadership behaviours are effective in particular situations (e.g., the nature of the task, the ability to exert power, attitudes of followers). Numerous studies of leadership have been conducted using the situational approach. We highlight two situational theories here: the Path-Goal Theory of Leadership and the Vroom-Jago Leader-Participation Model.

Path-Goal Theory of Leadership

In the Path-Goal Theory of Leadership the role of the leader is (1) to assist followers in attaining the followers' goals and (2) to provide the necessary direction and support to ensure that followers' goals are compatible with the organization's goals.[17] Effective leaders are those who clarify and clear the path for the followers to achieve those goals.

Leaders are effective when they provide a positive impact on followers' motivation, performance, and satisfaction. If the leader clarifies the links or paths between effort and performance and between performance and reward, and if the leader rewards the followers with things that they value (assists the followers in attaining the followers' work goals), then the followers will be motivated.

Four styles of leader behaviour are identified:

1. *Directive:* A directive leader explicitly lets followers know what is expected of them by scheduling work, maintaining performance standards, giving specific guidance about what and how work is done, etc.
2. *Supportive:* A supportive leader shows concern for followers, is friendly and approachable, and treats members as equals.
3. *Participative:* A participative leader consults followers and uses their suggestions in making decisions.
4. *Achievement oriented:* An achievement-oriented leader sets challenging goals and expects high-level performance with continual improvement.

In order to determine which of these leadership styles is appropriate, two situational variables must be considered: the personal characteristics of the followers and environmental factors. The personal characteristics of the followers that are deemed important in determining the appropriate leadership style are:

1. The followers' perceptions of their ability: whether the followers perceive that they have the relevant experience and ability to do a given task;
2. The followers' locus of control: whether the followers believe that their actions can have influence; and
3. The followers' level of authoritarianism: whether the followers are willing to accept the influence of others.

Environmental factors are beyond the control of followers, but they are important to the followers' satisfaction and ability to perform effectively. The factors considered are:

1. The formal authority system in the organization—The extent to which the system is well defined through rules and a clear chain of command.
2. The nature of the work groups—The extent to which group norms and dynamics allow followers to receive necessary cues to do the job and desired rewards from someone other than the leader.
3. The nature of the tasks—The extent to which the task is clearly defined, and routine.

An effective leadership style is one that complements the personal characteristics of the followers and the environmental factors. For example, if the followers do not perceive that they have the necessary ability to do the task, they have an external locus of control (they believe that events arounds them are shaped by forces beyond their control), and/or they are willing to accept the influence of others, then a directive style would be appropriate. If, however, the task is clearly defined and routine, then it is unlikely that a directive style of leadership would be desired by the followers — followers are already very aware of what it is they are to do, thereby making this style redundant. Similarly, if there is no clear chain of command or if there are group norms of autonomy, then followers would not welcome a directive style. This theory assumes that the leader can portray different styles more or less simultaneously, as required by different environmental factors and follower characteristics.

Vroom-Jago Leader-Participation Model

The Vroom-Jago leader-participation model[18] suggests specific means for determining effective leader behaviour. It provides a set of rules to follow in selecting the form and amount of participation in decision making for a given situation. The model incorporates eight questions and five alternative leadership styles in the form of a decision tree (see Figure 2). The answer to each successive question in the decision tree points the leader to a particular end or leadership style. This model also assumes flexibility of leaders in adjusting their styles to different situations. The leadership styles are:

- *Autocratic I:* The leader solves the problem or makes the decision alone, using available information.
- *Autocratic II:* The leader obtains necessary information from subordinates and then solves the problem or makes the decision alone. The leader may or may not inform the subordinates of the reason for the information requested. The leader does not engage the subordinates in generating or evaluating solutions.
- *Consultative I:* The leader shares the problem with subordinates individually and obtains their ideas and suggestions. The leader makes the decision alone, and the decision may or may not reflect the subordinates' input.
- *Consultative II:* The leader shares the problem with subordinates in a group situation and obtains their ideas and suggestions. The leader makes the decision alone, and the decision may or may not reflect the subordinates' input.
- *Group II:* The leader shares the problem with subordinates in a group situation and has the subordinates generate and evaluate alternatives. The group attempts to reach a consensus on the solution. The leader facilitates the group discussion by keeping it focused on the problem and the critical issues to be resolved. The leader does not try to convince the group to adopt his/her solution.

This model shows that leaders use participatory methods when the quality of the decision is important, the acceptance by subordinates is important, and the subordinates are trusted to pay attention to organization or group goals over their own preferences. However, the model only focuses on work-related decisions at one point in time. It also assumes that leaders possess the necessary skills to use each of the leadership styles.

Transformational Leadership

In contrast to the above "transactional" approaches to leadership, in which leaders establish what is required of their followers, the conditions that must be abided by, and the rewards that will be received when the requirements are fulfilled, Bernard Bass presents another view of the transformational leader.[19] Bass's transformational leaders achieve superior results from their employees by employing some or all of the following four components of transformational leadership:

FIGURE 2
Vroom-Jego
Leadership-
Participation
Model

QR	Quality Requirement:	How important is the technical quality of this decision?
CR	Commitment Requirement:	How important is subordinate commitment to the decision?
LI	Leader's Information:	Do you have sufficient information to make a high-quality decision?
ST	Problem Structure:	Is the problem well structured?
CP	Commitment Probability:	If you were to make the decision by yourself, is it reasonably certain that your subordinate(s) would be committed to the decision?
GC	Goal Congruence:	Do subordinates share the organizational goals to be attained in solving the problem?
CO	Subordinate Conflict:	Is conflict among subordinates over preferred solutions likely?
SI	Subordinate Information:	Do subordinates have sufficient information to make a high-quality decision?

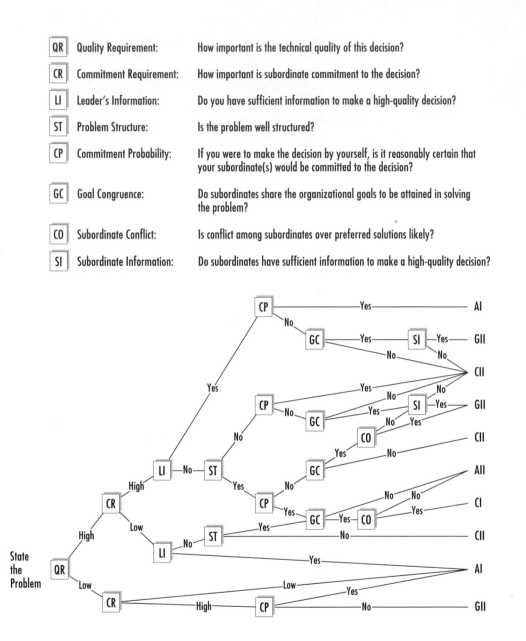

Adapted and reprinted from *Leadership and Decision Making,* by Victor H. Vroom and Philip W. Yetton, by permission of the University of Pittsburgh Press. © 1973 by University of Pittsburgh Press.

1. *Charismatic leadership:* Leaders are perceived as having extraordinary capabilities, persistence, and determination; are willing to take risks; are consistent; are highly ethical and moral; and are admired, respected, and trusted.

2. *Inspirational motivation:* Leaders provide meaning and challenge to their followers' work; arouse team spirit and enthusiasm; clearly articulate a vision for the future; and demonstrate clear commitment to goals.

3. *Intellectual stimulation:* Leaders stimulate followers to be innovative and creative by questioning assumptions, reframing problems, and using and encouraging novel approaches to situations.

4. *Individualized consideration:* Leaders pay special attention to followers' needs for achievement and growth by acting as coach and mentor and personalizing their interactions. Followers are continually encouraged to reach higher levels of achievement, and new learning opportunities are created within a supportive climate.

Thus, transformational leadership goes beyond merely fulfilling the transactional aspects of leadership. It occurs when "leaders broaden and elevate the interests of their employees, when they generate awareness and acceptance of the purposes and missions of the group, and when they stir their employees to look beyond their own self-interest for the good of the group."[20]

THE IMPORTANCE OF EFFECTIVE LEADERSHIP

Studies of leadership have a common thread — to determine what makes a leader effective. As the preceding discussion has revealed, there is no clear-cut answer — it depends on the situation. Yet for any organization there are many unforeseen situational factors that must be dealt with, including unexpected changes in the environment and differences in organizational members' goals. Thus, it is important to the organization that its leaders have the ability to influence organizational members appropriately.

SECTION

FOUR

POWER AND INFLUENCE

Power is a fundamental concept in the study of organizational behaviour. Many authorities argue that the effective use of power is the most critical element of management.[21] Harvard professor John Kotter, who teaches a course on power, has the following to say:

> It makes me sick to hear economists tell students that their job is to maximize shareholder profits. Their job is going to be managing a whole host of constituencies: bosses, underlings, customers, suppliers, unions, you name it. Trying to get cooperation from different constituencies is an infinitely more difficult task than milking your business for money.[22]

Simply defined, power is the ability to mobilize resources to accomplish the work of the organization. Although we often associate power with domination or exacting behaviour under duress, power is not negative in and of itself. How it is used is critical in understanding its effects. Power is an essential issue for managers, since their success is fundamentally shaped by how effectively they use power. Managers who either do not have power or who cannot use it effectively ultimately are judged as poor managers.

In this section we consider different sources of power, the conditions for using power, and various influence strategies for using power.

SOURCES OF POWER

John French and Bertram Raven have identified five sources of power: reward power, coercive power, legitimate power, referent power, and expert power.[23]

1. *Reward power.* If a person controls rewards that someone else wants (e.g., pay or promotion), then that person is able to exert reward power. Reward power can be exerted only if the potential recipient values the rewards and believes that the power holder has the ability to give or withhold the reward.

2. *Coercive power.* If a person can punish someone (e.g., place a written warning in a personnel file or revoke privileges), then that power holder is able to exert coercive power. Coercive power can be exerted only if the other person dislikes the punishment and believes that the power holder has the ability to administer or terminate the punishment. Continued punishment or threat of punishment is necessary to maintain influence; if punishment or its threat is not present, then the effects will only be temporary.

3. *Legitimate power.* If a person is perceived as having the right to influence another, then that power holder is able to exert legitimate power. Typically, legitimate power is based on the position within the formal organizational hierarchy, whereby superiors have the right to influence subordinates' actions. Legitimate power can be exerted only if subordinates respect the formal hierarchy.

4. *Referent power.* If a person is well liked by others and has personal qualities or characteristics that are admired, then that person is able to exert referent power. For example, individuals can exert referent power when other people seek their approval.

5. *Expert power.* If a person has information or knowledge relevant to a particular problem that another person does not have, then the power holder is able to exert expert power. In order for expert power to be used, others must acknowledge that the person actually possesses the critical information and skills. Furthermore, expert power is limited in influence, since it is situation specific.

Reward, coercive, and legitimate power are often referred to as position power — because of individuals' organizational positions, they have the ability to influence others through these avenues. Referent and expert power are often referred to as personal power — owing to individuals' attributes, they have the ability to influence others through these avenues.

CONDITIONS FOR USING POWER

Pfeffer identifies three necessary conditions for the use of power: interdependence, scarcity, and heterogeneous goals.[24]

1. *Interdependence.* Interdependence is a necessary precondition to the use of power. If individuals can do their work relatively independently, there is little opportunity for power to play a role. For example, if individuals have easy access to all the resources required to do their task or if they have a great deal of latitude in decision making, then they have considerably reduced (1) their reliance on other people, (2) the likelihood of conflict, and (3) the opportunity for others to exert influence over them. Conversely, as an individual's dependency on others increases, there is more opportunity for conflict and for others to use power in the relationship.

2. *Scarcity.* Scarcity is closely connected to the issue of interdependence. If there are no alternative sources of supply for a required resource and the supply is limited, the resource is deemed scarce. In situations of scarcity, dependence increases on the supplier of that resource. The situation of dependency, as noted above, results in the opportunity to exert power.

3. *Heterogeneous goals.* If everyone agrees on goals and if there is no ambiguity about these goals, the opportunity for the use of power is decreased. Under these circumstances there is likely to be little conflict or need to influence individuals' actions. However, this situation is highly unlikely in any organization. The more typical organizational situation is one where individuals or groups have different goals they wish to achieve and the goals are ambiguous. This sort of situation will likely lead to disagreements and conflict, thus allowing for the use of power.

INFLUENCE STRATEGIES

Power is a necessary precondition for influence. Without power one cannot hope to secure the consent of others to accomplish organizational objectives. However, power must be converted to influence so that the consent of others is gained in ways that minimize their resistance and resentment. Influence strategies used by managers fall into three broad categories: retribution, reciprocity, and reason.[25] Each influence strategy relies on different mechanisms to secure compliance.

Retribution

This strategy relies on coercive and reward power — on an explicit or implied threat to either impose a punishment or withhold a reward if the manager's request is not obeyed. This strategy is effective in producing the desired behaviour immediately and to the manager's exact specifications. It is best used when there is a significant imbalance in power between the manager and the subordinate, when commitment and quality are not important, or when resistance is likely anyway. However, this strategy also has significant drawbacks. It inevitably creates resentment on the part of the target, it often creates resistance to future requests, it requires the escalation of threats over time to maintain the same level of pressure, and it significantly reduces the target's levels of commitment and creativity. Effective managers use this technique sparingly — only in crises or as a last resort when other strategies have failed.

Reciprocity

This strategy works to satisfy the interests of both parties and is based on reward power. It has both direct and indirect forms. The direct form appears in the context of negotiation in which the parties bargain over the transaction they are making so that both are able to extract what they want from the deal. The indirect form appears as ingratiation, whereby the manager or subordinate grants favours to incur social debt or obligations that can be called on when help or support is needed. Examples in organizations include an employee's agreeing to work overtime in exchange for time off later or a subordinate doing small favours for a boss in exchange for the ability to take longer lunch hours on occasion.[26] The benefit of the reciprocity strategy is that it generates compliance without resentment or resistance. The main drawback of this strategy is that it tends to create an instrumental view of the workplace. It encourages people to believe that every request made of them is open for negotiation. The result is often that the individual will eventually do what the manager asks only when something is offered in return. It is a strategy that is best used when the parties are mutually dependent, when each has resources desired by the other, and when the parties have time to negotiate.

Reason

In exerting influence based on reason, the manager argues that compliance is warranted because of the inherent merits of the request. This strategy is most likely to be effective if subordinates see the manager as knowledgeable or as possessing attractive personal characteristics; in other words, the manager relies on expert and referent power. The major benefits of the reason strategy are the higher levels of compliance and internalized commitment it engenders, which, in turn, reduce the need for supervision and control and often increase subordinates' levels of initiative and creativity. The major drawback to this strategy, however, is the considerable time that is required to develop the necessary relationship and trust on which a reason strategy is based. It is best used when the parties have an ongoing relationship, common goals and values, and mutual respect.

Research has evaluated the effectiveness of these different strategies. Managers who rely largely on reason and logic to influence others are rated as highly effective by their superiors. In addition, they report low levels of job-related stress and high levels of job satisfaction.[27] In contrast, managers who use other strategies to accomplish their objectives tend to receive lower performance ratings from their bosses and experience higher levels of both personal stress and job dissatisfaction.

MOTIVATION

The motivation of employees is critical for all managers. Managers want employees who are highly motivated — who are willing to persist in their efforts to achieve particular goals. To motivate employees, it helps to have a basic understanding of the nature of human motivation, a topic that has been the subject of considerable research over the years. Attention has been paid to what energizes people in terms of their needs and desires and how the process of motivation works.

McCLELLAND'S NEED THEORY

The most supported theory of what energizes people in terms of their needs and desires is McClelland's need theory.[28] McClelland identifies three fundamental needs that are important to understanding motivation in organizational settings: the need for achievement, the need for affiliation, and the need for power. People high in any of these needs are likely to be motivated by situations in which they perceive they can satisfy these needs.

The *need for achievement* is characterized by a drive to excel. Individuals with a high need for achievement like personal responsibility for performance results, rapid feedback on performance, and moderately challenging goals. In particular, these people seek to do things better than others and to rise to challenges. If goals or tasks are too easy, such individuals are not challenged and will want to move on to something new. If goals or tasks are too difficult, such individuals will not want to engage in these tasks since they feel they will be unsuccessful. When working in a group situation, they like feedback about their task performance and they like knowing whether they are doing better than others. They care little about how well they get along with group members and are too focused on their own performance to notice the achievement orientation of others in their group.

People with a high need for achievement tend to be interested in and do well at business. Business requires dealing with moderate levels of risk, assuming personal responsibility, being innovative, and paying attention to performance feedback in terms of profits and costs. These people are particularly good at sales and entrepreneurial activity, since they are focused on managing their own performance. Nonetheless, people high in need for achievement are typically ineffective managers. They find it hard to focus on others and to delegate since they like to take personal responsibility for their tasks.

The *need for affiliation* is characterized by a desire to interact with other people. Maintaining or establishing close, friendly interpersonal relationships is what drives such individuals. People who are high in need for affiliation work harder and get better outcomes when their manager is warm and friendly. When working in groups, they prefer feedback on how well the group is getting along as opposed to feedback on how well the group is performing the task. They also learn social relationships more quickly, typically engage in more dialogue, and act to avoid conflict when possible.

Individuals with a high need for affiliation tend to be less successful as managers. Managers often must act competitively, try to influence others, and make decisions that hurt other people's feelings. These activities are difficult for people with a high need for affiliation who prefer to avoid conflict. However, if the manager's job is to be an integrator — to help people to resolve their differences and to get along — those high in need for affiliation are more successful.

The *need for power* is characterized by a desire to influence others. Being in charge, being influential, and having an impact drive individuals high in this need. Individuals who are high in the need for power prefer situations where they can influence others, and they tend to collect symbols of power (prestige possessions). When working in a group, people with a high need for power behave in ways that make them more visible to other group members and prefer to take on dominant, controlling roles. They also prefer to surround themselves with less known or less assertive individuals who can be led. Not surprisingly, those with a high need for power are not best liked, nor are they considered to have contributed most to getting the job done. They are, however, judged to be influential and to have talked a lot. Individuals who are seen as effective managers tend to have a relatively high need for power and a lower need for affiliation.

EQUITY THEORY

Equity theory[29] is what is known as a process theory of motivation — a theory concerned with how individuals become motivated. Equity theory predicts that we will engage in certain activities to the extent that we perceive the situation to be fair and equitable. In general, we compare what we receive in return for our efforts with what others in similar situations receive relative to their efforts. If this comparison of input to output ratios is equal, then we perceive equity and will continue with the activity. In assessing inputs we consider factors such as effort, performance level, education, and time. In assessing outputs we consider factors such as pay, recognition, and other rewards.

Situations can be perceived as inequitable for two reasons: we are being overrewarded or we are being underrewarded. Often people are more comfortable with being overrewarded than with being underrewarded. Nonetheless, in situations of overreward, people may feel guilty and be motivated to try to decrease the imbalance. The common means of decreasing the imbalance is to increase the level of input by increasing either the amount or the quality of the work done.

When we perceive that we are underrewarded, we are motivated to alter the level of input to bring the situation into balance either by working less or lowering the quality of our work. In more extreme instances, we simply quit. People also may be motivated to try to alter the outcome side of the equation by seeking raises or other forms of recognition.

Although the theory seems relatively simple, the difficulty for the manager reveals itself when we recognize that equity is based on people's perceptions. People can perceptually distort either their performance or the comparison person's performance to produce equity.

Regardless of the accuracy of my perceptions of my inputs and outcomes or the other person's inputs or outcomes, I will make an assessment of the equity of the situation. I may not, in fact, know all of your inputs, nor may I weigh all the inputs in a similar fashion to you or to the manager as I am doing my mental calculations of equity. Unfortunately for the manager, though, the perceptions of equity or inequity influence how people are motivated and, hence, how they behave.

EXPECTANCY THEORY

Expectancy theory,[30] another process theory of motivation, is a relatively complex probabilistic model of motivation. It can be summarized by the following equation:

$$\text{Motivation} = \text{Expectancy} \times \text{Instrumentality} \times \text{Valence}$$

Expectancy is the probability that a certain level of effort will lead to a certain level of performance as assessed by the individual; *instrumentality* is the probability that a certain level of performance will lead to a certain level of the reward as assessed by the individual; and *valence* is the attractiveness of the reward to the individual.

The model suggests that for each activity a person will assess the likelihood that his or her efforts will lead to performance, that his or her performance will lead to the reward, and that he or she values the reward. If any of these relationships are assessed to be zero, there will be no motivation to engage in that activity. The activity that the person will be motivated to engage in is the one in which the product of these relationships is the greatest.

It may be somewhat difficult for managers to use this theory to motivate subordinates, since they may not know all of the activities an employee is considering engaging in or exactly what each employee values. Nonetheless, managers can ensure that the link between effort and performance is clear or attainable (increasing expectancy). They can also clarify the link between performance and reward (increasing instrumentality). Finally, they can try to determine what rewards their employees will value (increasing valence).

Motivating employees is a complex activity. Managers must think not only about how the process of motivation works but also about what motivates their employees, neither of which is easy to ascertain. However, if managers can try to understand what their individual employees need or value and try to deliver rewards that are equitable, they can go a long ways toward improving their employees' motivation.

Cognitive Differences

Cognitive differences importantly shape behaviour in organizations. They affect how we see the world and respond to various stimuli. As a manager, it is important to understand such individual differences in order to foresee how others might respond, to structure tasks so that they will be readily accepted, and to understand your own preconceptions in dealing with others. In this section, we highlight three important cognitive differences: personality, learning style, and perception.

Personality

Research on personality has been extensive. However, researchers in this field continue to debate a number of questions, including, How is one's personality determined? and, What are the critical dimensions of personality? What can be agreed upon, however, is that personality is defined by the stable, personal characteristics that lead to consistent behaviour. Furthermore, researchers have largely come to agree that these characteristics are inherited as well as learned and that personality is defined early in life.

Hundreds, if not thousands, of personality traits have been identified and investigated over time. We focus here on one that has been extensively studied and that has obvious organizational implications: locus of control. Locus of control refers to the degree to which individuals believe that they can control events affecting them. Individuals with a high internal locus of control believe that they largely (but not totally) determine events in their lives. In contrast, people with an external locus of control believe that events around them are largely shaped by forces beyond their control — by other people, chance, or fate.

An individual's locus of control has been shown to be significant in predicting some aspects of job behaviour.[31] For example, people with a high internal locus of control have been shown to perform better in work that requires complex information processing and learning, that requires initiative and independent action, that requires high motivation, and that provides valued rewards in return for greater effort. In contrast, when the work requires compliance and conformity, individuals with a high external locus of control perform better.

Learning Style

It is also important for a manager to be aware of an individual's learning or cognitive style. Often confused with a measure of personality, the Myers-Briggs Type Indicator (MBTI) test classifies individuals into one of 16 categories based on a set of four bipolar dimensions:

Extroversion (externally directed)   –   Introversion (introspective)
Sensing (relies on facts)   –   INtuitive (explores possibilities)
Thinking (logical and analytical)   –   Feeling (emotional and sympathetic)
Judgment (structured and organized) –   Perception (adaptable)

(The boldfaced letters are used as abbreviations for the dimensions and are combined to indicate a person' category for each of the four dimensions.)

Research on the MBTI suggests that certain types (such as INTJ or ESFP) are better suited for particular occupations.[32] For example, on the sensing–intuitive dimension, over 80 percent of steelworkers, police detectives, and factory supervisors prefer S over N. In contrast, over 80 percent of research assistants, social scientists, writers, artists, and entertainers prefer N over S.

The extroversion–introversion dimension also has organizational implications. Extroverts need stimulation in the form of social activity, frequent change in their environment, and intense colours or noise. Introverts, in contrast, require little stimulation from the external environment. They may perform better than their extroverted counterparts on repetitive tasks or in environments that provide little sensory stimulation.

To be effective, managers need to recognize and be able to adapt to the learning styles of their subordinates. For example, learning style may affect how and the extent to which managers organize their subordinates' tasks — high Js prefers structured tasks, whereas high Ps prefer a more unstructured work environment. Similarly, a manager of a high S may need to provide the subordinate with sufficient information to accomplish the task, while a manager of a high N may not need to provide such information, but rather may allow the subordinate more latitude in exploring a range of possibilities.

PERCEPTION

All of us continuously engage in the process of perception. We are constantly bombarded with sensory stimuli, but we pay attention to only a small portion of them. It is through the process of perception that we organize, interpret, and give meaning to our environment. The perceptual process affects what we notice and how we interpret or make sense of our observations. Our perceptions are influenced by who we are, what we are perceiving, and the situation. Thus, different people perceive different things, and different people perceive the same thing differently.

Our motives, our experiences and expectations, and our attitudes and beliefs all influence the way we perceive targets (objects, people, or events). For example, if you are hungry and everything you see reminds you of food, your perceptions are being influenced by your motives (in this case, hunger). Similarly, if every time you complete a task your boss finds fault with it and you start to think your boss is just someone who likes to find faults no matter what

FIGURE 3   *Perceptual Tendency to Group Based on Proximity (a) and Similarity (b)*

```
        + +        X X X X      O X O X

        + +        O O O O      O X O X

        + +        X X X X      O X O X
```

Source: David Cherrington, *Organizational Behaviour: The Management of Individual and Organizational Performance* (Boston: Allyn & Bacon, 1994).

the situation, your perceptions are being influenced by your past experiences and expectations. In fact, if your boss praises you, you will likely be surprised.

In addition, characteristics of the target influence our perception. If the target stands out in some way, owing to appearance or some other attribute, we are more likely to notice or perceive it. For example, advertisers often use moving or blinking signs to promote their products because they realize that we are more likely to pay attention to those signs than to ones that are not changing or moving. Also, items are often perceived as belonging together because of proximity or other similarities in features. Figure 3 provides a simple visual example. In these examples, we tend to perceive three rows of "+" rather than two columns, and we tend to perceive rows of Xs and Os on the left half of the second example and columns of Xs and Os on the right half. These same principles apply to our perceptions of other objects, people, and events.

Finally, the situation will influence whether and how an object or person is perceived. For example, if a person has a very loud voice, it is possible that he or she will go unnoticed at a large party but it is very likely that he or she will be noticed in the library. Thus, the background or the situation affects how the figure or the target is perceived. Similarly, the type of organizational context in which people work will influence how they perceive events and the actions of other people. If a new employee in an organization that is very cooperative displays a self-serving behaviour, not only will that behaviour be noticed, but it may also be frowned on.

Sources of Perceptual Errors

Because we are faced with so much information from our environment, we tend to use shortcuts to help process information faster. Unfortunately, many of these shortcuts result in misreading the situation, since we are making judgments using only a portion of the information available to us. Some of the sources of perceptual errors are selectivity, assumed similarity, stereotyping, the halo effect, and the recency and primacy effects.

Selectivity occurs when we attend to only a portion of the information available based on our interests, experiences, and expectations. As a result, we may miss important information that could help us to more accurately interpret events in our environment. In organizations, it is not uncommon for departments to narrowly focus on resolving issues from the perspective of their own department, as opposed to using a broader approach. In doing so, the solution may fit well within the context of the one department, but it may lead to a different set of problems for another department that it must deal with.

Assumed similarity occurs when we project our beliefs, attitudes, or motives onto others. For example, if managers decide that they should give their subordinates more challenging jobs because the managers like to be challenged, they are operating under the assumption of assumed similarity. If, in fact, the subordinates do not want more challenging jobs, they may be unhappy with the changes to their work.

Stereotyping occurs when we judge others based on the group they belong to. This grouping can be on the basis of age, gender, race/ethnicity, occupation, or any other characteristic that is seen to distinguish one group of people from another. The danger with stereotyping is that there are many ways in which people may differ, despite having one area of obvious similarity. For example, one researcher found that a number of the managers in her study thought that women should be happy to receive emotional rewards in place of monetary rewards because women were motivated by noneconomic, emotional factors.[33] Clearly, making decisions based on stereotyping can lead to erroneous conclusions!

The *halo effect* occurs when we generate a general impression about someone based on a single positive characteristic. The reality may be that the person is good at that particular activity, but he or she may not be good at all other activities. For example, if a manager notices that an employee is very good at organizing his or her thoughts on paper, it would be erroneous for the manager to assume that the employee would necessarily be good at delivering a speech to a large audience. The skills required for these two activities, although overlapping, are somewhat different.

The *recency effect* occurs when we weigh the most recent information about a person more heavily than the other information that we have. The *primacy effect* occurs when we use the limited information from our first meeting with a person to form stable impressions about that person. In both cases, we are using limited information to draw general conclusions about a person which we cannot be certain will hold true over time or in different situations.

Attribution

When we try to explain the behaviours of ourselves and other people, we are making attributions. Attribution theory attempts to explain how we judge people based on the meaning we give to a behaviour.[34] There are two basic explanations of why people behave as they do:

1. *Dispositional attributions:* People behave the way they do because of factors under their control, such as their personality, ability, effort, or level of knowledge.

2. *Situational attributions:* People behave the way they do because of factors in the situation beyond their control, such as luck, chance, or something specific about the nature of the environment.

The general tendency of observers is to perceive that other people's behaviour is internally controlled, or due to disposition, when outcomes are unfavourable. Yet, we tend to attribute our own unfavourable outcomes to the situation. In contrast, when we explain our own favourable outcomes, we are more than willing to attest that they were due to our disposition. For others, however, we attribute their success to the situation.

If we asssume that a problem behaviour is internally controllable, we make a dispositional attribution and then focus our responses on trying to "fix" or replace the person. If, on the other hand, we assume that a problem behaviour is externally caused, we make a situational attribution and then focus our responses on the organizational systems that may have contributed to the situation. Such attributions typically occur when we lack sufficient information about other people. To make more accurate attributions, managers should consider the following factors:

- *Distinctiveness:* Does the person display different behaviours in different situations? If the answer is yes, then the current behaviour is likely a result of the situation. If the answer is no, then the current behaviour is likely a result of the person's disposition.

- *Consensus:* Do other people display similar behaviours in a similar situation? If the answer is yes, then the current behaviour is likely a result of the situation. If the answer is no, then the current behaviour is likely a result of the person's disposition.

- *Consistency:* Does the same person display similar behaviours in the same or similar situations? If the answer is yes, then the current behaviour is likely a result of the person's disposition. If the answer is no, then the current behaviour is likely a result of the situation.

Managers need to understand the potential sources of differences in how individuals see, interpret, and respond to the world around them. By understanding people's personality characteristics and individual learning styles, a manager can ensure that job assignments and leadership styles are appropriate to the individual. Managers also gain by understanding how we make attributions about people's behaviours.

DIVERSITY

The composition of Canadian organizations today is more diverse than it has been at any other time in history. Several factors have come together to produce this unprecedented diversity. First, the dramatic inflow of women into the work force in the 1960s and 1970s constitutes one of the most significant events in recent economic history. In 1951 only 10 percent of married women worked outside the home; by 1981, 51 percent of married women did so.[35] By 2000, women will make up 50 percent of the work force.[36] Second, changes in patterns of Canadian immigration have been equally dramatic. In the 1950s, 80 percent of immigrants came from Great Britain or Europe.[37] By the 1980s, almost 85 percent of immigrants into Canada came from the Third World, radically changing the racial and ethnic makeup of Canada's cities, as well as its organizations. By 2006, when Canada's population is slated to move over the 30 million mark, it is estimated that 18 percent of the population will be made up of visible minorities.[38] Third, demographics have played an important role in changing the makeup of Canadian organizations. As the baby boom has moved through the work force, organizations' members have aged, on average. The median age in the Canadian population has increased by nearly 11 years since the early 1970s.[39] Gender, race and ethnicity, and age are just three important dimensions of diversity that affect relations within organizations.

More than ever before, it is critical that this diverse work force be managed effectively to ensure organizational success in today's highly competitive environment. Recognizing individual differences, their sources, and their likely impacts can help a manager be more effective in this regard. The purpose of this section is twofold: to outline some core dimensions of diversity and how they may affect individual behaviour in organizations and to present evidence of the implications for organizational competitiveness of managing diversity well.

SOURCES OF DIVERSITY

Researchers in the field of diversity studies differentiate between core and secondary dimensions of diversity.[40] Core dimensions include age, gender, and race and ethnicity. Secondary dimensions include a much wider ranging set of characteristics, such as education, family status, sexual orientation, work experience, geographic location, religion, first language, organizational role, and communication style. We focus on core dimensions in this discussion.

Race/Ethnicity

Changing immigration patterns have had an enormous impact on the makeup of Canadian organizations. The integration of these diverse populations into the work force creates two sets of challenges for managers. The first is the challenge of integrating people who bring diverse experiences, attitudes, assumptions, and beliefs to the organization. The second is the challenge of managing and overcoming racism — whether it is overt and intentional or not. Racism discounts or prevents the contributions by organizational members who are seen to be inferior to the dominant group.

Gender

The unprecedented entry of women into the labour force over the past three decades has led to profound organizational changes. Although they now constitute nearly half the work force, women are still underrepresented in top-management positions, making up only 6 percent of such positions in the industrialized world.[41] Recognition of this disparity is motivating many organizations to change how women are treated.

Gender role stereotypes have limited women's mobility within organizations. Attitudes about the managerial effectiveness of women may affect how women's performance is assessed. They may also influence the granting or withholding of developmental opportunities. Organizations tackling diversity issues have sought to address such stereotyping through workshops, mentoring programs, and leadership development programs especially for women.

In addition to the challenges posed by stereotypes, women face a set of constraints related to their gender. Women remain the predominant primary caregivers for children and for the elderly. These extraorganizational constraints often mean that women require additional flexibility in terms of hours, travel demands, and time off for bearing and raising children. Accommodating this set of needs requires organizational adaptation in order for an organization to access and use the talents and abilities of women to full effect. Interestingly, innovations designed mainly for women (such as the so-called Mommy Track, in which women are able to take their careers onto a slower track while in the midst of their childbearing years) have helped men too. There are increasing numbers of men who share in the care of their young children or who are raising children themselves as single parents. Both women and men benefit from such policies, as do their organizations, which gain their added attention and commitment.

Age

The demographic makeup of Canadian society is reflected inside Canadian organizations. Three major age groups are currently in the work force, and a fourth will begin to enter in the next few years. Each cohort brings distinctive interests to the workplace.[42]

The Blessed Ones, Born 1930–1945, Population 4.3 Million

People in this small cohort were born lucky; with no competition in the job market, they couldn't help but make it. The unprecedented economic boom of the 1950s and 1960s benefited this generation immeasurably.

Baby Boomers, Born 1946–1966, Population 9.8 Million

The defining demographic cohort of Canadian life, the baby boom actually has two phases:

The Woodstock Generation, Born 1946–1960, Population 5.6 Million

This group made it to the job market before Generation X, but the competition resulting from their sheer numbers forced them to embrace the world of debt.

Generation X, Born 1961–1966, Population 4.2 Million

This group was demographically cursed. With spotty employment opportunities, Gen-Xers are often found living in basement apartments.

Baby Busters, Born 1967–1978, Population 5.3 Million

Born in the wake of the baby boom crest, members of this cohort like to paint themselves as disaffected. They face roomier job market opportunities as they grow older — their McJobs will eventually turn into something meatier.

Baby Boom Echo, Born 1979–1994, Population 6 Million

Relatively high numbers in this group will make competition for jobs stiff.
Perhaps the critical age-related tension that faces managers is the tension between Baby Boomers and Baby Busters. The two groups often hold stereotypes of the other, leading to dysfunctional working relationships. For example, Baby Busters perceive that Baby Boomers have achieved their positions and status simply by being born at the right time. In contrast, Baby Boomers perceive Baby Busters as cocky, unwilling to pay their dues, disloyal, and uncommitted to the organization.[43]

IMPLICATIONS OF MANAGING DIVERSITY FOR ORGANIZATIONAL COMPETITIVENESS

Taylor Cox and Stacy Blake, from the University of Michigan, have reviewed the research literature to assess the effects of successful management of diversity on organizational competitiveness. Among their findings are the following highlights. Cox and Blake cite Kanter's study, which finds that companies that have done a better job than most in eradicating sexism, racism, and classism and that have tended to employ more women and members of visible minorities are more innovative than comparable others.[44] The conclusion drawn is that minority views can stimulate alternative approaches and generate new insights in task groups. Groups exposed to minority viewpoints are more creative than are more homogeneous groups.[45]

Similar studies on groups of varying degrees of homogeneity find that more diversity (up to a point) produces decisions of better quality than more homogeneous groups. Cox and Blake summarize, "Decision quality is best when neither excessive diversity nor excessive homogeneity are present."[46] Where a minority view is present, a larger number of alternatives are considered, assumptions are more carefully scrutinized, and possible implications of various alternatives are more carefully thought out.

Finally, the effective management of diversity enhances organizational flexibility. This occurs for two reasons. First, it appears that women and racio-ethnic minorities tend to have more flexible cognitive structures than do white males. Research has indicated, for example, that women tend to have a higher tolerance for ambiguity than do men, which has been linked to factors related to flexibility, such as cognitive complexity and the ability to excel in undertaking ambiguous tasks.[47] Moreover, there is evidence that as the organization becomes more tolerant of diverse viewpoints based on age, gender, and racio-ethnic diversity, it becomes more open to new ideas in general, making it in turn more fluid and adaptable.[48]

SUMMARY

In this chapter we have introduced you to a number of theories and concepts that you will find useful in thinking about managing people in organizations. As this chapter has pointed out, the job of a manager requires knowledge not only of the structures and culture of the organization, but also of how people are motivated, led, and persuaded to work toward the goals of the organization. Moreover, as the workplace becomes more diverse and competition more intense, the job of the manager is made increasingly complex. An understanding of individual differences — both cognitive and demographic — becomes even more important in understanding how to manage people effectively. As you approach the challenge of management, we hope you will use this knowledge to think creatively about approaches to various individuals and situations and will be well equipped to manage people effectively.

NOTES

1. Nitin Nohria, *Note on Organization Structure* (Boston: Harvard Business School Publishing, 1991).
2. David A. Nadler and Michael L. Tushman, *Competing by Design* (New York: Oxford University Press, 1997).
3. Edgar H. Schein, "Organizational Culture," *American Psychologist*, Vol. 45, No. 2 (1990), 109–19.
4. Mary Kay Ash, *Mary Kay* (New York: Harper & Row, 1981).
5. Charles O'Reilly and Jeffrey Pfeffer, *Southwest Airlines* (A) (Stanford, Calif.: Stanford University Graduate School of Business, 1992).
6. Roger Hallowell, "Southwest Airlines: A Case Study Linking Employee Needs Satisfaction and Organizational Capabilities to Competitive Advantage," *Human Resource Management*, Vol. 35, No. 4 (1996), 513–34.
7. Charles A. O'Reilly and Jennifer A. Chatman, "Culture as Social Control: Corporations, Cults, and Commitment," in *Advances in Organizational Behavior*, Vol. 18 (Greenwich, Conn.: JAI Press, 1996), 157–200.
8. John Van Maanen, "People Processing: Strategies of Organizational Socialization," *Organizational Dynamics*, Vol. 7 (1978), 18–36.
9. Eileen D. Watson, *Four Seasons* (A), No. 9-88-C007 (London, Ont.: Richard Ivey School of Business, 1988).
10. O'Reilly and Pfeffer. 1992. *Southwest Airlines* (A).
11. Harrison Trice and Janice Beyer, *The Cultures of Work Organizations* (Englewood Cliffs, N.J.: Prentice-Hall, 1993).
12. John P. Kotter and James L. Heskett, *Corporate Culture and Performance* (New York: The Free Press, 1992).
13. Gary Yukl, *Leadership in Organizations*, 3rd ed. (Englewood Cliffs, N.J.: Prentice-Hall, 1994), 256.
14. Ralph M. Stogdill, *Handbook of Leadership: A Survey of the Literature* (New York: Free Press, 1974).
15. Robert L. Kahn and Daniel Katz, "Leadership Practices in Relation to Productivity and Morale," in D. Cartwright and A. Zander (eds.) *Group Dynamics: Research and Theory* (New York: Row, Peterson & Co., 1960).
    Steven Kerr, Chester A. Schriesheim, Charles J. Murphy, and Ralph M. Stogdill, "Toward a Contingency Theory of Leadership Based upon the Consideration and Initiating Structure Literature," *Organizational Behavior and Human Performance*, Vol. 12 (1974), 62–82.
    Ralph M. Stogdill and Alvin E. Coons, *Leader Behavior: Its Description and Measurement*, Research Monograph #88 (Columbus: Ohio State University, 1957).
16. Gary Yukl, *Leadership in Organizations*, 72, 69.
17. Robert J. House and Terence R. Mitchell, "Path-Goal Theory of Leadership," *Journal of Contemporary Business*, Autumn (1974), 81–97.
18. Victor Vroom and Arthur Jago, *The New Leadership: Managing Participation in Organizations* (Englewood Cliffs, N.J.: Prentice-Hall,1988).
19. Bernard Bass, *Leadership and Performance Beyond Expectations* (New York: The Free Press, 1985).
    Bernard Bass, *Transformational Leadership: Industry, Military, and Educational Impact* (Mahwah, N.J.: Lawrence Erlbaum Assoc., 1998).
20. Bernard Bass, *Leadership and Performance Beyond Expectations*, 70.
21. David Whetten and Kim Cameron, *Developing Management Skills*, 4th ed. (Reading, Mass.: Addison Wesley, 1998).

22. Eric Gelman, Vicki Quade, J.M. Harrison, and Peter McAlevey, "Playing Office Politics," *Newsweek* 16 September 1985, 56.
23. John R.P. French and Bertram Raven, "The Bases of Social Power," in D. Cartwright and A. Zander (eds.) *Group Dynamics: Research and Theory*, 2nd ed. (Evanston, Ill.: Row, Peterson, 1960), 607–23.
24. Jeffrey Pfeffer, *Power in Organizations* (Marshfield, Mass.: Pitman Publishers, 1981).
25. David Whetten and Kim Cameron, *Developing Management Skills*.
26. A.R. Cohen and D.L. Bradford, "Influence Without Authority: The Use of Alliances, Reciprocity, and Exchange to Accomplish Our Work," in Barry M. Staw (ed.) *Psychological Dimensions of Organizational Behavior* (New York: Macmillan, 1991), 378–87.
27. D. Kipnis and S.M. Schmidt, "Upward-Influence Styles: Relationship with Performance Evaluations, Salary, and Stress," *Administrative Science Quarterly*, Vol. 33 (1988), 528–42.
28. David C. McClelland, *Human Motivation* (Cambridge: Cambridge University Press, 1987), 9.
29. Stacey J. Adams, "Inequity in Social Exchange," in L. Berkowitz (ed.) *Advances in Experimental Psychology* (New York: Academic Press, 1965), 267–99.
30. Victor H. Vroom, *Work and Motivation* (New York: John Wiley & Sons, 1964). Frank J. Landy and Don A. Trumbo, "Instrumentality Theory," in R.M. Steers and L.W. Porter (eds.) *Motivation and Work Behavior* (New York: McGraw-Hill, 1983), 72–81.
31. J.B. Miner, *Industrial and Organizational Psychology* (New York: McGraw-Hill, 1992).
32. Isabel Briggs Myers and Mary H. McCaulley, *A Guide to the Development and Use of the Myers-Briggs Type Indicator* (Palo Alto, Calif.: Consulting Psychologists Press, 1985).
33. Rosabeth Moss Kanter, *Men and Women of the Corporation* (New York: Basic Books, 1977).
34. Edward E. Jones, David E. Kanouse, Harold H. Kelley, Richard E. Nisbett, Stuart Valins, and Bernard Weiner, *Attribution: Perceiving the Causes of Behavior* (Morristown, N.J.: General Learning Press, 1972).
35. Morley Gunderson and Craig Riddell, *Labour Market Economics* (Toronto: McGraw-Hill Ryerson, 1988).
36. Trevor Wilson, *Diversity at Work* (Etobicoke, Ont.: John Wiley & Sons, 1996).
37. Ibid.
38. C. Taylor, "Building a Case for Diversity," *Canadian Business Review*, Vol. 22, No. 1 (1995). 12–15.
39. Ibid.
40. Marilyn Loden, *Implementing Diversity* (Chicago, Ill.: Irwin Professional Publishing, 1996).
41. R.J. Burke and C.A. McKeen, "Do Women at the Top Make a Difference? Gender Proportions and the Experiences of Managerial and Professional Women," *Human Relations*, Vol. 49, No. 8 (1996), 1093–1104.
42. *The Impact of Demographic Change.* Ministry of Education, Skills and Training, Province of British Columbia. Online. Available: http://www.est.gov.bc.ca:80/randa/lmi/making.content/chap2pd.htm#secl
43. Don Hellriegel, John W. Slocum, Jr., Richard W. Woodman, and N. Sue Bruning, *Organizational Behaviour*, 8th Canadian ed. (Toronto: ITP Nelson, 1998).
44. Rosabeth Moss Kanter, *The Change Masters* (New York: Simon & Schuster, 1983).

45. Charlene Jeanne Nemeth, "Differential Contributions of Majority and Minority Influence," *Psychology Review*, Vol. 93 (1986), 23–32.
46. Taylor H. Cox and Stacy Blake, "Managing Cultural Diversity: Implications for Organizational Performance," *Academy of Management Executive*, Vol. 5, No. 3 (1991), 51.
47. Naomi G. Rotter and Agnes N. O'Connell, "The Relationships Among Sex-Role Orientation Cognitive Complexity, and Tolerance for Ambiguity," *Sex Roles*, Vol. 8, No. 12 (1982), 1209–20.
     David R. Shaffer et al., "Interactive Effects of Ambiguity Tolerance and Task Effort on Dissonance Reduction," *Journal of Personality*, Vol. 41, No. 2 (1973), 224–33.
48. Taylor H. Cox and Stacy Blake, "Managing Cultural Diversity," 45–54.

■ ■ ■ CASES FOR PART 4 ■ ■ ■

CASE 4.1 Anna

■

CASE 4.2 Big Brothers (BB)

■

CASE 4.3 The Canadian National Bank

■

CASE 4.4 Consulting for George Lancia

■

CASE 4.5 The Food Terminal

■

CASE 4.6 A Glossary of Industrial Relations Terminology

■

CASE 4.7 Hibbs's Webb

■

CASE 4.8 A Johnson & Johnson Company

■

CASE 4.9 Medictest Laboratories

■

CASE 4.10 Ottawa Valley Food Products

■

CASE 4.11 Royal Hardware

C A S E 4.1   ANNA

By Elizabeth Grasby and Sonya M. Head

At 7 o'clock on a warm spring night, an unsuspecting Morris Secord prepared to step through the door of the Grand Boardroom and into the path of Anna Head's fury.

Anna's exasperation was the culmination of a series of incidents that began when she was first hired. She had been waiting for two hours to confront Morris, mentally reviewing the events that had led to tonight's crisis.

REPORTING STRUCTURES

Morris Secord was a senior middle manager in a prestigious public relations firm, headquartered in New York. Branch offices were located in most major cities on the eastern seaboard. The company had recently established a new division, Executive Placement Services (EPS). Anna Head was one of four consultants who made up the new EPS group. Ray Harris was Anna's direct supervisor. Harris reported to Secord.

THE FIRST EPISODES

Ray Harris and Anna Head had been hired five years ago, within two weeks of each other. Both reported to Jim Hunt, assistant vice-president of client development, when they first joined the company. Hunt spoke about Anna:

> I tried to take her "under my wing," to show her the ropes. But Anna was too independent. I could tell she thought me persnickety. I am the kind of manager who wants all of the bases covered. I don't like surprises. She had no time for the details.
>
> One time, she told me to quit pointing my finger at her and then stalked out of my office. I gave her a few minutes to cool down and then I went to her office. I had just started talking when her husband walked into the room. He wouldn't leave us alone until he was convinced that she was all right. Anna had telephoned her husband, upset, after she left my office.

Anna thought she knew it all. She had every angle worked out in her mind and only presented me with alternatives from which to choose. Whenever I questioned the technicalities that led to her options, she implied that I was finicky, that I was wasting her time on trivia.

She told me that I acted like her father and that she didn't need a second father. Granted, I may have been a little soft. My wife was sick at the time and I may have projected my wife's fragility onto Anna. You would think that Anna would have appreciated my indulgent attitude toward her, but no, she wanted to be treated objectively, like she was "one of the guys."

During my last performance appraisal of her, I asked her to outline a five-year career plan. She responded that she wanted to be in middle management within five years. I told her she would never make it because she had no "people sense," no savvy. As a minor example of her naiveté, I characterized her deportment. I told her that she walked like a monomaniac with a mission. In fact, I could hear her stomping her way to my office long before she appeared at my door.

I also told her that she smiled and giggled too much. Only an idiot smiles all of the time. Her laugh disclosed her insecurity and immaturity. Her demeanour grated on my nerves.

When the EPS group was formed, I was one of a panel of three managers who interviewed the candidates for four new consulting jobs. Anna scored very high with the other two managers on the panel. In fact, and despite my reservations, I ranked her second in the whole group of applicants. Nevertheless, I wanted to test her mettle. So I called her into my office after all of the interviews were finished and I told her that she had scored fifth. In other words, there were four candidates who ranked above her. She would not get one of the jobs. My purpose was to test her commitment. For all I knew, Anna might have applied for the job on a whim.

Anna called in sick the next day. Since she had been upset about not getting one of the new jobs, I telephoned her home. I asked her if she wanted me to "pull some strings" in order to get a fifth position created for her in the new group. She declined, but then she went out of her way to go to the personnel office the next day, where she reviewed her employee file. Through that file, she discovered that she had been ranked first by the other two managers. Then she came to my office and confronted me.

Just to get her out of my office, I conceded that she had earned one of the new jobs and I bade her good riddance. She was a thorn in my side, and I was glad when she was gone.

RAY HARRIS'S VIEWPOINT

About seven months ago, I went to work on Monday morning and discovered that Anna was no longer working out of the New York office. She had moved to Boston and was servicing her clients from an office there.

When I questioned Morris Secord about the secrecy surrounding Anna's transfer, he told me that he, too, had just found out about the transfer. One of the vice-presidents told him, nonchalantly, in a shared taxi from the airport. Morris was as surprised as I was. I was Anna's supervisor; Morris was my immediate superior, and neither of us knew about Anna's move until afterward. Apparently she sold the idea, privately, to the vice-president. We were expected to just go along with it.

About three weeks after Anna's move, I went to see the vice-president on an unrelated issue. I took the opportunity to ask how things had happened so easily for Anna. The vice-president explained that Anna's accounts were all near Boston, and she felt that Anna had successfully commuted to New York headquarters for every administrative meeting.

ANNA'S VIEWPOINT

Ray Harris and I worked together when I first started at this company. In order to achieve my new consultant's position, I went through a rigorous screening process. I was quite surprised when Ray just showed up as my boss without having to go through the same interview mechanism. However, I had begun to accept anomalies in this company as standard fare.

I first met the vice-president when she visited some of my clients with me on a preliminary check of my effectiveness in the community. Within a few hours, she befriended me. She was like a kindred spirit. I told her about some of my problems at work, and I told her that my husband was starting the MBA program at Harvard that autumn. I felt that she understood when I explained how much I wanted to be with my husband. Despite the fact that I had personal reasons for wanting to move to Boston, I justified a transfer on the basis of its feasibility to the company, not solely on the basis of private reasons. She spoke to the president on my behalf and my transfer to Boston was approved. The vice-president was thrilled, actually, because my move represented a tangible link, a beginning of an effort at regional consolidation.

My communication problems with Ray began in earnest about three weeks after I moved to Boston. I was on that damned train, commuting to New York, sometimes five days a week. Some days, Ray would call a meeting and then cancel it after I arrived in New York. Other times, I would arrive in New York with the files that Ray had requested, and he would claim to have asked for totally different files, files that were still in Boston. I spent 60 percent of my time on the train and in New York. I felt like I was neglecting my clients.

I requested a private meeting with Ray in order to clear the air. We held the meeting, but it did nothing to resolve the situation. Ray concluded that I was threatened by him. After that meeting, Ray went on a "faxing" campaign. He faxed so much information to me that I thought the machine would burn up. Then, he started calling my clients and visiting them without my prior knowledge. My clients began to realize that there was a problem, that there were differences between Ray and me.

I went to see the vice-president several times while the situation continued to degenerate. I wanted advice. I wrote three or four letters to her. Her response was, "Hang in there. You will learn to grow with people like Ray." Things got worse.

A month ago, I wrote a letter to Morris Secord and requested a meeting with him to discuss the apparent problems between Ray and me. I never heard back from him.

Today, I commuted to my regular meeting with Ray and the other three consultants. During the meeting, Ray announced with an authoritative tone in his voice that he wanted to see me in his office after the meeting. We met in his office about 4 o'clock, whereupon he told me that my behaviour lately was unacceptable and that the letter I wrote a month ago to Morris was inexcusable. I couldn't believe that Morris had shown my letter to Ray. I felt violated. I was furious.

I found out that Morris was in another meeting.

I have been waiting outside the Grand Boardroom for two hours, all the time thinking about how my health and my home life have disintegrated over the past few months, and feeling like I am obsessed by my work, but just too driven to quit....

THE SHOWDOWN

The door to the Grand Boardroom opened and Morris Secord stepped out. "Don't you like my work?" Anna snapped at him. "Are you trying to force me to quit?" Despite her determination to maintain a professional presence, Anna began to sob. "Why don't you do something?"

Morris knew he would have to do something soon.

C A S E **4.2**   BIG BROTHERS (BB)

By Elizabeth Grasby and Sonya M. Head

Glen Mitchell, Executive Director of Big Brothers of London Inc., reviewed 1994's annual report and knew changes would have to be made. Volunteers were so scarce that total matches between big and little brothers had dropped by 40 percent over the past two years, to 119 paired companions. At the same time, 110 boys marked time on a waiting list, anticipating matches with big brothers, a wait that sometimes consumed two years.

Recruitment and retention of volunteer big brothers were now crucial issues for the organization. As well, Big Brothers of London relied heavily on funding from the United Way Campaign,[1] a funding agency that distributed monies based on results achieved by recipient organizations. In order to increase donations from the United Way, Glen needed to improve the number of matches and to demonstrate the organization's effectiveness in meeting its objectives.

THE CONCEPT

BB was part of a national nonprofit agency that attempted to provide boys, aged 6 to 16 from father-absent homes with consistent adult male companionship. Because of a paucity of volunteers willing to become big brothers, the London organization concentrated its efforts on the age group from 7 to 13 years.

For the most part, the boys had shared only negative experiences with adult males. Although some boys had never known a dad, many others had witnessed family violence. Many boys carried emotional scars resulting in poor attitudes toward men in general. When they were matched with a big brother, the boys were able to see that "there were men (out there) who didn't drink excessively, didn't hit women, and who provided an adult male influence they could hold in high esteem."[2]

HISTORY

In 1903, Irvin Westheimer, a Cincinnati businessman, found a young boy rummaging through trash in an alley. He befriended the boy and found out that the boy was fatherless. Mr. Westheimer's friends and associates agreed that boys like this could benefit from interested men who would act as a big brother to them.

Big Brothers originated in 1909 in New York City when 40 men agreed to each initiate a relationship with a boy who had been in trouble with the law. This original group believed that many boys who ran afoul of the law came from father-absent homes, and they concluded that a male influence might help to redirect these boys toward a better path in life.

Big Brothers began in Toronto in 1913. The Canadian operation focused its efforts on fatherless boys who had appeared in juvenile court. Over the years, the original concept was altered. In 1950, the agency widened its mandate to any boy lacking consistent adult male identification, not just those who had encountered trouble with the law. Championed by a provincial court judge, Big Brothers of London incorporated in 1971. By the late 1980s, the number of London boys who were matched with big brothers had increased to 200 per year from an initial 50 per year. There was an overabundance of volunteers willing to make a two-year commitment to a father-absent boy, and as many as 90 matches were made annually.

In 1994, 213 men inquired about becoming a big brother; however, the number of volunteers who applied plummeted to 41. Despite the fact that a stipulated commitment for volunteers was reduced from two years to one, the number of matches dropped to 32; Glen expected there would be less than 25 matches made in 1995.

CURRENT SOCIO-ECONOMIC CLIMATE

The city of London, like many other cities, had not fully recovered from a recession early in the decade. This economic slowdown displaced many white- and blue-collar workers to other occupations or to the ranks of the unemployed. The remaining employees who survived widespread corporate downsizing experienced additional pressures with added responsibilities becoming part of their workload; therefore, it was not surprising to find that market research on existing and potential volunteers indicated that a "lack of time" was the single most frequently cited reason for refraining from becoming volunteer big brothers.

To counter a broad-based fear of having to create extra time in an already overloaded week, Glen tried the following tactic in print promotions and information sessions: *"In reality, most volunteer Big Brothers involve little brothers in their routine activities (e.g., auto repairs, biking, mall trips, etc.) much the way a parent will spend time with their own children."* Despite this message, the number of volunteers continued to plunge. Glen speculated that there were other reasons for the decline. Some potential volunteers claimed that unemployment had left them with little time for activities other than job searches. Newly unemployed men faced the likelihood of relocation to another city, presenting the possibility that they would be unable to fulfill the year's obligation to a boy.

A portion of London's population was transient. Thirty thousand students attended the University of Western Ontario during the months September through April. As well, the city was home to many service-oriented corporations that frequently relocated employees who were adult males in their 20s and early 30s, the prime age for volunteering to be a big brother. Glen found that more established men in the community were usually married and preoccupied with young families of their own.

The fear of being accused of sexual abuse was more prevalent in society in general and, in particular, in the city of London. Local law enforcement officials recently garnered intense publicity over an investigation into a child pornography ring. Media attention to allegations of abuse, whether true or false, threatened careers and families, making many men hypersensitive to the risk of associations with unrelated children.

Big Brothers of London attempted to confront the issue of false allegations of sexual abuse at its information sessions, providing strict rules of conduct. The process to become a big brother was so rigorous that the possibility of truth to allegations of sexual abuse was negligible. Nevertheless, fear prevailed.

Universally, the number of single-parent households headed by women had grown significantly in the past few years. Many social service agencies, like the Children's Aid and CPRI,[3] weathered cutbacks that led to reduced programs. Many organizations had pared back to minimal numbers of legally mandated policies. Problems that did not fit their core agenda were sometimes referred to volunteer agencies like Big Brothers. This trend to downsizing, increasingly evident throughout the public sector, put ever-increasing pressure on volunteer social service organizations.

Consequently, while there was a glut of existing and potential little brothers and an unprecedented need for agencies like Big Brothers, there was a dearth of volunteers willing to become adult companions.

FUNDING

In 1995, close to 58 percent of the London agency's receipts came from the United Way's annual fundraising drive. The balance of funding came from private donations and other Big Brothers activities like the annual "Bowl for Big Brothers" event, which brought in over $37,000, slightly short of the committee's $45,000 goal. See Exhibit 1 for the agency's schedule of receipts and disbursements for fiscal 1995.

London Big Brothers paid 2.75 percent of their annual receipts to the national parent organization to support national advertising, workshops, conventions, and public relations. Otherwise, in most operating and policy matters, London Big Brothers Inc. was autonomous.

The extent of funding and the continued commitment of donors and donor agencies was dependent on the viability of the organization. Many organizations competed for dwindling donor dollars. An increase in the number of matches would improve Big Brothers' image and its chances of benefiting from larger donations and United Way allocations. In turn, greater revenues would allow the organization to hire additional staff to support existing caseworkers.

**ORGANIZA-
TIONAL
STRUCTURE**

Exhibit 2 shows an organization chart for the London agency, including a list of committees to which a cross-section of board and staff members and other volunteers belonged. A volunteer board of directors formed committees to direct and oversee Big Brothers functions. Each committee established its own goals and objectives.

In addition to their screening and matching functions, the two caseworkers currently employed by Big Brothers functioned as expert sources for longer-term big brothers who needed to further explore problems in their match or to discuss other issues related to their role. The only prerequisite for the caseworker's job was education and experience in social services. Both caseworkers held a bachelor of science in social work (B.S.W.), and one had worked with a Children's Aid Society before joining Big Brothers.

Periodically, the London agency accepted placements of social work students from local postsecondary institutions to assist their caseworkers. Other volunteer aids helped caseworkers on an as needed basis, usually keeping contact by telephone with the big and little brother matches and reporting any problems to the caseworkers.

**LITTLE BROTHER
PROFILE**

Little brothers were boys aged 7 to 13 who had little or no male companionship. They had been often disappointed by broken promises from "unreliable" fathers or other adult males. They came from homes in which contact with a father or other adult male was once a month or less. The majority of the agency's contacts were mothers of these boys. It was not uncommon that when the agency blitzed for volunteers or sponsored a major fundraising event, the numbers of boys on the waiting list grew because single mothers contacted the agency during these promotional efforts.

A 1994 study[4] investigated the long-term impact of Big Brothers of Ontario on little brothers who had been matched as of December 31, 1980. Statistics showed that in 1980, children from families headed by women were economically disadvantaged. In fact, 32 percent of the little brothers came from homes in which the sole source of income was social assistance. The employment earnings of the remaining mothers was estimated at 38 percent of the average income of two-parent families with children. The poverty rate for Ontario's female-led single-parent families was 55 percent compared with less than 9 percent for two-parent families.

The study showed, with statistical significance, that former little brothers had fared quite well compared with the rest of the population. Over 80 percent of them attained at least a secondary school diploma, compared with 60 percent of the other people in their age group. In addition, there was an observable advantage for those little brothers who were matched the longest with a big brother.

With regard to social psychological attitudes, it was found that an "excellent" relationship with a big brother disproportionately tended to result in higher educational attainment for the little brothers; in turn, these higher levels of education disproportionately resulted in higher self-esteem. With regard to other attitudinal variables, former little brothers who felt that they would personally make good parents disproportionately tended to highly respect authority and believed in a heightened sense of right and wrong.

Lately, more boys presented the agency with multiple problems: school troubles, hyperactivity, emotional problems, and difficulty in relationships with peers and adults. Many of these boys were referred by social service agencies that were under financial pressure.

BIG BROTHER PROFILE

Anyone over the age of 18 was eligible to become a big brother. In 1995, market research on London's big brother volunteers indicated that 27 percent were in the age group 20 to 29. Another 27 percent were aged 30 to 34, with the balance split equally among the 35–39, 40–44, and 45–49 age groups. Approximately half of the volunteers had children of their own. The primary reason for becoming a volunteer was to "help people." The majority chose Big Brothers because they knew an existing big brother or discovered by word-of-mouth that volunteers were needed. London's matches had historically averaged two and a half years in length.

Most big brothers took between two months and three years before reaching the decision to become a volunteer. Thirty-six percent took between one and three years to make their decision. Close to half of the surveyed big brothers indicated that they lacked confidence in making the decision to get involved or were unclear of their expected role as a big brother. Only 4 percent were previous little brothers.

ONE BIG BROTHER'S EXPERIENCE

One volunteer who had been a big brother for four years offered to be interviewed. When living in Toronto, Gerrard (not his real name) had volunteered weekly in an institution for the physically and mentally challenged. When he began his job in London, four years previously, Gerrard approached BB on his own and explained that he wanted to "live a balanced life" and, by volunteering, he would be able to "give something back to society." He reported that, over the years, he had procured at least two other successful big brothers for the London agency through his own work and social contacts.

When he had a new baby, his first child, Gerrard's little brother came to his home and blended with family activities every second week. In the intervening weeks, Gerrard and his little brother pursued one-on-one activities like attending sports events, going to a movie theatre, fishing, or attending an agency-sponsored event. Gerrard had discussed this revised visiting plan with his little brother before the new baby arrived. He offered to see his little brother every second week at an activity of the little brother's choice, or to visit in the intervening weeks at Gerrard's home. His little brother chose weekly contact, and so far, the little brother had adjusted well to this new schedule. He was enthusiastic about helping Gerrard with the baby, the household chores, and minor repairs.

When asked hypothetically if he would become a big brother to a boy with more challenges like hyperactivity or emotional complexities, Gerrard was not interested, adding that if he were younger and without a family of his own, he would consider a more challenging little brother.

Gerrard was a white-collar executive. He held a university degree, enjoyed a good lifestyle, and presented himself as a thoughtful, sensitive, composed individual in his mid-30s. Like many big brothers, he had very little contact with other BB volunteers. Despite his financial comfort, Gerrard understood how economics could discourage some volunteers from becoming big brothers. His suggestion for overcoming this problem was that the agency create and staff a general purpose room in its headquarters. Gerrard thought that a staffed and renovated room at the house or in another central location could function as a general meeting place to hold games like dominoes or cards or to show videos. One or several matches could use the facility simultaneously. With this general purpose room in place, most big brothers would be able to utilize public transportation, and they would be able to reduce the cost of activities with little brothers to almost nothing, eliminating much of the out-of-pocket cost of movies, sports activities, and meals or snacks. Big Brothers of London wholly owned a renovated house located centrally in the city. At present, the small house, stationed on a tract of land that provided limited parking, was almost totally consumed by offices and a small reception area.

One concern for the agency was the budget constraint of hiring additional staff and security. Big Brothers could access outside facilities like the Boys' and Girls' Club for the sole use of Big Brothers for special events.

THE PROCESS OF BECOMING A BIG BROTHER

Once a volunteer made a decision to become a big brother, the process (Exhibit 3) took three to four months. Each candidate completed an application form with references, and each was submitted to a police check to ensure they had a clear police record for the past five years. As well, the agency discussed the application with the volunteer's partner, if appropriate.

A caseworker then conducted a lengthy interview with the volunteer. This meeting covered the volunteer's family background, education, employment, social life, interests, and activities. During this same interview, the caseworker initiated discussions of sexual orientation, drugs, and alcohol usage. They also reviewed Big Brothers' Sexual Abuse Prevention Program with the potential candidate.

If the applicant were recommended for a second interview, he met at a later date with the agency's Executive Director, Glen.

Once the applicant was matched with a little brother, he was expected to keep regular contact with his caseworker in order to discuss his experiences, for better or worse. The big brother was required to visit his little brother regularly for three or four hours a week. Volunteers were asked to stick to a one-on-one format during visits, to limit the involvement of their family or friends, and to keep their visits as active as possible, like throwing a ball around a park rather than watching television together. No overnight trips were allowed for the first three months of the relationship, and after that, big brothers were to contact the caseworker if an overnight trip were planned.

THE MARKET FOR VOLUNTEERS

Big Brothers of London competed for volunteers with many nonprofit organizations, all of which had recently experienced a decline in numbers. Statistics Canada reported that half of all volunteers were in the 25 to 44 age group. The participation rate of volunteers tended to increase with age (to peak at the 35 to 44 age group) and with education (those with a university degree were most likely to volunteer). Surprisingly, Statistics Canada also reported that 60 percent of volunteers enjoyed an annual income of greater than $60,000, and that half of all volunteers became involved with an organization when someone within the organization approached them. Only 17 percent sought out the organization on their own initiative.

Market research in London indicated that many community members were willing to help the agency in many ways, but extremely few wanted to become big brothers. Even when told that they would spend only 3 to 4 hours per week, 70 percent said that they would still not become a big brother, nor would they become a big brother for just the months of July and August with no future obligations. Justification varied from specific problems, like a lack of transportation, to general issues, such as family and time constraints.

THE BIG BUNCH PROGRAM

The agency's Program Committee decided to pursue a new concept during the upcoming year, the Big Bunch program, designed for boys on the waiting list. Each month, BB would host one agency activity, assigning several (a bunch of) boys from the waiting list to two or three volunteers for the monthly special event. There would be no one-to-one contact; however, the plan would support the interests and the hopes of the boys on the waiting list. Volunteers would be asked to make a six-month commitment to the program.

Volunteers for this program would still be required to go through the same intensive screening process as big brothers, except for the last few steps involved in matching. Glen hoped to target the student population at Western, encouraging them to apply in the spring (March/April) and then to join the Big Bunch program when they returned in the autumn. During the students' summer vacation, the agency could process applications, check references, and be ready to accept the volunteer when he returned in September for his education.

THE FUTURE

The 1995 market research group recommended an aggressive marketing plan that involved hiring a marketing coordinator to implement an augmented recruiting effort. They suggested a direct mailing campaign and telephone follow-up. A colour photograph of a man and a boy "having fun together" would be sent to a list of prospective males, procured through a marketing firm's database.

The plan was costly, and Glen wondered if the "fun" message, also depicted in BB's logo (Exhibit 4), was the most appropriate appeal that could be made to potential volunteers. The first step in his action plan would be to motivate existing committees and volunteers to raise more funds for the marketing campaign, which would ultimately render an increased number of matches, which, in turn, would generate more funds for the purpose of hiring another caseworker.

Recently, the national Big Brothers organization had contracted Angus Reid to conduct a survey of matches before, during, and after closure. Glen wondered what sorts of questions would be appropriate to help measure the many positive benefits for little brothers and big brothers resulting from a match. Statistics from evaluations like this held potential to bolster his ability to point to positive outcomes from matches in promotional efforts.

With all of this in mind, Glen sat down to prepare a plan for the organization, including a strategy for augmenting recruitment and for the retention of volunteer big brothers.

NOTES

1. The United Way was an agency that solicited corporate and individual donations on behalf of several volunteer organizations. Membership in the group of United Way agencies precluded these recipient organizations from soliciting corporate donations for operations. Corporate donations could be directed to assets or special projects.
2. Quote from a Big Brother's caseworker.
3. The Child and Parent Resource Institute (CPRI) formerly ran many support programs such as anger counselling.
4. *Project Impact: A Program Evaluation of Big Brothers of Ontario*, April 1994, the Social Planning and Research Council of Hamilton and District.

Exhibit 1

STATEMENT OF CHANGES IN FUND BALANCES
for the Year Ending March 31, 1995

REVENUE

United Way donations	$138,000
Bowl for Big Brothers campaign	24,329
General	8,381
Hole-in-One	3,943
Net Bingo proceeds	11,939
City of London grant	8,550
Nevada income	3,567
Interest	1,808
	$200,517

EXPENDITURES

Salaries	$137,612
Employee benefits	17,450
Recruitment and education	9,484
Stationery and office expenses	7,241
Affiliation fees	5,788
Property taxes	4,756
Telephone	3,434
Promotion	3,294
Postage	3,196
Insurance	3,021
Travel allowance	2,743
Audit and legal	1,700
Utilities	1,500
General expenses	1,328
Repairs and maintenance	923
Recreation	338
	$203,808

Net increase (decrease) in fund	($ 3,291)
Opening fund balance	$ 71,083
Fund balance — March 31, 1995	$ 67,792

Exhibit 2
Organizational
Chart

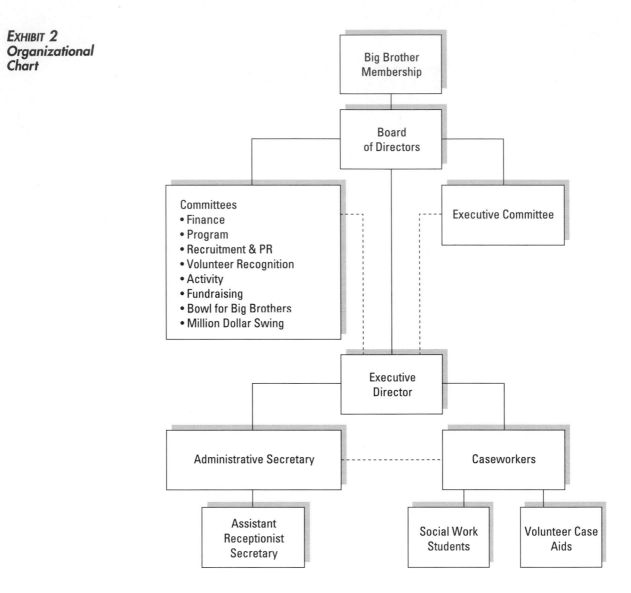

**EXHIBIT 3
Application
Process**

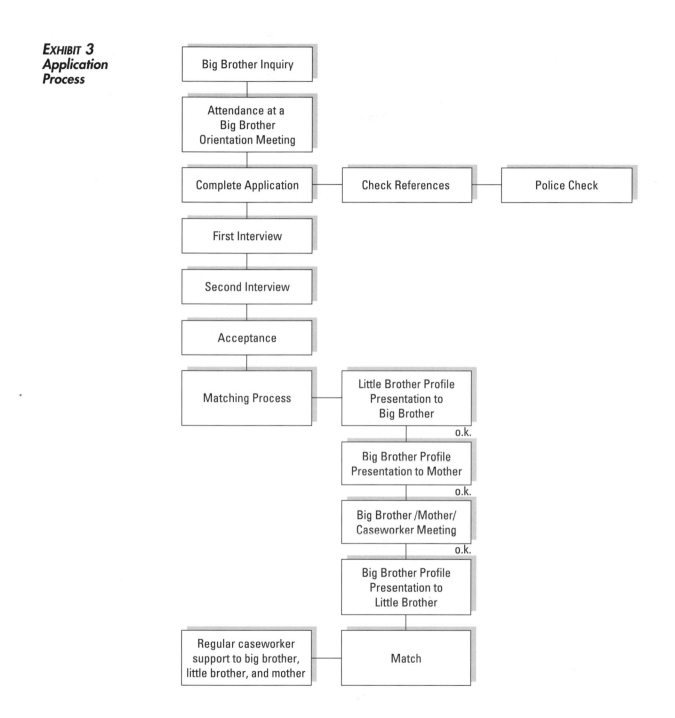

EXHIBIT 4
The Agency
Logo

C A S E 4.3   THE CANADIAN NATIONAL BANK

By Elizabeth Grasby and Cara C. Maurer

It was 10:00 a.m. on February 26, 1997, and Lesley Mahon, manager of customer service at the Chatham Branch of the Canadian National Bank, had just completed a phone conversation with Robert Aronson, the manager for all branches of the bank in the Chatham region. Lesley was alarmed about the news that Pam Stewart, one of the Chatham branch's customer service representatives, had complained in a formal written statement to the National Committee for Employee Concerns (NCEC) at head office that Lesley was impeding Pam's personal and professional development by not allowing her to take business courses. Lesley and Pam had had several conflicts since the first day of Lesley's appointment. Lesley was shocked and upset about this serious allegation and wondered what action, if any, she should take.

THE CANADIAN BANKING INDUSTRY

All banks that operated in Canada were chartered by Parliament and regulated by the Bank Act. Under the Act, these banks were required to be incorporated, to hold sufficient bank reserves, and to follow a set of general banking rules as guidelines. The largest chartered banks in Canada, all with a nationwide network of branches, were Canadian Imperial Bank of Commerce, Bank of Montreal, Canadian National Bank, Bank of Nova Scotia, Royal Bank of Canada, Toronto Dominion Bank, Laurentian Bank of Canada, National Bank of Canada, and Canadian Western Bank. Up to now, the Bank Act had kept the "four pillars" of the financial service sector separate from each other. These pillars were banking, insurance, trust, and securities.

Recent Changes in Banking

Recent deregulation of the financial services industry had produced many changes for the Canadian banking industry. Cross-ownership between the four pillars was now possible and was becoming increasingly common as the industry moved toward greater consolidation. For the chartered banks this meant competition from new entrants into the banking industry. Most banks were trying to acquire other financial services businesses to gain competence in the nonbanking

IVEY Cara C. Maurer prepared this case under the supervision of Elizabeth Grasby solely to provide material for class discussion. The authors do not intend to illustrate either effective or ineffective handling of a managerial situation. The authors may have disguised certain names and other identifying information to protect confidentiality. Ivey Management Services prohibits any form of reproduction, storage or transmittal without its written permission. This material is not covered under authorization from CanCopy or any reproduction rights organization. Copyright © 1997, Ivey Management Services.

areas of financial service, especially insurance and securities. The pace of these changes was further accelerated owing to technological innovations and rising customer expectations. In an effort to meet these demands and remain competitive within the industry, banks were driven to offer financial advice on a widening range of products and services, more flexible hours of operations, and more convenient banking services (e.g., automated banking, telephone banking, and home banking). These initiatives had allowed the banks to increase their revenues on a per customer basis; however, there was also continued pressure within the banking industry to increase overall profits through the control of internal costs and efficient use of the banks' resources.

THE CANADIAN NATIONAL BANK

The Canadian National Bank, with 1996 revenues of $16.5 billion, net income of $1.4 billion, assets of $218 billion, and 1,600 branches nationwide, was one of the six dominant chartered banks in Canada. The Canadian National Bank offered a full range of commercial, corporate, international, investment, private, and retail banking (see Exhibit 1 for the Canadian National Bank's organizational chart).

Each branch was jointly administered by the manager of customer service and the manager of personal banking, whose performance evaluations were to a large extent evaluated by the branch's financial performance. Consistently good performance was essential for a manager's career with the bank (see Exhibit 2 for Lesley Mahon's job description). While the manager of personal banking was responsible for attracting new business to the bank in the form of loans and financial services, the manager of customer service was in charge of controlling costs and ensuring the overall quality of customer service.

During the past year, the Canadian National Bank had introduced several initiatives to increase revenues per customer and to reduce internal costs. The introduction of various distribution channels (e.g., automated banking, home banking) was making the bank more readily accessible to its customers. Additionally, to increase revenues, customer service representatives were required to be familiar with the entire range of the bank's products and services. This knowledge would enable customer service representatives to refer customers to other services offered by the bank. These referrals were deemed to be crucial to the bank's future growth and profits.

Customer Service Capacity Management

Internal cost control was equally important to increasing profits as was revenue generation. One of the main initiatives introduced to manage internal resources more efficiently was Customer Service Capacity Management (CSCM). This system was designed to create a more cost-effective match of fluctuating customer traffic with the number of customer service representatives scheduled at any given time (see Exhibit 3 for a further description of CSCM). Previously, service schedules had been developed manually. Under the new system the schedule was developed by head office and then implemented and administered by the manager of customer service at the local branch. For customer service representatives in most branches this initiative meant reduced hours, flexible schedules, and sometimes shared jobs. Training and counselling to deal with these changes were readily available for anyone who desired them.

THE CHATHAM BRANCH

With a staff of only 12, the Chatham branch was considered a small branch (see Exhibit 4 for the branch's organizational chart). Customers and employees knew one another through contact in the bank and through the community of Chatham, a mid-sized city in southwestern Ontario.

Over the past three years there had been three managers at the Chatham branch. Lesley's predecessor, a middle-aged, well-educated male, had been the manager of customer service for two years. Prior to that, a female manager had left the branch owing to personal problems after a few months.

Lesley Mahon

Lesley Mahon had been the manager of customer service at the Chatham branch since October 1996. She was expected to stay at this branch for 18 months, at which time she would be able to apply for a position at any other branch of the Canadian National Bank.

Lesley graduated from the honours business administration program at the Richard Ivey School of Business in the spring of 1996. During the four summers between school years, Lesley had been enrolled in a special training program in all aspects of retail banking with the Canadian National Bank. The purpose of this training program was to develop promising candidates during their formal education for management positions after graduation.

Lesley was 24 years of age, single, and described by her peers and subordinates as considerate, calm, and competent. Lesley described herself: "I see myself as a fairly laid-back manager who appreciates her employees and believes that they can do a good job if I give them enough support. I love working for this bank because I see opportunities for growth and because people are treated with respect and fairness." After a few more years as customer service manager, Lesley was hoping to work for the treasury department at head office.

Pam Stewart

Pam had joined the Canadian National Bank as a customer service representative after receiving her high-school diploma and had been working for the Chatham branch ever since. She was 43 years of age, married, and had two teenage daughters. Her colleagues described her as stern, very exacting, and professional. Some were intimidated by her because she always found and pointed out any mistakes or oversights. Everyone valued her in-depth knowledge of all the operations of the bank and her many years of experience. Her performance evaluations over the last five years indicated above average ratings in all criteria of her job description (see Exhibit 5 for Pam's job description). Two years earlier, Pam had applied for the position of customer service manager at the branch. She was not hired for this position. Lesley suspected Aronson had chosen another applicant for the position because that applicant had a formal business degree and some management experience.

LESLEY'S FIRST WEEK

On October 21, 1996, her first day at the Chatham branch, Lesley received a warm welcome from all the employees of the branch.

The previous manager briefed her on the recent performance of the branch and the employees, including the following comment:

Lesley, I wish you all the best. I know you are going to do a fine job with this branch. Just watch out for Pam Stewart; she can be difficult to manage and does not seem to agree with all the performance expectations that the bank has introduced in the last few years.

The next day, Lesley met with all branch employees individually in her office to brief them informally on her goals for the immediate future:

I told all of them that I had high hopes for this branch because I believed that all the recent changes the bank had introduced would make the bank more profitable and more efficient. All employees seemed committed to the bank's goals of excellent service and growth. I think they were quite relieved to see that I was positive about the future and was going to support them.

Pam Stewart was the only one who reacted negatively to this first meeting with Lesley. Lesley recalls the conversation as follows:

Lesley:

Pam, I am looking forward to working with you, and I am confident that your experience will be crucial to our team's success. The bank has introduced a lot of new initiatives to our operations, and I would like all of us to work together to implement these as best possible.

Pam shrugged her shoulders and replied coldly:

You may think that you can walk in here and make all kinds of changes just because you have a degree, but you will not change anything about my job. I have been here for 25 years, and I know from my experience how things around here work best.

Lesley, taken aback by this outburst, replied calmly:

Pam, I am not planning on making any major changes by myself. Most of what is currently changing was decided by head office two or three months before I came to this branch. My job is to make sure we implement these changes here as painlessly as possible.

Pam adamantly said:

I don't care what your plans are, this branch does not need you. We have gotten rid of the other managers before, and we will also get rid of you.

Without any further explanation, Pam stormed out of the office. Lesley felt very uncomfortable about this confrontation so early in her new job, but she told herself that she would be able to work it out over time. Lesley documented the incident and placed it in the personnel file. Lesley was surprised to find that the file contained no other documentation about Pam's behaviour prior to Lesley's arrival.

FOUR DAYS LATER

On Friday, October 25, Lesley was collecting the referral sheets from each customer service representative to compile the summary of referrals that had to be sent to the area manager. She noticed that Pam's referral sheet was the only one missing. Lesley went over to Pam to talk to her. Lesley recollected the conversation as follows:

Lesley:

Pam, I noticed that your referral sheet for this week is still missing. You know that I am going to collect them every Friday for the summary report.

Pam replied sharply:

I have not made referrals for 25 years, and I am not going to start now.

Lesley:

Pam, I know that it is not easy for anyone to change, but it is very important that we refer financial products. Customers need our recommendations to make the right kinds of financial decisions. If you like, you could get some extra training for referrals, and you can count on my support as well.

Pam, breathing heavily, replied:

Forget it. I am a bank customer service representative, not a salesperson. I am not going to sell anything to my clients, and you cannot tell me what to do.

Without any further explanation, Pam walked away briskly.

After Pam had left her office that day, Lesley recalled her initial training. She wanted to continue to be lenient with Pam because she thought that Pam might have personal problems underlying her uncooperative behaviour in the office. She was also perplexed: How could Pam have received above-average performance evaluations over all these years without making any referrals, considering the heavy weight of referrals in her job description? Lesley was wondering if the former managers had felt intimidated by Pam's behaviour.

PAM'S REQUEST

On Monday morning, October 28, there was a letter from Pam on Lesley's desk requesting a change in her job description back to a customer service representative position exclusively. Pam was currently rotating on a weekly basis between her customer service representative job and a utility clerk position. In September, Pam and another customer service representative at the branch, Sarah Wright, had signed an agreement to share these two positions. This change had been made after Sarah's full-time position had been eliminated at the branch because of a CSCM recommendation.

Sarah Wright was 45 years of age, married with two adult children, had a high-school education, and had also been with the Chatham branch for 25 years. Sarah was very content with her job at the branch, experienced and very capable. Two years earlier, she had won the national customer service award as the employee who had demonstrated the most outstanding customer service during the year. Her colleagues described her as very likeable, smart, and uncomplicated.

The rotation schedule between the two positions had allowed both Pam and Sarah to stay with the branch and receive development training as customer service representatives. The utility clerk position was less desirable because it involved looking after many odd jobs in the branch, such as ordering supplies and restacking brochures, and it provided fewer opportunities for personal development. Pam had complained that it was stressful to switch between two jobs and that it usually took her a full day to get back into the clerk's duties. She was often not able to complete all assigned work during her week as the utility clerk. During her week as the utility clerk, Sarah worked quickly and was able to complete her own work as well as the work Pam had left behind.

Pam's letter stated that she no longer wanted to do the utility clerk's job because of the stress involved in switching between two positions. An attached doctor's note attested to Pam's claim that her job was too stressful for her. From her own experience of working both jobs, Lesley could not understand how this type of work was too stressful for anyone.

After lunch, Lesley asked Sarah to come into her office. Lesley asked Sarah if she would be interested in working as the utility clerk exclusively. Lesley recalls the conversation:

Sarah responded in a quiet and friendly voice:

Well, I am quite happy with the current arrangement and if it is no trouble for you I would like it to continue. I would really miss the daily customer contact I have as a customer service representative if I were only to look after odd jobs.

Lesley nodded and replied:

The reason I am asking is that Pam would like to have the customer service representative position for herself since the rotation between the two jobs is causing her a lot of stress. However, I will not want to agree to this if it makes you unhappy.

Sarah paused for a moment before answering:

Pam and I have been very close friends for the last 15 years and I know that she is feeling a lot of stress, especially these days. You know, her younger teenage daughter just had a child out of wedlock, and Pam and her husband are taking care of the child now. I do not think that her husband is too thrilled with that decision. Although I understand her problems, I also need to look after my own welfare.

Lesley:

Okay, Sarah. I will talk to Pam as well and then I will leave it to you and Pam to find your own solution. You may take until February 28 to find a better arrangement.

After Lesley had spoken to Pam, they agreed that Pam and Sarah would work out a compromise between themselves and get back to Lesley with their proposal. There were no further problems in the branch until mid-November.

PAM TAKES STRESS LEAVE

On the morning of November 11, Lesley found a note on her desk from the receptionist informing her that Pam had taken short-term disability leave because of unbearable job-related stress.

Lesley was concerned about who would take over Pam's job while she was gone. She also knew that Pam's disability leave would be a substantial cost to the branch, affecting the branch's financial performance for the year.

Over the next four weeks the atmosphere in the bank was very cooperative and friendly, despite some occasional resentment by the employees about the extra work. Lesley was pleased that all staff worked well together in this situation and were able to keep the number of referrals constant. When Pam came back on December 9, she seemed well rested and friendly. Pam and Sarah had still not made a proposal to Lesley about their shared jobs but were sharing the two positions without any interruptions.

THE FINAL CONFRONTA- TION

Prior to Lesley's arrival, in September 1996, the Chatham branch had received its centralized CSCM schedule from head office, which required one position to be downsized and increased the hours for all staff until September 1997. It took a lot of fine-tuning and careful planning by the customer service manager at the time to staff the schedule. Everyone had adjusted quickly to the new hours that required many of them to work late one day of the week. Lesley understood that Pam had agreed to be scheduled to work until 8 p.m. on Thursdays without mentioning any time conflicts.

On February 24, 1997, Pam came to Lesley's office to talk to her. Pam:

I am no longer able to work on Thursday evenings because I want to take an accounting course on Thursday nights, starting next month. The course would allow me to develop myself further. The only other day the course is offered is Fridays, but on Fridays I am committed as a Brownie leader, which I cannot change.

Lesley tried to remain calm, remembering that she wanted to be supportive toward Pam because of the difficulties in her private life.

Lesley:

Pam, I understand that all these things are very important for you, but the schedule has been set and is not meant to be changed for at least seven months. You are cross-trained in many special areas and there is no one single person I could use as a substitute for you. Since the course does not directly relate to your job at the branch, I suggest that you either wait until next September or until the accounting course is offered at another time.

Pam nodded her head and replied:

Okay, I'll wait. Thanks.

As Pam left the office, Lesley thought the issue had been resolved.

Lesley felt that these confrontations with Pam were leaving her more and more exhausted. She thought back to the job posting she had seen in the cafeteria that day for customer service manager at a branch of the Canadian National Bank in her home town of Sarnia, Ontario.

FEBRUARY 26   Now it was February 26, and Lesley was trying to understand what she could have done to prevent the crisis situation with Pam, of which Robert had just informed her. Lesley mulled over Robert's comments:

Pam Stewart came to me for a confidential counselling meeting yesterday. She said that she felt harassed by you because of her emotional problems and that you were intentionally blocking her development. I also found out that she had officially complained to the NCEC about you. She really should have talked to you or me before writing to the committee. [See Exhibit 6 for the complaint procedures within the bank.] Lesley, I've known you for several years, and frankly, this just does not sound like you. This is a very serious allegation that I thought you should know about.

Lesley sat back in her chair. Looking through the *Employee Rules* and the *Guidelines for Corrective Action Procedures* (see Exhibits 7 and 8), she was wondering what she should do.

EXHIBIT **1**
Organizational Chart of the Canadian National Bank

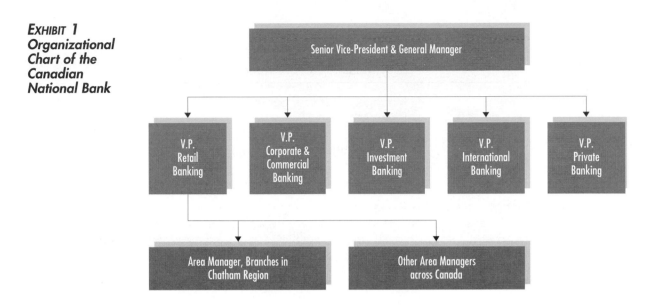

Source: Company documents.

Exhibit 2

Lesley Mahon's Job Description

Position Title: Manager, Customer Service
Incumbent: Lesley Mahon
Date: October 1, 1996
Reports to: Area Manager, Chatham Region

Purpose:

To support the Manager, Personal Banking, in maintaining a premium level of customer service in the branch. Responsible for ensuring high levels of productivity through close control of noninterest expenses. To contribute to the overall branch growth and profitability through effective product sales and cross-selling initiatives and by providing a wide variety of transactional services.

Key Result Areas:

Quality Service — 25 Percent

- Promotes service improvement through designing and implementing quality service initiatives.
- Effectively manages client complaints.
- Continuously improves the match between customer expectations and branch service

Human Resources Management and Leadership — 25 Percent

- Communicates and monitors performance expectations and branch guidelines to staff.
- Facilitates ongoing training and development of staff to ensure future staffing needs.
- Ensures coaching, counselling, motivation of staff to facilitate any changes.
- Ensures strong morale and teamwork in the branch.
- Completes quarterly performance appraisals.

Business Management and Profitability — 25 Percent

- Supports branch goals by implementing an effective referral system, including weekly coaching, goal setting, tracking of results, and recognizing achievements.
- Assists Manager, Personal Banking, with implementation of sales programs.
- Maximizes efficient match between customer service needs and staff availability.

Productivity and Operations Quality — 25 Percent

- Ensures cost control of noninterest expenses.
- Implements innovations to increase productivity.
- Efficiently manages all resources.
- Assumes responsibility for branch security.

Source: Company documents.

Exhibit 3

Customer Service Capacity Management

Purpose:

To better meet customer traffic needs without overstaffing resources. Actual data are used to forecast client traffic and design an ideal customer service representative schedule. The main benefits are better customer service, fewer scheduling uncertainties for branch management, and generally fewer wasted resources.

How It Works:

---

1. A centralized information group collects data from the branches. These data measure the number of transactions made by customer service representatives during a day and the amount of down time between transactions.
2. These data are then compared with the actual branch schedule that was set manually by branch management. This comparison will detect any excess or lack of customer service representatives on schedule at any given time.
3. The centralized group then factors in any other client information (e.g., peak periods before holidays, demographic makeup of branch customers and their traffic patterns to the branch — high senior traffic, families, young professionals), forecasts a schedule for the branch for the next 12 months, and makes recommendations as to the skills and demographic makeup needed from the customer service representatives.
4. Branch management receives the centralized schedule and completes the actual scheduling of individual customer service representatives. Branch management assigns staff to the schedule who have qualifications and skills that are forecast to be needed.
5. Information group monitors the schedule by collecting actual data on customer matches.

Source: Company documents.

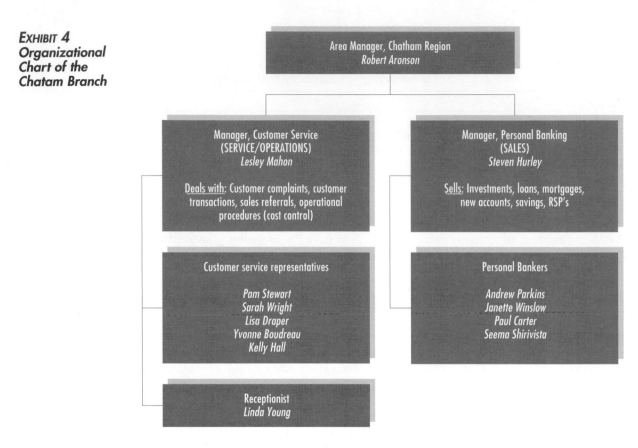

Exhibit 4
Organizational
Chart of the
Chatam Branch

Source: Company documents.

Exhibit 5

Pam Stewart's Job Description

Title: Customer Service Representative
Incumbent: Pam Stewart
Date: September 1, 1995
Reports to: Manager, Customer Service

The following criteria are reviewed quarterly and evaluated on a seven-point rating scale:
Customer Service — 25 Percent

- Provides friendly, personal service to all customers.
- Deals with customer needs in a time-efficient manner.
- Ensures client needs are complete when client leaves the branch.

Quality Referrals — 35 Percent

- Suggests products that match client needs and refers to the appropriate officer.
- Maintains accurate product knowledge.
- Strives toward goals set by Customer Service Manager.

Rating	No. of Referrals per Month
1	0–40
2	41–80
3	81–120
4	121–160
5	161–240
6	241–320
7	321+

Team Work — 20 Percent

- Shows initiative and self-motivation.
- Accepts changes within the branch in a positive manner and provides constructive criticism to management.
- Demonstrates interpersonal ability to get along with clients and other branch employees.
- Supports all branch/bank campaigns.

Operational Skills — 20 Percent

- Continually looks for ways to increase revenue enhancement opportunities.
- Follows all branch policies, guidelines, and procedures.
- Completes transaction with less than 10 errors per quarter.

Source: Company documents.

Exhibit 6

Complaint Procedures within the Bank

If you have a concern or complaint, please follow the following guidelines:

1. Talk to your supervisor or manager first.
2. Talk to your manager's manager if (a) you are not comfortable talking to your own manager, or (b) the conversation with your manager did not resolve the issue.
3. Talk to the Human Resources Department if steps 1–2 could not resolve the issue.
4. Write to the NCEC if (a) steps 1–3 could not resolve the issue, or (b) the issue is too serious in nature.

To register a formal complaint with the NCEC, type a detailed report on the confidential complaint form and send to the committee. This process is absolutely confidential. Only the coordinators of the program will know your name. No one except you and the committee know about the complaint unless you choose to discuss your subject with a qualified person who is required to keep the information confidential unless you specify otherwise.

Source: Company documents.

EXHIBIT 7

Employee Rules

Employees must abide by the following rules. Any intentional violation will require the appropriate corrective action to be taken, outlined in the guidelines for corrective action.

1. Upholding the law
   - Complying with all banking laws and regulations**
   - Upholding confidentiality of inside information**
   - Protecting software or other copyrights**
   - Not using drugs and alcohol
   - Not smoking in nonsmoking areas

2. Ensuring confidentiality**
   - Protecting client privacy**
   - Protecting employee privacy**
   - Protecting proprietary bank information**
   - Not soliciting nonbank information

3. Demonstrating fairness
   - Not discriminating
   - Encouraging free competition

4. Showing corporate responsibility
   - Demonstrating social responsibility

5. Honouring trust
   - Avoiding misappropriation**
   - Preventing improper banking transactions
   - Reporting banking irregularities and dishonesty
   - Attending work promptly and regularly
   - Promptly complying with all instructions received from a supervisor**

6. Showing objectivity
   - Declining improper gifts, payment, or entertainment
   - Avoiding conflict of interest

7. Demonstrating integrity
   - In all communications, telling the truth and not misleading directly or indirectly**
   - Completing records with integrity
   - Demonstrating unquestionable honesty and integrity inside and outside the bank

8. Assuming individual responsibility
   - Not harassing others (through verbal abuse or threats, unwelcome remarks or jokes, innuendo, or taunting)
   - Being dressed and groomed in a manner appropriate to the banking environment

---

Exhibit 8

Guidelines for Corrective Action Procedures

The bank recognizes that the majority of employees are conscientious and responsible and play a positive role in the company's operations. Motivated by self-respect, they conduct themselves in a disciplined manner and perform satisfactorily on the job. In situations where an employee's conduct is unsatisfactory, the bank believes that in most cases the problem can be corrected without punitive action, using a progressive positive approach. The bank's objective is to implement a corrective system that identifies and corrects the cause of unsatisfactory employee behaviour in a positive manner, encouraging improvements in the employee's conduct by ensuring that the employee clearly understands his/her responsibilities.

Cases of minor infringement of the employee rules should be dealt with by the employee's immediate supervisor by way of informal discussion, resorting to the formal procedure provided below if this fails to correct the problem. It is the bank's intent that written warnings be used only when verbal reprimands have failed to produce the desired results or when misconduct is serious enough to warrant action at a more advanced stage of the corrective process. While not an exhaustive list, gross misconduct includes things such as theft, fraud, or willful disobedience and warrants immediate dismissal.

All incidents that could reasonably be viewed as dishonest or deceitful acts by an employee must be placed in correspondence or discussed with the Human Resources Department before any corrective action is taken.

Basic Procedures

A. The employee shall be informed at the outset of the grounds of the complaint, and the employee should be accompanied in any interview on the subject by a co-worker, preferably one having knowledge of the matter being discussed.
B. The employee must be given an opportunity to present the case from his/her point of view before any decision is reached.
C. Once the decision is made, the employee is to be informed in writing of the action being taken (e.g., written warning, final warning) and the reason thereof.

Corrective Action

A. A first breach of an employee rule not identified by a double asterisk will be dealt with by a formal verbal warning. The warning should follow the violation as soon as is practical, and the employee should be advised that this represents the first normal corrective action step. A notation of the warning should be placed in the employee's file.
B. If the violation recurs the employee should receive a first written warning. The warning should include a time frame within which the employee's performance is expected to meet acceptable standards. Prior to issuing the written warning, the incident should be discussed with the National Human Resources Department. Copies of the written warning should be kept in the employee's files for one year and thereafter destroyed if the employee has not been subject to any other corrective action

Exhibit 8 (cont.)

Guidelines for Corrective Action Procedures

C. If the above measures fail to correct the problem, a decision-making leave should be ordered in conjunction with a final written warning. The immediate supervisor will meet with the employee to review the problem, clearly outline the bank's expectations, and instruct the employee to return home to consider what the employee will do to correct the problem. The maximum one-day leave must be with pay. If the employee decides to meet the bank's expectations, he/she should compile a written document that indicates the employee's commitment to change, and outlines specific steps to correct his/her behaviour. If the employee fails to commit to change, this should be noted in the final written warning, and the employee should be made aware of the bank's corrective action in case of another recurrence of the problem.

D. In the event of gross misconduct (rules labelled with a double asterisk) the employee is subject to immediate dismissal. Dismissal is also appropriate if the employee's unacceptable behaviour recurs after all above steps have been taken. No dismissal should be issued without prior consultation with the Human Resources Department.

Source: Company documents.

CASE 4.4 CONSULTING FOR GEORGE LANCIA

By Elizabeth Grasby and Michelle Linton

Cam Matthews shook his head as he looked over the financial statements in front of him. It was June 1993, and he had been hired as a consultant to bring George Lancia's organization under control. George, who wanted a break from the management of his various businesses, was concerned about the successes of his investments. Cam, a 24-year-old recent business graduate, knew upon reading the statements that the financial position was worse than George realized. Cam's foremost concern was how to manage and to relate to George. Cam believed significant changes would have to be made. He wondered what problems he should anticipate.

GEORGE LANCIA

George Lancia was the 45-year-old owner of the organization. He had worked on his own in order to support himself through high school. Upon graduation, he worked as a surveyor's assistant for two years, after which he sold securities for five years. At various times during these years he had owned a movie theatre, a drive-in theatre, and a restaurant. He had also begun to buy and sell real estate, including rental properties, and had created a substantial amount of wealth through these dealings.

In 1985, George was approached by Kevin Gibson with the idea of leading a syndicate to invest in several fast food restaurants in Eastern Ontario. George agreed to invest in this venture. By 1988, the restaurants' performances had failed to improve and George was forced to buy out the other investors.

Three years later, George was approached with another investment opportunity, a nursing home and retirement lodge in the small town of Sterling, Ontario. George responded with an offer that was accepted in principle; however, the actual agreement was still being completed by the lawyers.

George built a new house in 1991. By this time, all of his cash was tied up in six restaurants, the retirement home, the rental properties, and the new house.

MANAGEMENT STRUCTURE

George's investments were set up as individual, numbered corporations. In theory, this structure was intended to protect him from personal liability and to

IVEY Michelle Linton prepared this case under the supervision of Elizabeth Grasby solely to provide material for class discussion. The authors do not intend to illustrate either effective or ineffective handling of a managerial situation. The authors may have disguised certain names and other identifying information to protect confidentiality. Ivey Management Services prohibits any form of reproduction, storage or transmittal without its written permission. This material is not covered under authorization from CanCopy or any reproduction rights organization. Copyright © 1995, Ivey Management Services.

save the structure from problems in a single unit. However, two sources of exposure could not be avoided. Both George's reputation and his borrowing ability within this very small town would be hindered if any of the individual corporations were to go bankrupt. The banks and creditors had recently begun to ask for personal guarantees on any new debt requested by George.

In general, George made all decisions and approved all spending. His primary source of control was monthly financial statements, which he often viewed several months late and did not trust the accuracy of. He seldom had direct contact with his front-line employees.

George's secretary, Sharon, was 23 years old and had received a college diploma in bookkeeping. Sharon had been named the controller of the company. She prepared financial statements, managed the payroll, and handled supplier relationships. Her assistant, Caroline, who was 24 years old with a commerce degree from Brock University, helped Sharon prepare the financial statements. Both women had a difficult time remaining productive during the day; statements were occasionally late or inaccurate. George was aware of this situation but wondered how the office computers would be run and the filing and banking handled without Sharon and Caroline. Because George wished to avoid any conflict, Sharon had an effective veto on the decisions in her area.

Restaurants

Kevin Gibson was the general manager of the restaurant operations. He was 22 years old when he started working for George. Kevin had no formal management education but had managed fast-food restaurants since the age of 18. George had given him full control over decisions at first, claiming that he "would totally step aside and let Kevin do his thing." When commenting on his own management approach, George said he "preferred to sell an idea rather than tell people what to do." George would review the monthly financial statements and then hold "grilling sessions" during which he would ask Kevin for explanations of any apparent poor results. Kevin would then be asked to project the next month's results. George would write down these projections and file them to be pulled out and pointed to during next month's "grilling session." George received other information informally from time to time, in the form of phone calls from banks, suppliers, employees, or the franchiser, whenever there were problems.

For various reasons, Kevin was unable to provide positive results over time, causing George to lose patience and to take back the formal authority. Currently, Kevin had no authority to make any decisions without George's approval; however, he did anyway. Most of the restaurant staff and suppliers had never heard of George and assumed Kevin was the owner. George wondered who would manage the restaurants if Kevin left and therefore did not want to create any friction between himself and Kevin. Additionally, George hoped Kevin would repay the money he had loaned him on a handshake to finance Kevin's house.

Jeff Cranney, a 35-year-old with no management education or former management experience, managed the restaurant in Cobourg. He had invested a substantial amount of cash to build the store in 1991 and currently held 49 percent of the shares. However, this restaurant was not managed effectively and had significant operating problems. George was worried that he would be forced to buy Jeff out if these concerns were addressed.

John and Lucy Wilson approached George in September 1992 and asked him to sell them the restaurant in Peterborough. They provided two houses as a down payment and intended to pay the rest over time. From the perspectives of the bank, the employees, and the landlord, George remained responsible for the asset. John and Lucy were middle-aged with no management education or supervisory experience. John worked as a linesman for a power company; Lucy was a health care aide. George wanted to avoid any conflict here as well to prevent "being left with a real mess."

The Sterling Manor

The Sterling Manor was a nursing home and retirement lodge that housed 62 residents and employed close to 50 employees. The negotiations between George and the retirement home's initial owners, the Vaughans, were intense. The Vaughans, the Ministry of Health, and the bank had expressed considerable doubt about George's ability to run the home successfully. It was expected that any additional conflicts or problems would further hinder their perception of him.

At the same time, major changes in the industry were pending. The government had developed stricter regulations to increase the level of quality and service in the industry. These regulations stipulated how the funding should be allocated among nursing, food services, and housekeeping. These changes would reduce net profit considerably, and management would face a much greater challenge than before, when financing was plentiful and regulations minimal.

Linda Baxter was the administrator of the Sterling Manor. She had been a nursing assistant for 25 years and had a diploma in long-term care management. Linda was very personable and concerned about doing a good job. However, she lacked several important technical skills regarding computers, time management, and supervising. She had been hired by the Vaughans and continued to report to them on a regular basis. Whenever she and George disagreed, Linda stated that she still worked for the Vaughans and threatened to seek their decisions. The administration of the home was very disorganized. Phones went unanswered, and Linda's desk was piled with paperwork and mail dating back to 1989. Linda lacked focus or direction and felt that she was accomplishing very little. With the pending regulations, Linda was worried that others would question her competence; therefore, she reacted defensively when anyone attempted to get involved in her work.

Heather Irvin was the director of nursing at the Manor. She was a registered nurse with 30 years' experience. Heather found it difficult to organize and run a staff while dealing with all the conflict and confusion among George, Linda, and the Vaughans. She recognized the importance of management control in a nursing organization, where health and lives are at stake. It was her opinion that Linda did not understood how to operate a health business. So, in order to protect her own position, Heather refused to listen to Linda. Instead, she complained constantly to George about Linda. Because George knew very little about nursing, he could not effectively evaluate Heather's work. He worried about what would happen if she quit. He had not heard any negative comments from anyone else about her work, so he basically gave her complete freedom.

Real Estate

Margaret Dennett managed the apartment building in Belleville. She had been given authority to make decisions about the tenants and daily operations but continually called George about problems she encountered. George did not have the time to find a replacement for her and therefore, to prevent upsetting Margaret, did not attempt to change the situation.

PERFORMANCE

Restaurants

The restaurant operation had performed poorly for the past three years. The stores had reached their overdraft limit several times, and George had been forced to inject $70,000 from his personal line of credit. Labour productivity was low, quality and service were substandard, current marketing activities were expensive and ineffective, and relations with banks, suppliers, and the franchisers were very poor. In the spring of 1993, Kevin had diverted $70,000 cash from the restaurants to secure equipment and working capital for an ice cream store, a venture that had lost $3,000 per month since its inception.

The Sterling Manor

The Sterling Manor had been barely breaking even for the past several months and was near its overdraft limit. The new union was in the midst of contract arbitration that, when completed in late 1993, would likely expose the home to a retroactive wage settlement of between $200,000 and $500,000. Whenever George accumulated money in the business, the Vaughans withdrew it as advance payment on the Manor's purchase price. George did not want to jeopardize the sale and was therefore reluctant to approach the Vaughans about this.

George did not understand the Ministry of Health's new funding model and did not know whether the home would be a good purchase, or even if it would survive, under the new system. George did not seem aware of the severity of the Manor's financial position.

George had almost reached the limit of his personal credit line and could not count on significant cash flows from his businesses in the short term. He had pledged to limit his withdrawals from the Manor; there were minimal funds coming from the restaurant operations; and recent vacancies had eliminated any positive cash flow from his rental properties.

GEORGE AND CAM

George and Cam had met several times during the spring of 1993. By this time, George was tired and wanted nothing more than to hand over the reins of his business to someone else and step back for awhile. He wanted to remove himself from day-to-day management of all assets and to remain merely as a hands-off investor. In June, George hired Cam as a consultant, asking him to prepare a plan to bring the organization under control, specifically, to "find a way to clean up all the junk on my plate."

Cam had graduated in 1992 with a degree in business administration from Wilfrid Laurier University and had started working as a consultant to medium-sized businesses. His experience consisted of co-op positions[1] with large companies, part-time restaurant management during school, and research and consulting since his final year of school.

During their initial meetings together, George repeatedly said to Cam:

> I've promoted myself to the level of my own incompetence. I know that now, and so from here on, I'm going to be like Henry Ford — I'm going to hire the expertise that I lack myself. That's where you come in — you have the education that I missed out on. I'll give you the benefit of my 25 years' experience in business, and you give me the benefit of your education.

Cam knew from the start that it would be a grave mistake to underestimate the value of George's "school of hard knocks" education, but felt that he, too, had several significant contributions to make. Cam wondered where to start. He wanted to make sure he had a good understanding of the organization and its problems before he made recommendations or attempted any changes. Cam also wondered if he should expect any problems in dealing with George.

NOTE

1. The university offered a business program that combined regular course work with work terms at various companies.

CASE 4.5   THE FOOD TERMINAL

By John Graham and Leo Klus

In July 1991, three months after graduating from the Western Business School, 23-year-old Mike Bellafacia knew that he was in for a rough ride.

> When I arrived at the store, the staff morale was terrible. The previous manager had made a mess of things, the recession was hitting home, sales were spiralling downward quickly, and my store was losing $10,000 per week. To make matters worse, most of the key people in the company felt that I didn't deserve the store manager's position.

As the recently appointed store manager of the newest Foodco location in St. Catharines, Ontario, Mike knew that he had to turn the store around by improving its financial performance and the employee morale. He also knew that something had to be done immediately because the losses at this store were seriously affecting the entire company.

FOODCO LTD.   Foodco Ltd. (FC), with its head office located in St. Catharines, Ontario, was a large player in the Niagara Peninsula grocery retailing industry. FC, a retailer in this market since 1962, was currently made up of seven stores: three St. Catharines locations, one Welland location, one Port Colborne location, and two Lincoln locations. Most of the ownership and key management positions were held by Frank Bellafacia, Tony Bellafacia, and Rocco Bellafacia, as shown in Exhibit 1. Selected financial ratios for FC are shown in Exhibit 2.

FC had created a powerful presence in this industry by developing and refining a strategy that worked. Their product offering was that of any typical supermarket: groceries, meats, bakery and dairy items, packaged foods, and nonfood items. Each store carried eight to ten thousand different items. FC planned to widen the selection available by adding more lines and to follow a general trend in consumer preferences toward an increased percentage of nonfood items in the product mix. Central to FC's strategy was a well-managed marketing effort. Weekly flyers were distributed that highlighted five or six items. FC priced these items below cost to draw customers. The rest of the flyer's products were representative of all the product groups. FC's ability to differentiate itself from the other competitors centred on its corporate vision: low food prices and fast, friendly service. Central to the FC competitive strategy was the mandate to be the low-price leader among conventional supermarkets, during good and bad economic times. Mike Bellafacia stated: "This is a no frills and low price store for a no frills and low price clientele. Most markets are shifting in this direction." FC had developed aggressive expansion plans with six stores being considered for development.

THE RETAIL GROCERY INDUSTRY

The job of managing the store and the staff became crucial to the overall success of FC, given the demanding challenges in the industry. The industry was shifting from a simple mass market to a spectrum of distinct, serviceable segments. A recent statistic stated that 30 percent of consumers switch stores every year. Moreover, a new Food Marketing Institute study found that consumers buy on the basis of the following criteria (ranked in decreasing priority): service, quality products, variety, and low prices. Thus, there was now more opportunity for competitive differentiation based on service and on quality than on price alone.

There were tremendous opportunities for niche players to enter the market, and such entrants had been observed. Health and organic food stores, fruit markets, and independent single-commodity stores (i.e., pet food stores) emerged and were servicing their target segments more effectively than the supermarkets were willing or able to do. Consumer demands varied from region to region, and many small independent retail grocers emerged to meet these demands both in the Niagara Peninsula and across all of Ontario. These independents managed not only to survive, but to take sizable portions of market share from the major chains. This shift toward niche marketing and catering to the local market outlined the need to employ store managers who understood how to please and retain the local customer.

THE ROLE OF THE STORE MANAGER

The success of FC depended upon each of the seven store managers operating his/her store consistently with the corporate strategy. Traditionally, the road to store manager (SM) began within one of the stores at a lower management position. The family culture within each food terminal location was very important to FC management. Thus, store managers were selected from within the company to ensure a leader who understood the FC vision and values. Five managers reported directly to the SM, as shown in Exhibit 3, and their development was an important job for the SM. The SM position became increasingly more important at FC. Many of the current SM functions that used to be handled by the head office were delegated downward to the store level to allow head office to focus on overall company strategy. The stores were now more attuned to the local market they serve. An SM was responsible for the following:

1. Ensuring that merchandising skills were strong among all department managers;
2. Monitoring local market information;
3. Focusing staff on organizational goals (such as sales, gross margin, and profit goals);
4. Organizing weekly staff meetings;
5. Developing all employees and encouraging staff training;
6. Generating and producing sales, gross margin, and profit objectives;
7. Meeting cost objectives (motivating the staff to be cost conscious);
8. Analyzing the performance of each interstore department; and
9. Attending FC "Top Management Meetings" (TMMs).

MIKE BELLAFACIA'S BACKGROUND

Mike Bellafacia graduated from the University of Western Ontario with an Honours Business Administration degree (HBA). During his summers at university, he was assigned special projects from his father that focused on a variety of company problems. Mike would combine the analytical skills developed in the business school with his knowledge of the family business to address these issues. In his last year in the HBA program, Mike and a team of student consultants spent the year focusing on the long-term strategy and competitive advantage of FC. They examined every aspect of the company and developed many strategic recommendations for the top management at FC.

Upon graduation, Mike decided to work for FC. He planned to start off working in some of the various departments (i.e., the produce department) and at different stores within FC to work his way up in order to get the experience he needed to manage a store. This would have allowed him the opportunity to work under some of the most knowledgeable managers in the company. He didn't expect to be store manager so soon.

THE SCOTT AND VINE LOCATION: THE FIRST MONTH

Mike's career at FC was supposed to begin in one of the departments in the company. Both Mike and FC management felt strongly about that. However, while Mike was on vacation in May, FC management made a chancy decision. As of June 1, 1991, Mike Bellafacia would take over the SM position at the Scott and Vine location from the existing SM. The store's performance was deteriorating, and Mike was expected to change things. Mike reflected on the first week at the three-month old location:

> When I first started I was extremely nervous. The district supervisor brought me to the store to have a meeting with the department managers, and I could see the look of disappointment in their eyes. Most of these managers had been forced to move to this new store from other locations. The staff morale was definitely low to begin with. Combined with the fact that I am the boss's son, they probably assumed that I was sent to check on them.

After getting settled in, Mike began to realize that something was terribly wrong at the Scott and Vine food terminal. The store was not producing a bottom line, and many of the 95 employees were not performing well. Mike commented:

This building used to be a Food City that was on the verge of closing down. We acquired it and picked up where they left off. The task I had was to get above average performance from an average staff. They were just not driven to succeed, were poorly trained, and many of them, especially the managers, didn't want to be there.

The previous manager had performed poorly by FC standards. Although he had been an SM at other grocery stores, he was unable to create a productive atmosphere at this one. When this location opened, the sales level was $160,000 per week, but by Mike's first month it had dropped by 17 percent. FC management expected this location to be operating at over $200,000 per week. The other St. Catharines stores were operating at over $350,000 per week. They had a long way to go.

What took place at the Scott and Vine location was a symptom of a more serious problem: the performance of FC as a whole. Mike explained the situation:

Some of what was happening here can be attributed to FC. They became fat cats and, in the process, they lost touch with the customers. Pricing had gone way out of line, cross-border shopping was cutting into our bottom line, and our marketing efforts were poor. The weekly ads that are developed by head office for all the stores were not drawing in customers like they used to. As a result, we had no word-of-mouth advertising, which is so essential to a retail outlet. When our sales across the board went down, we had only ourselves to blame.

SORTING THROUGH THE DISORDER

The job of managing the food terminal was overwhelming, and the problems were endless. Some of the more prevalent problems are listed below:

1. Product rotation (a job monitored by department managers and very important for customer satisfaction) was handled improperly.
2. It was not uncommon to find empty counters and shelves.
3. The staff paid very little attention to cleanliness. (Customers complained about this.)
4. Customers were not treated with respect by those employees who had frequent contact with them.
5. Department managers were doing a poor job of managing and motivating the employees in their departments.
6. Department sales and gross profit results were poor. (See Exhibit 4 for a breakdown of departmental sales and gross profit figures.)

Difficulties arose within the staff that made the SM job even more strenuous. Mike described the situation:

There were a lot of people problems that I had to face. The weekly staff meetings we had together were a joke. Instead of a time to interact and solve problems together, it was just a waste of time. As well, the entire staff was demoralized due to the continual failure to meet monthly performance goals since the store opened. We had the worst performance in the FC organization. The controller of the company told me that the Scott and Vine location was hurting the entire company. I felt as though head office was blaming me for the store's poor performance, and I knew that I had to set some goals that we could all rally behind.

For the first month I was very autocratic. I had to be! I replaced all the cashiers that month, because of the numerous customer complaints about their attitude, but that was just the beginning of my problems. The part-time staff were continually standing around doing nothing. The receiver was not handling the deliveries very well. I found it tough to get along with the department managers. My worst employee problems came from the produce and meat managers. They just were not doing their jobs well. I tried going over the product orders with them, developing schedules, and assisting with their product display plans. I even brought in some of FC's department experts to go over things with them. They would not listen to any of my suggestions. Even though I had some problems with my grocery manager, I began to see that he had real potential for managing. There was some resentment toward me for being a family member and getting the SM position so young, and as a result, people would not open up to me. I also knew that some of the other SMs at other locations didn't want me to succeed, and I found myself conveniently left out of important SM meetings. To make matters worse, after two months here, the general manager of FC made it known that I should be pulled out of this job.

FACING THE FUTURE

It was a tough season to compete in the retail grocery business. Mike Bellafacia found this out after only two months at the food terminal, and the situation was now grave. The Scott and Vine location was losing over $10,000 per week, and the sales level was stagnant. The staff morale had changed very little. Customers were not responding to advertisement efforts, and things looked as if they were going to worsen. Mike reflected on what had happened during these last two months and where things were going. He wondered if he was responsible for the mess the store was in — had he mismanaged his managers, thereby making the situation worse? Had FC made a big mistake putting him in the position of SM. Thinking back on his education, Mike commented:

> The business school helped me understand the decision-making process. I'm not afraid to make decisions, do analysis, and pin-point problem areas. But it didn't teach me how to get the job done, the execution of a decision. More importantly, I was not prepared to deal with people who didn't have the training I did, or the desire to succeed as I did.

Although he was unsure about these issues, he focused on what he should do to get the Scott and Vine food terminal operating profitably, with good management and with a growing customer base. As he looked over the financial data, he wondered if he should lay off some employees to bring the wages expense down. Mike reflected on this: "We didn't have the sales to support the exorbitant number of employees we had at the store." He was concerned about how he would handle these layoffs. He also thought about the serious morale problem. Many of the employees were lazy and demotivated, and customers complained regularly about cleanliness and service. He wondered if there was a way to use the weekly meetings to his advantage. Things seemed just as complicated as they did in June.

EXHIBIT 1
Personnel
Organization
Chart

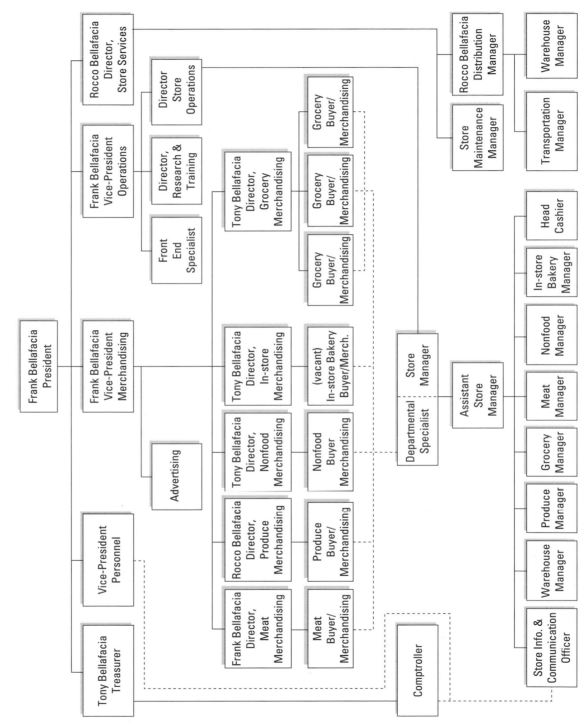

EXHIBIT 2

Selected Financial Ratios					
	1986	**1987**	**1988**	**1989**	**1990**
PROFITABILITY					
Cost of goods sold	81.2%	80.2%	79.7%	78.7	78.3%
Operating expenses	19.4%	18.7%	19.1%	19.6%	19.8%
Net income before tax	–1.1%	0.5%	0.3%	0.7%	0.7%
RETURN					
After tax return on equity	0.0%	715.0%	n/a	725.0%	94.2%
STABILITY					
Interest coverage[1]	1.28X	1.36X	1.05X	1.19X	2.3X
LIQUIDITY					
Net working capital ($000)	–1,447	–2,051	–13	–316	–243
GROWTH					
Sales		26.0%	10.7%	14.1%	15.5%
Assets[1]		16.7%	3.8%	11.2%	9.6%
Equity[1]		–0.35	1.2%	4.9%	19.55

1. Denotes a ratio calculated from the statements of Bellafacia's Consolidated Holdings Inc.

EXHIBIT 3
Scott and Vine
Organizational
Chart

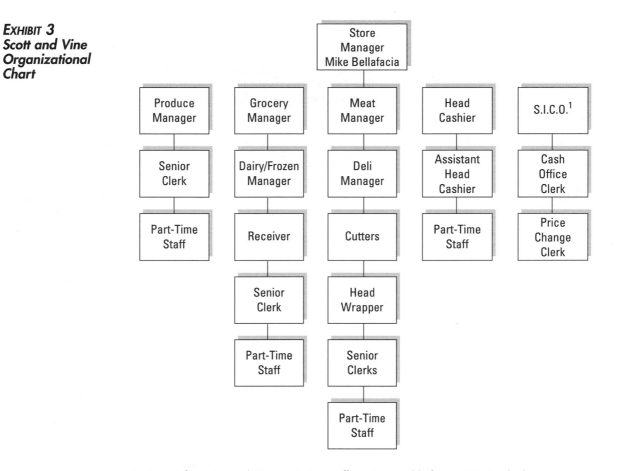

1. Store Information and Communications Officer. Responsible for maintaining the lines communication between the store and head office

Exhibit **4**

	Selected Financial Indicators **Scott and Vine Location** **for the Week Ending June 9, 1991**		
	Department Performance		
DEPARTMENT	**SALES($)**	**GROSS PROFIT($)**	**% OF SALES**
Produce	22,677	4,602	20.3
Grocery	77,363	12,467	16.1
Meat	32,963	7,629	23.1
Nonfood	4,784	1,228	25.7
IS-Bakery	2,337	934	40.0
TOTAL	140,124	28,850	19.2

Overall Store Performance (One Week)		
WEEKLY INDICATORS	**BUDGET ($)**	**ACTUAL ($)**
SALES	155,000	140,124
GROSS PROFIT	33,683	26,860
EXPENSES:		
Wages	16,483	19,600
Supplies	1,895	1,410
Other Expenses	17,091	16,257
TOTAL EXPENSES	35,469	37,267
NET INCOME	(1,786)	(10,407)
# OF CUSTOMERS	7,723/WEEK	

C A S E 4.6   A GLOSSARY OF INDUSTRIAL RELATIONS TERMINOLOGY

By Elizabeth Grasby and Lisa Luinenburg

According to most authors, *industrial relations* is an all-encompassing expression that consists of utterly every form of interaction between employers and employees. This includes relations between unions and management, unions themselves, management and the government, and unions and the government. Ergo, industrial relations is a complex field, one that many researchers have spent years investigating and characterizing. Our current survey of this theme will be limited to an introduction to some of the jargon and a few of the concepts.[1]

INDUSTRIAL RELATIONS TERMINOLOGY
Labour Relations/Union–Management Relations

This term refers to the interaction that takes place between employee organizations (unions) and employers (management/owners). You may have heard the relationship described as "strained" or alternatively as "positive," depending on the particular organization under review and the specific period of time under study.

Union

A labour union or a trade union is an association of workers, usually employed in the same company or industry or practising a similar trade that is recognized under the terms of a labour relations act. In some circumstances, powerful national or international unions such as the Canadian Auto Workers Union will attempt to organize dissatisfied employees in smaller, nonrelated industries. Generally, the more powerful unions are more persuasive with managers and employers. They can bring their collectively greater membership and greater expertise to bear in any negotiations between labour and management. When a company's employees threaten to join one of the larger unions, management will normally make sincere efforts to avert the unionization.

Despite the negative image that management sometimes paints of unions, the primary purpose of a union is to improve the conditions of the workplace for its members by addressing issues such as wage rates, job security, and working environment. As well, the union provides support and guidance for employees who may feel that they have been treated unfairly by management or the hierarchy.

Workers join unions because:

- The collective power of employees is exerted;
- It increases an employee's sense of economic security;
- An official certification of the union as bargaining representative has already occurred (no choice); and
- People enjoy membership in groups.

Types of Unions

- *Craft*: Members carry on the same craft or trade (e.g., International Association of Firefighters).
- *Industrial*: Members usually include most of the workers eligible for union membership in a particular organization or industry (e.g., International Chemical Workers' Union).

Local Unions

Unions are also differentiated according to their jurisdiction (international, national, or local).

The local union is the lowest level of a union. Most activities are centred at the local level; that is, workers join the local union and pay dues to the local union, and they interact with members of the local union more often than they would with the larger body. All members are allowed to vote on union matters. The membership elects representatives who handle the administration of the union.

The functions of local unions include the following:

- Local union members elect delegates to represent all of the unionized workers in collective bargaining talks with management.
- The local union administers the collective agreement that is reached with management, ensuring that the company abides by the provisions in the agreement.

Parent Unions

The parent union is the final authority over the actions of the local union. The parent union can be regional, national (e.g., the Canadian Union of Public Employees or the Canadian Auto Workers), or international (e.g., the Steelworkers or the Longshoremen).

The functions of parent unions include the following:

- The executive sets major union policies.
- Parent unions aid locals in legal strikes[2] by sending strikers to the picket lines,[3] strike fund control, research, and collective bargaining.
- They lobby government to promote the interests of labour.[4]

Collective Bargaining

Collective bargaining is the process by which employees negotiate the terms of their employment with their employer. Before negotiations for an agreement can commence, the company and the union establish their respective bargaining committees. The company negotiating committee usually includes the industrial relations manager, a plant/operations manager or representative, and other specialists needed for negotiations, such as wage negotiation specialists.

The union negotiating committee usually consists of a select group of union representatives such as the president of the local, the vice-president, and the chief steward. Once a written agreement has been accepted, each party must honour it. Deadline procedures are put in the document to prevent either party from stalling to fulfill its commitments to the collective agreement.

Collective Agreement

A collective agreement is an contract in writing between an employer and the union representing the employees. The agreement usually contains provisions respecting conditions of employment, rates of pay, hours of work, rest periods, safety and health standards, and the rights or duties of the parties to the agreement. Ordinarily, the agreement is for a definite period, such as one to three years.

Shop Steward/Union Committee Person

A steward is the union person, usually elected, who represents workers in a particular shop or department. He/she collects dues, solicits new members, announces meetings, and receives, investigates, and attempts the adjustment of grievances.

Grievance

An employee/employer can file a grievance for a disagreement respecting the interpretation, application, administration, or alleged violation of the collective agreement. In every collective agreement, the grievance procedure outlines clearly the steps that must be followed to settle an alleged violation of the agreement. The initial steps usually involve the employee's supervisor and possibly the shop steward.

Arbitration

Arbitration is the procedure by which an arbitrator (board/single person), acting under the authority of both parties to a dispute, hears both sides of the controversy and issues a written decision, which may also include a compensatory award. The decision is, ordinarily, binding on both parties. Arbitrators are usually appointed by the parties concerned, but under special circumstances they are appointed by the minister of labour (the elected official who heads the federal labour ministry).

There are two main types of arbitration: interest disputes and rights disputes. Interest disputes arise between an employer and a union when a fundamental disagreement occurs during the negotiation of a new collective agreement. A rights dispute is one that occurs between an employee and a union. A rights dispute involves the interpretation, application, or administration of the collective agreement that governs the employer–employee relationship.

Compulsory arbitration can occur as a last step in the grievance procedure set out in a collective agreement. Only a small percentage of grievances result in this last step.

Notes

1. Definitions from "Glossary of Industrial Relations Terms," Ministry of Labour, Ottawa, 1992.
2. A strike is the act of stopping work in order to put pressure on an employer. A strike-breaker is a person who is engaged to do a striker's work or a company that supplies workers to an employee during a strike.
3. A picket line is a group of workers posted to dissuade other workers or clients from entering their place of work during a strike.
4. A lobby is a group of people that pressures legislators to pursue policies favourable to its interests. Lobby is also a verb meaning to influence in favour of a certain policy by constantly seeking interviews, writing letters, and exerting pressure. A lobbyist is one person engaged in lobbying.

CASE 4.7   HIBBS'S WEB

By Elizabeth Grasby and Sonya M. Head

Frederick Fontaine, West Coast division manager for the Uvex Corporation, knew he needed to take action before nine o'clock the next morning. Otherwise, it was highly probable that Alex Fuhrman would commence a lawsuit against one of his division's employees, Christopher Hibbs, and against the Uvex Corporation itself. A lawsuit risked press coverage and conjecture that could diminish the success of Uvex's next public stock offering, due to be underwritten early in the new year.

THE COMPANY

The Uvex Corporation started as a small family-owned medical centre on the southwest coast. The original owners were a father and son team of physicians who seized an opportunity to develop a private medical health-care facility. Over the years, the two men recruited only the best physicians in their fields to expand the enterprise across the nation. Last year, this strategy paid off in revenues of $750 million. Uvex specialized in pioneering treatments for cancers and ancillary surgical procedures for cosmetic recovery. The company's research labs were at the leading edge of cancer research in North America.

ALEX FUHRMAN

Immediately after graduating from an MBA program, Alex Fuhrman had joined the Uvex Corporation as its director of accounting and finance. At that time, nine years ago, the corporation was still a small family-owned business with centres primarily on the west coast. The business flourished, increasing revenues almost exponentially after Alex became involved in restructuring for expansion.

ORGANIZA-TIONAL STRUCTURE

Nine years ago, Uvex was organized along geographical lines. Each of its medical centres engaged in all types of treatments and undertook to collect and receive all payments from patients. Payroll and accounting were handled by Alex's staff at head office in San Francisco. The original organizational structure is depicted in Exhibit 1.

Five years after Alex joined Uvex, the company went public[1] in order to fund a monumental expansion into cancer research and treatment. At that time, Uvex rationalized all of its cancer procedures to the San Francisco location. The com-

IVEY Sonya M. Head prepared this case under the supervision of Elizabeth Grasby solely to provide material for class discussion. The authors do not intend to illustrate either effective or ineffective handling of a managerial situation. The authors may have disguised certain names and other identifying information to protect confidentiality. Ivey Management Services prohibits any form of reproduction, storage or transmittal without its written permission. This material is not covered under authorization from CanCopy or any reproduction rights organization. Copyright © 1994, Ivey Management Services.

pany built a state-of-the-art facility for cancer treatment and research in the foothills of San Rafael, 25 km from the existing facility. The old San Francisco site was renovated into executive suites for vice-presidents and their staff.

The new San Rafael facility was highly capitalized with sophisticated radiation therapy units. The close proximity of research talent to treatment devices effected rapid and creative exchange of innovative techniques. Cancer patients from all other Uvex centres were transported to San Rafael for treatment. The company's reputation flourished.

In order to better service its patients from the central part of the country, Uvex looked forward to installing state-of-the-art radiation therapy units in Salt Lake City. The Salt Lake centre currently administered chemotherapies only. In order to fund this new equipment, Uvex would issue another public stock offering early next year.

Uvex's newest organizational design is shown in Exhibit 2. Vice-presidents for marketing, human resources, and financial planning were now located at the company's head office in San Francisco. There were regional managers in charge of specific geographies, and all cancer facilities and treatment planning were managed through the San Rafael facility.

THE SAN RAFAEL GROUP

The final aspect to be formulated at San Rafael was the research facility. Uvex was considered to be the vanguard of cancer research because its staff was the best and the brightest in the country. The research group consisted of a core of leading scientists with doctoral degrees in biochemistry. These supervisory investigators were assisted by lab technicians, nutritionists, and mental health professionals with varied backgrounds. Most of the treatment centre's medical doctors were involved in part-time clinical studies in conjunction with the full-time scientists. Pay scales at San Rafael were commensurate with experience and were the highest in the industry.

The San Rafael centre enjoyed abundant donations from grateful patients and their families. As well, many private and public groups and businesses contributed significant funds to specific researchers or research endeavours.

Despite their accomplishments, the staff in the cancer centre were prone to mental fatigue and stress. Managing this group's creativity and intensity required extensive people skills, empathy, and attention to team spirit. Alex Fuhrman was the ideal choice to head the administration of the cancer research and treatment division. Alex was a competent, sensitive "people" manager and a talented financial administrator, who chose to maintain an office in the San Rafael centre in order to be close to the staff.

As was the case with the reorganization of Uvex's other divisions, an accounting manager was hired for the West Coast division. The accounting manager was to compile monthly expense statements for each department, and to handle simple receivables, payables, and payroll functions with a staff of two or three clerks. Alex was involved in the initial screening process of the candidates. The final decision to hire Christopher Hibbs was made by Frederick Fontaine.

Hibbs had previously worked as a bookkeeper for the city of Sacramento. His former boss offered high praise of Hibbs in his letter of recommendation.

Alex's last act within the accounting division was to set up systems for reporting expenses to the various department heads within the San Rafael centre. After that, department heads would set their own budgets for operating funds and capital expenditures. To aid their estimates, each department head now received monthly statements from the accounting manager.

In order to foster a smooth transition to responsibility centres in the cancer facility, Alex conducted seminars for the department heads who were, primarily, long-term employees and usually the only doctoral degrees in their departments. As a general rule, the scientists viewed budgeting as secondary to research. Consequently, the first seminar was lightly attended, even though Alex ordered pizza for the lunch-hour meeting. After Alex's first seminar, there was widespread shock in the research centre. The next seminar was highly enlisted and the budgeting process was hotly debated. Department heads did not want to take responsibility for budgeting and controlling expenses. Alex persisted and, after about a month's lapse in time, the department heads appeared to mellow.

THE MEMO

Frederick Fontaine harboured some early reservations about Hibbs because the new accounting manager seemed to want to make numerous changes to the accounting system that Alex installed. Frederick was not convinced that Hibbs was adequately qualified to alter the process; however, as time passed and the department heads appeared placated, Frederick forgot his worries. Besides, finance and accounting were not particular strengths of Frederick's, and he preferred to avoid dealing with them. Hibbs sent his financial reports directly to the executive controller of Uvex.

One Friday night when he was working late, Frederick requested security to give him entry into the accounting manager's office so that he could retrieve a requisition for a specialized piece of equipment. While he was in Hibbs's office, Frederick noticed a memo that sat in the middle of Hibbs's desk. The memo was addressed to the controller and dated the week previous. It read in part:

> ... In the general and research accounts, I have found several thousands of dollars discrepancy. It may be that there are funds missing. I thought you should know that Alex Fuhrman was the only person who had access to the accounts prior to my arrival at the centre.

The next morning, Frederick called the controller's office and asked about the memo. The controller admitted to receiving the memo from Hibbs and expressed some mystification about it. He explained that after nine months with the company, Hibbs's first fiscal year-end report was due within the next two weeks. The controller expressed a belief that Hibbs had encountered problems trying to reconcile accounts when he began to compile results for the centre's fiscal year-end. So far, the controller had not taken time to challenge Hibbs about the memo.

Frederick then drove to the research centre and stopped by Alex's office, without announcing his arrival. He brought with him a photocopy of the memo. After reading the note, Alex was outraged and insisted on an immediate meeting with Hibbs, the controller, and Frederick.

THE MEETING

A meeting was hastily organized for that afternoon. During the confrontation, it became apparent that the centre's department heads had become alarmed when they received their first monthly statements from Hibbs. Subsequently, they plied considerable pressure on Hibbs to do something to relieve their fears about budget cuts. Hibbs had succumbed to the pressure and decided to alter the centre's methods for depreciation in order to understate the expenses. As well, Hibbs decided to defer some expenses to future periods and to recognize revenues when treatment services were rendered rather than when the cash was received from the patients. These modifications amounted to acceptable accounting practices when they were disclosed; however, the net result was that the centre reported a much higher profitability than in previous years. Hibbs had become confused when he was unable to reconcile the statements at year-end with the systems that Alex had instituted.

The controller asked: So, you put together fraudulent statements and then sent them to me?

Hibbs responded haughtily: With a broad stretch of the imagination, you could call the statements fraudulent, but I don't like that term.

Alex spoke to Hibbs heatedly: And then you wrote a letter to the controller at the executive suites, and you implicated me in what you termed "missing funds."

Hibbs was remorseless: Well, you didn't do such a hot job, Alex.

He paused to pick up a departmental budget and waved it under Alex's nose: The department heads were devastated by the budgeting process. They didn't understand it all.

Alex shot back: Did you try to explain it to them?

Hibbs looked smug: That was your job, Alex, and you did not do it well.

Alex insisted that Hibbs submit a written retraction to the staff at the executive offices, an explanation to the department heads, and an apology.

Hibbs flatly refused and launched into a tirade of righteous indignation.

Frederick suddenly stood up and left the room. He was exasperated by the situation. The controller mopped his brow and stared silently at the ceiling while Hibbs mercilessly elaborated his resentment at being asked to apologize.

Before Hibbs could finish his speech, Alex left the room abruptly and without further comment.

At six o'clock that night, Frederick received a telephone call from Alex's lawyer:

> Mr. Fontaine, my client and I believe that Christopher Hibbs's memo is slanderous toward Alex Fuhrman. Unless you dismiss him and put into writing a retraction of the allegations that he has made, we will file a libel suit against him and the Uvex Corporation. We will be in court when it opens tomorrow morning at 10 o'clock.

NOTE

1. To "go public" means to sell shares of the company to outside investors on the public stock exchange.

***Exhibit* 1
*Former
Organizational
Structure***

***Exhibit* 2
*New
Organizational
Structure***

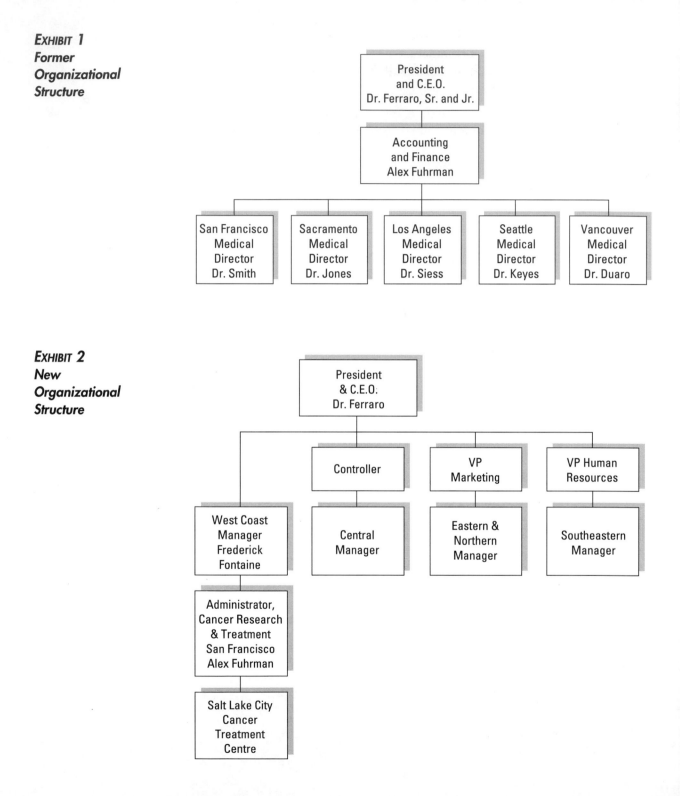

CASE 4.8 A JOHNSON & JOHNSON COMPANY

By John Graham and L. Davidson

On Wednesday January 4, 1989, Mark Simpson, manager of human resources for a Johnson & Johnson Company (J & J), was deeply concerned. He had just spoken with Doug Bishop, the supervisor of the maintenance department, and learned that an employee had physically assaulted another employee eight days earlier during the Christmas shutdown. Doug had just learned of the incident from the victim. This J & J Company had never before had an incident of violence in the workplace. Mark now faced one of the toughest problems he had encountered in his first six months with J & J. He knew it was imperative that he act quickly.

Johnson & Johnson Worldwide was the world's largest health care company. It had three divisions: Consumer, Pharmaceutical, and Professional. By 1988, Johnson & Johnson Worldwide was operating in 47 countries, had approximately 81,000 employees, sales of $9 billion, and net earnings of $974 million. This J & J company was one of the 13 members of the Johnson & Johnson family of companies in Canada.

THE COMPANY

J & J's facilities included offices and a plant, in total employing about 400 nonunionized, salaried employees in 1989. J & J produced and sold various consumer products.

J & J's management believed that the company's success was due to the attention it paid to four key groups: (1) the trade and, ultimately, the end consumer, (2) its employees, (3) the community, and (4) its shareholders. The company's credo articulated J & J's responsibilities to these groups (see Exhibit 1).

Management believed that employee productivity was dependent on both physical and mental health. Therefore, management believed its role was to commit to the well-being of its employees. Studies have indicated that employee health is a major productivity issue for companies. The annual costs to businesses for absenteeism, lateness, substandard work performance, negligence, and other actions resulting from poor employee health, either emotional or physical, are staggering (see Exhibit 2).

J & J took its responsibility to its employees seriously. It initiated a comprehensive "LIVE FOR LIFE" wellness program which included an on-site exercise facility with fitness classes, an extensive health and safety program, and an Employee Assistance Program (EAP). The EAP offered confidential counselling for all employees. It had various programs for problems, including physical or emotional illness; financial, marital, or family distress; alcohol or drug abuse; and legal or other concerns. Employees were also encouraged to use the EAP if they were concerned about a fellow employee and wanted advice. Exhibit 3 outlines the EAP. In addition, there was a health services supervisor on staff.

J & J tried to hire individuals who would fit into its corporate culture. In the words of Mr. Perry, the vice-president of human resources, "We try to hire people who care about people, because it is difficult to teach someone to care." Mr. Perry was well liked and respected by J & J's employees, because it was obvious that he cared. The staff in the human resources department enjoyed working for Mr. Perry. Mark described Mr. Perry in the following manner: he is progressive, he is a strong believer in empowering people (delegation), he has a strong commitment to the company's credo, and he is an outstanding leader in his functional area and in the community at large. One of management's practices was to give perks, such as tickets for sporting, arts, and cultural events, to provide spontaneous recognition to employees for outstanding performance.

J & J had progressive hiring policies. The company met its responsibility to the community by hiring people with special needs, such as the mentally challenged. In order to follow this policy, J & J used Adult Rehabilitation Centre (ARC) Industries. ARC was a nonprofit organization that trained approximately 200 handicapped adults. The centre had two objectives: to provide training and extended-term work programs for those who were not currently able to compete for community employment and to provide training and vocational guidance for those who were preparing for competitive employment in the community. ARC sponsored three programs: Community Contract Placement, Work Experience Placement, and Employment Placement.

ARC's six-week "Work Experience Placement Program" allowed an individual and a prospective company to determine whether further employment would be mutually beneficial. The work experience placement provided a worker with the opportunity to test his or her capabilities.

In April 1985, J & J participated in the Work Experience Program. ARC supplied a candidate, Cheryl McNeil, to work in the labs. ARC also provided a community placement services supervisor to J & J to initially help get the work term in action. As a result of a successful six weeks, Cheryl was hired as a permanent part-time worker (27.5 hours/week) in July 1985. The placement services supervisor remained involved for a three-month follow-up period. In addition, after Cheryl was hired, ARC Industries supplied personnel to augment the previous training provided to the lab employees. The training was used to address the employees' questions about Cheryl's abilities, needs, and behaviour patterns.

Furthermore, the trainer focused on the employees' fears and discomfort associated with working with a mentally challenged individual. This process was necessary because the company wanted to ensure that the integration of Cheryl would not interfere with the existing operations. Initially, some problems were encountered, but, through coaching and counselling, Cheryl became a productive employee.

In late 1985 another opportunity to use ARC surfaced. The human resources group approached the cafeteria company, which was contracted to provide J & J's cafeteria food services, and suggested it sponsor a candidate for the Work Experience Program. J & J's arrangement with the cafeteria company required this company to manage the food staff; however, J & J ultimately paid the wages of the staff. The cafeteria company decided to participate and, once again, ARC Industries was asked to supply a candidate.

The candidate ARC sent to the cafeteria company was Tom Phillips. The six-week trial period was successful and, in December 1985, the cafeteria company offered Tom a full-time position as a dishwasher in the cafeteria. Tom's job resulted in daily contact with most employees and, consequently, he became well known within the organization. Employee attitudes toward Tom were positive; people wanted him to succeed.

After working for the cafeteria company for one year, Tom applied to a job posting for a maintenance position on the second shift at J & J. His application was accepted because Tom was considered capable of performing the same work as the existing employees. He was hired in December 1986. It was decided that the maintenance staff did not require the training provided by ARC to facilitate Tom's integration because they all knew him.

MAINTENANCE DEPARTMENT

The maintenance staff consisted of the supervisor, Doug Bishop; the second shift lead technician, Frank Cromwell; Dave Thompson; Tim Hudson; Bob Clark; and now Tom Phillips. Doug and Dave worked the first shift from 7:30 a.m. to 3:30 p.m. When conflicts arose in the department, Doug's approach to problem solving was to tell employees "work this out or you will all be in trouble." Doug reported to Jason Sommers, manager engineering.

The other four men worked the second shift from 4:30 p.m. to 12:30 a.m. During the second shift, Frank, the lead technician on that shift, had been responsible for supervision and job assignment. On a daily basis he monitored and redirected activities in line with priorities and manpower availability. See Exhibit 4 for a work history of Doug and the second shift workers.

As the men on the second shift had gotten to know each other better, they had started to pull pranks on each other. Unknown to Doug, they jumped out of lockers, threw water at each other, and put salt in each other's pop. Tom, being a newcomer, had not taken part in the pranks when he first started working with the group.

TOM PHILLIPS   Shortly after being hired full time by J & J, Tom decided that he did not need to maintain contact with ARC; subsequently, he severed his ties with ARC. His work performance was satisfactory, although, unknown to management, he also participated in the horseplay. Tom was not always able to distinguish the serious from the silly. His mood swings would lead him to withdraw, and he would go for several days without talking to a particular individual, in response to a comment or a prank. His fellow workers would try to coax him out of his "moods," but, if they were unsuccessful, they would then choose to ignore him.

His co-workers were always supportive and concerned about his welfare: they provided him with a ride to work; they would speak to management if they were concerned about his well-being; they monitored his eating habits and sometimes supplied him with lunch if he was short of money.

THE INCIDENT   On Wednesday, December 28, 1988, during the Christmas plant shutdown, Tom had thought that Bob was playing a joke on him by asking Frank to assign Tom to a different job than the one Tom wanted to do. Tom had wanted to vacuum the carpet in the eating area; this task had not been assigned by Frank and was not a priority, given the holiday. Tom apparently wanted to perform this task because he wanted to be near the people who were watering plants in the cafeteria. He had been chatting with them earlier and they had been very friendly.

When Frank insisted that Tom do the job he had been assigned, Tom lost his temper and assaulted Bob, punching him in the chest and mouth. Tom's actions thoroughly surprised his co-workers because he had never done anything violent before, nor had he ever threatened to do anything. As he was considerably stronger than Bob, Frank and Tim had to intervene to pull Tom off Bob. Bob, who was upset and angered, demanded to know what had provoked Tom. The misunderstanding was quickly resolved; Tom apologized, and the four men decided not to report the incident because Bob said he was not hurt.

Eight days later, on January 5, 1989, when all employees had returned to work following the Christmas holidays, Bob visited the company's health services because he was concerned about the bruise that had developed on his chest. Upon discovering the source of the bruise, the nurse convinced Bob to report the incident to his supervisor. The following day Bob informed Doug; Doug then spoke to his boss, Jason Sommers. Subsequently, Mark Simpson was called because of the seriousness of the incident.

Mark wanted to recommend a solid course of action to Mr. Perry. As he had only worked at J & J for six months, he wanted to demonstrate his human resources skills through the careful management of this problem. His previous work experience included employee relations responsibilities for a large multi-plant automotive operation.

Mark knew that he faced a very complex problem. This was a difficult situation to handle, especially because there had never been anything like it before at J & J. He wondered what criteria he should consider before making recommendations to Mr. Perry. He thought of a few potential alternatives: (1) follow the performance improvement procedures (see Exhibit 5); (2) use the company's EAP services; (3) get ARC Industries involved; (4) suspend Tom with or without pay for an appropriate period of time (Mark considered a four-week suspension without pay to be the minimum industry practice for this type of incident); or (5) fire him in accordance with the company's position on violent behaviour (see Exhibit 6). As Mark sat down to formulate an action plan he wondered if there were any other alternatives he should consider.

EXHIBIT 1

Our Credo

We believe our first responsibility is to the doctors, nurses and patients,
to mothers and fathers and all others who use our products and services.
In meeting their needs everything we do must be of high quality.
We must constantly strive to reduce our costs
in order to maintain reasonable prices.
Customers' orders must be serviced promptly and accurately.
Our suppliers and distributors must have an opportunity
to make a fair profit.

We are responsible to our employees,
the men and women who work with us throughout the world.
Everyone must be considered as an individual.
We must respect their dignity and recognize their merit.
They must have a sense of security in their jobs.
Compensation must be fair and adequate,
and working conditions clean, orderly and safe.
We must be mindful of ways to help our employees fulfill
their family responsibilities.
Employees must feel free to make suggestions and complaints.
There must be equal opportunity for employment, development
and advancement for those qualified.
We must provide competent management,
and their actions must be just and ethical.

We are responsible to the communities in which we live and work
and to the world community as well.
We must be good citizens—support good works and charities
and bear our fair share of taxes.
We must maintain in good order
the property we are privileged to use,
protecting the environment and natural resources.

Our final responsibility is to our stockholders.
Business must make a sound profit.
We must experiment with new ideas.
Research must be carried on, innovative programs developed
and mistakes paid for.
New equipment must be purchased, new facilities provided
and new products launched.
Reserves must be created to provide for adverse times.
When we operate according to these principles,
the stockholders should realize a fair return.

Johnson & Johnson

EXHIBIT 2 *Our Personal* *Problems Do* *Affect Our Work* *Lives*	**The Canadian Mental Health Association reports:***

- 1/3 of the population will struggle with a serious emotional problem
- 2/5 will be hospitalized to treat illness resulting from emotional problems
- 50% of marriages will end in divorce
- 60% of women and 10% of men will be victims of sexual assault by the time they reach the age of 19
- 22% of adults suffer from alcohol or drug problems
- Personal problems don't play favourites
- Recognition of the overlap between our personal and work lives
- 33% of employees in one London organization reported personal family problems that had adversely affected their work performance in the previous year
- 65–80% of employee terminations are due to personal or interpersonal factors rather than technical factors

*Statistics as of October 1989.

EXHIBIT 3
Employee
Assistance
Program

Johnson & Johnson recognizes that a wide range of personal problems can have an adverse effect on job performance. In most instances, the employee will overcome such personal problems independently. In other instances, good management techniques will serve either as guidance or motivation to resolve the problems so that the employee's job performance can return to an acceptable level. In some cases, however, the efforts of the employee and the supervisor fail to have the desired effect, and unsatisfactory performance persists over a period of time.

We believe it is in the interest of both our employees and the Company to provide an Employee Assistance Program (EAP) to help with these lingering problems.

The Employee Assistance Program is designed to retain employees with personal problems by assisting them in arresting the further advance of those problems. If left unattended, they might otherwise render the employee unemployable.

EAP POLICY GUIDELINES

1. Johnson & Johnson recognizes many human problems can be successfully treated, provided they are identified in the early stages and appropriate referral is made. This applies whether the problem is physical or emotional illness, financial, marital or family distress, alcohol or drug abuse, legal or other general concerns.
2. Johnson & Johnson recognizes alcoholism as an illness which can be treated.
3. Employees with personal problems will be given the same opportunity for treatment as employees with any physical illness. It must be recognized, however, that successful resolution of such problems requires a high degree of personal motivation on the part of the employee.

EXHIBIT 3
(cont.)

4. This program is preventative and is intended to correct job performance diffi-culties at the earliest possible time. It is in no way meant to interfere with the private life of the employee. The concern of the Company with alcoholism and personal problems is strictly limited to their effects on the employee's job per-formance.

5. Where indicated, sick leave will be granted for treatment or rehabilitation on the same basis as is granted for other health problems.

6. Since family problems can impair job performance, referrals can also be made for a family member. An eligible family member is a spouse or a depen-dent child. An employee's parents, brothers and sisters are also included if they are members of the employee's household.

Confidentiality

Employees are assured that their job security and future promotional opportunities will not be jeopardized by utilizing the Employee Assistance Program. All records with respect to personal problems are completely confidential.

Types of Referral

1. Self Referral
   Employees or family members who feel they have a problem are encouraged to seek help on a voluntary basis through the EAP Administrator. A decision on the part of an employee to seek help voluntarily will not be reported to management or entered into personal records.

2. Management Referral
   This is to be based on documented, persistent deteriorating job performance as noted by the immediate supervisor. The employee will be referred by the supervisor to the EAP Administrator, who will make an evaluation and, where appropriate, either provide treatment or suggest referral for treatment or assis-tance.

Employee Responsibility

1. The employee is expected to maintain job performance and attendance at an acceptable level.

2. Where there is a problem detrimentally affecting work performance and appropriate treatment is obtained, the employee is to continue with the treat-ment program to completion.

3. If the employee refuses the help that is offered and his job performance and attendance do not improve, or continue to deteriorate, the employee is subject to normal disciplinary procedures.

4. Where the employee cooperates with assistance and/or treatment, but, after a reasonable period of time, is still unable to bring work performance up to an acceptable level, normal disciplinary procedures will also apply.

Exhibit 3 (cont.)

Employer Responsibility

1. To maintain, wherever possible, full job benefit protection for the employee undergoing treatment.
2. To make every possible effort to provide time, where necessary, for the employee to receive treatment by appointment.
3. To provide the time for periodic EAP educational seminars for all employees.
4. To ensure full confidentiality of all EAP records.

Exhibit 4
Work History

Doug Bishop—Supervision	
June 1985	lead technician
March 1988	supervisior, maintenance

Frank Cromwell—Lead Technician	
December 1986	technician
May 1987	lead technician, second shift

Bob Clark—Technician	
July 1987	technician

Tom Philips—Technician	
December 1986	technician

Tim Hudson—Technician	
October 1988	temporary technician (1-year control)
December 1988	permanent technician

EXHIBIT 5

EMPLOYEE HANDBOOK

Performance Improvement Procedures
Performance improvement includes the following three stages:

1. Verbal Discussion
At least one verbal discussion with the employee outlining the aspects of performance which are below standard. Your Supervisor may choose to record this discussion, depending on the severity of the incident.

Employees are encouraged to discuss differences, including contributing circumstances, with their supervisor.

2. Performance Improvement Plan
The second stage is to provide the employee a written Performance Improvement Plan. This plan must outline specific improvements which you will be expected to attain within a specified period of time, and an outline of the probable consequences if improvement is not demonstrated.

3. Suspension/Dismissal
If an employee has not achieved the improvements outlined by the Performance Improvement Plan, suspension or termination may result.

EXHIBIT 6

EMPLOYEE HANDBOOK

Actions Subject to Termination
The following actions may result in the immediate termination of an employee:

- Possession of a dangerous weapon on Company property.
- Refusal to follow job responsibilities or duties other than when safety is a factor.
- Falsification of records.
- Illegal purchase, manufacture, transfer, use, sales, consumption or possession of non-prescribed chemical substances on Company property or while on Company business.
- Violent or threatening behavior.
- Harassment of any kind.
- Behavior that threatens another individual's character or reputation.
- Unauthorized disclosure of Company or confidential information.
- Misappropriation of Company funds.
- Theft, unauthorized use of or negligence of Company property or products.
- Conviction for careless or impaired driving if assigned a fleet vehicle.

C A S E 4.9   MEDICTEST LABORATORIES

By Elizabeth Grasby and Michelle Linton

In April 1994, Jean Kelly, manager of the Southwestern Ontario region of Medictest Laboratories, faced a tough situation in Sarnia, Ontario. The Ontario government had imposed funding cutbacks to the Ontario Health Insurance Plan (OHIP),[1] for all testing centres in the province, creating a severe need for cost cutting. Over the past two years, Medictest Laboratories had reduced costs by improving work-flow efficiency. However, further cost reduction was necessary and required a review of the supervisory structure. Jean had designed a new organizational structure that streamlined management and furthered the company's objectives for augmenting employee decision-making power, but this structure would require the dismissal of five long-term supervisors. Jean wondered how to implement these changes without a negative impact on morale, productivity, and motivation.

THE INDUSTRY

The technology-based health care industry was rapidly changing. In particular, the testing laboratories industry was experiencing significant streamlining due to funding cutbacks and the impacts of new technology and automation.

Labs received testing orders from doctors, hospitals, and medical centres. Upon filling each order, the labs would bill OHIP, which paid a specified amount for each type of test. Labs were responsible for controlling their costs in order to achieve a profit. As the Ontario Government attempted to decrease its expenses, funding for health care came under severe pressure. The compensation provided by OHIP[1] for testing was significantly reduced. The laboratories were faced with a 17 percent decrease in funding for completion of the same work; this placed tremendous pressure on the profit margins. Many testing laboratories attempted to adapt by restructuring, downsizing, and streamlining. Further funding reduction was expected over the next two years. The Ontario Ministry of Health offered a restructuring credit, based on market share, for those testing centres that reduced their costs beyond industry standards and invested significantly in new technology.

Each medical laboratory was required by law to have a medical doctor on the Board of Directors to be accountable for medical care. Although usually not directly involved in the operation of the lab, this person approved all major decisions before they were implemented and facilitated the relationship between the for-profit labs and the public hospitals.

MEDICTEST LABORATORIES

Medictest Laboratories' head office was based in London, Ontario, and operated a chain of private medical laboratories in Canada. It was composed of labs and specimen collection centres throughout Canada. These centres determined the most appropriate tests to be performed and then executed the tests.

As stated in the 1993 annual report, the company's commitment was "to seize the opportunity to serve the needs of the health care marketplace, to persevere in innovation, to achieve the defined objectives and to realize the shared vision of leadership in health care." Medictest's future objective was to become more automated through the integration of state-of-the-art technology. In general, Medictest had a reputation for its ability to make excellent decisions. It was also known as a nonunionized, people-oriented company that truly cared for its employees and believed in its values (see Exhibit 1). Upon hiring dedicated and hard-working employees, Medictest was considerate and thoughtful toward them, recognizing them as a valuable resource. The company placed high priority on enabling employees to develop to their full potential and to advance within the organization. The employees were very close and tight-knit among the Ontario labs, often remaining with the company for long employment periods.

Medictest had begun to establish goals to augment empowerment, teamwork, and shared responsibility. These concepts were gradually being implemented by restructuring leadership teams and by choosing leaders who fit with these objectives. Former pyramid-style systems of authority were being replaced with new structures for decision making. A self-directed team approach was designed to empower employees to make decisions. The intent of the restructuring program was to realign resources in order to operate more effectively and efficiently.

Because of funding changes and the company's goals for empowerment, head office began to review the leadership and support staff structure across Ontario. Recent changes had been made to the upper management structure, including consolidating four regional management positions into one. Medictest Sarnia was a target of consideration for restructuring because of the large size of its management team. Discussion about these changes had begun two years ago.

MEDICTEST SARNIA

The Sarnia location was a large laboratory, processing thousands of specimens daily, operating on a 24-hour basis. This testing facility served physicians, patient centres, hospitals, and other Medictest locations, handling one-third of Medictest's testing in Ontario. Most of this testing was for southwestern Ontario, although some tests were also completed for clients in other regions. Because of the high volume of work done at this location, the Sarnia lab had a great impact on the perceived quality of service provided by Medictest in general; therefore, there was significant pressure on the management at Medictest Sarnia.

Medictest Sarnia currently operated with 12 supervisors and 234 employees, many of whom had been with the subsidiary since its origin 20 years ago (see Exhibit 2). Most of the testing was completed at one main location, but there were also several smaller nearby sites that were part of the same operation.

Within the past two years, measures had been taken to improve work-flow efficiency. Six months ago, it had become evident that, although costs needed further reduction, no additional improvements were possible within the current structure.

Jean Kelly had worked for Medictest for two years. In her former position as operations manager, she had been responsible for all operations done by this laboratory. Recently, her position had expanded to manager of southwestern Ontario, which also gave her the responsibility of market share and revenue generation within this region. Upon graduating from Leeds University in England with a post-graduate degree in medical microbiology, Jean had worked for six years as a laboratory manager at Toronto East General Hospital. Over the past few years, she had taken business courses through continuing education. Jean was asked by head office to review the current supervisory structure and develop a revised one that would cut down on costs and facilitate the goals of empowerment. Jean found the ensuing changes exciting and challenging. She had been given a few months to report the structural changes to the regional manager.

Jean's objectives for redesigning the current structure were to reduce costs, to ensure profitability, and to build a new organizational team that would support empowerment through responsibility and leadership. Although there was some teamwork already in place, the supervisory structure was so large that there was no need to be interdependent or even to meet regularly. Jean thought that a leaner management team, with different responsibilities than the existing team, would be better equipped to carry out these new interdependent roles. The revised structure had to "make sense" by providing a logical connection among the departments. Jean also hoped to better integrate the testing facilities with client services and improve relationships with other Medictest locations. In developing a different supervisory team, Jean had to choose leaders who possessed the core technical competency and, more importantly, displayed the appropriate leadership skills to fit the new objectives.

Effects on Management

Before Jean made any changes, she gave the supervisors the option to take part in designing a new structure, either directly or indirectly. They were given three options: to be directly involved in the design; to fine-tune the structure after it had been designed; or to be told after the decisions were made. They chose to have no active involvement, reasoning that they were too close as a group, and preferred to be told about the changes once they were decided upon by upper management. Jean had expected this because the individuals would have felt that they were negotiating for each others' jobs. Although this eliminated some valuable input, Jean believed it would be less painful for the supervisors.

While Jean analyzed the current structure, some interesting dynamics began to take place among the supervisors. Each supervisor was competent and hard working, having worked for Medictest for an average of 18 years, with minimal movement or change in responsibility or position. They knew each other well and were comfortable with their roles and work environment. They had known for the past two years that changes were going to be made. Six months ago, they became aware that these changes would be structural and would affect their positions. Anxiety levels escalated. They wanted to hear about the changes as soon as possible and were uncomfortable with the delay. Although productivity was unaffected by the anxiety, some supervisors began to protect their turf by emphasizing the size and importance of their particular unit at every opportunity.

The supervisors realized that there would be a smaller leadership team and thus began inwardly to assess their own strengths and weaknesses, reasoning whether their style of leadership would be one of those desired for the new roles. Each supervisor's individual level of anxiety depended on his or her personal situation; most of them could determine from their own intuitive comfort level whether they would be chosen to stay.

Jean held one-on-one discussions with the supervisors. The two supervisors of specimen collection began increasingly to inquire about the severance package, alternative careers, and retirement options. It appeared to Jean that they were prepared to leave Medictest.

Even those supervisors who felt strong in their role experienced high anxiety. Résumés were prepared and other job opportunities were considered. While work performance continued normally, the supervisors behaved differently. They were quieter than before and vigilant for signals of what changes would be made. Jean had to be extremely careful of her actions. For example, she occasionally had to delegate meetings to supervisors if she could not attend; her choice of supervisor now took on new meaning for the supervisors. Another time, when Jean discussed the severance packages with the group of supervisors, she had to be careful with whom she made eye-contact.

Effect on the Staff

Great lengths had been taken by management to prevent the staff members in Sarnia from knowing about the pending structural changes, in order to keep the situation manageable for the supervisors. Within the past few weeks, the staff members had found out that a review of the supervisory structure was taking place. They were anxious about the effect these changes would have on them and were concerned that the "right" supervisors be chosen to stay. Several employees who were fond of their supervisors discreetly approached Jean, encouraging her to "bear in mind the right person for the job."

Additionally, the staff were aware that the largest laboratory, located in London, was expanding due to automation. This knowledge created the fear that the lab in Sarnia would be closed because of its proximity to London.

DEVELOPING REVISED STRUCTURE

Jean saw several opportunities for effective change to the current structure at Medictest Sarnia.

The lab service representative was basically responsible for new business, while the client service representative was in charge of keeping current business. Jean decided that these positions could be consolidated due to marketplace changes.

The courier supervisor had taken early retirement in January 1994 with a separation package. His position had not been filled since his departure, and this had not created any problems. There was some apparent overlap and excess supervision of the specimen collection centres and courier operations. Jean concluded that the courier and collection centres staff could be streamlined under one supervisor, instead of the previous four. However, this would require a strong, energetic supervisor who was capable of handling the increased responsibility.

The supervisors of Testing Centres 1 and 2 currently shared the same staff; Jean decided their positions could be merged into one with few problems.

Testing Centre 3 was highly complex and completed 80 percent of the tests. It currently had a strong supervisor with potential for interregional liaison with other Medictest locations.

Testing Centre 5 was of low complexity but high importance and was highly interdependent with Testing Centre 4. These centres could logically be merged.

The customer service department dealt with customer requests and communicated testing solutions to customers. This department operated within a vacuum, separate from testing. The lack of communication regarding customer requests negatively affected the level of service provided to the customers. Jean saw the opportunity to address this concern by linking it with Testing Centres 1 and 2, under one supervisor.

Billing was closely audited by OHIP every two years. OHIP subtracted a percentage from revenue for each minor error found. Each billing form had to contain specific and correct information (e.g., the ordering doctor's name) in order to prevent this direct loss of revenue. Because of the high cost of error, it was important that this department be well managed. The current supervisor had high expertise in this function, which could be utilized throughout the region. By separating billing from customer service, this supervisor could focus externally on the reduction of error rates throughout the specimen collection centres in various locations.

Based on the above observations, Jean developed a new structure that reduced the number of supervisory positions by five (see Exhibit 3). Working closely with Helen Hoi, the head office director of human resources, Jean now had to evaluate the current supervisors. Helen had previously been a manager at Medictest Sarnia and had worked with these supervisors several years ago.

The best candidates had to be chosen for these new positions. Jean would need leaders who would be willing and able to move forward with twice as many staff members as before. Because of the closeness of the group, it was difficult to evaluate the supervisors without disclosing any information. After a thorough evaluation of the current supervisors, their skills, assurance, and ability to take on increased responsibility, Jean and Helen developed a list of six supervisors to form the revised leadership team.

THE NEXT CHALLENGE

Head office and the medical director agreed to the structural changes. The next challenge Jean faced was the communication of the decisions and the logistics involved in that process. How should the changes be conveyed to the supervisors leaving, to those supervisors staying, and to the staff? Where should the discussions be held? Who should communicate the decisions? In what sequence? What should the physical setup be? How should head office be involved? There were many questions that would have to be thoroughly addressed before the plan was implemented. Jean wanted to develop a clear, specific plan that would maintain employee morale, enable the operations to continue, maintain self-confidence in those chosen to stay, and redirect those not chosen in such a way that their dignity would be preserved. Jean wondered what reactions to expect from the supervisors and the staff. She wanted to effect the changes within the next month. It was important for this process to be recognized in the future as a natural change effect, instead of a "Black Day."

Note

1. OHIP is a program run by the Ontario government that provides free basic health services to Canadian citizens and landed immigrants living in Ontario.

Exhibit 1
The Values of Medictest

QUALITY
Doing the right things the right way.

COMPETENCE
Having the appropriate attitudes and abilities.

CARING
Showing genuine concern for others.

RESPECT FOR THE INDIVIDUAL
Treating people as individuals, with the same understanding and appreciation we seek for ourselves.

MUTUAL TRUST AND OPENNESS
Having confidence enough to rely on others and to be open to new and different people and ideas.

INTEGRITY
Being reliable and accountable in word and behaviour.

TEAMWORK
Accepting a "hierarchy of roles with equality of persons" willing to work together as "we."

COMMUNICATION
Listening is the key.

BALANCE
Keeping home and work in perspective, recognizing that one helps the other.

SIMPLICITY
Maintaining humility, humour, and a common-sense approach to work and life.

What is expected of all individuals can be summarized as Competence and Mutual Trust.

EXHIBIT 2
Current
Structure—Sarnia

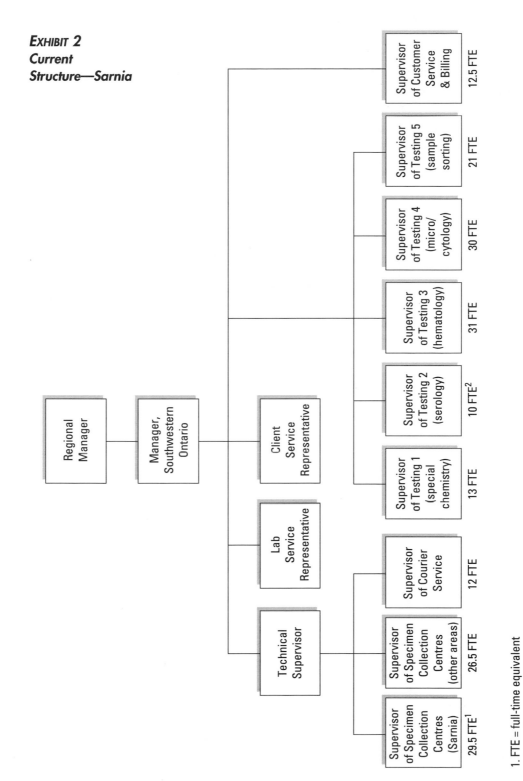

1. FTE = full-time equivalent
2. Note: Testing centres 1 and 2 share the same staff

Exhibit 3
Proposed
Structure—
Sarnia

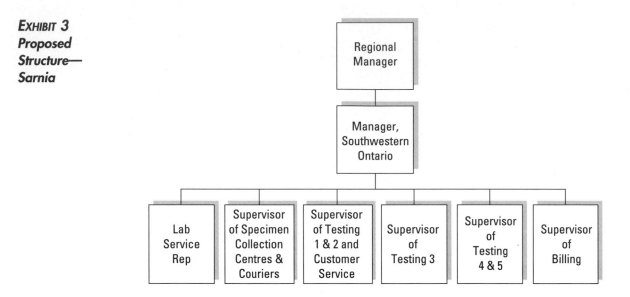

CASE 4.10 OTTAWA VALLEY FOOD PRODUCTS

By Elizabeth Grasby and Sonya M. Head

At 2:30 on the afternoon of February 13, R.J. Jennings received a hand delivered note from Karen Russell, a highly respected and well-liked administrative assistant. The note explained that all of the executive assistants in the company had vacated their respective posts in support of Mary Gregory, and were gathered in the employees' lounge. Earlier that day, Jennings had told Gregory that her employment would not be continued at the end of her six-week probationary period because she was unable to handle the duties necessary to be his administrative assistant.

THE COMPANY

Ottawa Valley Food Products (OVFP) manufactured and distributed a line of low calorie and diet food products to national grocery chains. The company was located in Arnprior, a small town about 65 km southwest of the nation's capital. OVFP employed 100 production workers and 18 management and support staff.

R.J. JENNINGS

Jennings had worked for OVFP for 31 years, beginning as a production line worker at the age of 23. He was ever-respected by his contemporaries for his plant management expertise. Administration at OVFP felt that much of the company's success could be attributed to Jennings's dedication to operating the most efficient production process in the Ottawa Valley.

Jennings's high expectations for all employees were surpassed only by his own personal standards. It was common to find him working at his cluttered desk past 8 p.m. and on weekends.

Although Jennings was eligible for early retirement in one year, he had indicated no desire to exercise that option. When approached by the personnel department on the issue of retirement, Jennings had quipped that he was too busy to retire.

ELLA ARNOLD

After 10 years as Jennings's assistant, Ella Arnold had taken early retirement at the beginning of January. Her eyesight had deteriorated and, at 58 years of age,

Ella felt she could afford to take life easier. Over the years, Ella and Jennings had become close friends. Ella was willing to work overtime, often without pay, frequently breaking previous personal commitments. In Jennings's opinion, his long-time assistant had a sixth sense for her job. She knew when things were building up for Jennings and would go out of her way to shield him from distractions to his work. Ella often ran errands for Jennings, even on her lunch hours. When Ella retired, the personnel department replaced her with Mary Gregory.

MARY GREGORY   Mary started to work as Jennings's assistant on January 16. She had graduated the previous spring with a bachelor's degree in administrative studies from a well-known Canadian university. For the next few months, Mary had travelled extensively throughout Europe and the Far East before returning to her family home in Arnprior to start her job at OVFP. She was 24 years old.

The initial episode in a series of events leading to today's predicament occurred on her first day. About an hour into the morning's work, Jennings called Mary on her interoffice line and asked her to bring him coffee and the morning newspaper on her way back from her break in the staff lounge. This request was a morning routine he had practised for almost 10 years. Mary refused, claiming that she was quite busy. However, Jennings had purposely given Mary a light workload on her first day. Nonetheless, he fetched the coffee and newspaper himself and dismissed the incident as first-day jitters.

The second incident was more disturbing to Jennings. For several months, OVFP had pursued an order from a national chain that did not previously carry OVFP's products. The chain's purchasing agent had requested a meeting with Jennings to discuss production and shipping schedules prior to signing a contract with OVFP.

On the day of the meeting with the purchasing agent, Jennings walked into his office late and found Mary chatting to the agent about her previous weekend's activities. Jennings, surprised to find her in his office and shocked by her chatty attitude toward this important client, bluntly asked Mary to leave the office. Within hearing range of the purchasing agent, Mary not only refused Jennings's request, she elaborated that she had not been drafted into the armed services, finished her anecdotal dissertation to the purchasing agent, and only then left the office, slamming the door behind her.

Jennings was humiliated and sensed the embarrassment of the agent. When the purchasing agent left, Jennings called Mary into his office and demanded an explanation.

Mary simply repeated her earlier comments:

I wasn't drafted into the army. You're not my drill sergeant. I was having a pleasant conversation with a very friendly client, and you were very rude to ask me to leave like you did. That's all there is to it.

This morning, Mary refused to file the previous day's production reports in a filing cabinet that was inside Jennings's office, far away from her desk. He had called her away from her work, into his office, to ask that she file the reports.

"No bloody way," she snapped and stomped out of his office.

Jennings believed he had worked too long and too hard to achieve his current level of respect, and he was not about to hand over control to a "green" college kid. He was a senior manager at OVFP and he felt that his time was better spent on pressing company problems. Ella Arnold had never refused a request, even on her own time.

THE NOTE

Jennings turned his attention to the note he had been handed by Karen Russell. He read it three times before the message hit home. Either he backed down and reversed his decision to release Mary at the end of her probationary period, or all 10 of OVFP's administrative assistants would travel to Ottawa to publicize their grievances on the Canadian Broadcast Corporation's (CBC) six o'clock newscast. The producer of the evening news had promised to air the women's complaint if it was not resolved by show time.

It was now 2:40 p.m. The women had threatened to leave the lounge for the trip to Ottawa by 3 o'clock. Jennings had less than 20 minutes to take action, if he felt action was necessary.

CASE 4.11   ROYAL HARDWARE

By Elizabeth Grasby and Sonya M. Head

John Kurtis, president and majority shareholder of Royal Hardware Company Limited, decided it was time for action. His company was in the midst of an internal reorganization, but Ernie Lamb, one of his oldest friends, was thwarting the success of the transition. Every day, John received more complaints about Ernie's lack of cooperation.

THE COMPANY

Royal Hardware was located in Hartsville, 80 km from a major industrial and commercial centre. The company manufactured and distributed doorknobs, shelving, miscellaneous hardware products, and gaskets for industrial use. Royal also distributed a line of small consumer appliances.

Industrial and wholesale buyers could choose from 520 hardware items, some with up to 10 colour and material variations. Royal was widely known in the industry for its custom work. The company could copy any competitor's product or manufacture any product to a customer's specifications. John Kurtis summarized Royal's production strategy:

We will produce anything, in any amount, as long as we have an order for it.

GROWTH AND STRATEGIC PLANNING ISSUES

Royal's hardware line had grown vigorously in the past decade; however, it was not expected to grow as rapidly in the future. Trends in the industry indicated that cost cutting and price competition would become greater factors in the home and industrial hardware markets.

To date at Royal Hardware, there were many inefficiencies. Salespeople sometimes brought in orders for delivery of discontinued lines. Inventories became obsolete. In the past year, $192,000 of inventory had to be written off. Production workers often complained of poor quality parts, which led to constant adjustments of assembly tasks. Because of scheduling problems, parts for orders were often not available, and work-in-process inventories built to very high levels. Employees consumed too much time searching for parts.

Royal produced and assembled most of its own parts. Its competitors were dependent on separate suppliers for unassembled parts. Recently, and consistent with prevailing trends to just-in-time (JIT) inventories, Royal's competitors had begun to carry smaller amounts of raw materials and work-in-process inventories, sometimes holding only an hour's worth of materials on hand.

Mr. Kurtis believed it was crucial for Royal to reorganize, to develop better operating information and systems, and to institute better controls over inventories. He appointed Stan Burns to the production supervisor's role and gave him the task of developing a production system for Royal. He hired Will Hilton to develop a materials requisition system. Kurtis asked Ernie Lamb to help coordinate the various activities required for the reorganization.

PERSONNEL

In the Hartsville plant and head office, Royal employed 72 people. Fifty-seven were hourly-rated production workers, eight were salaried office staff, and seven were members of the management team. On the shop floor, 41 people were employed in the control of inventory, shipping, receiving, stamping, degreasing, plating, and painting. Sixteen people were employed on design, component manufacturing, and assembly.

The average age of the workers was 44 and there was a four-to-one ratio of women to men in the plant. Key plant jobs were held by senior employees. There were no back-up personnel to replace them if they left or if they were absent.

In general, worker–management relations were satisfactory. Royal had very low absenteeism (and turnover), which employees attributed to an "acceptable" wage, the infrequency of layoffs in the plant, and the fact that jobs were neither too difficult nor too demanding. Employees attributed high morale to the fact that the union had recently agreed on a new contract with higher wages, wages that were slightly above the standards of other Hartsville plants. As well, they felt that purchase of new equipment had made some jobs easier, and the recent hiring of more women increased the seniority and security of many workers.

Stan Burns believed that the workers, especially the older ones, felt that there was no reason to do above-average work, since there was no pay or other incentive for doing so. Management wanted to develop an incentive program, but one could not be introduced until proper work standards had been established. At one time, management did try to introduce a piece-work plan, but the labourers rejected the offer due, primarily, to an inadequate inventory system that caused them to spend excessive amounts of time searching for parts.

REORGANIZATION ISSUES

Will Hilton summarized his frustrations:

> Ernie says he is always too busy in the plant (where Stan is supposed to be in control) to help me out. This is the same story everyone else gets. Most of the production workers still go to Ernie for advice and help. Old customers keep asking for Ernie, and that doesn't help either.

Previously, Ernie Lamb had been responsible for inventory, production, scheduling, and shipping, as well as general plant upkeep. Overall, Lamb was to make sure that the plant could produce what was demanded by the sales force and to get the products out to meet delivery deadlines. With reorganization, two new positions — scheduling and controlling — were created, and the old position of plant supervisor was eliminated. Instead, there was now a production supervisor, Stan Burns. The scheduling and control functions were given to Will Hilton and Keith Holland, respectively.

Lamb was assigned the task of comparing theoretical standards against actual labour standards and making appropriate recommendations to Ned Learner, the costing coordinator. As well, Lamb was asked to work with designer Stew Morris and Ned Learner in developing accurate material lists for costing purposes, to work with Keith Holland and Will Hilton to develop a requisition system for purchasing, and to be available to Stan in an advisory capacity related to production problems.

Ernie had not been carrying out these tasks. He acknowledged the extent of the problems associated with reorganization; however, he said:

> I can't see the relevance of these jobs they want me to do. I'm a people person, not a paper person.

About Stan Burns, Ernie said:

> What's the use of going to Stan when he doesn't have the answers? Stan will have to learn it the same way I learned it ... he will have to make his own decisions.

About his lack of attention to his new tasks:

> I can't concentrate on my new job since daily problems take up too much time.

Ernie's lack of cooperation had divided the plant into two factions. An older worker summed up the sentiments of the more senior workers:

> Stan's been trying hard to get things running the way he thinks they should, by using all his new ideas, but Ernie's the only one here who knows how this place really works. We make this place run and Ernie knows that.

Another employee summarized the feelings of the younger labourers:

> It's good at last to have someone at the controls who's got some new ideas in his head. You've got to change with the times — Stan can, but Ernie's been here too long.

THE DILEMMA Management agreed that Royal's systems problems needed to be addressed. But, before the bigger issues could be solved, John Kurtis had to do something about Ernie Lamb. Ernie had indicated an interest in retiring within two years, but there had been questions raised about his value to the company if his behaviour continued to hinder the reorganization.

Exhibit 1

Management Personnel Data

STAN BURNS

Position:	Production Supervisor
Age:	43
Years with company:	1
Background:	Design and metal works foreman
Responsibilities:	Maintain and improve production, handle personnel function for plant
Education:	Engineering diploma from U.K.

WILL HILTON

Position:	Production Coordinator (Scheduling)
Age:	37
Years with company:	2
Background:	Production planning supervisor in clothing industry
Responsibilities:	Scheduling, inventory control, purchasing for some parts
Education:	Grade 12 and production planning courses

KEITH HOLLAND

Position:	Controller
Age:	34
Years with company:	1.5
Background:	Sales management and office administration in drug industry
Responsibilities:	Office management, development and operation of control systems
Education:	Attended university for three and a half years, Certified Management Accountant

Exhibit 1 (cont.)

NED LEARNER

Position:	Costing Coordinator
Age:	47
Years with company:	21
Responsibilities:	Costing and standards development, maintaining and updating material and labour standards, costing and production
Education:	Grade 12

ERNIE LAMB

Position:	Plant Manager
Age:	58
Years with company:	40
Background:	Worked his way up through the plant
Responsibilities:	Developing purchasing controls, pricing, updating standards, establishing information flows
Education:	Grade 10

GORD PULDING

Position:	Vice-President and Sales Manager
Age:	69
Years with company:	31
Background:	Selling and administration
Responsibilities:	Development and sales territories, account administration, sales force management, pricing
Education:	Attended university for three years

JOHN KURTIS

Position:	President and majority shareholder
Age:	53
Years with company:	31
Background:	Commissioned officer in the RCAF, purchasing of some parts, personnel administration, public relations

PART

AN INTRODUCTION TO
MARKETING MANAGEMENT

The role of marketing in any organization, whether it is a business or a nonbusiness,[*] is to improve the performance of the organization. Good performance is achieved through a disciplined focus on creating, developing, and maintaining profitable relationships between customers and the organization. Marketers have so many different ways to accomplish this result that the practice of marketing is much more complicated than any short discussion of it can convey. There is far more to the marketing profession than the unfortunate stereotypes of fast-talking salespeople and manipulative advertisers. In this chapter, we will attempt to explain the major choices that professional marketers face and the ways in which marketing decisions are made, in order to prepare you for the cases in this section. Preparing a marketing plan is not a simple, repetitive exercise of filling in the blanks of a checklist, so there is no simple 1-2-3 approach to marketing. Rather, each circumstance requires you to decide which analysis and decisions are appropriate.

Marketers are at the intersection of the firm and the market. This means that they have the dual responsibility of representing the market (customers, competitors, and trade) to the other members of the company and of representing the company to the market. For example, a marketer helps other managers understand what customers want and how this affects managerial decisions. A marketer also makes promises to customers about what the company has to offer. In the final analysis, marketing is more about people than about products or techniques. The marketer's job is to understand, influence, and serve people.

---

[*]Throughout this chapter, reference is made to business marketing. The special issues of non-business marketing are briefly discussed at the end of this chapter.

DEFINING THE MARKETING CHALLENGE

There are many ways to approach marketing. The best place to start as a marketer is with a clear understanding of what performance one is trying to effect. For example, suppose you were operating a store and you wondered how to improve it with marketing techniques. Before examining all the marketing options, you would want to know what exactly you are trying to achieve. Do you need more people to come through the door? Do you need to convert more of the current browsing traffic into paying customers? Do you need to find a way to get each customer, on average, to spend more? These questions matter greatly in terms of what marketing plan you would develop. For example, if the marketing challenge were to get more people to come into the store, you might focus attention on media advertising to ensure people know about your store. On the other hand, if the marketing challenge were to convert more browsers into customers, you might focus attention on your sales associates: Do they need more training, a different compensation scheme, or what? Or perhaps the store isn't carrying the right kind of products and thus browsers can't find what they want to buy. On the other hand, if the marketing challenge were to increase the transaction size of customers, you might rearrange displays to encourage more related item purchases (a technique often used in clothing stores) or consider changes in the selection of products carried.

You would want to know, as well, if you should focus on deciding which strategy to undertake (the direction to go in), on implementing a strategy (the execution), or both. This means you would need to determine first whether the strategy is appropriate (and change it, if it needs improvement) and second, whether the strategy is being properly implemented (and work on that, if it needs improvement).

In other words, there are so many possible marketing activities that it is critical that you define the marketing challenge at the outset. Not only does this help decide what to do, but it also makes it easier to gauge success later. After all, marketing activities cost money and management wants to know if the money was well spent.

ASSESSING MARKETING PERFORMANCE

The usual measures of performance that concern marketers are as follows:

Total sales: This might be expressed in dollar or unit volume

Sales per customer: This might be expressed in dollars or units per customer, share of a customer's total purchases in a category (e.g., books) over time, or frequency of purchase.

Market share: This is usually expressed as a percentage of the total sales (by all competitors) in this category in a specified market area accounted for by the firm.

Sales growth: This indicates the trend, usually expressed in percentage terms, from one period to another.

Total profitability: This is expressed either as the dollar gross profit (margin) or dollar net profit.

Customer profitability: This is expressed as the average dollar profit per customer or by customer group.

Awareness: This is expressed as the percentage of the target market who are aware of the firm or specific things about the firm.

Loyalty: There are a variety of measures used, but the idea is to express what percentage of customers are repeat customers versus new customers.

We will examine these measures in greater detail later in the chapter. There are many other measures of performance that marketers use, both to set objectives and track progress. The point is to establish what the marketing effort is supposed to accomplish and then use that as a guide for what to do and how to measure results.

<table>
<tr><td>

■
SECTION
■
TWO
■

</td><td>

IDENTIFYING MARKET OPPORTUNITIES AND SELECTING TARGET MARKETS

A continual challenge for any marketer is to find market opportunities. Marketing is much more than simply selling what the company makes or advertising what the company has. Marketing is about deciding what to do and for whom. In other words, marketing should lead the firm's strategy by determining that the firm will make what can be sold, not sell what can be made.

</td></tr>
</table>

EXHIBIT 1

The Gap

The Gap began in 1969 in San Francisco. Initially it was intended to serve the "generation gap" (the baby boomers in their teen years) with a wide variety of jeans (especially Levi's) and a limited selection of casual, "basic with attitude" clothing at moderate prices. If the Gap's management had thought marketing was just selling what they had, they would never have become such a retail winner. Over the years, the Gap has responded to a changing market (the boomers are now pushing 50) by broadening its assortment and its appeal. They continue to attract today's teens, but they have not lost the teens' parents, the boomers. New lines, higher price points, fashionable advertising, more stores, and above all a strong focus on associating its brand with a contemporary "cool" lifestyle image have all contributed to its remarkable success.

Marketers are always looking for customers. *Prospects* are individuals, households, or organizations that a marketer thinks might be converted into customers — *customers* are those people who actually buy. *Consumer* is another term often used to describe members of a market, but more accurately these are the people who actually use a product or service.

CUSTOMER ANALYSIS

Customers buy products and services to satisfy their needs and wants, so it only makes sense that marketers must work hard to understand what these needs and wants are, through what is typically called a customer analysis or consumer analysis. Marketers want to know what customers are looking for and how they go about making their own choices of which marketers to patronize and which products and services to buy from them. In other words, the marketing challenge is to be chosen over competitors.

For this reason, many marketers start their thinking by considering individual potential customers or groups of customers (also known as segments, discussed later in the chapter). Some usual questions marketers pose about potential and current customers are as follows:

> What wants and needs are people trying to satisfy? What is particularly important to them? For example, is lowest price more important than product performance? Are these needs and wants strong or weak?

> What motivation lies behind the choice of a product or service? For example, what is the reason that they are interested in buying a sport utility vehicle when the car they have is working just fine?

> Where do they get information about products, services, stores, and so on, as they proceed through a process of considering a purchase? Where do they shop, and why there? For example, why are some shoppers purchasing books on the Internet rather than from book stores?

> When do they go through this shopping/purchasing process? For example, do shoppers make their weekly grocery trip on Thursday or Saturday?

All of these questions are designed to discover insights into how the marketer can influence this shopping/purchasing process so that the marketer gets the business. In other words, research and analysis about prospects and customers are conducted not to uncover interesting facts, but rather to find actionable ideas.

MARKET SEGMENTATION

Market segmentation is a concept with great power for marketers. It is very helpful in the process of target market selection and in making other marketing decisions. The basic idea is very simple: people differ, so divide them into different groups of similar people. Because people differ, some segments will be far more attractive to the marketer than others. Consider the difference between "tweens" (7–12 year olds) and "the mature market" (over 50 years old) for a marketer of cosmetics. Preferences for colours and fragrances, how much they are willing to pay, and much more will vary tremendously between these two segments. In other words, the customer analysis questions posed above will be answered differently for each segment.

<table>
<tr><td>EXHIBIT 2</td><td></td></tr>
</table>

Kool-Aid

Kool-Aid appeared in 1927 as a successor to Fruit Smack. This powdered drink mix remained at five cents for over 30 years. Positioned as "for 5–12 year old kids who are looking for a fun, hip, tasty drink with lots of flavour variety that Moms find inexpensive," Kool-Aid has been a long-term marketing success, with a dominant share in its category. Its competitors include other powdered drinks of all kinds, as well as soft drinks and juices. More than 2,600 million litres of Kool-Aid are consumed in a year worldwide. Its yearly sales in packages, laid end to end, would go around the equator twice.

The practice of segmentation can be complicated. For example, if the challenge were to segment the bicycle market, the marketer might begin by bicycle types (a product-based segmentation approach) and thus separate children's bicycles, touring road bikes, off-road mountain bikes, and so on. Or the marketer may begin by considering different users (a customer-based segmentation approach) and thus separate weekend users, enthusiasts, racers, and so on. The point of segmentation is to find groups that make marketing sense. If the marketer chose to focus on children's bicycles, the rest of the marketing program should be consistent with everything he or she knows or suspects about this segment of the market. For example, if the marketer knows that children's bikes are usually purchased by their parents and that parents are especially concerned about safety, he or she might emphasize safety in product selections, advertising, in-store merchandising, and so on. In other words, a marketer's understanding of segmentation leads to target market selection, which in turn leads to the rest of the marketing decisions.

TARGET MARKET SPECIFICATION

Early on in the process of making marketing decisions, the marketer must deal with the question, Who are we trying to serve? In other words, a major marketing decision is the selection of a target market. A target market does not necessarily mean that a business won't sell to people who don't fit the target characteristics, but rather that the marketing offer is being designed with a particular audience in mind. A target market enables a marketer to focus the offer and the delivery of that offer.

The idea is to select the part of the market that represents an attractive opportunity for the marketer because the marketer may be able to serve it better than competitors and hence build a profitable business. The alternative, not specifying a target (which is trying to be all things to all people), is rarely successful in today's competitive, crowded marketplace. For example, many full-line department stores were once the one-stop shopping places for the majority of the population. However, they have been outmanoeuvred and outperformed by specialist retailers such as Toys "R" Us who target segments of the public with more compelling, more narrowly defined offers.

There are as many ways to specify target markets as there are to describe people. For example, one might select:

> A certain age group (such as teenagers);
>
> An income group (such as $50,000–$100,000 in household income);
>
> An attitudinal or behavioural group (such as those who ride motorcycles);
>
> A geographic group (such as those who live in a particular city); or
>
> A psychographic group (such as those whose lifestyle involves experience rather than accumulation of possessions).

With such a broad range of options for describing a target market, the marketer should be wary of simplistic target market specifications such as "women between the ages of 25 to 34."

The key is to meet the following criteria in selecting a target market:

> Does this definition include a large enough market to be worth serving? This is the important issue of substantial market size (and its potential growth).
>
> Is the target accessible to the marketer? For example, specifying "all Canadians" as the target market makes little sense if one is able to distribute only to those who live in Halifax.
>
> Does the target specification provide us with a different way of thinking about customers than our competition? Does it identify a group we can serve in a differentiated, better way than competitors?
>
> Does the target specification provide guidance for the rest of the organization in terms of obtaining the performance outcomes desired? For example, specifying a target customer who has "blue eyes and feels young at heart" may not help the marketer find, reach, or affect such customers. This criterion of actionability is very important.

While examining alternative target markets, the marketer considers ways to improve marketing performance. There are four major approaches:

> *Market penetration:* Focus on current customers — can we sell them more of what they are already buying from us? Can we increase their usage of our product or service, such as by convincing them to use our product at new times of the day (e.g., drinking a cola with breakfast instead of coffee or tea)?

New product/service offerings: Seek to sell something new to current customers, such as a related product or service. In this instance, the marketer would build on the current relationship as a supplier (e.g., a retailer might add new products to her store).

New segments/market areas: Seek new customers for the current product or service (e.g., enter a new geographic area).

Diversification: Seek new customers and offer them new (to the marketer, anyway) products and services.

The relative merits of these approaches can be assessed in part through an understanding of the market, which is to say a careful assessment of customers and prospects in the light of competition for their attention. (Part 7 elaborates on these four approaches.)

COMPETITIVE ANALYSIS

An important part of target market selection is competitive analysis. Who else is seeking the patronage of various segments of the market, and how successful are they? Are there any exploitable deficiencies in competitive products or services, in their service, in their prices, in anything that matters to the target customer? For example, if the competition is slow to respond to service calls, perhaps a company can differentiate itself by providing rapid response. It is important, however, to focus on factors that matter to customers, not simply to marketers. The key is to look at everything from the customer's perspective. From the customer's perspective (those in the target segment) how does one offering compare with competitors'? Competitive analysis includes such comparison of marketing programs and marketing performance. If the competition has a much greater share of market, much greater financial resources, and so on, then they will have significant advantages that a marketer must overcome to compete directly. Perhaps the business should find another market to focus on. Finally, what changes are expected in the competitive environment (new competitors, new ways of competing) that will affect a business's performance?

Understanding, anticipating, and dealing with competition is a core part of every marketer's job.

DECIDING ON PRODUCT/SERVICE OFFERING

SECTION

THREE

Marketing means taking into consideration what customers need and want, how they make decisions about how to satisfy themselves, and so on, and then doing something with that knowledge. The decision of what to offer for sale in the marketplace should be made not just by considering what one can offer. Simply trying to convert into cash what one can and wants to make is not marketing; it is merely selling. From a marketing perspective then, we should think about the product or service offering as a "package of benefits" that customers find worth their time, energy, and money. In this way, we realize that people want *solutions to their problems* (they don't want a can opener for its own sake, but rather they want opened cans) and *answers to their wants* (they subscribe to a wireless phone because they want to talk to people when on the move).

Typically, a marketer must decide exactly what to offer in the way of products and services—and what not to offer. How many variations are needed? What branding should be created (own name or someone else's)? What packaging should be used? For example, consider the number of individual products that might be produced to satisfy one style of jean: 8 waist sizes × 8 leg lengths × 3 colours = 192 different products. The number of products can quickly increase, thus adding complexity to the marketing challenges. Furthermore, in almost all product categories there is an amazing number of new product entries every year, which means a marketer has to think about product decisions continually.

There are many considerations when making product or service decisions. What features or characteristics are most important to potential and current customers? What are they willing to pay for the package of benefits they want? Is a business underachieving or overachieving in relation to that "ideal"? How can it differentiate its offering from that of competitors so that customers will prefer its offering? Can it sustain a competitive edge over time?

Exhibit 3

FedEx

FedEx wouldn't exist if Fred Smith believed the C grade he got from his economics professor for a business proposal over 25 years ago. Undaunted, he went ahead with his ideas and changed the parcel delivery industry to become the world's largest express transportation company. The success of the FedEx brand is undisputed; in fact, recognition and use of the FedEx brand name was so successful that it became synonymous with "ship it overnight." The company had to alter its advertising and promotion campaign to avoid losing control of the slogan "FedEx it."

The success of FedEx is often attributed to Fred Smith's foreseeing how information technology could be applied to change traditional business practices and principles with respect to inventories, order processing, and distribution in parcel delivery. FedEx has avoided the temptation to engage in price wars, steadfastly remaining focused on customer service as a means to create and sustain competitive advantage. Through the use of information, FedEx has improved customer satisfaction and profitability by understanding the needs of its customer segments and consequently developing products and services to satisfy them better than the competition.

Products and services that have a short life are usually referred to as *fads.* Toy items frequently last only one season. On the other hand, some products and services have a long life cycle. The Boeing 747 has been around for decades. The projected length of the *product life cycle* and where the product or service currently is in its life have a big impact on the remaining marketing decisions that a manager will make. For example, if a product appears to be nearing the end of its life cycle, a manager may lower its price to clear inventory, offer it to different distributors, and so on. The fashion business is a good example of the impact of the life cycle on marketing decisions.

At a conceptual level, products and services are quite similar, but there are some important differences to bear in mind. Most services are performed and consumed at the same time. This means that they cannot be inventoried, so managing demand to match the service provider's capacity is a key marketing challenge. For example, a hair stylist cannot inventory haircuts and would prefer to spread demand over a week rather than have all customers appear at the same time. Another distinguishing feature of services is that many are intangible, that is, they cannot be touched like products. This intangibility creates challenges for the marketer in communicating about services and challenges for the customer in choosing among competing services. For example, a visit to a museum is intangible and therefore it is difficult for the museum marketer to communicate what a visit will be like to a potential visitor.

DISTRIBUTION APPROACHES

Distribution refers to the movement of the product or service to the customer. There are many methods of distribution, typically called channels of distribution. The marketer must decide which channel(s) to use. The entire business "system" includes all participants, from the raw materials provider to the end customer. A marketer may find him- or herself at different locations in the total system. For example, a vendor of fabric will be a marketer to apparel manufacturers, an apparel manufacturer will be a marketer to retail stores, and a retail store will be a marketer to the end consumer. Those marketers who sell to the end consumer are called consumer marketers, while those who sell to other businesses are called industrial or business-to-business marketers. This classification sometimes helps explain differences in marketing challenges (e.g., selling to a business may require a price quotation process) and differences in marketing programs (e.g., a business-to-business marketer may rely more on a direct sales force, while a consumer marketer may rely more on media advertising). Notice that all participants in that distribution system need to understand the end consumer and do their part to satisfy that buyer. If the end customer doesn't buy, the whole system is stopped.

When trying to understand a distribution system in a particular industry or product category, it is usually helpful to prepare a diagram of it. This allows you to examine who does what for whom — for example, who carries inventory, who ships the product, who collects market information, and who provides after-sale service. Generally, there are a variety of distribution tasks such as the above which are divided among several intermediaries (members of the distribution system). In return for performing these tasks, the intermediaries take a portion of the ultimate sales dollar (called their margin). The calculations for this margin, the marketing arithmetic, will be discussed later in this chapter.

DISTRIBUTION ALTERNATIVES

Some of the many distribution alternatives include:

> Selling direct through one's own sales force or stores;
>
> Selling direct through mail order or telemarketing;
>
> Selling direct through the Internet; and
>
> Selling to wholesalers (or other distributors such as agents), who sell to others in turn.

Deciding which combination of channels to use is a major marketing decision with long-term implications. Distribution is usually the most difficult dimension of the marketing program to change quickly. Considerations include what distribution tasks need to be performed to add value to the product or service, who can perform these tasks most cost effectively, what the financial implications are, and what the management implications are. On this last point, anytime a marketer deals with an intermediary between her- or himself and the ultimate customer, he or she gives a measure of control over what happens to that intermediary. For example, a manufacturer of jeans cannot dictate the ultimate retail selling price a retailer charges for those jeans or control what the retail sales associate says to potential customers. By the same token, the manufacturer may not be able to perform those distribution tasks at the same cost as the retailer, so doing them instead of the retailer may not be an option. This means that a major issue in distribution decisions is power and control over the marketing efforts of other channel members.

Distribution channels change over time. An alert marketer seeks channels that make sense for his or her target market and does not simply accept historical practice in the industry. Challenges to conventional industry practice have given us new approaches and major success stories, such as FedEx (hub-and-spoke courier service) and Dell Computers (direct sales of personal computers). At the same time, we have seen the demise of catalogue showrooms and the struggles of conventional department stores.

EXHIBIT 4

Chapters

Chapters is the major bookseller in Canada and operates through several distribution channels. Its SmithBooks and Coles stores are primarily located in malls. These stores are typically about 140 square metres and carry a limited selection of books. On the other hand, the Chapters book superstores are approximately 3,250 square metres in size. These stores carry 10 to 12 times as many books as the mall-based stores, plus CDs and other items. Chapters stores are freestanding, often near major malls or in downtown locations. While catalogues and special orders have long been possible ways to buy books with Chapters, in 1998 Chapters began selling on the Internet. Chapters.ca is now a major venture for the company, representing a new channel of communication and distribution.

MARKETING COMMUNICATIONS (HOW TO ATTRACT CUSTOMERS)

Some people erroneously think that marketing simply means advertising or promotion. Certainly, advertising and promotion are very visible aspects of a marketing program, but these activities are but a part of the whole program. Marketers need to communicate incentive to buy, and they do this through a variety of communication methods, including the following:

Advertising: The use of mass media such as broadcast (e.g., radio, TV), print (e.g., newspapers and magazines), and electronic (such as Web sites and banner ads);

Promotion: The use of coupons, samples, sales, contests, and other sales incentives;

Point-of-purchase displays: The use of in-store techniques such as shelf signs;

Direct mail: The use of materials sent through the regular postal system;

Telemarketing: The use of the telephone to contact customers via voice or fax;

Packaging: The use of graphics and other packaging elements;

Personal selling: The use of people to speak for the product or service; and

Publicity: The use of the media to provide free coverage in their stories related to their product or service.

Many other techniques are used to reach out and speak with customers and prospects. In each instance, typical decisions include whom to target, what the purpose is (the objectives), what to say (the message), how to say it (the execution), who will convey the message (media), when it will be done (the schedule), how much will be spent (the budget), and how it will be assessed (the evaluation).

COMMUNICATION OBJECTIVES

The first step is to establish objectives that are consistent with the overall marketing challenge being faced. Here are some possible examples:

Communicate attributes, benefits, product/service improvements;

Make service tangible, more understood;

Introduce extensions, incentives, special deals;

Increase amount or frequency of use;

Decrease frequency of use;

Increase uses;

Attract new users; and

Motivate/educate staff service providers.

MESSAGE DESIGN, BUDGET, AND MEDIA

The next step is to design the message, which some call the creative strategy. To design the message, the marketer considers the target market, the desired response from that target, the basic selling proposition, the desired image and tone of the message, and the attention-getting techniques that might be used (e.g., a product demonstration or testimonial from a well-known athlete).

Deciding how much to spend is difficult. Typically, there are several aspects to a communications campaign, and a marketer must decide how much to spend on each part of the campaign. Some marketers use rules of thumb, such as an "advertising to sales ratio," while others use an "all we can afford" approach. Some set a total amount and then divide it into pieces, while others establish what each piece might cost and the amounts to create a total budget. In short, there is no common agreement on how to decide on a budget.

Media choices include deciding which media to use (e.g., TV or radio), the placement within each medium (e.g., the section of the newspaper) and scheduling (e.g., when an outdoor ad should appear). Each choice involves many considerations, such as the ability of the medium to deliver colour, the costs to reach the target, the media's audience characteristics, when the medium is available, and what media competitors use. Each medium usually provides some statistics to help marketers decide whether the prices charged are worthwhile. Here are some common audience measurement terms:

Circulation: In print media, circulation measures the one-time physical distribution of the publication to any individual or household. In broadcast media, anyone tuned in once or more often to a station in a week is in that station's weekly circulation.

Reach: This measures the cumulative, unduplicated target audience exposed to the advertiser's message, by media, expressed as a percentage of the target group population in a defined geographic area (also known as penetration).

Frequency: This means the average number of occasions that the persons reached have been exposed to an ad during a given period of time.

Impressions: The number of impressions equals the total number of ads scheduled times the total target audience exposed to each occasion.

If all of this suggests to you that making marketing communication decisions is a complex business, you are correct. The basic rule is to evaluate as much as possible before, during, and after any marketing communication campaign because the answers as to what to do are in the marketplace, not in a book.

Exhibit 5

BMW

In the early 1900s, Bayerische Motoren Werke AG (BMW) was a maker of aircraft engines. In 1922, the company began producing motorcycles, and in 1928 the first BMW car was introduced. Over the years BMW has become a global company and also a global brand. As new models were introduced, the company continued to focus on quality, engineering, and performance. The quality reputation earned by BMW is grounded in the company philosophy that the driver is an integral part of the car itself. Generally, the target segments for BMW cars are 35- to 55-year-old drivers who value handling performance with a degree of luxury and are willing to pay for a quality car.

The consistency in marketing is evident in the strong identity and image that BMW has developed. The personality of the brand is one of performance. The continuing slogan of the brand, first introduced in 1975, is "The Ultimate Driving Machine." The emblem of BMW contributes to the image and reaches back to the beginning of the company: a roundel from an aircraft propeller provided the inspiration in 1917. BMW has also developed secondary associations with their brand of their technical superiority in aircraft, automobile, and motorcycle design and manufacture and their country of origin.

Advertising has been a critical component of BMW's brand building. Its "Ultimate Driving Machine" tagline, which allowed BMW to dominate the performance sedan category, has remained through numerous executive changes, agency changes, and economic downturns. The company has won countless advertising awards. Jim McDowell, vice-president of marketing for BMW North America, has said that their ads don't sell cars — they reinforce the brand and position it against competitors. "Once we get them behind the wheel, we'll likely sell them a car," said McDowell. With this in mind, Ultimate Driving Experience Test Drives and performance driving instruction programs are held around the country and are by invitation only. The corporate Web site has interactive features designed to encourage the driving experience. As part of their direct marketing efforts, people are invited to dealerships to test drive the cars, and BMW donates one dollar for each mile of test driving to the Susan G. Komen Foundation for breast cancer research. Every promotional program is designed to get people behind the wheel.

In addition to charity sponsorships, BMW reaches an audience through participation in motorcycle and auto racing. BMW's product placement in recent James Bond films has also garnered broad awareness for new product launches. BMW provided vehicles, as well, for the Olympic Torch Run, and their cars transported Olympic athletes in a caravan from Los Angeles to New England and then Atlanta. Recent ads include copy such as "Happiness is not around the corner. Happiness is the corner."

EVALUATING COMMUNICATION EFFECTIVENESS

Evaluating communications can be tricky because so much else is occurring at the same time in marketing. With the exception of carefully controlled direct marketing campaigns (such as direct mail), most communications are difficult to relate directly to sales results. Typically, marketers begin their evaluation of a communications idea qualitatively, asking questions such as:

Does it focus on benefits important to customers?

Is it believable and compelling?

Is it clear and memorable?

Is it true and in good taste?

Does it stand out from competitive campaigns?

Does it represent the company appropriately?

Then, the marketers typically move to more quantitative evaluation of communications to answer the basic question "Does it pay off?" Measures used include:

Nonbehavioural measures:

Awareness of company, product, or message,

Aided and unaided recall of the advertising, and

Opinions, attitudes, and intentions.

Behavioural measures:

Inquiries,

Traffic (e.g., number of people coming into a store), and

Sales (e.g., trial and repeat rates, dollars spent, frequency of purchase).

PERSONAL SELLING

Unlike mass media or direct communications, personal selling requires people to interact with prospects and customers. Personal selling can range from simple transaction processing at a cashier's desk in a grocery store to complex team selling in a business-to-business situation. For some companies, personal selling is their prime marketing communications approach.

There are many ideas about how to effectively sell. Conventional wisdom about personal selling dictates that the marketer follow these steps:

Do your homework first (know the product, know the customer), then

Approach the customer (the opening),

Present to the customer (focus on the benefits), and

Ask for the order (the close).

Sales training helps a salesperson learn what to say about a product or service and the company (e.g., what can be promised about delivery and installation) and helps a salesperson learn selling techniques. Selling techniques include learning how to deal with customer resistance and objections. For example, Xerox's selling techniques suggest providing evidence for one's claim when a prospect expresses doubt or objection, offering endorsement when a prospect expresses agreement, and probing when a prospect expresses indifference. Highly effective salespeople typically say that they ask and listen well before they talk and show, that they focus on the customer as an individual rather than doing a canned presentation, and that they focus on product/service benefits, not features.

The sales management task is to establish and support the sales force. The sales manager often has little time for selling. Much of the sales manager's job involves recruiting, selecting, training, organizing, deploying (e.g., allocating territory), motivating, and compensating salespeople and working on the sales strategy.

SECTION

SIX

PRICING

Pricing decisions are rarely made first when putting together a marketing program. Price decisions involve much more than costs. The two major types of pricing decisions are establishing initial prices and margins and making changes to prices and margins.

Pricing is a powerful marketing tool that is often highly visible to customers and competitors alike. Prices can be changed very quickly relative to other marketing decisions (such as distribution method), and the impact of pricing changes can be seen directly on financial performance.

When establishing price, a good rule of thumb is to think of it as a representation of what the total product/service "package of benefits" is worth to the customer. For example, a customer may be willing to pay more for diapers at midnight at a convenience store than during a regular grocery shopping trip. If so, the convenience store is justified in charging more, which in turn helps pay for the cost of being open for longer hours than the grocery store. In general terms, the marketer should think about establishing price within a range where the ceiling is what customers are willing to pay and the floor is what the marketer is willing to accept, given costs and other constraints.

Prices may be fixed or negotiable. In many countries, negotiated pricing is more common than in North America. In North America, negotiation tends to occur only with high price consumer products (cars, houses, etc.) and in business-to-business marketing. Another variation in establishing prices is the distinction between bundling all options into a package or unbundling them. For example, some car manufacturers offer a series of options that the customer may add, with prices for each option, while other car manufacturers bundle options together into an "all included price."

PRICING OBJECTIVES

Deciding on what price to charge depends, in part, on one's objectives. For example, pricing objectives may include the following:

> Obtaining quick market penetration (a high volume, low margin approach called "penetration pricing");

> Obtaining high margins and slower penetration (called "skimming the market" with low volume and high margins);

> Discouraging new competitors from entering the market or encouraging existing competitors to quit;

> Discouraging competitive price cutting; and

> Matching demand to capacity.

METHODS OF ESTABLISHING PRICE

A price may be based on cost (less than, same as, or more than costs), on competition (higher, the same, or lower than), on customer value (what the customer is prepared to pay), or on what one is allowed to charge when the market is regulated. It may seem odd that sometimes price is set lower than cost (called *loss leader pricing*), but this strategy is used to draw customers to the marketer in the hope that the customers will buy other, higher margin items at the same time. Some marketers set their prices lower or higher than competitors as a matter of strategy. For example, Wal-Mart is a discount mass merchandiser that prides itself on finding ways to lower, not raise, its prices. On the other hand, some cosmetics marketers charge very high prices, regardless of the actual cost of their products — they want the image of exclusive, fashionable products and believe that higher prices contribute to that image.

There are many notions about pricing. For example, some marketers believe that customers who lack product knowledge will use price as an indicator of quality. For example, when confronted with a wine list of unknown wines, a customer may think that the prices indicate the relative worth of the wines and will choose a bottle accordingly. Also, some believe that price endings are important influencers of consumer behaviour. For example, odd endings like 7 or 9 are used to indicate value, whereas even endings like 0 are meant to convey that price is not critical. Similarly, "sale" is often used with pricing to indicate that there is a bargain to be had, as in "regular price $19.95, sale price $14.99." There are so many ways to express price that sometimes customers have difficulty comparing competitive offerings; some marketers like this confusion, but others do their best to avoid it. The issues in pricing calculations will be dealt with in Section Eight, "Assessing the Marketing Program."

EXHIBIT 6

Chanel No. 5

When Gabrielle "Coco" Chanel, a fashion designer for the rich and famous, set out to create her first perfume in 1922, she knew that, in the same way that she had revolutionized the way women dressed, she would change the way women wore their fragrance. At the time, perfume was the domain of the parfumiers, and women habitually doused themselves in heavy floral scents, the only fragrances available. These natural scents were highly concentrated and faded quickly, because of their unstable molecular structure, causing the wearers to overapply them, rather than letting their own "natural fragrance" emerge. Chanel wanted a perfume that smelled like a woman, not like a flower — an abstract fragrance that enhanced, rather than masked.

After much experimentation and consultation, she was presented with ten samples. She chose No. 5 — the fifth sample, and Chanel's lucky number. This was to become the name of the perfume, as far removed as possible from the fanciful names currently in use. Chanel was told that because this perfume contained over 80 elements, including a great deal of the pricey jasmine essence, it would be extremely expensive. At that, Chanel ordered, "In that case, add more of it. I want to create the most expensive perfume in the world."

Chanel brought small bottles of No. 5 back to Paris with her to give to her most eminent clients as gifts, claiming that she barely remembered where they came from. She spritzed her fitting rooms and the air around her at social functions, knowing that her fragrance was like no other. She created a frenzied demand for the scent but claimed that it was unavailable, all the while preparing to launch its sale. When the perfume was ready for sale, Chanel at first made it available only to a few of her most privileged clients, and only through her salon. As word of the perfume spread and demand skyrocketed, she kept tight control of its distribution, and therefore of its exclusivity. She also ensured that, by distributing it to a select class, she was creating a brand association with that class.

The first and only slogan ever associated with Chanel No. 5 was "Share the Fantasy," implying that even if you are not part of the upper class, you can join it by wearing the perfume. It is, and always has been, an exclusive product and is priced at a premium (although it is no longer the most expensive — that distinction belongs to Jean Patou's Joy).

A price war occurs when competitors change price to match or undercut one another because they believe that there is an advantage to be gained. Price wars often occur when there is excess capacity relative to demand (e.g., of gasoline), when a market matures or demand is slackening (e.g., end-of-season fashion items), and when one competitor achieves a lower cost position and wants to exploit it. Price wars can be extreme. They end when all competitors stop dropping their prices because they decide there is no longer an advantage to be gained from price cuts.

Governments impose rules and regulations on pricing, which vary from country to country. Two Canadian laws are particularly noteworthy. First, it is illegal to conspire to fix prices; that is, it is illegal to get together with one's competitor to set prices. Second, it is illegal to set or attempt to impose a resale price. That means that a manufacturer cannot dictate or control the price at which a retailer sells its product; it is legal to suggest a resale price, but not to require it.

Developing and Retaining Customers

A marketer can focus attention on acquiring new customers (called prospecting) or on developing existing customers (called development and retention). Customer acquisition costs money; studies have consistently shown that it costs more to acquire a customer than to keep a customer. Retained customers often can be developed into even more valuable customers than new customers. For these reasons, it is not surprising that savvy marketers try to balance their attention between customer acquisition and customer retention and development. In these ways, marketing performance can be dramatically improved.

One way to think about customer retention (the opposite is customer defection or "churn") is in terms of the value of a customer over time. A single visit to the grocery store may only mean a transaction value of $100, or a profit of $1.50 (a net profit of 1.5 percent is considered good in grocery stores). However, that customer is worth a great deal to the store over several visits, over several years. No wonder grocery stores and other marketers have devised so many different schemes to reward their loyal, repeat customers. These loyalty programs are intended both to retain customers and to provide information about customers so that the marketers can do an even better job of attracting and serving them.

The concept of customer development means increasing the value of a customer. For example, if a customer purchases a computer printer at a computer store, that store wants to develop the customer further by selling computer software, printer cartridges, paper, and other supplies.

More than Loyalty Programs

The key to customer retention and development is not simply a clever loyalty program. Loyalty programs differ greatly. For example, a "buy 10, get the next one free" paper punch card does not provide much marketing information, whereas a sophisticated loyalty program that identifies a customer with a purchase can help develop a valuable customer database.

Customers stay and buy more from a particular marketer if they believe this gives them more value than switching their patronage to someone else. Smart marketers constantly look for ways to understand what customers expect of them (e.g., What does the customer think is good service?) and what customers want more of (e.g., Is it possible to speed up the checkout process?). With these insights, marketers can continually refine their marketing programs and maintain competitive advantage.

SECTION

EIGHT

ASSESSING THE MARKETING PROGRAM

As a marketer decides what to do to acquire, retain, and develop customers — all profitably — a marketing program is established. This program, often called a marketing plan if it is future oriented, expresses the strategy and implementation of the company's marketing effort. Fully developed, such a program says what the company is trying to do, how it will do it, and why it is worth doing. It is important to realize that there is no one "right" format for a marketing program or plan; however, there are three key criteria for assessing a good program.

DOES IT MAKE MARKET SENSE?

The first test of a proposed marketing program is whether it makes sense for the market. Is there reason to believe that the target market will respond favourably and in sufficient numbers? Is there reason to believe that consumers will regard the offer as better than competitive offers? Is there reason to believe that the trade (all members of the distribution system) will respond favourably? In other words, a marketer does a market analysis not simply for interest's sake, but rather to determine whether there is an adequate market opportunity and then to determine how to obtain it. Market information should be looked at for its implications for marketing decisions and performance. For example, if one learns that a competitor has just lowered prices 10 percent, the questions are, What does that mean for us? What are we going to do?

IS IT COMPLETE AND CONSISTENT?

The second test of a proposed marketing program is its completeness and internal consistency. Do the parts fit together well? For example, if the intent is to excel in customer service, is there adequate provision in the program for recruiting, training, and managing customer service personnel? Or if the intention is to seek customers who value high performance, does the product measure up?

DOES IT MAKE FINANCIAL SENSE?

The third test of a proposed marketing program is its financial feasibility. Marketing decisions always have financial implications, and it is important for the marketer to figure these out. Marketing activities (such as sending direct mail or deploying salespeople) cost money and are intended to bring in revenues. A marketing program should be translated into the costs expected, the investments needed, and the returns expected.

Calculating the costs involved requires a careful estimation of all the costs and then a classification of those costs into different categories. Some costs are directly related to unit volume and are called *variable costs*. For example, if each item sold required $30 of raw materials to make, that $30 is a variable cost. Or if each time an item is sold a commission of $10 is paid to the sales force, that commission is a variable cost. On the other hand, some costs do not vary (at least within a broad range) by unit volume sold; these are called *fixed costs*. For example, the marketing manager's salary may be $100,000 and not vary with changes in volume sold. The test for variable versus fixed is whether within a reasonable range the costs vary with each unit of volume. The categorization of costs helps in doing some simple calculations of feasibility, which we'll get to in a moment.

Sometimes the financial implication of a marketing decision is a change in costs; other times, it is a change in investments. For example, if the proposed marketing program requires that additional inventory be carried, that means an additional working capital investment. If additional cars or facilities must be purchased, these are fixed, depreciating investments. The test is whether the additional expenditure will appear on the income statement (a cost) or on the balance sheet (an investment). Advertising and other communication expenditures are regarded as costs, not investments. A marketer should be able to respond to the question, What will the plan require financially to undertake it?

FORECASTING

The marketer is constantly being asked to forecast sales revenue because that estimate is so crucial to every other forecast for a company, yet sales forecasting can be difficult to do with any accuracy, particularly in new situations. Sales forecasts can be prepared based on several approaches:

Previous experience (last year's results plus a change factor);

What experts say will happen (pooling of individual salespeople's forecasts);

What has happened in test markets (extending results to a bigger area); and

Judgment (what the manager thinks might happen, all things considered).

There is seldom a perfect method to forecast sales, but it is usually required of the marketer when undertaking a marketing program.

CONTRIBUTION ANALYSIS

A key question asked about a proposed marketing program is, How will this affect profitability? One way to answer this question is to prepare detailed projected statements (income statement, cash flow statement, and balance sheet) as discussed in Part 2. A faster way to do this is through contribution analysis. Both techniques should give you the same results, provided you use the same numbers and assumptions. The value of the contribution approach is that it provides a quick and straightforward way to examine relationships between price, costs, volume, and thus profit. The financial impact of a marketing program will boil down to what happens to these items.

Here are the steps to do contribution analysis:

1. Calculate the contribution per unit in dollar terms.

$$\text{Contribution per unit} = \text{Unit selling price} - \text{Unit variable costs}$$

For example, if raw materials cost $10 per unit, processing costs $20 per unit, and the selling price was $50 per unit, then the contribution per unit would be $20. Note: If dealing with a distribution system, you may have to calculate selling price and costs at various levels, perhaps to find a missing value. For example, suppose a retailer sells an item for $100 that cost it $70 to buy from a wholesaler whose margin was 25 percent. What was the manufacturer's selling price? The way to calculate this price is by constructing a logical flow diagram as follows:

	Margin	Margin
Retail selling price	$100.00	
– Retail margin	$ 30.00	30%
= Retail cost = Wholesale selling price	$ 70.00	
– Wholesaler margin	$ 17.50	25%
= Wholesaler cost = Manufacturer selling price	$ 52.50	

In other words, you construct the diagram, then calculate the missing value.

Margins are usually expressed as a percentage of selling price. Sometimes margins get expressed as a percentage of cost. It is important to ask which way a percentage margin is being expressed; in the cases in this book, unless stated otherwise, margin is expressed in terms of selling price.

2. Calculate the total fixed costs.

For example, if advertising costs were $25,000, the sales manager's salary $75,000, and the corporate overhead $200,000, then the fixed costs would be $300,000. It would be inappropriate to divide these costs by a projected unit sales volume and express them on a per unit basis as if they were variable costs. These costs do not change with volume sold (at least within a reasonable range) and thus should be treated as fixed costs.

3. Calculate the profit target.

A profit target means the amount the marketer wants to make beyond covering costs. Some people advocate doing a "break-even analysis," which means setting a profit target of zero, but rarely does a marketer want to undertake a program that returns zero profit. The profit target may be expressed in dollar terms, such as $10,000, or it may be in percentage terms, such as 10 percent of revenue. If no profit target is given, you may wish to make an assumption you regard as reasonable.

There are two approaches:

- If the profit target is expressed as total dollars, add this amount directly to the total fixed dollar costs.

- If the profit target is expressed as a percentage of revenue, calculate this percentage, add it to the unit variable costs, and recalculate the unit contribution. This has the effect of lowering the dollar contribution per unit figure.

4. Calculate the volume required to meet the profit target.

$$\text{Required volume (in units)} = \frac{\$(\text{Fixed costs} + \text{Profit target})}{\$ \text{ Unit contribution}}$$

5. Interpret the result of this scenario.

An example may help. Suppose the manufacturer's selling price is $52.50, variable costs per unit are $35, fixed costs are $100,000, and the profit target is $10,000. How many units must be sold to reach this profit target?

1. Contribution per unit = $52.50 − 35 = $17.50

2. Total fixed costs = $100,000

3. Profit target = $10,000

4. Target + Fixed costs = $10,000 + 100,000 = $110,000

5. Required volume = 110,000 / 17.50 = 6,286

Interpretation: 6,286 units sold at $52.50, costing $35 each, will cover $100,000 in fixed costs and provide $10,000 profit. We could also multiply 6,286 units by $52.50 to arrive at the required sales in dollars (which is $330,015).

SENSITIVITY ANALYSIS

The advantage of the contribution analysis approach is the speed and ease with which you can calculate another scenario. For example, what would happen if you changed the selling price to $60 and kept everything else the same? The impact would be an increase in the unit contribution of $60 − $52.50 = $7.50. This should mean that fewer units would need to be sold to cover the same fixed costs and profit target. All you have to do is calculate 110,000 / 25.00 = 4,400 units, a decrease of 30 percent in volume required.

Trying several different numbers, that is trying different contribution scenarios, is called a *sensitivity analysis*. The intent is to find out what happens to the relationships among the numbers as they are changed. For example, does increasing the selling price 10 percent have as much impact as decreasing costs by 10 percent?

Sensitivity analysis can be quickly done, for example, to assess the impact of an increase in advertising spending. Suppose the current ad budget is $300,000 and the contribution per unit is $20. A proposal is put forward to increase advertising to $440,000. How many more units must be sold to make that increase worthwhile? This analysis can be done incrementally. The proposed increase is $140,000. The $20 contribution can be thought of as the contribution toward fixed costs + profit target + incremental advertising spending. The calculation would be 140,000 / 20 = 7,000 units. In other words, the incremental advertising spending has to bring in at least an additional 7,000 units in sales to pay for itself; if it is unlikely that the additional advertising will increase sales by 7,000 units, it is not a good idea to spend it.

The usual elements to look at in a sensitivity analysis, one element at a time, are the following:

What happens if there is a price change?

What happens if there is a change in variable costs?

What happens if there is a change in fixed costs?

What happens if there is a change in the profit target?

A scenario can be constructed for each change. This helps the marketer assess whether making the change is a good idea or how a possible change (such as an increase in manufacturing costs that might be anticipated) will affect the financial feasibility of the marketing program.

WHAT MIGHT HAPPEN VERSUS WHAT WILL HAPPEN

None of the calculations in contribution analysis and sensitivity analysis are forecasts or guarantees of what will happen. They are only numbers calculated in relation to one another. For example, when we calculated above that we needed to sell 6,286 units at $52.50 to hit the profit target, this doesn't mean this will actually happen. Interpretation and judgment are required to see if this is the likely outcome. If, for example, the total market is estimated to be 100,000 units per year, we could calculate target market share at 6,286 / 100000 x 100 = 6.3 percent share.

Is this reasonable to expect? If no competitor has over 5 percent share and we are new to the category, this may be a stretch. If, on the other hand, test market results showed a 40 percent preference for our product over all others, this may be achievable. It is a judgment call until it is actually tried.

The important point is to try to figure out the financial implications of marketing decisions. There is considerable uncertainty about such forecasts, but nonetheless they help everyone in making firm plans for the future.

LEARNING FOR NEXT TIME

Marketing is not a science. It is impossible to anticipate all the things that happen in the marketplace and to sort out all the factors that affect marketing performance. For these reasons, a savvy marketer constantly endeavours to learn from experience. What happened last time, and most important, why? Even partial answers help the marketer make better decisions in the future.

One major set of tools for decision making is market research techniques. Marketing research may be used to explore, to explain, to predict, or to monitor marketing. For example, marketers might use focus groups (small groups of about eight people at a time) to explore how customers think about a product or a store and thus gain some insights into how to improve. Or they might use a survey to gauge satisfaction with service performance and thus predict retention of customers. Or one might track repeat purchase rates through a customer database driven by point-of-sale systems to assess a loyalty program. In each instance, the marketers are asking focused questions about the market or the marketing program and seeking answers in a systematic way. There are a host of research methods, but the essence is providing good answers to questions that help marketers make better decisions. This detective work is a critical part of the marketer's job. Good marketing programs always have a market research component so that learning about the market is continuous.

EXHIBIT 7

The Special Case of Social and Nonprofit Marketing

At the outset of this chapter, mention was made of nonprofit marketing, but the chapter has focused on profit-oriented marketing. Marketing is an approach to deciding what to offer to whom — a set of activities to make promises and to deliver. In that sense, marketing can apply to art galleries, symphonies, blood donor clinics, political candidates, and charitable drives. There are five major differences between profit and nonprofit marketing management.

1. The performance dimensions often differ. Whereas a profit-oriented marketer may wish to sell as much product to make as much money as possible, a social marketer may be trying to change behaviour (e.g., promote wearing condoms for safe sex) and an arts marketer may be trying to educate (e.g., expose a certain percentage of the public to an exhibition and thus educate them about an aspect of history). Marketers need a purpose (a performance objective), but it need not be profit.

2. Most profit-oriented marketers gain their revenue by selling something to a customer, who gives them money in return. In nonprofit marketing, often the exchange

of money is less straightforward. For example, a museum marketer may engage in fundraising to gain revenue from sponsors in order to provide a program to a public that pays little or nothing for admission. This separation of sponsorship from benefits to clients is very common in nonprofit marketing and means that such marketers require multiple marketing programs, for example, to attract sponsorship and to attract audience.

3. Many nonprofit organizations are resistant to using marketing terminology. Arts organizations and social agencies prefer to think about clients, audience, and visitors rather than customers, to think about information campaigns rather than advertising and promotion, and so on.

4. Many nonprofit organizations are not organized in the same way as profit-oriented organizations. Instead of a marketing or sales manager, there may be someone in charge of programming who also deals with marketing. More commonly, there may be several people who have overlapping interests in the marketing function and, thus, need to coordinate their marketing efforts.

5. Many nonprofit organizations have few resources explicitly available for marketing activities. The challenge in such situations is either to persuade other people to reallocate money (e.g., in a museum, to take money from exhibit development and use it for audience attraction) or to find creative ways to accomplish marketing objectives with little money (e.g., to harness volunteers as salespeople).

SUMMARY

Marketing is all about connecting an organization to customers. It requires:

> *Discipline,* to remember that customers are not all alike (and usually quite unlike the marketer) and to go through the analytical steps to ensure good understanding of the marketing situation and alternative approaches;

> *Creativity,* to discover new ways of attracting and developing customers; and

> *Courage* to take action in an uncertain, competitive environment.

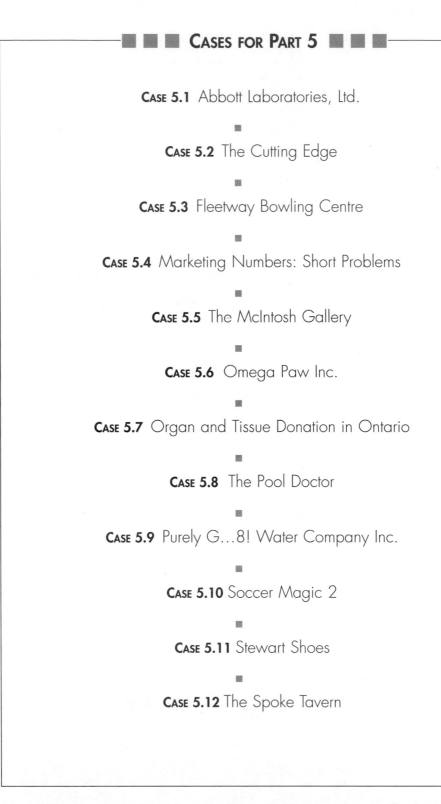

■ ■ ■ CASES FOR PART 5 ■ ■ ■

CASE 5.1 Abbott Laboratories, Ltd.

■

CASE 5.2 The Cutting Edge

■

CASE 5.3 Fleetway Bowling Centre

■

CASE 5.4 Marketing Numbers: Short Problems

■

CASE 5.5 The McIntosh Gallery

■

CASE 5.6 Omega Paw Inc.

■

CASE 5.7 Organ and Tissue Donation in Ontario

■

CASE 5.8 The Pool Doctor

■

CASE 5.9 Purely G…8! Water Company Inc.

■

CASE 5.10 Soccer Magic 2

■

CASE 5.11 Stewart Shoes

■

CASE 5.12 The Spoke Tavern

CASE 5.1 ABBOTT LABORATORIES, LTD.

By Elizabeth Grasby and Kristina Krupka

It was early March 1996, and Andrew Kerr, senior product manager at Abbott Laboratories, Ltd., in Montreal, had to quickly develop an appropriate marketing plan to launch Abbott's ground-breaking drug, Norvir, into Canada. Norvir, which had just been released in the United States, was used to treat patients with the human immunodeficiency virus (HIV). Canadian legislation prevented drug companies from marketing products directly to the end consumer, and Kerr knew this would have implications for his marketing plan.

HEALTH CARE IN CANADA

Canada had a publicly financed, privately delivered health care system known as Medicare. When Canadians needed medical care, they went to the physician or clinic of their choice and presented their personal health insurance card issued to all eligible residents of a province. Canadians did not pay directly for insured hospital and physicians' services. Medicare was financed primarily through taxation, in the form of provincial and federal personal and corporate income taxes.

Pharmaceutical companies made every effort to ensure that their products were paid for by either the government drug plan or the private firm plans, such as insurance companies or drug plan companies. When a new drug was launched, each provincial government decided whether to place that drug on formulary — the list of drugs that the government would pay for. Every provincial formulary was different, and applications had to be made in every province. In Ontario, the government paid for seniors' and welfare and social assistance recipients' drugs. If a patient in Ontario did not fall into one of these categories, then the patient had to pay for the drugs personally and submit for reimbursement by his or her insurance company or company drug plan. The provinces of Quebec and British Columbia had universal drug coverage — all drugs were paid for by the government plans for all residents of that province, as long as the drug was listed on the provincial formulary. Approximately 80 percent of HIV and acquired immune deficiency syndrome (AIDS) patients' drugs were paid for by government formulary plans.

HIV/AIDS PATIENTS

The largest group of persons living with HIV were men between the ages of 25 and 40. In 1995, the largest-growing segment of HIV-infected persons included women and children.

Once diagnosed with HIV, patients relied heavily on pharmaceutical products to help slow the progression of the disease to prolong life. Some patients would take as many as 20 to 40 pills a day. Many of these pills had specific dosage requirements, causing frustration for the patient. For example, some drugs required that a patient fast before or after taking them, while others had to be taken with food. Most drugs had to be taken at a specific hour and perhaps with certain water requirements. If the regimen was not strictly adhered to, the patient could experience severe side effects or the patient's immune system could become resistant to the drugs. These regimens created much confusion among patients; thus, many stopped taking their medication when the quality of their life was significantly affected. Patients preferred taking as few pills as possible with the least side effects so that their treatment left them able to lead as normal a life as possible. Most pills were quite large, and this made it difficult for children and for those patients with advanced AIDS to swallow their pills. These patients preferred liquid oral solutions.

HIV AND AIDS

AIDS is a disease that gradually destroys the body's immune defence system and makes the body vulnerable to opportunistic infections, such as pneumonia or bronchitis. It is caused by infection of HIV. An individual's immune system may fight HIV for a number of years before that person develops full-blown AIDS. Currently, there is no known cure for HIV.

To date, an estimated 20 million people worldwide have been HIV infected. Within Canada, from 1985 to 1995, 33,520 HIV positive cases were detected, with 46 percent of cases detected in Ontario, 18 percent in British Columbia, and 24 percent in Quebec. Recent data indicated that the number of AIDS cases in Canada had levelled off in the period 1993–1995, and the 1996 AIDS incidence showed a decline for the first time in history. It was believed this trend reflected new treatments, preventive education, and overall better management of the disease.[1]

HIV/AIDS HEALTH CARE COSTS

In 1994, it was estimated that treating an AIDS patient in hospital cost the public health system $1,000 per day, and the average hospital stay was 15 days.[2] It was difficult to predict whether the cost of AIDS care would rise or fall in the coming years. Although the number of AIDS cases had levelled off, health care costs could rise as new treatments became available and patients lived longer. On the other hand, costs could just as easily fall, since patients were increasingly being treated in residential settings, where care was approximately $500 a day less than a hospital stay.[3]

ABBOTT LABORATORIES, LTD.

Abbott Laboratories, Ltd., (Abbott) incorporated in 1900, was one of the world's leading health care companies. With operations in more than 50 countries, Abbott researched, developed, and marketed pharmaceutical, diagnostic, nutritional, and hospital products. Abbott's Canadian sales of pharmaceutical products were $135 million in 1996, placing it 11th in total sales among its competitors.[4]

HIV/AIDS TREATMENT

Although there was much to learn about HIV and AIDS, research had made important progress in treating those people infected. One category of HIV/AIDS treatments included drugs using new protease inhibitors.

In the drug class of protease inhibitors, there were three products being prepared for launch in Canada:

Norvir

Norvir was discovered in Chicago by a team of Abbott researchers in 1995. The drug was considered a breakthrough in treatment and received (at the time) the most expedient drug approval in the history of the United States Food and Drug Administration. In a six-month study of 1,090 patients in the United States, Europe, and Australia, Norvir decreased disease progression or delayed death by approximately 50 percent. Abbott had acquired patent protection on Norvir until the year 2015.

Norvir was available in capsules and in an oral solution. Patients were required to take a total of 12 pills a day. A major advantage of Norvir was its simple dosage requirements: Norvir could be taken with or without food and needed to be administered only twice daily, compared with similar drugs that required dosage every eight hours. Norvir had to be refrigerated when not being taken. This was a disadvantage because it created some inconvenience for the patient and had implications for the distribution and storage of the product.

It was recommended that Norvir be used in combination with other drugs for maximum benefit. When launched into the marketplace, the total cost per year for the patient would be $5,848.

Norvir had recently been launched in the United States. Side effects, which included nausea, vomiting, and diarrhea, were considered transient and dose related; however, Norvir's competitors, who were still in the prelaunch phase, were flooding the market with news that Norvir could not be tolerated. Patients and physicians were becoming leery of the product because of these reported side effects. In order to help patients cope with these side effects, a more gradual dosage schedule was developed. Even with the new dosage schedule, it was expected that sales representatives would have difficulty convincing doctors and patients that side effects could be managed.

Crixivan

Abbott's main competitor of Norvir was Crixivan, developed by Merck Frosst, the third-largest multinational pharmaceutical company in the world. Crixivan had been in its prelaunch phase for one year now, was being prepared for an October 1996 launch in Canada, and was due out the next month in the United States.

Crixivan was as efficacious[5] as Norvir, but Crixivan had to be administered every eight hours with both food and minimum water requirements. It was being positioned as the "no side effects" drug, because it did not have the side effects of

Norvir; however, kidney stones could develop in the long term in some patients. Crixivan would be priced at $5,900 per patient per year.

Invirase

Hoffman-La Roche had also developed a protease inhibitor, named Invirase, expected to be in the Canadian market by April 1996.

Invirase had been prelaunched in a Compassionate User Program in Canada in 1995. In this program, 1,000 patients were given Invirase free of charge. These programs acted as clinical studies so that more information could be acquired on the drug, its side effects, and interactions with other drugs. When the program terminated, and if the results were positive, the pool of test patients would become a market of 1,000 paying consumers.

Invirase had to be administered every eight hours. Its side effects were limited, but its results showed that it was not as efficacious as Norvir or Crixivan. It was estimated that Invirase would cost the patient $5,950 per year.

Kerr estimated the current market for protease inhibitors to be 10,000 patients. He knew the actual market was greater than 10,000 patients; however, some patients had not yet been diagnosed, others had been diagnosed but were healthy and thus did not require powerful drug treatments, and still others were using alternative forms of treatments (i.e., nonpharmaceutical products).

OTHER STAKEHOLDERS

Advocacy Groups

Since it was illegal in Canada for pharmaceutical companies to advertise directly to consumers (it was legal to do so in the United States), patient advocacy groups became important partners for drug companies. Pharmaceutical companies educated these advocacy groups about diseases, drug developments, side effects, and so on, and promoted the merits of the company's products so that, in turn, patients could be educated about new treatments. Most of this information was transferred through newsletters or the Internet. The provision of corporate funding for education and research, as well as the sponsoring of AIDS events, enhanced the reputation of a pharmaceutical company from the advocacy groups' perspective.

Physicians

All physicians relied on the results of clinical studies, published research, recommendations by specialists at major conferences, or first-hand experience with the drug (if any) before deciding on the appropriate drug therapy.

HIV and AIDS Specialists

HIV and AIDS specialists included either researchers in HIV or infectious disease specialists. Specialists were key to educating the entire medical community, since they were viewed as leading researchers in the disease area. Specialists would frequently make presentations to the medical community about disease and treatments and were usually paid an honorarium by the pharmaceutical company for this presentation.

Pharmacists

Pharmacists were an important group of purchasers of pharmaceuticals. Pharmacists were influenced by sales visits and pharmacy education programs, in which leading pharmacists would lecture on a particular class of drugs.

Government and Insurance Companies

In an effort to reduce health care costs, provincial governments were beginning to restrict the number of drugs placed on formulary each year. In order to be placed on formulary, pharmaceutical companies had to demonstrate the efficacy, safety, and cost effectiveness of their new drug; that is, the cost of the medication should offset other health care costs, such as hospital stays and doctors' visits. The pharmaceutical firm's marketing department and market access personnel were instrumental in preparing and presenting the cost effectiveness data, as well as building relationships with government, insurance, and drug plan officials.

THE LAUNCH

Abbott's objectives for Norvir were aggressive — to achieve a profit and gain 30 to 40 percent market share within the first year of launch. With the full launch of Norvir only six months away, Kerr was faced with a daunting task. He had to determine how Norvir would be positioned relative to its competition to develop the marketing message.

The annual Vancouver AIDS Conference was scheduled for July. Health care professionals and resource people from across North America convened at this event to exchange the latest information on the spread of the disease, prevention, and counselling and treatment of patients and families affected by AIDS. In addition to attending this conference, Kerr had several ideas about how to boost customer relations, including providing funding and sponsorship money to patient advocacy groups, developing patient and clinical educational materials, and setting up Abbott's home page on the Internet with current drug use information.

Kerr wondered what his campaign should entail. Specifically, what should the marketing message be, which promotional activities should he undertake, and on which key stakeholders should efforts be concentrated?

NOTES

1. "AIDS in Canada: Quarterly Surveillance Update," *Health Canada*, May 1997, 1.
2. "Updated Forecasts of the Cost of Medicare for Persons with AIDS, 1989–1994," *Public Health Reports*, Vol. 105, No. 1, 1994.
3. "Where All That AIDS Money Is Going," *Fortune*, 7 February 1997.
4. *Canadian Pharmaceutical Industry Review 1996*, IMF Canada, May 1997.
5. Producing the desired effect.

C A S E 5.2   THE CUTTING EDGE

By Greg Mason and Michael R. Pearce

During the school winter break of 1991, Greg Mason was sitting at his desk and looking at the movie posters around the office. Although he had joined Metro Goldwyn Mayer (MGM) as a marketing intern less than a week ago, he had already been given leeway in creating new promotions for the upcoming MGM release *The Cutting Edge*. Sharon Kasey, publicity and promotions director, had instructed Greg to obtain "free" promotions through numerous organizations by giving away advance screening passes. Greg was enthusiastic about being able to use his creativity in this assignment.

MGM AND THE MOVIE INDUSTRY

The extremely competitive film industry released an average of three new movies every Friday to audiences worldwide. Warner Brothers, Paramount, Columbia Tri-Star Pictures, Alliance, Universal, Twentieth Century Fox, and Buena Vista were all fierce rivals who spent millions of dollars each year producing major motion pictures. A lower budget film cost under $10 million to produce, and the most expensive film to date, *Terminator II: Judgement Day*, had cost over $110 million. An average film cost $28 million. Lower grossing films generally played in major urban centres for an average of four weeks, with higher grossing films often lasting for over 20 weeks. Films were later released on videocassette and shown on pay-television channels. Timing for video releases depended on the success of the film.

MGM began making motion pictures in 1924 and was legendary for its trademark, Leo the lion, roaring at the beginning of each of its films. Making films under its philosophy, "Make it good. Make it big and give it class," MGM was a film industry giant and had brought hundreds of film classics to the big screen, including *Gone with the Wind, Singing in the Rain, The Wizard of Oz, Dr. Zhivago,* and *Mutiny on the Bounty*. In the 1960s the company began to boast that "MGM has more stars than there are in the heavens." United Artists, which fell under the MGM umbrella, created all James Bond, Pink Panther, and Rocky motion pic-

---

tures. In recent years, MGM had produced many highly successful films, including *Thelma and Louise, Rain Man, A Fish Called Wanda,* and *Moonstruck.*

MGM CANADA

Although based in Los Angeles, California, MGM had offices worldwide. Film titles, posters, and previews were created in Los Angeles, and regional offices implemented these marketing tools. All marketing for Canadian releases was coordinated at the Toronto office, which was divided into three areas: sales and accounting, advertising, and publicity and promotions. Sales arranged theatre release locations and preview screenings across Canada, while advertising coordinated all radio, print, and television advertising.

Publicity and promotions handled all press coverage areas by providing print and electronic press kits. In addition, this department created "free" promotions. An organization or retailer would often gladly display posters or be supportive of an MGM film in return for passes that it could give away to its clientele. For example, MGM could give passes to a radio station in return for free on-air "plugs" from the station's disc jockeys as they gave the passes away. These passes, each of which admitted two people, were then used to provide audiences for advance screenings, which created awareness of the film prior to its release. This system provided lots of publicity for new films. Ideally, MGM sought publicity that would include in-store signage (posters), point-of-purchase displays in high traffic areas, and contests to give away the advance passes. The department had two full-time people devoted to these functions: Sharon Kasey, director; and David Brand, coordinator.

MARKETING INTERNS

Publicity and promotions accepted unpaid student interns, who were given an exclusive opportunity to design cross-Canada promotions for movies, as well as receiving free movie passes and posters. For MGM, the student interns provided fresh ideas and new perspectives toward promoting films. In return, MGM provided its successful interns with excellent recommendations and assisted in placing them in starting positions within the film industry.

Greg Mason, a 1993 honours bachelor of arts candidate in business administration at the Western Business School (now the Richard Ivey School of Business), had a strong interest in marketing. Over the winter break in 1991, he joined MGM as a student intern with the intention of gaining marketing experience to build his résumé.

On his first day, Sharon Kasey informed him that he would be setting up promotions for the upcoming winter release *The Cutting Edge*. Exhibits 1 and 2 show scenes from the film. She showed Greg the one-sheet (movie poster), which had been designed in Los Angeles, and she also gave him a copy of the press release in order for him to become more familiar with the film. The following section contains excerpts from the press release:

THE CUTTING EDGE

Doug Dorsey is the star of the United States Olympic hockey team. Combining power and skill with a competitive spirit and a brash attitude, he is usually treated to a front row seat in the penalty box. His shot at Olympic gold and a bright future in the National Hockey League, however, is fleeting. Blindsided by an overzealous opponent, losing his peripheral vision, Doug now skates on his local small-town hockey team, his life punctuated by apologetic rejection letters from once beckoning NHL teams.

Kate Moseley embodies the athleticism and grace that have spotlighted her as one of the most talented and beautiful pairs figure skaters in the world. Off the ice, however, her sharp tongue, prima donna behaviour, and hopelessly high standards have made it impossible for her to keep a partner. One is too tall, one too short; one sweats too much, one not enough ... Her coach, the legendary Anton Pamchenko, has reached the bottom of the barrel, so he looks in another barrel — and finds Doug.

The pairing of Moseley and Dorsey changes the face of figure skating forever. In a sport that demands cooperation and harmony, the only thing these two headstrong athletes do in unison is fight. Through the rigorous training and tedious practices, to the scenic drama of the 1992 Winter Olympics figure skating competition, a "rink rat" rivalry of comic and romantic proportions ensues.

PROMOTING THE CUTTING EDGE

The Cutting Edge, which would be released on March 27, 1992, had been filmed in Hamilton and Toronto during the summer of 1991, under the direction of Paul Michael Glaser of TV's Starsky and Hutch. The stars were D.B. Sweeney and Moira Kelly; however, the fact that they were both relative unknowns made promotions all the more difficult, as movies were often driven by the stars' reputations. This film was aimed at a young audience, mostly teenagers, who would be attracted by the poster's slogan, "The Ultimate Love/Skate Relationship." Success would be rated on a province-by-province basis.

David Brand explained that the advance screenings would be held in Canada's seven major markets: Montreal, Ottawa, Toronto, Winnipeg, Edmonton, Calgary, and Vancouver. There were 45 advance screenings planned, as outlined in Exhibit 3. These would be held in downtown and suburban theatres, with capacities ranging from 180 to 400 seats. The number of passes given out was adjusted according to a theatre's capacity, but not everyone who received an advance pass would use it; therefore, MGM would give away significantly more passes than there were available seats. This practice is termed "filler," and the degree of filler varies depending on the film. David Brand suggested that The Cutting Edge would require 180 percent filler for early screenings and would drop down to 110 percent as advertising and awareness of the film increased for screenings closer to the release date.

After showing Greg a video with excerpts from The Cutting Edge to increase his familiarity with the film, David Brand instructed him to give away as many passes as he wished under at least one of the following criteria:

1. Passes were to be given away to create advance awareness. Therefore, they should be given to groups and organizations that would likely enjoy the film's content.

2. Passes were to be given to groups that would provide exciting, new free promotions, such as giveaways, and in so doing, reach the target market.

Greg had to determine whom to approach and how. As well, he had to decide how many passes he should give away. In addition, he had received other promotional items that would increase awareness for the film, including pens, jerseys, and mini-posters. Recalling the MGM philosophy of "Make it good. Make it big and give it class," Greg knew that *The Cutting Edge* provided him with an excellent opportunity to create exciting promotions. Not knowing where to begin, he asked David Brand what type of promotions were usually done. David responded, "It's always something new every time. Be creative and have fun."

EXHIBIT 1
Scenes
***from* The**
Cutting
Edge

Source: MGM, Publicity and Promotions, Toronto.

EXHIBIT 2
Scenes
***from* The**
Cutting
Edge

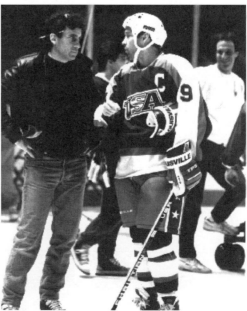

Source: MGM, Publicity and Promotions, Toronto.

EXHIBIT **3**

Advance Screenings Schedule				
February	13	Toronto Montreal Winnipeg	Vancouver Calgary	Edmonton Ottawa
	19	Toronto		
	20	Toronto Montreal	Vancouver	
	26	Toronto		
	27	Toronto Montreal Winnipeg	Vancouver Calgary	Edmonton Ottawa
March	2	Toronto Montreal	Vancouver	
	4	Toronto		
	5	Toronto Montreal	Vancouver	
	9	Toronto		
	11	Toronto Montreal Winnipeg	Vancouver Calgary	Edmonton Ottawa
	16	Toronto	Vancouver	
	18	Toronto Montreal		
	23			Ottawa
	25	Toronto Montreal Winnipeg	Vancouver Calgary	Edmonton

C A S E 5.3   FLEETWAY BOWLING CENTRE

By Elizabeth Grasby and Lisa A. Luinenburg

In early March 1994, Harvey Katz, member of the ESAM Group and manager of Fleetway Bowling Centre in London, Ontario, was approached by his bowling alley software supplier about a new program that could combine bowling with the game of bingo. Harvey wondered if "Bingo-Bowling" would be a good move for Fleetway, considering the negative public perception toward bingo. If he chose to go ahead with supplying the program for his 12 five-pin lanes, many decisions regarding the marketing plan would have to be resolved, including whom to target, what media to choose, and whether this opportunity would be financially attractive for Fleetway.

GENERAL BACKGROUND

The ESAM Group, a commercial development firm, was established in the late 1950s by Sam Katz and a partner. ESAM took over Fleetway Bowling Lanes in 1959, when the previous owners could not cover rental payments. During the next 30 years, Fleetway encountered financial problems as bowling continuously declined in popularity since the mid-1970s. Little was done in the way of marketing and improvements to the operation. Fleetway was perceived as an unclean, old, and "boring" place to go. Sam continued to support the lanes because of his interest in the game and his desire to provide a recreational facility for ESAM's many tenants in the surrounding area.

In 1976, Sam moved Fleetway from its strip mall location to an area just west of ESAM's housing developments. The new and much larger facility, Fleetway 40 Bowling Centre (Fleetway), offered 40 five-pin lanes. With increased marketing efforts, Fleetway eventually showed small profits in 1989. Prices reached an all-time high in 1994 of $2.75 per game (adult), $2 per game (children) for five-pin and $3 per game (adult), $2 per game (children) for ten-pin. In addition to this cost, bowling shoes could be rented for $1.75 (adult) and $1 (children). These costs were comparable to Fleetway's competitors' prices.

HARVEY KATZ

After graduating from the administrative and commercial studies program in Finance at the University of Western Ontario, Harvey Katz briefly worked as a life insurance salesman. Persuaded by his father to join the family business, Harvey soon took over as manager of ESAM's many properties. In 1990, he became responsible for Fleetway's operations.

Harvey looked forward to the challenge of changing Fleetway's image. He wanted to create a recreational facility that was fun for the whole family and for all age groups. He believed that, with the right marketing mix, there was no reason why the facility could not become very profitable.

Upon assuming his new position, Harvey discovered three things: the importance of a clean and updated facility, the consumer's expectations for computerized automatic scoring, and the growing demand for ten-pin bowling in Canada. To address these needs at Fleetway, Harvey hired an interior designer to redecorate and create a more "family" type of atmosphere. He constantly changed and improved Fleetway's surroundings with biannual renovations and new decor. The highest standards of cleanliness were demanded from Fleetway's employees inside and outside the building. Computerized scoring was introduced to each lane, making Fleetway the second bowling alley in London with such technology. Lastly, Harvey switched over 12 lanes from five-pin bowling to ten-pin bowling.

More changes followed with the introduction of billiard tables, a profitable snack bar (with 40 percent margins on the average selling price), monthly draws for Blue Jay tickets or weekend vacations, free giveaways, Halloween and New Year's Eve parties, and "Midnight Madness" bowling — a feature in which bowlers competed for prizes by making designated shots. These changes accompanied a new focus on customer satisfaction and service that led Harvey and Fleetway to win the "Best Quest Gold Award" in 1993, a local award granted for exceptional customer service. Profits increased in the early 1990s, reaching an all-time high in 1992.

THE BOWLING INDUSTRY: 1950s TO PRESENT

Typically known as a blue-collar sport, bowling achieved its peak popularity in the 1950 to early 1960s. During this period, bowling alley construction flourished in North America. The sport became a favourite social event for North American families, both through leagues and through recreational activity. Its popularity was the result of its appeal to all age groups and its relatively inexpensive price. Additionally, bowling was one of only a few alternatives available for social recreation at this time.

Participation in bowling declined and many alleys were forced to close throughout the following decade. The sport was considered an "uncool" and "boring" thing to do, especially by the younger generation. Since alleys were forced to increase their prices to cover higher fixed costs, bowling quickly became too expensive for the average worker and his or her family.

Consumer appeal increased slightly in the mid-1970s when "automatic pin set-up" technology was introduced. Demand eventually levelled off and weakened in the 1980s and early 1990s. Bowling was now competing with many other pursuits for the recreational dollar in a declining economy.

THE CONSUMER

Bowlers spanned all ages, with the majority occupying the 35 to 59 age group. This adult category was the largest, constituting approximately two-thirds of all bowlers. The golden age group (65 years or older) was the second-largest adult category, representing 18 percent of all bowlers. (See Exhibit 1 for a consumer profile of bowlers in Canada.)

There were two types of participants: league players and recreational/open play bowlers. In 1993, there were approximately 130,000 five- and ten-pin league bowlers and 1.9 million recreational bowlers in Canada. Both groups shared similar demographics. The main differentiation distinguishing these groups was frequency of play. While league players played on average 1.2 times per week, recreational/open play bowlers bowled as infrequently as once per year, often in groups as part of a social event organized by a church, high school, university, club, and so on. Canadian league play had been steadily declining in popularity since the mid-1970s, whereas recreational bowling had been rising.

Leagues consisted of both five- and ten-pin games. A typical league season consisted of 32 weeks from September to April. While the standard ten-pin game was the preferred league sport around the world, Canadians favoured the five-pin game. Invented in 1905 by Canadian businessmen, five-pin bowling was a faster-paced game that could be played over the lunch hour. It was also an easier game for women, since the ball size was significantly smaller. In 1994, 70 percent of all league bowlers in Canada were five-pin bowlers. Accordingly, the ratio of ten- and five-pin lanes across Canada was 30:70.[1]

COMPETITION

In 1994, competition for the London bowling dollar was intense. Of the eight competitors, three offered ten-pin bowling exclusively, three offered only five-pin, and just two offered both games. (For competitors' geographical locations, see Exhibit 2.)

Fleetway's major competitor was Southland Bowling Alleys. As part of a large U.S. chain that also manufactured bowling equipment, Southland had the financial support and marketing expertise of its head office. An extremely large facility with 32 ten-pin lanes, Southland was the first fully computer-automated bowling facility in London. Its management was staffed with professional bowlers who had a solid understanding of market trends. Southland housed many strong leagues and open bowling. It also offered a bar and pinball facilities.

Fleetway's other ten-pin competitors — Huron Bowl, Centre Bowlarama, and Royal Bowl — had various advantages and disadvantages. Huron, the third to fully computer automate its facilities, had strong league play, affiliation with a large parent company, 32 ten-pin lanes, a bar, and pinball facilities. It did very little marketing, and the building had not been updated for many years. Centre Bowlarama had 12 computer-automated ten-pin lanes and 12 standard five-pin lanes, good management, chain affiliation, a liquor licence, and excellent merchandising and marketing skills. Royal Bowl, with 32 ten-pin lanes, was the newest competitor, having been only a year in operation. It was a fully computerized and modernized licensed facility with a great location. Each ten-pin competitor had unique weaknesses, ranging from poor marketing; stale, outdated facilities or upstairs facilities in poor locations (economically depressed areas of London); and poor management.

Fleetway's competitors in the five-pin game were Fairmont, Eastown Lanes, and the London Bowl-A-Rama. Fleetway and its competitors appeared to be suffering from the decline in popularity of the five-pin game. Fleetway's competitors were fully licensed and had pinball facilities with manual scoring. Fairmont was a friendly, family-operated business with a good location in the basement of a plaza with strong league play. Eastown, with 16 lanes, was also located in a plaza. The last competitor, London Bowl-A-Rama, with 24 lanes, was well managed and appeared to be holding its own in five-pin play. Recently, another exclusive five-pin competitor, Plaza Lanes and Billiards, had gone out of business. Fleetway's five-pin competitors faced some disadvantages, including old furnishings and outdated decor, poor locations (customers had to climb stairs), and outdated equipment.

BINGO-BOWLING

The game of "Bingo-Bowling" was a computerized team sport played across two or more bowling lanes. Unlike regular bowling in which an individual tried to achieve the highest score, Bingo-Bowling required participants to block out their lane's bingo card faster than their competitors (see Exhibit 3 for a sample card and rules). Each lane's team consisted of one to six players. Whenever a certain point combination was achieved (strike, spare, 13 points, etc.), the required element was erased automatically on the electronic bingo card. Bingo-Bowling was a much faster-paced game than regular bowling, since it was a race to beat your competitor in blocking out your card. The amount of time spent per game depended on the bingo card selected, as they ranged in the level of difficulty.

Harvey believed that Bingo-Bowling could help solve some of his current problems. A growing consumer preference for ten-pin was leaving five-pin lanes unused, especially on weeknights after 9:00, when league play finished. Fleetway was also having problems attracting young adults to the facility. Harvey saw a great opportunity to tap the university market, since the University of Western Ontario (UWO) serviced 28,000 full- and part-time students and was only kilometres from Fleetway. According to a survey of this market conducted for Fleetway, students were not recurrent bowlers (see Exhibit 4). Most participants in the survey characterized bowling as an "uncool way" to spend an evening. However, when asked to rate their enjoyment after a bowling experience, students described it as "fun," "entertaining," and "a completely different experience from a regular night out." Although Harvey believed it would be very difficult to change this group's general attitude toward bowling, he thought the more competitive game of Bingo-Bowling might entice them to become more frequent patrons of Fleetway.

In order to measure student reaction to the game, Harvey initiated a focus group study with six groups of university students. After coming in for a free trial of Bingo-Bowling, they filled out a questionnaire (see Exhibit 5 for their responses). Overall, the feedback was favourable. In particular, the participants enjoyed competing against their friends and acquaintances.

THE DECISION   Harvey wondered if Bingo-Bowling should be introduced at Fleetway. He was concerned about the image that Bingo portrayed: "When I think of Bingo halls, I think of smoky, unclean, shady establishments full of people playing a game they can't afford." Since Harvey believed many others agreed with his perception of Bingo, he didn't want to introduce a game whose name could jeopardize the family image he had tried to develop at Fleetway. Harvey stated:

> I'm scared of doing things without a thoroughly thought-out plan. Public perception is so important in this business, as word-of-mouth spreads so quickly. If we introduce this game in a hard-sell campaign with lots of advertising and promotion and there are still kinks in the game, we may never be able to recover. However, I don't know if a slow and soft sell approach will get people in to try it.

Other decisions included developing some type of schedule for the lanes: Should Bingo-Bowling be offered nightly or on designated days or nights? Should prizes be awarded to the winners? Harvey wondered what pricing strategy to pursue for this new game. Although regular bowling was priced by the game, this might not be appropriate for Bingo-Bowling. A game of Bingo-Bowling, depending on the card, could take anywhere from 20 minutes to 1 1/2 hours. In addition, if Harvey decided to take a more aggressive approach in targeting university students, he would need to formulate a marketing scheme attractive to these students. One possibility Harvey was considering was using the London Transit Commission to bus students to and from the university to Fleetway, at a cost of $100 an evening. It sounded like a good idea, but he didn't know if it would work. Harvey believed he currently didn't have the connections on UWO campus to do an effective job marketing to student groups. He thought hiring a student coordinator might provide Fleetway with a closer relationship with UWO clubs, residences, and faculties. He had no idea what to pay this person or what this position would entail.

The cost of supplying Fleetway's 12 lanes with the Bingo-Bowling software program would be $50 per lane. The lanes could still be used for five-pin bowling at any time. Harvey spent $30,000 on advertising last year and had no idea how much to allocate to Bingo-Bowling. Other costs would include promotion, advertising, and prizes (See Exhibit 6 for a list of options).

Decisions needed to be made soon if Fleetway was to proceed. Harvey would have to decide on a price, determine whether the product should be aimed at league or recreational bowlers, plan a promotional campaign, and formulate a successful implementation plan. He wondered what would be the most effective plan to introduce Bingo-Bowling to the London market. He wanted to have the plan in place by September for the university market.

NOTE

1. Canadian Five-Pin Association and Ontario Five-Pin Association.

EXHIBIT 1

CANADIAN BOWLING DEMOGRAPHICS
(League and Recreational)

AGE

Group	%
3 to 24	7
25 to 34	10
35 to 59	65
60+	18

MARITAL STATUS

Status	%
Single	29
Married	71

INCOME GROUPS

Income	%
Under $20,000	6
$20,000 to $40,000	36
$40,000 to $50,000	4
$50,000+	27
No response	25

OCCUPATION

Type	%
Sales	8
Homemakers	18
Administration	14
Trades	22
Farming	2
Service	4
Executives	6
Retired	10
No response	10

GENDER

Sex	%
Female	50
Male	50

EDUCATION LEVEL

Level	%
Attended high school	33
Finished high school	33
Attended postsecondary	16
Finished postsecondary	8
No response	10

Source: Canadian Five-Pin Association.

Exhibit 2
**Competition in
the London
Bowling Market**

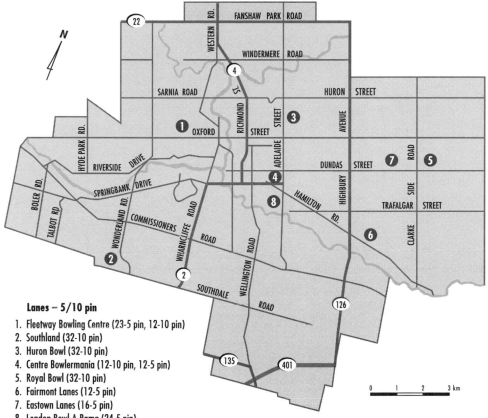

Lanes – 5/10 pin

1. Fleetway Bowling Centre (23-5 pin, 12-10 pin)
2. Southland (32-10 pin)
3. Huron Bowl (32-10 pin)
4. Centre Bowlermania (12-10 pin, 12-5 pin)
5. Royal Bowl (32-10 pin)
6. Fairmont Lanes (12-5 pin)
7. Eastown Lanes (16-5 pin)
8. London Bowl-A-Rama (24-5 pin)

Exhibit 3

Bingo-Bowling Sample Card and Rules

OBJECT: The object of Bingo-Bowling is to clear your lane's bingo card faster than any other competing lane.

RULES
1. Divide yourselves into teams of equal size.
2. Player one shall attempt to score one of the point combinations on his/her bingo card with up to three balls.
3. If the score is a strike or a spare, the square will be deleted from the card automatically. However, if the score is one of the other possible point combinations, and the player wishes to delete this square, he/she must press the reset button firmly for 2–3 seconds.
4. The next player follows the same procedure, bowling up to three balls.
5. This continues until one lane clears their entire card. When this is achieved, they must shout "Bingo" and they are the winners.

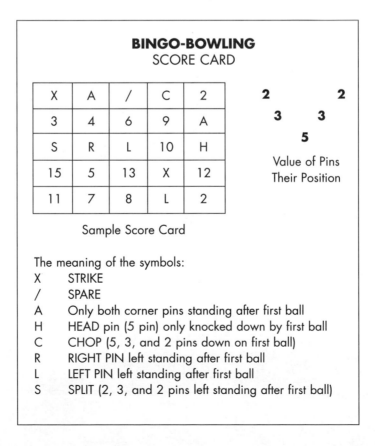

BINGO-BOWLING
SCORE CARD

X	A	/	C	2
3	4	6	9	A
S	R	L	10	H
15	5	13	X	12
11	7	8	L	2

Sample Score Card

2   **2**
  3   **3**
     5

Value of Pins
Their Position

The meaning of the symbols:
X   STRIKE
/   SPARE
A   Only both corner pins standing after first ball
H   HEAD pin (5 pin) only knocked down by first ball
C   CHOP (5, 3, and 2 pins down on first ball)
R   RIGHT PIN left standing after first ball
L   LEFT PIN left standing after first ball
S   SPLIT (2, 3, and 2 pins left standing after first ball)

*Exhibit **4***

UWO Student Bowling Questionnaire

---

1. How often do you bowl?

Never	**Few times/year**	**Once/month**	**Once/week**
31%	63%	6%	0%

2. Do you prefer five- or ten-pin bowling?

Five-pin	**Ten-pin**
33%	67%

3. How many games do you bowl in one visit to a bowling alley?

One	**Two**	**Three**	**More than three**
6%	29%	47%	18%

4. How much do you budget to spend when you bowl?

Less than $5	**$5 to $6.50**	**$6.50 to $8**	**$8 to $9.50**	**More than $9.50**
18%	29%	50%	3%	3%

5. Do you purchase any food or drinks when you bowl?

Yes	**No**
69%	31%

6. How much did you spend?
Avg. $3

7. How large is your group when you go bowling?

1	**2**	**3**	**4**	**5**	**6**	**7**	**8**	**9**	**10**	**More than 15**
0%	6%	12%	60%	19%	3%	0%	0%	0%	0%	0%

8. What night(s) of the week do you bowl?

Monday	**Tuesday**	**Wednesday**	**Thursday**	**Friday**	**Saturday**	**Sunday**
6%	4%	31%	0%	50%	0%	9%

Source: Study completed by Benjamin Katchen and Robert Stoller.

Exhibit 5

Student Bing-Bowling Questionnaire

---

1. Do you consider yourself a competitive person?

Yes	**No**
88%	12%

2. Do you prefer to compete on an individual basis or as part of a team?

Individual				**Team**
1	**2**	**3**	**4**	**5**
25%	6%	0%	31%	38%

3. Do you prefer Bingo-Bowling to regular five-pin or ten-pin bowling?

Bingo-Bowling				**Regular Bowling**
1	**2**	**3**	**4**	**5**
44%	12%	19%	12%	13%

4. How hard was the game?

Easy				**Hard**
1	**2**	**3**	**4**	**5**
4%	20%	44%	32%	0%

5. Would you prefer to design your own bingo card?

Yes	**No**
19%	81%

6. What would be the ideal number of teams to compete against?

1	**2**	**3**	**4**	**5**	**6**	**7 to 10**	**More than 10**
0%	12%	0%	44%	12%	0%	19%	12%

7. Would you pay more to play Bingo-Bowling than normal bowling?

Less				**More**
1	**2**	**3**	**4**	**5**
0%	3%	88%	3%	6%

8. Would you prefer to play by the hour or by the game for Bingo-Bowling?

Hour	**Game**
52%	48%

9. Would you prefer to play Bingo-Bowling against others in your group, or would you rather play against strangers?

Friends and Acquaintances	**Strangers**
81%	19%

Exhibit 5 (cont.)

STUDENT BINGO-BOWLING QUESTIONNAIRE

---

10. Do you need some sort of prize to motivate your team to win?

Yes	**No**
56%	44%

11. What sort of prizes would you suggest?
    Cash, Recognition (Picture), Free bowling, Gifts, Drinks, Gift certificates

12. Would you pay proportionately higher to cover the cost of this prize?

Yes	**No**
43%	57%

13. Would you rather bring your own prizes than pay a little more?

Yes	**No**
37%	63%

14. Now that you are aware of Bingo-Bowling, will you bowl more often?

Yes	**No**
40%	60%

15. What would be the best ways to inform UWO students to the existence of Bingo-Bowling?
    (Scale of 1 to 5)

Flyer	**Coupons**	**Poster Advertising**	**Gazette***	**By Faculty**	**Student Council**
2	4	1	5	2	4

16. Give a three- to four-line overview of your experience this evening.

   ■ "Fun, exciting. I like being competitive and being with friends at the same time."
   ■ "This was a fun experience. I don't bowl, but something that must be stressed here is that the machinery be maintained more carefully (i.e., the reset button). The game requires speed and the button put some teams at a disadvantage."
   ■ "Good entertainment for UWO students."
   ■ "Fun, but at first it is hard to understand."
   ■ "It took a while to learn the meanings of the letters, but we had fun doing it."
   ■ "The more people the better. I've never heard of Bingo Bowling so advertising is going to be vital."
   ■ "It would be nice to have a board that the winning team could have their picture taken and placed on."
   ■ "Well done — a fun, new, innovative way to bowl."

---

*The University of Western Ontario student newspaper.

Source: Study completed by Benjamin Katchen and Robert Stoller.

EXHIBIT 6

Various Promotional/Advertising Options				
NEWSPAPER				
Paper (copies/week)	**1/8 page**	**1/4 page**	**1/2 page**	**3/4 page**
The Gazette (four times/week)	$212/ad	$ 375/ad	$ 718/ad	$1,054/ad
Western News (once/week)	$ 91/ad	$ 170/ad	$ 365/ad	$ 550/ad
London Free Press (daily)	$820/ad	$1,657/ad	$2,485/ad	

RADIO

Breakfast	AAA	Monday to Saturday	6:00 a.m. to 10:00 a.m.
Drive	AA	Monday to Friday	3:00 p.m. to 7:00 p.m.
Midday	A	Monday to Friday	10:00 a.m. to 3:00 p.m.
Weekend	A	Saturday	10:00 a.m. to 6:00 p.m.
Evening	B	Monday to Friday, Sunday	7:00 p.m. to midnight

Station (30-second spots)	AAA	AA	A	B
CJBK (youth/teenagers)	$245	$ 227	$210	$194
CKSL (youth/teenagers)	$207	$ 175	$170	$160
CHRW and 106.9 FM (university and college)	$ 14			

PRIZES

	Cost to Fleetway
Hats	$2.00
T-shirts	$3.50
Coupons, printing	$0.02
Drinks	$0.10

OTHERS

Billboard	$1,000/artwork
Flyers	$0.02 + mailing
Bus Rental	$100/evening

C A S E 5.4   MARKETING NUMBERS: SHORT PROBLEMS

By Michael Pearce and Liz Gray

The exercises below are intended to provide practice in the typical arithmetic challenges faced by marketers. Accordingly, you should focus on the numerical analysis required, disregarding the shortage of other information that you would wish to have before making final decisions.

Exercise 1

A ballpoint pen manufacturer had the following information:

Plastic tubes: top and tip	.12 per unit
Ink	.02 per unit
Direct labour	.02 per unit
Selling price	.40 per unit
Advertising	$80,000
Managerial and secretarial salaries	$200,000
Salespeople's commissions	10 percent of selling price
Factory overhead	$120,000

Total available ballpoint pen market is 10 million pens (near this selling price)

Calculate:

a. unit contribution
b. break-even volume in units
c. share of total market to break even
d. total profit for the company if three million pens are sold
e. volume in units required to generate $500,000 profit

Exercise 2

Jones Toy Store sells toys purchased from a wholesaler, who buys them from a manufacturer. The wholesaler gets a 20 percent margin on its selling price, and Jones gets 40 percent markup on cost. If the manufacturer sells a toy for $5, what is Jones' selling price to consumers?

Exercise 3

Leaven's Box & Label is evaluating the feasibility of manufacturing a new product. The plant it owns has a capacity to produce one million units of the product. Fixed costs associated with this product are $2,000,000, and the maximum selling price that the market will tolerate is $10 a unit. If variable costs are 85 percent of selling price, should Leavens pursue its idea and do further market analysis?

Exercise 4

Using the following information, calculate unit contribution:
a. Advertising = $50,000
b. Break-even sales revenue = $450,000
c. Salaries = $40,000
d. Selling price = $3 per unit
e. Overhead = $60,000

Exercise 5

Last year, consumers spent $1,200,000 on a product called Wipe-It-Clean. Wipe-It-Clean costs a retailer $2, and normal retail margins are 33 percent for this kind of product. The manufacturer of Wipe-It-Clean is about to launch a nationwide advertising campaign, which will bring its fixed costs up to $200,000. Wholesaler margins are 25 percent, and manufacturer margins are 66 percent. Margins are calculated as the percentage of each company's own selling price. What market share must Wipe-It-Clean capture for the manufacturer to break even? What market share must Wipe-It-Clean capture for the manufacturer to achieve a profit of $150,000?

Exercise 6

The manufacturing costs, all variable, for a product are $1.50 per unit. Wholesaler margins are 50 percent, and retailer margins are 75 percent (both calculated as a percentage of their respective selling prices). The manufacturer wants to make a minimum of $100,000 profit over and above fixed costs of $50,000. What will be the minimum retail selling price if the manufacturer produces only 10,000 units?

Exercise 7

Richard Miller was preparing a new product analysis for Brand A. Based on his market research, his decision was to sell at $10 retail. Retailers customarily expected a 40 percent margin and wholesalers a 20 percent margin (both expressed as a percentage of their selling price). Brand A's variable costs were $2/unit and estimated total fixed costs were $28,000. At an anticipated sales volume of 9,000 units, would Richard's Brand A make a profit?

Exercise 8

Brilliance Toothpaste sells at retail for $1.50 per tube. The manufacturing cost is $0.25 per tube, and the fixed costs total $20,000. The manufacturer's margin is 50 percent, and the retailer's margin is 33 percent. All margins are calculated on selling prices. On sales of 200,000 units, calculate the manufacturer's profit, the wholesaler's margin, and the retailer's margin.

Exercise 9

Joe needed a job to at least cover his university tuition next year. Acme Vacuum Company would hire him to sell its vacuum cleaners door-to-door. The company estimated that Joe's variable cost per sale (which included paying Acme for the vacuums) would amount to approximately 60 percent of the selling price of the cleaners. Joe's fixed costs for the summer (including his apartment rent and spending money) would amount to $2,500. Joe figured that he needed $4,500 to cover tuition next year. Acme estimated that a keen salesperson could sell $15,000 at retail of vacuum cleaners in a four-month period. Joe knew that he could return instead to his old summer job in a factory. Although his salary would be assured at this factory job, Joe understood he would be able to save only $3,500 for his schooling. Which job should Joe take? What factors did you consider when making your decision?

Exercise 10

A children's puzzle costs $3 to manufacture. Manufacturer margins are 25 percent, wholesaler margins 20 percent, and retailer margins 50 percent (all calculated as a percentage of their respective selling prices). What price would this mean for consumers in the stores?

Exercise 11

Jane Murray was wondering whether to increase her advertising expenditures or hire more salespeople. Her overall sales last quarter were $750,000, and her cost of goods sold was $500,000. She currently had five salespeople, who cost her $250,000 in compensation and expenses per year. Her advertising budget was $240,000 on an annual basis. Her other fixed costs she calculated to be approximately $500,000 annually. Jane had recently been experimenting with increased expenditures in sales effort and advertising. A three-month test using a temporary additional salesperson at regular rates had resulted in additional sales revenues of $75,000. A one-month test in one city using a 20 percent increase in advertising resulted in increased sales revenue of 10 percent. Jane knew these tests were inconclusive, but she wondered how she might spend her $600,000 planned marketing budget next year based on them.

Exercise 12

Management of Michelle's Lingerie were considering several packaging and pricing alternatives for their style 4D5. Currently 4D5 was packaged in individual units and was offered in white or pastel colours. Last year, Michelle's sold 72,702 dozen white and 27,975 dozen coloured 4D5, contributing $97,421 and $33,570, respectively, to general overhead and profit. For the past year, 4D5 had been selling to retail accounts at $12.60 per dozen, for a suggested retail price of $2.50 each. Several retail customers had indicated that they thought Michelle's should double-pack 4D5, so management explored the costing situation. It was estimated that double-packing would save about $0.50 per dozen. Management had decided that if they went to a double pack, they would offer only white at the outset. Four suggestions had been made, but the merchandise manager wanted to examine the implications for Michelle's contribution and volume, as well as the implications for retailer's margins. Which of the following suggestions do you favour?

		Wholesale	**Retail**
A	White	$12.15	2/$4.70
	Colours	$12.60	$2.50
B	White	$12.10	2/$4.95
	Colours	$12.10	$2.50
C	White	$12.35	2/$5.25
	Colours	$12.35	$2.60
D	White — 1	$12.60	$2.50
	White — 2	$12.10	2/$4.95
	Colours	$12.60	$2.50

Exercise 13

Mr. R.P. David, associate dealer of the Dominion Tire Store in Brandon, Manitoba, was considering the purchase of toy tow trucks for the Christmas season. The tow truck was a well-designed durable toy that operated on two 1.5-volt dry cells. The truck, without batteries, had retailed for $9.95 the previous year in his store and in the local department store. A local discount store had sold the trucks "on special" the week before Christmas for $8.95. Batteries varied in retail price according to their length of life and brand name, but Mr. David estimated on average a consumer spent $2.50 per truck for batteries.

David's total sales last year amounted to $2 million with profit after tax of 3 percent. He stocked toys heavily only at Christmas. Last year, he sold $75,000 worth of toys, virtually all in the months of November and December.

Yesterday, during his visit to the Dominion Tire Winnipeg regional warehouse, Mr. David noticed a stock of 400 toy trucks left over from last year. He found that the line had not moved as well as had been expected, and since each truck had been imprinted with the Dominion Tire insignia, they could not be returned to the manufacturer. The warehouse manager stated that they had sold only 350 toy trucks the previous year and did not intend to order any more. They hoped to move the stock in bulk and offered the complete stock to Mr. David at $3.25 per unit, or half the stock at $4 per unit. Mr. David asked for one day to think it over.

On his return to Brandon, Mr. David stopped in at the local department store and saw that they were offering the same truck without insignia at $9.95. When he returned to his office, he looked in his records and found that last year he had ordered and sold 50 trucks in the two and a half months prior to Christmas. His cost had been $6 per unit. He decided he would not order any trucks unless he could be reasonably sure of at least doubling last year's total gross profit on trucks.

The space he would use would mean that he would carry less of another toy. The toy truck would potentially cannibalize another toy vehicle that was planned to go in the space the tow truck would need. This toy would cost $5 and sell for $7.75; 100 units had been ordered, but the order could be cancelled at a cost of $50.

As he thought about likely price levels, Mr. David reasoned he could sell 50 trucks at $9.95, 75 trucks at $8.95, and 100 trucks at $7.95, all without any advertising support. Based on other toys he had carried, he felt that about $250 of advertising (sharing space in his store ads) would increase sales by 50 trucks over no advertising.

Mr. David's son, who was second-in-command at the store, disagreed. "Last year we left money on the table by not taking a big enough inventory risk right up to the end of the Christmas season. I would prefer to sell them at $8.49. We could then sell at least 150 trucks without advertising and at least 200 with about $250 on advertising."

Mr. David did not envisage any other costs. If he was stuck with trucks at the end of the Christmas season, he figured he could mark them down 50 percent and move them all out in January without difficulty.

1. Calculate all contributions, required volumes, and other projections for every price level mentioned.
2. What incremental volume must advertising generate to be worthwhile at each price level?
3. Considering both pre-Christmas and post-Christmas sales, what would you recommend? Why?

Exercise 14

A large shampoo and toiletries manufacturer was trying to decide whether to introduce a new product onto the market — Product X. Sarah Jones, the branch manager, was responsible for the final decision. She had the following information on Product X:

Cost of product/unit	$0.73
Freight and delivery/unit	$0.03
Selling and other head office expenses/unit	$0.08

There were other somewhat similar products on the market but they were cheaper in quality and cost to produce. Retail margins were expected to be equal to the competition, at 25 percent of the selling price to consumers. In this case,

Sarah's company would sell directly to the retailers. The drugstores would also expect a cooperative advertising allowance of 5 percent of their selling price. In similar situations, the manufacturer usually offered price-reducing allowances to the drugstores (at least five times per year) so that they could pass this savings on to their consumers. These deals were in the order of 10 percent of retail selling price and accounted for approximately 65 percent of the annual volume.

Sarah knew that $450,000 of equipment would have to be purchased to manufacture Product X. Other fixed costs allocated to the product would reach $100,000 before advertising plans were included. These advertising program options would range from a high of $1 million to a mid-range of $500,000, to a modest program launch of $150,000. In future years advertising programs would probably level out at $300,000.

Sarah needed to decide on the best retail selling price. Three options seemed available:

$1.95 per unit	Selling price to reflect the superior quality of the product
$1.65 per unit	Selling price to stay on target with the competition
$1.25 per unit	Selling price to underbid the competition in an attempt to gain increased volume

She knew that management expected a break-even position on new products in the first year and a 10 percent return on total investments in each of the following years. Sarah had projected that the total market for Product X would be 18,560,000 units but that the relevant market in which it would be positioned would be approximately 6,750,000 units. These markets were expected to grow at approximately 8 percent per year.

a. What price should Product X be? Why?

b. What level of advertising should be used in the first year? Why? Is there other information you would like to know? What information?

c. What share of the total market will Product X have to attain to meet the corporate objectives?

d. What share of the relevant market will Product X have to attain to meet the corporate objectives?

C A S E 5.5   THE McINTOSH GALLERY

By Elizabeth Grasby and Marilyn Campbell

In the early 1990s, the McIntosh Gallery in London, Ontario, was experiencing a problem in inspiring attendance and interest. Kevin Kung, volunteer promotion director, was handed the task of improving the situation as quickly as possible.

BACKGROUND

The McIntosh Gallery was a public, nonprofit art gallery situated on the campus of the University of Western Ontario. It served the university and surrounding community. Built in 1942 with a bequest from the estate of Wilhelmina Morris McIntosh, it was the oldest university art gallery in Canada. From 1960 to 1969 the programs were administered by artists-in-residence. Since 1969, the university had provided the principal financial support for the operation of the gallery and the program of exhibitions, films, videos on art, lectures, and other events. Additional funding was provided by the government of Ontario through the Ontario Arts Council, the Canada Council, the William Abbott Fund, the McIntosh estate, and the McIntosh Gallery membership.

The mission of the gallery was to collect, exhibit, research, and interpret exemplary visual art with an emphasis on contemporary Canadian art. Its expressed aims were:

- To collect and preserve Canadian visual artistic heritage in public trust now and for future generations;
- To cultivate the appreciation of art;
- To make art part of the everyday life on campus;
- To encourage visual literacy and critical visual awareness; and
- To make Canadian visual heritage accessible to all.

COMMUNITY

The city of London, population 316,000 as of 1993, was part of the densely populated region of southwestern Ontario. Over five million people resided within a 300-mile radius. London was also midway on a direct, well-used corridor from the United States to Toronto. McIntosh Gallery audiences included the university community of 26,000 students, faculty, and staff; the broader London area community of 350,000; a general audience that was increasingly exposed to images of the contemporary art world through the mass media; and the more specialized community of artists, art and museum professionals, critics, writers, dealers, collectors, and teachers who also supported and contributed to the dialogue.

GOVERNING AUTHORITY

The director was the secretary of the McIntosh Gallery Committee, the governing body, which was a standing committee of the University Board of Governors. The director was also accountable to the vice-president (external) for operations as a budget unit head, with other external colleagues in advancement and development, alumni affairs, university relations and information, and Foundation Western. Institutional decisions regarding policy and acquisitions were made by the McIntosh Gallery Committee and the Acquisitions Committee, as approved by the University Board of Governors. Operational decisions were made by the director under the authority of the vice-president (external). Three full-time staff reported to the director: a curator, installations officer/registrar, and secretary. There were also two part-time gallery attendants and 25 to 30 volunteers.

Responsible for gallery operations, programs, collections, budget, and planning, the director's primary ongoing task was to maintain institutional identity and self-determination as a public art gallery within the university context (which often perceived the gallery as a service that was less than central to the academic mission). This was becoming a bigger and bigger task as the university was constrained by tightening resources, forcing every department and facility to "do more with less." The university was also undergoing a shift to "total quality service" at this time, and this would bring even more responsibilities to the director, Arlene Kennedy, and the curator, Catherine Elliot Shaw.

A volunteer force was formally initiated in September 1990. Over 17 individuals, primarily students, volunteered as tour guides, gallery attendants, researchers, and public relations and general assistants. Most commitments were tied to terms of study and seasonal student workload; however, two nonstudent volunteers continued to give generously of their time every week. An abundance of special projects was accumulated on file for volunteers as an opportunity for direct participation and public gallery experience. Governing committee members were also volunteers, some of whom were faculty.

Volunteer contributions for 1992–93 were:

8 volunteer gallery attendants	406 hours
5 research volunteers	396 hours
3 special events/planning assistants	378 hours
2 miscellaneous volunteer tasks	80 hours
volunteer committee members	135 hours
	1,395 hours

There were also 108 members of the gallery.[1]

The gallery was open 12 months a year and regular weekly hours were:

Mon. closed	Fri. 12–4 p.m.
Tues. 12–7 p.m.	Sat. 12–4 p.m.
Wed. 12–7 p.m.	Sun. 12–4 p.m.
Thurs. 12–7 p.m.	

COLLECTION

There were approximately 1,700 objects in the McIntosh Gallery's permanent collection. About 25 percent of the permanent collection (valued at over $10 million) was on display throughout the campus and in public outdoor sites. An average of 25 works were donated annually. At least one exhibition was curated from the collection each year and provided a historical context/counterpoint to concurrent exhibitions of contemporary works. The collection, records, and reference library were also a resource for artists, collectors, educators, students, curators, and researchers.

To enhance the visitor's movement from familiar to more challenging work, the gallery provided a constellation of educational vehicles: exhibitions, educational/interpretive activities, and original research and documentation. Information packages, which included such reference materials as biographies, reviews, and bibliographies, were available for casual consultation. Gallery Notes, often including artists' statements, offered ideas, insights, and open-ended questions as an approach to the exhibitions. "Meet-the-artist" videotaped interviews provided additional primary information in an informal and nonthreatening manner. Informal walking tours, called "walkabouts," facilitated a more personal forum for discussion of the work and, where possible, first-hand experience of the artist. Tours for adult and school groups were requested and scheduled on a regular basis. The gallery promoted scholarship relating to visual art practice and, when limited resources allowed, produced more extensive publications as a contribution to the existing body of knowledge.

VISITORS

The McIntosh Gallery conducted annual in-depth audience surveys of those who visited the gallery from 1989 to 1993. These surveys were broken down into categories of age, residence, and frequency of visit. Exhibit 1 is a synopsis of significant results from the 1993 audience survey. The overall responses from this survey are highlighted in Exhibit 2. Exhibit 3 shows additional visitors' comments that were also collected. Kevin hoped that this information would help him to better understand his audience and to ensure that his promotion recommendations would reach them.

A small focus group was also conducted with an introductory business class, Catherine Elliot Shaw, Kevin, and the instructor. The students revealed many interesting thoughts and opinions. Overall, there was a widespread awareness of the McIntosh Gallery, but only four out of approximately 60 students had actually been in the gallery. Interestingly, the reason many of the students knew of the gallery, they said, was because of its red front door (the only red door on campus). Many students said that they passed by on their way to class but did not have time to enter, or that the door was closed and they did not know if it was open, even though the hours were posted outside the gallery.

After the focus group concluded, Catherine Elliot Shaw shared some of her insight from research that she had done surrounding the type of people that a gallery attracts and maintains. Some of the highlights of this study showed that galleries were often assumed to be the domain of the elite and frequent visitors, who appreciate quiet time to be alone and absorb the artistic work. Less frequent visitors equated museums with a "monument to the dead," while frequent and regular visitors likened it to a library. Catherine believed that a more sports-focused group was less likely to visit a gallery frequently than a quiet, more contemplative group of people.

COMMUNICA-TIONS

The McIntosh Gallery had two advertising accounts. The operating advertising account paid for information campaigns for the gallery in general: $2,500 for 1993. The program account paid for advertising specific to gallery programming: $1,600 for 1993. Paid advertising was placed in art specialist periodicals and campus publications with a broad distribution (e.g., the campus phone directory). This was supplemented with a host of free promotional opportunities: public service announcements in the *London Free Press* (the gallery could not afford to advertise in it), electronic media, news releases distributed through the university's media channels, and appearances on cable television. The *Western News* (a campus newspaper directed at faculty, administration, and students) had been a consistent supporter in listing its activities, and the students' newspaper the *Gazette* covered it from time to time. The Gallery Bulletin was deposited at various pickup points around the campus and throughout London (libraries, galleries, etc.) and included with letters sent on other gallery business as a point of interest and information.

THE CHALLENGE

Kevin was enthusiastic about the many possibilities to increase the exposure, knowledge, and attendance of the McIntosh Gallery. He saw a potential for greater exposure through the newspapers and wondered about the possibility of having gallery volunteers write reviews on pieces of the permanent collection. In this way, the permanent collection would become better known and the gallery name would appear in the papers more frequently. Other promotional ideas included placing tent cards at residence dining rooms and at campus food outlets (see Exhibit 5). Use of internal campus memos as invitations to openings and as a reminder of new exhibitions was also being considered.

Last year's attendance (1993–94) was 10,400 visitors. Catherine Elliot Shaw wanted to increase this figure to 15,000 visitors. Kevin knew that he had a formidable challenge ahead. He had to design a promotional strategy that considered his audience, budget, and the aims of the McIntosh Gallery. He had to be clear on his objectives, and the timing of each plan was important. His strategy had to meet with the approval of the director and the curator.

NOTE

1. The segmented results are available from the McIntosh Gallery for further study.

EXHIBIT 1

SYNOPSIS OF SIGNIFICANT RESULTS FROM AUDIENCE SURVEYS, 1993

Age and Population Spreads

78.8% of all gallery visitors were 15 to 45 years of age
54.8% of once-a-month visitors were age 15 to 25
42.2% of all gallery visitors were students
45.2% of once-a-month visitors were students

Residence

41.0% of London visitors were from the north end of the city
30.1% of all gallery visitors were from off-campus
41.5% of first-time visitors were from off-campus
44.0% of off-campus visitors came with the sole purpose of visiting the gallery
40.0% of first-time gallery visitors came to see an exhibition
72.8% of all visitors indicated that they were supportive of the expansion of the gallery

Exhibit 2

McINTOSH GALLERY AUDIENCE SURVEY, 1993*

Responses:

All responses are listed in descending order. The total number of audience surveys is 166. This is the second survey tabulated under the new hours.

1. Visit Frequency

first-time visitor	39.2% (65)
once a month	18.7% (31)
2–3 times per year	15.1% (25)
every 2–3 months	14.5% (24)
less than twice/year	10.8% (18)
other	1.8% (3)

2. Visit Pattern

no response	53.0% (88)
Tues–Fri 1–4	16.3% (27)
Tues–Fri 12–1	12.0% (20)
Sat–Sun 12–4	10.8% (18)
Tues–Thurs 4–7	10.2% (17)
other (various)	4.2% (7)

3. Reason for Visit

exhibition	53.6% (89)
other	22.3% (37)
habit	15.1% (25)
public event at gallery	9.0% (15)
visit to library	9.0% (15)
no response	7.8% (13)

---

*Percentages do not add to 100% due to multiple responses.

EXHIBIT 2 (cont.)

McINTOSH GALLERY AUDIENCE SURVEY, 1993* (cont.)

---

4. Publicity Effectiveness

word-of-mouth	29.5% (49)
Western News	25.9% (43)
The *Gazette*	23.5% (39)
gallery light box	18.7% (31)
no response	15.7% (26)
Visual Arts dept.	13.9% (23)
posters	13.9% (23)
gallery bulletin	13.3% (22)
other sources	7.8% (13)
London Free Press listing	6.6% (11)
London Free Press review	4.8% (8)
membership mailing	3.0% (5)
TV London	1.2% (2)
tourism brochure	0.6% (1)
Cable 13	0.0% (0)

5a. Comparison of Population

student	42.2% (70)
visitor	30.1% (50)
visual arts student	11.4% (19)
faculty	8.4% (14)
staff	7.2% (12)
no response	1.2% (2)

5b. Visitors: Purpose to visit gallery?

no	56.0% (28)
yes	44.0% (22)

6. Age Ranges

15–25 male:	21.1%	(35)	female:	29.5%	(49)	(84)
26–35 male:	9.0%	(15)	female:	9.0%	(15)	(30)
36–45 male:	4.2%	(7)	female:	6.0%	(10)	(17)
46–55 male:	6.0%	(10)	female:	4.8%	(8)	(18)
56–65 male:	3.6%	(6)	female:	2.4%	(4)	(10)
Over 65 male:	1.8%	(3)	female:	2.4%	(4)	(7)

*Percentages do not add to 100% due to multiple responses.

EXHIBIT 2 (cont.)

McINTOSH GALLERY AUDIENCE SURVEY, 1993* (cont.)

7a. London Resident

permanent	42.2% (70)
temporary	36.7% (61)
other (i.e., outside London)	12.7% (21)
no response	8.4% (14)

7b. Area of Residence
(Calculated only for London residents.)

northwest	17.6% (23)
north	16.8% (22)
no response	16.8% (22)
central	14.5% (19)
campus	6.9% (9)
old north	6.1% (8)
west	5.3% (7)
northeast	4.6% (6)
southwest	3.8% (5)
east	3.1% (4)
south	2.3% (3)
old south	2.3% (3)

8. Transportation

foot	57.8% (96)
car	27.1% (45)
bus	12.0% (20)
bike	7.8% (13)
no response	4.8% (8)
taxi	0.0% (0)

9. Support for Expansion Plans

very supportive	36.7% (61)
somewhat supportive	36.1% (60)
indifferent	16.3% (27)
no response	7.8% (13)
other	3.0% (5)
opposed	0.0% (0)

---

*Percentages do not add to 100 percent owing to multiple responses.

Exhibit 3

APPENDIX: VISITOR COMMENTS

I am a first-time visitor to the gallery. I have heard a lot about it in the last year. As an alumna, I hope I will be back to visit. Thanks.

A fine little gallery! The exhibit was wonderful!

A good idea (to tie the exhibitions together, presenting more challenging, unusual and interdisciplinary exhibitions, and provoking more thought and discussion), but I haven't paid much attention until recently. I will do so in the future.

Less tripe and more thought, please.

I haven't been around to notice the changes, but I feel that the gallery I saw today accomplished these goals.

I like to follow the work of Ontario artists, particularly those of the '50s and '60s, some of whom I knew.

I have noticed how thought-provoking your exhibits are, although I've never had the opportunity of participating in a discussion of the exhibition except for those offered in my art classes. Advertise about your lectures/discussions more!

(I have noticed these changes) but the period of rotation has greatly decreased and therefore so has exposure to this type of art!

I miss the talks and films.

I see no reason to tie all exhibitions together.

The quality of exhibitions is somewhat less appealing than in the past.

Please show real art, NOT the productions of the Faculty of Visual Arts.

I am somewhat disappointed with the parking situation on the weekends. I would rather have my money go to the gallery than to the university for parking.

Keep up the good work! Thank you.

I am not a serious art enthusiast, I just like to see what happens here every so often. I am in physics and often I go to the UCC, so usually I stop by when I have the time.

I enjoy visiting the gallery on a regular basis. Good work!

Exhibit 3 (cont.)

APPENDIX: VISITOR COMMENTS

I have only been here for three years, but in these three years I have often been disappointed with the shows. I would be more supportive if the criteria for show selection were modified some of the time. Art accessible to a wider cross-section of the public is what I would like to see. The gallery should be satisfying for more than just university art students. I'm sure this would generate more support with a wider base to draw from. Art both intellectually challenging and accessible on a level of the "average" interested person does exist. Finding it may benefit both the gallery and the London population.

All exhibits are interesting and thought-provoking.

It's great! I hope the people who hand out the cash figure this out soon!

(Have you) ever thought of renting artworks to corporations or special functions to raise money? Perhaps the insurance coverage would be too much. The McIntosh does a pleasurable job!

I find the taste in art I see here is frequently tacky and cliché in its attempt to be contemporary and modern. I think a stronger blending of traditional and historical elements in our artistic culture would be advisable. Usually I don't like the exhibits. Their quality is significantly less than the beauty of this little building deserves.

I would like to see more of your permanent collection on display.

Keep up the good work. I liked some of the talks given here last year as well. I would like to see more contemporary works by Canadian artists. The old stuff from the permanent collection I didn't care for too much.

I am in third-year science. I do enjoy, however, a bit of *culture!*

I've always found the exhibitions thought-provoking.

I am not very pleased that I have to pay $2 just to park here on the weekends. It doesn't make sense to have to pay when it is the least busy.

I feel the exhibitions could be more challenging. I realize it is necessary to mount student and faculty shows and show the permanent collection, but this takes up space that could be used better, I think.

(I) appreciate the stimulation — mental — generated by the works.

Greater clarity and more information needed in some presentations.

Impressive as is. Keep it simple.

Exhibit 3 (cont.)

APPENDIX: VISITOR COMMENTS

I have generally thought your exhibitions to be amongst the best in the area for a good number of years. Though this past year has not been as interesting as previous years, perhaps because of the political context (words) that would be on the whole better to read sitting down than to stand reading … the limitations of the medium does not allow for much development of thought. Generally I prefer works that stimulate visually not literally.

I would say so (i.e., noticed the changes in programming), although I find I usually learn from most displays at the McIntosh. I like to look at new and different art, but sometimes I wish it were a bit more accessible.

The McIntosh is a lovely, quiet haven for peaceful afternoon visits. Have you considered using parts of the space for music or theatrical performance?

I very much enjoy the various displays you present. However, I am not steeped in art history and wouldn't mind seeing some earlier works as well as current creations.

I always enjoy the exhibitions of graduating classes, including Fanshawe. How about an exhibition similar to the annual Art Mart?

Those who visit and know the gallery have noticed the changes; those who don't come haven't and probably never will unless they break out and become visitors. Anyway, keep up the good work!

I prefer Renaissance paintings, which are very seldom displayed at the McIntosh.

I have enjoyed your exhibits!

I certainly appreciate a challenge to my frighteningly ethnocentric views on art. Provoke! Provoke!

I belong to the Faculty of Engineering Science; the engineering art exhibition is an excellent idea.

I have only visited the gallery twice, as I am a new student. I feel it is a great asset to have a gallery on campus.

This exhibit is interesting but appears to be more documentation of an event that should have been seen at the time. I felt some of the presentation unprofessionally presented, but it did intrigue me!

The display space is well laid out presenting the exhibitions to the viewer.

No free parking??

Source: Survey tabulated by Janette Cousins, August 1993.

EXHIBIT 4

EXHIBITIONS

McIntosh Gallery

The University
of Western Ontario
London, Ontario
Canada N6A 3K7

Tel: (519) 661-3181
Fax: 661-3292

January 7 – February 6, 1994

EXHIBITING CULTURE

Western society has entrusted to its museums the task of collecting, preserving and interpreting its cultural history. Over the centuries of a treasure-house tradition, these institutions have developed a codified "museum experience", the combined effect of architectural environment and exhibition design on the individual objects displayed. In an age of specialist institutions, museums are also moving from encyclopaedic collecting to more focussed acquisitions. This month's exhibitions examine the museum/art gallery experience, its collecting function, and its influence upon our understanding of material culture.

TWO PAVILIONS: MUSEUM AND A TENT FOR THE EXPLORATION OF A DARK CONTINENT

This installation by Regina artist Lorne Beug presents two environments in which we are invited to consider the ambiguous relationship between architectural atmosphere and the objects placed within them. The installation is divided into two sections or "pavilions". The first simulates a Euro-centric museum complete with imitation stone and marble walls and filled with an assortment of pseudo-relics from ancient civilizations. The second, a nylon structure reminiscent in part of medieval European tents, is covered in images collaged from an orientalized view of "exotic cultures". The resulting juxtaposition questions the depiction of non-Western cultures within the prescripted Western perception of the museum environment.

WEST
WING

GETTING TO THE OBJECT

Despite fundamental changes in the philosophical frame-work of exhibition design, the concept of placing an object within a specially designated space continues to define our understanding of that museum object. From traditional floor-to-ceiling hanging to the "white cube" of contemporary gallery spaces, the lighting, spatial proximity, and other incidental details all influence the assimilation of the visual information. This exhibition features some of the presentation practices used in today's museums but in a skewed manner that emphasizes how the viewer's perceptions of the objects are altered by the display.

EAST
WING

VALUING ART

Public art galleries collect art as a record of our cultural heritage in the visual arts. Since 1942, the McIntosh Gallery has been devoted to collecting and exhibiting the artwork of our time, a collection which has grown to over 1,700 objects. The value of a public art collection, however, lies in its use as a resource to its community. It is a public trust which demands accountability in the efficient and effective use of limited resources. Selections from the McIntosh Gallery Collection will illustrate some of the motivations for collecting and the costs associated with this universal activity.

LOWER
FLOOR

Gallery Hours
Tuesday-Thursday 12-7 pm
Friday-Sunday 12-4 pm
Closed Mondays
Free Admission

EXHIBIT 5

Exhibit 5

Discover the McIntosh Gallery

EXHIBITIONS

March 24 - April 10, 1994

THE UNIVERSITY OF WESTERN ONTARIO DEPARTMENT OF VISUAL ARTS GRADUATION EXHIBITION
This annual exhibition presents work of students who leave in the past 3 or 4 years studied visual communications through the traditions of art making and critical inquiry.

Opening: Thursday, March 24, 7:30 p.m.
Free Public Walking Tour of the Exhibition:
Friday, March 25, 12:15 - 12:50 p.m.

Gallery Hours
Tuesday-Thursday 12-7 pm
Friday-Sunday 12-4pm
Closed Mondays
Free Admission

Discover the McIntosh Gallery

EXHIBITIONS

March 24 - April 10, 1994

THE UNIVERSITY OF WESTERN ONTARIO DEPARTMENT OF VISUAL ARTS GRADUATION EXHIBITION
This annual exhibition presents work of students who leave in the past 3 or 4 years studied visual communications through the traditions of art making and critical inquiry.

Opening: Thursday, March 24, 7:30 p.m.
Free Public Walking Tour of the Exhibition:
Friday, March 25, 12:15 - 12:50 p.m.

Gallery Hours
Tuesday-Thursday 12-7 pm
Friday-Sunday 12-4pm
Closed Mondays
Free Admission

The University of Western Ontario

Gallery Hours
Tuesday-Thursday 12-7 pm
Friday-Sunday 12-4pm
Closed Mondays
Free Admission

CASE 5.6   OMEGA PAW INC.

By Elizabeth Grasby and Jannalee Anderson

Michael Ebert, president of Omega Paw (Omega) and inventor of the Self-Cleaning Litter Box, reflected on the progress of his company, based in St. Marys, Ontario. In September 1996, after being in business for just over a year, Omega had reached a sales level of $1 million. Ebert knew that with Omega's current resources, the company could potentially target a much larger market. His goal was to "grow the business quickly," and in order to achieve these goals, Ebert knew Omega would have to expand its marketing initiatives and consider alternative channels of distribution.

THE CAT OWNERS MARKET

In the mid-1990s, North America was home to approximately 66 million cats — 60 million in the United States and six million in Canada. In 1996, approximately 33 percent of the 10 million households in Canada had, on average, two cats. The cat population had risen by 7 percent between 1994 and 1996, and it was estimated to continue growing at an annual rate of 4 percent for the next few years. A survey conducted by the American Pet Products Manufacturers Association, Inc., cited, as reasons for the growth, the increased trend in apartment and, more recently, condominium living. In addition, the survey pointed to the ever-increasing mobility of the work force, the rising average age of the Canadian population (the typical cat owner was older than other pet owners), and the ease of care and maintenance for cats relative to other popular pets as reasons for the continued growth.

The typical cat owner spent approximately $520 annually on his or her feline pet. Forty-four percent was spent on food and 23 percent on veterinarian visits. Cat supplies, such as litter, litter boxes, bowls, etc., accounted for 13 percent of the yearly budget, while 20 percent was spent on flea and tick supplies, grooming, and toys. Just over 50 percent of owners bought presents for their cats, of which the majority (88 percent) were purchased and given during the Christmas season.[1]

IVEY Jannalee Anderson prepared this case under the supervision of Elizabeth Grasby solely to provide material for class discussion. The authors do not intend to illustrate either effective or ineffective handling of a managerial situation. The authors may have disguised certain names and other identifying information to protect confidentiality. Ivey Management Services prohibits any form of reproduction, storage or transmittal without its written permission. This material is not covered under authorization from CanCopy or any reproduction rights organization. Copyright © 1999, Ivey. Management Services.

OMEGA PAW'S CONSUMER GROUPS

Based on experience and knowledge, Omega Paw had divided cat owners into three main consumer groups. The first group, 5 percent of the total cat owner market, was the "new pet owner." These were consumers who had just acquired a cat or a kitten and who needed all the applicable pet care and maintenance products. They often did their own pet and product research, wanted good quality, long-lasting products, and usually purchased items at the local pet stores or at the veterinarian's office.

The "existing cat owner," 80 percent of the total cat owner market, was the second identifiable market. Having owned cats for some time, these consumers were experienced in caring for their cats and were well stocked with the traditional cat care and maintenance supplies. They purchased their cat products at a variety of locations, such as pet stores, the veterinarian's office, household supply stores, and grocery stores.

The remaining 15 percent of the cat owner market was labelled as the "grey zone." Most of this segment lived in the country and owned a variety of outdoor pets, such as dogs and cats. Cats in this segment were not only one of many pets, but they were also free to roam outside, and, as a result, the owners usually did not concern themselves with purchasing specific cat products other than cat food.

THE SELF-CLEANING LITTER BOX

Two years ago, Ebert's brother and sister-in-law had gone on vacation, leaving Ebert to care for their cats. "There's got to be a better way," Ebert had thought as he held his nose while cleaning the cats' litter box. By September 1996, not only had Ebert "found a better way" by inventing a self-cleaning litter box, but he had set up a new company to distribute this product and other pet care products through pet store distribution channels across North America.

The Self-Cleaning Litter Box was a moulded plastic box with rounded edges that allowed the cat to enter and leave through a large opening at the side. The box was available in two sizes, and the larger size was ideally suited for large or multiple cats. To clean the litter box, the cat owner would first roll the box onto its back, allowing all of the litter to pass through a filter screen and collecting any clumped litter separately in a long, narrow tray. The owner would then roll the box back to its normal position and allow the clean litter to flow back through the filter to the litter tray. At this point, the narrow tray could be removed by its handle, and the used cat litter could be dumped out. Exhibit 1 illustrates the simplicity of the process: roll back, roll forward, remove the tray, and dump the waste.

THE COMPETITION

Direct Competition

The first of three main North American competitors, the Everclean Self Scoop Litter Box, was an open litter box with rounded edges. In order to clean it, the rounded cover had to be attached and the box rolled. This allowed clean litter to fall through the filters and collected the clumped litter in the top half of the box. Following this, the entire top of the box was taken off, carefully maneouvred over a garbage can, and then angled so that the litter clumps would fall into the garbage. When finished, the top of the box was left detached and had to be stored until the next cleaning.

First Brands Corporation, the manufacturer of the Everclean Self Scoop Litter Box, retailed its product for between $53 and $63.[2] It spent a lot of money advertising to pet stores via trade magazines and had North America-wide distribution. First Brands also manufactured well-known home, automotive, and pet-care products and recently reported annual sales revenues of just over $1 billion.

The second direct competitor, Quick Sand, used a series of three trays — each with slanted slots on the bottom of the tray. These trays were layered in such a way that the slanted slots of the top and bottom were going in the same direction, and the slanted slots of the middle tray were facing the opposite direction. This layering technique formed a solid bottom to the litter box and prevented the clean litter from filtering through the trays prematurely. In order to clean the litter box, the first tray was lifted and sifted. Clean litter filtered down to the second tray, leaving the clumped litter in the top tray. The used litter was deposited in the garbage and the empty tray was replaced under the bottom until the process needed to be repeated.

The whole box required carrying and emptying, which was awkward, and trays had to be replaced underneath each other with care so that litter did not leak onto the floor. However, Quick Sand was competitively priced at $29 retail. In addition, it was shorter in length than other litter boxes and, as a result, was easier to place in a secluded spot. Introduced in March 1995, the product was endorsed by Dini Petty, a Canadian morning talk show host. It did not receive much attention, however, until Smart Inventions, a U.S. company, bought the product in 1996 and launched an extensive media campaign. They spent between $200,000 to $300,000 per week for six months and gained exposure throughout Canada and the United States.

The last main competitor, Lift & Sift, was very similar to the Quick Sand product. It was priced at $29 and also used the three-tray method. In addition, both products incorporated easy-to-follow directions as part of their packaging design. Although Lift & Sift had been on the market for three years, it had limited advertising exposure. However, in 1996 it benefited from Quick Sand's extensive advertising, and actually beat it into mass distribution outlets like Wal-Mart.

Indirect Competition

Despite the increasing number of "owner-friendly" cat litter boxes, many cat owners continued to favour the basic model. These products retailed for $10 to $15, were sold at numerous locations, and represented the majority of the litter box market (approximately 90 percent). Although cat litter boxes could be purchased in a variety of colours and sizes, compared with the more recent offerings they were awkward, messy, and smelly.

At the other end of the spectrum, a product named Litter Maid had also made its way into the market. With the aid of electric eyes and an automatic sifting comb, this computerized self-cleaning litter box combed through the litter, collected the waste, and deposited it into a container at one end of the tray. The electric eyes reacted quickly, and the litter box was cleaned within minutes of the cat leaving the box, thereby eliminating almost any odour. Its hassle-free process, benefits, and one-year manufacturer's warranty had all been heavily advertised on TV and in national magazines. Litter Maid could be purchased via mail order for US$199.00.

FROM AUGUST 1995 TO PRESENT

Ebert realized that with such heavy competition, Omega would have to think carefully about its marketing campaign. Specifically, as it attempted to expand distribution, it would have to think carefully of the company's success and failures over the past year.

In August 1995, after four months of advertising the Self-Cleaning Litter Box via magazine advertisements (mail-order) and TV commercials, Omega presold 2,500 units. These units were shipped to the customers as the orders came in; however, production problems with the initial moulds caused delays, and instead of the actual product, Omega had to send out letters stating that the product would be ready in a few weeks' time.

In late August 1995, the management group at Omega decided to end the "direct to customer" mail-order experiment and instead to target pet stores via distributors. Omega contacted Canadian Pet Distributors (CPD) in Cambridge, Ontario, who responded favourably and picked up the Self-Cleaning Litter Box line immediately. CPD distributed nationally and required a 40 percent markup on the manufacturer's selling price; the pet stores, in turn, required a 100 percent markup on the distributor's selling price.

CPD continued to sell Omega's prototype to pet stores in Canada from August through to December 1995. However, the initial run of products was not yet perfect and, as a result, slightly dented Omega's reputation. When asked why Omega continued to sell these prototype products, Ebert answered, "At that point we were happy to sell to anyone."

By December 1995, the "new and improved" Self-Cleaning Litter Box was ready. Omega sold it for $18. The variable costs for each box were $6.00 for production, $1.50 for shipping, and $1.38 for packaging. Since CPD only sold in Canada, Omega started looking for a distributor in the United States. After being introduced to the product at a trade show that Omega's management had attended, six of seven distributors contacted picked up the product right away. Interestingly, this favourable response made Omega the only self-cleaning litter box on the U.S. market in late 1995.

By January 1996, the management at Omega realized that they could not possibly continue their direct selling technique to the many potential pet store distributors across the United States. Instead, they chose to use the skills and industry contacts of manufacturer representatives. Manufacturer representatives required 6 percent commission (on the MSP), and in return added Omega's product line to their existing product line portfolio for sale to pet store distributors across the United States.[3]

Throughout 1996, Omega continued to attend U.S. industry pet trade shows. The manufacturer representatives were working out very well for Omega and had secured 60 distributors across North America. By September 1996, Omega had sold approximately 50,000 Self-Cleaning Litter Boxes, totalling $1 million in sales.

ALTERNATIVES FOR THE FUTURE

After being in business for just over a year, Omega had reached impressive sales levels. Ebert hoped to continue this favourable trend and aspired to reach sales of $1.7 million by the company's December 1996 fiscal year-end, $3 million by December 1997, and $5.7 million by December 1998. He knew that such aggressive growth would not be easy and wondered, "Where do we go from here? Should we continue as we are, increase our penetration into pet stores, revisit mail order channels, pursue mass markets, or expand into grocery stores?"

Ebert wondered what changes to the existing strategy would be necessary to achieve market penetration and increased sales. Should Omega consider using different advertising mediums to attract attention, or should it simply increase the amount of existing advertising? Ebert knew of two or three good trade magazines that offered a one-shot deal (one month/one issue) at a cost of $3,000 to $4,000, including a one-time production fee. However, he wondered if there were any other creative marketing initiatives that could help increase sales among pet stores.

A mail order/TV campaign would cost $20,000 for an initial run. This cost included producing the commercial, a 1-800 phone number, the hiring of a company to answer the calls, and another company to collect the money. As a result of previous difficulties with mail order, a trial run would be conducted. Since Americans tended to be more receptive to mail order than Canadians, the trial would be launched on national television in the United States and would initially run for a two-week period. Then, if the trial went well, the TV campaign would continue. Ebert noted that under this alternative, Omega would produce and ship the product directly to the customer.

If Omega sold its Self-Cleaning Litter Box to mass distribution outlets such as Wal-Mart or Kmart,[4] it would cost an estimated $50,000 for additional tooling, different packaging, and increased advertising. If this option was pursued, Ebert wondered what changes would have to be made to the product and how this might affect the product's selling price, image, and promotional plans.

If mass distribution outlets were pursued, there was also the decision of which trade route to use. With small to medium-sized accounts, Omega could continue using its existing manufacturer representatives to sell to the different stores. However, with large accounts, called "house" accounts, Omega would have to sell directly to the specific mass distribution buyers. The product would then be shipped by the buyers to store distribution centres, and only then would it be sent out to the individual stores. In addition to the added complexity of this trade route, Ebert was especially concerned about meeting the demands of buyers who required a 40 percent markup (on the MSP), ample quantities, and on-time deliveries.

With 80,000 grocery stores in the United States alone, this relatively untapped market had considerable potential. However, if grocery store placement was pursued, Ebert knew the demands on Omega would be many.

In order to sell to grocery stores, Omega had to sell through a national broker, a regional broker, the distribution centres, and finally the grocery stores. The members of this trade channel respectively required the following:

- The greater of a 4 percent margin on the MSP, or a $2,000 monthly retaining fee (national broker);
- A 4 percent margin on the MSP (regional broker);
- A 20 to 25 percent markup on the MSP (distribution centres); and
- A 40 percent markup on the distributors' selling price (grocery stores).

In addition to the required margin, grocery stores wanted 10 percent for cooperative advertising and for setting up point-of-purchase displays. Omega estimated a further cost of $3 to produce each of these displays.

Before he could seriously pursue this option, Ebert questioned whether the grocery industry was ready to accept "hard-good"[5] products. He knew some of the more aggressive stores, approximately 10 percent, were expanding their pet sections, but would customers be willing to make an impulse buy of $30 as part of their weekly grocery shopping? It was evident that this distribution option had high potential, but Ebert questioned whether he wanted to be the one to develop it.

DECISION TIME   Omega had achieved considerable success to date, and the company's current financial resources and production capabilities positioned it well to service a larger market. A marketing budget of $100,000 was available, and the manufacturing facilities had a capacity of 3,500 units per week. With all of this in mind and the options to consider, Ebert wondered what decisions he should make to best position Omega Paw for the future.

NOTES

1. "1996–1997 APPMA National Pet Owners Survey (Revised), American Pet Products Manufacturers Assoc., Inc.
2. All prices are in Canadian dollars unless noted otherwise.
3. U.S. distributors and pet stores required the same markup as distributors and pet stores in Canada. (Distributors required 40 percent markup on MSP. Pet stores required 100 percent markup on DSP.)
4. Wal-Mart and Kmart each had 2,200 stores in the United States alone.
5. Hard goods are generally more durable products, giving benefit to the consumer over an extended period of time.

Exhibit **1**

Omega Paw's Self-Cleaning Litter Box

C A S E 5.7 ORGAN AND TISSUE DONATION IN ONTARIO

By Elizabeth Grasby and Liz Gray

When you're a parent and your child is awaiting a life-saving transplant, every week seems like a month, every day seems like a week.
— *Penny Priddy, B.C. Health Minister*

A recent study by the House of Commons Standing Committee on Health identified a severe lack of organ donors throughout all provinces and territories in Canada. This report spurred the committee, in May 1999, to urge the federal government to boost awareness of the need to increase organ donations across Canada. The question now facing each provincial government was how to increase awareness.

ORGAN AND TISSUE DONATION

An individual can choose to be a living donor or a cadaveric donor. A living donor chooses to donate an organ or tissue that is not critical to his or her survival to someone in need. A cadaveric donor is an individual who donates organ(s) and/or tissue(s) once deceased.

Cadaveric Organ Donation

To qualify as a cadaveric organ donor, the deceased must have suffered brain death.[1] This means that the body may continue to function with the aid of a mechanical support system, but the patient will never regain consciousness. Brain death occurs most frequently in patients who have suffered a brain aneurysm, massive head trauma, a brain tumour, or a lack of oxygen to the brain. Because the heart remains active with mechanical support, the flow of blood to the organs has not ceased and they can still function properly. Among organs that can be transplanted are the kidneys, liver, pancreas, heart, lung, and bowel. A donor can be any age, depending on the specific organ, and many transplants have been successful using organs over 80 years old. The liver can regenerate itself once transplanted, and age does not necessarily dictate the health of the organ.

Provided there are no underlying diseases within the organ and the deceased did not suffer from an acquired disease such as HIV or hepatitis, the organs can be successfully transplanted. Rigorous tests are performed on the organ to ensure it qualifies before it is transplanted. After transplantation, most recipients lead normal, active lives (see Exhibit 1 for transplant success rates by type of organ).

Cadaveric Tissue Donation

A patient does not need to suffer brain death to qualify as a cadaveric tissue donor. Heart valves, cornea, bone, and skin are among the tissues that can be successfully retrieved from the deceased and transplanted to a patient in need. Tissue donations undergo the same rigorous disease testing that organ donations do, but the criteria for tissue donations are different.

DONORS AND RECIPIENTS

A recent study undertaken by the House of Commons Standing Committee on Health[2] presented the following information on Canadian donors and recipients:

- Most cadaveric donors were multiorgan donors (79.1 percent in 1996).
- The most common cause of death for organ donors was an intracranial event such as a cerebral bleed (48 percent).
- Traumas such as motor vehicle accidents or gunshot wounds accounted for approximately 33 percent of donor deaths.
- The average age of a cadaveric donor was 36 years.
- The most common transplant recipient was a middle-aged Caucasian male.
- Eighty-seven percent of recipients were between the ages of 18 and 64, and 65 percent were male.
- Males constituted 84 percent of heart transplant recipients.

ORGAN DONATION IN CANADA

Organ donation was a major item on the agenda of the House of Commons Health Committee and was a topic well known in Ottawa. Provincial governments across Canada shared one common problem — a severe lack of organ donors. It was so severe that Canada's rate of donation had fallen to "one of the lowest rates in the industrial world at 14.4 donors per million population."[3] It was because of this poor rate that an estimated 140 Canadians died each year awaiting organ transplants.[4] In fact, less than half of those who needed a transplant ever received it.[5] Organ donor statistics varied greatly across Canada and worldwide (see Exhibit 2 for national and international donor rates).

Because the process saved lives, most major religions accepted organ donation; however, there remained strong opposition by some religions that were guided by the belief that to be clinically dead was not necessarily to be spiritually dead and that a cadaver should not be intruded upon until the soul had had time to depart the body. Other factors contributing to low donor rates included the following:

- People mistrusted the medical system — it was believed by many that hospital officials would not make as much of an effort to save a life if it was known that the patient had agreed to organ donation.
- There was little knowledge about the need for organs.
- There was little knowledge about the success rate of organ transplants.
- Superstitious beliefs existed that death would occur soon after the donor card was signed.
- There was a high cost for a hospital to identify and maintain organ donors.
- Health care professionals' attitudes and the methods they used to approach families of the deceased were not liked.
- There was inadequate recognition and/or compensation for donating organs.
- Families believed that organ donations would affect funeral arrangements and that the body might be disfigured or endure more suffering.

ORGAN DONATION IN ONTARIO

Provincial Support

Prior to issuing new driver's licences on one credit-card size plastic card, the provincial government of Ontario printed an organ donation section directly on the paper portion of the licence. The driver wishing to become an organ donor could fill out this area and sign it, and it remained as a part of the driver's licence. Currently, the Ministry of Transportation included a separate donor card with the new plastic driver's licence. Interested individuals could sign the card and were asked to keep it with their personal belongings in their wallet or purse. Individuals would also receive a donor card form with their new picture identification health card from the provincial government that could be filled out and mailed in (see Exhibit 3).

Family Involvement

Despite the fact that an individual had registered as an organ donor, the family of the deceased always had the power to veto this decision. This was reported to have occurred in as many as 35 percent of all cases;[6] however, sources in the field believed the figure to be much lower. The family also had the power to allow retrieval of organs even if the individual had not preregistered in the program. Under Resolution 518 of the Public Hospitals Act passed in June 1990, "all hospitals in Ontario must have policies and procedures to identify potential donors and approach their families."[7] How well hospital officials were trained often determined how successful they were when approaching those who had recently lost a family member.

Multiple Organ Retrieval and Exchange Program (MORE)

There were five regional transplant centres across Ontario. Located in London, Hamilton, Toronto, Kingston, and Ottawa, the regional centres were the hubs of all retrieval and transplantation activity for the province. In an attempt to better manage the flow of information between the centres, the Multiple Organ Retrieval and Exchange Program (MORE) was established in 1988. MORE was the communication liaison between transplant units across Ontario. The centre, located in downtown Toronto, collected and managed data relating to organ donation activity and statistics on a central computer system with the intent to ensure that all organs were shared among waiting recipients in an efficient and fair manner. In 1999 MORE was changed to ODO.

**Organ Donation
Ontario (ODO)**

Once a patient was identified as a candidate for organ transplantation, the patient's name and vital information were confidentially entered into the computer system at the regional site and were also stored in the provincial database. When a family whose loved one had suffered brain death agreed to organ donation, the deceased's information was put into the ODO system, and based on need and compatibility, the system produced a list of potential candidates from which the transplant surgeon selected the best match. Retrieval surgeons from one of the regional centres then travelled to the location of the organ donor and performed the operation to remove the donated organs. The organ(s) were then placed in a preservation solution and transported as quickly as possible to the waiting recipient(s), where transplantation surgeons performed the operation(s).[8] The organ and tissues donated by one individual could save the lives of as many as seven patients.

City Donor Rates

Within Ontario, it was believed that Toronto's donor rate was the lowest because of its highly diverse population. In addition, it was suspected that Toronto's rates might be lower owing to the large number of hospitals scattered across a wide geographical area that made the dissemination of information and procedures more difficult (see Exhibit 4 for city donor rates within Ontario).

London's rates, on the other hand, were considered relatively high. One reason for this high rate was the presence of the London Health Sciences Centre, a champion in organ donor awareness. "Don't take your organs to heaven … heaven knows we need them here" was the slogan showcased across the line of clothing, posters, calendars, and events all aimed at increasing organ donation in the city. See Exhibit 5 for an example of these marketing efforts.

**THE CURRENT
SITUATION**

Spurred on by the federal health committee's interest in boosting awareness of the need to increase organ donations across Canada, provincial governments knew a strong marketing communications plan would be necessary to improve on the results of the most recent poll: as many as 90 percent of the sample population indicated they supported organ and tissue donation; however, only 27 to 30 percent of that same group had signed their organ donor form.

Notes

1. Total cessation of brain function as manifested by the absence of consciousness, absence of spontaneous movement, absence of spontaneous respiration, and absence of all brainstem functions.

2. *Organ and Tissue Donation and Transplantation: A Canadian Approach,* Report of the Standing Committee on Health.
3. CFRA news talk radio, 26 April 1999. This rate calculates the number of actual organ donations that are made per million people.
4. *Toronto Star,* 12 March 1999.
5. "Wanted: Spare Parts," *Maclean's,* 3 May 1999.
6. *Toronto Star,* 3 March 1999.
7. Online. August 1999. http://www.transplant-ontario.org
8. Surgeons are responsible either for retrieving organs or for transplanting them.

Exhibit **1**

Success Rates by Transplant Organ

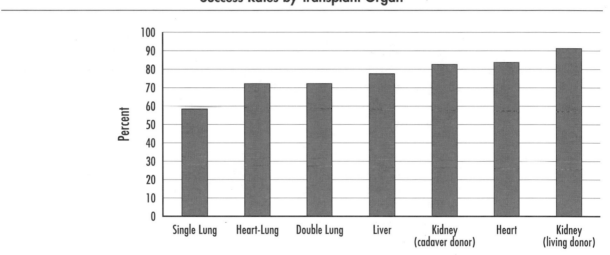

Source: London Health Sciences Centre Multi-Organ Transplant Service.

Exhibit **2**

National Donor Rates, 1998

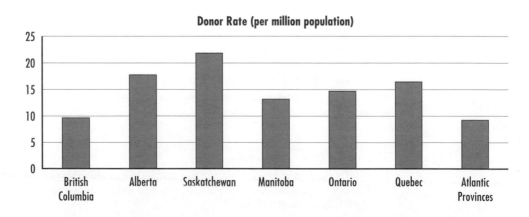

Source: *Transplant Perspectives,* March/June 1999.

EXHIBIT 2 (cont.)

Inernational Donor Rates, 1998

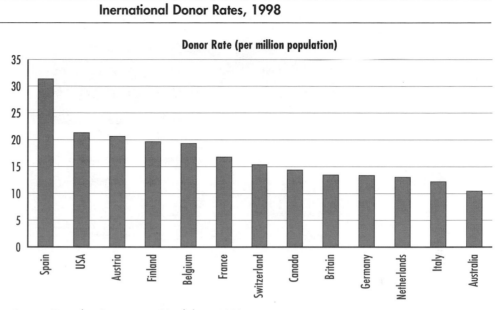

Source: *Transplant Perspectives,* March/June 1999.

EXHIBIT 3

Ontario Donor Rates, 1998

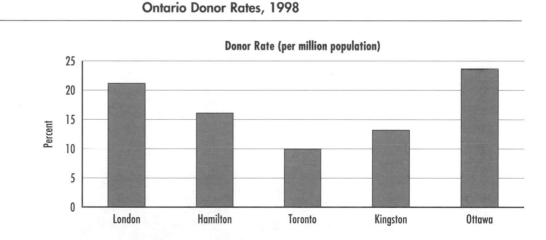

Source: *Transplant Perspectives,* March/June 1999.

Exhibit 4

MORE Organ Donor Card

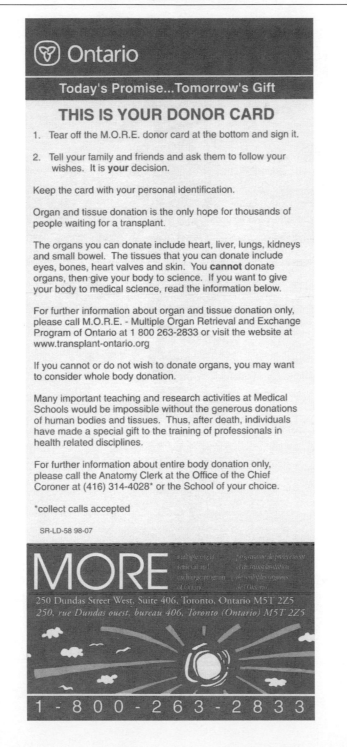

EXHIBIT 5

London's Organ Donor Campaign Materials

Exhibit 5 (cont.)

London's Organ Donor Campaign Materials

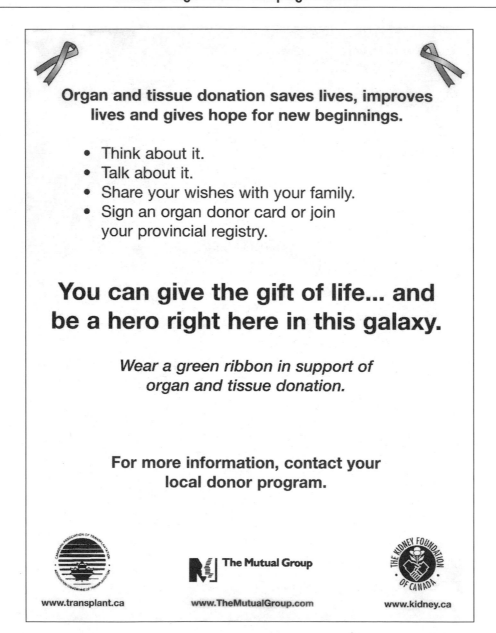

Organ and tissue donation saves lives, improves lives and gives hope for new beginnings.

- Think about it.
- Talk about it.
- Share your wishes with your family.
- Sign an organ donor card or join your provincial registry.

You can give the gift of life... and be a hero right here in this galaxy.

Wear a green ribbon in support of organ and tissue donation.

For more information, contact your local donor program.

The Mutual Group

www.transplant.ca   www.TheMutualGroup.com   www.kidney.ca

CASE 5.8   THE POOL DOCTOR

By Jeff Golfman, Michael Pearce, and John Hulland

In mid-December 1989, Jeff Golfman sat down in front of his laptop computer in order to close off his books for the previous summer and to start preparing for the upcoming swimming pool season. A meeting was scheduled with his bank manager for the first week of January, and he had to present his strategy for the following year at that time.

Many strategic issues remained unresolved. For example, Jeff was still unsure of how he should market his business during the coming year and whether or not he should remain with his current chemical supplier. In addition, he did not know which services he should offer in order to achieve maximum profits and long-term success for the Pool Doctor.

THE POOL DOCTOR

The Business Concept

During its first two years of operation, the Pool Doctor developed a reputation for offering excellent, professional, and friendly service to the Winnipeg swimming pool market at very reasonable prices. The company had been established to cater to the needs of pool owners who wanted to use their swimming pools throughout the summer but who did not want to do the maintenance jobs themselves. The Pool Doctor offered a complete package of routine pool maintenance, pool summerizations, winterizations, and repairs.

Customers' pools were serviced three times per week (including water analysis, chemical balancing, vacuuming, skimming, backwashing, and a routine equipment check). In addition, each pool was visited once a week by a quality control manager from the company to ensure top-level performance by the labour force. Furthermore, the Pool Doctor ran a chemical delivery program for its clients on an "as needed basis," which allowed the pool owners to avoid stocking pool chemicals.

The History of the Company

During the summer of 1988, Jeff Golfman and Alan Secter formed a partnership under the Pool Doctor name. Originally, they had planned to sell ionization water purification systems. This idea was dropped when the ionization units did not per-

---

form to the partners' expectations. Early that summer, Jeff and Alan printed and hand delivered fliers to pool owners in order to solicit customers (see Exhibit 1). They also approached Aristocrat Pools N' Spa to establish a source of supply for pool chemicals. The partners maintained their customers' pools with the help of one worker, and by the end of the summer had a client list with more than 30 names on it. In addition, they generated a total profit for the summer of over $8,000 (see Exhibit 2).

During the summer of 1989, the company's client base increased to more than 60 customers, including 23 of the previous season's customers, and four commercial accounts. An office was leased, and eight students were hired as service technicians for the summer. The partners divided the duties between themselves, with Alan handling the purchasing, arranging for client repairs, and completing government forms, and with Jeff handling the bookkeeping and office systems management functions. The training, hiring, firing, marketing, and quality control functions were shared between the two partners.

During that same season, the Pool Doctor became the largest residential pool-cleaning company in Winnipeg. The business was computerized for all of the accounting functions, and many procedures and business systems, as well as standards, were established. The Pool Doctor was supported by an interest-free loan from the Federal Business Development Bank and by a wage subsidy from Employment Development Services. In addition, the Pool Doctor was invited to join the Canadian Swimming Pool Association in recognition of its previous success.

For the 1989 season, the Pool Doctor generated revenues totalling $87,468. This netted an operating income of $7,223 for the period May 1 through September 30, 1989. (See Exhibit 3 for the 1989 income statement and Exhibit 4 for the closing balance sheet.) Following the 1989 season, Alan decided to continue his studies overseas, and a buy-out agreement was drafted in order to dissolve the partnership.

THE POOL SERVICES CONSUMER

Jeff believed that the typical Pool Doctor customer was a dual-income family with children. With the increased incidence of dual-income families and women entering the work force, many home owners needed to hire extra help around the house. These people tended to retain the services of a lawn maintenance company, a snow removal company, and a maid. The next logical step was to have someone take care of their swimming pool. The higher costs associated with buying and maintaining a summer cottage had led many people to turn to their own backyards for their weekend retreats. Thus, new pool installations over the past five years had been quite steady despite fluctuations in the economy, and the number of pool owners hiring someone else to maintain their pools had increased steadily during the same period.

During the 1989 season, a "Mid-Summer Evaluation" was sent to 65 Pool Doctor customers (see Exhibit 5). The purpose of this survey was to determine their purchase criteria, to assess their overall satisfaction with the service, and to identify areas that needed improvement. Of the customers surveyed, 91 percent rated their overall satisfaction as either very good or excellent, and 87 percent were completely satisfied with the number of cleanings per week, the time of day servicing was conducted, and the politeness and disposition of Pool Doctor staff. When asked why they had decided to use the Pool Doctor, 40 percent stated that they found pool cleaning to be too time consuming. Furthermore, 26 percent of the customers surveyed stated that they had switched from another company to the Pool Doctor for pool servicing, citing price, reliability, and quality as the major reasons for making the switch. Finally, when asked for suggestions for improvement, 26 percent wanted to see more mechanical/technical know-how, 13 percent wanted a faster response to emergency situations, 21 percent wanted better accommodation of their special needs, and 26 percent indicated that they felt the price charged was too high.

Jeff had found during the previous two summers that new pool owners were not a good source of Pool Doctor customers. This situation was true whether the pool was newly constructed or was older but recently bought by people who had not previously owned a pool. Jeff attributed this behaviour to a number of factors. First, pool stores did not service the pools that they sold, preferring to let owners do so on their own. This eliminated additional low-margin work, led to increased chemical sales, and helped release the stores from any warranty work. Second, after spending thousands of dollars to purchase a pool, the last thing most new pool owners wanted to do was spend additional money. Finally, because new pool owners were unlikely to realize that caring for a pool was a full-time job, they were prepared to carry out the task by themselves.

After spending a few summers fighting with their pools and spending sunny Sunday afternoons cleaning them instead of swimming in them, most pool owners became very frustrated. They quickly realized that the pool stores did not want to teach them how to maintain their pools, as this training would result in lower chemical sales and after-sales service work. The short pool season and the long, cold winters experienced in Winnipeg led to further frustration. Every year, each pool had to be drained and winterized in the fall, and then summerized and chemically re-balanced in the spring. This process caused a lot of wear and tear on the pool liner, equipment, and piping and fittings.

The pool stores viewed these yearly tasks as opportunities to charge high prices while providing minimal guarantees on workmanship and parts. An all too common pool store practice involved telling a customer that a certain part needed replacing. When the customer purchased a new part, the pool store then turned around and sold that customer's part as a used one to someone else. Occurrences like this had increased consumer distrust in the industry. Furthermore, pool owners received little communication, know-how, or prompt service from the pool stores. In an extreme case, one pool store initiated a "VIP Service" program, which required pool owners to pay the store $100 at the beginning of the season in order to become a VIP customer and thus receive quicker service on repairs.

After a couple of years, most pool owners were frustrated, and many wished that they had never purchased a pool in the first place. Most found themselves to be either too busy, too lazy, or too intimidated by their pools and the pool stores to provide proper care for their pools on an ongoing basis. At this point, many purchased automatic cleaning devices and automatic chlorinating mechanisms in search of an easy solution. When they soon discovered that these methods worked only in conjunction with a routine maintenance program, they quickly became discouraged again. It was at this point that Jeff thought the pool owner was ready to try a pool servicing company like the Pool Doctor.

Near the end of the 1989 pool season, Jeff went through the Pool Doctor's client list and determined the number of clients that he felt would return with the company for the following summer. He estimated that 80 percent (50 customers) would definitely return for the 1990 pool season, while he considered the remaining 20 percent questionable. In reviewing the summer of 1989 figures, Jeff estimated that the cost of acquiring each new Pool Doctor customer during that year had been approximately $80. Furthermore, he calculated that the company had billed an average customer $1,329 during the 1989 season ($560 for chemicals and the balance for labour).

COMPETITION

The pool servicing companies operating in Winnipeg could be divided into two distinct categories: independents and pool stores. Although there were seven major pool stores in Winnipeg, only two (Krevco and Aqua-Pleasure) maintained swimming pools themselves. Most pool storeowners thought that the returns from servicing pools did not justify the additional effort involved. The pool stores were primarily concerned with swimming pool installations, chemical sales, repair work, and pool openings and closings.

Jeff estimated that there were more than 10,000 swimming pools in Winnipeg. Of these, approximately 353 owners had their pools serviced regularly by a maintenance company. An estimated client base for each company and their respective market shares are shown in Exhibit 6.

Both Krevco and Aqua-Pleasure had lost the majority of their regular maintenance customers over the past few years as a result of high prices and poor service. Many customers complained of cloudy pools, large chemical bills, rude treatment, and slow or nonexistent problem-solving capabilities.

The independent pool maintenance companies (e.g., CVB and Aqua-Clear) tended to concentrate their efforts on the pool summerization, winterization, and repair businesses. Although this provided them with very high margins, they were in direct competition with the pool stores using an after-sales service strategy. Most of these companies had small routes, and they rarely competed directly with the Pool Doctor.

The Pool Clinic was a pool servicing company competing directly with the Pool Doctor. The Pool Clinic, which had been in operation for four years, had an established clientele of approximately 30 full-time customers. Jeff believed that the company concentrated its efforts in the "once per week service" and the "vacation service" segments of the market. It also actively pursued pool openings and closings, as well as repair work. In order to obtain greater company exposure, it used a large milk truck with the company's name written on the side. However, four of the Pool Clinic's customers switched over to the Pool Doctor during 1989.

Duguay Pool Services was an established company that had been in business for many years. It concentrated on pool opening, closing, and repair work and had a small but established route of full-time customers. The business was concentrated in the St. Boniface and St. Vital areas of Winnipeg. The Pool Doctor had not yet entered these areas, focusing instead on River Heights and Tuxedo. As a result, competition with Duguay had been minimal.

In addition to these more established firms, several new people tried to enter the pool maintenance business each summer. This occurred because of the low cost of entry into the market and because many individuals had a desire to work outdoors and to be their own boss. Due to the considerable exposure that had been generated for the Pool Doctor over the past two summers, Jeff anticipated that new competitors would start up during the summer.

During the 1988 season, a former Pool Doctor employee had left to start The Pool Pros. This business was a direct copy of the Pool Doctor operation, but since the Pool Doctor did not have a noncompetition agreement with this employee, Jeff could do little about the matter. The Pool Pros, after building up an estimated client base of 20 customers during 1989, was expected to continue operations during the 1990 season. However, the company had not been able to take any business away from the Pool Doctor.

PLANS FOR THE 1990 OPERATION

Goals and Objectives

For the 1990 season, Jeff had a number of corporate and personal objectives in mind. He expected the Pool Doctor operation to generate sales of $100,000 and an overall profit of $22,000. This would be achieved by establishing a customer base of 80 customers and by ensuring little or no customer turnover. Jeff would focus on reducing bad debt and repair expenses, eliminating inventory write-offs, and changing strategy from growth to maintaining and extending the value of each customer by providing a wider range of services. Jeff believed that he could reduce unnecessary overhead expenses by about $11,000 in 1990. On the personal level, Jeff's primary goals were to gain valuable business experience, to work during summers and travel during winters, to avoid monotony and stagnation, to set his own hours and work at his own pace, and to live a balanced lifestyle. In addition, he was prepared to sell the business if the right price were offered.

Besides establishing goals and objectives for the upcoming summer, Jeff had also given considerable thought to a number of operational issues. He planned to operate the Pool Doctor himself, along with a general manager. The general manager was to be responsible for all of the internal controls and bookkeeping functions, including computer data entry (payroll, invoices, accounts payable and receivable), inventory management, and filing and telephone answering duties.

The general manager would receive $5,000 for the summer (April 15 to September 1) plus 20 percent of any profits in excess of $13,000. Jeff had already hired an individual for this position for the upcoming summer. This person had worked at Aristocrat Pools N' Spas for the past three summers and was currently in his fourth year at the University of Manitoba.

While the general manager supervised the office, Jeff planned to spend his time focusing on the hiring, training, firing, marketing, and quality control functions of the business. He also planned to visit each customer's home once a week in order to ensure high quality work. In order to respond quickly to client requests or complaints, he planned to purchase a portable cellular phone including free air-time for the summer months.

Selecting and Training Staff

The Pool Doctor would hire eight university students from both the University of Winnipeg and the University of Manitoba as technicians for the summer. Posters would be placed throughout both campuses in February 1990 in order to stimulate interest in a summer position. Because more than 50 applications had been received by the Pool Doctor from students for positions during the summer of 1989, Jeff did not anticipate any problems in finding eight good people for 1990. During the month of March, Jeff planned to interview all of the applicants. He was looking for responsible, motivated, caring, and independent problem solvers. While Jeff felt that prior work experience helped, he did not view it as a prerequisite for the job. Instead, he believed that a genuine concern for the customer was the most important attribute a potential employee could have.

Once hired, employees would participate in a training session lasting two weeks, from April 30 to May 13. During this time, all of the technicians would be taught about water chemistry, pool mechanics, pool safety, and each pool product to be used. The training sessions would employ a combination of classroom discussions, how-to videotapes, and hands-on techniques.

In order to service 60 to 80 swimming pools during the 1990 pool season, the Pool Doctor planned to employ eight students who would each be responsible for the upkeep of between eight and ten swimming pools. Situated in a proximate geographical area, the pools were to be maintained on a six-day schedule, from Monday to Saturday (assuming a total of ten pools were assigned). Each pool was to be visited by each technician a minimum of three times per week. Daily duties for each pool visit included vacuuming, performing a chemical analysis, skimming debris, monitoring chemical supply, making minor equipment checks, and wiping down pool coping. It was expected that the swimming pools would be kept in a clean and swimmable state at all times. However, during periods of unfavourable weather conditions, it was possible that the pools might temporarily become out of balance.

When visiting a pool, each employee was to be responsible for completing a Pool Doctor quality control sheet. This sheet acted as a checklist for the technician, outlining every task that needed to be completed at the client's home. It covered all aspects of water chemistry, pool mechanics, and appearance of the pool water and the surrounding areas. Upon completion of the duties on a customer's pool, the technician was to fill out the quality control sheet and rate the pool on a 30-point scale. One copy was to be left at the client's home, and a second copy was to be taken back to the Pool Doctor office so that both Jeff and the general manager could assess the state of every pool serviced by the Pool Doctor on a regular basis.

Quality Control   In order to ensure that all pools were in a clean and chemically balanced state, Jeff planned to visit every client's home once per week. During these inspections, each pool would be rated on a 30-point rating scale using the quality control sheets. The 30 points consisted of 12 for the chemical balance of the water, 12 for the appearance of the water, and six for the general cleanliness of the pool shed, deck, and yard. In order to pass an inspection, a minimum rating of 24 points had to be achieved. A failure meant that Jeff considered the pool to be in an unswimmable state. A technician receiving a rating below 24 points would be informed of this fact and would then be responsible for getting the pool back into a swimmable state as soon as possible.

Jeff believed that ongoing service quality was of great importance to most of the Pool Doctor's customers, and that the quality control system that he had instigated provided the company with a competitive advantage. In order to maintain this advantage, Jeff planned to hold regular staff meetings and to offer bonuses based on superior quality performance. During the summer season, all staff would be required to attend a quality control meeting at 4 p.m. every Monday. These meetings would provide a forum for problem solving and building morale, as well as permitting the presentation of an employee-of-the-week award. This employee would be selected on the basis of a bonus system (described below). These bonuses would take the form of tickets to Blue Bomber football games, cases of beer, rock concert tickets, or cash. In addition, the person receiving the highest average quality control rating for the entire summer would receive an additional bonus of $250.

Each employee was to be rated weekly on a fairly detailed rating scale incorporating three distinct, equally weighted measures. The first measure was the average quality control rating given by Jeff that week. The second was to be a rating based on soft goals for the company, and the third was to be a biweekly quality control rating given by each customer. These three measures would then be averaged to give the technician's weekly rating. The soft goals making up the second part of the rating scale included no firings, submission of all quality control sheets, no customer complaints, no bad debts, and ongoing client communication.

In addition to these performance-based bonuses, each technician who remained with the Pool Doctor for the duration of the summer would receive a $250 bonus. This latter payment was included to discourage technicians from quitting during the last two weeks of summer in order to have a break before returning to school. The Pool Doctor had employed this bonus during the previous summer and had found that it was successful in preventing early departures.

SELECTING A 1990 CHEMICAL SUPPLIER

During the 1988 and 1989 swimming pool seasons, the Pool Doctor had purchased its pool chemicals from Aristocrat Pools at a discount. The average margin received from this arrangement was 36 percent, but no contribution was gained on pool summerizations, winterizations, repairs, or accessories. Furthermore, the relationship with this retailer was less than perfect, and Aristocrat's reputation in the industry was poor.

For these reasons, Jeff wondered if he should find a new source of supply for the upcoming summer. If he left Aristocrat Pools, the Pool Doctor would no longer receive leads from Aristocrat's staff for potential customers. In addition, he would not be invited to attend their customer appreciation show, which attracted more than 2,000 pool owners to a one-night pool show featuring Aristocrat's products as well as the services of various pool companies that worked in conjunction with them.

In order to assess the feasibility of switching suppliers, Jeff had gathered price lists from many pool chemical manufacturers, distributors, and retailers. After reviewing this information, Jeff felt that the choice came down to two suppliers: Aristocrat Pools or Capo Industries, located in Burlington, Ontario. Capo was a large chemical supply company that sold pool chemicals and provided limited ongoing technical support to a wide variety of retailers, including Aristocrat Pools. The annual chemical consumption level for a typical pool, along with the two suppliers' chemical costs, are shown in Exhibit 7. The total retail value of these chemicals to the Pool Doctor would be $543.10.

Although Jeff thought that a higher margin could be obtained by switching suppliers, he was unsure whether this potential increase in contribution would outweigh the potential costs. His primary concerns were that (1) the company's logistical problems might increase with the supplier being out of town and having to buy bulk chemicals, (2) the company would now have to stock inventory, and (3) he would lose the pool store as a knowledge and customer source.

SERVICE SELECTION

In addition to regular pool maintenance, Jeff was working on a number of projects that would help the Pool Doctor grow by providing more services to pool owners. However, he was not sure which ones should be pursued during the 1990 season and which ones should be scrapped or postponed. Four projects that Jeff was particularly interested in involved offering private swimming lessons, selling ozone devices, installing fibreglass coatings, and expanding the Pool Doctor operation to new markets.

Results from the 1989 customer survey indicated that 17 percent of all Pool Doctor clients would be interested in having private swimming lessons taught in their backyards. A former Pool Doctor employee who had expressed interest in this concept was prepared to develop it further for the coming summer if the company offered lessons.

The customer survey had also shown that 34 percent of the Pool Doctor's customers would be interested in purchasing an ozone emitting device.

Ozonators allowed a pool to be operated without the use of chlorine, by emitting O3 into the water. Although these devices eliminated the need for all chemicals when used in whirlpools, Jeff had found through trial and error that they were only effective in eliminating O3 in larger swimming pools. Water Environment Technology, the manufacturer of these devices, would give the Pool Doctor approximately $200 for each unit that it sold.

Jeff had had recent discussions with Pool-Tech, a new company located in Trenton, Ontario. He was potentially interested in becoming an exclusive supplier of a new type of fibreglass pool coating that this company produced. The coating was applied like paint but allowed the pool owner to enjoy a smoother finish, with no cracks or staining, no algae build up, 10 percent lower heating bills, and 15 to 20 percent lower chemical costs. The process, which took three individuals two days to complete, would generate a profit for the Pool Doctor of more than $2,000 per installation. Furthermore, Pool-Tech would provide a 10-day training seminar coverings all aspects of pool mechanics, water chemistry, and installation.

Jeff also wanted to consider the possibility of expanding the Pool Doctor into new markets. With either a company-owned or franchised outlet, the Pool Doctor could be operated in more than one city by providing the same set of services to pool owners. Alternatively, the company could continue to focus on Winnipeg but more aggressively seek clients from all regions of the city.

THE 1990 MARKETING PLAN

In order to solicit customers, the Pool Doctor had utilized a direct-mail advertising campaign for the past two seasons. However, the response rate for the 1989 advertisements had been quite low, and Jeff wondered how the marketing plan could be changed for 1990 in order to make it more effective. In considering possible modifications, he first reviewed the 1989 plan.

The Pool Doctor began the 1989 year by sending season's greetings cards to all of its 1988 customers in early December. Letters were then sent to these same customers in February, in an attempt to get them to make an early commitment to return with the Pool Doctor for the 1989 swimming pool season. The company set up a booth at the Aristocrat customer appreciation show on April 18. The Pool Doctor was the only pool-servicing company at the show and donated one month of free pool cleaning for a draw held during the show. In addition, a joint mailing with Aristocrat Pool N' Spa was sent to 5,000 pool owners in early April. (See Exhibit 8 for a copy of the flier employed).

During the summer, the Pool Doctor was able to obtain significant newspaper coverage from both the *Winnipeg Free Press* and the *Jewish Post*. In addition, the company placed six advertisements in the weekly issues of the Jewish Post during April and May. Finally, the Pool Doctor's name was listed in the Yellow Pages, but no advertisement was submitted.

The 1989 customer survey indicated that 30 percent of the 1989 customers had heard about the Pool Doctor from a friend, another 30 percent had received a flier at their homes, 17 percent had been referred by Aristocrat Pools, 13 percent had read a *Jewish Post* advertisement, and the remaining 10 percent had heard about the Pool Doctor by other means.

Jeff noted that the industry typically used the Yellow Pages, direct mail, billboards, print, and radio in order to create demand for their products and services. The expected costs of using these various media in 1990 are indicated in Exhibit 9. Jeff also wondered if he should change the message and the copy that he had used on the 1989 flier or use a cheaper, less professional looking ad similar to the one employed in 1988. Finally, he considered printing Pool Doctor T-shirts and hats to give to pool owners in order to generate additional word-of-mouth and to stimulate demand.

LOOKING AHEAD

The meeting with his bank manager was quickly approaching, and Jeff needed to prepare a business plan for the upcoming summer. He wanted to ensure that the Pool Doctor would be successful during 1990 so that he could travel during the following winter months and repay his student debts. To this end, he began to analyze the options available to the Pool Doctor and wondered what he would have to do in order to meet his profit objective. He was particularly concerned with the choice of a chemical supplier, the mix of services and products to be offered, and the company's marketing plan for 1990.

Eхнiвiт 1

1988 Promotional Flier

THE POOL DOCTOR

"RELIABLE POOL SERVICING AT AFFORDABLE PRICES"

- WATER ANALYSIS
- CHEMICAL BALANCING
- VACUUMING
- SERVICE 3 TIMES WEEKLY

$40 / week

FOR MORE INFORMATION, CONTACT:

JEFF GOLFMAN	ALAN SECTER
489–8150	**475–2804**

* EXCLUSIVE DISTRIBUTORS OF WATERTROL IONIZATION PURIFICATION SYSTEMS–FOR A CHLORINE-FREE SWIMMING POOL / SPA.

EXHIBIT 2

	Income Statement **for the Year Ending August 3, 1988**	
Revenues		
Total		$ 20,886
Expenses		
Advertising	$ 249	
Bank service charges	59	
Office supplies	65	
Miscellaneous supplies	127	
Telephone	256	
Miscellaneous	367	
Purchases	8,877	
Wages	2,367	
Loss on equipment	184	
Total expenses		12,551
Profit		$ 8,335

Exhibit 3

INCOME STATEMENT
for the Year ending September 30, 1989

REVENUES

Service		
Pool servicing — regular	$43,950.99	
Pool servicing — commercial	6,071.06	$50,022.05
Chemical sales		
Pool chemical sales	36,385.56	
Pool accessories	322.63	36,708.19
Other		
Government grant	2,791.80	
Freight revenue	69.84	2,861.64
Sales discounts		
Returns and allowances	(352.24)	
Discounts	(1,771.27)	(2,123.51)
Total revenue		87,468.37

EXPENSES

Administration		
Advertising	$ 779.65	
Bonuses	2,150.20	
Fliers	1,439.17	
Marketing and promotion	1,095.80	
T-shirts and clothing	917.73	
Other[1]	14,277.65	20,660.20
Labour		
Quality control management	3,332.80	
Technicians' wages and benefits	29,744.90	33,077.70
Costs of goods sold		
Pool chemicals	22,297.38	
Pool accessories	628.32	
Other	3,581.74	26,507.44
Total expenses		80,245.34
Net income		$ 7,223.03

1. Other was made up of 41 additional administrative categories, none of which has a significant impact on the decisions in the case.

Exhibit **4**

**Balance Sheet
for the Period Ending November 22, 1989**

ASSETS

Current assets:			
Cash		$(8,673.02)	
Accounts receivable		3,179.19	
Inventory	2,367.88		
Less: write-off	(2,478.27)		
Net inventory		(110.39)	
Total current assets			(5,604.22)
Fixed assets			
Equipment		2,700.00	
Goodwill — AJS buyout		5,128.14	
Total fixed assets			7,828.14
TOTAL ASSETS			$2,223.92

LIABILITIES AND EQUITY

Current liabilities (pst payable)			$ 115.40
Long-term liabilities			0.00
Equity			
Capital contributions			
Golfman, capital	2,701.00		
Less: JJ. Golfman withdrawals	(8,190.07)		(5,489.07)
Earnings			
Retained earnings			0.00
Current earnings			7,597.59
Total equity			2,108.52
TOTAL LIABILITIES AND EQUITY			$2,223.92

Exhibit 5
1989
Mid-Summer
Evaluation

THE POOL DOCTOR
Professional Pool Servicing

POOL DOCTOR—MID-SUMMER EVALUATION FORM   **July 10, 1989**

NAME: _____   PHONE : _____

ADDRESS: _____   POSTAL : _____

OF TIMES SERVICED/WK.: _____   TECHNICIAN:_____

SECTION 1

ON A SCALE OF 1 TO 5 (WITH 1 BEING THE LOWEST) PLEASE RATE THE FOLLOWING:

1.	Your overall satisfaction with the Pool Doctor	1	2	3	4	5
2.	Your satisfaction with the number of cleanings per week	1	2	3	4	5
3.	The time of day that your pool is serviced	1	2	3	4	5
4.	The fairness of our fixed weekly fee structure	1	2	3	4	5
5.	The politeness and disposition of your technician	1	2	3	4	5
6.	The politeness and disposition of other Pool Doctor personnel	1	2	3	4	5
7.	The willingness of the Pool Doctor to accommodate any special needs	1	2	3	4	5

SECTION II

PLEASE ANSWER THE FOLLOWING BY CIRCLING EITHER YES OR NO

– The Pool Doctor is considering expanding the breadth of its services;

1. Would you be interested in private swimming lessons and/or water aerobics classes, taught in your pool by qualified instructors?   YES   NO

2. Would you be interested in receiving information on how you could maintain a virtually chlorine-free pool and/or spa through the use of an Hydro-Pure ozone generator?   YES   NO

1501 Chevrier Blvd., Winnipeg MB, R3T 1Y7   PH: (204) 452-7272   FAX: (204) 786-8544

Exhibit 5 (cont.)

THE POOL DOCTOR

Professional Pool Servicing

POOL DOCTOR EVALUATION FORM

PLEASE ANSWER THE FOLLOWING IN GREATER DETAIL IF POSSIBLE:

1. How long have you been a client of the Pool Doctor? Why did you decide to use us?

    _____

    _____

2. How did you first hear about the Pool Doctor?

    _____

    _____

3. Have you ever had your pool serviced regularly by another company? If yes, which company, and why did you decide to switch?

    _____

    _____

4. What suggestions could you offer to help us improve our service?

    _____

    _____

    _____

    _____

    _____

Thank you for your cooperation. The Pool Doctor commits itself to satisfying your pool servicing needs.

Jeff & Allan

1501 Chevrier Blvd., Winnipeg MB, R3T 1Y7   PH: (204) 452-7272   FAX: (204) 786-8544

EXHIBIT 6

	Market Share of Selected Pool-Cleaning Companies	
Company	Number of Full-Time Customers in 1989	Market Share
Pool Doctor	65	18.4%
The Pool Clinic	30	8.5%
Duguay Pool Services	30	8.5%
Krevco Pool, Patio, and Spa	35	9.9%
Aqua-Pleasure Pool Service	18	5.1%
CVB Pool & Spa Care	25	7.1%
Aqua-Clear Pool Care	30	8.5%
Pool Pros	20	5.7%
Other	100	28.3%
Total	353	100.0%

EXHIBIT 7

	ALTERNATIVE SUPPLIER COSTS FOR CHEMICALS	
Average Annual Chemical Consumption per Pool	Aristocrat Unit Cost	Capo Unit Cost
3 CHLORINE (71 kg)	$55.73[1]	$40.81
1 HTH (11.4 kg)	58.12	37.04
1 OXYOUT (7 kg)	45.71	50.00
2 PH BOOST (2.5 kg)	5.12	1.50
3 PH REDUCER (3.5 kg)	6.52	2.52
2 ALGEE 500 (1 kg)	11.97	5.95
2 STABILIZER (1 kg)	6.52	4.06
2 ALKA PLUS (2 kg)	5.79	1.79
TERMS:	F.O.B. WINNIPEG	F.O.B. WINNIPEG
MINIMUM ORDER:	–	$1,000

1. An average customer's pool would require the use of three 71 kg units of chlorine during the year. The cost of this chlorine to the Pool Doctor would be $167.19 (3 x $55.73) if supplied by Aristrocrat.

EXHIBIT 8

1989 Joint Mailing Flyer

DON'T ALLOW YOUR POOL TO RUIN YOUR SUMMER ...THIS YEAR

Let Professionals maintain it, so that you can enjoy it!

How?
- Complete Pool maintenance 3 times weekly;
  with vacuuming, skimming, water analysis and chemical balancing
- Pool openings and closings
- Free chemical delivery
- Residential and Commercial Service

Why?
- Fully Insured
- Canspa member (Cdn. Swimming Pool Assoc.)
- Very affordable prices and guaranteed satisfaction
- Save time, money, headaches and prolong the life of your pool

Call **452-7272** Anytime
POOL DOCTOR
"The Pool Care Specialist"

Exhibit 8 (cont.)

Swimming Pool Maintenance Guide
DAILY

1. Check the chlorine and PH levels with a test kit
- Be sure to accurately line up the water level with the fill line on the test kit
- Replace reagents each year and do not store them in the sun

2. Adjust the chlorine and PH levels as needed
- Keep the chlorine level in the desired range; 1.5 – 2.5 ppm
- Keep the PH level in the desired range; 7.4 – 7.6
- Add Ph down when the level is above 7.6, and add Ph up when it is below 7.4. See the label on the chemical bottle for dosages.
- Always mix chemicals in a bucket of water before adding them to the pool. Never add water to chemicals!

3. Backwash the filter for 2 – 3 minutes

4. Check the water level. Try to keep it halfway up the skimmer intake on the side of the pool

5. Vacuum when necessary. Be sure to vacuum the walls, wipe down the ring around the water level, remove any leaves from the surface, and empty the filter and pump baskets whenever they have debris in them

WEEKLY (e.g., every Saturday)

1. Add an algicide to the pool (check the label for dosage)

2. Add a shock treatment to the pool (either chlorine or non-chlorine, and check the label for dosage)

MONTHLY

1. Have the pool water professionally tested:
- Check hardness, Alkalinity and Stabilizer levels and maintain them in the desired ranges
- Hardness   50 – 300 ppm
- Stabilizer   30 – 60 ppm
- Alkalinity   110 – 140 ppm

HELPFUL HINTS

- Have the sand in your filter changed every 4 years as it loses its effectiveness, and can cause cloudy water.
- Attend to the pool regularly! If you neglect it, the water can turn green and cloudy and will take more time and money to rectify it and restore clarity
- Have the water professionally tested if water problems arise
- Call the pool doctor at 452-7272 if you have any questions

Exhibit 9

SELECTED 1990 MEDIA COSTS

- Winnipeg Yellow Pages advertisement (average size): $40 per month
- Direct mail: $0.55 per household
- Daily Newspapers:

	MAL Rates[1]		
	B/W	**3 Colours**	**Paid Circulation**
The Winnipeg Free Press	$4.91	$8.10	172,191
The Winnipeg Sun	$1.55	$2.08	48,445

- Weekly Community Papers:[2]

	MAL Rates	**Circulation**
The Herald	$ 0.99	42,000
The Metro	1.08	55,050
The Lance	1.20	53,800
The North Times	1.00	39,150
The Jewish Post	0.78	3,735

1. MAL stands for Modular Agate Line, which is a unit of space 1/14 inches high by 2 inches (1 column) in width. A full-size newspaper has 1,800 MALs.

2. The four area-based community papers were delivered weekly to the following regions:

Herald:	East and North Kildonan, Trancona, Elmwood
Metro:	St. James-Assiniboia, Westwood, Crestview, Silver Heights, River Heights, Charleswood, Ft. Rouge, Lindenwoods, Tuxedo
Lance:	St. Boniface, St. Vital, Windsor Park, Southdale, Island Lakes, River Park South, Fort Garry, Fort Richmond, Waverly Heights, Richmond West, St. Norbert
North Times:	Garden City, Tyndall Park, The Maples, The West End, West Kilodan, The North End

- Radio:

CIFX-AM

60-Second Spots	**1x**	**5x**
Class "AAA"	$212	$165
Class "AA"	201	156
Class "A"	127	95

Exhibit **9** *(cont.)*

SELECTED 1990 MEDIA COSTS

---

30 Seconds (75 Percent of 60-Second Rate)

Class "AAA"	5:30 a.m.–10:00 a.m. Monday to Saturday
Class "AA"	10:00 a.m.–8:00 p.m. Monday to Saturday
Class "A"	8:00 p.m.–1:00 a.m. Monday to Saturday
	6:00 a.m.–12:00 p.m. Sunday

- Transit Shelters:

Number of Units	Cost per 4–week period
9	$4,248
18	8,100
28	12,600

- Transit (Exterior):

Number of Buses	Cost per 4–week period
30	$2,905
60	5,415
92	7,685

C A S E 5.9   PURELY GR...8! WATER COMPANY INC.

By Elizabeth Grasby and Kristina Krupka

"Pure water is liquid gold and I think we're sitting on a gold mine," Romil Reyes, vice-president of operations of Purely Gr...8! Water Company Inc. (Purely) of Scarborough, Ontario, Canada remarked to his marketing consultant, Sandra Hawken. It was June 1997, and Sandra Hawken was meeting with her new client, Romil Reyes. Reyes was confident about the future of Purely, but Hawken knew that the company's current marketing strategy would have to be overhauled if new markets were to be successfully penetrated. Since Reyes was anxious to begin market expansion, Hawken had less than a week to prepare her recommendations.

SANDRA HAWKEN

Sandra Hawken, 24, completed a bachelor of commerce (honours) degree in 1995 at Queen's University in Kingston, Ontario. She graduated top of her class and was quickly recruited by an award-winning advertising agency in Toronto. She enjoyed much success in her position as account executive and was being considered for a promotion to account supervisor after only two years with the firm.

Hawken's long-term goal was to establish her own marketing consulting firm. But until she had acquired the start-up capital to do so, Hawken decided to do some freelance consulting during her spare time to gain more experience and to start building a client base. She had heard of Purely's marketing dilemma through a friend and as a favour had volunteered her services.

HENRY AND ROMIL REYES

Henry Reyes, 49, immigrated to Canada from the Philippines in 1987. His previous work experience included owning a janitorial service company, and more recently, working as a sales associate for Simply Water Co. Ltd. When this company went bankrupt, Henry decided to start his own premium purified bottled water company, calling it Purely Gr...8! Water Company Inc. The company was incorporated in August 1996 by Henry Reyes and his son, Romil. Henry believed that there was great demand for premium purified bottled water and he already had a solid customer list. Although Henry did not have much personal capital, he obtained a bank loan and offered Romil a 20 percent partnership.

Romil Reyes, 24, graduated from the accounting program at George Brown College in 1992 and from a three-year computer science program at the Devry Institute in Toronto in 1996. He was employed as a shipper at an office supply company but had recently quit that job to devote himself full time to the role of Purely's vice-president of operations.

Romil hoped to make a lot of money quickly from the business and wanted to buy out his father in a year or two. Romil planned to expand the business quickly to new markets and eventually export globally. He also had goals to expand Purely's product line through the development of soft drinks and juice, using Purely's premium purified water.

However, Romil's father enjoyed servicing Purely's small clientele and did not share Romil's vision for the business. Henry knew his customers well, who were predominantly Filipino, and understood the market. He had developed a good reputation and, thus, was anxious about taking risks that might jeopardize his business.

Romil believed that with Sandra's help and with a solid marketing plan, Henry could be convinced that market expansion was key to sustaining the business.

THE BOTTLED WATER INDUSTRY

Consumers

American and Canadian consumers were increasingly using bottled water and home water treatment systems to avoid direct tap water. Many people were questioning tap water quality and were becoming suspicious of its health effects. The public's consciousness of water quality was raised due to several widely reported incidents in the United States of public drinking water endangering health and even causing death.

In Canada, consumers had been more fortunate. Historically, Canadians had extensive supplies of good drinking water, and water-related illnesses were virtually unknown; however, many of these waters were losing their unspoiled quality. In 1990, a Metro Works survey revealed that 25 percent of the population of Toronto did not trust the quality of their tap water, which came from Lake Ontario. Among those who did drink tap water, nearly 40 percent used a home filtering device.[1]

Although health and safety were foremost among water quality concerns, consumers' main reason for avoiding direct tap water was that they objected to the taste and/or smell of tap water. Additionally, North American culture had become more health and weight conscious since the 1980s, and bottled water naturally became a healthy substitute for caffeinated or alcoholic beverages. By the early 1990s, bottled water had become a booming business. According to the Canadian Bottled Water Association, estimated sales of bottled water totalled $292 million in 1996, a 13 percent increase over the previous year.

There were two distinct consumer groups that used bottled water: residential users and commercial users. Of total bottled water sales, 90 percent were sold to residential users, and 10 percent to commercial users.

Residential Users

Residential users could be further divided into distinct groups based on, for example, similar demographics or psychographics (image, lifestyle, etc.). The bottled water market itself was also divided into three main categories based on price: premium, mid-priced, and private label.

Premium residential users of bottled water drank imported water, as they believed it to be a superior tasting product. Although some used bottled water only for drinking, others insisted on using bottled water for cooking, making other beverages, ice cubes, baby formula, pets or plants, and even for brushing their teeth and washing their hair and face. Fifteen percent of bottled water sales were made to this consumer group of premium users, and they were highly influenced by image-based advertising.

Consumers who purchased mid-priced bottled water were more price conscious than the premium residential users and might use the water for not only drinking but for one or all of the uses previously mentioned. This group purchased the imported brands only when they were priced competitively. These consumers were influenced by bus board advertising and radio and print promotions positioning the water as a family product. Thirty-five percent of bottled water sales were made to this consumer group.

The remaining 50 percent of bottled water sales were made to those consumers who purchased private label brands. These consumers sought value and purchased their water in larger quantities at grocery stores. They were influenced primarily by print advertising in flyers, point of purchase displays, and coupons.

Commercial Users

In the commercial sector, businesses required large 20-litre bottles and water dispensers for their customers and employees. Premium quality water may not be of paramount concern. Many businesses provided bottled water in the workplace as an alternative to coffee and/or to make customers feel comfortable and invited. The cost of the water and the dispenser was a main concern, and businesses would usually shop around before settling on one supplier. Service and delivery were also important.

Types of Bottled Water

As bottled water fell under the authority of the Health Protection Branch in Canada, all contents had to be clearly listed on labels. The purity of water was measured in parts per million (ppm) of total dissolved solids (TDS), where TDS was simply the dissolved matter in water. There were several types of bottled water currently on the market.

Mineral Water

Mineral water contained over 500 ppm of TDS of inorganic particles (lead, copper, mercury and fluoride, to name a few). It was usually bottled at the water source and could be filtered or processed for bacterial removal.

Spring Water

To be declared a spring water, such as Volvic or Evian, the water had to have an inorganic mineral count of less than 500 ppm of TDS. Spring water was usually transported to its bottling location and could be processed to remove all classifications of contaminants.

Distilled Water

Distilled water was the steam condensed when water was boiled. This process left the heavier contaminants in the water. Additionally, contaminants that boiled at less or close to the same temperature as water would then be filtered, using an activated carbon-based filter, from the condensed water.

Pure Water

Pure water was defined by the International Bottled Water Association (IBWA) as having less than 10 ppm of TDS and was virtually free of detectable levels of water contaminants (including bacteria and parasites, inorganic materials, pesticides, and herbicides). Some or all of these contaminants could be harmful to a person's health.

Advertising messages for bottled water had misled consumers about the purity of their bottled water. While this was true for some types of bottled water, this was not the case of for all bottled water. According to a competitive product survey in 1994 (see Exhibit 1), Evian had more ppm of TDS than the city of Scarborough's tap water; however, that did not necessarily mean that Scarborough's water was better tasting or better smelling.

THE COMPETITION

Major Players

Of the approximately 900 bottled water companies in the United States and Canada in 1996, the market was dominated by two foreign conglomerates with enormous financial resources and marketing muscle — Evian and Perrier. Evian, a unit of Swiss-based Nestlé Inc., was the leader, with more than half of the U.S. market and 25 percent of the Canadian market. Close behind Evian was Perrier, a unit controlled by France's Danone Group.

When ranked by a panel of expert tasters for The Toronto Star, Perrier's Valvert was chosen as the winning spring water. It was described as fresh, smooth, and bright, and would be a perfect water with a nice meal. However, Valvert was also one of the most expensive waters, retailing at $2.25 for a 1.5 L bottle. Evian received average reviews in the same taste test. Evian was described as refreshing and smooth without strong flavours. Its retail price was competitive in the mid-priced bottled water category at $1.79 per 1.5 L bottle. President's Choice spring water retailed for $0.89 per 1.5 L bottle but was described as bitter, heavy, and metallic.

The market became even more competitive in July 1996, when Coca-Cola Enterprises Inc. purchased Nora Beverages Inc. of Mirabel, Quebec, the largest producer of bottled water in Canada. Since the purchase, Coca-Cola had been heavily promoting its spring water sold under the trade name Naya. Naya was being targeted to the young, athletic market through television advertisements that focused on fast-paced sports. In the 1.5 litre and smaller category of spring water, Naya had 18 percent of the market in Canada, second to Evian's 25 percent share.[2]

Minor Players

The magnitude and continued growth of the market enticed hundreds of smaller companies to market their own brand of bottled water. Given the industry's capital intensive nature and the domination of Evian and Perrier, smaller bottled water companies rarely set their own price in most markets.

Crystal Clear Springs (Crystal) and Gold Mountain Water Inc., two smaller bottled water companies, presented direct competition for Purely in the pure water category. Crystal had been servicing 8,000 homes and offices in the greater Toronto area since 1985. Crystal sold pure water in sizes ranging from 350 mL bottles to 18 L containers of natural and added fruit flavours. Crystal's domestic sales for 1996 were in the $5 million to $10 million range, with export sales in the $100,000 range.

Gold Mountain Water Inc., also based in Toronto, sold two labels of pure water: Gold Mountain, which was a unique pure water with an expensive price tag, and Canadian Mountain, which was less expensive but considered equally unique in its taste. Marketing efforts concentrated on residential users only. The company had received accolades from the IBWA for "Prestigious Excellence in Manufacturing" at a conference in October 1995. Gold Mountain Water Inc. was currently seeking a distribution network to further penetrate Canadian, U.S., and global markets. Domestic sales for 1996 were in the $2 million to $5 million range.

PURELY GR...8! WATER COMPANY INC.

The Product

Henry and Romil Reyes believed Purely to be "the purest of the pure waters," containing less than 8 ppm of TDS. Purely used an eight-step purification process that began with regular tap water, which through reverse osmosis, was purified to remove most contaminants. Experts had proclaimed this process to be the best way to produce pure water. Most tasks were done by hand, such as putting caps on bottles and applying labels. The family prided itself on using extreme care and surpassing sanitation standards.

In the 10 months that Purely had been in business, the company had experienced tremendous growth. The company's successful sales growth had been achieved primarily by targeting the Filipino residential user in the greater Toronto area. Purely's best-selling item was a case of 12 bottles of 1.5 L to this segment, since this size was easy to carry and store in the refrigerator. The company's secondary target market had been the commercial sector, representing 15 percent of sales. The family attributed the company's success to its premium product, exceptional customer service, and persuasive door-to-door selling tactics.

Sales Visits

During a sales visit, the company representative would warn potential customers of the health risks associated with dehydration and would stress the importance of drinking eight glasses of water daily to maintain good health. Following this, the sales representative would then conduct a demonstration that involved testing the home user's tap water. During the demonstration, the contaminants in tap water were highlighted so that the customer saw bright orange matter floating in the water. This same test was then conducted on Purely's product, with the results showing that Purely's water was virtually free of containments and dissolved matter. Purely promoted the idea that "your body deserves the best" and the comparative safety and health benefits of pure water over other water types. The sales visit concluded with the distribution of price lists (see Exhibits 2 and 3).

Sales Force

Purely employed six sales representatives who were each paid a salary of $30,000 per year (no commission). The sales representatives were responsible for selling. Henry would collect the accounts receivable and a warehouse worker would deliver the water. Romil estimated that the sales representatives were responsible for approximately 40 percent of sales.

The remaining 60 percent of sales were made by 12 sales associates who were independent sales representatives. The associates were responsible for obtaining the product from Purely, selling, delivering, and collecting any accounts receivable. The sales associates expected a minimum margin of 20 percent; however, some associates would discount the product to move more volume. The price that the end consumer paid could vary anywhere from $10.50 per case of 12 (1.5 L) bottles to $17.00 per case. Romil was concerned about the inconsistent pricing strategy and wondered what impact this had on the consumers' perception of their product. It was also unclear to Romil what the associates stressed in their sales pitch.

Variable costs, including raw materials, direct labour, and overhead, were estimated at approximately $6.70 per case of 12 (1.5 L) bottles.

FUTURE PLANS

Even though Romil Reyes was anxious to expand into new markets, Sandra Hawken knew that the company was severely financially limited. During her plant tour, Hawken noted that all equipment was working at full capacity to meet the current demand. Romil mentioned that an additional $150,000 was needed to finance new machinery and a delivery van and hoped that if a solid business plan was presented to the bank, a loan could be obtained. However, the company's profitability could not be accurately determined because business and personal expenses had been mixed together. An accountant was currently working on the records to try to prepare statements for the bank. All personal and business assets had been pledged to secure the first business loan of $300,000. If financing was obtained, Purely's current industrial complex could not house the new equipment. Rent on the new complex would increase Purely's yearly expenditures by $5,500.

As Hawken reviewed this information, she knew the company could not afford an elaborate promotion strategy. The current advertising efforts (door-to-door sales, word of mouth within the Filipino community, brochures, and occasional newspaper advertising in Filipino-targeted publications) totalled $2,000 annually. Hawken had contacted a friend, a media buyer, and had received listings of advertising and promotional costs (Exhibit 4).

CONCLUSION

With the marketing plan due within the week, decisions concerning product positioning, pricing, promotion, and distribution needed to be resolved. Hawken knew that Romil expected her to set the advertising budget and justify its feasibility. In addition, Hawken knew that her recommendations would have to satisfy both Romil's goals of quick market expansion and Henry's goals of conservative growth within the current target market. This consideration created its own challenge, and Hawken wondered how the new marketing plan could build clientele without confusing the existing customer base.

Notes

1. Metro Works, "Water Quality Update," 1990, ii.
2. *The Montreal Gazette*, 20 August 1996.

Exhibit 1

Bottled Water Parts per Million (PPM) of Total Dissolved Solids (TDS) Competitive Product Survey 1994

Ballygowan (Irish Spring)	*480 p.p.m.*
Spring Valley	*386 p.p.m.*
Crystal Spring	*369 p.p.m.*
White Mountain (Canada Dry)	*368 p.p.m.*
Evian	*310 p.p.m.*
Alpine	*244 p.p.m.*
Mount Claire	*245 p.p.m.*
Naya	*200 p.p.m.*
Fern Brook	*194 p.p.m.*
Arctic Clear	*190 p.p.m.*
Tap Water (Scarborough	*210 p.p.m.*
Tap Water (Woodbridge)	*190 p.p.m.*
Crystal Eau de Source	*160 p.p.m.*
President's Choice	*120 p.p.m.*
Purely Gr....8! Water Company Inc. less than	*8 p.p.m.*

Water with less than 10 p.p.m. is classified as Pure Water. It is the *healthiest* water you can drink but the most *difficult to find*.

PURE WATER IS LIQUID GOLD

Source: Purely Gr...8! Water Company Inc.

Exhibit 2

Water Bottle Price List

We offer three different sizes of water bottles with competitive pricing:

Refundable deposit on the 18.9 L (5 U.S. gallons) **bottles**	$ 9.00

Individual prices:

18.9 L (5 U.S. gallons)	$ 6.00
1.5 L Bottles	$ 1.50
500 mL Bottles	$ 0.75

Package prices:

10 or more 18.9 L (5 U.S. gallons)	$ 5.00
12 bottles of 1.5 L	$ 12.00
24 bottles of 500 mL	$ 12.00

* All prices include applicable taxes *
Price may change without notice

Exhibit 3

Water Dispenser Price List

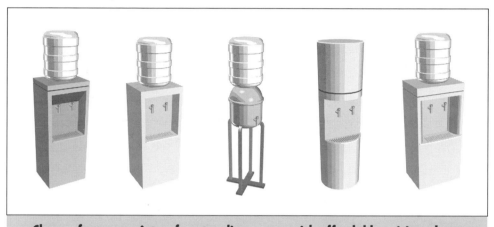

Choose from a variety of water dispensers with affordable pricing plans:

All dispensers are available in white or almond colour

Hot and Cold	**$ 480.00**
Cook (room temperature) **and Cold**	**$ 330.00**
Counter Top with Cook (room temperature)	**$ 90.00**
Battery-operated pump	**GOING PRICE**

Or

We offer a rent-to-own plan:			
	Hot & Cold	Cook & Cold	Counter Top
3 months	$160.00	$110.00	$30.00
6 months	$80.00	$55.00	
12 months	$40.00	$27.50	
18 months	$27.00		

($27 for 17 months & $21 for 18th month)
* All prices include applicable taxes *
Price may change without notice

Source: Purely Gr....8 Water Company Inc.

EXHIBIT 4

ADVERTISING AND PROMOTION COSTS FOR THE TORONTO AREA

TRANSIT[1]

Bus Stop Benches	$200 per bench per month $150 per bench for artwork/setup/installation
Transit Shelters (4 x 5 feet)	$500 per shelter per month $220 per shelter for artwork/setup/installation

TRADE SHOWS

The Food Show Toronto (once in February)	$5,000 per booth $1,000 for brochures

NEWSPAPERS

Globe and Mail (1/8 of a page)	$259 per weekday $490 Saturdays
Toronto Star (1/8) of a page)	$385 per weekday $529 Saturdays

---

1. Gallop + Gallop Advertising.

C A S E 5.10   SOCCER MAGIC 2

By Elizabeth Grasby and Liz Gray

In June 1999, Ralph DeBlois, the new program director at Soccer Magic 2 (SM2) in London, Ontario, sat at his desk and reflected on the company's performance to date. Financial statements indicated that the company did not break even that year and would, in fact, fall short of projections by $270,000. DeBlois wondered why this had happened and what could be done to ensure that head office's goals would be met in the next fiscal year.

SOCCER IN CANADA

Since 1990, the total number of registered soccer players across Canada had increased by 70 percent[1] and it had continued to be among the fastest-growing sports in North America. The Canadian Soccer Association (CSA) reported that in 1997 there were over 585,000 registered soccer players, representing a 9 percent increase over 1996 primarily owing to increased female participation. By comparison, hockey, historically Canada's premier sport, had 536,000 registered players in 1997 and had experienced declining growth rates.

SOCCER MAGIC INC.

Soccer Magic Inc. (SMI) was formed in January 1997 as "a recreation company established to capitalize on the growing demand for indoor soccer facilities." The company designed an indoor sports facility consisting of an air-supported dome that fully enclosed two indoor fields. SMI opened two indoor sports facilities, the first in Kingston, Ontario, in December 1997 (Soccer Magic), and the second in London, Ontario, in February 1998 (Soccer Magic 2). Soccer Magic and Soccer Magic 2 were primarily designed for soccer players but could also support the play of many other sports. While the SMI head office, located in Concord, Ontario, retained ultimate financial and managerial control, those in charge of the individual facilities were responsible for their own daily operations and local marketing campaigns.

Soccer in London

As of June 1999, the population of London was approximately 331,000 and had been growing at an average rate of 8.5 percent per year over the last 25 years.

London, Ontario, was home to more than 25,000 soccer players[2] registered with the Ontario Soccer Association (OSA). The OSA officially governed the game of soccer in Ontario. In this capacity, the OSA made and implemented any necessary rule changes, scheduled tournaments for their registrants, and supplied coaches and referees. All amateur soccer teams registered under the OSA and had their games scheduled by this organization.

In order to participate in organized soccer, London players were required to register with the Elgin Middlesex Soccer Association, the local division of the OSA, for a fee of $4.25. This fee provided each player with insurance in the event of injury. After registering, players could join a team within the league of their choice. The team then decided where they would play.

SOCCER MAGIC 2

Soccer Magic 2 was located at the far east end of the city of London, near the city's airport in a highly industrialized, nonurban area. The facility was built on 0.8 hectares of land and consisted of an air-supported dome that housed two 1,350 square-metre soccer pitches with spectator seating and a batting cage. The playing surface on the soccer pitches was FieldTurf, an innovative product that prevented injuries that often would occur on artificial turf. FieldTurf, produced in Montreal, was used in a number of outdoor and indoor locations around the world. FieldTurf felt like grass, and the soccer ball rolled and bounced on it in the same manner as it would on grass. The facility also included a licensed snack bar (subcontracted to a local establishment), four change rooms, and a large parking area.

Because of intense competition from outdoor pitches and the high temperatures within the dome during the summer months, SM2 had historically operated from mid-October to mid-May. Fortunately, due to structural problems, the vendor agreed to replace the existing dome during the summer of 1999 with an opaque version that would reduce the temperature to 15 degrees below that of the outside environment. The facility could also be heated during the winter months.

First Year of Operation

Soccer

Once registered with the OSA, a soccer team could join regular league play at SM2 at a cost of $1,500 per season. The various leagues included the men's premier league designed for above average soccer players, both women's and men's competitive and recreational leagues, the co-ed league, and the youth competitive league. SM2 would help any registered player find a suitable team if he or she did not already belong to one. All teams were limited to a maximum of 18 players and, on average, most teams consisted of 12 players. Play began in October each season and ran at various times throughout the week, with the exception of Saturdays. Each team played an average of 20 games per season. Soccer Magic provided OSA-certified referees for each game and administered and posted the standings of all leagues. During the 1998–1999 season, SM2 operated at 35 percent capacity with registration consisting of 35 percent adults and 65 percent youth players, of which 65 percent were male and 35 percent were female.

In addition to regular league play, SM2 ran several other soccer activities (listed below) during the season in an attempt to boost revenue.

Youth Recreational

SM2's youth recreational league was open to children aged six to 18 for both fall and winter sessions. Each team played one 45-minute game each Saturday for 12 weeks. One season (fall and winter) cost $184.95 per child; this amount included awards, referees, and team jerseys. In addition to arranging for a team coach, SM2 ensured all children were placed on the appropriate team given their ages. The youth recreational league drew 750 players, and registration was expected to jump to over 1,000 players for the 1999–2000 season.

March Madness

SM2 coordinated and hosted a competitive soccer money tournament[3] in March 1999. This tournament drew men's and women's soccer teams from Toronto, Hamilton, Kingston, Ottawa, and Michigan and was the largest of its kind that London had ever experienced.

Soccer Academy

"The stars of Canadian soccer tomorrow are the youth players of today!" was the slogan advertising Skills-n-Drills, SM2's soccer program for young players. Open to boys and girls between the ages of eight and 15, Skills-n-Drills was an eight-week course designed to teach young players fundamental soccer techniques. The course began in early February and ran on Thursdays from 5:30 p.m. to 6:30 p.m. at a cost of $88 per child.

Other Activities

In addition to soccer, the pitches were used for women's field hockey one day of the week. This required no alteration to the facility.

In addition to the pitches, SM2 also housed a batting cage. Batting cage prices were $40 for 60 minutes, $22 for 30 minutes, or $10 for 40 balls. SM2 also rented out its pitches for baseball practice at a charge of $125 (plus GST) per hour. Baseball teams could also rent the batting cage for an additional charge of $25.

THE COMPETITION

Currently in London, there were no indoor soccer facilities comparable to SM2. A local Optimist Community Centre offered indoor soccer on a hardwood floor at a rate of $78 per hour, and a local golf club offered its indoor area to soccer teams at a rate of $900 per season. The golf club's floor covering was Astroturf, since the facility was primarily designed as an indoor driving range. League play was restricted to 9:30 p.m. to 11:30 p.m. three nights a week and 7:30 a.m. to 9:30 a.m. on Saturdays and Sundays because other activities were held at the facility.

There were 38 outdoor soccer pitches owned and operated by the city's Parks and Recreation department. Players paid between $95 to $150 per season, and owing to expanding leagues and limited fields, it was expected these teams would average 12 games per season.

THE FUTURE

DeBlois certainly had a lot on his mind. He believed the greatest challenge facing the facility was exposure. London was home to the Henderson Memorial Soccer Tournament, which attracted 160 teams each year, and SM2 had set up a booth on the grounds in the past at no charge. Due to limited staffing, DeBlois believed he could not attend the tournament in 1999, but SM2 could instead place an ad costing $200 in the event program. He wondered what the ad should look like and what message should be conveyed.

SM2 had also advertised in London's major newspaper and had gauged the response rate to be less than 1 percent. DeBlois believed that a television campaign could be effective, but it would cost $5,000 to produce a 30-second spot in addition to the cost of running the ad. He wondered how effective a billboard advertisement might be and what it should look like. Alternatively, would a promotional campaign be more appropriate, and if so, what would it entail?

Furthermore, since SM2 could provide play for various other sports, DeBlois wondered whether he should turn it into a multisport facility. If so, which sports would be offered, and when would they be offered?

Overall, DeBlois knew that in order to break even, SM2 would need to operate at 70 percent capacity during the months that the facility was open, but he was unsure how to create the awareness to achieve this goal with a limited marketing budget.

DeBlois wondered if he should collect more information before making any decisions. He did, however, know one thing: something had to be done differently in the year to come if SM2 was going to be a profitable venture.

NOTES

1. VSDOC, International Trade Administration, IMI 970630.
2. Of this number, 71 percent were children/youths and 29 percent were adult players.
3. The teams paid a cash entry fee and the winners received a cash prize.

C A S E 5.11   STEWART SHOES

By Michael R. Pearce

Founded in 1953, Stewart Shoes had grown to six similar sized outlets by 1990, headquartered in Nova Scotia. For the past year, management had been debating the value of money being spent on advertising and promotion.

"I'm convinced we should simply stop advertising altogether," said Malcolm Gibbings, the controller. "We're facing tough times and all that money could simply go to the bottom line. John hasn't shown us that it really pays for itself."

"Well, I don't know how I can convince you, Malcolm," said John Andrews, the marketing manager, "but I can't imagine maintaining our presence in our markets without advertising. Our major competitors all advertise about the same percentage of sales that we do, as best we can figure out. And how would our customers ever learn about our special sales? No, we shouldn't cut advertising — we should increase it by 50 percent."

"That's a lot more money, about $285,000 if I'm not mistaken," said Lynn Graham, manager of stores. "Why not put more of our emphasis on direct mail efforts or even just do a better job with our in-store signs and displays? We've got 53,000 names on our total mailing list. It's pretty evenly divided across the stores. We could mail to them for a lot less than we spend on advertising and probably have a bigger sales impact. It costs us about 65 cents to send a simple letter to each person. And our in-store merchandising can be done for about $28,000 per event, about $10,000 in production and $2,000 per store to implement."

"I'm tired of this disagreement," said Janet Stewart, president. "It's time we resolved this. We've got our Father's Day event coming up in six weeks and there are a couple of products we were going to promote heavily. Then there's the Canada Day sale a little after that. Let's try some testing of these ideas around these two week-long events to find out just which way is best for us to spend our advertising, direct mail, and merchandising dollars. Now, I know that none of our store managers or buyers will want less than a total ad and promo effort for their area, but I think we can convince them if we have a good test design. We had originally set aside $40,000 for advertising and $28,000 for merchandising in total for these events. John, please design a test or two and get back to me by the end of the week."

C A S E 5.12   THE SPOKE TAVERN

By Michael R. Pearce and Paul Harte

In early April 1990, Ted Remillard, recently elected vice-president finance, sat in his office in the University Community Centre contemplating the exciting year ahead. Ted, a second-year law student at the University of Western Ontario, had decided to take a year off school to take advantage of the opportunity to serve as a vice-president on the University Students' Council (USC). One of his top priorities for the year was to turn around the ailing student bar — the Spoke Tavern. The once-popular campus drinking hole had been experiencing a significant decline in attendance and profitability. He was sure that something could be done to reverse this alarming trend, and he was willing to bet his political reputation on it.

USC BACKGROUND

The University Students' Commission was created in 1930 to synthesize the efforts of the existing arts, sciences, and medicine student organizations. In 1947, the name was changed to the University Students' Council. The USC was the central, single voice of students on campus until the mid-1950s, when the graduate business students formed the M.B.A. Association, which later became a fully autonomous council. In 1963 the Council of Graduate Students was formed to represent those concerns unique to the graduate student body.

In 1965, the USC incorporated as "the representative body of the full-time undergraduate students of the University of Western Ontario." The reference to full-time undergraduate students was subsequently eliminated to reaffirm the USC's original mission to represent the interests and concerns of all students. At the same time, a business manager was hired and provisions were made to pay the president for the summer. Previously, the USC was staffed entirely by part-time volunteers.

In 1968, John Yokom became the first USC president to serve as a full-time staff member. In 1987, the vice-presidents also became full-time employees. The USC budget for fiscal 1990 was in excess of $3.5 million (see Exhibits 1 and 2).

THE SPOKE TAVERN

The Spoke Tavern began as an operating unit of the USC. The tavern, located in Somerville House on the university campus (see Exhibit 3), was originally established to provide a source of revenue for the USC.[1] This revenue had been used in the past to support the extensive programming undertaken by the students' council. In addition, the Spoke was given a mandate to provide employment for students, to encourage responsible drinking habits, and to provide entertainment to students on campus. Nevertheless, the principal objective of the Spoke was to generate a stream of revenue to support USC operations. In the absence of this revenue the council would likely shut down this operation.

The Spoke's contribution, after rising year upon year since its inception, began a steady decline in 1989 (see Exhibit 4). USC projections for the 1989–90 academic year indicated a loss of as much as $10,000.

SPOKE MANAGEMENT

Prior to April 1, 1990, Joanna Dunton, USC controller, supported the Spoke in an accounting function, while the operations of the Spoke were handled by the vice-president, operations. On April 1, after the operations portfolio was dropped, Dunton, a Western M.B.A., became responsible for both the financial and daily operational status of the Spoke. The political responsibility for the Spoke Tavern was transferred to Ted Remillard, vice-president finance, who was ultimately held accountable for the campus bar (see Exhibit 5).

The Spoke manager oversaw the daily operation of the Spoke. Over the period from September 1988 until April 1990 three individuals had held this position. Rich Culley, the last of these managers, joined the tavern in August 1989. Rich remained excited about the Spoke's potential despite the often frustrating performance during the 1989–90 academic year. Rich brought with him significant knowledge of the bar business in London; prior to taking up his job at the Spoke, Rich had been employed with the Keg Restaurants in British Columbia and Ontario for seven years. Rich had lived in London for five years and had excellent connections in the bar business in London.

Peter Standbridge, entertainment productions manager, was also actively involved in the management of the Spoke and selected and scheduled the tavern's live entertainment.

OPERATIONS

The Spoke was more a night club than a pub. It served draft and bottled beer, house brand liquor, liqueurs, wine, and pop (see Exhibit 6). No food was served, although the management team were considering adding a kitchen. The bar catered to younger undergraduate students, primarily those in first and second year. It was a high energy live entertainment venue. The decor was plain. The Tavern had a maximum capacity of 400 (300 seated and 100 standing). There was one dance floor, which could hold about 150 people. The Spoke operated a patio in the summer and early fall; hamburgers were served from a barbecue located on the patio.

It had been open Monday through Saturday from 12:00 p.m. to 1:00 a.m. However, after consistently poor attendance during the afternoon periods in the first term, the tavern reduced its hours in January 1990 — opening at 7:00 p.m., except on Fridays, when the doors continued to be open at noon.

Attendance, and hence revenues, were very seasonal (see Exhibit 6). For example, the bar typically closed for a portion of the summer. In addition, business was very slow during the holiday periods both at Christmas and during reading week (mid-February). Revenues also varied depending on the night of the week (see Exhibit 7). For example, weekend nights (Thursday, Friday, and Saturday) were significantly more popular evenings than Monday, Tuesday, or Wednesday. Of particular concern, however, was a steady decline in attendance on Thursdays. Thursdays had been a particularly popular night, but revenues had been falling since early in the 1989–90 academic year as students began frequenting other bars.

**WEEKLY
PATTERNS**

Monday

As with many bars, Monday was slow at the Spoke. The bar was usually empty from 7:00 p.m. until 10:00 p.m. There was rarely live entertainment. A disc jockey played records, but patrons rarely danced. A cross-section of students arrived after night class (10:00 p.m.) to unwind over a beer or two. They typically left around midnight. This short period became known as "attitude adjustment hour" among the patrons.

Gross revenues:	$50 to $400
Attendance:	maximum 25
Drinks per person:	2 to 3
Door charge:	none

Tuesday

Tuesday at the Spoke was comedy night. Two or three comics from Yuk Yuks International would take the stage around 9:00 p.m. and entertain until 11:30 p.m. Students arrived around 9:30 p.m. and rarely stayed beyond midnight. In past years comedy night attracted an excellent crowd, often filling the bar on an otherwise slow evening. However, comedy night during the 1989–90 school year had been running at a substantial deficit despite the Spoke's constant effort to advertise and promote the previously successful event. The patrons who did attend represented a fair cross-section of students.

Gross revenues:	$1,000 to $1,500
Attendance:	maximum 150
Drinks per person:	2 to 3
Door charge:	$3

Wednesday

Wednesdays were much like Mondays. Students arrived late and left early, drinking very little. Gross revenues were somewhat higher than Mondays. Occasionally, a fraternity or other special event held in the Spoke would increase revenues. These events were infrequent.

Gross Revenues:	$60 to $500
Attendance:	maximum 30

Drinks per person:	2 to 3
Door charge:	none

Thursday

Thursdays had always been "pub night" at Western. Correspondingly, the Spoke had always done a brisk business on Thursdays. In the first term of the 1989–90 year crowds had consistently been at capacity, but in the second term attendance had shown a clear reduction. The Spoke, known as a live entertainment venue, had a band performing 90 percent of the time on Thursdays. The Spoke had its own house band, Glider, who performed Top 40 covers and kept the dance floor crowded. Glider was supplemented regularly with touring acts selected by Standbridge. Culley, the manager, had a sense that the crowd was made up, primarily, of first- and second-year students from the nearby residences.

Gross revenues:	$3,000 to $5,000
Attendance:	300 to 350
Drinks per person:	4
Door charge:	$3

Friday Afternoon

The Spoke used to be packed on Friday afternoons. On average, the bar did between $1,000 and $1,500 business. Sales were predominantly draft beer, served in pitchers. A wide cross-section of students would come to start the weekend early. However, pitchers of draft were banned by a campus regulatory body, who felt that pitchers contributed to alcohol excesses. As a result, the Spoke stopped serving pitchers and business began to decline. The Spoke remained open on Friday afternoons, but attendance declined dramatically, as did the average number of drinks per person. Culley suggested that the typical student dropped into the Spoke for a quick beer and perhaps a game of pool and then went home or to another bar.

Gross revenues:	$300 to $400
Attendance:	max 50
Drinks per person:	1 to 3
Door charge:	none

Friday Night

Fridays had always been the Spoke's highest revenue night. Students arrived early and left late. The bar reached capacity by 9:30 p.m. and would have lineups until after 11:00 p.m. The Spoke's staff, who knew many of the patrons, characterized the crowd as young — first- and second-year residents and off-campus students.[2] As with Thursday nights, a dance band played 90 percent of the time. The second term of 1989–90 had shown a slight decline in average revenues, but overall, Friday's profitability remained strong.

Gross revenues:	$4,500 to $7,000
Attendance:	Capacity (400)

| Drinks per person: | 5 |
| Door charge: | $3 |

Saturday

Saturdays were much like Fridays. There was always live entertainment. Revenues were generally slightly lower than Fridays, as the lineups tended to begin somewhat later in the evening. The staff, on average, saw fewer off-campus students than they would on a Friday.

Gross revenues:	$4,000 to $6,000
Attendance:	Capacity (400)
Drinks per person:	5
Door charge:	$3

THE SPOKE CUSTOMER

Culley felt that the students frequenting the Spoke were generally first- and second-year students (Exhibit 8). Certainly, first-year students visited the Spoke. They came to the Spoke to dance, drink, and meet with friends.

Culley also believed that, prior to the 1989–90 year, price pulled in these students. Starting in 1988 prices moved continuously upward as a result of strict regulation by APAG (Alcohol Policy Advisory Group), the campus alcohol watchdog. What was once an inexpensive drinking hole became simply a student drinking hole. The price sensitivity of these students varied throughout the year. Dunton speculated that as their bank accounts dwindled toward the end of the year, students become somewhat more price conscious. There also seemed to be a trend, especially on-campus, toward decreased alcohol consumption (see Exhibit 9), although a study performed by Student Services had indicated that almost 55 percent of first-year students drank at least once per week (Exhibit 10).

The management team was of the general opinion that students tended to go where their friends were. Therefore, if the Spoke was not busy, students might be inclined to turn away. Consequently, the team considered the Spoke's physical size (400-person capacity) both an asset and a liability. On a good night the Spoke could accommodate a large crowd of paying customers. However, on a mediocre night, the Spoke's size swallowed up the few customers that were there, turning away other potential customers. Thus, when the Spoke was busy, it was really busy, and when it was quiet, it was dead.

Another significant change that might have affected the Spoke was the implementation of several changes to the education system in Ontario, the most important of which saw the elimination of grade 13. As a result, students were coming to the university at a much younger age, often one or two years under the legal drinking age.

REGULATION

The increasing liability associated with drunken students, combined with a social change that supported responsible drinking, resulted in the formation of APAG as the campus watchdog and regulatory body. The Spoke was heavily regulated and frequently monitored by both APAG and the Liquor Licensing Board of

Ontario (LLBO). The Spoke was often visited twice a week by the LLBO inspector. In addition, other groups on campus, including the student newspaper, The Gazette, monitored the operations of the bar closely. As a result of the close scrutiny that the Spoke received, the breweries stayed clear of the campus when considering promotions. For example, Culley, through his involvement in the London bar business, understood that the Spoke used to receive kickbacks in the form of a free keg for doing a certain volume of business. Although this practice was clearly illegal, Culley felt that it had become an integral part of doing business in London and was taken into consideration by owners in the operation of their bars. This practice was stopped at the Spoke prior to 1989. However, downtown bars continued the practice.

As a result of regulation (see Exhibit 11), the Spoke was forbidden to advertise off campus. In addition, it was given a price list for all its products, from which the Spoke could vary only marginally within a given range (often less than 10 percent). The Spoke's product line was also carefully monitored. For example, the selling of draft beer in pitchers was stopped as a result of campus regulators who became concerned about the image that such a product created. This regulation severely hampered the ability of the Spoke to respond to competitors in offering innovative products such as shooters.

ADVERTISING AND PROMOTION

The Spoke communicated to its target audience through poster distribution on campus, including the residences, and in several student publications such as the Gazette. This advertising copy was closely regulated by campus regulatory bodies such as APAG: The Spoke also allowed the manager to offer free "promo" drinks to certain customers at his discretion to increase customer loyalty. This form of promotion was not frequently used. Rich had considered other advertising and/or promotion to raise awareness of the campus bar, such as selling merchandise with the Spoke logo at low cost, but had yet to come to any conclusions about the benefit of these programs. The Spoke budgeted $12,000 to $13,000 for advertising.

PERSONNEL

Except for the manager, the Spoke was staffed entirely with part-time students (see Exhibit 12). The staff often stayed on for several years and was a tight social group. There was an extremely low personnel turnover during the year, although up to 40 percent left at the end of each year as students graduated.

The relationship between staff and customers had been good but could be improved. In particular, during slow periods the staff were frequently observed talking among themselves rather than serving the few customers in the bar. Also, over the years an anti-USC attitude had developed within the staff. This attitude resulted from a series of events over a number of years in which members of the USC used their power to obtain free services or goods from the Spoke for their own use. Both Ted and Rich recognized that this area of staff relations needed work.

COMPETITION

The Spoke competed with a number of bars off campus as well as with the Elbow Room, the only other on-campus bar. The Elbow was run by the University Community Centre Directorate (UCCD). The UCCD operated independently from the USC and, as a result, the Elbow and Spoke competed directly with each other for the student dollar.

The Elbow Room presented the Spoke's most difficult competition. The Elbow served drinks in a lounge atmosphere. It was a significantly smaller bar with only a small dance floor. In addition to drinks, it offered a limited food menu, which attracted a sizeable lunch-time crowd. The Elbow also had a small stage and provided live entertainment. Generally, this entertainment was on a somewhat smaller scale from that being showcased at the Spoke. For example, Rick McGhee, an acoustic guitar player, often performed at the Elbow. However, the Elbow did offer a comedy night on Tuesdays.

The Elbow was planning a major expansion, which would see the bar more than double in size. Plans included a restaurant, pub, games room, and dance floor. Over a million dollars had been budgeted for this expansion, which was expected to be ready for September 1991.

The Spoke's competition with bars off campus was entirely one-way, since the Spoke was unable to advertise off campus. Therefore, the off-campus bars were able to take student business away from the Spoke, while the Spoke remained unable to attract nonstudents.

There were a number of off-campus bars that competed for the student dollar. The Ceeps was, for many years, a rundown building that served extremely inexpensive draft and became somewhat of an institution over many years of operation. In the summer of 1989, the Ceeps completely renovated its facility. The Ceeps remained a drinking-only venue. On a typical Thursday night the lineup began well before 8:00 p.m. and lasted all night long.

Joe Kools was another popular student bar in London. It provided both a dining area and two stand-up bars. Joe Kools' advertising boasted the worst service in London. Ad campaigns featured the copy "Joe Kools, where you're always welcome, unless you're a jerk." Kools was crowded throughout the week, and more so on the weekends.

The Bavarian was also quite close to campus. Located in a mall 15 minutes from the university, the Bavarian was both a restaurant and bar. A buffet was served from 4:00 p.m. until about 8:00 p.m., when a disc jockey would start the music. A movable wall separated one part of the bar and was opened later in the evening as lineups began to develop. The Bavarian had three dance floors, two bars, and several dozen large tables.

During the 1989–90 academic year the Spoke faced an increasingly competitive market. The Ridout Tavern, which had been previously known as a biker bar, was also renovated during the summer of 1989. In addition, the owner provided free drinks and steak dinners for leaders in the fraternity and sorority community.

As a result of these aggressive marketing tactics, the Ridout's popularity grew dramatically. This may have affected the Spoke, particularly on Thursday nights.

The Spoke had experienced tremendous difficulty in competing in its regulated environment. In particular, it was unable to lower its prices substantially to meet the draft prices of its competition. Indeed, its prices were also above those on other campuses in Ontario (Exhibit 13). It was also unable to meet the competition's innovative product line, such as shooter bars.

KITCHEN PROPOSAL

The Spoke management team was considering installing a small kitchen to offer food to its patrons as early as September 1990. The cost of installing the kitchen was estimated at approximately $40,000. Dunton thought that as much as $75,000 could be made available for improvements to the Spoke if justifiable.

THE DECISION

As Ted considered what action he should support, he realized that the only way to turn the Spoke around was to keep the bar filled, thus spreading the high cost of rent over more profitable transactions. To this end he thought that the addition of food to the tavern would generate significant business during the day and would bring people in early at night. But more importantly, he thought that the Spoke needed a changed image. He wanted to create a bar where people went to be seen — where the "in" crowd went.

NOTES

1. The Spoke Tavern rented space owned by the university for $5,800/month. This figure included all maintenance and cleaning.
2. Off-campus students referred to those students who did not live on the campus in student residences.

Exhibit 1

| University Students' Council of |
| The University of Western Ontario |
| (Incorporated without Stated Capital under the Laws of Ontario) |

BALANCE SHEET
as at May 31

ASSETS

	1989	1988
Current assets:		
Cash	$ 305,195	$ 292,908
Accounts receivable	70,045	66,395
Inventories	32,000	35,563
Prepaids	26,962	23,721
Due from Radio Western	–	7,630
Total current assets	434,202	426,217
Fixed assets	463,792	449,744
Total assets	$ 897,994	$ 875,961

LIABILITIES AND OPERATING CAPITAL

	1989	1988
Current liabilities:		
Accounts payable and accrued charges	$ 118,161	$ 89,939
Due to:		
Radio Western	13,709	–
Affiliated councils	66,565	56,894
Clubs and organizations	41,147	55,404
Current portion of obligation under capital lease	7,052	30,270
Total current liabilities	276,634	232,507
Long-term liability:		
Obligation under capital lease	61,266	84,762
Operating capital	560,094	558,692
Total liabilities and operating capital	$ 897,994	$ 875,961

EXHIBIT 2

	1989	**1988**
University Students' Council of **The University of Western Ontario**		
Statement of Revenues and Expenses **for Year Ended May 31**		
Revenues:		
Undergraduate fees	$ 1,101,614	$ 997,021
Graduate fees	5,424	6,213
Interest	43,814	33,204
Organizations and programs[1]	2,316,694	2,288,147
Other	7,567	9,467
Total revenues	3,475,113	3,334,052
Expenses:		
Organizations and programs[2]	2,526,824	2,423,992
Portfolio and administrative costs		
Corporate	389,422	383,578
President	46,812	43,566
Finance	14,847	9,554
Communications	25,656	18,737
Operations	17,443	5,573
Programming	–	3,344
External	38,870	36,172
Student affairs	15,897	5,989
Grants and association fees		
Ontario Federation of Students	61,859	59,758
Charity ball donations	33,000	36,000
Radio Western	143,630	109,214
Councils	79,379	80,355
Clubs	16,343	15,658
Student award grants	6,000	6,000
Day care centre grant	20,620	19,857
Community legal services	36,084	34,750
Total expenses	3,472,686	3,292,097
Excess of revenues over expenses from operations	2,427	41,955
Loss on disposal of fixed assets	1,025	16,085
Excess of revenues over expenses	$ 1,402	$ 25,870

1. This number includes revenue generated by the Spoke Tavern's operations.
2. This number includes the expenses of the Spoke Tavern's operations.

Exhibit 3

Spoke Tavern Flyer

Exhibit 4

Income Statements **for the Years Ending May 31**				
	1987	1988	1989	1990[1]
Revenues:				
Draft	$ 99,913	$171,986	$157,986	$124,285
Bottled beer	226,876	237,489	194,458	131,059
Liquor	149,352	153,428	111,671	93,939
Liqueurs	26,716	34,987	58,061	30,846
Wine	3,498	10,401	7,110	3,340
Pop/juice/coffee	4,361	8,183	6,196	3,667
Bar food	0	0	6,195	1,460
Less: sales tax	47,869	55,866	48,535	36,254
Total sales	462,846	560,606	493,141	352,343
Cost of sales	160,526	214,827	199,854	130,812
Gross margin	302,319	345,779	293,287	221,531
Operating expenses:				
Salary and wages	126,427	155,084	162,916	112,940
Staff benefits	1,385	718	2,510	980
Taxis	0	302	787	310
Travel	37	12	210	60
Meetings	6	119	216	238
Telephone rental	827	1,157	1,190	885
Long distance	613	550	860	508
Postage	25	33	40	2
Copying/printing	1,226	1,124	849	664
Advertising	11,144	10,263	9,135	8,269
Equipment	991	1,857	1,136	875
Supplies	1,618	1,739	2,162	1,387
Occupancy	61,231	66,153	67,512	52,805
Maintenance	6,273	6,179	6,107	6,556
Glassware	5,885	6,689	4,623	5,100
Linen supplies	664	1,090	845	579
Delivery/telegram	493	210	1,307	210
Records/albums	348	1,372	300	710
CAPE	446	550	729	1,000
Depreciation	1,490	1,263	1,141	12,959
Special events	15,375	18,909	17,445	277
Miscellaneous	550	748	65	237
Total operating expense	237,054	276,120	282,083	207,552
Operating Contribution	65,265	69,658	11,204	13,979
Programming				
Bands	28,981	25,839	9,890	(16)
Comedy	(1,242)	2,751	(2,566)	(14,767)
Special events expense	(996)	(1,393)	(1,507)	0
CAPAC/PRO fees	0	675)	(1,234)	(805)
Total programming	26,744	26,522	4,583	(15,588)
Misc. revenue	5,022	5,345	5,610	2,763
Total contribution	$97,031	$101,526	$ 21,398	$ 1,154

1. 1990 figures include operating data up to February 28, 1990.

Exhibit 5

USC Structural Chart

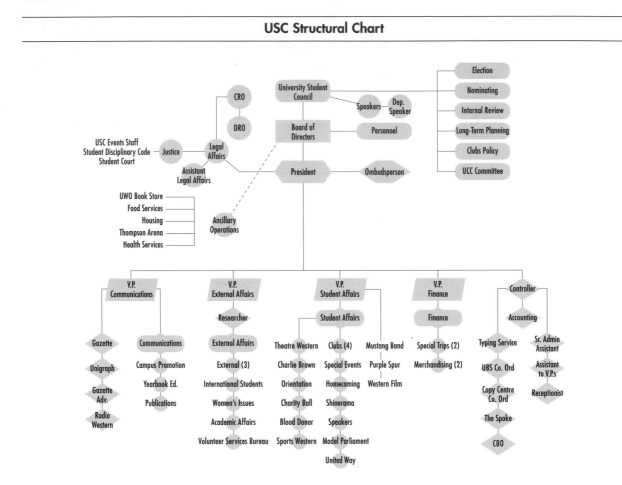

EXHIBIT 6

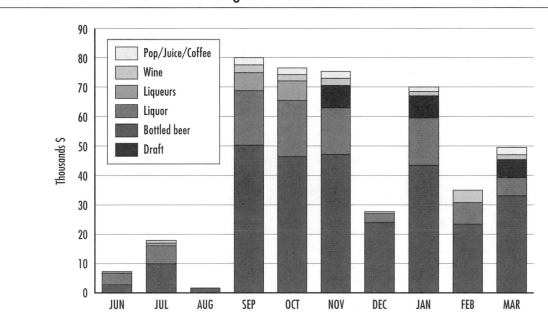

Beverage Sales 1989–90

EXHIBIT 7

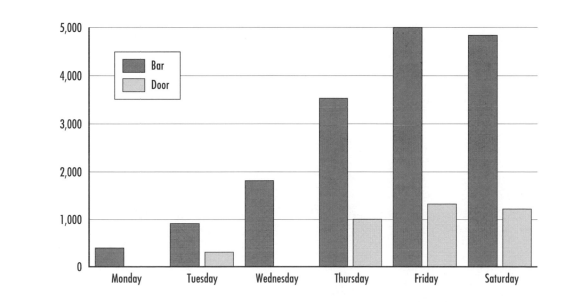

Average Revenues 1989–90

EXHIBIT 8

CAPE Program Survey: Selected Questions

Have you attended campus bars/special pubs?

	1984	**1985**
YES	83.8%	82.4%

If Yes, which of the following?

	1984	1985
Elbow Room	83.8%	63.2%
Spoke Tavern	72.7%	62.2%
Pub Nights	64.1%	57.2%

Does differential pricing influence your decision to buy light beer?

	1984	1985
YES	20.7%	13.3%

Source: Progress on Campus: Evaluation of the CAPE Program (1987), Addiction Research Foundation.

EXHIBIT **9**

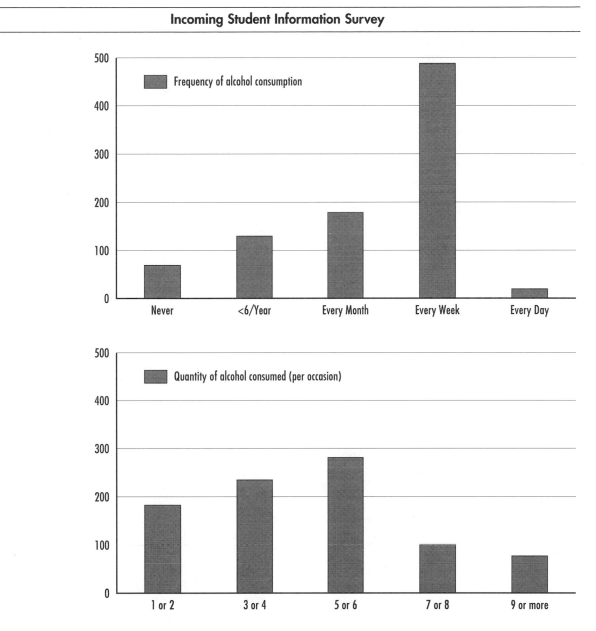

Incoming Student Information Survey

Source: Incoming Student Information Survey (1988), UWO Student Services.

Exhibit 10

Excerpt from the *Gazette*, 20 March 1990

Less student drinking dries up bar revenues

by Elliotte Friedman of the Gazette

Students are drinking less and Western's three bars are suffering.

The Graduate Centre was expected to make $9,000 this year, but assistant manager Nick Panter said the pub will only break even.

The Spoke was to have a total profit of $11,849, but by February it had cleared only $1,153.

The Elbow Room was projected to net $100,000 this year, a figure that was lower than previous year, according to Habeeb Al-Aidroos, University Community Centre director.

After what manager Mark Wellington called "a rough first term," the budget was adjusted to expect only $78,000. But a strong second term should allow the Elbow to meet original projections, he said.

"There is no question that consumption has declined, but it is nowhere near the extent it has been reported," he said, adding the overall drop in alcohol revenues can be attributed to a "lack of competitiveness among Western's bars."

Wellington said the success of off-campus bars shows there is not a huge decline in drinking. "Both of the on-campus bars are out of date. We simply cannot compete with Dr. Rockits, the Ceeps, or the Ridout."

Al-Aidroos agreed that the Elbow Room is at a disadvantage, but said students' thoughts on drinking have plenty to do with the situation.

"There are a host of factors for why the Elbow Room is having problems. The location is a main reason. It has a dreary ambiance, and sits next to garbage. There is also the problem of poor food. But the pressure on students to do better and get jobs has increased as well."

"The Elbow Room will be moved to Platters old position in exactly one-and-a-half years, but it would not make sense to put capital costs into the Elbow Room in its present position since it will be there for only one more school year," Al-Aidroos said.

Alcohol awareness programs, such as Western's "Can We Talk?" have also helped the slowdown in alcohol consumption. This program was created by Ardath Hill, nurse-educator of Student Health Services. The program goes to Western residences in the fall and reaches about 1,000 students.

"We are more concerned with showing students how their decision-making process is affected by consuming alcohol and teaching them that controlling stress by getting blasted is not the answer. But today's students seem to be much more conscientious about their studies," Hill said.

Exhibit 11

Sample of APAG Alcohol Policies

	Adopted	Adopted in Principle
Alcohol Accessibility Policies		
#1 Increases in the number of outlets, the capacity of outlets and the hours of operation should be limited.	X	___
#2 There should be limits on the number of special licenses events on campus.	X	___
#3 Drink sizes should be controlled by establishing "shots" of one ounce only and eliminating "doubles" and "pitchers".	X	___
Responsible Serving Practices		
#4 All servers of alcohol on campus should be trained in responsible serving practices, including the monitoring of patrons' age, consumption, and behaviour.	___	X
#5 In the provision of alcohol on campus, non-alcoholic alternatives should be promoted.	X	___
#6 Campus bars should discontinue selling alcohol before closing, while retaining the availability of non-alcoholic specials.	___	X
#7 Campus alcohol outlets should not take multiple drink orders at the closing of the bar.	X	___
Substitution Policies		
#8 When alcohol is sold on campus, light alcoholic beverages should be readily available.	X	___
#9 In providing beer on campus, the only type of draft should be light beer.	X	___
#10 Provisions should be made for non-alcoholic beverages and high-protein, non-salty foods.	X	___
#11 Throughout each academic year, the post-secondary institutions should ensure that there are a greater number of interesting, non-alcohol activities, particularly during orientation.	___	X
#12 When alcohol is sold on campus, the base price should be at parity with off-campus prices.	___	X
#13 The sale of alcohol on campus should entail differential pricing according to alcohol content.	___	X
#14 In providing non-alcoholic beverages, the price should be lower than that for the least expensive alcoholic beverage	X	___
#15 When alcohol is being sold on campus, comprehensive price lists should be available to ensure that patrons understand price differential between alcoholic and non-alcoholic beverages.	X	___
Management Policies		
#16 In allowing the sale of alcohol, efforts should be made to reduce the extent to which campus organizations rely on alcohol sales as a source of revenue.	___	X
#17 In allowing the sale of alcohol, the post-secondary institutions should ensure that alcohol promotions and advertisings comply with the law and campus standards.	X	___
#18 Since alcohol is available on campus, the post-secondary institution should ensure that there is adequate enforcement of provincial laws and campus policies.	___	X
#19 To assist with responsible management of alcohol on campus, the security staff should receive adequate training.	___	X

Exhibit 12

Staff

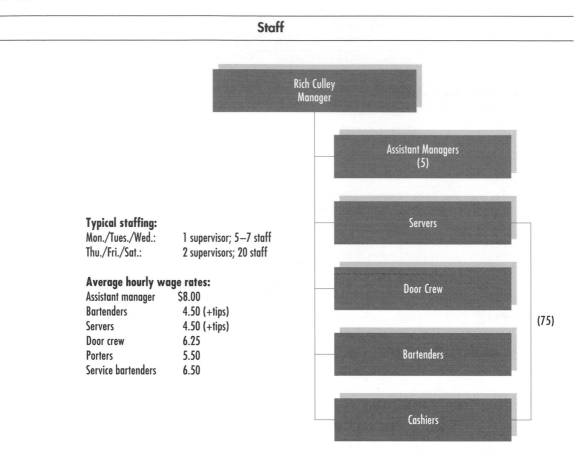

Typical staffing:
Mon./Tues./Wed.:   1 supervisor; 5–7 staff
Thu./Fri./Sat.:   2 supervisors; 20 staff

Average hourly wage rates:
Assistant manager $8.00
Bartenders   4.50 (+tips)
Servers   4.50 (+tips)
Door crew   6.25
Porters   5.50
Service bartenders   6.50

Exhibit **13**

Letter to the Editor, the *Gazette*, 30 March 1990

BEER TOO EXPENSIVE

To the Editor:

The article "Less student drinking dries up bar revenues," printed in *The Gazette* on March 20, discusses the fact that campus bars are falling well short of their profit objectives for this year. To explain this, its author claims that "students are drinking less," while in the same article quoting Elbow Room manager Mark Wellington as saying that campus bars cannot compete with off-campus establishments.

Whether students are drinking less (or not) is virtually impossible to say, but it is quite obvious that they are drinking less at campus bars. I think that this problem can be directly attributed to the fact that Western's bars are not competitive; not because of location, not because of food (although it definitely could be better); but simply because of price.

Traditionally, campus bars at Canadian universities have attracted business because of cheap alcohol. I believe that this year's increases in prices of draught beer here at Western bars is almost entirely responsible for the slide in profits. Although these increases were designed with admirable intentions, i.e., responsible drinking, sobriety, etc., they have already been proven unsuccessful. If Western's bars continue to lose business to off-campus competition, thus decreasing university revenue by tens of thousands of dollars, students can expect to compensate in tuition increases.

Western should learn by experience and example. At Alfie's, the popular campus bar at Queen's, students pay only $7.10 for a pitcher of draught (and that's after raising the price only 20 cents this year). The result: Alfie's is packed with students from Wednesday to Saturday nights. The Elbow, or Spoke, cannot expect to see such overwhelming response if prices of $2;75 for a regular draught and $3.60 for a large, served only on Fridays, are maintained.

I am not endorsing lower prices to promote drunkenness. I am suggesting only that Western's policy makers should realize what the realities of the bar market are, and adjust prices accordingly. That way the students can't lose.

Erik Schatzker
English/History II

PART

AN INTRODUCTION TO OPERATIONS
MANAGEMENT

Operations is one key to any organization's success. Along with marketing, operations, often called production, is where an organization adds value and makes money. You all have experience with operations through your day-to-day lives. The goal of operations is to produce goods and services efficiently and effectively. To help you develop an effective operating point of view and decision-making skills related to operations, this chapter explores four fundamental aspects of all organizations:

1. The purpose and components of operations;
2. The key tasks that operations managers must manage for their respective organizations to do well;
3. The types of operations systems and their management requirements; and
4. Some tools to help you diagnose and solve operations problems.

THE PURPOSE AND BASIC COMPONENTS OF OPERATIONS

One common way to describe operations is the input-transformation-output model shown in Figure 1. According to this model, the organization "purchases" inputs from suppliers, changes them in some way, and then "sells" the outputs to customers. Although the core of operations is the transformation process, the scope of the operations function usually includes purchasing and often distribution. One key message in the sections that follow is that operations is where the action is: it makes things happen.

465

Operations is everywhere, all around each of us every day. All parts of every organization have an operations component, which is often critical to financial success. Although we normally associate operations with mines, factories, and food processing plants, we also see it in everyday settings such as restaurants, hotels, airlines, universities, hospitals, banks, and stores. Exhibit 1 gives some examples.

Exhibit 2 lists six conclusions drawn from Exhibit 1 and Figure 1. First, some enterprises transform materials, others transform customers, and others transform information. Although almost every organization transforms a mixture of inputs, one type usually dominates. Steel companies concentrate on transforming materials — iron ore, lime, and coal. Dentists, doctors, theatres, and universities transform customers (patients or students). Researchers or financial managers transform information. Restaurants transform materials in the kitchen and customers in the dining room. Investment managers transform information to make decisions and transform customers through their conversations and the results of their decisions.

Second, operations is everywhere. Accounting departments need a process to transform transactions into financial records. Marketing departments need a process to capture information from customers. Personnel departments need processes to hire, train, evaluate, promote, motivate, discipline, and lay off staff.

Third, inputs and outputs are a matter of perspective. The iron mine's output, iron oxide concentrate, becomes a major input to the steel mill. In turn, its steel output is purchased by parts manufacturers who produce body panels, wheels, engines, and the like, for sale to automobile assemblers. They sell their finished products to dealers who, in turn, sell them to consumers. Sale to the final user might end the chain, or, as is common in the case of automobiles, there might be active markets in used goods or scrap. Scrap is particularly interesting in this case because a steel company's output might well become one of its own major inputs some time later when the steel is recycled. To deal with the potential ambiguity, the analyst must carefully define the operations system by deciding where its boundaries are, keeping in mind that although such boundaries are necessary, they are almost always artificial.

Fourth, operations adds value. Banks buy money from depositors (by paying interest on deposits) and sell it to borrowers (by charging interest on loans). They survive because there is a spread of several percentage points between these two interest rates and because they provide security, information, and pools of funds unavailable to lenders and borrowers who might interact directly. Real estate brokers are able to bring buyers and sellers together because they know the local market. Paper mills link forestry companies to newspapers because they can transform wood into paper.

Fifth, breaking an operation down into its many steps can help in understanding and analysis. The examples in Exhibit 1 tend to be rather large — at the factory or company level. Thus, iron oxide concentrate, limestone, and coal are

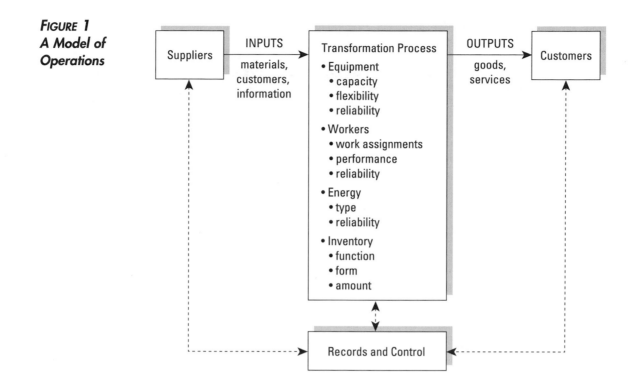

FIGURE 1
A Model of
Operations

put in and steel is taken out; thousands of parts are assembled and an automobile is driven away; food is purchased and a meal is prepared. But an automobile assembly plant might have 1,000 work stations, and everyone knows that preparing a meal, such as a breakfast of a boiled egg, coffee, orange juice, and toast, involves many steps. Each of the four items on the menu could be considered as a single step — boil the egg, make the coffee, pour the juice, toast the bread. But, consider the egg boiling step. It too can be broken down into a series of separate steps — get out the pot, pour in enough water, get the egg from the refrigerator, add it to the pot of water, put the pot on the stove, turn on the heat, wait, set the timer, and so on. Furthermore, the step of getting out the pot can also be broken down into such steps as walking to the cupboard, reaching forward, grasping the handle, pulling the cupboard door open, locating the pot, reaching in, grasping the handle, and so forth. The level at which you perform such analyses depends entirely on the sorts of decisions you want to make. For kitchen design decisions, a detailed sequence would be useful, but to decide how much to charge customers for the labour content in such a breakfast, a much broader scope would be appropriate.

Exhibit 1

Examples of Operating Systems			
Organization	Inputs	Transformation Process	Outputs
Iron mine	iron ore	drilling, blasting, separating, crushing, concentrating	iron oxide concentrate, waste rock
Steel mill	iron oxide pellets, lime, coal, scrap steel	smelting, pouring, oxy-genating, rolling, forming	steel ingots, slabs, sheets
Parts manufacturer	sheet steel	pressing, punching, machining, painting, polishing	parts ready to assemble
Automobile assembly plant	parts	welding, bolting, riveting, painting, testing	finished automobile
Restaurant	foodstuffs, hungry customers	seating, order taking, preparing drinks and food, serving, cleaning-up, setting table	satisfied customers, waste food
University	knowledge, students	analyzing, sorting, writing, teaching, counselling, evalu-ating, planning, gathering data	skilled and knowledge-able graduates, new knowledge
Planning rock concert	available dates, necessary activities and required order, estimated times	organizing activities into a network, marshalling resources, scheduling, moni-toring progress	project completed on time and on budget
Investment management	interest rates, trends, yields, client preferences, network of contacts	analyzing data, matching client and portfolio, transac-tions	wealthier, satisfied clients
Personnel department	staff records, performance evaluations, department needs	scheduling, analyzing data, interviewing, discussing strengths and weaknesses	staff development plan, enhanced resources, satisfied staff
Marketing department	records of customer orders and inventory, production schedule, new products	market research, analyzing data, discussing strengths and weaknesses	market plans and incen-tive systems, successful product launch

Exhibit **2**

Some Conclusions about Operating Processes

---

1. Different organizations process (transform) different types of input.
2. Operations extends to all departments of the enterprise, not just the factory; the operations process for such departments can be a significant factor in the organization's competitiveness.
3. One organization's outputs often become another's inputs.
4. Operations links suppliers and customers by adding value for which customers will pay.
5. Virtually every process has a number of steps.
6. Information about inputs, outputs, and the process itself is required; this information must also flow to allow managers to control and evaluate the operation.

Sixth, operations needs information. The model in Figure 1 shows the flow of materials and services. Although this flow is central to any operating process, no process operates completely independently. You must make decisions: Should I start my egg, coffee, juice, or toast first? Should I fry my egg or boil it? How long should I cook it? How well is the process working? Questions such as these require information, and that information must also flow, as shown by the dotted lines in Figure 1.

OPERATING SYSTEM COMPONENTS

The transformation process usually involves equipment, people with a range of skills, inventories of goods to help smooth out the operation, and energy to make it all happen. These four elements are the normal components of operations (see Figure 1).

Equipment

Equipment includes the machinery needed to make production happen: lathes, milling machines, and grinders in machine shops; mixers, stoves, refrigerators, and cash registers in restaurants; aircraft, baggage-handling apparatus, and maintenance equipment in airlines; computers, printers, and automated teller machines in banks. In some operations, for example, a counselling service, there might be little, if any, required equipment. Capability, capacity, flexibility, and reliability are four important features of equipment, each of which has a number of important aspects.

Capability refers to what a piece of equipment can do. Drill presses are capable of drilling round holes but not square ones. In quality terms, capability refers to a machine's ability to perform reproducibly. In printed circuit board manufacture, component alignment is crucial to product quality. Thus, a surface mount technology machine that can place memory chips on printed circuit boards to within 0.03 mm of the desired location is more capable than one that can do the same task with an accuracy of 0.10 mm.

Capacity is different from capability. This word has two distinct notions: how much a piece of equipment can hold and the amount of material, number of customers, or quantity of information that can be processed or produced in a given period of time. Exhibit 3 gives some examples. As with many areas of our study, one key to understanding these different meanings of capacity is to keep the units straight. Note that the volume examples in Exhibit 3 have single units, whereas speed is always expressed as a ratio.

We normally discuss capacity in terms of *theoretical capacity* — what the equipment manufacturer designed and built the unit to do — and *operating capacity* — what happens in actual use. The extent to which theoretical capacity is achieved is one measure of the equipment's efficiency. Thus, a class of 62 students (operating capacity) scheduled for a classroom with 75 seats (theoretical capacity), has an equipment efficiency of 62/75 or 82.7 percent. A hamburger grill designed to produce 12 patties every three minutes (or 240 per hour) operating nonstop producing 220 per hour is 91.7 percent efficient (220/240).

Why don't we get 100 percent utilization? The reasons vary. In the beer kettle example we might be unable to stir a completely full kettle without spilling some of the contents. Dents or sensing and stirring devices installed inside the kettle also might reduce its effective volume. In the case of hamburger cooking, the operator might have to clean the grill periodically and must take time to remove cooked patties and replace them with raw ones. These times might not have been considered in calculating theoretical capacity. Although operating capacity is usually less than theoretical capacity, there are exceptions. Workers might speed up machines or change methods to get more than the theoretical capacity. Special equipment and tuning routinely give stock car racers speeds above the manufacturer's rating.

Exhibit 3

Types of Capacity			
Volume		**Speed**	
Beer-brewing kettle	7,000 L	Bottle capper	40 bottles per minute
Classroom	75 students	Airliner	1,000 km per hour
Car	5 people (including driver)	Computer	100,000 operations per second
Elevator	900 kg	Hamburger grill	12 patties every 3 minutes
		Worker	3 forms per hour
		Baseball pitcher	100 pitches per game

Flexibility refers to an operating system's ability to cope with changing circumstances with little penalty in cost, time, effort, or performance. Because the word *flexibility* refers to many things, it should be used carefully. It might refer to product range, rates of output, speed of change, and the like. General purpose equipment or skilled workers are usually very flexible. A lathe, for example, can often turn wide ranges of items that have different diameters and lengths and are composed of various materials. And a kitchen stove can cook almost anything. An oil refinery, however, is relatively inflexible — it is designed to handle only certain types of crude oil and put out a limited range of petroleum products. A bottling machine might be flexible in its ability to bottle almost any liquid, but inflexible because it can put it in only one size and shape of bottle. Although an automobile assembly plant might be able to produce cars with a wide range of colours and options, it can handle only a single body design and produce efficiently at only one car per minute without major line rebalancing. Labour contracts that spell out detailed job classifications often reduce flexibility by restricting the right to do certain types of work.

Reliability refers to the likelihood that a piece of equipment will perform as designed. Some equipment is extremely reliable; the two Voyager spacecraft launched in 1976 to explore the solar system performed both at much higher levels and much longer than expected. Other products never seem to achieve their goals, possibly from a design flaw (as with the Hubble telescope or software sold with bugs) or from failures of equipment, people, or systems (exemplified by the Chernobyl nuclear reactor, the Challenger Space Shuttle, or automobiles recalled by the manufacturer because of faults). High or increasing downtime and maintenance costs might indicate a decrease in reliability.

People

The above discussion of capability, capacity, flexibility, and reliability also applies to people who bring muscles, brains, and interpersonal skills to operations. Although most operations require some labour to operate machines, move materials, or perform operating tasks, physical labour is increasingly being reduced as tasks become automated or otherwise changed.

As muscle tasks become automated, the worker's ability to evaluate a situation and detect trouble and the ability to think become more prevalent. Instead of doing hard physical work, many operations employees are now there to watch dials or monitors, make periodic quality checks, stop the process, and make minor adjustments to machines. Thinking is needed in design, programming, and managerial tasks such as planning, controlling, motivating, and making decisions. The current trend is to automate intellectual tasks wherever possible.

In many services, operations workers interact directly with customers. In such a role, their interpersonal skills are an important determinant of the quality of service provided.

The people component brings the psychological concepts and theories of organizational behaviour face to face with the realities of assigning workers to tasks, assessing performance, and achieving reliability. In this area, operations and human resource managers must work together closely. Operations managers must consider several important aspects in assigning work. They must know what kinds of work and work sequences are needed to produce a satisfactory good or service. In this regard, they also need to be able to measure work so they know whether it is being done correctly. Job design and methods analysis techniques are tools to ensure that the transformation process is both effective and efficient. Many well-established firms, such as McDonald's, have removed many decisions of this sort from the managers of day-to-day restaurant operations by having teams of corporate experts develop standard procedures collected in extensive operating manuals.

So they can make better recruitment, hiring, training, development, and scheduling decisions, operations managers also need to know the skills and numbers of people required for the various jobs. Once a job is staffed, operations managers must assess machine and labour productivity and staff behaviour to get the right quality and quantity of output. Adequate measurement tools are needed, such as production rates, standards, quality levels, and customer satisfaction. Poor performance cannot always be blamed on workers. Management is responsible for designing jobs and for creating a productive work atmosphere that motivates people to do a good job. One way to do this, particularly in the service sector, is to allow and indeed expect front-line workers to make more of their own decisions.

Energy

Energy is a component of almost any operation. Normally, we don't think very much about it — it is just there. In other cases, however, energy is a major operations factor. Traditionally, our economy developed around energy sources, as many watercourses were exploited to run mills and factories. The number of towns with "Mills" or "Falls" in their name attests to that. The Niagara Falls area, for example, is still a major industrial site. With transportation and electricity now widely available, this argument for site selection has largely disappeared, although in recent times Arvida, Quebec; Kitimat, British Columbia; and Bluff, New Zealand, have risen to prominence because of their aluminum smelters. In addition to being relatively remote, these centres share three features: accessibility to large ocean-going vessels; isolation (thousands of kilometres) from the nearest bauxite (aluminum oxide) deposits; and proximity to large hydroelectric facilities. This last feature is no accident. Aluminum smelting requires huge amounts of electricity, and aluminum is thus one substance that is smelted not, as with most other kinds of smelting, near the ore body or the markets, but near another significant operations component, electrical energy.

Inventory

Inventory is an input, a component, and a product of most operating systems. Inventory can be defined as anything that is purchased or acquired for transformation or resale or that assists in the transformation of materials into saleable goods. Thus, we can talk about inventories of people, plants, equipment, capacity, or light bulbs. We will, however, restrict our discussion to inventories of items along the material flow shown in Figure 1.

There are three basic kinds of inventory: raw materials, work in process, and finished goods. Wendy's, for example, buys frozen hamburger meat and buns in batches — maybe several days' worth — which it stores as *raw materials inventory*. During a normal day the staff will frequently remove some of the materials from storage and process them. For example, they might put 12 hamburger patties on a grill, where they cook for a set length of time. Then, the patties sit, waiting for orders from customers. While they are sitting, they are *work-in-process inventory* — partially completed units. When a customer orders a hamburger, it is assembled quickly from a number of work-in-process inventories and delivered to the customer. Because Wendy's makes hamburgers to customers' orders (one, two, or three patties, and many combinations of toppings), it does not hold a *finished goods inventory* of hamburgers (although its salad bar items are finished goods). In contrast, McDonald's, whose production process is devoted to making to stock, does carry a small finished hamburger inventory ready for sale when customers order.

Why do organizations have inventory? The basic answer is that it is cheaper to have it than not. Inventories both cost and save money — inventory management involves managing these costs. Some of the costs are described in Exhibit 4. The major benefits can be summed up as helping to smooth the flow of materials and reduce the costs in going from the supplier through the production process and on to the customer.

As shown in Exhibit 5, inventory can serve many functions. A key concept is that just as an inventory item can be raw materials, work in process, or finished goods simultaneously (depending on your perspective), it can also serve more than one function at any given time. The key characteristic of *pipeline* or *transit inventory* is that it is moving. If the movement stops, for example, while a valve is changed or the truck driver has lunch, it is no longer purely pipeline inventory; it is still in the pipeline, but it now also has an additional purpose.

All sorts of things can happen outside the established boundaries of the production system to stop the flow of operations. For example, a shipment might be delayed for any number of reasons, customer demand is almost never completely predictable, or customers might demand products even when production is shut down. Inside the plant, a machine might break down or a worker might be absent, both of which disrupt operations. *Buffer inventories* can help operations continue despite these problems. *Decoupling inventories* are in place to separate steps that operate at different rates or with different patterns so that each can work smoothly on its own. Decoupling allows each step to be more efficient by

Exhibit 4

Costs and Benefits of Holding Inventory

Costs of Having Inventory

Financing	Cost of invested working capital
Obsolescence	Risk of loss of value before sale
Shrinkage	Damage, theft, or spoilage during storage
Holding	Cost of maintaining storage facilities
Scrap and rework	Cost of errors detected long after manufacture
Management	Cost of managing the resource

Costs of Not Having Inventory

Stock out	Opportunity cost of lost sales, present and future, to a customer
Idle resources	Opportunity cost of resources idled by lack of inventory
Expediting	Cost to rush an order through

For example, consider a company that makes a standard line of computer memory products. The question might be, What are the costs of having (and not having) finished goods inventory of a particular product? Although the result might be expressed in monetary units, it is commonly stated as a percentage of the cost of the item, which, although convenient, is less correct, as not all costs vary with changes in the item cost. The table below shows the results. Note that the numbers are inevitably rather soft estimates and that they are relevant only for this product.

Cost	Amount (%)	Source	Comments
Financing	20	Finance	Company's opportunity cost of capital
Obsolescence	8	Marketing	Frequent introduction of new models increases risk
Shrinkage	3	Accounting	Product has high street value and is easily damaged
Holding	5	Accounting	Holding area must be tightly secured
Scrap and rework	0	Operations	Products are tested extensively immediately after production
Management	1	Operations	
Total	37%		
Stock-out	25	Marketing	Customers value reliability; stock-outs will also affect future purchases
Idle resources	0	Operations	Finished goods inventory leaves no resources idle
Expediting	5	Operations	Cost of overtime and estimate of probability
Total	30%		

In this case, the cost of having inventory (37 percent) is estimated to exceed the cost of not having it (30 percent). Thus, this company should adopt a policy of carrying low amounts of finished goods inventory of this product.

EXHIBIT 5

Functions of Inventory			
Functions	**Rationale**	**Key feature**	**Examples**
Pipeline or transit	Materials must be transported between two points	It is moving	Oil in a pipeline Ore on ship between mine and smelter Parts moving between two work centres on forklift truck or moving belt
Buffer or safety stock	Buffer operation from external uncertainty	External disruption likely	Piles of ore, coal, and limestone at steel mill Finished hamburgers and fries at McDonald's Material between adjacent machines
Decoupling	Isolate steps that operate at different rates or patterns	Operations work at different speeds	Chassis between body welding shop (75 cars per hour) and final assembly (60 cars per hour) McDonald's hamburgers between cooking (batches of 12) and customer arrival (reasonably steady stream at much shorter intervals)
Seasonal	Production or use has well-defined season or anticipated event	Business activity has definite, predictable peaks and valleys	Harvested apples for sale during winter Salads prepared for lunch peak Texts in book store awaiting start of classes
Cycle	Allow operations or transport to function in economical lots	Something is produced, used, or shipped in a "batch"	Truckload of goods for sale Boat load of iron ore for smelting

keeping all of them running; no step is affected immediately by a disruption in another. Continuously moving assembly lines operate without decoupling inventory. Instead, each step is forced to operate at the same rate, or more correctly, to perform each step in the same, usually short, time period paced by the slowest step. Balance losses can be high.

Agricultural and fishing industries are well aware of the build-up of *seasonal inventory* because of well-defined seasons for planting, fertilizing, harvesting, and the like. A special form of seasonal inventory, closely related to buffer stocks, arises from the expectation that something might happen. The key difference between buffer and seasonal inventories is that, with the former, events are much less predictable.

The last reason for having inventory is to allow operations to function in economical lots. Whenever managers decide to buy or make something, they will incur an ordering or set-up cost. To avoid these costs, managers might batch the orders or jobs, creating *cycle inventory*.

Despite the usefulness of inventory, a relatively recent approach to production management called just-in-time (JIT), originating in Japan and discussed in more detail later in this chapter, argues that inventories are not beneficial. The essential argument is that the costs of having inventory are much higher than the costs of not having it. Inventory mostly just sits around costing a lot of money and adding no value of any kind. Do the Japanese live under a completely different set of economic rules? No, but they have found ways to eliminate the reasons for having inventory.

How can these reasons be eliminated? Exhibit 6 gives some examples. Many assembly plants have clusters of supplier plants very close by. Moreover, the whole complex might be near a steel mill and necessary services. This proximity reduces pipeline or transit inventory. Many of an organization's outside uncertainties are related to its supply chains. Parts that are of poor quality will stop production, unless sufficient inventory buffers production from the source of bad parts. Reducing these uncertainties helps to reduce buffer stock.

EXHIBIT 6

Some Ways to Eliminate Inventory	
Function	**Techniques to Reduce Level**
Pipeline or transit	Locate operations as close to each other as possible Move items between operation steps as fast as possible
Buffer or safety stock	Reduce pipeline inventories (and thus pipeline uncertainty) Establish close long-term working relationships with suppliers Ensure high quality material
Decoupling	Ensure careful machine design and worker training Accept idle time or use it creatively (possibly for cleaning or job analysis)
Seasonal	Work to develop sources of supply and demand that, collectively, extend seasons Develop processing capacity to meet peaks
Cycle	Work hard to reduce set-up times

SECTION

TWO

OPERATIONS TASKS

Operations tasks are what an organization must do to produce products and/or services to satisfy customers and realize its overall objectives. The main function of operations is to transform inputs into the desired outputs, using the necessary (and available) resources (see Figure 1). The goal is to provide the right product or service, in the right quantity, at the right price, in the right place, at the right time, every time, with an acceptable level of side effects. To understand the activities properly, it is necessary to consider the environment of operating managers. Although their main job is transforming inputs, operations is very much an integrating function because operations managers must also interact with managers in other functions.

A second operations task is managing people. The liaison between operations and its sources of employees is the human resources department, which helps to locate, hire, train, evaluate, and, if necessary, discipline staff; establish personnel policies; keep records; and so on.

Finance connects operations to the firm's treasury. Finance and accounting, often separate departments, should establish financial policies, help operations make investment decisions, measure the costs incurred in operations, and be prepared to provide the funds necessary to support effective production systems. The two departments (particularly accounting) maintain many of the records necessary to perform and measure operations and are also responsible for sending invoices and collecting and making payments.

These different departments are all interdependent: operations needs them and they need operations. But each of the various departments has its own agenda, priorities, and ways of doing things. The operations manager must deal with the inherent conflicts to which these distinctions will give rise in the internal environment. In addition, the manager must keep up with changes in the outside world — developments in equipment and ways of making things (technology), new materials, cost changes, and competitive developments, such as changes in capacity by suppliers or competitors.

Although one production task is to satisfy customers, marketing is the liaison between production and the firm's external customers. Marketing should help to translate customer needs and wishes into product specifications, forecasts of sales volumes, delivery schedules, and the like. Marketing should also be both aware of and geared up to sell what operations can pro-

Exhibit 7

Customer Needs with Some Implications for Operations	
Need	**Implications**
Function	Will the product do what the customer needs and wants it to do?
Quality	Will the product perform reliably?
Quantity	How much product should we make and when?
Price	How much should we charge for the product?
Service	What services will we provide to accompany the product?

duce. Note that in services, the operations and marketing functions tend to merge, as customers come into direct contact with production. One way to help to define the operations tasks is to consider operations from the customer's perspective — after all, customers really determine what products and services we should provide. Exhibit 7 outlines five important customer needs that have significant implications for operations.

FUNCTION

You expect a computer to have certain characteristics, the exact nature of which depends on you. It might be operating speed, working memory, hard drive size, adaptability, or something else. Function depends on design. A computer's failure to run Windows software might be the result of its design. Slide rule manufacturers have disappeared, not because they produced poor quality slide rules, but because calculators and computers made slide rules unnecessary. Home milk delivery, coal sales for home furnaces, and long-playing records disappeared for similar reasons: customers demanded different product and service designs to perform the different functions required by a changing world.

QUALITY

When you buy a computer, you want the quality to be high. You do not expect that it will fall apart after a year's use (unless, of course, you have some special, hard use in mind). Quality must be such that the product's functions will perform reliably. Manufacturing affects quality. For example, no matter how good the design, putting a faulty disk drive in a computer will result in a poor quality finished product.

QUANTITY

Quantity is an easily understood need. Customers want enough to satisfy their needs. If a man wanted to buy compact disc players for each of his five daughters-in-law for Christmas, he would not be satisfied if he could buy only two. Similarly, a university must ensure that it offers enough course sections of sufficient size to enable all its students to take a full load; a city must ensure that it has enough police, fire-fighting, hospital, and library services; and a railroad must see that it has enough space to carry all passengers or freight. Insufficiency in these services can lead to loss of life, to loss of business to alternative services, or, in the case of public services, to tax revolts or replacement of elected officials. On the other hand, overproducing goods and services results in higher than necessary costs. For operations, quantity demands require attention to customer needs and the timing of those needs.

PRICE

Price also appears to be a fairly simple idea. Most customers have limited income and are able or willing to spend only a limited amount on any specific product or service. Potential customers who perceive the price to be too high will either not buy or switch to an alternative. However, it is clear that price, particularly that of a single purchase, is not the sole purchase criterion. If it were, courier services, for example, would not exist. Value is a notion that comes closer to the mark. Consumers and organizations often buy more expensive items because they perceive them to be more valuable — providing more function, quality, or quantity per dollar. They might arrive more quickly (courier services), last longer (light bulbs), be more reliable (solid state electronics), or bestow more snob appeal on the buyer (luxury cars).

Although price and value are marketing concerns, they have a major effect on operations. Products or services that compete on the basis of low price must be produced at low cost or the organization will not make money. Similarly, those competing at high prices must have high quality and/or high functional utility to attract customers. Few organizations can manage to produce low cost products or services with a full range of features and high quality.

SERVICE

Service has many dimensions. Service might include advice on how to operate or maintain a product, financing arrangements, checkups, availability of parts, provision of qualified labour, or assurance that the manufacturer or service firm will survive the lifetime of the product or service. Once a manufacturer announces that it intends to stop making a product line, purchasers might not be keen to buy one. And who wants to deposit or invest their money in a weak financial institution, obtain a degree from a university that might close, buy a computer with a chip that might give arithmetic errors, even rarely, or buy a ticket from a tour company that faces bankruptcy?

Delivery is yet another facet of service. Delivery has several meanings. Some organizations, such as appliance and furniture retailers, deliver purchased goods to customers and use this fact competitively. Insurance salespeople make home visits. Some fitness clubs will send staff members to your home if you wish. However, the once-routine services of doctors who make house calls and grocery stores that deliver now make headlines.

Time is another dimension of delivery. We expect fast response from fire, ambulance, and emergency departments to save lives. We expect newspapers to include the latest news in their current editions. Every manufacturer gets the occasional call from a customer looking for a product in a hurry. Producing on time might be even more important than producing quickly. How useful are snowmobiles delivered to Canadian retailers in April, Christmas cards in February, completed income tax forms after the deadline, or lunch salads at 2:00

p.m.? Many people criticize VIA Rail and Canada Post not for genuine slowness, but because they perceive that they cannot rely on these services' advertised delivery times.

Competing on service requires that operations have a very flexible delivery system; often excess capacity; equipment, people, and suppliers that are fully competent, reliable, and at least somewhat interchangeable; and intelligent scheduling.

Achieving the Desired Outcomes

Why are we focusing all this attention on customers in a chapter on operations? The answer is in two parts: operations is responsible for supplying goods and services to satisfy specific customer needs, and the viability of the whole enterprise depends on how well this is done. Although well-managed operations can never guarantee corporate success — all functions must be in good shape and well coordinated throughout the company and with the external environment to ensure that — it is fair to say that it is extremely difficult to have good corporate performance if operations is poorly managed. Because operations often accounts for 50 to 70 percent of total costs and employs most of an enterprise's work force, it warrants close attention. Customer needs must be used to set objectives, and operations should be organized to meet them. In most well-run firms, these objectives are set jointly by operations, marketing, finance, and other key groups.

Function and quality come from the new product development group. The design must both do what the customer wants it to do and be manufacturable. Operations should be involved throughout the product development process. There are many examples of product designs handed to operations ("thrown over the wall"), as though their manufacture were automatic, that have turned out to be either impossible or too expensive to make. The result is usually unplanned design compromises or extremely high costs. Early integration can prevent such undesirable outcomes. Throughout the production process, targets should be set and measurements taken to ensure that the product design's quality needs are met.

Sometimes marketing alone translates customer needs into required product quantities; in more progressive companies, operations and other functions will also be involved. The problem is to match the quantity produced with customer demand in any given time period. Both producing too much and producing too little might result in losses.

Firms translate customer price requirements into a target manufacturing cost, on which company profits hinge. Thus, operations can be highly cost-oriented and many enterprises establish elaborate systems to measure and control costs to ensure profitable operation.

Organizations translate customer needs for delivery into operational time targets. They schedule and continually monitor where everything is in the whole operation so that each product will be completed by a certain time. They require information: What is ahead of schedule? Can it be delayed? What is late? Why? What can be done to expedite the items that are behind?

Organizations translate the need for other services much as they do the price need. Because many service aspects have implications for function, quality, quantity, and price, they can be considered as part of these objectives. However, it is not good enough simply to meet only some of these targets, even perfectly. Because the process must be repeatable and improvable, managers must manage operations to ensure that it is in harmony with overall company policies and objectives for continuity of the enterprise. They must also plan both for the short and the long term. It is not good enough simply to do well today — tomorrow and next year count at least as much. On the other hand, the short term cannot be ignored. A brilliant long-range plan is useless if the organization does not survive that long.

It is tempting to ask, Which of the needs is most important? The answer is simple but frustrating: It depends. Customer needs vary from one individual to another and depend very much on the situation. The operations manager's job includes determining what today's need is and having the flexibility to provide it. The ranking of those needs will dictate what the operations manager should emphasize. One restaurateur trains his staff to determine if customers are "eaters" or "diners." Although both groups choose from the same menu and receive food of the same quality, the serving staff make sure the eaters are served promptly and the diners have time to relax. The result is a higher portion of satisfied customers and a higher number of table turns from the eaters.

EFFECTIVENESS AND EFFICIENCY

The role of the operations manager is to accomplish these tasks as effectively and as efficiently as possible. Exhibit 8 describes and gives some examples of these two concepts. *Effectiveness* is related to quality. Operations is effective if it makes the product as designed, on time. Although a prescribed design is important, many service organizations are demonstrating their effectiveness in satisfying customers by expecting employees to go to whatever lengths are necessary to solve customer problems.

Efficiency is related to productivity. Operations is efficient if it produces with a minimum of cost, effort, and waste. Effectiveness and efficiency often seem to conflict — you can have one, but only at the expense of the other. In other words, it is possible for an operation to be efficient but not effective; or it can be effective but not efficient. Another possibility is that it might be neither effective nor efficient. Hospitals that operate with no slack capacity in their emergency departments or universities that encourage undergraduate classes of 250 students are focusing on efficiency — some observers argue that in these cases, efficiency comes at the expense of effectiveness. The same university might have graduate classes of only five students — in this case the class might be very effective, but it might cost as much as (or even more than) the 250-student class down the hall.

Exhibit 8

Effectiveness and Efficiency

Effectiveness	Doing the right thing: the extent to which an objective is realized
■ Railroad	Delivering all goods to a destination, within a designated amount of time, without damage, while remaining flexible to changes in future demand
■ Restaurant	Stocking sufficient goods to meet the published menu, taking customer orders accurately and promptly, preparing the meal as described or asked for by the customer, delivering it within a reasonable period of time, and performing all the necessary service functions politely so that the customer feels welcome and comfortable
■ Automobile assembly plant	Producing cars to design specifications (high quality) in a reasonable time after the order is placed
■ Retail store	Clerk who, on his or her own initiative, hires a cab to deliver a forgotten parcel to a customer's home
Efficiency	Doing things right: producing effectively while minimizing waste (cost, effort, time, etc.)

The ideal, of course, is to be both effective and efficient. Although this goal is not always possible, every organization should strive for it. The relative importance of efficiency and effectiveness depends on the organization's major objectives and required tasks. Effectiveness is usually considered to be much more important than efficiency in courier services; consequently, courier services are relatively expensive. The post office puts more emphasis on efficiency; costs are much lower, but the effectiveness (here measured by delivery speed and variability) suffers. In some cases, efficiency can develop into effectiveness. Many banks originally bought automated banking machines (ABMs) to reduce costs — an efficiency rationale. Recently, however, institutions are adding services to their ABMs to give customers more choice in services — making them more effective.

■
SECTION
■
THREE
■

TYPES OF OPERATING PROCESSES AND MANAGERIAL IMPLICATIONS

So far we have talked about operating processes as if they were all the same. Clearly, this is absurd. You have undoubtedly seen or can imagine several different kinds of production processes. But what is the best way to transform inputs into outputs to meet the demands on operations? What is needed to compete? Why would a customer want to buy a product or service from us rather than from one of our competitors? How should we classify production processes?

The following sections describe three types of production process along a continuous spectrum as shown in Exhibit 9. In reality, it is difficult to classify a particular production system as clearly one type or another because the differences are not always obvious and some organizations are hybrids because of

Exhibit 9

Operations Process Types				
Project	Job Shop	Batch Flow	Line Flow	Continuous Flow
Large construction projects	Small metal working shops	Clothing manufacture	Bottle-filling operations	Oil refineries
Repair of large machinery	Management consultancies	Beer brewing	Bottle making plants	Chemical plants
Staging a rock concert	Automobile body shops	University classes	Letter-sorting plants	Pulp mills
Organizing a wedding			Automobile assembly lines	Telecommunications (dedicated lines)
				Stock quote systems

mixing. Mixing is natural because production facilities might change process type over time. Despite classification problems, however, focusing on these three types is useful because they:

1. Stress the need to select a process according to the production tasks to be performed and

2. Represent very different kinds of production processes, each with its own critical characteristics that must be carefully managed.

CONTINUOUS-FLOW AND LINE-FLOW PROCESSES

In a *continuous-flow process*, inputs are transformed into outputs continuously. As Exhibit 9 shows, they are closely akin to *line-flow processes*. The differences between the two are largely matters of degree; one distinction is that line-flow processes tend to produce discrete units (that is, they can be counted one by one, such as cars or bottles), whereas continuous-flow processes produce products counted in units of measure (litres of benzene, tonnes of steel). Exhibit 10 shows some important traits of such processes.

Because all materials in production go through the same steps in the same order, a critical element to be managed is the smoothness of flow in and between the steps. A "break" in production at any place along the line effectively shuts down the whole line. Examples are everywhere: you are in a cafeteria line and someone ahead of you wants to wait for a special serving; you are on a crowded highway when two cars ahead of you collide; a work station on an automobile assembly line runs out of parts; a machine breaks down; a worker has to go to the washroom; one work centre (worker or machine) is slower than the rest.

Although the possibilities are endless, the result is the same: operations stop, or at least slow down, in some cases, for a long time.

To keep things moving, managers have to try to foresee some of these problems and take appropriate preventive measures. Rules forbidding special servings, great inventory management procedures, off-line places to put problems, and back-up people and equipment are some possibilities. A major concern in designing continuous-flow or line-flow operations is to make sure that each step takes the same amount of time. This process is called *line balancing* and is designed to control the number and location of *bottlenecks* that occur whenever one step in a connected sequence is slower than the others. Figure 2 provides an example.

For dishwashing on a camping trip, the times in Scenario A might not be a great concern. However, if you were paying the workers, you would pay for idle time. Although the amount might still be trivial in a dishwashing operation, in an assembly operation with 1,000 one-person work stations working 16 hours per day, five days per week, 52 weeks per year, and paying each worker $15 per hour, 33 percent idle time would cost $20.8 million per year.

One approach to dealing with this problem is to balance the line, that is, to reduce the idle time to zero. Only rarely can a continuous- or line-flow operation be completely balanced, of course, but it is worth getting the idle time as low as possible. In the dishwashing example, adding a second dryer (Scenario B) would help. Although it would shift the bottleneck to washing, it would reduce drying time to 7.5 seconds per cycle and reduce idle time. Redesigning the drying job might help too. Perhaps the dryer has a poor technique or an awkward layout in which to work. Maybe the washer could also stack, giving a completely balanced two-worker line. A basic technique called *process analysis* is very useful in determining the degree of balance in a process and in planning improvements. We will discuss process analysis and another useful technique, *trade-off analysis*, in Section Four. First, however, we will discuss some additional process types.

JOB SHOP AND BATCH PROCESSES

In *job shop* and *batch processes* work moves intermittently in batches. Exhibit 9 gives some examples. Processes can be of mixed type; although at McDonald's the overall operation is line flow, the chain cooks its hamburgers in batches. Processes can also be changed; traffic along a freeway moves continuously (at least until volume or an accident interrupts it); traffic lights convert the process into batch flow.

Major features distinguish job shop and batching operations from continuous-flow and line-flow operations. In the job shop and batching operations, each job uses a unique amount of resources at each step and produces a different product. In line-flow and continuous-flow operations, every unit goes through the same steps, in the same order, and at the same rate. In contrast, in batch operations, and particularly job shops, flow is jumbled.

Although one flow pattern might dominate, each job might take a different pathway through the process depending on scheduling needs or technical

FIGURE 2

An Example of an Unbalanced Line

Suppose you and some friends are on a camping trip and are washing dishes. The table below shows two scenarios: A, in which one person washes, one dries, and one puts the dry dishes away; and B, in which one person washes, two dry, and one puts the dry dishes away.

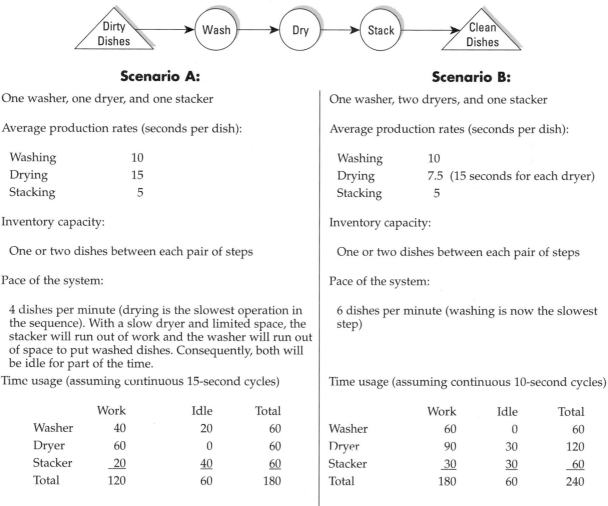

Scenario A:

One washer, one dryer, and one stacker

Average production rates (seconds per dish):

Washing	10
Drying	15
Stacking	5

Inventory capacity:

One or two dishes between each pair of steps

Pace of the system:

4 dishes per minute (drying is the slowest operation in the sequence). With a slow dryer and limited space, the stacker will run out of work and the washer will run out of space to put washed dishes. Consequently, both will be idle for part of the time.

Time usage (assuming continuous 15-second cycles)

	Work	Idle	Total
Washer	40	20	60
Dryer	60	0	60
Stacker	20	40	60
Total	120	60	180

Idle time: 60/180 = 33%

Scenario B:

One washer, two dryers, and one stacker

Average production rates (seconds per dish):

Washing	10
Drying	7.5 (15 seconds for each dryer)
Stacking	5

Inventory capacity:

One or two dishes between each pair of steps

Pace of the system:

6 dishes per minute (washing is now the slowest step)

Time usage (assuming continuous 10-second cycles)

	Work	Idle	Total
Washer	60	0	60
Dryer	90	30	120
Stacker	30	30	60
Total	180	60	240

Idle time: 60/240 = 25%

---

requirements. For example, a full-service automobile repair shop might have separate areas for welding, tuning up, and wheel alignment. Some cars might be welded first, then tuned up, then aligned, and, finally, given a road test. Others might bypass welding and wheel alignment. Others might be aligned before being tuned up. Routing is not entirely random — painting is always one of the last operations in a body shop. The wide range of potential products, customers, volumes, and tasks means that purchasing, inventory planning, work force planning, and scheduling often cannot be established in isolation from specific customer orders or inventory positions. For many, all these activities begin to interact only when a customer order is received or finished goods inventory drops to a set level (the reorder point).

The operations manager's main task is to manage conflicting objectives, such as both meeting customer needs and keeping costs low. Speed comes from processing each order through each work centre as soon as it appears. Unfortunately, this policy demands extensive facilities to handle periods of peak demand, increasing costs during idle periods. However, facilities designed for average demand cannot handle the load in peak periods. Batching operations are less exposed to this problem because they schedule production around a finished goods inventory. The manager might have to decide between customers in cases where not all of them can be satisfied.

The differences in operations, sequences of steps, and times greatly complicate the scheduling task, which should consider all jobs in the shop, their process requirements, and the current backlog at each work station, as well as orders expected but not yet received. There are some useful and common, but by no means perfect, scheduling rules, such as first come first served, shortest processing time, urgency, customer persistence, or customer importance. Many organizations use judicious combinations of these and other rules.

Another difference between job shop and batching operations and continuous- and line-flow operations is the type of equipment used. Job shop and batching operations use flexible, general purpose equipment rather than the more specialized machines common in line- or continuous-flow operations. A single drill press might be used to drill holes of all diameters and depths. The penalty paid for this flexibility is the cost of adjusting or setting up the equipment differently for each job. Set-ups might take from minutes to several hours or even days. Set-ups incur direct and indirect costs as they take machines out of production.

A final difference lies in the amount and type of inventory. Job shop and batching operations typically build up significant work-in-process inventories. In one company that uses batch production to make plumbing products, although the cumulative production time spent making a single part is only one or two hours, parts take eight weeks on average (320 working hours, 1,344 real hours) to go from raw materials to finished goods. The work-in-process inventory is large and costly. In contrast, line- and continuous-flow operations have relatively little work-in-process inventory but more raw materials and finished goods.

Although job shop and batching operations are similar, they are not identical. A key difference is their response to customer specifications. A job shop typically performs *custom work in response to customer orders*. Automobile repair shops, for example, work only when a customer brings in a vehicle; they perform the tasks requested by the customer and can identify the car with the customer at every stage. Individual orders might not be all that complex; the process of tuning an engine is reasonably standard. A batching operation more likely makes a *standard product line in response to inventory levels*. Although a restaurant, for example, might prepare many of its menu items to customer order, the chef will likely prepare a batch of the Irish stew special or garden salads in advance, based on a demand forecast. The product becomes identified with an individual customer only when it is actually served.

Decisions on the optimum batch size, work centre schedule, and size or mix of inventory occupy much of job shop managers' time. Despite their difficulty and frequency, these tasks are not the job shop manager's most important ones. Management must watch for changes over time in customer demand regarding the five basic needs (function, quality, quantity, price, and service). As the priority of these demands changes, the manager must be prepared to respond by changing the existing process. This decision is difficult because the changes are subtle and gradual. An automobile repair shop doing a variety of repairs might become known for reliable, fast muffler replacement. The manager might notice that the services most in demand have changed. The shop now has a high portion of muffler jobs and requests for this service are steady. The number of these jobs has increased; the expected delivery time is probably shorter than for most jobs; and inefficiencies of scheduling these jobs around larger jobs might well be increasing overall cost. Changing the operation from a job shop to one in which at least its muffler jobs are done in a line-flow system might well be important to future profitability.

PROJECT PROCESSES

Some products are unique or very complex. In these situations, a somewhat different approach to production, a *project process,* is most efficient and effective. Economies of scale and specialization do not apply. Often, the organization is "product-dedicated," with the job often being stationary and having resources brought to it. Exhibit 9 gives some examples.

Projects resemble job shops in that both handle special custom orders. Projects are unique because of their size, complexity, and the presence of a number of steps that must be completed in a clearly defined order. Because the key cost components are investments in materials and human resources, producers and customers are both interested in early completion. A critical task is scheduling the various steps of the project so that they are finished just as they are needed. The goal is usually to reduce cost by minimizing the overall completion time and the investment in the components of the project. A number of methods that identify the project's longest or *critical path* have been developed to help project managers in these tasks. Many commercial computer programs will perform the necessary calculations.

Exhibit **10**

	Process Characteristics		
	Project	Job Shop and Batch	Line and Continuous Flow
Product Characteristics			
■ mix	special, small range of standards	special to many	standard
■ designed by	customer	customer and company	company
■ range	wide	wide	narrow to very narrow
■ order size	small	small	large to very large
■ company sells	capability	capability	products
■ order-winning criteria	delivery, quality, design capability	delivery, quality, design capability	price
■ qualifying criteria	price	price	quality, design
Process Characteristics			
■ technology	general purpose	universal to specialized	dedicated
■ flow pattern	no pattern, often no flow (movement)	jumbled to dominant	rigid
■ linking process steps	loose	loose to tight	tight to very tight
■ inventory	mostly work in process	raw materials, work in process, and finished goods	mostly raw materials and finished goods
■ notion of capacity	very vague	vague, measured in dollars	clear, measured in physical units
■ flexibility	high	high	low to inflexible
■ volumes	very low	low	high to very high
■ key operations tasks	meet specifications and delivery dates, scheduling, materials management	meet specifications, quality, flexibility in output volume	low cost production, price

Adapted from R.W. Schmenner, *Production/Operations Management: Concepts and Situations*, 4th ed. (New York: Macmillan, 1990), Chapter 1; and T.J. Hill, "Processes: Their Origins and Implications," *Operations Management Review*, Vol. 8, No. 2 (1991), 1–7.

Choosing a Process

Although there are exceptions, observers have noted a strong correlation between the characteristics of the product and the process used to make it. The product characteristics are typical of the product life cycle, which describes changes in product volume and other traits over time. Most products start life as prototypes. They are produced in low volumes, often with radical product changes between one unit and the next, and sold at a premium price. Customers are paying for design features, for speed of delivery, and, in many cases, for flexibility — the producer's ability to customize the design to meet customer needs.

After a product moves through the rapid growth phase to maturity, volume is usually high, the product design has stabilized, and the price has levelled off. The products now compete on such features as price, reliability, quality, and product features. In extreme cases, the product becomes a commodity. These two scenarios, infancy and maturity, are quite different and demand a different approach to operations. Yet although changes in product characteristics should be matched by changes in the process, most organizations cannot afford to change processes frequently; consequently, they might choose to tolerate processes that are not ideal and live with the resulting inefficiencies.

The answer to the question, What is the best way to make clothes? can really be answered only by more questions. What type of clothes? Who will buy them? How will they compete? What volume is expected? What features will they have? What quality is needed? After answering these questions (determining what features the product needs), managers are in a position to pick the process. For products early in their life cycles, job shops are typical. Flexibility, design, and quality are important characteristics to the customer, and job shops are ideally set up to provide them. As a product becomes more stable and volume increases, the job shop might well give way to a batching operation, which is less flexible, more price competitive, and more able to produce in volume. At maturity and high volumes, a line-flow or continuous-flow process is most appropriate.

In the clothing industry, a large producer of off-the-rack ladies' wear would probably use some form of line-flow process requiring specialized machinery and relatively unskilled labour, possibly from a Third World country. In contrast, a producer of custom clothing, for whom design and quality are paramount and volumes are low, would use a quite different operation. In this case, mechanization would be low, those hired would have to be skilled, and, typically, it would be located near the customer. Intermediate product characteristics would demand an intermediate process — batching.

Figure 3 shows the relationship between product and process characteristics. According to this model, successful organizations are found in or near the diagonal band; those found significantly above or below it are uncompetitive. Think about how you would make a line of family cars versus a high-performance race car, or how you would set up a cafeteria as opposed to an *haute cuisine* restaurant.

FIGURE 3
The Product–
Process Matrix

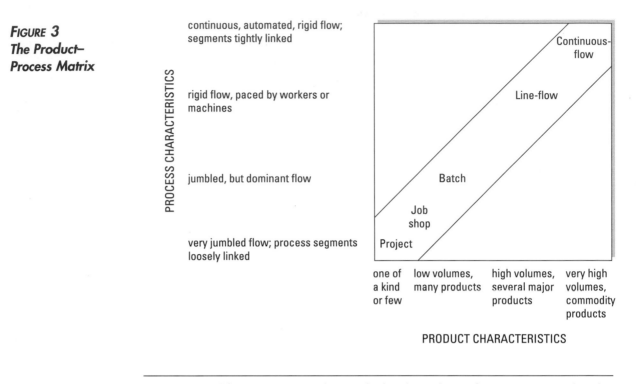

continuous, automated, rigid flow; segments tightly linked

rigid flow, paced by workers or machines

jumbled, but dominant flow

very jumbled flow; process segments loosely linked

PROCESS CHARACTERISTICS

Continuous-flow

Line-flow

Batch

Job shop

Project

one of a kind or few

low volumes, many products

high volumes, several major products

very high volumes, commodity products

PRODUCT CHARACTERISTICS

Source: Adapted from R.H. Hayes and S.C. Wheelwright, "Link Manufacturing Process and Product Life Cycles," *Harvard Business Review*, Vol. 57, No. 1 (1979), 133–40.

OTHER MANAGEMENT DECISIONS

Obviously, operations managers need to do more than simply choose a suitable process type and change it as the product traits change. Exhibit 11 gives examples of the sorts of decisions managers must make during design and start-up as well as on a day-to-day basis. This chapter's cases and problems will give you more practice in applying the principles of operations and other functions to some of them.

Each of these and many other decisions must consider the production tasks and the firm's internal and external environments. Available company resources will constrain many choices; the type of output desired will restrict others. Some decisions, such as location, represent long-term commitments, others are medium term (investment in equipment), and yet others are short term (purchasing policies). Particularly when making major decisions, managers must bear in mind both the current circumstances and anticipated future developments. Changing major decisions, such as plant location and primary machinery layout, is always expensive and disruptive and can sometimes threaten the firm's future. One of a university's most important decisions is classroom design. Although people,

Exhibit 11

Operations Decisions	
Decision Area	**Typical Decisions**
Purchasing	Order frequency and size, source, relationship with suppliers
Maintenance	Repair or preventive maintenance
Scheduling	Job priority, planning horizon
Subcontracting	Making versus buying
Location	Near supplies or markets
Layout	By machine groups, by production steps, for customer convenience, or for some other goal
Equipment	Renting or buying, specialized or general purpose, standard or technologically innovative
Job design	Specialized or general jobs, rotation between jobs
Research and development	Making versus buying

courses, course materials, and teaching methods come and go, the concrete and walls tend not to be changed once they are in place. A classroom designed for lectures to 250 students is unsuitable for case teaching to classes of 70.

■

Section

■

Four

■

Process and Trade-off Analyses: Two Basic Analytical Tools

Process Analysis

As much as possible, operations managers must ensure that the units of product proceed through the process as scheduled. In continuous- or line-flow processes, production is usually either on or off; when it is on, each unit moves along at essentially the same even or level rate. In job shops or batch operations, this is usually not the case. Flow is intermittent, and the rate of any one step can change frequently, leading to bottlenecks that keep changing. To determine the location of bottlenecks and the degree of balance in the process, we must perform the key operations tool of process analysis. Typically, it proceeds as shown in Exhibit 12.

EXHIBIT 12

Typical Process Analysis Steps

1. Determine the system boundaries.
2. List all steps, in order.
3. Draw a process flow diagram using standard notation (see Figure 4).
4. Decide what units of measure to use, and be consistent.
5. Determine theoretical capacities and required output.
6. Factor in known inefficiencies.
7. Locate the bottleneck step (the slowest).
8. Determine the effect of a stoppage.
9. Decide how to improve the process.

Depending on the questions you want to answer, the boundaries of your analysis might be the whole plant, a particular department, a specific machine, or a small sequence on that machine — making one of the many different parts, for example. The list of process steps should include relevant movement, storage (inventory), inspection, and transformation steps. The required output is often based on customer demand, either forecasted or known. Inefficiencies restrict process output. Some processes work at 100 percent for a while and then stop completely, possibly for set-ups, preventive maintenance, or cleaning. Others work all the time but at only a fraction of theoretical capacity. The output of every process is limited by one step. Even so, how much excess capacity do the other steps have? How much inventory buffers them from other steps? How long will it be before adjacent steps (in each direction) are affected? How you improve the process depends on what types of questions you want to address. If you have a line-balancing problem, try to even out the outputs of each step. If you have an overall output problem, determine where to add resources. If the output problem is timing, find out where attention should be directed to smooth out the flow.

Figure 5 shows an example of process analysis, including a partial process-flow diagram with the capacities for four of the steps and the required output. The process boundaries are set as the dishwashing operations in this department, excluding cutlery, and the rate is measured in dishes per day. Because of the hospital's inventory of dishes, average rates are quite sufficient for our analysis. If it did not have this number of dishes, the exact timing of dish use and return would be much more important and we would have to analyze dishes processed per hour, or even per minute. Although we do not know of any machine inefficiencies, we do know that the workers work for only seven hours per day after breaks are accounted for. The process bottleneck is in the two machine operations (washing and drying) at 6,300 dishes per day (seven hours). In fact, because these two operations take place sequentially in the same machines with no human intervention, they might even be combined in this analysis — unless, of course, we were considering replacing one of them with two machines, one to wash and one to dry. Depending on how the work is scheduled and whether machines must

FIGURE 4
Process Analysis
Notation

Symbol	Event
⟶	Movement
△	Storage
☐	Inspection
○	Operation
D	Delay
┈⟶	Information

be watched at all times when they are running, the effective workday for machines might be eight hours.

With a required output (demand) of 6,304 dishes per day, we are really tight on overall capacity. Demand is close enough to capacity to warrant a close look at the accuracy of the figures. Although in this example working a small amount of overtime would be an attractive alternative, if capacity were to be increased, it is clear that the first place it should be added is to the washing machines — our bottleneck. The system is not balanced. The worker operations, particularly scraping, rinsing, and stacking (operation 1), have excess capacity. Could we get by with one less worker in this operation? Overall, we need five to six workers (5.57) at the stated work rates (Figure 5). Could we do this by sharing a person between the two worker operations? How good are the work rate and demand figures? How much slack do we want to have to cover contingencies? Is there something else that these workers could do? These and similar questions should serve as a signal to management to look more closely. There might be enough money at stake to make more accurate answers worthwhile. Of course, changing or eliminating jobs would involve the human resources department. The answers to some of these questions will involve a second fundamental operations tool, trade-off analysis.

TRADE-OFF ANALYSIS

Trade-offs arise when you must choose because you cannot have everything. Everyone makes trade-offs every day. For example, you might want to spend the evening with your friends at a popular pub, but because you also want to do well on your exam at the end of the week, you decide to spend the evening studying. You might like to study business and also medicine, but having to choose a limited number of courses forces you either to eliminate one option or to extend your academic studies. In some cases, the trade-off is black or white — medicine or business. In others, it is progressive — you could study for one, two, or three hours and then go to the pub — with varying costs and benefits. Trade-off analysis helps managers decide what the "best" compromise is. Like process analysis, trade-off analysis involves a logical sequence of steps that will not guarantee success but might prevent disaster. Exhibit 13 shows the steps.

Figure 5

The Process of Washing Dishes in a Hospital

SALIENT FACTS

Beds: 361
Meal volume: 3 per patient day
Dish inventory: 1 day's demand
Hours: 8 per worker day
Equipment: 2 20-year-old washer-driers

Average utilization: 97%
Average dish usage: 6 per patient meal, plus associated cutlery
Staffing: 7
Breaks: 30 minutes for lunch plus 2 15-minute breaks
Cycle time: 60 minutes per batch, including loading

PROCESS FLOW

Sequence of steps	Flow diagram	Rate of production (capacity)
Dirty dishes input from hospital wards		
Storage (raw materials)	△	
Hand-scrape, rinse, stack	①	8,400 dishes/day (4 people @ 300 dishes/person hour)
Storage (work in process)	△	
Load machine and wash	②	6,300 dishes/day (2 machines @ 450 dishes/machine cycle)
Machine dry	③	6,300 dishes/day (2 machines @ 450 dishes/machine cycle)
Inspect	☐	
Unload machine and stack	④	7,350 dishes/day (3 people @ 350 dishes/person hour)
Storage (finished goods)	△	
Deliver clean dishes to dietary		

DEMAND

3 meals per person day × 6 dishes per person meal × 361 person beds × 0.97 persons per bed = 6,304 dishes per day

STAFFING LEVELS

Operation	Capacity (dishes/worker day)	Workers required for 6,304 dishes/day
Hand-scrape, rinse, stack	2,100	3.00 (6,304/2,100)
Unload machine and stack	2,450	2.57

Exhibit 13

The Steps Involved in Trade-off Analysis

1. Seek decisions that involve trade-offs.
2. List the various alternatives open to management.
3. Specify the qualitative and quantitative pros and cons of each alternative.
4. Express as many of the advantages and disadvantages as possible in a common unit.
5. Decide on a course of action that you think will give you the largest net gain.

In Step 4 of Exhibit 13, although monetary units are particularly common and useful, output units and processing rates are also used. This step is not easy and will involve estimates. Although determining a monetary value for a qualitative benefit such as better customer service or happier workers is not always possible, it is a bigger mistake to ignore such factors. One way to begin is to perform a sensitivity analysis and to determine how large or small the value would have to be before it would make a difference to the decision. The answer will tell you how close your estimate has to be. The entire activity will necessarily involve a lot of sound managerial judgment because many of the costs and savings will be qualitative or uncertain.

Our hospital dishwashing example demonstrates the trade-off process. Our process analysis of this operation revealed some idle labour time in two of the four steps (see Figure 5). We might ask, Is there a better way to process the dirty dishes, that is, can we make the process more efficient while maintaining our effectiveness in cleaning just over 6,300 dishes per day? Apparently, demand peaks are not a problem here, and outputs determine inputs as dishes are cycled through this process (6,300 clean dishes return as 6,300 dirty dishes — with occasional losses from breakage). For the purpose of illustration, we will consider only two of the many possible alternatives:

1. Leave the current system alone (that is, do nothing).
2. Reduce scraping, rinsing, and stacking staff by one; reassign workloads so staff perform all operations on a rotating basis; separate labour and machine operations by work-in-process dish inventory.

Exhibit 14 summarizes estimates of the costs and benefits of these alternatives.

The cost of the first alternative is the quantitative savings of the second alternative — the yearly wages plus benefits of one worker. However, laying off a worker and reassigning work does not come cost-free. Staff idle time gives an operation flexibility that might be useful if, for example, one of the machines breaks and washing dishes by hand becomes necessary, surprise menu changes for a special occasion require seven dishes per patient meal, or a worker is absent. How will the remaining workers react to the new workload? As a manager, you might judge the annual value of these costs at $24,000, $15,000, and $50,000, respectively. Making the second two estimates is obviously difficult and subjec-

Exhibit 14

Comparison of Dishwashing Alternatives			
Option 1		**Option 2**	
Annual Savings	Annual Costs	Annual Savings	Annual Costs
	$24,000	$24,000	Lost flexibility ($15,000)
			Possible labour unrest ($50,000)
Net annual saving: –$24,000		Net annual saving: $24,000 – 15,000 – 50,000 = –$41,000	

tive. One way might be to ask how much you would be prepared to pay for insurance to avoid the cost altogether. Depending on your judgment, you will choose one of the alternatives or continue to investigate others, along with their associated trade-offs. In this example, note that departments other than operations are, or should be, involved.

Several questions increase substantially the complexities and challenges of managing this simple example:

- What are the hospital's policies to replace dishes that are broken, lost, or stolen?
- What happens if a washing machine breaks down?
- How are sudden increases or decreases in demand handled?
- What is the best way to schedule the job of picking up dirty dishes from the wards?
- Is too much or too little money invested in the inventory of dishes?
- Should we replace one or both of the existing washing and drying machines?

Performing a process analysis to gain a good understanding of how a process works and careful consideration of relevant trade-offs will put you in a good position to make operations decisions. The problems and cases at the end of this chapter will allow you to practise using these and other analytical tools to develop your managerial skills.

SECTION

FIVE

RECENT DEVELOPMENT IN OPERATIONS

Like all fields, operations is constantly developing. The recent past has seen revolutionary changes in attitudes toward quality, inventory management, and timing, which affect all departments in an organization.

QUALITY

The changes in quality originate in how it affects an organization's competitiveness, how it is defined, and how it is achieved. Industries go through phases in which one competitive factor or another dominates. From time to time it might be access — such as to a patented product or process or one requiring special skills or a secret recipe — the ability to produce at low cost, the ability to produce high quality, or the willingness and ability to provide superior service. Many organizations have been able to produce high quality goods and services, forcing participants in their industries to devote significant attention to this area to maintain their market share.

Some see quality as an inherent characteristic that cannot really be defined but is recognized when seen. For example, you might judge the quality of a car by its shape. Art, wine, and services that rely on interpersonal interactions are other examples. Others see quality as a measurable characteristic inherent in a product — more, or less, represents higher quality. Thus, you might judge the quality of a car by its horsepower rating, top speed, or acceleration. Others view quality as conformance to specifications — deviation from specifications means bad quality. A fleet manager might judge the quality of cars by the degree of similarity between units. Still others consider quality to be whatever the user or customer says it is. You and a friend might have radically different views about the quality of a new album, course, or car. Your view might well depend on your circumstances. Underlying the whole notion of quality is a trade-off between quality and cost — extra quality is available, but only at a cost. Although different managers view quality differently, increasingly it is left up to customers to define it. Needless to say, this shift affects operations by placing extra emphasis on flexibility and communication.

Some organizations, such as artistic ventures and professional services, rely on artisans and craftspersons to build a high quality product or service. Others rely on objective measures and statistical rules to separate acceptable batches of product (or input) from unacceptable ones; the relevant factors include the costs of testing and of making errors — accepting bad units and rejecting good ones. However, ensuring high quality by inspecting and separating out unacceptable output is expensive. More advanced organizations use statistics to help build quality through statistical process control (SPC). This technique requires regular collection and analysis of relevant quality data. Even though quality problems show up in the products, the focus of controlling quality is on the processes that make them.

Current thinking on quality focuses on a philosophy rooted in Japan known as total quality management (TQM), which builds on SPC in two ways. First, its real goal is to enhance competitive performance in all areas: costs, productivity, market share, and profits, as well as quality. Second, TQM is all-inclusive. It means improving an organization by eliminating waste in every activity — not only production, but also design, purchasing, inspection, marketing, sales, service, research and development, financial controls, personnel management, and the like. TQM treats every function as a process, which it sets out to analyze and improve. Although TQM uses several simple SPC tools to diagnose quality problems, TQM is not a set of techniques or even a state — it is a philosophy, an attitude, a never-ending journey. Exhibit 15 shows its philosophical bases.

EXHIBIT 15

Philosophy of Total Quality Management

1. Quality is customer driven.
2. The environment is data rich.
3. Processes are never perfect.
4. Problems require quick response.
5. Employees, particularly at low levels (operators) are an organization's most important assets.
6. Organizations, including suppliers and customers, are like families; we should reduce uncertainty by developing friendly, mutually supporting, partnership relationships them and share information freely with them.
7. Quality and error prevention should be part of product and process design.

Exhibit 16 describes some of the significant implications of TQM. Because it concentrates on processes, TQM recognizes a series of supplier-operator-customer groups connected in chains, with attention focused on the links between activities. Almost everyone is simultaneously in all three roles. This environment requires effective and frequent cooperation and communication along the chains. Constantly seeking perfection leads organizations to search for and study the best possible examples of relevant processes (benchmarking), wherever they occur. They then use the information to redesign (improve) their own processes. TQM links processes and involves everyone, including top management, in managing quality.

TQM requires dramatic change in many organizations. It is hard to establish a culture of cooperation when the traditional supplier-customer relationships, both internal and external, have been adversarial. However, the benefits — higher quality inputs and outputs, reduced variability, and delegated decision making — are real. To get results, organizations must invest in training, development, and technology and adopt an attitude that change is good. Managers often see this change as threatening because:

- Their jobs change from gathering information, making decisions, and using incentives and punishments to manage the work force, to consulting and coaching, and
- Organizations widen their spans of control and reduce layers of management.

Exhibit **16**

The Traditional Model of the Firm in Contrast to TQM		
	Traditional Model	**TQM Model**
Organizational goals	Maximizing shareholder wealth through maximizing profits	Serving customer needs by supplying goods and services of the highest possible quality
Individual goals	Individuals motivated only by economic goals; maximizing income and minimizing effort	Individuals motivated by economic, social, and psychological goals relating to personal fulfillment and social acceptance
Time orientation	Static optimization: maximizing the present value of net cash flow by maximizing revenue and minimizing cost	Dynamic: focusing on innovation and continual improvement
Coordination and control	Managers have the expertise to coordinate and direct subordinates; agency problems necessitate monitoring of subordinates and applying incentives to align objectives	Employees are trustworthy and are experts in their jobs, hence, there is emphasis on self-management; employees are capable of coordinating on a voluntary basis
Role of information	Information system matches hierarchical structure: key functions are to support managers' decision making and monitor subordinates	Open and timely information flows are critical to self-management, horizontal coordination, and a quest for continual improvement
Principles of work design	Productivity maximization by specializing on the basis of comparative advantage	System-based optimization with emphasis on dynamic performance
Firm boundaries	Clear distinction between markets and firms as governance mechanisms, firm boundaries determined by transaction costs	Issues of supplier-customer relations, information flow, and dynamic coordination common to transactions within and between firms.

Source: R.M. Grant, R. Shani, and R. Krishnan, "TQM's Challenge to Management Theory and Practice," *Sloan Management Review*, Vol. 35, No. 2 (1994), 25–35.

Above all, TQM is an integrating philosophy that focuses the whole organization's attention on the single goal of satisfying customers. The changes are sufficiently sweeping to alter the very notion of why firms exist. The traditional model sees a firm's overriding goal as maximizing shareholders' wealth by maximizing profits. In contrast, TQM views satisfying customers as a firm's prime goal; shareholder wealth is a logical outcome of customer satisfaction, not a goal in its own right.

With reference to Figure 3, on page 492, through reduced set-up times, TQM has shifted the attractive band of production from the rigid diagonal shown, toward the lower right-hand corner. It has allowed job shops and batching operations to operate more like line-flow or continuous-flow operations. It is an attractive, radical departure from traditional North American and European thinking.

TQM proficiency is now recognized by a number of well-known awards, such as the Deming Prize (Japan), the Malcolm Baldrige National Quality Award (United States), and the ISO 9000 family of standards (international). The goal of these awards is to promote quality and productivity, which are essential to successful business. In general, the focus of these awards is on management systems, rather than on product specifications; thus, although extremely unlikely, an awarded organization could produce low quality products. The awards promote process standards in all departments and functions to help organizations continuously achieve quality for their customers.

JUST-IN-TIME MANUFACTURING

TQM arose from a more fundamental Japanese movement, just-in-time (JIT) or zero inventory (ZI) manufacturing, which is largely responsible for Japan's striking post–World War II success. JIT has at least two distinct meanings. On a micro level, the term literally is taken to mean that something arrives just as it is needed — no sooner and no later. Factories manage to achieve this goal by using an effective information system. Despite the widespread use of computers in production, the system used is low-tech: a visible signal (*kanban*) authorizes a worker to do something, for example, work on one or a few more parts or move one or a few parts to the next work centre. The rules are simple — no *kanban*, no action. When a machine breaks or production flow stops for any reason, the flow of *kanban*, and thus production, stops. Because there are only a few *kanban* between any two work centres, the system is very responsive to disruptions. In contrast, traditional North American and European systems expect workers to work on the next part, if at all possible, and these systems will not stop until workers run out of parts to work on. Because the systems are designed to keep workers occupied, there are always lots of parts and it takes a long time for the system to stop.

Stopping production quickly would lead to lost efficiency if nothing else happened. But, in Japanese eyes, stopping work allows workers to identify and solve real production problems and prevents the accumulation of costly inventories, which hide opportunities for improvement. If work was stopped because of a poor quality part produced in an earlier operation, it is hardly wise to keep producing more just to keep workers occupied. The advantages of JIT production have to be balanced against the need for demand stability.

On a macro level JIT means eliminating waste — the TQM philosophy of continual improvement. Non-TQM plants often believe that operations, once debugged, are running optimally and that changing things will only cause problems. TQM recognizes that no matter how well something is running, it is never perfect. Under this philosophy, everyone, including managers, tries to find production problems (waste) and eliminate them. A useful start is to reduce inventory, which mostly just sits around, costing a lot of money and adding no value of any kind. As described earlier in this chapter, JIT operators have found ways to eliminate the reasons for having inventory.

FLEXIBILITY AND OPERATIONS CONTROL

In the past few years, customers have started to demand exactly what they want from manufacturers. Typically, they want something different — perhaps colour, size, flavour, or shape — and they want it fast without a price penalty. This phenomenon, termed "mass customization," is more common in some industries than others. In some markets — such as those for commodities — customers place little value on the possible custom features. Other markets might be restricted by law from customizing. Although mass customization can be expected to increase production costs, there are significant advantages to producers that can manage it, especially if they can charge a price premium.

For example, one small Japanese bicycle manufacturer can produce several million different variations based on model, frame size, colour, and so on. The company's electronic communications connect the store, where customers are measured, with the factory. Its computer-aided design (CAD) system designs the product. The plant itself, however, is not extensively automated. Although the company promises delivery of custom bicycles within two to three weeks, it can complete them in only 150 minutes (compared with 90 minutes for its standard lines). The custom bicycles sell at a considerable premium above the standard models. The company can use the skill it has developed in responding rapidly to market demands to help sell all its products and keep inventory levels low.

Mass customization differs from providing variety in one important respect: it means economically manufacturing in response to a customer's order instead of trying to meet customer needs through inventory. The requirements of mass customization are both a major challenge and a significant opportunity for manufacturers. The task is simultaneously to obtain both low cost and flexibility. With reference to Figure 3 the question becomes, How can manufacturers combine the traditional scale of line- and continuous-flow processes with the nimbleness of job shops?

There are various ways to deal with this problem. First of all, it pays at the design stage to plan products and processes so that customized versions can be built from standard modules (held in an electronic database) from which the product can be rapidly created. It also helps to keep customer orders moving as quickly as possible from product design, through process planning, to creation and delivery of the product or service by linking all the processes needed to plan, manufacture, and deliver a product. A third way to increase flexibility is to ensure that all the steps from suppliers through to delivery to the customer (the supply chain) are as short as possible. It doesn't make much sense to be able to design a product and a process to make it within hours of receiving a customer order if it takes weeks to get the material or to free up capacity in the supply chain. Typically, responsive supply chains have relatively few steps, low set-up times, and excess capacity.

Many mass customizers dedicate a team to design, produce, and deliver a customer's order. Flexibility requires that such teams be established quickly and work together from the start, implying a cooperative organizational culture. It also helps to seek and capture customer feedback about both the product and the process. An enterprise can use such information for its own planning, particularly in deciding how to deal with a specific customer in the future. Lastly, computers can help improve flexibility by capturing data in an electronically retrievable and editable form, which can be transferred across the world instantaneously. Thus, product design can be accomplished much more quickly. It is common for designs created in North America to be transferred to manufacturers in Southeast Asia, who immediately start manufacture. Computers are vital to the operating steps themselves as both their physical and mental aspects are increasingly automated.

Computers are also being used in operations planning and control in a technique known as *manufacturing resource planning* (MRP). The main notion behind MRP is that the needs for materials and other resources are interconnected rather than independent. Once a fast-food restaurant manager has a forecast of hamburger sales, he or she no longer has to estimate how many hamburger buns (or meat, relish, worker hours, electricity, and so on) will be needed and when to order them. These demands can be calculated because fast-food restaurants do not sell these components except as complete hamburgers. MRP's goals are to have the right amount of the right part, in the right place, at the right time, every time; to minimize inventories, especially work in process; and to improve customer service by avoiding stock-outs. MRP allows a way around the conflict between minimizing inventories and improving customer service. By connecting manufacturing to accounting, purchasing, marketing, and other functions, advanced MRP systems are information systems that integrate all functional areas of the organization.

MRP and TQM use quite different means toward the same ends. In production controlled by *kanban*, problems quickly stop the flow — production is *pulled* through the system. Think about a string attached to a toy; stop pulling, and the toy stops instantly. In production controlled by MRP, production is *pushed* through the system. MRP production is thus relatively insensitive to stoppages in flow unless the MRP program is recalculated. Try stopping a rolling toy by pushing on the string. MRP's aim is to control the current system using computer programs and databases as tools. In contrast, TQM's aim is to discover problems in the existing system so that the system can be improved by eliminating the problems. Referring to Figure 3, computerization in manufacturing can increase flexibility. It can reduce set-up costs per run, making production of small lots of mature products viable (the lower right-hand corner).

SUMMARY

This chapter was designed to broaden your knowledge of operations situations by discussing five aspects of operating systems:

1. The input-transformation-output notion and the basic transformation components of equipment, labour, materials, and energy;

2. The key operations tasks of function, quality, quantity, price, and service;

3. The basic process types (continuous-flow, line-flow, batch, job shop, and project processes) and their management requirements;

4. The two basic operations analysis tools of process and trade-off analysis; and

5. Recent developments in quality, inventory management, and timing.

The chapter also emphasized that operations is all around us, all the time. Each of us is involved in operations daily in our professional and personal lives. Operations cannot meaningfully be dealt with in isolation from the other functions in the organization, nor can these functions ignore operations. Although operations problems vary in their difficulty and scope, we believe that understanding the points discussed in this chapter will help you to make a significant start in dealing with the complexities and accepting the challenges.

APPENDIX D

Operations Questions and Problems[1]

1. Your sandwich-making company has just received two orders for tomorrow. The first, from the local daycare, is for 300 peanut butter and jam sandwiches. The second, from the city council, is for 100 roast beef sandwiches.

   a. Perform a task analysis for each of these customers, supporting your positioning of the variables on the continuum of process types.

   b. How could you or other managers use this information to make operating decisions?

2. Give one example of an operation *not in the text* that would efficiently operate under each of the following processes:

   a. Project

   b. Job shop

   c. Batch

   d. Line flow

   e. Continuous flow

List the characteristics in your processes that support your classification.

3. Jim, a baker, was shaking his head in disgust as he was putting some of the week-old cakes out in the trash. "I just don't understand it," he said. "Last week I sold out of my carrot cakes in only two days. Now I'm throwing half of them out! I must be doing something wrong!"

Jim tried to offer his customers a selection of at least 10 different types of cake at any one time. He changed this selection each week. Because the bakery was closed on Sundays, Jim set this day aside to make enough cakes to last the week. The number of each type he baked depended on Jim's estimate. He threw out any unsold cakes at the end of the week. Unfortunately, Jim was throwing more and more away, and he was starting to feel this loss in his weekly profits.

   a. Where does Jim's cake production fall on the production process continuum? Support your answer.

   b. Is this the best position? Why or why not?

   c. Advise Jim of at least *two* different options in making his cakes, and state the pros and cons of each.

4. Liz Lawton, operations director of the Mitchell Company, was trying to decide what to do about the capacity of the production line. If the current sales trend continued, demand would soon exceed capacity. Liz was considering replacing some of the company's current equipment with a new, high-speed machine. Although the projected investment of $15 million was high, the equipment was expected to have a useful life of 13 years. Despite the increase in depreciation, Liz expected the investment to reduce annual fixed costs from $540,000 to $490,000. Unfortunately, she expected that the old equipment, which had worked faithfully for decades, would have no resale value. According to the manufacturer, the annual capacity of the new machine would be 40,000 units higher than that of the equipment it would replace. Mitchell Company realized a contribution of $50 from each unit sold. From a purely quantitative point of view, does this potential investment make economic sense? What other factors might Liz want to consider?

5. Classify each of the following examples of inventory by form (raw materials, work in process, finished goods) and by function (decoupling, pipeline, and so on).

   a. Sausages in boxes moving along a conveyor to the frozen goods warehouse where they will await shipment to customers

   b. Passengers walking from the plane from which they have just disembarked to the baggage carousel to wait for baggage

   c. Spare parts (made in-house) for repair of the machines used in the production of pipeline welding equipment

   d. Patients waiting in a doctor's office for their scheduled appointments

   e. Bins of castings awaiting machining in a facility manufacturing plumbing supplies (taps and fixtures)

   f. A large pot containing potatoes peeled and sliced for fries at 11:30 a.m. in a downtown restaurant that caters primarily to the work force of a large office building

6. For the examples in question 5, how could the inventories be reduced to make the operations more like a just-in-time system?

7. In order to satisfy customers, a small manufacturing firm found that over the past several months it had slowly increased the variety of its component parts, lot sizes, and lead times. Discuss the effect such changes to the product line would likely have on the production process.

8. Because of a large increase in demand, Outwest Drillpress was considering expanding its automatic precision drilling operation, for which it charged its customers $30 per hour. The process was automatic except for setting up the controls, placing the part in a jig, and removing it after drilling.

   Outwest officials were surprised to find that the cost of this type of equipment had doubled since they had purchased the original machine. The precision driller now cost $109,000, including a $3,000 installation charge. Maintenance on the present machine totalled $2,000 per year, and electricity cost $1 per hour. Any new equipment would incur similar expenses. With operator wages costing $15 per hour and a 6,000-hour lifespan on these machines, the company was not sure if it should expand.

   As a consultant to Outwest, would you advise them to purchase the new machine?

9. Raoul Ramsay had just graduated from high school and would soon start university. On his recent visit to the campus, he stopped at the bookstore. He was

interested in his options for buying a book for his introductory business course. The text for the course was available from the bookstore in two formats, bound for $65 and unbound for $28. Bound copies were also available from the used bookstore for $40. Raoul discovered that, at the end of the year, he would probably be able to sell either a new or used bound copy for $25 if he placed a $15 advertisement in the student newspaper. Alternatively, the used bookstore would buy bound books from him, paying $25 for a book purchased new and $15 for one purchased used. From these prices, the used bookstore would deduct a 40 percent commission. Unfortunately, the unbound version of the book would have no resale value. From a purely economic viewpoint, which option is best for Raoul?

10. A predicted phenomenal surge in the popularity of Leanne's Liquid Beverage would increase weekly demand to 8,000 cases of six 350-mL bottles. The production manager was worried that the process would be unable to handle increased demand.

The mixing operation was capable of producing 3.5 L of Leanne's Liquid Beverage per minute. The bottling machine's effective capacity was 300 bottles per hour. Workers applied labels by hand; each worker could apply labels to 1,920 bottles per day. The capping machine could cap up to 600 bottles per hour. The final machine in the line, the packager, could package 1,600 cases per day. The plant's productive time was eight hours per day, five days per week.

Leanne's production manager informed her that the cost per week of doubling the output at each of the five operations would be:

mixing $ 550
bottling $1,975   (Note that each time you increase the output of the
labelling $1,200   bottling machine by 300 bottles per hour, it costs $1,975)
capping $ 900
packaging $1,500

The current rate of production is 2,000 cases per week. The unit contribution per case is $2.

a. What is the current capacity of this system?

b   Can the current system handle the increased demand?

c. If not, what changes will have to be made?

d. Should Leanne invest in the new equipment? Why or why not?

11. Laurie Kay was trying to choose between two manufacturing options. The firm for which she worked sold its product for $1 per unit. Although Laurie estimated that demand would be 200,000 units, she was not at all certain about this value because the environment was rather turbulent. The costs of the two options were:

	Alternative 1	**Alternative 2**
Material	$0.40 per unit	$0.30 per unit
Direct labour	0.20 per unit	0.10 per unit
Variable overhead	0.10 per unit	0.10 per unit
Fixed overhead	50,000 per year	100,000 per year

a. What is the breakeven volume for each alternative?

b. What is the profitability of each alternative at sales levels of 180,000, 200,000, and 220,000?

c. At what point are the two alternatives economically identical?

d. Which is the better alternative quantitatively?

12. In her home town of Peterborough, Ontario, Vanessa was reviewing the operations of her small business: baskets filled with gift items. Although sales had been up from last year, she remembered several occasions when she had completely stocked out of baskets and was unable to meet the needs of her customers. Sales for the upcoming year were forecasted at 20,000 baskets and varied significantly from week to week. Reviewing some financial data, Vanessa discovered the following costs:

Cost of gifts placed in the basket	$3.00
Cost of the basket	0.50
Direct labour per basket	0.50

Currently, Vanessa carried two weeks' worth of both raw materials and finished goods inventory at an inventory carrying rate of 20 percent. The baskets sold for $5 each. Vanessa was wondering whether she should increase the finished goods inventory from two weeks to three weeks.

a. Assuming she carries two weeks' worth of both finished goods and raw materials, what will Vanessa's inventory carrying cost be for both next year?

b. How much is she losing with every basket that is *not* sold because of stockout?

c. What would be the *extra* cost of carrying an additional week of finished goods inventory?

d. Would you advise Vanessa to carry the extra week? Why or why not?

13. Brianna Butler, who lived in Centreville, wanted to spend a few days visiting her grandmother in Fosterburgh, and she had to decide how to get there. The two cities were connected by good roads and convenient bus, train, and plane service. One option Brianna was considering was to rent a car for $90 plus $0.06 per km. With her student discount, Brianna could buy return, nonstop tickets as follows: bus, $120; train, $240; plane, $400. Although Brianna could walk to the nearby bus station or the car rental agency, she would have to take a cab to the airport or the train station. Brianna estimated the cab fares at $20 and $10, respectively. Her grandmother would happily pick her up from her arrival point in Fosterburgh. Because Fosterburgh was in a foreign country 1,275 km from Centreville, Brianna would need a visa, which would cost her $40. Brianna estimated that she could drive the distance at 120 km per hour and stop for a total of one hour each way en route. The train was scheduled to take 12 hours 45 minutes from departure from Centreville to arrival in Fosterburgh. The bus was scheduled to make the trip in 14 hours 10 minutes, and the journey by plane was scheduled to take 2 hours 55 minutes. Brianna estimated that she would have to leave her apartment at least 60 minutes before scheduled departure time to catch the plane. Similarly, she would have to leave 30 minutes early to catch the train but only 15 minutes early to catch the bus or get to the car rental agency. Time was a concern to Brianna because she was trying to save as much as possible from her summer job. She worked in the bar at the Centreville Hotel. Although the wages of $6.50 per hour weren't great, her job did allow her to work whenever she wanted. Regardless of which travel option she chose, she knew that she would spend seven full days with her grandmother. Which option is best for Brianna?

14. Return to the example given near the end of this chapter concerning a hospital dishwashing operation. A manager in the hospital has discovered that disposable dishes can be purchased for about $0.08 each.

   a. Would disposable dishes be a viable option?

   b. What factors would be important?

   c. What other possible solutions warrant investigation?

15. After a tour of the plant, Sue Barnes, the general manager, called Fred Dirkin, foreman of the frame-building section in the Sentsun Stereo factory. She said: "What was your section up to this afternoon, Fred? When I walked through, more than half of the workers seemed to be doing nothing. We can't really afford to have workers sitting around idle, you know. And I don't really understand why your section always seems so close to missing your target of 500 frames per hour with all that excess labour. Take a look at it and let me know what gives."

The section, which was responsible for some of the first steps in the stereo production process, employed two types of workers. Nine workers assembled frames; an experienced assembler could produce 60 frames per hour. Fifteen other workers installed heat sinks (an electrical component). Their job was more complex; installing a heat sink took an experienced worker about 75 seconds.

Fred wanted to measure the efficiency of each type of worker and prepare his answer for Sue Barnes. He also wanted to ensure that people were not idle the next time she came around.

16. The local Italian Club had established a tradition – its weekly Really Old Times Latin Night, when it sold nothing but bloody caesars from 7:30 to 11:30. In

fact, the night was so popular that members usually ordered about 1,900 bloody caesars. To speed up production, the bartenders specialized their activities. They stood in a row behind the bar. Sabrina, the first one in line, took a glass, dipped the rim in lemon juice, and rolled it in celery salt. Sabrina could prepare 500 glasses per hour. Kevin took a prepared glass, filled it with ice, and added vodka from a dispenser. He averaged seven seconds for this task. Candice put two drops of Worcestershire sauce and one drop of Tabasco sauce into the vodka; she could complete 15 glasses per minute. Brandon filled the glass with Clamato juice and garnished it with salt, pepper, a slice of lime, and a stalk of celery. It took him 6.5 seconds to complete these steps. Sarah handed the drink to the customer and took the drink ticket. Sarah could handle 2,100 customer per night. The bartenders were helped by others who washed glasses, prepared celery, lime slices, etc., and sold tickets.

a. What is the bottleneck for the drink preparation operation?

b. If each bartender starts work at exactly 7:30, what is the earliest time that Sarah can complete the sale to the first customer?

c. If all staff stop work at exactly 11:30, what is the nightly capacity of this operation?

d. If each bartender works at capacity for four hours and sales are steady, how much inventory will the system contain?

e. The club just got word from the social committee that next week several guests would attend from a sister club, thus raising demand to about 2,400 bloody caesars. Would adding a sixth bartender, Enzo, help the operation meet this demand? Conceptually, how might Enzo be used?

NOTE

1. Based in part on problem sets created by John Cummings and Liz Gray, Richard Ivey School of Business, The University of Western Ontario.

■ ■ ■ CASES FOR PART 6 ■ ■ ■

CASE **6.1** Bankruptcy

■

CASE **6.2** Central Insurance Canada

■

CASE **6.3** Garlic's

■

CASE **6.4** Hempline Inc.

■

CASE **6.5** Introducing New Technology at General Motors

■

CASE **6.6** The Mongolian Grill

■

CASE **6.7** Off Broadway Photography

■

CASE **6.8** Steelway Building Systems

■

CASE **6.9** Universal Pulp and Paper

■

CASE **6.10** The University of Western Ontario Book Store

■

CASE **6.11** WhiteWater Specialities Limited

C A S E 6.1 BANKRUPTCY

By Michael R. Pearce and Stephannie A. Larocque

Bernita Graf had just been assigned the new job of production manager — games and toys for the Exemplar Manufacturing Company. For the past seven years, Bernita had worked as a supervisor in another division of Exemplar. Exemplar had several well-established product lines and was beginning to diversify into new areas. Bernita's superior, the general production manager, asked her to work with the new products manager on the latest product, code-named *Bankruptcy*. *Bankruptcy* was a new adult game that the marketing department seemed to think would be an immense success, competing with board games such as *Trivial Pursuit* and *Pictionary*.

An Exemplar staff member, John Duncan, informed Bernita that the basic tasks to be performed were assembling components purchased from other manufacturers. The assembly operations could be performed in any order. In repeated attempts John was able to assemble completed versions of *Bankruptcy* in 15 minutes. He also found that if three workers performed only two assembly operations each, instead of all six, each operation could be completed in half the time. Thus, although one person working alone could produce 32 games a day, a team of three people working together could produce 192 games of *Bankruptcy* per day. Bernita received details on the time requirements and material costs of the various components for each operation, as shown in Exhibit 1.

All materials could usually be obtained within one week of being ordered. On occasion, materials could take up to two weeks to be delivered. The vice-president of finance recently had sent a memo to managers asking that all inventories be kept at minimum sizes because costs for the company had risen substantially. The vice-president asked to be informed of all investment needs exceeding $40,000.

The community had a good supply of semiskilled personnel. The starting rate at Exemplar was $8 per hour (including benefits): normal hours were 7:30 to 16:00, with 30 minutes for lunch. Thus, each worker was paid an average of $64 per day. Considering that on average there were 20 working days in a month, this worked out to $1,280 per month. Bernita was told she could hire as many workers as she thought she needed and pay them on whatever basis she wished, so long as she did not exceed the plant average of $12 per hour regular time for semi-skilled labour. Overtime, if used, was calculated at time and a half.

Bernita was allotted a plant space of 20 by 5 metres and told she could arrange her operations as she saw fit. The department would be charged $48 per square metre annually for the allotted space. Extra space beyond the allotted 100 square metres was also available but would be charged to her operation at $72 per square metre annually. The raw materials inventory (at $20 per unit) and finished goods inventory (valued at material cost plus labour cost) would require roughly the same volume. Because the boxes were fairly bulky, she could store the equivalent of 60 units of *Bankruptcy* on each square metre of floor space, assuming she piled them as high as possible. John Duncan told Bernita he figured they would need 50 square metres for assembly operations, including tables, work stations, lockers, etc. Other fixed manufacturing overhead costs associated with *Bankruptcy* were estimated to be $4,120 per month.

The new products manager told Bernita that the forecasted demand for Bankruptcy for at least the first year was 3,600 units per month, with a range from 3,000 to 4,000 in any given month. He stressed that he expected Bernita to avoid stock-outs because *Bankruptcy* would primarily be an impulse purchase, and stock-outs would be very costly. The intended selling price was $25 per unit. Marketing estimated its fixed costs (mostly for packaging design, advertising, and point of purchase displays) at $40,000.

Bernita was also told that one of her suppliers, Hutchison Ltd., had sent in a quotation of $23 per completed unit to produce the year's requirements of *Bankruptcy* for Exemplar. Their quality was not considered as good as Exemplar's, but they were prepared to provide units on any schedule desired. Unfortunately, they added, the delivery time could vary from one to four weeks depending on how busy they were.

EXHIBIT 1
Time and Material Costs

Assembly Operation	Time Required (Minutes)		Material Cost
	For One Person Alone	For a Three-Person Team	
A	1	0.5	$ 1.00
B	4	2	2.50
C	2	1	0.50
D	2	1	1.00
E	3	1.5	5.00
F	3	1.5	10.00
	15	7.5	$20.00

C A S E 6.2   CENTRAL INSURANCE CANADA

By John Haywood-Farmer and Tim Silk

When Mark Rutherford, supervisor of administration services for Central Insurance Canada (CIC), returned to his Toronto office from vacation on April 12, 1997, he received some disturbing news. Céline Lefevbre, one of the corporation's underwriters, explained that a policy holder had cancelled her policy after having been forced to pay Canada Post for a letter that had been mailed from CIC's Toronto office with insufficient postage. The marketing department wanted Mr. Rutherford to find a way to prevent sending mail with insufficient postage to policy holders before the next promotional mailing scheduled for June 23.

CENTRAL INSURANCE CANADA

Central Insurance Canada, with annual sales of nearly $250 million, was one of Canada's 25 largest insurance companies. CIC provided automobile, home owner, and business insurance to its customers and sold primarily to Canadian adults. CIC's parent company, Central Insurance International, operated in over 20 countries and was among the five largest insurance companies globally.

Administration Services Department

The administration services department managed all activities that were not considered part of insurance operations. The list included purchasing, finance, accounting, and other support services such as mailroom operations.

Mark Rutherford

Mr. Rutherford had been with CIC for 18 years. As supervisor of administration services, he reported directly to the vice-president of finance and administration. His direct responsibilities included purchasing and supplier management and coordinating the mailing of promotional materials sent to policy holders with policy statements.

The Mailroom

The mailroom, with six employees, was one of the most time-pressured departments in the Toronto office. Each year it spent nearly $400,000 in postage and processed approximately 620,000 units of outgoing mail (i.e., envelopes with inserts). All policy statements (invoices), promotional materials, and broker mail flowed through the mailroom. Promotional materials were processed using the

IVEY Tim Silk prepared this case during the 1997 Case Writing Workshop and under the direction of Professor John Haywood-Farmer solely to provide material for class discussion. The authors do not intend to illustrate either effective or ineffective handling of a managerial situation. The authors may have disguised certain names and other identifying information to protect confidentiality. Ivey Management Services prohibits any form of reproduction, storage or transmittal without its written permission. This material is not covered under authorization from CanCopy or any reproduction rights organization. Copyright © 1997, Ivey Management Services.

Kamai Quickpost mail inserter, a $350,000 machine that was effectively a small automated assembly line. The machine grasped an envelope at the start of the line and inserted various promotional insert pages into the envelope as it moved down the line. Once all sheets had been inserted into the envelope, the machine placed postage on the envelope and sealed it. Because it was critical that the correct postage be applied to each envelope to adhere to Canada Post's strict postage regulations, determining the weight of the envelope and its contents was a critical step in processing the envelopes. To do this, Mr. Rutherford took samples of each insert, recorded its weight, and added the weights. He then set the Quickpost's postage meter accordingly. For example, because a mailing that included an envelope (eight grams), a policy statement (five grams), and insert #2 (10 grams) would be expected to weigh 23 grams, he would set the postage meter manually for 45¢ postage (see Exhibit 1) and all envelopes in that mailing batch would receive postage of 45¢. Exhibit 2 lists the various weights of page inserts.

CANADA POST PROCEDURES

Most of CIC's mail fell into one of three Canada Post postage categories for letter-size envelopes. Exhibit 1 shows these categories; Exhibit 3 shows CIC's percentage of mail sent by category. An envelope that was even one-tenth of a gram over the weight limit would be bumped into the next postage category.

Exhibit 4 outlines Canada Post's process for handling mail. After collecting mail from senders, Canada Post transported it to sorting plants, which, in addition to sorting mail, checked it for correct postage. Canada Post would not deliver mail with insufficient postage. If the plant detected a piece of mail with insufficient postage, it would normally return it to the sender. Canada Post sorting plants also spot-checked bulk mailings sent by businesses. If Canada Post found samples to be over-weight (insufficient postage), it would reject the entire bulk mailing and either return it to the sender to have the appropriate postage placed on each envelope or contact the sender to discuss the matter. Sorted mail was transported to postal stations for delivery. If a piece of mail with insufficient postage was detected at this stage, the postal station notified the addressee that it was holding mail; it would not release the mail until the addressee had paid the balance owing. For example, a customer receiving a piece of mail weighing 56.3 grams with postage of 71¢ would have to pay 20¢ (90¢ — 71¢ + 1¢ GST[1]). Canada Post was unable to say what portion of errors it detected at each stage. It gave no credit for mail with excess postage.

Customers who believed that a Canada Post error had caused damages could file a claim with Canada Post's customer service claims department. Canada Post required a sample of the mail, a statement of what had gone wrong and Canada Post's liability, and verification from a third party.

THE RACHEL SIMMONS INCIDENT

Rachel Simmons was a 42-year-old legal secretary who worked for a prominent Toronto law firm. Both she and her husband had been CIC policy holders for some years, insuring their automobiles and jointly owned home and cottage. The

Simmons had always paid their premiums, which totalled about $3,600 annually, on time; their infrequent claims had been for relatively small amounts.

On April 7, 1997, Ms Simmons received a call from Canada Post informing her that it was holding an envelope for her at the postal station. When she arrived at the postal station, she found a letter from CIC. Canada Post demanded a payment of 28¢ to make up the 26¢ difference between the 45¢ stamp attached to the envelope and the 71¢ stamp that Canada Post claimed CIC should have used. Ms Simmons was annoyed by this incident and further irritated by having to pay the 2¢ GST. Her annoyance quickly turned to rage when she discovered that the envelope contained her automobile policy statement indicating the outstanding balance of $864.50 she owed CIC. Furious that CIC had had the audacity to make her pay for a letter that contained her bill, Ms Simmons called her broker later that day, cancelled her automobile policy with CIC, and purchased a new policy from a competing insurance company.

Mark Rutherford's Response

Upon hearing the news on April 12, Mr. Rutherford immediately sent a letter of apology to Rachel Simmons, along with a $5.00 book of stamps, and then proceeded to find out what had gone wrong. The bar code of the envelope sent to Ms Simmons indicated that it should have contained the policy sheet and inserts #4, #5, and #7. Thus the total weight, including the envelope, should have been 29 grams. The postage of 45¢ should have been sufficient. Mr. Rutherford later discovered that Canada Post had made an error in its central sorting plant in Markham, Ontario.

However, he also discovered that it was likely that some mail was being sent out over the weight limit. There were three possible reasons for overweight envelopes. First, Quickpost could malfunction and insert multiple copies of a single insert into an envelope, thereby pushing the weight over the limit. Second, he found that the weight of inserts varied by as much as 0.5 grams per page because of variances in paper thickness, humidity, and ink weight. Third, not all policy holders received the same combination of inserts. Therefore, some envelopes in a batch might be over 30 grams (the 45¢ weight limit), but would still be stamped at 45¢. The implications of this problem were serious: lost customers, a poor reputation, and the costs associated with restamping mailings rejected by Canada Post. The problem also jeopardized CIC's promise to policy holders that policy statements would be received within one week of the policy date.

As a short-term solution, Mr. Rutherford calibrated the Quickpost machine to stamp all mail at 71¢ until he could find a permanent solution. This adjustment would ensure that all mail previously stamped at 45¢ would have more than enough postage. However, he had to find a permanent solution and decided to contact vendors for quotes on equipment that would solve his problem.

VENDOR AND EQUIPMENT INFORMATION

Mr. Rutherford identified two suppliers that could provide solutions to his problem. Kamai, manufacturer of the Quickpost system, had developed a software package that could be used with the Quickpost machine. The software enabled the Quickpost to calculate the weight of each stuffed envelope and apply the correct amount of postage. The software was priced at $18,500. In addition to the purchase price, Kamai charged $700 per year thereafter as a mandatory contract for future software upgrades.

A second alternative was the Digi-calc machine, an envelope-weighing machine manufactured and marketed by Edelbrook to compete with Kamai's Quickpost software package. The Digi-calc machine, priced at $23,900 and compatible with CIC's existing Quickpost machine, used a digital scale to weigh each envelope and apply the correct postage. Edelbrook also offered an optional service contract of $1,200 per year to maintain the equipment.

Customer service was a factor in evaluating the alternatives. Machine downtime created costly processing delays. Kamai had a good reputation for quick response time to requests for service and was capable of fixing 75 percent of machine malfunctions within six hours. Edelbrook's service record was less admirable. On average, it took Edelbrook 12 hours to correct machine malfunctions. However, a recent industry study showed that Edelbrook equipment experienced an average of seven malfunctions per year, compared with 11 malfunctions per year for Kamai equipment. Kamai informed Mr. Rutherford that the software could be installed and functioning by June 18. Edelbrook could have the Digi-calc installed by May 15. Both the Kamai and Edelbrook approaches would provide significant excess capacity and could be operated by the current work force.

Mr. Rutherford needed to reach a decision that would solve the problem for the company. Because mail was being sent to policy holders on a daily basis, he wanted the problem solved quickly. The vice-president of finance and administration would expect to see a report that justified his decision.

NOTE

1. The goods and services tax (GST) was an unpopular federal tax applied at the wholesale and retail levels to most goods and services sold in Canada. In 1997 the GST rate was 7 percent.

EXHIBIT 1

Canada Post's Postage Categories	
Weight Category (grams)	**Postage Required**
0.1 to 30	45¢
30.1 to 50	71¢
50.1 to 100	90¢

Source: Canada Post.

EXHIBIT 2

Insert Weights	
Insert	**Weight (grams)**
Envelope	8
Policy Sheet	5
Insert #1	2
Insert #2	10
Insert #3	3
Insert #4	4
Insert #5	4
Insert #6	8
Insert #7	8

Source: Company files.

EXHIBIT 3

Percentage of Central Insurance Canada's Mail by Postage Category	
Postage Category	**Portion of Mail Sent**
45¢	30%
71¢	65
90¢	5
	100%

Source: Company files.

Exhibit 4

Canada Post's Mail-Handling Procedure

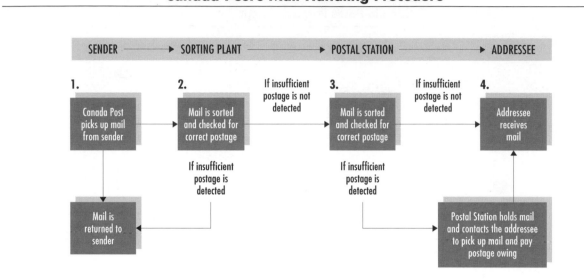

Source: Canada Post.

CASE 6.3   GARLIC'S

By Elizabeth Grasby and Andrew Fletcher

In January 1994, Kathy Burns, owner of Garlic's Restaurant in London, Ontario, had to make some decisions to ensure her first month's high sales figures would translate into long-term success. In particular, she wanted to improve the current dinner reservation system, which she believed was hindering customer service. Burns also wondered if any other changes should be made.

COMPANY BACKGROUND

Kathy Burns finished her MBA at the Western Business School in April 1993. Before entering the MBA program, she had worked 10 years in the restaurant and beverage industry, including six years at Western Food Services at The University of Western Ontario. She had always dreamed of owning a restaurant; her dream came true on December 2, 1993, when the doors of Garlic's opened. Garlic's, considered a bistro, focused 60 percent of its menu items on garlic and international cuisine. Burns's vision was to serve excellent food at a reasonable price and provide superior customer service in an informal, comfortable ambience. Her business plan outlined some goals of Garlic's: in the short term, she wanted to provide customer and employee satisfaction and maintain a 10 percent return on investment; in the long term, she wanted to grow through expansion to other locations. The restaurant was situated two doors north of the Grand Theatre, London's major theatre, on Richmond Street, in downtown London. London had a population of 315,000 and was located along Highway 401, the major east–west artery through southern Ontario. The city was home to The University of Western Ontario and the head offices of many companies, including Labatt's Brewery and Canada Trust. Richmond Row, approximately eight blocks of Richmond Street from Oxford Street to Queen's Avenue, consisted of many restaurants and retail shops and was generally considered to be the trendy part of town. Burns believed Garlic's close proximity to the theatre would provide a stable dinner crowd and the many office buildings in the downtown core would provide a stable lunch crowd.

THE GRAND THEATRE

The Grand Theatre season was from October to May and attracted not only Londoners, but also out-of-towners. All evening performances started at 8 p.m. and

---

Wednesday and Saturday matinées started at 2 p.m. Patrons of the theatre had formerly been middle-age with middle to upper income levels, but over the past few years the theatre clientele had changed to reflect the general population. For example, the Grand Theatre produced children's plays as well as provocative productions to mature audiences and targeted students with discounts on ticket prices.

THE CONSUMER

Burns offered high quality food combined with a reasonable price to fit with the 1990s customer perception of value. (Garlic's menu is shown in Exhibit 1.) In addition, for a restaurant to be successful it had to combine the food and price with an appealing atmosphere. Various atmospheres ranged from classy and elegant fine dining to lively, relaxed, and casual dining. The atmosphere of Garlic's was considered informal, comfortable, lively, and cosmopolitan. During the day, Garlic's clientele were business people with a one-hour lunch break. Burns noted that some of her business lunch customers also visited Garlic's for dinner. Dinner customers, the majority being the pre-theatre crowd, usually took two hours to dine as they ordered drinks and coffee and, in many cases, ordered dessert. Dinners and lunches represented 70 percent and 30 percent, respectively, of Garlic's sales.

FOOD PREPARATION AND SERVICING CUSTOMERS

The food was prepared for anticipated demand. For example, pasta was bought in individual portions, and when an order from the server was brought to the kitchen, the pasta was cooked to order in a spaghetti magic machine. The longest preparation time for any menu item was pizza, which took 10 to 12 minutes. Burns wanted to serve as many customers as possible while still giving the customer an enjoyable experience. Burns believed that an enjoyable experience created word-of-mouth advertising and generated repeat business. Burns's time estimation of a dinner for two is shown in Exhibit 2.

HIGH SALES IN DECEMBER

Sales in December totalled $80,000, surpassing optimistic expectations by $24,000. Burns believed that the restaurant's success in December was due to several factors. First, Garlic's was the first new downtown restaurant to open since the Blue Plate had opened in September 1992. (Location of Garlic's and competitors is shown in Exhibit 3.) Second, the location of Garlic's on Richmond Street gave it high visibility, not only to Grand Theatre patrons, but also to walk-by traffic. Third, December was traditionally a busy time of year for restaurants because of the celebratory mood of people. From her 1994 projected income statement, Burns projected fixed costs of $285,000 and a net profit after tax of $79,000, assuming an optimistic sales figure of $600,000. Variable cost was projected at 35 percent of sales.

THE RESERVATION SYSTEM

Garlic's used a reservation system that booked all 25 tables. Currently, Burns or any staff member answering the phone recorded the customer's request on the reservation time-table. When a dinner party first arrived at Garlic's, they would either be seated by the host or asked to sit at the bar until their table was ready. There were 12 bar stools to accommodate waiting patrons. Burns described some difficult moments during the dinner hours in December:

We were pretty much booked solid Thursday, Friday, and Saturday. We had situations in which five people were coming in and we had reserved a table for two people. We had people claiming they had a reservation, but we didn't have anything in our books. We had people showing up Saturday and their reservation in our book was for Friday. As well, we had people complaining that, even though they had booked a week and a half ago, they had terrible seats by the washrooms.

One of Burns's experienced waiters had suggested that Garlic's not reserve tables at 7 p.m. Although 7 p.m. was the most popular time to dine, the next available time the table was vacant, 9 p.m., was too late for people to start dining. In addition to not reserving tables at 7 p.m., Burns thought she should decrease the number of reservations to desirable seating only. Garlic's seating capacity was limited to approximately 80 seats. Changing reservations would be a trial and error approach, and the first step was to decide which seats were undesirable. (Garlic's seating plan is shown in Exhibit 4.)

OTHER CONSIDERATIONS

During December, Burns gave menus and business cards to customers turned away at the door and encouraged them to phone and make reservations the next time they wished to dine. The menus were rolled with a bow and cost $0.30 each. One thousand business cards cost $189.75. Burns gave out 210 cards and menus in December. She gave menus to potential customers with the hope that they would see the value and return at a later date.

Other options to meet or suppress demand included raising prices or expanding upstairs. If she raised prices, Burns wondered how high to raise them to match the competition. Garlic's nine major competitors and their prices are shown in Exhibit 5. The cost of renovating the upstairs would be about $30,000 and would be ideal to cater to large groups. Garlic's had received many calls from patrons requesting office parties, and Burns was unable to accommodate these requests because she wanted Garlic's to be available to the public on a daily basis. The only stairway to the second floor was through the next-door neighbour's antique store, and Burns would need to solve this problem if she expanded.

There were other concerns. Some customers had complained that the food was not always hot enough when delivered to the table. Burns thought she might need a plate warmer at the cost of $125 and/or a bus person to help in the food delivery. This bus person would work on Thursday, Friday, and Saturday from 5:30 p.m. to 10:30 p.m. and would earn $5.80 per hour.

Burns was unsure which options she should implement, but she knew she wanted to make her first month's high sales totals the first step to long-term success. While Burns, married with two daughters, welcomed the high sales, she wondered how long she could sustain working 90 hours a week. Yet, in such a competitive market Burns knew she had to ensure customer satisfaction and keep the customers coming back. She commented:

> We've been very successful to date; however, people are curious about new restaurants. I want to ensure Garlic's future and keep our customers returning for many years.

EXHIBIT 1
Garlic's Menu

MENU

DIPS & BREADS

TZATZIKI
a garlicky cucumber & yogurt dip originally
from Greece $3.95

CROSTINI
a baguette topped with a savory mixture of black olives,
pine nuts and garlic, baked in our oven $3.95

BRIE AND GARLIC TOASTS
roasted garlic and brie spread on a french stick and
melted under the broiler $4.25

BAGNO CALDO
a warm anchovy and garlic dip characteristic
of Northern Italy $4.95

BRUSCHETTA
tomatoes, fresh herbs and crushed garlic
served warm on a baguette $4.50

SMALL PLATES

SAKE STEAMED MUSSELS
12–14 mussels steamed with sake, garlic
and ginger $6.95

FIVE THAI SHRIMP
with cilantro pesto $5.95

TRADITIONAL SMOKED SALMON
cured and smoked in Garlic's kitchen $6.50

FOUR SPRING ROLLS
served with our own
apricot-mustard sauce $3.95

SUNDRIED TOMATO & BRIE TRIANGLES
four phyllo pastries served with a
lemon-sage sauce $3.95

SOUPS

CREAM OF GARLIC SOUP .... $2.50   CONCH & GARLIC CHOWDER $3.95

SALADS

GARLIC'S CAESAR
with lemony-garlic croutons $3.75

GRILLED CHICKEN & SHRIMP SALAD
with fresh fruit and a raspberry vinaigrette $6.25

MIXED GREENS SALAD
with tarragon dressing $3.95

CRUSTACEAN CAESAR
mussels, scallops, shrimps and crab $6.95

FULL PLATES

GARLIC CRUSTED LOIN OF SPRING LAMB
with madeira sauce $12.95

BEEF TENDERLOIN
with oyster mushrooms $12.95

POACHED SALMON
with red pepper butter $10.95

BURMESE-STYLE PORK CURRY
with fresh ginger, rice and our own mango chutney $9.95

CHICKEN BREAST
with roast garlic and rice stuffing and an apricot-mustard sauce $9.95

FULL PLATES ARE SERVED DAILY FROM 5 P.M. TO 1

Exhibit 1 (cont.)

GOURMET PIZZAS

SMOKED SALMON
Smoked salmon with bocconcini and mozzarella cheese, red onions, capers, dill and red peppers $6.95

CAPACOLA
Capacola, oyster mushrooms, green peppers, black olives, plum tomatoes, and mozzarella $6.25

PESTO
Sundried tomatoes, artichoke hearts, grilled eggplant, roasted red peppers, mozzarella and pesto sauce $5.95

THREE CHEESE
Asiago, mozzarella, parmesan cheeses with slices of elephant garlic and tomato $5.50

WHEN COOKED, GARLIC NOT ONLY LOSES ITS PUNGENT AROMA AND MUCH OF ITS INTENSE FLAVOR, BUT SOME OF ITS MOLECULES ARE ACTUALLY CONVERTED INTO COMPLEX MOLECULES THAT ARE APPROXIMATELY SIXTY-THREE TIMES SWEETER THAN THOSE OF TABLE SUGAR.

SANDWICHES

ALL OF OUR SANDWICHES ARE SERVED WITH GARLIC'S CRISPY POTATOES.

SHAVED ALBERTA BEEF
served on a baguette, au jus. $4.95

GRILLED CHICKEN
chicken breast, roasted garlic, grilled sweet peppers and swiss cheese served open-faced on a kaiser $5.95

MAPLE CURED HAM
shaved ham, grilled peppers and swiss cheese served open-faced on light rye $5.95

SANDWICH OF THE DAY
ask your server for today's special $4.50

SANDWICHES ARE SERVED DAILY UNTIL 3 P.M.

CRUSHED GARLIC HAS ABOUT THREE TIMES THE IMPACT OF CHOPPED OR MINCED.

PASTAS

SMOKED SALMON FETTUCINI
Fettucini with smoked salmon in a lemon, garlic and saffron cream sauce $7.50

CHICKEN LINGUINI
Linguini with chicken, snow peas, and sundried tomatoes in a light cream sauce $6.95

EGGPLANT RAVIOLI
Ravioli stuffed with eggplant served with slivers of crispy onions and drizzled with a lemon-sage sauce $6.25

ROASTED GARLIC PENNE
Penne with roasted garlic, peppers, wild mushrooms and black olives, in a basil pesto sauce $6.25

SEAFOOD FETTUCINI
Fettucini with jumbo shrimp, scallops and mussels in a tomato sauce $7.50

EXHIBIT **1** *(cont.)*

DESERTS

ALL OF OUR DESSERTS ARE AVAILABLE IN FULL OR HALF PORTIONS WITH
THE EXCEPTION OF THE ICE CREAMS AND THE CHEESE PLATE.

FOR CHOCOLATE LOVERS

CHOCOLATE PATE
a slice of Belgian chocolate mousse accompanied by raspberry and passion fruit sauce $3.95

TUXEDO SWIRL
a creamy white and dark chocolate filling in a macaroon pastry crust $3.95

ORANGE CHOCOLATE TORTE
layers of chocolate and white cake with an orange bavarian cream filling $3.95

DEATH BY CHOCOLATE
a three layer chocolate cake with creamy icing—imported from Cakewalkers $4.95

ON THE LIGHTER SIDE

ASSORTED SORBETS AND ICE CREAMS
please ask your server to describe the flavours of the day $1.95

SEASONAL FRANGIPANE
a warm slice of seasonal fruit flan with a crumbly topping $3.50

ASSORTED CHEESES & FRESH FRUIT PLATE $4.50

AND FINALLY ...

PECAN PIE $4.25

CHEESECAKE
New York style with pralines $4.50

GARLIC ICE CREAM
served with chocolate dipped roast garlic—an adventure worth sampling $2.50

BEVERAGES

COFFEE / TEA $1.50	CAPPUCCINO $2.50
MILK $1.50	POP $1.25
JUICE $1.50	ESPRESSO $1.75

Exhibit 2
Timing of Dinner
for Two

Time	Process
0:00	guests arrive
0:01	guests seated with menus
0:04	water served and drink order taken
0:10	drinks delivered
0:11	guests ask questions and order food
0:14	food order processed in computer
0:22	appetizers are delivered
0:37	appetizer dishes are cleared and drink refill offered
0:42	entrées are delivered
0:46	server performs quality check
1:02	entrée plates are cleared
1:05	dessert menus are delivered and coffee is ordered
1:10	coffee is delivered and dessert order is taken
1:11	dessert order processed in computer
1:19	dessert orders are delivered and coffee is replenished
1:35	dessert plates are cleared and final coffee is offered
1:40	bill is delivered
1:45	bill is processed — change is made or credit card is processed
1:50	guests leave

Exhibit 3
Map of
Competitors —
Downtown
London

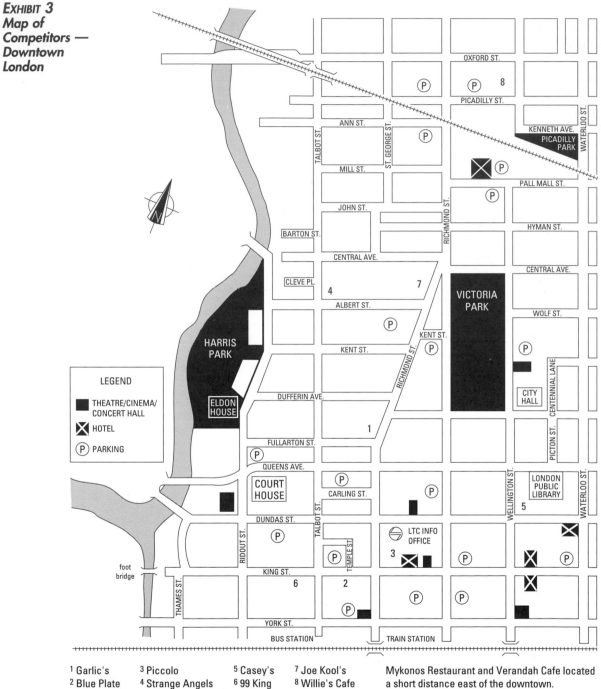

OXFORD ST.

PICADILLY ST.

8

ANN ST.

KENNETH AVE.
PICADILLY PARK

MILL ST.

TALBOT ST.

ST. GEORGE ST.

WATERLOO ST.

PALL MALL ST.

JOHN ST.

RICHMOND ST.

HYMAN ST.

BARTON ST.

CENTRAL AVE.

CENTRAL AVE.

CLEVE PL.

4

7

ALBERT ST.

VICTORIA PARK

WOLF ST.

HARRIS PARK

KENT ST.

KENT ST.

RICHMOND ST.

CITY HALL

CENTENNIAL LANE

LEGEND

■ THEATRE/CINEMA/CONCERT HALL
✕ HOTEL
Ⓟ PARKING

ELDON HOUSE

DUFFERIN AVE.

1

PICTON ST.

FULLARTON ST.

QUEENS AVE.

COURT HOUSE

CARLING ST.

WELLINGTON ST.

LONDON PUBLIC LIBRARY

WATERLOO ST.

5

DUNDAS ST.

RIDOUT ST.

TALBOT ST.

LTC INFO OFFICE

3

TEMPLE ST.

foot bridge

THAMES ST.

KING ST.

6

2

YORK ST.

BUS STATION

TRAIN STATION

1 Garlic's	3 Piccolo	5 Casey's	7 Joe Kool's
2 Blue Plate	4 Strange Angels	6 99 King	8 Willie's Cafe

Mykonos Restaurant and Verandah Cafe located a short distance east of the downtown.

**EXHIBIT 4
Seating Plan**

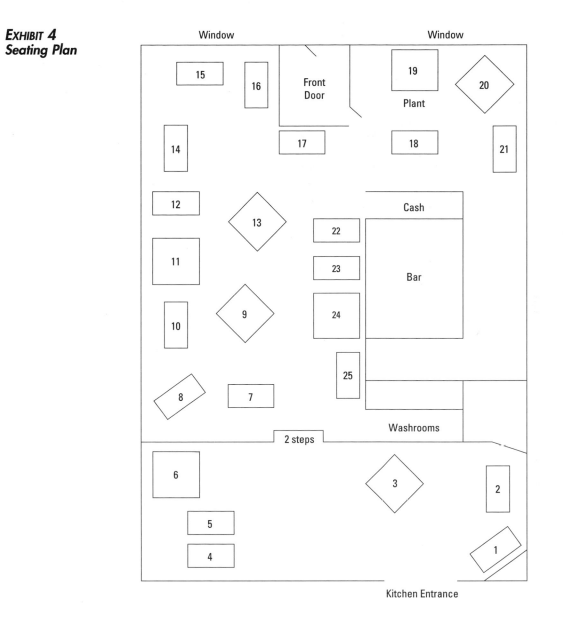

Exhibit **5**

Competition Price Comparison ($)				
Restaurant	**Appetizer**	**Lunch**	**Dinner**	**Dessert**
Blue Plate	2.95 – 5.95	4.95 – 6.95	4.95 – 6.95	3.50 – 4.95
Piccolo	4.25 – 6.75	6.50 – 7.25	6.95 – 7.75	4.50 – 4.75
Mykonos	3.15 – 6.95	2.65 – 7.65	7.95 – 13.95	
Strange Angels	3.50 – 8.25	6.95 – 14.50	6.95 – 14.50	
Casey's	2.49 – 8.99	3.99 – 7.49	7.99 – 14.99	2.99 – 3.99
99 King	3.00 – 7.00	7.00 – 13.00	11.00 – 22.00	4.25 – 4.95
Verandah Cafe				
Joe Kool's	2.50 – 5.95	3.95 – 9.95	3.95 – 9.95	
Willie's Cafe	3.25 – 5.45	3.25 – 5.25	N/A	N/A

1. Fixed price includes appetizer and entrée.

C A S E 6.4   HEMPLINE INC.

By Elizabeth Grasby and Andrew Fletcher

On April 15, 1995, Geof Kime, co-owner of Hempline Inc., had many decisions to make before planting his company's second crop of hemp in as many years. He had only one week to determine the costs of harvested hemp before travelling to Oregon to meet a company about their request for 200 tonnes of hemp for research purposes in the wood panel industry. Many questions had to be answered, including the amount of land to rent, the number of machines to rent, the number of workers to hire, and the financial feasibility of this research request and future requests. Finally, the most time-consuming activity would be obtaining a licence from the federal government to grow this newly requested crop of hemp before the planting season in three weeks.

HEMP

Hemp,[1] of the species *Cannabis sativa L.*, was an annual plant that grew from seed to a height ranging from 2 to 5.5 metres, with a stalk diameter between 0.5 and 5 centimetres, depending on variety and climate. Hemp was grown for its fibrous stalk and seeds and was not to be confused with marijuana. Marijuana, also of the species *Cannabis sativa L.*, referred to the mixture of leaves and flowers that contained, on average, 3 to 5 percent tetrahydrocannabinol (THC), a psychoactive ingredient. Hemp contained a very low level of THC, typically less than 0.3 percent, and thus could not be used as a narcotic. Canada had prohibited production of hemp since 1938 under the Opium and Narcotics Control Act. The United States had also limited production of hemp since 1937. Only during World War II did the Canadian and U.S. governments lift restrictions on hemp production to provide materials for the war effort. Hemp was experiencing a resurgence as a potential crop in Canada because of the world's dwindling resource base. Hemp had two types of fibre: core and primary bast fibre (Exhibit 1). It was the core fibre that was attracting the attention of wood panel manufacturers, as it could potentially offset some use of wood fibre in production. Both fibres could be used in different end consumer products by allowing a process called retting to take place.

IVEY Andrew Fletcher prepared this case under the supervision of Elizabeth Grasby solely to provide material for class discussion. The authors do not intend to illustrate either effective or ineffective handling of a managerial situation. The authors may have disguised certain names and other identifying information to protect confidentiality. Ivey Management Services prohibits any form of reproduction, storage or transmittal without its written permission. This material is not covered under authorization from CanCopy or any reproduction rights organization. Copyright © 1996, Ivey Management Services

For retting to occur, the harvested hemp was subjected to moisture to allow the primary bast fibres to separate from the core fibres.

Hemp products could potentially offset the use of wood in paper and building materials, of chemically intensive cotton in textiles, and of petrochemicals for a wide variety of products. Hemp oil could be used in cooking, burning, cosmetics, paints, varnishes, and precision lubricants. Environmentally, hemp was favoured over many existing products. For instance, the bast fibre had a lower lignin content than wood fibre, which provided better opportunities for nonchlorine bleaching, and hemp could produce more fibre per hectare for paper production than most species of trees based on a 20-year growth period. Hemp also required limited pesticides because it grew quickly and had few pests. In fact, in Europe and China, where the majority of the world's 122,400 tonnes of hemp was grown, little or no pesticides were used.

A Highly Regulated Industry

In Canada, a licence from the federal government had to be obtained to cultivate hemp and the harvested product could be used only for research purposes. On February 2, 1994, Bill C-7, the Controlled Drugs and Substances Act, was introduced by the ministers of health and justice to bring Canadian law in line with international accords. The bill, if passed, would replace the Canadian Narcotics Control Act (passed in 1961) and Parts III and IV of the Food and Drugs Act to allow regulations for the commercial production of hemp. However, Hempline did not expect the Bill to pass for the 1995 growing season because other issues, not directly related to hemp, would slow the bill's progression. As a result, Hempline did not expect commercial licences to be granted until at least 1996. Geof estimated that future regulations would include growing area, security of the land, control of seed distribution, and the securing of a mandatory buyer to process the harvested product.

Growing Hemp and Current Opportunities

In climates such as southwestern Ontario's, hemp would be planted in the second week of May with growing time for fibre at 70 to 100 days or for seed at 90 to 150 days. When planted for fibre, yields ranged from 6.3 to 13.5 tonnes of dry stalk per hectare and for seed yields ranged from 780 to 1120 kilograms per hectare. Geof believed that 7.4 to 9.9 tonnes of fibre hemp per hectare would be attainable in southwestern Ontario. Wood-processing mills were interested in material supplements for wood and wastewood (i.e., sawdust) due to forecasted shortages. These mills produced composite wood panel products as medium-density fibre board (MDF), oriented strand board (OSB), hard board, and other composite materials such as fibre blocks. These products were used in building cabinets, desks, furniture, and house walls. Geof commented on the mills' interest in hemp:

> Supply of the current raw material used in these products, wood and wastewood, is diminishing in North America because reforestation of areas already logged has not happened quickly enough and trees are not yet large

enough to cut. Some mills are not close to suitable raw materials, making it difficult to produce wood panel products at a competitive price to other materials. As a result, these fibre-processing mills are trying to establish alternative sources of material. One company has actually evaluated a proposal to build a plant in Manitoba to produce particle board from flax and straw. These two materials are waste materials from producing linseed oil and grain and are usually burned in the field. These particle board producing mills need 200 to 300 tonnes of material each day with some very large mills using 1,000 tonnes per day. Hemp would be an ideal product for these mills because preliminary tests show hemp fibre to be just as strong as wood fibre.

HEMPLINE INC.

Hempline Inc. was formed in 1994 to reestablish hemp as a renewable resource in Canada. The co-owners were Joe Strobel, a long-time farmer and retired high school teacher, and Geof, a professional engineer. They wanted the company to be profitable using hemp as a commercial crop by 1997. Geof and Joe saw many opportunities in manufacturing processes, but currently the North American hemp industry was too young to firmly establish its direction. In 1994, Hempline had received a special licence from the Canadian Government to plant, grow, and harvest 4 hectares, under strict supervision, for research purposes only. This made Hempline the first company to grow hemp legally in North America since the 1950s. The company planted five different types of seeds to establish the best types of hemp to grow in southwestern Ontario. Hempline's research using the harvested hemp entailed cost and quality of a harvested crop to evaluate the market acceptance and competitiveness of a variety of hemp-based products (fibreboard, paper, fuel, textiles, and cordage). To continue the seed-type research, Hempline was planning to increase the types of seed from five to 10.

Hempline had incurred substantial losses in 1994. For the 1995 year, the Canadian and Ontario departments of agriculture had given Hempline a research and development grant through the tobacco diversification program. However, the grant was structured in such a way that Hempline would receive 75 percent of approved costs and 33 percent of approved equipment purchases or development. As well, the government would not reimburse any costs until incurred. Since the government took two months to reimburse Hempline, Geof wanted to include any interest expense on any working capital loan. He needed to evaluate how much investment he would need for the planting of crops since the remaining money would be used to research end-consumer products.

CURRENT SITUATION

For the 1995 year, Hempline had applied for a licence to grow 8 hectares of hemp for research purposes. However, an Oregon research and development company that consulted to wood mills had recently contacted Hempline to request 200 tonnes of hemp (whole stalk) for research purposes to potentially reduce some usage of wood in building products. Hempline had to quickly prepare a proposal to allow the Canadian government time to review the application to grow additional hemp. There was time pressure because Hempline needed to receive permission before the planting season. Over the past two years, Hempline had many meetings and presentations with government agencies and police to agree on the terms to allow research crops to be grown. Not only did Geof have to prepare quickly for the upcoming meeting in Oregon, but he also wanted to prove to Canadian authorities that hemp could be economically viable. Hempline estimated the industry would not consider paying more than $50 to $150 per tonne for baled hemp if hemp was to become a commercial crop used in wood panel products.

Interest in Oregon

Geof knew he could rent land in the Tillsonburg, Ontario, area for $125 per hectare but wondered how many hectares he should request on the application. Tillsonburg was located 300 kilometres east from the Windsor, Ontario–Detroit, Michigan, border. Located south of Highway 401, a major road artery through southwestern Ontario, Tillsonburg had land suitable for tobacco, corn, and other grain crops.

Geof also wanted to establish his production costs before meeting the Oregon firm next week. Under potential future commercial licences, Geof expected to receive $120 per tonne (delivered) for harvested baled hemp with a 25 percent premium for uniform chips. The Oregon firm, like all mills, wanted the product to be delivered in uniform chips, preferably in 2.5, 5, and 7.5 centimetre sizes. The Oregon firm would reluctantly accept baled hemp, but extra work to prepare the hemp in chip form would be needed. Geof felt he could develop a mobile chipping machine at a cost of $50,000. This machine would actually chip hemp in the field. Alternatively, a stationary chipper could be developed for $75,000 to $100,000. He wanted to evaluate seriously these potential investments, given the financial situation of his company. Hempline was confident that the Oregon firm would finance half of the machinery cost. Geof and Joe were quite excited about the request because the wood products industry had long been one of Canada's leading industrial sectors. The research on these 200 tonnes could provide credibility to hemp as a viable crop and lead to future acceptance.

PRODUCTION PROCESS

There were six steps to produce ready-to-manufacture hemp: planting, growing, harvesting (two stages), storing, and transporting. Geof would hire labour at $9.00 per hour for any of the six steps.

Planting

This step started in the fall by plowing the land. Assuming proper weather conditions, the seeds were planted and fertilizer applied in the second week of May. Geof estimated his costs (equipment rental, fuel, oil, seed, and fertilizer) for this process would be $595.52 per hectare. He would need 3.75 labour hours per hectare for this process. He estimated one-quarter of this time would be spent in the fall to plow the land and the remainder in May to cultivate, plant, and fertilize. The second week of May was quite hectic because this process needed to be finished quickly to take advantage of good weather conditions. Geof estimated he might need two to three successive days (assuming 16 hours per day were available) without rain to plant seed. Geof needed to estimate how many workers he would need to hire and how many machines to rent (one worker per machine).

Growing

Hemp is a very hearty plant and requires little or no maintenance while growing. Hempline would make various security inspections throughout the growing period for a total yearly cost of $23.50 per hectare.

Harvesting Stage 1 — Cutting and Drying

After growing for 70 to 100 days, the plant was cut down using either a side bar mower or a mower/conditioner. Then, the stalks were raked into rows and turned periodically to assist in drying. Geof needed to hire enough workers and rent enough equipment, at $25.00/hour, to perform the 2.5 hours of labour per hectare over two to three days of good weather. Fuel costs were estimated at $17.78 per hectare for this step. Alternatives to renting equipment included purchasing a new side bar mower for $3,000 or a used mower for $500 to $2,000.

Harvesting Stage 2 — Gathering and Packaging

At this point, the stalks had to be removed from the field. The harvesting would take place only between the hours of noon and 8 p.m. when the stalks were dry. Geof knew that he would have only two to three successive days of good weather, during a three- to four-week period, to coordinate people during this common harvesting time. Harvesting conflicts would need to be addressed well in advance, and Geof wondered how many machines and people he would need to schedule to finish this step. Hempline was faced with four alternative forms in which to deliver the required 200 tonnes: large square bales, large round bales, small square bales, and uniform chips. Unlike the other two alternatives, Hempline needed to schedule two workers (not one) if it pursued either small bales or chips. A custom chipper would have to be developed for the chip-harvesting option. A stationary model could be developed at a cost of $75,000 to $100,000, while a mobile model that could chip in the field would cost $50,000 to $75,000. Exhibit 2 outlines all costs and details if he rented or purchased equipment to harvest the crop.

Storage

The bales or chips would then be stored until further processing and transportation were required. Bales had to be stored under shelter to eliminate any formation of mould, and chips were stored in silos or covered piles. Geof knew he would not need to store any of the 200-tonne request as it would be shipped immediately after harvesting, but in the future this cost must be considered. If hemp were to be economically viable and competitive with other products, mills would have to receive regular shipments throughout the year. Exhibit 2 outlines the costs of storing the various forms of harvested hemp over a typical storage period.

Transportation

Geof estimated the following transportation costs for the four different forms of harvested hemp (all costs in dollars per tonne kilometre): large square bales $0.07, large round bales $0.11, small square bales $0.12, and $0.17 for chips. The cost per tonne kilometre was different for each harvested form due to different sizes and compaction densities. The Oregon research firm was located 3,940 kilometres from Tillsonburg.

Other Concerns

Since hemp was highly regulated, Geof had plenty of organizations with questions to answer. He commented on his management of the situation:

> I am in contact with up to 10 government agencies, five potential suppliers of seed, five to six consultants, lawyers, and accountants, the bank, and finally the media! As well, I am trying to plan research and development activities for new potential uses of hemp. Joe and I are seriously considering hiring a full-time person for $22,000. I am currently stretching my ability to maintain enough time in the day to manage this new venture with my full-time position.

CONCLUSION

Hempline had expended a tremendous amount of effort just to convince government agencies that they should be allowed to grow hemp. Since the industry was speculative due to the government's hesitancy to allow commercial hemp crops, combined with little infrastructure in the industry to produce hemp-based products, Geof wanted to analyze the various alternatives carefully to best decide on the harvesting approach for this year and to develop a strategy for following years. As well, he wondered how his analysis would help Hempline's proposals to various industries, farmers, and governments on the viability of hemp production in Canada.

NOTE

1. The source for most of the background information on hemp that is found in this case is Agriculture and Agri-Food Canada's Bi-Weekly Bulletin, Vol. 7, No. 23 (16 December 1994).

Exhibit **1**

Cross-Section of the Hemp

The hemp stalk is harvested for the fibre and hurds. Its centre is hollow except at the nodes where the leaves are attached. The hollow space occupies at least one-half the diameter in the best fibre-producing types of hemp. The main parts of the stalk are:

Core fibres (hurds): The woody core that is freed through a process known as retting, which breaks down the pectin.

Pectin: The natural glue that holds the primary bast fibres to the core fibres; the binding agent broken down in the retting process.

Primary bast fibres: Long fibres low in lignin, the most valuable part of the stalk.

In Ontario in August 1994, just 70 days after planting, Joe Strobel of Hempline, Inc., admires a 3-metre hemp plant, grown for the first time in over 40 years under a research licence issued by the federal government (photo © 1994 by Geof G. Kime).

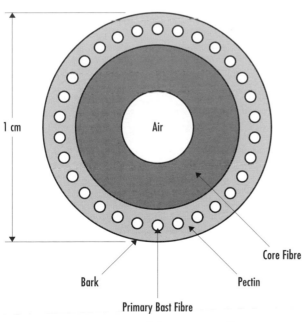

Cross-section of the Hemp Stalk

Source: Hempline Inc.

Exhibit 2

BALING/CHIPPING COSTS AND DETAILS				
	Large Square Bales	**Round Bales**	**Small Square Bales**	**Chips**
Equipment (including all labour) rental ($/hour)	$80	$50	$35	n/a
Machine capacity (tonne/hour)	10	7.5	5	n/a
Harvesting cost ($/tonne)	$ 8.00	$ 6.67	$ 7.00	$6.25
Purchase new machine	$90,000–120,000	$34,000	$14,000	Develop one of two machines
Purchase used machine	n/a	$7,000–16,000	$2,500–7,500	n/a
Storage ($/tonne) (average for six months of storage)	$5.00	$6.00	$8.00	$12.00
Equipment readily available to rent?	No	Yes	Yes	Develop one of two machines

C A S E 6.5   INTRODUCING NEW TECHNOLOGY AT GENERAL MOTORS

By John F. Graham and John W. Cummings

In May 1990, John Hare first recognized the opportunity to increase employee efficiency in the hood install operation at General Motors Truck Assembly Plant in Oshawa, Ontario. He believed that an overhead hoist could be used to lift the hood from the monorail carrier over to the trucks passing along the main production line. As process engineer for the truck plant, Mr. Hare was responsible for improving efficiency throughout the production process. An immediate savings in his mind was the elimination of at least one of the four employees involved in the hood install operation.

THE OSHAWA TRUCK PLANT

The Oshawa Truck Assembly Plant was the exclusive producer of full-size extended cab pickup trucks for General Motors Corporation (GM) and the American market. The plant was part of GM of Canada's Autoplex Complex, along with two car assembly facilities, and three parts fabrication operations. Combined, these plants employed over 15,000 people, both salaried and hourly rated.

The Truck Assembly Centre encompassed over 2.7 million square feet of floor space and had capacity to produce 215,000 units per year. The plant's 3,000 employees operated on two eight-hour shifts, five days a week, with the capacity of producing 441 units per shift. The facility had been utilized for the production of Chevrolet and GMC trucks since its construction in 1965, but many changes in layout and products had occurred since that time (including the production of buses and heavy duty trucks). In the most recent changeover (1986), state-of-the-art body and paint shops were constructed in an approximately $600 million project, adding one million square feet of floor space. Shop floor automation was enhanced in both of these areas through the introduction of robotics. Also, automatic guided vehicles and an electrified monorail system were implemented, making the truck plant one of the most highly automated vehicle assembly plants in the world.

THE AUTOMOBILE INDUSTRY

Despite a significant slowdown in the sale of cars, truck sales managed to maintain a fairly constant growth at approximately 5 percent annually during the

1980s. In December 1990, GM chose to shut down production at both Oshawa car assembly plants for four weeks because of excessive build-up of inventories. The truck plant remained producing at two full shifts. However, as a result of recent economic conditions, the plant eliminated the production of regular cab trucks, which were produced by two "sister" plants in the United States. As well, the line speed was reduced, bringing the production rate down from 61 to 53 trucks per hour. These combined moves resulted in the reduction of approximately 400 hourly rated employees.

The nature of competition in the automobile industry changed dramatically during the 1980s. The increased competition from foreign manufacturers such as Honda and Nissan created the problem of overcapacity, and the North American producers found themselves fighting to maintain market share. Consequently, sales incentives and competitive pricing were being used to attract customers, resulting in a profit squeeze for the automakers.

One further reaction of some North American producers was to build high-technology production facilities in newly industrialized countries (e.g., Mexico), in an effort to remain internationally competitive. The biggest savings occurred in terms of labour costs. Workers in Mexico received less than $1.50 per hour, compared to the $25 per hour received by North American autoworkers.

The presence of foreign competition was by no means of only short-term concern. The Japanese automakers, who had earned a reputation for building high quality automobiles, were continually establishing themselves in the North American market. By 1990, there were more Japanese models being made in the United States than were imported. It was expected that by 1991, Japanese-owned or -operated assembly plants in the United States could be producing two million cars and trucks a year.

The challenge was clear. If North American automakers wanted to achieve long-term survival, they were not only going to have to be competitive in price, but also meet the consumers' increasing demand for quality.

THE SITUATION   Mr. Hare first became aware of an opportunity to improve efficiency when he noticed the large amount of walking being done by the two hood carriers. After observing the operation for some time, he believed that an overhead hoist, similar to that being used by GM's sister plant in Pontiac, could be implemented to improve employee efficiency.

The entire hood installation procedure currently involved a total of four workers. For a detailed description of their individual tasks and time budgets, see Exhibit 1. The existing procedure required the two hood carriers to lift the hood from the carrier and carry it over to the truck passing down the main assembly line. The distance carried was approximately eight metres. In addition to this, each had other tasks to perform before returning to retrieve the next hood.

Mr. Hare believed that by introducing an overhead hoist, the hood could be secured and guided to the truck by only one worker. The hoist would use a suction cup device to secure the hood and would run on pullies to carry it over to the trucks. The single worker would have a small hand control to operate the hoist. Once the hood was above the truck, the two hood secure workers would assist in placing it in the proper position. After the hood was secured, the hoist could be released and taken back to retrieve the next hood. Mr. Hare estimated that it would now take 0.95 minutes for the single operator to perform this task.

Mr. Hare had done some rough drafting and believed the entire system could be installed at a cost of $85,000. The savings would be a reduction of one production worker. He knew, however, that before this worker could be released, each of the tasks that had to be performed would have to be covered by one of the three remaining workers. The plant paid workers about $55,000 per year. Remembering the goal of the new plant manager of increasing the employee work hours to an average of 55 minutes per hour, Mr. Hare wondered what impact any of these changes would have on this goal. Finally, because implementation of this project would result in the elimination of at least one job per shift, he wondered what reaction he would receive from the union.

Exhibit 1

Current Job Descriptions and Times (in minutes)[1] per vehicle		
Job	**Task Description**	**Time**
Hood carry (left)	■ obtain hood from carrier — carry hood to truck	0.42
	■ place rubber bumper inside left fender	0.14
	■ place plastic clip on front rad support	0.06
	■ secure harness in clip on inside left fender	0.08
	■ visual inspection of engine wire — front	0.10
	Total Time	0.80
Hood carry (right)	■ obtain hood from carrier, carry hood to truck	0.42
	■ press release pedal on floor to advance carriers[2]	0
	■ place rubber bumper inside right fender	0.14
	Total Time	0.56
Hood secure (left)	■ get tool, check hood hinge for proper width — bend if necessary	0.16
	■ get two bolts and nuts from bench, return to job	0.075
	■ secure hood to harness	0.25
	■ secure hood to hinge	0.28
	■ visual inspection	0.10
	Total Time	0.865
Hood secure (right)	■ get tool; check hood hinge for proper width — bend if necessary	0.16
	■ get two bolts and nuts from bench, return to job	0.075
	■ secure hood to harness	0.25
	■ secure hood to hinge	0.28
	■ visual inspection	0.10
	Total Time	0.865

1. Times were estimated by the case writer.
2. This operation can be done simultaneously with the above operation; therefore, additional time is not necessary.

C A S E 6.6 THE MONGOLIAN GRILL

By Tim Silk and John Haywood-Farmer

On May 20, 1997, John Butkus, owner of the Mongolian Grill restaurant in London, Ontario, was considering a major design decision for his second restaurant in Waterloo, Ontario. Although the first Mongolian Grill had been successful, Mr. Butkus was considering changing the preliminary design of the Waterloo location to increase its capacity and serve customers more quickly. Because he planned to open the Waterloo location on July 1, he had to finalize his operations decisions without delay.

TRENDS IN THE RESTAURANT BUSINESS

The restaurant business was extremely competitive. Customers were beginning to look for dining experiences that were entertaining and unique, rather than restaurants that simply provided good food. Restaurants with traditional themes struggled to keep up with the increasing demands of customers. Many restaurateurs began searching for unique concepts to satisfy those in search of something original. Trends seemed to indicate that customers wanted quality ingredients, healthier food offerings, and a variety of choices. They wanted value and were unwilling to pay inflated prices. A comfortable atmosphere and an accessible location were also important to customers.

THE MONGOLIAN GRILL CONCEPT

The Mongolian Grill was based on four features: an entertaining and interactive atmosphere, fresh and healthy food ingredients, unlimited food quantities, and customer involvement in meal preparation. Customers at the Mongolian Grill were involved directly in preparing their meals at three stations in the food preparation area: the food bar, the sauce, oil, and spice bar, and the cooking station. Exhibit 1 shows the floor plan of the London Mongolian Grill.

Immediately after entering the restaurant, customers were seated. A member of the serving staff explained the concept to first-time customers and took drink orders. Customers then made their way to the food preparation area. Customers selected meat and vegetables from the food bar and placed them in a small bowl. They then moved to the sauce, oil, and spice bar, where they added sauces, oil,

---

and spices to their bowl of food. Lastly, they moved to an available space along the counter of the cooking station, where they handed their bowls to a cook working around the large, circular (two-metre diameter) iron grill equipped with a vent hood. Once the cook had finished cooking the order, he or she placed the food in a clean bowl and handed it to the customer. Customers then returned to their seats. In the meantime, servers had brought the ordered drinks as well as warm tortilla bread and rice to complement the meal.

Customers paid a single price for the food, and drinks were extra; they could return to the food preparation area as many times as they wished. Dinner was priced at $11.95 per person; the average bill per person, including drinks, was approximately $15.00 before tax. The restaurant's profit margin was approximately 50 percent. The cooking station was the social centre of the restaurant where customers could share their recipes and food combinations while being entertained by the cooks who wielded long, wooden Mongolian cooking sticks to move the food around on the grill.

OPERATIONS AT THE LONDON MONGOLIAN GRILL

The London restaurant, with a seating capacity of approximately 130, was in Richmond Row, a popular downtown shopping and restaurant district in a city of some 350,000 people. Although many of the tables were for two people, it was easy to move tables together, if necessary, to form larger tables. The Mongolian Grill did not take reservations and was usually at full capacity on Thursday, Friday, and Saturday nights, especially during the busiest dinner hours of 6:00 to 10:00 p.m. The restaurant was open from 11:00 a.m. to 11:00 p.m. seven days per week. Although Mr. Butkus was pleased with the restaurant's popularity, he was concerned with how long customers had to wait in line at the food preparation area when the restaurant was full. He decided to observe the food preparation area and record how long it took customers to go through the three stations and return to their tables. Mr. Butkus recorded two sets of observations: on a Wednesday night when the restaurant was about half full and customers did not have to wait in line, and again on a Saturday night when the restaurant was full and customers had to wait in line. He timed three randomly chosen customers each night and then averaged the results. The variation between customers on each night was small. Exhibit 2 shows the averages for both sets of observations.

Mr. Butkus also observed that the average customer made three trips to the food preparation area during dinner and that on busy nights, the average group of four to six people spent 90 minutes at the restaurant from being seated to departure. The restaurant turned away many potential customers on busy nights. Mr. Butkus believed that, by either adding seating capacity or finding a way to serve customers more quickly, he could seat more customers over the duration of the evening, thus increasing sales.

One possible way to reduce the time for an average group to eat dinner was to expand the food preparation area so that customers would spend less time in line. Mr. Butkus calculated that if he could reduce each group's dinner time by 15 minutes, each table could seat four groups of customers rather than three during the busy 6:00 to 10:00 p.m. dinner period. Although a lack of available space made changes to the London operations impractical, the operations at the new Waterloo location had yet to be finalized. Mr. Butkus saw this as an opportunity to avoid the same problem in Waterloo.

OPERATIONS AT THE WATERLOO LOCATION

The Waterloo restaurant would seat 190. Waterloo was at the northern edge of a growing metropolitan area comprising the adjacent cities of Waterloo, Kitchener, and Cambridge and surrounding areas. The population within 40 kilometres was about 560,000. Mr. Butkus estimated that the Waterloo Mongolian Grill would likely turn away 20 to 30 people on Thursday nights and 30 to 40 people on Friday and Saturday nights if he could not reduce dinner times. Seating additional customers would lead to additional sales revenues and higher profits. Exhibit 3 shows Mr. Butkus' initial floor plan. However, he was considering two major changes to it: adding a second food preparation area and moving the location of the cooking grill. Exhibit 4 shows the floor plan of the Waterloo restaurant with the proposed design changes.

Adding a Second Food Preparation Area

Customer waiting time might be reduced by having two food preparation areas located close to the grill so that customers would not have to wait in line for a single food preparation area. Adding a second food preparation area would require the installation of a second food bar and a second sauce, oil, and spice bar. The food bar would cost $3,200, including installation. The sauce, oil, and spice bar was somewhat smaller and would cost $2,100 including installation. This option would require one additional kitchen employee to work an eight-hour shift on Thursday, Friday, and Saturday nights to keep the additional food preparation area stocked and clean. Kitchen staff cost $8.00 per hour (including benefits); they sometimes received a portion of the tips.

Mr. Butkus estimated that adding a second food preparation area would save approximately 90 seconds per trip for customers waiting in line at the food bar and 80 seconds per trip for customers waiting in line at the sauce, oil, and spice bar. He also estimated that because there would be fewer people at each station, customers would save approximately 60 seconds per trip selecting items from the food bar and 30 seconds per trip selecting items from the sauce, oil, and spice bar.

Although Mr. Butkus was confident that two food preparation areas would reduce waiting and item selection times, he was concerned that customers might be confused by the layout and not know where to go. He commented:

> I've noticed in other restaurants that when you have a choice between two food bars, the natural thing for people to do is to stand there trying to decide which one to go to. I'm worried that people entering the food preparation area will create a bottleneck because they are standing still and trying to decide where to go. We might reduce the time customers wait in line, but if they take longer to get to the food bar, it defeats the purpose.

Mr. Butkus was unsure whether this would be a major problem and wondered what he could do to prevent it from happening.

Moving the Cooking Grill

Mr. Butkus was also considering moving the cooking grill from the corner to a more central area inside the restaurant, which would increase the counter space around the grill. Mr. Butkus estimated that this move would save customers 80 seconds per trip waiting for an open space along the counter of the cooking station. Because this would increase the capacity of the cooking area, an additional cook would be needed during busy periods. Although the grill itself would not be a capacity constraint, because of the heat, working around the grill was very tiring. To alleviate this problem, two cooks would work in 30-minute intervals to cover a single five-hour cooking shift. Both cooks would be paid $12.00 per hour (including benefits) plus tips for the five-hour shift. The cost of the additional counter space would be $600.

THE DECISION

Mr. Butkus looked over the blueprints of the Waterloo restaurant and considered his options. He was unsure whether one, both, or neither of the options would be feasible. His objective was to decide on a design that would optimize the restaurant's profitability without compromising the dining experience of his customers.

EXHIBIT 1
Floor Plan of
the London
Mongolian Grill

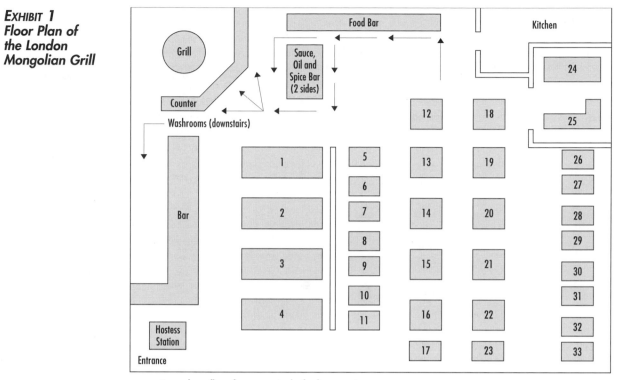

→ Arrow shows flow of customers in the food preparation area.
Diagram approximately to scale.

Exhibit 2

		Wednesday Night (half full)	Saturday Night (full)
Customer Throughput Times in the London Mongolian Grill Food Preparation Area[1]			
Area	Description	Time (sec)	Time (sec)
Tables	Customer walks from table to food bar	12	25
Food bar	Customer waits in line at food bar	0	106
Food bar	Customer takes bowl, adds selected items from food bar to bowl	88	161
Between stations	Customer walks from food bar to sauce, oil, and spice bar	3	12
Sauce, oil, and spice bar	Customer waits in line at sauce, oil, and spice bar	0	94
Sauce, oil, and spice bar	Customer adds selected sauces, oils, and spices to bowl	62	99
Between stations	Customer walks from sauce, oil, and spice bar to cooking station	3	10
Cooking station	Customer waits for open space at cooking station counter	0	80
Cooking station	Customer gives bowl to cook, watches as food cooks on grill	245	246
Table area	Customer receives bowl of cooked food and returns to table	15	33
Total time for a single trip		428 (7:08 min)	866 (14:26 min)
Total time for three trips[2]		1,284 (21:24 min)	2,598 (43:18 min)

1. All times are given in seconds unless otherwise stated.
2. Customers averaged three trips per meal.

Source: Company files.

Exhibit 3
Initial Floor Plan
of the Waterloo
Mongolian Grill

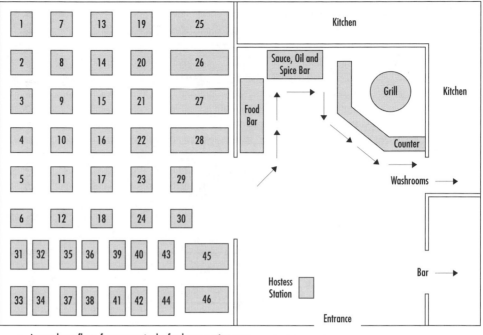

⟶ Arrow shows flow of customers in the food preparation area.
Diagram approximately to scale.

Exhibit 4
Floor Plan of
the Waterloo
Mongolian Grill
with Proposed
Changes

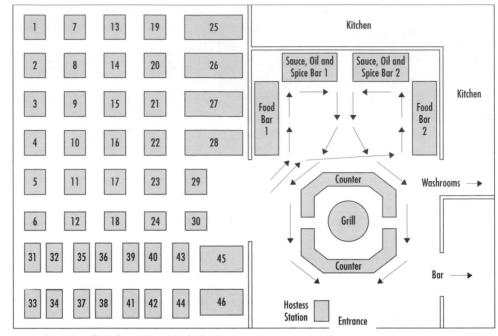

→ Arrow shows flow of customers in the food preparation area.
Diagram approximately to scale.

C A S E 6.7   OFF BROADWAY PHOTOGRAPHY

By Elizabeth Grasby and Jannalee Blok

Jim Hockings and Judy Cairns, photographers and co-owners of Off Broadway Photography (Broadway) in London, Ontario, were reviewing the company's year-end financial statements on January 5, 1998. Broadway's sales had grown from $64,000 in 1986 to $174,200 in 1997, with net profit levels of 30 percent and 22 percent, respectively. Hockings and Cairns wanted to improve both the sales and profitability levels in 1998 and were considering three options: purchasing bulk film, outsourcing black-and-white film development, and changing the proof format.

COMPANY BACKGROUND

task

Broadway was located amid trendy retail shops and restaurants on Richmond Row, an upscale shopping district near downtown London. Broadway set itself apart from the almost 70 photography portrait studios in and around London through its processing quality and service. Hockings and Cairns were responsible for the complete order, from start to finish. They made sure film, photographic paper, processing chemicals, and other materials were always in stock, of high quality, and within the freshness date. The retail store front, as well as the store windows facing Richmond Street, displayed some of Hockings' and Cairns' best portrait work. Each portrait was unique; the owners believed that it reflected the time and talent put into each customer order. The studio consisted of a retail store front, a studio, a lab, a framing room, and an office. Cairns and Hockings believed that it was well laid out and presented a professional yet relaxing atmosphere to the local clientele. Cairns remarked that Broadway specialized in anticipating and capturing "special moments." Currently, Hockings and Cairns were the only full-time staff at Broadway. They each worked an average of 55 hours per week over a six-day work week. As owners of a small business, Hockings and Cairns were responsible for every area of their business, including sales, consultations, photo shoots, developing, processing orders, and printing. A high school student helped out on Tuesday and Thursday afternoons.

IVEY Jannalee Blok prepared this case under the supervision of Elizabeth Grasby solely to provide material for class discussion. The authors do not intend to illustrate either effective or ineffective handling of a managerial situation. The authors may have disguised certain names and other identifying information to protect confidentiality. Ivey Management Services prohibits any form of reproduction, storage or transmittal without its written permission. This material is not covered under authorization from CanCopy or any reproduction rights organization. Copyright © 1998, Ivey Management Services.

Broadway's Customer Base

Job Shop

Thirty percent of Broadway's sales were commercial orders; additionally, these orders accounted for 75 percent of total sales for January, February, and March. These orders would typically be phoned in. These customers expected a competitive price, reasonable quality, and speedy delivery because they were usually working to a deadline. Hockings believed these clients were initially attracted to Broadway by its quality; however, he knew the purchase decision was primarily based on the price and quoted delivery time. Hockings had more commercial business than he could handle, and since he had estimated how much his time was worth, he had actually considered raising his prices.

Projects

Another 30 percent of Broadway's sales were from wedding orders. The work done by Hockings and Cairns was in such demand that wedding orders had to be booked 15 months in advance. Wedding clientele were typically much more demanding and had very high expectations of the amount of time to be spent consulting (both before and after the "sale"), the details, and the number, style, and distinctiveness of the actual wedding pictures. The average price of a Broadway wedding package totalled $2,200. Wedding sales were typically paid for in three installments: 25 percent when the order was placed, 50 percent when the wedding proofs were shown to the couple, and the remaining 25 percent when the final order of prints was placed.

task ⟹

The balance of Broadway's sales was made up of portrait orders, photo finishing, slide processing, and frame retailing. These customers expected good quality and service and reasonably fast delivery — Cairns expressed it as "doing it right the first time." Over the years, Hockings and Cairns had seen an increase in customer expectations regarding the speed of processing their order. Hockings stated that "customers are getting used to one hour for everything." As a result, Broadway had implemented rush charges for customers who insisted on having their order processed right away. This, of course, resulted in the bumping of other orders further down the priority list.

Broadway's slowest sales months were January, February, and March, and its busiest sales months were November and December. The slower season gave Hockings a chance to try out new products and processes in the market as well as time to develop some of his own new products and marketing strategies. However, in the busier fall months, Hockings and Cairns could barely keep up with the demand. Hockings commented that there was no need to advertise beyond the single ad in the Yellow Pages and the store window displays; they already had more work than they could handle and sometimes had to turn orders away.

OPERATIONS — FROM START TO FINISH

Order Taking

The "preservice" aspect of the photography business was very important to the success of the company. Some people phoned to inquire about the studio's services but most people would just drop in at the Richmond store location. Sales consultations lasted from 10 minutes for most commercial orders, to up to three hours for wedding orders. Once the order was placed, the date and place for the photo shoot would be set.

The Photo Shoot

Photo shoots were usually done at the Richmond Street studio but had also been held at customers' homes, churches, businesses, and parks. Before the photo shoot, the setting was prepared. It took approximately 15 to 30 minutes to gather and set up the right equipment, background, and materials before the photo shoot could begin. The actual photo shoot itself took from 45 to 120 minutes, not including travel time.

Developing the Negatives

The next step required developing the negatives. Hockings developed and proofed the black-and-white film, which represented 50 percent of Broadway's film. He separated the black-and-white films by type and then by size so that a batch of all the same type and size would be developed at one time. The other 50 percent of Broadway's film was colour. Broadway outsourced all of this for processing. Fifty percent of all colour films were from wedding orders, and Cairns sent most of these to Toronto for processing, with a return in 10 to 13 days. Of the remaining 50 percent of colour film, 75 percent was sent to a local London developer and was returned in "proof" format.[1] If the film was a normal size, the proofs would be returned to Broadway within a day; however, if the film was a larger size,[2] the order would usually take three or four days to be processed because the developer waited for several other large film orders before developing the orders. The remaining 25 percent of Broadway's colour film was returned in the negative format, which Hockings proofed (printed the proofs from the negatives) himself. Proofing usually took eight minutes per roll. Weddings used approximately 16 rolls, family portraits used three to six rolls, and commercial shots or single-person portraits used one to two rolls.

Proof Consultation with the Customer

Once the proofs were ready, Cairns collated, spotted, stamped the company logo onto them, and edited the entire order. These final steps usually took 20 to 40 minutes for commercial and portrait jobs and up to four hours for wedding jobs. An appointment was then made for viewing the proofs. Hockings believed in the "show big; sell big" marketing strategy and, therefore, chose one of the best proofs, enlarged it (usually 50 by 60 cm), and had it displayed when the customer came in for the viewing appointment. Customers were encouraged to borrow the large print, put it up in their home with stick-tack, and see how it looked. This marketing strategy often persuaded customers to purchase a larger than planned print. Customers usually took 30 to 60 minutes to look at the proofs and were given a discount if they placed an order that day.

Printing the Order

After the order was placed, Cairns took 10 minutes to put the order together (pull the negatives, write out the order, ensure that the correct photo paper was in stock, etc.). She then prioritized the orders, first according to deadlines, and then according to the chronological order in which they were shot. Hockings was responsible for printing the pictures, which required him to spend three of his six working days in his lab. Hockings was able to print the pictures in three days for commercial orders, nine days for portraits and other retail jobs, and two to four weeks for wedding orders. Again, as in the developing stage, Hockings batched and sub-batched the types of proofs before he started printing based on whether or not they were colour or black and white. When printing colour orders, the negatives were placed into an enlarger that projected the negative's picture onto colour photographic paper. The paper was then placed into a processor, treated with a variety of chemicals[3] for specific amounts of time, rinsed off, and dried. The final picture was then ready to be sorted and boxed. Black-and-white orders were produced using a tray process. First, the negatives were enlarged on a black-and-white enlarger and projected onto black-and-white photographic paper. The prints were then manually (using tongs or fingers) dipped into a series of three trays, each with a different chemical mix and each for a different length of time. The prints were then run through a water rinse container and finally placed into a dryer.

Final Check and Order Completion

The prints were then counted, stamped with the company's logo, spotted[4] for slight blemishes, and cut to the right sizes. The customer was then invoiced, the final order of pictures was bagged, and a call was made to the client that the order had been completed. This last step took an average of five minutes for commercial orders, two to three hours for portrait orders, and four to five hours for wedding orders. Customers with portrait or wedding orders usually came into the studio to pick up their order.

OPTIONS UNDER CONSIDERATION

Broadway had grown from 1986 sales of $64,000 to 1996 sales of $182,000, with a slight decrease in 1997 to sales of $174,200. Despite the $8,000 decline in sales, Broadway's net profit increased from 8 percent in 1996 to 22 percent in 1997. In March 1997 the studio lost a lab person, which meant that Hockings had to take time out of his shooting schedule to do more of the developing. As a result of one less salary, rent renegotiations, and fewer photo shoots, two things happened: Broadway's net profits increased substantially and sales decreased slightly. Hockings and Cairns wanted to improve sales and simultaneously increase operating efficiency to once again reach a 30 percent net profit level, as they had done a decade earlier. Their goal for 1998 was to bill[5] $575 in sales[6] every day and achieve a 28 percent profit level after all expenses.

Hockings and Cairns narrowed down the possible options to increase both sales and profitability to three: purchasing bulk film, outsourcing black-and-white film development, and changing the proof format. They had already ruled out buying more automated equipment, since the next level of automation would require an investment of millions of dollars.

Option 1: Purchasing Bulk Film

Broadway used 1,000 rolls of 35 mm film per year (only one of many types they used in total). Currently, this colour film, with 38 exposures per roll, was purchased directly from the factory in packages of 19 rolls for $160. This was by far the quickest and most convenient way to buy film. Broadway could purchase

30.5 m of bulk film, which was equivalent to 19 rolls, at $80 and roll it onto separate film cassettes. This alternative would require purchasing a bulk roller at a cost of $75, and film cassettes, at $1 per cassette.[7] Purchasing bulk film allowed Hockings and Cairns to customize the lengths of their film rolls. For example, the traditional factory roll had 38 exposures, but sometimes it was more appropriate for Cairns or Hockings to use a shorter or longer film. Additionally, Hockings could proof only 35 exposures at a time, so another advantage of buying bulk film was that it could be rolled to lengths of 35 exposures versus the factory roll of 38 exposures — in which case the last three exposures would be wasted. On the other hand, buying in bulk required more time to manually load the film onto the roller, roll the film onto the cassette, and finally label each cassette according to the film type. This process required about an hour for every 30.5 m bulk roll and would have to be done by Hockings or Cairns, since it was a fairly delicate procedure. If the bulk roller, which had to be loaded in the dark, was misloaded, $80 of film would be wasted. As well, care had to be taken not to scratch the film when loading and rolling it, and not to mislabel the finished cassette, and, since the film would be on reusable cassettes, the photographer had to be careful not to accidentally drop the cassette because the end would come off and a few of the frames would be lost.

Option 2: Outsourcing Black-and-White Film Development

Since black-and-white orders were approximately 50 percent of Broadway's business, outsourcing the film's development would free up some time for other demands. Hockings used 12 to 15 rolls of the Kodak traditional black-and-white film weekly. A roll of film cost $2.25 and developing cost $0.50 per roll. If Hockings were to outsource the development, he would have to use a different type of film — Chromagenic film — which cost $5.25 per roll and $3.75 per roll to develop.

Although Chromagenic film was more expensive, it had several advantages. First, and most importantly, since it was made of die base silver technology, it could be developed using a normal colour film processor. This meant that instead of needing both colour and black-and-white technology, a lab could invest in one (albeit more expensive) advanced colour processor, and all the film, whether colour or black and white, could go through the standard chemistry. Second, the end result was a cleaner and more consistently processed batch of proofs, decreasing the amount of time Cairns spent spotting the proofs. Third, the lab could cut the film into strips of five negatives each, thus eliminating yet another step. Finally, Hockings and Cairns estimated that outsourcing the black-and-white film would save them approximately 14 hours per week (three hours for the developing and 11 for processing).

Hockings had made a few inquiries and was considering negotiating an agreement with a photo-finishing business across the road from the store. The owner had assured him that he would be able to develop any number of orders Broadway had and promised a turnaround time of a day or less.

**Option 3:
Changing the
Proof Format**

During the proof consultation, Broadway usually enlarged and displayed one of the best proofs and had the other smaller proofs in a stack for the customer to look through. Since the large displayed proof was part of their marketing plan, Hockings and Cairns were not about to change it. However, they had begun to reconsider the format in which they produced and showed the rest of the proofs.

Currently, clients were given a stack of proofs, each 10 by 12.5 cm in size. Each of these proofs had to be collated and copyright stamped. Customers liked this format because the proofs were not only easy to look at and decide upon, but were also a usable product. However, some customers would copy the high quality proofs using a home scanner or frame the actual proofs instead of ordering the prints, thus cutting directly into Broadway's sales.

Hockings considered switching to an alternative method of developing and displaying proofs. This new format would use enlarged gang proof pages.[8] The customers could still easily view the proofs, since they were enlarged to 8.25 by 10.8 cm; however, now the proofs were all contained on one enlarged sheet, and the quality of the large sheet was not quite as high. Using the large sheets would not only save Cairns time, since collating was no longer necessary and only one copyright stamp was required (compared to 36 to 38 with the previous format), but it would also prevent customers from copying and using the proofs as pictures: the sheet was too large to fit into a scanner and the sheet was slightly spotted, had slight colour variation across the sheet, and was of a lower resolution.

When comparing costs, Broadway's local developer charged Broadway $0.30 each for individual proofs. Hockings could supply an enlarged gang proof with 35 proofs on it for $2.10 per page plus labour. Hockings currently developed six to nine sheets per hour and wondered if this would be an efficient use of his time. Hockings and Cairns wondered how this new format would affect sales levels. On the one hand, since customers would no longer be able to frame the proofs, they expected there would be an increase in print sales; however, on the other hand, they also knew that customers would not prefer this new format and wondered to what extent this would affect the number of phone inquiries and referrals the studio received. Hockings remarked that referrals often took place a year or two after the initial sale, and he wondered whether or not, and if so, how, Broadway should go about implementing the switch from singular proofs to the enlarged gang proof format.

Hockings and Cairns wanted to make any operational changes as soon as possible. They wondered which of the options would successfully lead them into a year of increased sales and profits.

NOTES

1. Proofs were preliminary prints that were shown to customers from which they chose the ones that they wanted made into the final picture product.
2. Approximately half of the film was of the larger size.

3. The first chemical solution was the developer, which made the exposed portions of image visible on the material. The second solution was made of acetic acid and stopped the developing process. The final chemical solution made the image permanent.

4. In spotting, the photographer checked for little white marks or blemishes on the proofs, which could be a result of a dirty negative, and made a note of those to be fixed in the final printing stage.

5. Hockings considered photo shoots, developing, printing, spotting, retouching, framing, and any other activity that could be linked to a specific order as billable time.

6. Hockings and Cairns' labour costs were estimated at 25 percent of the daily sales figure of $575.

7. The minimum bulk order size for cassettes was 100 cassettes. Each cassette could be reloaded an average of 12 times.

8. Proof pages, which contained the whole roll of proofs, were enlarged up to four times in order to produce the enlarged gang proof pages.

C A S E 6.8 STEELWAY BUILDING SYSTEMS

By Tracy L. Paul and John F. Graham

Glen White, owner and president of Steelway Building Systems (SBS), was in his office overlooking his production facilities. Lately, the flange line had been taking up a great deal of his thoughts. Mr. White realized that the competitive forces in the industry were changing. He believed that by adding more new technology he would improve his competitive position in the industry, but he wondered which system available to SBS would be the most cost-effective and productive to implement in the flange area.

STEELWAY BUILDING SYSTEMS

Steelway, located in Aylmer, Ontario, was incorporated in 1976 by Mr. White. Steelway had gradually expanded its capabilities to the point where it could now manufacture all the necessary components of an entire steel building.

SBS had grown from a one-person operation in 1976 to a company employing up to 100 people in its peak periods. The company was broken into four main areas: sales and customer service, design, production, and administration.

THE STEEL BUILDING INDUSTRY

Steel building manufacturers were affected by a number of pressing issues. First, the industry had become highly competitive. A small number of competitors affected SBS directly. Two of these, Canadian Building Systems and Robertson Building Systems, were located within Canada but were wholly or partly owned by companies from the United States.

Because of the Free Trade Agreement more and more competition was coming directly from the United States. There were approximately four major competitors without Canadian links that had generated strong sales penetration in the Canadian market.

These competitors had already begun to implement automated systems similar to the ones Mr. White had been evaluating for his own plant. If SBS were to survive through the 1990s, it had to keep up with the latest technological trends.

The general economic conditions were also a concern. The increasing value of the Canadian dollar and the recessionary times in 1990–91 had negatively affected the business.

THE PURCHASE PROCESS

The purchase of a steel building was not as straightforward as it might seem. The end consumer usually contacted a number of local contractors if the need for a new building arose. The contractors each had an already established relationship with a specific steel building manufacturer. The contractors then contacted their steel building manufacturer to get a quote. The contractors gave the end consumer an estimate to complete the construction of the steel building.

Contractors usually dealt with only one steel building manufacturer. For example, a contractor in the London area might deal exclusively with SBS. Another contractor in London dealt exclusively with Robertson Building Systems. SBS worked very hard to develop contractor relationships in many different locations around North America. A company like SBS created all the components for the building, and the contractor assembled the components at the location specified by the end consumer. Exhibit 1 illustrates the variety of projects in which SBS had been involved.

Timely delivery was important to the end consumer. If a grocery store was scheduled to open in May, the building had to arrive and be assembled on time. Just as important as delivery was service, especially the after sales follow-up. If there were any problem with the new building, the end consumer had to be able to contact the manufacturer or contractor. At this time SBS's customer service department became very important. Quality was definitely a concern. Mr. White expressed it this way: "If the quality isn't there, you can sometimes get away with it in the short run, but it will catch up to you in the long run."

Contractors were concerned with the delivery, because they had to assemble the building to a set schedule. Quality and price also had to be competitive for SBS to retain the contractor relationship.

SBS PRODUCTION

Key Success Factors

Mr. White explained the three key success factors for the manufacture of steel beams in SBS. First, the design had to be accurate and precise. Second, the purchase of the main raw material had to be efficient. It would be ideal to be able to purchase the cheapest steel possible. Third, SBS had to be "a good manufacturer," meaning that it had to be able to obtain the right equipment to process the most efficient material. It needed the ability to cut steel varying in length from a few inches in length up to 60 feet with a tolerance (accuracy) of 1/16 of an inch.

Beam Production

Mr. White had introduced CAD/CAM into his plant. CAD/CAM was really two separate pieces of computerization. CAD (computer-assisted (or aided) design) employed computer graphics to create designs of physical objects. SBS used CAD in the design of its steel buildings. Exhibit 2 shows a design of one section of SBS's production area, created using CAD technology.

CAM (computer-assisted (or aided) manufacturing) used computers to control the machinery on the plant floor. One computer could be used to control a number of different operations on the plant floor. CAD/CAM was the integration of the two.

The flange line was the area where flanges and connector plates were manufactured. The area was one part of the total production process for a steel building. Flanges were raised edges that protected the webs. Connector plates were the ends of a beam where other beams were connected to create a building. Exhibit 3 illustrates a steel building frame manufactured by SBS. Exhibit 4 focuses attention on a steel beam that forms part of the entire frame and illustrates the three components mentioned above (flange, connector plate, and web) in more detail.

The usual process began with raw materials (steel) being shipped to SBS. SBS could use two types of steel. It used sheet steel to produce webs — mini-walls between flanges. Sheet steel was made by primary steel companies, such as Dofasco. The other type of steel, made primarily from scrap steel, was called flat bar. It was melted down by steel mills, such as Lasco. Flat bar was more efficient than sheet steel because it did not have to be cut to width before the flange process began and there was less waste.

Flange Production

Once the steel was delivered, it was lifted by an overhead crane and placed onto the bar line. Once the flat bar was on the flange line it was manually welded, cut to the appropriate length, and holes were punched in it to facilitate assembly of the frames. Then the flange was manually moved to the next step of the process. The new technology Mr. White was considering adding would eliminate the overhead crane and replace it with a more manageable process.

Connector Plate Production

The flat bar also had to be cut to length for connector plates, which were considerably shorter than the flanges. The connector plates had to be taken manually from the flange area to the plasma area (see Exhibit 2) for the hole punching step. As a result, there was much more material handling than was necessary. Any of the new processes would eliminate the need to move the connector plates to the plasma area.

The entire flange production and connector plate production process involved a great deal of physical exertion on the part of the people on the shop floor, and the new automated processes could significantly reduce the number of injuries.

Numerous other operations were necessary to complete the production of all the components of the steel building, but the flange and connector plate production was the very first step in the entire process.

THE PROPOSED SYSTEM

Mr. White believed it was time for SBS to redefine its direction. He explained his reasoning in simple, yet decisive, terms: "I have no choice; it's a matter of do we survive or don't we?"

Mr. White saw the major advantages of changing his current system as the following:

- It would increase the quality of the product because the new computer software would increase production accuracy.

- It would improve customer service because the faster new process would decrease delivery time. Mr. White estimated that an 80 by 120 foot building currently took SBS 40 person-hours to complete. With the new system he estimated that the same building would take only 12 person-hours. As a result, there was an opportunity to decrease the production group by three workers. The people working on the shop floor made approximately $15 per hour (including benefits) and usually worked eight hours a day. These people were considered full-time employees.

- It would decrease the stress on workers because most manual aspects of the operation would be considerably reduced.

- Materials handling would be significantly reduced with any one of these systems installed.

- The estimated materials savings for any of the three options available to Mr. White would be $10,000.

OPTIONS AVAILABLE TO SBS

Mr. White was considering three options. He had quotes from two separate suppliers: Franklin Manufacturing Company and Washington Manufacturing Company. Alternatively, SBS could assemble the whole system itself from a group of suppliers. Mr. White saw the most critical components of any new system to be accuracy, flexibility (in particular, the ability to cut steel varying widely in length), and compatibility with his current IBM hardware.

The Franklin Manufacturing Company Quotation

Mr. White had contacted Franklin Manufacturing Company for a quotation to improve SBS's flange line.

The computer component of the system would use a software package compatible with IBM computers. Franklin described it as the world's fastest processor and the software as highly accurate and reliable. Franklin stated that finished flanges could be from 4 feet to 50 feet in width with a tolerance of plus or minus 1/16 of an inch, meaning that the width could be programmed to within that amount of variance. To reach the capability of cutting lengths to a few inches Franklin would add an extra $100,000 to the price.

Franklin's basic system cost $198,295 and included the following:

- the computer system mentioned above
- welding assembly
- hydraulic press

The delivery period for the basic machine would be 14 to 16 weeks from receipt of the purchase order. If any extra equipment was required (for example, infeed/outfeed equipment), the delivery period would be negotiated.

Purchasing infeed equipment, which fed raw materials (steel) into the press, from Franklin would add an extra $13,750 to the base purchase price. The outfeed equipment, which mechanically pulled the connector plate or flange out of the press, would add an extra $16,285 to the base purchase price. The machinery would be sent to SBS with no start-up assistance. There was a one-year warranty. Mr. White wondered how necessary start-up assistance was.

The Washington Manufacturing Company Quotation

Mr. White also had a quote from Washington Manufacturing Company, which used software that it developed itself. SBS might have to purchase a new computer to run the software. No mention was made of tolerances.

The price quoted for this system was $245,800, which included the following:

- infeed equipment
- weld bar assembly — this piece of machinery lifted the steel into position and performed the welding operation
- 350-ton hydraulic press and three-position die set — the press and die set were the heart of the operation where the steel was shaped to create bars that support the rest of the steel building
- outfeed equipment
- start-up assistance — this would include one person for three days to help Steelway assemble and operate the new system

The delivery period was 20 to 24 weeks from receipt of the purchase order; a one-year warranty would apply.

The Do-It-Yourself Option

This would entail SBS buying parts of the system from various suppliers and putting the pieces together itself. The do-it-yourself option was attractive because it was relatively inexpensive. Mr. White believed SBS might also be able to make some of the necessary components in its shop. Mr. White realized that this route would take a great deal of time and effort.

One potential pitfall was that if one part of the system was faulty or broke down, the suppliers could blame it on other pieces of equipment from other suppliers. Another pitfall was that the suppliers might think that the in-house assembly of the system lacked the necessary expertise. Exhibit 5 outlines the costs involved in SBS creating its own system. There was also the question of how contractors would react to this change in the Steelway production process.

Mr. White sat with the options spread over his desk. He knew that he had to examine the costs and benefits of each system along with the advantages and disadvantages of the three options. He was also pondering the short-term implications of adding one of these systems to the current production process. He wondered what the priorities should be and what the long-term ramifications would be.

EXHIBIT 1
Samples of SBS
Product Lines

Exhibit 2
Partial
Production Area
Created Using
CAD Technology

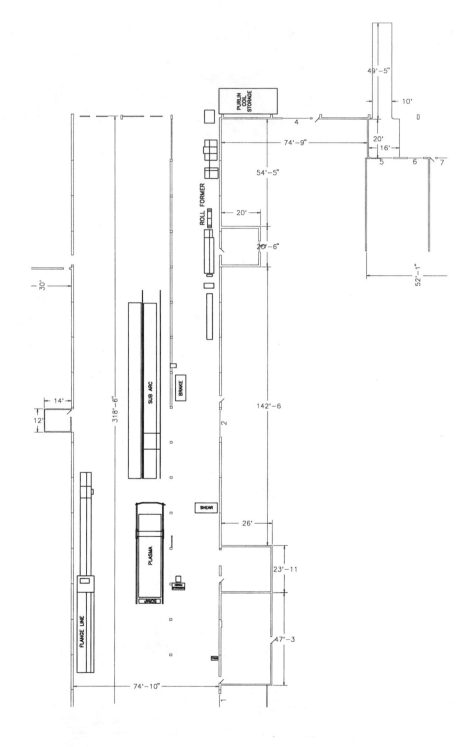

EXHIBIT 3
Steel Building
Frame

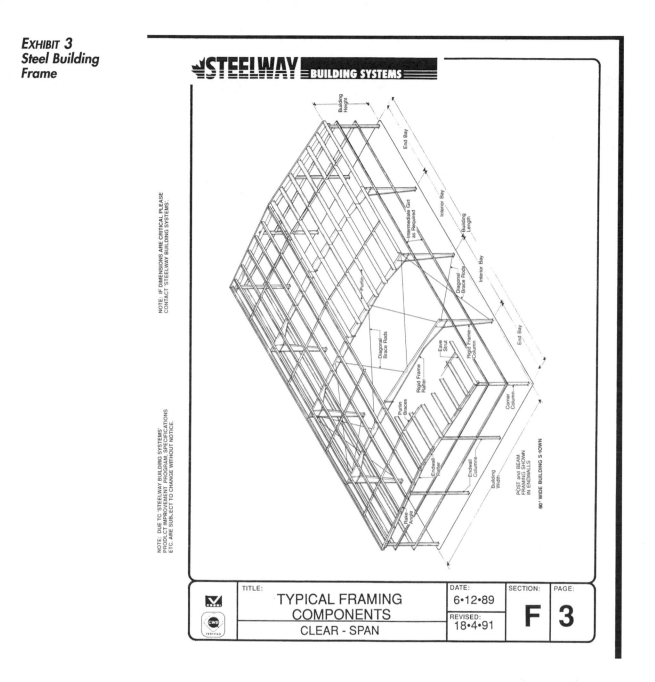

Exhibit 4
Close-up of Rigid Frame Column, Illustrates Flange, Web, and Connector Plates

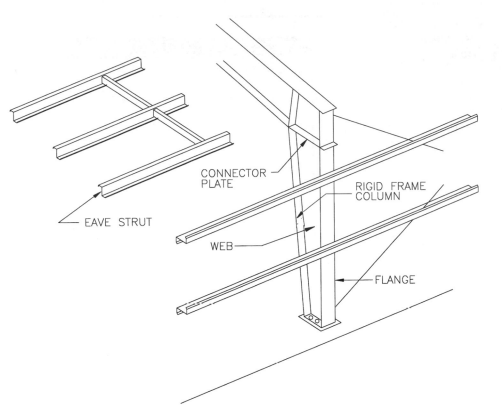

CONNECTOR PLATE

EAVE STRUT

RIGID FRAME COLUMN

WEB

FLANGE

EXHIBIT 5

	Costs of Do-It-Yourself Option	
	Flange Line Budget	
	Capital Cost	**Completion Date**
Pick and place	$ 5,000	Apr. 15/91
Input conveyor and centring device	5,000	May 15/91
Weld station	2,000	May 15/91
Shear[1]	50,000	Sept. 30/91
Punch[1]	50,000	Sept. 30/91
Output conveyor and stacking	3,000	Nov. 30/91
Measuring system[1]	25,000	Feb. 15/92
Total	$140,000	

1. The solution was still being reviewed for these components. The quoted cost was a maximum; a reduction of up to 30 percent was possible.

568

C A S E 6.9   UNIVERSAL PULP AND PAPER: WEST COAST DIVISION

By Jeffrey J. Dossett and Richard Mimick

Mike Garfield, the new plant manager of the West Coast Division of Universal Pulp and Paper, had just received a disturbing telephone call from his superior located at the company's head office. The head office staff had received several complaints from customers supplied by the West Coast Division. These complaints concerned inferior product quality and increasingly late deliveries. Given only two weeks in which to investigate and report back to his superior, Mike Garfield wondered what, specifically, could be done quickly to improve the overall operating efficiency and effectiveness of the plant.

THE WEST COAST DIVISION

The West Coast Division was a manufacturing operation involved in the processing of cut timber (wood) and the production of various paper products. The company's sales and marketing effort was carried out through the head office. Sales orders received by the head office were transmitted via a sophisticated computer communications network to the most "appropriate" plant. Two factors were considered in determining the appropriate plant for the order. First, proximity to the customer was important. The closest plant to the customer was often selected in an attempt to minimize the high transportation costs associated with the industry. Second, and more importantly, most plants were designed to produce only a small range of paper products. Therefore, depending on the type of product ordered, only certain plants were capable of manufacturing products that satisfied the customers' specific requirements.

The West Coast Division plant was a fully integrated operation, in that it produced and processed all of the wood pulp (raw material) it required for its manufacture of paper products. In the simplest terms, the plant or mill was designed to accept cut timber at one end of the plant, and to ship large rolls or "logs" of paper out of the other end. These large rolls of paper were then transferred to the customer's plant for final processing into finished paper products. A more detailed description of the production process appears later.

THE CONSUMER   Although an endless number and variety of paper products were sold at the retail level, the West Coast Division plant supplied companies that produced or used paper products for two basic purposes.

1.   Approximately 95 percent of the plant's production was newsprint, used primarily in the production of daily newspapers. End consumers of this product (newspaper readers) thought little of the actual newsprint, unless it was of unusually high or low quality. Only reasonable quality was expected. The newspaper chains, however, were characterized by the marketing staff as extremely price conscious and very concerned about delivery schedules. Recent financial analysis received by Mike Garfield indicated that 98 percent of the West Coast Division's net profit after tax resulted from sales to this segment.

2.   The remaining 5 percent of the plant's production was used for specialty writing paper products. This paper was high quality and was produced to widely varying customer specifications. Sales to this segment had begun only two years ago. The marketing staff had identified the specialty writing paper products segment as a small, but poorly served, market "niche" or segment. The marketing staff believed that *any* sales, however small, would be a bonus to add to the larger newsprint sales.

End consumers of these paper products tended to buy infrequently and in small quantities. These consumers were willing to pay a premium price for image or status qualities such as unique sizes, shapes, colours, and textures. Financial records indicated that only 2 percent of net profit after tax resulted from sales to these customers.

Mike Garfield recalled that although the West Coast Division plant was originally designed primarily for the production of high volume, low-to-medium quality newsprint, machine adjustments could be made to enable the equipment to produce a range of product types. However, this often resulted in shorter, more costly production runs, as a result of significantly increased machine downtime.

THE PRODUCTION PROCESS   The production process was quite complex at the West Coast plant but could be simplified into three key components: wood processing, pulp production, and paper production. The total investment in plant and equipment was approximately $2,340 million (see Exhibit 1 for details).

Wood Processing   The entire production process began with the receipt of wood logs. Upon receipt, these logs were weighed and sorted by tree species (e.g., spruce, pine, hemlock) and stored separately in an area known as the wood yard. As needed, specific log species were floated in water passageways to two de-barking machines. In the de-barking machines, the tree bark was removed by tumbling the logs against one another vigorously in log de-barking drums.

Once de-barked, the logs were moved to a "chipper" machine. Within several seconds, a large de-barked log was reduced to a pile of wood chips or fragments. The wood chips were then stored in large silos (storage bins). Once again, there were separate silos for different tree species. Separate storage of wood chips by species permitted the controlled mixing of chips into precise combinations or "recipes" required for the particular paper products being produced.

The entire wood processing component of the production process could provide 730 tons of wood chips per hour. Wood processing operated 24 hours per day, 365 days per year.

Pulp Production

Pulp, the key raw material for the production of paper, was produced using a complicated chemical process known as the Kraft process. Two tons of wood chips were required to produce one ton of pulp. The Kraft process worked by dissolving the lignin, or the "glue" that bonds wood fibres together. This "ungluing" was accomplished in two tall pressure-cookers known as digesters, by cooking the wood chips in a chemical solution of caustic soda and sodium sulphide.

Upon leaving the digesters, the digested chips entered a machine known as a blow tank. The blow tank was maintained at a significantly lower pressure than the digesters. This pressure difference caused the wood fibres to "blow apart" as lignin, the bonding glue, was no longer present in the wood fibres. The resulting wood fibre pulp was cleaned and bleached to remove unwanted impurities that might later affect the quality of the paper. The refined pulp remained in temporary storage where chemical additives could be mixed in to further prepare the pulp for paper production.

The pulp production facilities were capable of converting as much as eight million tons of wood chips into about four million tons of pulp per year.

Paper Production

The two paper-making machines in the West Coast plant were extremely large and involved an investment of about $500 million each. Each paper-making machine could be used to convert up to 2,250,000 tons of pulp into 2,250,000 tons of paper per year. (One ton of pulp could be converted into approximately one ton of newsprint or specialty paper.) Contribution per ton of newsprint was estimated by the finance department to be $80.

A paper-making machine had a wet end (where the diluted wood fibre pulp entered the process) and a dry end (where the completed paper was wound onto very large rolls or logs of paper). Paper orders of a similar nature were run at the same time to minimize the machine set-up time. Except for this set-up downtime, the paper-making machines ran as close to 24 hours per day as possible.

The paper-making process was highly complex and required the monitoring of many variables, such as temperature, chemical content, and machine speed. In total, approximately 75 technical measurements had to be made every 30 minutes. Currently, about 50 of these measurements were made automatically by computerized process controls. These controls constantly adjusted the machine settings based on "correct" values as predetermined by the production engineers. The remaining 25 measurements were made by a team of eight inspection employees. There was a team for each of the three shifts. These workers, all members of the Canadian Paperworkers Union, earned an average of $22.65 per hour.

Mike Garfield recalled a report prepared by the director of computer services indicating that a computer program was available that could enhance the present system so that all 75 measurements could be computer controlled. The report cited increased accuracy and labour savings as the major benefits of such an acquisition. The program would cost $450,000. To Mike, it seemed to be worthwhile, but he wondered why his predecessor hadn't authorized the expenditure.

If machine capacity was at the root of the complaints, Mike knew that a report recently prepared by the production engineers would be most helpful. The report included cost estimates for increasing capacity at various points in the production process. Exhibit 2 provides excerpts from the report.

THE COMPLAINTS

To better understand the source and cause of the recent complaints, Mike held a meeting with the chief production supervisor, Charlie Robertson. When asked about his understanding of the situation, Charlie responded:

> It's not my fault! It's those idiots in sales/marketing that keep sending me those stupid, small fancy orders ... I don't want them! Never used to get them. My guys are constantly shutting down to make machine adjustments ... by the time the order is completely through the process, we're just beginning to figure the proper settings!... About those late deliveries, what do you expect? If we keep accepting those special orders, the newsprint just has to wait its turn! Really, Mike, it's *your* problem.

With demand for newsprint expected to increase from three million tons of paper this year to 3,680,000 tons next year, Mike knew the current complaints might be a sign of worse days ahead. As plant manager, Mike knew he was ultimately responsible for the efficiency and profitability of his plant. With this in mind, he set out to prepare his report to his superior at head office.

Exhibit **1**

Plant and Equipment Investment (in Millions of Dollars)	
Paper-making machines	$1,000
Digesters (2)	420
Chipper machine	150
Blow tank	130
De-barking machines (2)	106
Storage silos	94
Low weighing and sorting equipment	74
Miscellaneous plant and equipment	366
TOTAL	$2,340

Exhibit **2**

Capacity Enhancement Cost Study Results
1. Wood Processing — $830,000 to increase production by 100,000 tons of wood chips per year.
2. Pulp Production — $1,330,000 to increase production by 100,000 tons of wood fibre pulp per year.
3. Paper Production — $49,500,000 to increase production by 225,000 tons of paper per year.

C A S E 6.10 THE UNIVERSITY OF WESTERN ONTARIO
BOOK STORE

By John Haywood-Farmer and Andrew Fletcher

On April 5, 1993, John Woolsey, director of University Book Store, The University of Western Ontario, was trying to decide how the Book Store should respond to a recent customer survey that had revealed student dissatisfaction with long lineups and the hours of operation. Mr. Woolsey had many options, including the purchase of a retail management system and opening on Saturdays. He wanted to decide which options to pursue before the staff met in one week to begin planning for the annual September rush. Michael Gourley, vice-president administration, had recently been actively encouraging all operating units to adopt total quality service (TQS) in their operations. Mr. Woolsey wondered how its principles might apply to his current decision.

THE UNIVERSITY OF WESTERN ONTARIO

The University of Western Ontario (UWO or Western) was located at the north end of London, Ontario, a city of 315,000 located along Highway 401, the major east-west traffic artery through southern Ontario. Western catered to 19,000 full-time and 2,300 part-time undergraduates, and 2,750 graduate students. Three colleges affiliated with UWO, situated within a short distance of the main campus, increased the student population by another 4,000. Like all Ontario universities, Western was facing budgetary constraints. For some years, the Ontario government had reduced funding in response to its fiscal deficits. Western officials believed that fiscal restraint would continue in the foreseeable future; consequently, for the 1993–94 fiscal year (beginning May 1) UWO reduced all operating budgets by 1.6 percent and reduced administrative unit budgets by an additional 0.5 percent. As a result of continued financial restraints, Western had called on its nonoperating units (such as the Book Store) to show a profit to support Western's operating budget. In addition, UWO had raised the fees it charged them for administrative support, such as accounting services. These financial concerns came at a time when UWO believed it was at capacity. In addition, the Ontario government would not allow

IVEY Andrew Fletcher prepared this case under the supervision of John Haywood-Farmer solely to provide material for class discussion. The authors do not intend to illustrate either effective or ineffective handling of a managerial situation. The authors may have disguised certain names and other identifying information to protect confidentiality. Ivey Management Services prohibits any form of reproduction, storage or transmittal without its written permission. This material is not covered under authorization from CanCopy or any reproduction rights organization. Copyright © 1995, Ivey Management Services.

universities to increase tuition fees beyond the authorized 7 percent for each of the next two years. Student leaders believed that, with summer jobs hard to find, these increases would be a burden to many students.

THE UNIVERSITY BOOK STORE

The University Book Store, located in a prominent location in the University Community Centre (UCC), was a full-service facility; it considered students, faculty, staff, and the general public to be its customers. Exhibit 1 shows its layout. Mr. Woolsey believed that the Book Store was typical of those at other North American universities similar in size and nature to UWO. The Book Store was an ancillary operation under the portfolio of Gordon Smiley, assistant vice-president (registrar and student affairs), who in turn reported to Mr. Gourley.

It sold textbooks for all courses on the main campus and in the affiliated colleges, academic reference books, children's books, general books, stationery, and UWO-branded merchandise, including clothing, knapsacks, and rings. On average, books returned a gross margin of 21 percent, whereas the nonbook merchandise margins were somewhat higher. The Book Store relied on the merchandise sales to offset the high cost of selling textbooks and to meet its financial targets. The sales breakdown was textbooks, 70 percent; stationery, 7 percent; general books, 13 percent; and merchandise, 10 percent. The store carried approximately 10,000 textbook titles, 30,000 general book titles, 5,000 different student supply items, and a few thousand different units of general merchandise. Mr. Woolsey estimated that a full-time student spent $350 to $700, averaging about $400, on textbooks each year. Exhibit 2 shows the Book Store's return policy.

TQS PRINCIPLES

TQS, the principles of which arose in total quality management but which had been modified for service industries, is a management style that imposes a customer-driven culture of continuous improvement within an organization. The principles of TQS include developing and managing processes to serve customers and training employees to become customer focused. Measuring, benchmarking, and seeking feedback from customers and front-line employees are important TQS practices.

TQS AT UWO

Mr. Gourley came to Western in 1992 as a firm believer in TQS. He believed that UWO's services must be improved to meet customer needs. He often told the story of how his first experience at Western encouraged him to promote TQS:

> The first person I met was a parking attendant, prior to my interview with the university's president for my current position. I explained to the attendant that I had been told to come to his booth, as parking arrangements had been made. The attendant replied: "Nobody told me. Nobody tells me anything." I asked if I could park in the lot. He said: "Park over there between the yellow lines." The attendant said he didn't know where the president's office was and that no one had ever told him he needed to know. It was clear to me that this person's job was to police the parking lot. He performed well at that task, but I didn't believe anybody should have a poor first impression of this uni-

versity. Fortunately, I got to my interview despite the poor signage. I knew Western needed a paradigm shift, not only in parking but in all its services.

As a result of the new TQS focus, training seminars were organized for Western's managers, including Mr. Woolsey. Of the four days, two were spent on an overview of TQS and two on TQS theory.

JOHN WOOLSEY AND NORM LAVOIE

John Woolsey graduated from McMaster University with a bachelor of commerce degree. Since that time, he had been involved with course materials operations at the correspondence-focused Athabasca University in Edmonton, Alberta. He came to Western in 1988 after managing the book store at Brock University in St. Catharines, Ontario, which had a total of about 9,000 full- and part-time students.

Norm Lavoie, manager of administrative services at the Book Store, would also be heavily involved in any change process. Before coming to UWO in 1990, he had worked at Canada Post's headquarters in retail operations, systems development, and training; before that he had managed the Christmas mail rush at Canada Post in Orillia, Ontario.

COMPETITION

No other book store in London matched the Book Store's extensive line of textbooks. However, the University Students' Council operated a used book store in the UCC, which offered used textbooks at discounts of up to 75 percent. Students also sold used textbooks privately using poster board advertisements throughout the campus. Competition for nontextbook merchandise was more significant. Picadilly (The Pic), a general store located directly across the hall from the Book Store, sold UWO merchandise, stationery, consumer packaged goods, and pharmaceutical products. As well, many stores in the vicinity of the campus sold UWO merchandise.

THE SEPTEMBER RUSH

During September, the busiest month of the year, the Book Store completed as many as 10,000 customer transactions in one day. Mr. Woolsey reflected on past Septembers:

> Many days it's wall-to-wall people most of the time and very difficult to move. Not only does this congestion make it hard for our customers, but it also puts our staff under a lot of stress. Obviously, it also doesn't help us in stocking the shelves either!

The Book Store's two levels were separated by about one metre vertically; customers entered on the upper level, where they left their bags, etc., and exited from the lower level. Shelving separated and divided the sales areas and restricted vision. When the Book Store was packed to capacity, security guards limited access, trying to match the entry rate to the exit rate. Once inside, the process was typical of any self-serve retail establishment: customers went to the relevant sections of the store to locate the required items. During the September rush, the Book Store installed a cash register at the entrance to deal with returns. Each year it handled book refunds or credits equivalent to about 6 percent of total book sales; about 51 percent of the year's refunds occurred in the month of September.

CUSTOMER SURVEYS

In February 1992, October 1992, February 1993, and March 1993, the Book Store management had conducted a standard statistically valid and reliable customer survey used in university book stores across North America. From the results, Mr. Woolsey targeted slow checkouts and hours of operations as the most common complaints that he believed the Book Store could improve. In 1992, during the busiest time of the day during the first week of classes, the Book Store measured waiting times. A staff member gave a time trial form explaining the process to a customer at the end of a line. The staff member recorded the time he or she distributed each numbered form. Upon leaving the store, the customer handed the form to a security guard who recorded the time. The Book Store thanked all participating customers with gifts such as a Western T-shirt. The longest lineup measured was 18 minutes. Mr. Woolsey was uncertain what an acceptable waiting time was and what target waiting time the Book Store should set.

ANDRÉE BOURGON'S EXPERIENCE

Andrée Bourgon, a first-year student at Western, commented on her first experience at the Book Store in September, 1992:

> It was early afternoon and I decided not to wait in the queue to enter the Book Store. My friend, Bob Wood, and I bought a coffee and waited for the line to diminish. Customers continued to join the line and it wasn't until 45 minutes after I bought that coffee that I saw an opportunity to enter the store without waiting. Once I was in the store I started my hunt to find 11 books, a plastic Western calendar, and a corkboard. It took me approximately 30 minutes to find all the books after asking for directions and finding the different subject areas within the store. It took another 30 minutes to check out. The lineup to check out extended almost the entire length of the store. The line never was at a standstill but continued to move at a slow pace. While I was in line, a few people knocked books off the high stack of books resting in my arms. Bob had to help me hang onto some of the items. We actually felt lucky, as we had estimated it would take two hours to complete buying our books.

POSSIBLE ACTION

Installing a Retail Management System

Mr. Woolsey was considering purchasing a retail management system. He and his selection committee had spent a considerable amount of time setting specifications and collecting bids from suppliers. Mr. Woolsey knew that the Book Store made purchases of this importance only every 10 to 15 years. It was significant because of the size of the proposed investment, the long-term commitment and training required to use the new hardware and software effectively, and the fact that it would change the way the Book Store did business in some areas. He cited the following situations as examples of the savings and the potential benefits of the system:

One feature of the retail management system we are looking at is bar code scanning. Currently, a check-out clerk has to enter the price of every item purchased into a cash register. It takes us an average of two minutes to check a customer out of the store. Queen's University in Kingston, Ontario, uses a bar code scanning system and has the check-out time down to an average of one minute. Also, if we used bar codes, we wouldn't have to put prices on every product we stock. Currently, 30 to 35 percent of one employee's time (at a rate of about $26,000 per year) is spent on this task. However, I think that maintenance on the computer system would offset any salary we could save.

The system's software also promises to provide us with a tremendous amount of customer information, including comprehensive sales data on all our products. As well, it will provide daily information of gross profit and information on product shrinkage. The current system allows us to collect sales data under only two accounts, books and merchandise, and we have to wait until after year-end inventory counts to estimate profit and shrinkage information. Because the new computer system would give us access to the university's main computer, we could process interdepartmental charges electronically instead of sending the business forms to each department like we do now. The new system would also reduce our telecommunication costs by about $3,000 per year because we would need fewer telephone lines to access the university's main frame computer. The system's new printers would also offer us the possibility of quicker credit card authorization.

Our purchasing would also benefit. The faculty member or department for every course provides us with a requisition for all books students will need. Of course, they come from hundreds of publishers. The new system would allow us to consolidate our purchase orders instead of sending a purchase order for each individual faculty requisition. Each year we return 12 percent of the books we purchase to publishers. It takes us the equivalent of one employee month of labour to complete the paperwork. By being able to consolidate, we could save that much and reduce the shipping costs to return books.

The system will also allow us to improve our inventory management. Because the software uses reorder flags, we should have more precise control and thus reduce both inventory overstocking and stockouts. We might save $15,000 to $16,000 per year on inventory carrying costs.

For three weeks in September it is a real zoo here; we are open from 9:00 a.m. to 9:00 p.m. Monday to Thursday, 9:00 a.m. to 5:30 p.m. Friday, and 11:00 a.m. to 3:30 p.m. Saturday. During that time, we need 20 cashiers for the first two weeks and 18 cashiers for the third week. During the rest of the year, we only need two or three cashiers. We hire the extra cashiers on a temporary basis through an employment firm for $11 per hour. The new system would allow us to reduce our cashier needs by four for each of our busy three weeks.

Although these benefits are quite attractive, I wonder if they make economic sense. I have estimated the necessary investment, annual operating costs, and savings (see Exhibit 3). They are large, and if we decide to go ahead there will be no turning back.

Providing Entertainment

The noise level, the image of the Book Store, and complaints from staff and customers concerned Mr. Woolsey. He believed that providing entertainment would make waiting in and around the Book Store more enjoyable and could increase customers' shopping experience, keep people's minds off the price of the textbooks and the long queues, and thus decrease the number of complaints the Book Store received. Granada, a home entertainment rental company, was willing to loan four televisions to the Book Store in return for the right to distribute literature at the Book Store exit. By tuning into the Much Music station, the Book Store could allow customers to watch music videos while they waited in line. The Intercollegiate Athletics Department was also willing to donate the time of a volunteer to play J.W., the Western athletics mascot, who could hand out candy (for about $50 for the month) and otherwise entertain customers.

Publishing Book Lists during the Summer

The Book Store did not provide book lists. However, Mr. Woolsey believed that if it did, students could buy their books earlier, thus reducing the mad rush of textbook sales in September. Such a move would allow students to check prices faster at the used book store and start reading earlier. He estimated that it would cost $1,000 to print the lists and would also involve some staff time to compile the lists using a computer program. He did not know how much suitable software would cost to develop or purchase, and he also wondered where the book lists should be placed if he decided to go ahead with this possibility. One potential location was outside the store. Placing them inside might be better service but could put an extra burden on staff if they became involved in interpreting student registration information to match textbook needs with specific courses or sections. Currently, staff were ill-equipped for such a role.

Opening on Saturdays

The Book Store opened on Saturdays only during the three-week September peak. Mr. Woolsey wondered if Saturday openings during the rest of the year would make sense. Opening on Saturdays from 10:00 a.m. to 3:00 p.m. would require seven or eight employees at $9 per hour each, plus at least one management staff member at no additional cost. Based on his perceptions, Mr. Woolsey believed that staff would oppose working on Saturdays instead of the customary Monday–Friday schedule. In earlier discussions, some staff had argued that Saturday openings would not increase sales but simply spread them over six days a week instead of five. In 1992–93, the Book Store had decided to stay open until 7:00 p.m. on Wednesday evenings from September to March to serve the part-time evening students who were unable to visit the Book Store during its regular hours. Mr. Woolsey learned that the Book Store could operate on Wednesday evening with only a skeleton staff but had not tracked sales in the evening period. However, he had heard reports of barely trained part-time and student staff struggling with complex systems and trying to offer expert service. He noted:

> Faculty and other customers demand sophisticated answers to their queries on publishing and authors.

Mr. Woolsey wondered if he should evaluate the Saturday opening proposal differently than the Wednesday evening opening.

Mailing Information to First-Year Students

Each year since 1990 the Book Store had mailed a brochure to the 5,000 first-year students, at a total cost of $3,500 to 4,000 per year. Students were often shocked when they encountered textbook prices; Mr. Woolsey wanted to decrease this financial surprise by informing students well in advance of the high prices of textbooks, as well as advertising the Book Store and its UWO merchandise. He wanted to re-evaluate the cost of this option against its benefits.

CONCLUSION

Mr. Woolsey had many ideas about increasing the quality of service to students and wondered which ideas he should implement to decrease the customers' concerns of long lineups and hours of operations while keeping his costs in line.

EXHIBIT 1
Floor Plan of the
University of
Western Ontario
Book Store

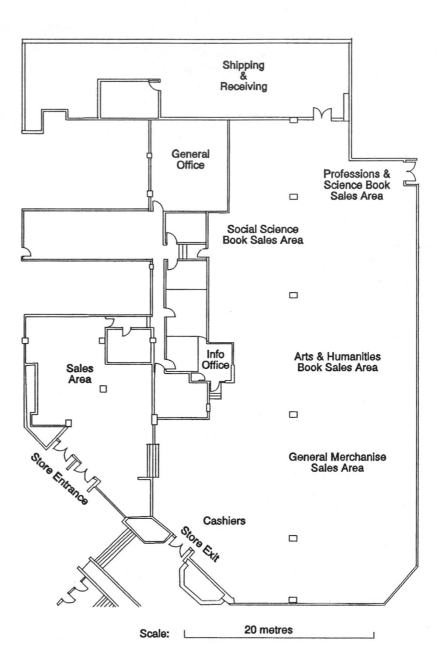

Source: Book Store files.

Exhibit **2**

The Book Store's Return Policy[1]

1. Refunds only within SEVEN DAYS of purchase
2. Cash register receipt must be presented
3. Merchandise must be in mint condition
4. There are no refunds or exchange on used or reduced books
5. Sale merchandise on exchange only

1. The Book Store informally extended its refund period during September.

Source: Posted publicly in the Book Store.

Exhibit **3**

Estimated Financial Costs and Benefits of a Retail System			
Year	Initial Investment	Annual Operating Costs	Annual Savings
1	$270,000[1]	$ 0	$ 0
2	50,000	29,000	16,000
3	16,000	50,000	122,000
4	10,000	52,000	165,000
5	3,000	54,000	170,000

1. Made up of hardware, $167,000; software, $56,000; training, $20,000; and price data conversion, renovation, financing, and miscellaneous costs, $27,000.

Source: Book Store files.

CASE 6.11 WHITEWATER SPECIALITIES LIMITED

By John Haywood-Farmer and Andrew Fletcher

In August 1993, Peter Winford, general manager of WhiteWater Specialties Limited, of Kelowna, British Columbia, was trying to decide whether to continue to pursue a potentially large order of fibreglass fascia signs from Consolidated Industries, a major Canadian retailer. Although the order would certainly allow WhiteWater Specialties to fulfill its mandate to diversify its product line, it might also result in almost quintupled sales. Mr. Winford wondered if such growth was appropriate for the company and its parent, WhiteWater West Industries Ltd.

BACKGROUND   WhiteWater West Industries Ltd. had been incorporated in 1981 to own and operate its own water slide. Geoffrey Chutter, the company's president, spent his childhood in British Columbia and subsequently lived in France and Ontario as his father, an executive in a multinational firm, changed locations. After graduating from university he obtained his chartered accountant designation while working in Toronto, Ontario. When Mr. Chutter was 28 years old, his entrepreneurial spirit and his desire to return to British Columbia led him to move to his accountancy firm's Vancouver office, where he began looking for business opportunities.

In 1980 he purchased a trailer park and campground in Penticton, a resort and agricultural city of 49,000 at the south end of Okanagan Lake in British Columbia's Okanagan Valley, and left the firm. In 1981 he decided to develop a small parcel of unused trailer park land located on a major street that ran beside the trailer park property. On this land, he designed and constructed a water park consisting of pools, water slides, whirlpools, a suntanning area, and service buildings. After the 1981 summer season, Mr. Chutter decided that he preferred designing, engineering, and manufacturing new parks, rather than selling tickets and hot dogs. Therefore, he decided to sell his property and concentrate on designing, manufacturing, and installing water slides. Since 1982 WhiteWater West had become significantly vertically integrated and offered a wide product line. The main services the company offered its customers included master planning, conceptual design, detailed engineering, detailed design, product manufacture, and construction. These activities involved taking into consideration the topography of the customer's land, designing a suitable variety of water slides; manufacturing the water slides, wave equipment, and interactive water play systems; and installing these products. Reaching sales of $13 million in 1994, WhiteWater West was the world leader in developing water parks.

WhiteWater West purchased WhiteWater Specialties and its fibreglass plant with vertical integration in mind. Originally the plant had supplied recreational vehicle manufacturers with parts and tractor trailer manufacturers with truck hoods. In 1990 and 1991 revenues had been $4.8 million and $4.2 million, respectively, but in 1992 they had dropped to $3.8 million. Mr. Winford expected that 1993 would see a turnaround in sales to $4.8 million, dominated, as usual, by sales of water slides to WhiteWater West. Exhibit 1 shows Specialties' actual and forecasted monthly revenues for 1993 by product category.

THE KELOWNA PLANT

WhiteWater Specialties' sole manufacturing facility was on the outskirts of the central Okanagan Valley city of Kelowna, population 124,000. The plant comprised about 4,275 square metres, within which the company employed 90 workers and used three different production processes: open fibreglass moulding, plastic rotomoulding, and polyurethane. Fibreglass is plastic reinforced by fine glass fibres. Conceptually, the product is similar to concrete strengthened by reinforcing steel bars (rebar). Fibreglass is formed by mixing the glass fibres into a plastic monomer, often a liquid, which is formed into the desired shape and then allowed to polymerize (set) to form a solid.

Mr. Winford described the 24-hour open fibreglass moulding process:

> The night shift sprays a gel coating on the mould. A few hours later the day shift applies the fibreglass with a spray gun. The fibreglass spray consists of liquid polyester resin and glass. The glass starts as a long thread, which then gets chopped into two-inch filaments by a chopper gun. The resin and glass combine as a spray and hit the mould simultaneously. After the fibreglass is applied, it cures for a few hours, during which it sets and dries. The afternoon shift applies a second fibreglass coat, which also has to cure. Finally, the night shift pulls the parts from the moulds, trimming and repairing the parts as needed. They then start the process all over again.

Should WhiteWater Specialties produce the Consolidated Industries fascia, it would use the open fibreglass moulding process. In total, the facility had about 200 moulds, 40 of which were the most common for manufacturing various water slide sections.

The polyurethane process was very similar to that used for open fibreglass moulding. In rotomoulding, plastic resin was placed in a closed mould, which was then heated and rotated to form the product. Mr. Winford believed that rotomoulding was an attractive area of growth for the company in the Kelowna area.

After they were completed, water slide parts were stored in crates to protect them from scratches during transportation. Once the parts for an entire order had been completed, the crates were shipped out by truck. Overseas orders were shipped through Vancouver by sea to their destination; North American orders were trucked directly to the site. Custom orders, including recurring orders — for example, computer assisted tomography (CAT) scanner shells — were handled similarly.

Because water slide components were produced in a wide variety of shapes and colours, it was not practical to store them in finished goods inventory. Project teams for water park contracts worked closely with WhiteWater Specialties to ensure timely delivery of the components at the construction site. Because most park owners wanted installation to be complete for the summer season, construction was usually finished in the spring. Although the usual lead time for slide construction at a water park was six to eight weeks, very large parks might need up to three to four months lead time.

Mr. Winford commented on the plant's capacity:

> It is hard to say what our capacity really is because the parts vary so much in size. Our dollar capacity can be reduced if in one particular week we are making very large, labour-intensive parts. Right now we work five days per week around the clock. We are comfortable producing 60 parts per day, which is enough to fill two or three containers and generate $20,000 to $30,000 in sales. Sometimes we get up to $600,000 a month, but that starts to stretch our capabilities. And, in a few extraordinary months, we have even produced sales of $700,000 to $800,000.

PREVIOUS EXPERIENCE WITH DIVERSIFICATION

Mr. Chutter wanted Mr. Winford to diversify from water slides to take advantage of the high capacity available in the summer and autumn months. Water slide production peaked from November to May in preparation for water park construction each spring. Although the company had tried many new products in the last few years, few had been successful. The list included environmentally friendly toilets, stretcher boards, satellite dishes, floating docks, CAT scanner shells, and soft-tub bathtubs. Mr. Winford commented on some of them:

> We are very flexible in being able to handle all sorts of designs of large fibreglass pieces. For instance, a new slide idea that was brought to our attention required us to combine our tube slide with our free fall slide. The tube slide is a covered water slide, while the free fall slide is a long and steep ride. Since we build our own moulds and use an open mould process, we can respond to changes in the customer's design. We can respond with quality and consistency.
>
> In the past we obtained the rights to a soft bathtub and an environmentally friendly toilet, two fibreglass products for which we are the sole manufacturer and marketer in Canada. The soft bathtub is a wonderful product. Once you try a bath in a cushioned tub, you will never return to a conventional one. We make them using our polyurethane process. Even though they are

price competitive with high quality tubs and jacuzzis, sales have not reached our expected level. We need a major advertising campaign to move it, but we just don't have the resources to inject into such a campaign.

The environmentally friendly toilet posed a different problem. It is only 10 percent fibreglass production, with the rest made up of electronics, packaging, seats, stickers, and labels. Unfortunately, because the design was poor, the toilet didn't work as planned, so we had little success in producing a high quality product.

We have struggled with the other processes associated with a product, as was the case with the environmentally friendly toilet. Unlike the toilet, however, we have been able to include the other nonfibreglass steps within our existing production process when producing truck hoods. The hoods have been quite successful for us, as have the CAT scanner inserts we make on contract for the Japanese market.

We also got into producing large satellite dishes. In this case the market collapsed with competition from cable and smaller dishes. We just couldn't become cost effective with the large dishes.

THE CONSOLIDATED INDUSTRIES OPPORTUNITY

Mr. Winford described the Consolidated Industries opportunity:

Last April an anonymous company asked us to bid on an order of large rounded pieces of fibreglass for a feasibility study. The request specified the dimensions and colour. To us it looked a lot like a small version of a water slide. Although the customer requested production using closed moulding, we recommended our open moulding process, as we could adjust the specifications of the order at a lower cost. Closed moulding would produce less expensive units, but until the customer was happy with the finished product we recommended the flexible open moulding. It wasn't until after a small British Columbia firm won the bid that we found out the customer was Consolidated. I predicted there would be problems, as the expertise of the firm that won the bid is research and development, not production. I knew this R & D firm was small and not considered a high volume producer.

I have been in touch with Consolidated and I know we can handle their needs. If possible, they would prefer to work with a single supplier. They want a flexible company that will work with them to modify the design as their business plans change or new information becomes available. They plan an entire renovation of their retail outlets. The fibreglass piece they want is a small, highly visible component of fascia that will surround the top of each retail outlet. It is similar to a water slide except the outside [convex] surface will be facing outward. This fascia will have some process steps different from those followed in manufacturing water slides, but we can incorporate them into our existing process with little loss in efficiency. I now realize that they don't want just a low cost fascia. They want to work with someone and get the signs on the retail outlets with a minimum of hassle over a two-year period. They want a company that will change with their plans, if necessary, and construct the new retail outlets with few or no problems. Consolidated's goal is to change their image with new, bright retail outlets. As a result, they will want to roll out the plan quickly. These are attractive products for us. Each retail outlet will use about $25,000 of fascia, the production of which would cost us about $8,750 in materials, $5,000 in direct labour, and $6,750 in direct overhead. The costs of our other products vary. Of our polyurethane sales, about 50 percent is taken up just in materials, another 20 percent is labour, and a further 20 percent is overhead. Our transfer price for water slides is set to allow us the same margin as other fibreglass products. Most of the pieces for Consolidated will be exactly the same shape and size, so the moulds can be used over and over. That should cut our fixed costs a little. There will be a few problems with corners and exact lengths, though. Although the fascia is very visible, after it is installed no one can get close enough to touch it or examine it closely. Each water slide is different enough so that moulds have limited use. And water slides have to fit perfectly on the inside [concave] surfaces because any edge sticking up just a little bit where the sections join would cut the users to shreds.

The challenge for us will be to keep up with demand. With our current excess capacity in the off-season for water slides [June to October], we could produce enough pieces each week for three retail outlets. If they rolled out the plan quickly I would have to make some major changes. However, Consolidated isn't sure they will invest in the changes as quickly as they originally planned. Recently, they have been downsizing considerably. They are going to reduce the number of retail outlets they refurbish from the 3,200 they estimated a year ago to 2,000. They are considering targeting specific test cities to see if the new retail outlets increase sales. The way I see it, Consolidated has three options they might pursue. They could only project the new image at new retail outlets. This would result in an order for $1 million of fascia. They could target specific cities and just change their image in those isolated areas. This would result in an order for $3 million of fascia. Or, they could do a complete rollout at a cost of some $50 million for fascia spread out over four or five years.

I am not convinced that this order is ideal for us, however. We are looking for products that have a completely opposite seasonal sales cycle. This order will require steady production year round.

CONCLUSION

Mr. Winford wondered if the Consolidated Industries order was appropriate and what impact it would have on WhiteWater Specialties and its parent company. He knew that Mr. Chutter would not want to walk away from a potentially huge contract. Consolidated Industries would expect facilities to be available to produce and deliver the fascia in a timely manner. WhiteWater Specialties had a number of options available to handle increased production. Because of the commonality of the fascia, it was possible to produce to finished goods inventory. Alternatively, it could rent a new production facility; 930 square metres of suitable space could be rented for $40,000 to $50,000 per year. Paint and spray booths for such a facility would require an investment of $100,000 to $150,000.

Mr. Winford wondered if WhiteWater Specialties should be diversifying in this manner and how he should plan for the potentially large order.

EXHIBIT 1

SALES AND FORECASTS FOR 1993
(in Thousands of Dollars)

	Actual							Forecasted[1]					Total
	Jan	Feb	Mar	Apr	May	Jun	Jul	Aug	Sept	Oct	Nov	Dec	
Fibreglass													
Water slides	$350.0	$388.7	$591.8	$490.3	$450.1	$183.5	$266.2	$ 50	$ 50	$100	$350	$400	$3,670.6
Medical equipment			21.5			21.5		20	20	20	0	20	123.0
Other	6.0	6.3	16.4	17.9	15.6	10.9	7.4	75	100	80	35	35	405.5
Total	356.0	395.0	629.7	508.2	465.7	215.9	273.6	145	170	200	385	455	4,199.1
Polyurethane	15.0	37.5	20.9	11.1	31.7	29.1	42.1	25	25	30	20	15	302.4
Rotomoulded	25.0	26.5	27.6	30.0	30.2	46.2	30.0	20	30	30	24	15	334.5
Total	$396.0	$459.0	$678.2	$549.3	$527.6	$291.2	$345.7	$190	$225	$260	$429	$485	$4,836.0

1. The forecast was made in June 1993.

Source: Company files.

PART

An Introduction to General Management

"No man is an island, entire of itself; every man is a piece of the continent, a part of the main ..."

—*John Donne, 17th-century poet*

General management integrates all of the functional areas with a view to making decisions that are coherent and consistent for the entire firm. The meaning of general management can vary. In a small, one-person business, the chief decision maker *is* the all-round general manager responsible for long-term planning as well as daily "fire fighting." There is no delegation of these responsibilities to specialized staff. In larger firms, the general management tasks are essentially the same but more complicated, and key decisions are shared by a management team. Titles used to describe the individuals vary from company to company: chief executive officer (CEO); chief operating officer (COO); managing director; vice-president administration. In this chapter, the title general manager will refer to the individual or people who are primarily responsible for the business or a major unit of the business.

The general manager differs from a manager of one of the functional areas described in earlier chapters in that the general manager is responsible for integrating the functional areas. For example, in assessing a firm's capabilities, a general manager would need to take into account all functional areas, including financial resources, human resources, and operational capability. The general manager also needs to have a marketing perspective to assess customer needs. As companies move to drive accountability to lower levels in the organization, with profit centres that manage both revenues and costs, more and more managers need to shift from a functional perspective to a general management perspective.

One of the key mechanisms that general managers use to integrate and coordinate the functional areas is strategy. Strategy, whether an explicit plan or implied from a set of actions, represents the choices made about how scarce human, physical, and financial resources are applied in opportunities that enable and sustain high performance. We call these choices *strategic decisions*.

Regardless of where you sit in the organization, having a general management perspective is extremely valuable since it enables you to take decisions and actions that are consistent with the overall strategy of the organization. Perhaps more importantly, it enables you to contribute to strategy discussions given your unique perspective. For example, you may have valuable information about customers, competitors, or suppliers that helps the firm understand the competitive environment. Or you may have important input that can be used to assess resources and capabilities.

This chapter begins with a strategy model that provides an overview of the key elements the general manager needs to consider when making strategic decisions. Each area of the strategy model is then discussed, starting with the identification of what a firm needs to do, followed by an assessment of what it can do, and concluding with an assessment of what managers want to do. Types of strategic choices are then presented. Building on Part 3, "An Introduction to Financial Management," a section on valuation is presented to assist you in the financial analysis associated with acquiring a firm. Part 7 concludes with an overview of a strategic decision-making process.

STRATEGY MODEL

SECTION

ONE

Strategic choices require identifying and resolving the tension between what a firm *needs* to do, given the competitive environment; what it *can* do, given its organization, resources, and capabilities; and what management *wants* to do, given management preferences, as shown in Figure 1. There is often no perfect fit between what a firm needs to do, what it wants to do, and what it can do. Through strategic analysis, the degree of stretch or tension between the elements is identified, and once the strategy is put in place, action plans need to address how to close any gaps. For example, many firms overextend their financial or human resources to go after new market opportunities — what they need and want to do may exceed their capacity to deliver on it. In this case, the stretch created by the strategy needs to be resolved through action plans to develop the resources.

The strategic tension can perhaps best be understood by applying it at a personal level. Every person faces the same kind of tension. Take career choice as an example. The job market may suggest that particular types of jobs are in abundance and quite lucrative. Those jobs will require a certain set of skills and abilities. It may be quite clear what you need to do, but it may not fit with what you can, or want to do. Many of you have pursued education as a means to enhance

FIGURE 1
Strategic
Management
Tension

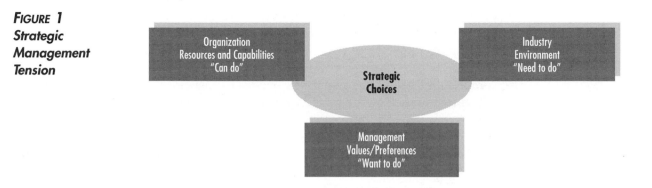

what it is you can do. However, the reality in career choice, as in strategic choice, is that identifying what you need to do, want to do, and can do is not easy. A key challenge is carrying out the analysis to assess each area before making the ultimate decision on how to resolve the tension. As you try to assess career opportunities and what you need to do to achieve them, you are trying to enhance your skills and capabilities around what you can do, while also trying to figure out what it is that you really want to do. It is complex for individuals, and even more complex for organizations.

SECTION

TWO

INDUSTRY ANALYSIS: ASSESSING WHAT YOU NEED TO DO

Assessing what a firm needs to do requires analyzing the industry in which the firm operates to answer three key questions: What are the key threats and opportunities? What are the key success factors in the industry? and, Is the industry attractive for future investment? Threats and opportunities are specific areas of analysis that stand out as having significant implications for the company. Key success factors are the aspects of the industry analysis that surface as the most important and critical elements that affect company performance. Industry attractiveness, as will be described later, relates to the overall profitability of the industry.

The early warning signs for threats and opportunities in the industry come from the political, economic, social, and technological forces in the industry, called PEST factors. These broad factors have a direct or indirect impact on the key players in the industry — suppliers to the industry, competitors in the industry, and customer demand.

PEST ANALYSIS

Political, economic, social, and technological forces can create fundamental industry change, such as the introduction of robotics to the automotive industry, the introduction of microchip processing, the deregulation of the airline industry, or the opening up of Eastern Europe to world markets. Such uncontrollable changes create and destroy major industries and market dominance quickly by offering new opportunities and/or imposing severe constraints. As well, many companies compete in international markets, making strategic analysis more complex because of the numerous business practices and cultural differences. When defining or revising strategy, general managers must identify the threats and opportunities from this PEST analysis and the implications for the decisions they face.

The political factors relate largely to the regulatory environment, and there are often implications for all elements of the system from the supply of products, to the nature of competition, through to the overall customer demand for products or services. For example, the Surgeon General's warning about cigarettes and the restrictions on their advertising have had a dramatic effect on sales of cigarettes in Canada and the United States. In Europe and many developing countries that do not have the same political intervention, sales of cigarettes are booming. Changes in regulation generally take time, and managers need to be aware of pending legislation and be proactive in dealing with regulations that will affect their business.

Economic forces include broad economic trends that affect demand, such as recessions or robust economic times. Managers also need to take into account such factors as interest and exchange rates, which may have significant implications for their business. For example, many companies have found themselves in a difficult financial position when conducting business with foreign countries whose currency has devalued rapidly.

Social trends relate to broad societal preferences and values that shift over time. For example, the trend toward fitness developed over many years. One of the major drivers of social trends is demographics. Demand for primary or secondary schools can be determined well in advance through birthrate data. In contrast, the death care industry has increased significantly in recent years owing to an aging population and the inevitable need for funeral services.

Technological factors have had a profound effect on industries as evidenced by the Internet and electronic commerce. However, it is important to note that technology is neither developed nor adopted overnight. Managers need to be aware of and track technological developments to understand the implications for their business.

It is helpful to examine each of the PEST factors to assess their implications — whether they will affect the industry, and if so, how, as shown in Figure 2. In addressing how they will have an impact on the industry, it is useful to examine how the factor may affect supply, competitors, or customer demand. A factor may affect all three in different ways. For example, in the death care industry, the aging of the population has increased demand for funeral services, although there are also social trends that have increased the demand for cremation relative to the traditional burial service. Competition has shifted significantly in the industry, with

Figure 2
Industry
Analysis
Framework

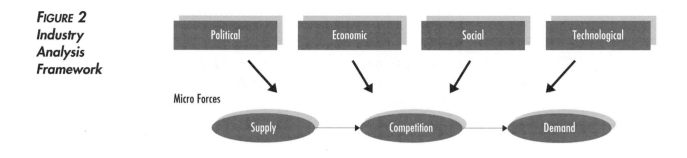

funeral home consolidators buying up independent funeral homes to achieve economies of scale in running funeral homes in geographic clusters. As the industry has consolidated, suppliers to the industry, including casket makers, have found their margins being squeezed given the pressure to lower prices. As a result, some have bypassed the funeral home and are attempting to sell directly to the end customer.

CUSTOMER DEMAND

Part 5, "An Introduction to Marketing Management," described the importance of segmentation and how to conduct a consumer analysis. Consumer analysis provides critical information for the marketing strategy with respect to product features, pricing, distribution, and advertising, for example. The consumer analysis can also be used to inform the overall strategy. Consumer analysis can help to determine industry attractiveness through detailing the nature of customer demand. Industries with high growth, strong demand, and few substitute products are more attractive. The consumer analysis can also help to assess threats and opportunities, such as the cost of an investment in equipment for a product known to have a very short life cycle because of rapid technological advancements. Finally, the consumer analysis will help to identify the key success factors (quality, speed of delivery, price, and sales and support services) involved in improving the firm's competitive stance to gain consumer acceptance and to make a profit. The key success factor in door-to-door cosmetic marketing, for example, is a very large, highly motivated sales force, and the key success factor in a basic commodity industry that is price competitive, such as sugar, is being a low cost producer.

THE COMPETITION

Part 5 also discussed the importance of understanding the strengths and weaknesses of competitors. This analysis of the current competition's existing and potential strengths and weaknesses will point to threats and opportunities, such as the following:

- A gap or niche for a product or service in the marketplace, perhaps as a result of a major competitor announcing a change in strategy, may become evident. This opportunity may match specific company skills, be easy to introduce, and involve little risk of inducing a competitive reaction.

- Competitive trends developing in terms of pricing, marketing, technology, number, and sophistication of competitors may surface.

- A back-up plan may be needed to help differentiate the company's product or service from its competitors. This is a direct attempt at minimizing the impact of competitive reactions.

- Producing a standardized product at low cost for price-sensitive consumers may be shown to provide the company with a competitive edge.

- The company's current marketing plan may need to be modified as a result of additional information gained from an analysis of the competition. Increased competition from foreign companies may lead a firm to market its product differently. A more specific example of this occurred in the Swiss watch industry:

> When confronted with inexpensive Japanese quartz technology, it was impossible for Swiss companies to compete with the new technology, and some businesses were driven to the brink of collapse. But the industry managed to look at its product as a fashion item rather than merely a high-precision timekeeper. This new outlook revolutionized the industry and the Swatch was born.[1]

With a sensitivity to these points the general manager should be able to thwart threats and seize potential opportunities.

SUPPLIERS

Part 5 described distribution channels. Wherever a company sits in the distribution channel, it will have suppliers and customers. Although farmers sell to food processing companies who are their customers, they also have suppliers from whom they buy seed, fertilizer, and equipment to grow and harvest crops. Even professional service firms, such as law, accounting, and consulting firms, need to consider the supply of human resources with the required expertise or the supply of other services, such as technology and graphic design.

The general manager needs to assess how PEST factors will influence supply of product or services to identify any risks or opportunities. For example, Mars Incorporated anticipated low prices on cocoa and increased the size of its chocolate bars as a preemptive move to gain market share. The whole supply chain can be altered as companies find new ways to get product to market, and the impact of changes in the supply chain can be significant. Many hardware companies have found it difficult to compete on price with Home Depot, whose strategy is to buy direct from manufacturers, cutting out the distributor. However, such strategic decisions also have significant impact on the resources and capabilities of the firms involved. For example, suppliers to Home Depot need to add capability in distribution, while Home Depot itself needs the capability to deal directly with the manufacturer.

INDUSTRY ATTRACTIVENESS, THREATS AND OPPORTUNITIES, AND KSFs

At the beginning of Section Two, three questions were posed. Assessing industry attractiveness is important because the profitability of many businesses depends more on the industry than on the firm's competitive position within the industry. Some industries generate higher profits than others, and it is necessary to understand how attractive an industry is for future investment. The assessment of threats and opportunities helps to focus the industry analysis on the critical areas, while the assessment of key success factors provides a point of comparison for subsequent analysis that will address the firm's resources and capabilities to deliver on the key success factors.

Assessing industry attractiveness requires examining the full business system from supplier to customer to understand the dynamics of the industry. Michael Porter, a well-known professor of strategic management, suggests that industry attractiveness depends on the power of suppliers, the power of buyers or consumers, whether there are other products or services that can act as substitutes, the degree of competitive rivalry in the industry, and whether new competitors can enter. The pharmaceutical industry is presented as an attractive industry, since there is little power on the part of suppliers or buyers. On the supply side the raw materials are widely available commodities. Buyers often are unable to differentiate between drugs, and in the case of prescription drugs, the physician makes the choice. Often there are no substitute products, particularly where a patent exists. The competitive rivalry in the pharmaceutical industry is not destructive to the companies in the industry because there is little price competition. Barriers to entry for new competitors are extremely high, given the cost of research to develop and test new drugs. The industry lost some of its attractiveness, however, with the advent of generic drugs.

The assessment of threats and opportunities and key success factors draws together all of the elements of the industry analysis to highlight the most important points. For example, after examining PEST factors and their impact on supply, competition, and demand, a manager might realize that the key threat for a particular company is one of a substitute product that will affect demand, or there could be significant regulatory changes that may impact competition. In addition to identifying threats and opportunities, it is important to summarize the key success factors in order to assess whether the company can deliver on them. Key success factors define what it is that a company needs to do to be successful in the industry. In contrast, threats and opportunities focus on key elements that will affect the company either negatively or positively.

COMPANY ANALYSIS: ASSESSING WHAT YOU CAN DO

A general manager must assess the various activities of the firm and evaluate the strengths and weaknesses in each functional area. This assessment will address how well the firm has performed in the past, assess how well competitors are performing, and estimate potential performance in light of the firm's resources, capabilities, and objectives. It is important to determine why performance in each aspect of the firm was as good as it was and why it was not better. If there was less than satisfactory performance, was it the result of incorrect strategy, poor execution, or a mixture of both? Each of the functional sections described earlier in the text was designed to enable the general manager to complete this analysis. For example:

1. In *finance,* an analysis of past and projected financial performance was undertaken, and sources and types of additional funds were discussed. This analysis will point to the company's financial flexibility and to the financial feasibility of implementing a new or existing strategic plan.

2. In *marketing,* understanding and predicting the response of consumers and competitors to changes in a company's product offering were studied. Companies now have the technical know-how to quickly react to their competition's offerings through slight variations of the product, improved product quality, and the sourcing of lower manufacturing costs resulting in a selling price advantage; consequently, they can quickly introduce these products to the consumer. These accelerated competitive reactions can effectively shorten the life cycle of products or eliminate a product's life. Therefore, the *sustainability* of the company's products or services in the marketplace is more tenuous than ever.

3. In *production/operations management,* the various processes a company may use to produce goods and services and the techniques to improve its production efficiency and effectiveness were examined. For example, how will a new strategy affect current capacity levels? What process changes will be required? Should the company switch from a continuous flow operation to a job shop operation?

    Technological improvements will continue to have a direct impact on how a company operates; most auto parts inventories no longer exist in the auto industry since the introduction of JIT computer capabilities; consequently, the manufacturing plant's scheduling has been adapted to this delivery system. Improvements such as the value added by research and development will affect the product's quality, the quantity produced, the cost of production, the design, and the delivery of the goods to the consumer.

4. In *human resources,* ways to understand individuals, groups, and organizations in order to accomplish tasks through the efforts of other people and ways to anticipate employee reaction were reviewed in addition to leadership styles. The existing skills/expertise of employees and the appropriate align-

ment, or "fit," of individual values and goals with the organization's goals and objectives was also reviewed.

Regardless of the assessment of the industry that defines what a firm "needs" to do, the general manager needs to provide an overall assessment of company capabilities to determine what "can" be done. If there are gaps between what needs to be done and what the company can do, it is necessary to assess whether the gap can be closed. For example, can obtaining a bank loan close a financial gap? Can a gap in operations be remedied? If there is a gap in human resources, can people be hired or developed to close the gap?

MANAGEMENT PREFERENCES: ASSESSING WHAT YOU WANT TO DO

Although it is challenging to resolve the tension between what a firm needs to do and what it can do, the situation is made more complex by adding the human element of motivation and aspiration, which captures what people want to do. At the simplest level, this analysis tries to take into account management preferences in making strategic decisions, because if management is not behind the strategy, it will go nowhere.

However, understanding management preferences is somewhat more complex. In entrepreneurial firms, management preferences may be the driving force behind strategy. There are many examples of entrepreneurs whose management preferences have had a profound impact on the company, including Henry Ford, Steve Jobs in the early stages of Apple Computer, and Bill Gates at Microsoft. In more mature, often larger organizations, where ownership of the company and management of the company are separate, many would argue that management preferences should not matter — management is hired to work on behalf of shareholders. The reality, however, is that people give their best only when they are motivated and inspired to do so. Therefore, strategic decisions that fail to take into account management preferences will likely suffer greatly on implementation.

Although management preferences need to be taken into account, the strategy is not dictated by what managers want to do. As in the case of the capabilities discussion, if there is a gap between what managers need to do and what they want to do, the general manager will need to assess whether there is a way to close the gap. Perhaps managers oppose a new strategic direction because they fear for their jobs. The general manager needs to identify ways to address concerns in order to close the gap.

Often, there is no single stated management preference. A major problem is that different people want different things. The strategic analysis needs to recognize the diversity of preferences and deal with them. The models of motivation and leadership presented in Part 4, "An Introduction to Managing People in Organizations," will assist you in understanding and reconciling differences in management preferences.

Management preferences need to be taken into account at the outset of the strategic analysis as you consider the role you are adopting as the decision maker in the case. What are your goals? How do they fit with the goals of others in the organization? Is it clear what you want to do? Although you may be considering several options, you may favour one over another in the absence of any analysis on what you need to do or what you can do.

Strategic Choices

The previous sections reviewed the analysis of each element of the strategy model. However, general managers may need to carry out this analysis in the context of the strategic choices facing the firm. While there are many types of strategic choices, we will review several common types in this section.

Choice of Products and Markets

Part 5 initiated discussion on product/market scope. A way to think about the choice of products and markets is to array the two against each other, as shown in the matrix in Figure 3.

1. *Market penetration.* The general manager improves the efficiency and effectiveness of resources devoted to the marketing and the production/operations for current products in order to increase the market penetration in current markets and to increase profitability. Marketing efforts will try to create increased demand for the product or service based on either tangible characteristics, such as differentiating technical features and financing, or intangible qualities, such as a prestige image. If a company is marketing milk and wants to convince current customers to use more of the company's product or to use it more frequently (market penetration), marketers might try an overall strategy of suggesting more occasions when milk drinking is appropriate or find new uses for milk, such as in cooking.

   It should be noted that the basis on which differentiation may be pursued and its success varies with the product's life cycle. Early in the life cycle it is easy to differentiate a product based on its unique features and, perhaps, based on patents, copyrights, or brand preference. But:

   > In the latter stages of the life cycle, it becomes more difficult to differentiate products in any sustainable way, so many companies focus on reinforcing an established position and using it as the base-point for incremental activities as competitive advantages are usually based on price and cost. Consider, for example, Coca-Cola's brand extensions into Diet Coke and Caffeine-Free Coke. Without a basic advantage of the long established product to build on, the new initiatives would be relatively meaningless, since they would be easy to copy on a purely technical basis. Thus, short of breakthroughs in product development, late cycle competition turns on price and cost.[2]

FIGURE 3
Strategic Choice:
Product/Market
Scope

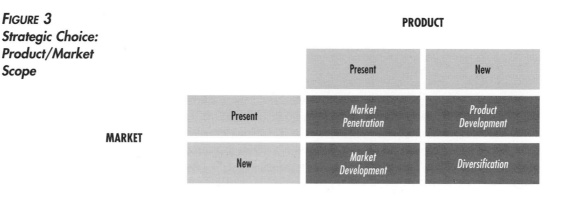

Source: H.I. Ansoff, *The New Corporate Strategy* (New York: John Wiley & Sons, 1987), Chapter 6.

2. *New market development.* A classic strategic decision firms face is whether to expand into new geographic markets. Applying the strategic tension model, the general manager needs to assess the competitive environment of the new geographic market to assess whether it is receptive to the current product. The general manager also needs to assess whether the firm has the capabilities and resources to enter the new market. For example, when Mark's Work Wearhouse was looking to enter the U.S. market, management underestimated the challenge of securing the supply of product they needed at the price point they needed to sell it. The competitive environment in the United States was different from that in Canada. Applying existing products to new markets also refers to seeking new market segments, as Cow Brand Baking Soda did with its line of deodorizing products for carpets and refrigerators.

3. *New product development.* The general manager proposes the development of new products to serve existing markets. For example, a large toy company, highly successful and well known for manufacturing safe and durable toys, introduced a new product line including baby strollers, playpens, and cribs. This line's products had many "child-proof" and "child-friendly" features not currently offered by its competitors, guaranteed the same standards of safety and durability as the toy line, and were researched and developed with the toy firm's existing knowledge of children's behaviour and children's and parents' needs. Prior to the introduction of this new line, large furniture companies distributing through major retail chains dominated the market. These same retail chains also carried the toy firm's toy products line. The toy firm's management team had identified a group of consumers who were in need of a product that offered more features and was "user-friendly."

4. *Diversification.* The general manager proposes the development of new products for new markets. Adding new but related products or services is referred to as *related diversification.* Wal-Mart's introduction of hypermarket stores, which combined supermarket and general merchandise at discount prices under one roof, is an example of related diversification. Adding new, unrelated products or services is referred to as *unrelated diversification.*

Reasons for unrelated diversification may include saturation of current products in existing markets, antitrust legislation, or an attractive investment opportunity.[3] A major automotive corporation purchasing a large mortgage insurance company is an example of unrelated diversification. The boundary between related and unrelated diversification is often quite fuzzy, particularly as firms have broadened the umbrella under which they operate to suggest that they are a "transportation company" or a "communications company," for example. The critical issue in related diversification is whether the company leverages a core competence or capability into new business opportunities, as Disney has done in leveraging its collection of characters into theme parks, movies, retail outlets, and hotels.

VERTICAL AND HORIZONTAL INTEGRATION

In addition to product/market choices, firms need to decide how much of the development and delivery of a product or service they do themselves versus buying or selling from others. This often involves a choice in the degree of integration.

Vertical integration can be either forward, which is closer to the final customer by developing or acquiring distribution outlets or retailers, or backward, which is closer to supply sources by developing or acquiring the firm's suppliers of materials or parts. Most major oil companies are totally vertically integrated, being involved in several stages of the industry supply chain. These companies explore for oil, extract it, refine it into gas and other products, warehouse, distribute, advertise, and market these products to consumers.[4]

Companies choose to forward or backward integrate to gain control over a particular part of the business system. Control may ensure a source of supply in the case of backward integration or a guaranteed customer in the case of forward integration. Vertical integration can also provide control over product quality and delivery, and it may even provide some cost advantages.

Integrating horizontally — buying ownership in or increased control over competitors — is often used as a growth strategy. Horizontal integration may provide some economies of scale if companies are able to share resources. Economies of scale arise when a company is able to lower its overall unit costs (economies) as it increases its size (scale). For example, when Nestlé acquired Rowntree they were able to consolidate the distribution network so that the cost of the joint distribution network was less than the cost of the two independent networks. In addition to potential cost savings, horizontal integration may also restore profitability to an industry as competitors no longer fight for market share. Air Canada and Canadian Airlines, for example, spent years arguing that there was not enough room in the industry for two domestic competitors, and in December 1999 finally merged.

MERGERS AND ACQUISITIONS

Sometimes, firms will diversify through *acquisitions,* when a large firm purchases a smaller firm or vice versa, or *mergers,* when two firms of comparable size combine into one firm. When appropriate, the acquisition of needed knowledge and expertise, new products or services, or new markets can provide a firm with rapid growth to gain a competitive edge in the marketplace. Acquisitions or mergers can take several forms: joint ventures, alliances, hostile takeovers, and buyouts. Most acquisitions or mergers are the result of a need to "round out" a product line or to diversify, leading to less dependence and, therefore, less risk on a single business or industry. Firms may also acquire other firms or merge in an effort to stabilize earnings. For example, Labatt Breweries acquired a significant stake in the Mexican brewery Femsa. This investment was intended to capitalize on market opportunities in Mexico, the United States, and Canada, thereby reducing Labatt's overall dependence on the domestic market.

It is important to note that the choices of products and markets, vertical integration, and mergers and acquisitions are not mutually exclusive. For example, a firm could enter new markets by acquiring a firm. Vertical integration is likely to occur through a merger or acquisition, although a company could achieve vertical integration by starting an entirely new operation from scratch. In the case of mergers and acquisitions, general managers need to estimate the company's economic value to assess whether the alternative makes financial sense.

SECTION

SIX

VALUATION

Three common methods of valuation are described below. As will be discussed, the methods are not mutually exclusive, and all three are often performed.

NET BOOK VALUE

Net book value is the difference between the total assets and total liabilities. This method does not account for the prevailing market value of the firm's assets or for any intangible assets, such as brand recognition, not captured in goodwill or superior human resources. Net book value is calculated using the most recent balance sheet.

ECONOMIC APPRAISAL

Economic appraisal is similar to net book value since it focuses on the value of the assets on the current balance sheet. It differs from the net book value in that it uses the current economic value, rather than the value listed on the accounting books.

For example, land may appear on the books at its original cost of $105,000. A real estate company may determine through an appraisal, however, that the market value of the land at the time of appraisal is $245,000. Appraisals may be based on replacement value or liquidation value. Consider a machine for filling bottles. To buy a new one to perform the same function may cost $100,000, but if the current machine were sold, especially if buyers knew the company was anxious to be rid of it, only $40,000 might be received. In other words, the economic value placed on a firm's assets depends largely on the reason for valuation and the circumstances of the firm. Assets are nearly always worth more if the firm is considered an ongoing business than if it is about to be liquidated. To arrive at the economic value of the firm, liabilities are deducted from the sum of the asset appraisals.

CAPITALIZATION OF EARNINGS

Capitalization of earnings differs from net book value and economic appraisal in that it focuses on the income statement instead of the balance sheet. This method of valuation is used when the buyer is interested in the cash flow or earnings generated by the business. In practice, this is a complicated and sophisticated calculation. We will simplify it here to provide you with a general sense of how it is calculated and why it may differ significantly from the other methods.

In its basic form, capitalization of earnings takes the projected net income after tax and uses a multiple (referred to as the price earnings multiple) to arrive at the overall value for the firm. Projected earnings are calculated as described in Part 2, "An Introduction to Financial Statements." You will need to look at the projected earnings using a "no change" scenario and the projected earnings given changes. This is particularly important because the projected earnings under the current management/owners with a no change scenario could be either higher or lower than under a projected scenario incorporating changes. For example, if there is a fear that the buyer may be unable to retain the current customer base, the business may be worth more to the seller than to the buyer. The reverse may occur as well. New management may be able to improve operations, and hence the business may be worth more to the buyer than to the seller. There may be large discrepancies between the two firms that need to be understood in order to assess the viability of the acquisition. In addition, an understanding of the differences is critical to the negotiation process.

The calculation of the multiple is more complex in practice than we will present here. In some respects, you can think of the multiple as the number of years it will take to pay back the investment. A multiple of 10 would suggest a 10-year payback. There is a wide range of multiples, from lows of 1 to highs of over 50. The multiple is affected by two primary factors: growth increases the multiple, whereas risk decreases it. In the case of growth, a high multiple reflects the fact that the earnings used to project the overall value will likely be understated if the company is undergoing dramatic growth. For example, the value of a firm whose earnings are going to double every year is significantly higher than one whose earnings are fairly stagnant. Similarly, if a firm is in a risky industry or is in a risky position within the industry, the multiple will be lower, since there is no guarantee of a continuous earnings stream — the firm could be out of business in two years. In practice, analysts often refer to multiples used in other acquisitions as *benchmarks*. For companies in mature industries, with fairly stable earnings, multiples generally range from 5 to 15. For companies in high growth industries, such as software, multiples often exceed 20.

The following demonstrates the calculations of the three valuation methods. Since you do not need to calculate a projected balance sheet to calculate the net book value or economic value, Exhibit 1 provides the current balance sheet for the LMN Retail Company, as shown in Part 2. Exhibit 2 presents the projected income statement for the LMN Retail Company (also provided in Part 2). We will use them to demonstrate the three methods of valuation.

Exhibit 1

LMN Retail Company Ltd.
Balance Sheet
as at January 31, 2000
(in 000s of Dollars)

Assets		Liabilities	
Current assets:		Current liabilities:	
Cash	$ 15	Accounts payable	$178
Net accounts receivable	200	Notes payable—bank	108
Inventory	450	Taxes payable	12
Total current assets	$665	Accrued expenses	20
Fixed assets, net (including $50 land)	80	Total current liabilities	$318
Total assets	$745	Long-term liabilities	25
		Total liabilities	$343
		Equity	
		Common stock	$ 37
		Retained earnings	365
		Total equity	$402
		TOTAL LIABILITIES AND EQUITY	$745

Net Book Value Method

$$\text{Net Book Value} = \text{Total Assets} - \text{Total Liabilities}$$

$$= 745{,}000 - \$343{,}000$$

$$= \$402{,}000$$

Economic Value Method

ASSETS		Appraisal	LIABILITIES		Appraisal
Current assets:			Current liabilities		
Cash	$ 15	$ 15	Accounts payable	$178	$178
Net accounts receivable	200	(80%) 60	Notes payable–bank	108	108
Inventory	450	(75%) 338	Taxes payable	12	12
Total current assets	$665	$513	Accured expenses	20	20
			Total current liabilities	$318	$318
Fixed assets, net		(land triple)	Long-term liabilities		
(including $50 land)	80	180	Total liabilities	25	25
Total Assets	$745	$693		$343	$343

$$\text{Economic Value} = \text{Total Assets (appraised)} - \text{Total Liabilities}$$

$$= \$693{,}000 - \$343{,}000$$

$$= \$350{,}000$$

Even though the land was valued at triple the current value on the books, the realized value of the accounts receivable and inventory reduced the overall value of the firm from the $402,000 net book value. This is only one example of how assets might be appraised. If this business were purchased as an ongoing operation, the accounts receivable and inventory might be valued at 100 percent. You need to use your judgment in understanding the circumstances of the case to determine what the realized or economic value of the assets would likely be. In most instances, the value of the liabilities will not change.

Exhibit **2**

LMN Retail Company Ltd.
Current and Project Income Statements
for the Years Ending January 31, 2000, and 2001
(in 000s of Dollars)

Item	Estimate for Projection	Current	Projected
Sales	20% growth from 2000[1]	$2,715	$3,258
Cost of goods sold	77.5% of sales[2]	2,105	2,525
Gross profit	22.5% of sales	$ 610	$ 733
Less operating expenses	G&A 8.7%, selling 10%, depreciation same as in 1996[1]	555	644
Net operating expenses		$ 55	$ 89
Less other expenses		8	10
Net income before tax	.3 % of sales[1]	$ 47	$ 79
Tax	25 % of net profit before tax[3]	12	20
Net earnings		$ 35	$ 59

1. *Manager's estimate.*
2. *Last year's best estimate.*
3. *Supplied by accountant.*

Capitalization of Earnings Method

(In the following example a multiple of 10 is used for illustrative purposes.)

   a. No Change Scenario

   Capitalization of Earnings   = Net Earnings x Multiple
                                = $35,000 x 10 = $350,000

   b. With Changes

   Capitalization of Earnings   = Net Earnings x Multiple
                                = $59,000 x 10 = $590,000

Different Results Using Different Methods

It is important to note that each of the methods is likely to generate different results, as shown in the following example:

Net Book value	$402,000
Economic appraisal	$350,000
Capitalization of earnings	
No change scenario	$350,000
With changes	$590,000

Banks, creditors, and buyers who may be interested in selling the assets of a business will be more interested in the valuation derived from the balance sheet methods. And most buyers intending to acquire a company solely for its assets would be more interested in the economic appraisal than the net book value, since they want to know what they could realize for the assets at the time of sale.

Buyers who are interested in the ongoing value of the firm will be interested in the income statement method looking at the capitalization of earnings. As can be seen in the example above, if the growth objectives of the projected income statement are achieved, the firm is worth $590,000, almost $200,000 more than the value of the assets. It is not uncommon to see that the earnings generated from the ongoing business exceed the value of the assets, particularly in knowledge intensive industries where there are few physical assets.

Overall, valuation is an important part of the financial analysis toolkit. General managers are often faced with decisions to buy and sell companies. Even an entrepreneur could face this kind of decision. Understanding the economics of the decision is a critical aspect of the analysis. Earlier, we referred to Labatt's acquisition of equity in the Mexican brewery Femsa. The qualitative analysis supporting that decision was excellent. The industry analysis suggested that it was a good idea, providing a great fit with Labatt's capabilities and resources. However, the decision became far more difficult when examining the economics of the decision and the value of the Femsa brewery. Both the qualitative and quantitative analysis need to be taken into account when making strategic decisions.

STRATEGIC DECISION-MAKING PROCESS

SECTION

SEVEN

Although there is no framework that can capture the complexity and judgment required in the strategic decision-making process, the following captures the broad areas of analysis.

As stated in Section Four, you should begin your analysis by identifying your role in the case, the issue or decision you are facing, and your own preferences or goals. Often, decision makers identify some constraints or concerns that could be listed at the outset but that will likely be addressed in the subsequent analysis, whether they have been explicitly stated or not. For example, the decision maker may question whether they have the financial resources to carry out the course of action or whether a loan might be required. Assessing financial capability and resources would need to be addressed in the assessment of capabilities, whether or not the decision makers state it as a consideration.

After assessing what you want to do, the analysis can proceed to address what you need to do, as described in Section Two, and what you can do, given your capabilities and resources. You then need to apply the analysis to address the alternatives. When analyzing strategic choices, all of the analysis needs to be integrated. The alternatives can often be framed around the type of strategic choice. Regardless of the type of strategic decision, it will most certainly involve a recognition and reconciliation of the tension arising from your previous assessment on the "need," "can," and "want" front. As you assess the alternatives, you need to draw this analysis together to discuss the pros and cons of each option. For example, you may need to decide whether to expand into new markets or penetrate the existing market. You may have a strong management preference for growth and expansion; however, the resources of the company may be quite constrained. Ultimately, you will need to decide how constrained resources are, whether or not you can close the gap, and how important market expansion is to the firm.

As you generate, evaluate, and rank, strategic alternatives, you must be aware of the skills and resources required to implement each of these strategies within the appropriate and necessary time frame. There will likely be differences in the degree of risk associated with each of these alternatives and differences in the expected payoffs to the company; these differences are what make strategy formulation difficult and interesting. A solid and thorough analysis of the strategic alternatives will enable you to formulate an action plan relatively easily because the action plan should practically "drop out" of the analysis. Action plans need to address *what* the key priorities/actions are, *who* will be responsible for them, *how* they will be achieved, and *when* they will be achieved.

This action plan must be consistent with the firm's corporate goals and objectives. It is the general manager's job to ensure that the functional areas, such as finance, marketing, production/operations, and human resources, fit together into an integrated whole to provide structure and processes, constituting the overall corporate strategic action plan.

In summary, one useful way to assess an idea for change is to compare the projected results of that change with the projected results without that change — in other words, to project the firm's performance first under a no change scenario and then compare that with the change scenarios. Another good test is to try to persuade a skeptical person that the plan of action makes sense. As a general manager, you should be able to explain both *what to do* and *why it is worth doing*.

SUMMARY

General managers should systematically formulate, implement, and evaluate the strategic direction of the firm. It is essential that the general manager review the firm's strategies, which can become obsolete. This process entails identifying and reconciling the tension between what a firm needs to do, wants to do, and can do. All strategic plans should include the monitoring of results. Measuring individual and organizational performance requires the utilization of solid accounting functions and reliable reporting systems, such as financial statements, market share reports, and ROI calculations, which must be in place to evaluate the plan's relative success and to aid in the analysis and corrective action of issues or problems.

A thorough and complete strategic analysis and implementation plan may not be sufficient; many strategists believe that companies must also be able to anticipate change and to be proactive, as well as to react quickly and decisively to the marketplace. Therefore, general managers need, through the organization's structure, its employees, and its management's leadership, to improve the organization's speed and flexibility; that is, for the firm to have strategic competence it must be nimble and more adaptive to changes in strategy. This process of continuous reevaluation drives the firm's management team to regularly reappraise the firm's current strategy in light of industry and corporate change.

NOTES

1. Kathryn Dorrell, "Comedy Shows Companies How to Improvise," *Western News*, 20 January 1994, 12.
2   Joseph N. Fry and J. Peter Killing, *Strategic Analysis and Action* (Scarborough, Ont.: Prentice Hall, 1985), 131.
3. Fred R. David, *Strategic Management*, 2nd ed. (Columbus, Ohio: Merrill Publishing Company, 1989), 69.
4. Jeffrey S. Harrison and Caron H. St. John, *Strategic Management of Organizations and Stakeholders: Theory and Cases* (Minneapolis, Minn.: West Publishing Company, 1994), 123.

■ ■ ■ **CASES FOR PART 7** ■ ■ ■

CASE 7.1 Blackshop Bistro

■

CASE 7.2 The Body Shop Canada

■

CASE 7.3 Braddock Manufacturing Maquiladora

■

CASE 7.4 English Center for Newcomers

■

CASE 7.5 The Greek Cosmobob

■

CASE 7.6 Inn at the Falls

■

CASE 7.7 Mail-Order in Canada

■

CASE 7.8 Mondetta Everywear

■

CASE 7.9 Rampac Distributors

■

CASE 7.10 Silk Route Oriental Rugs Ltd.

■

CASE 7.11 SWO Service

C A S E 7.1   BLACKSHOP BISTRO

By John Haywood-Farmer, Lisa Luinenburg, and Kirsten Fear

In November 1991, Alec Cerny was discussing a business opportunity with his father, Jan, who owned Blackshop Bistro in Cambridge, Ontario. The current facility offered little opportunity for sales growth. Jan proposed to relocate and expand their family business into a small business development nearby. Alec knew that such a move would have significant implications for the company's current strategy as well as for operations, marketing, finances, and human resources.

Alec realized that a restaurant on the scale proposed would allow him to stay in the family business and use some of his newly acquired skills if he wanted to. On the other hand, if Blackshop Bistro did not expand, there would be no position open for him. He wanted to make a decision and be able to present his father with a solid action plan as soon as possible. The developer needed an answer in the next two weeks. Alec knew that if he decided not to proceed, his father would ask him for some realistic options.

CAMBRIDGE, ONTARIO

Cambridge, Ontario, was about 100 km southwest of Toronto, adjacent to Kitchener. Highway 401, a multilane divided highway that served as the major traffic artery through southern Ontario, ran through the northern part of Cambridge. About 575,000 people lived within 40 km of Cambridge. Exhibit 1 shows maps of the area. The Kitchener-Waterloo and Cambridge area was a major Ontario industrial centre and home to many manufacturing and service firms. It boasted a large multicultural pool of skilled and semiskilled labour, particularly those of German, Italian, and Portuguese descent.

The population of the Kitchener, Waterloo, and Cambridge communities was growing at about twice the growth rate for Canada as a whole.[1] Its per capita income and retail sales figures were about 8 percent above and 2 percent below the respective Canadian averages. The average household in the area had 2.8 people and spent about $1,665 per year on restaurant meals.[2]

BLACKSHOP BISTRO

After working for three years at restaurants in London and Cambridge, Jan Cerny acquired financing and in 1983 opened Blackshop Restaurant in a 100-year-old house that he had renovated. He hoped to provide his family with a stable business for the future. The theme of the restaurant was that of an old blacksmith shop, hence the company's name. Jan chose dark decor to augment this theme and used antiques to create a sense of history. The restaurant always played recorded classical music to create an atmosphere of intimacy. The menu featured a combination of ethnic Czechoslovakian cuisine and dishes that Jan had seen served in Canadian restaurants in which he had worked, and included seafood, beef, and chicken dishes. The concept proved to be very attractive to Cambridge residents. The restaurant enjoyed a busy first year with sales of just over $175,000. Jan hired an additional waiter and a dishwasher to make operations run more smoothly.

However, the concept eventually lost its lustre. Czechoslovakian food was greasy and heavy, characteristics that conflicted with the 1980s trend toward healthy and sensible meals. As a result, revenues levelled off. In response, the Cernys removed the Czechoslovakian food from the menu in 1986. Except for this change, the menu remained largely intact.

In 1988, revenues levelled off again for no apparent reason. Jan raised prices only to see revenues drop. After consulting his staff, he realized that the menu needed to be more North American. He hired a new chef and introduced new, lighter menu items to reflect French and Italian influences in main courses, appetizers, desserts, and beverages; consequently, business improved again.

The Christmas period in 1988 was slow, and in 1989 revenues again began to stagnate. In response, they renovated the facility internally by raising the lighting level, removing the metal decor, painting the interior in bright colours, using peach-coloured table cloths, and enlivening the atmosphere by introducing recorded jazz as background music. A new name, Blackshop Bistro, as well as a lighter menu reflecting Australian and Californian influences, accompanied these changes. Despite these changes, the Cernys were able to retain the facility's family atmosphere and consistently high quality food and service. Jan believed that this reputation was key to his business's success. Once again, sales returned to their former levels.

Current Operations

Blackshop Bistro was truly a family-run operation. Jan, who acted as the waiter, oversaw all operations. His wife, Eva, a dietician, did all the bookkeeping and helped out the chef, who had emigrated from Czechoslovakia in 1989. Their younger son, John, was a certified chef and was considering entering the University of Guelph's hotel and food administration program. Both sons helped out on evenings and weekends.

Alec believed that the cuisine at Blackshop Bistro was top quality and priced at a premium. In late 1991, the average price for a full-course meal was $15 per person at lunch and $40 per person at dinner. He commented:

> We are by no means a cheap meal out. Our reputation is for excellent but expensive food. Middle-class customers consider us to be a restaurant suitable for special occasions. Only well-off people become regular clients. This

really reduces the size of our market. Customers won't just walk in for a light meal or a cocktail. They would feel intimidated.

Although change had been slow in Blackshop Bistro's early history, more recently the Cernys had adjusted their lunch and dinner menus every six to eight months to reflect changing customer demands and to offer variety to their very loyal clientele. Jan was proud of his efforts to consult his customers. He believed that this effort proved essential in recognizing problems early. Alec explained:

You have to keep changing in this business. This encompasses many aspects, including decor, menus, specials, music. You don't want to run the risk of your customers getting bored. If they don't enjoy the product, you can be sure that they'll tell two friends, and so on.

Blackshop Bistro, which relied heavily on word-of-mouth advertising and did little additional marketing, soon developed a strong base of loyal customers. At least 40 regular customers frequented the restaurant on a weekly or biweekly basis. The economy was booming and Blackshop Bistro was successful. Exhibit 2 shows some financial information.

Providing good service was the priority among Blackshop Bistro's staff of one chef, two waiters, and two dishwashers. They emphasized friendliness and efficiency, rather than pretentiousness. Jan hired only expert staff. The waiters and dishwashers received minimum wage — standard practice in the restaurant industry. The restaurant paid the chef an average wage. However, because the chef had limited ability in English and had no Canadian certification papers, Alec realized that his alternative opportunities were limited. Jan believed that customers appreciated the familiarity of having the same person servicing them time after time, and thus, that high turnover caused poor service and inconsistent quality.

The main business district in the Galt section of Cambridge lay east of the Grand River between Park Hill Road and Warnock Street, on the right-hand side of the map shown in Exhibit 3. Blackshop Bistro was on Ainslie Street on the northern edge of this district in a one-floor house of about 71.5 square metres, for which the Cernys paid an annual lease of $204.50 (1991) per square metre. The original lease specified annual rent increases of 10 percent; the Cernys expected further increases at the same rate. The building was at the back of the lot behind a real estate office. Ainslie Street was one way (north) and had a corner just south of the restaurant. The recessed location of the restaurant and the characteristics of Ainslie Street made the restaurant difficult to see. The lot had about 12 parking spaces available for Blackshop use, some of which were used by employees. Parking was not allowed on either Ainslie Street or Park Hill Road. There was a major grocery store immediately across Ainslie Street from the restaurant; it had complained to the Cernys about restaurant staff and patrons using its parking lot.

The restaurant had 32 seats. It was open for lunch from 11:30 a.m. until 2:00 p.m., Tuesday to Friday, and for dinner from 5:00 p.m. until 9:30 p.m., Tuesday to Saturday. The average table of two to four people took one hour for lunch and two to two and a half hours for dinner. Blackshop Bistro remained open until the last customer left, even if it was after 9:30 p.m. Although customers did not require reservations for either lunch or dinner, the restaurant recommended that customers have them. Lately, seats had often been heavily booked two weeks in advance for Friday and Saturday nights; consequently, the necessity of reservations on weekends ensured profitable business but deterred walk-in customers. Because the restaurant was small, the tables were too close together for business people to conduct business. The restaurant was not available for parties of more than 10. Blackshop Bistro was unable to meet the demand for this service, which was significant, especially around Christmas.

Dinner Ordering Process

The process was typical of full-service restaurants. When customers arrived, a staff member greeted them at the door, hung up their coats, escorted them to a table, and seated them. The waiter brought them menus and bread, described the daily specials, and took their drink orders. While the customers decided what food to order, the waiter filled the drink orders. This process usually took around 10 minutes. Most customers ordered appetizers as well as a main meal. The waiter took the appetizer orders to the kitchen, where the chef spent between five and eight minutes preparing them. The waiter took the appetizers to the customers' table, where they were consumed usually in 10 to 12 minutes. The waiter then returned to the kitchen and said "pick-up," which signalled the cooks to begin preparing the main meal. Following the preparation time of seven to 10 minutes, the meals were served and consumed in about 15 minutes. After clearing these dishes the waiter offered customers coffee and dessert. When the customers had finished their meal, the waiter brought the bill, which the customers paid at the table. The process was similar at lunch but faster.

THE RESTAURANT MARKET

Alec believed that Blackshop Bistro was a fine-dining restaurant whose customers wanted top quality food and service, in a relaxed environment. Although most of their clientele were business and affluent people in the Cambridge area, the Cernys knew that some customers came from Kitchener-Waterloo, Guelph, Brantford, and other communities within 40 kilometres of Cambridge.

The Restaurant and Food Association identified five industry segments, based on differences in price and quality:

Table 1: Industry Segments

Segment	Quality	Price	Portion of Restaurant Spending[3]
Fine	High	High	3%
Casual	Medium-high	Medium	15%
Family-style	Medium	Low-medium	13%
Fast food	Low-medium	Low	55%
Convenience	Low	Low	14%

THE COMPETITION

Alec discussed Blackshop Bistro's competitors:

> We have three main competitors in the fine-dining segment. Two of them are right near us (see Exhibit 3); the other one is farther away. Scallions has about 40 seats and is very similar to us. Two Italian brothers operate it. They are great chefs and take pride in knowing their customers, but they seem to lack business sense. Their home-made food is good and their prices are similar to ours. However, I think their service is inconsistent and they don't pay enough attention to their surroundings. It seems to look dirty.

> The Cambridge Mill is our most expensive competitor. Its average cheque is about $25 per person for lunch and $45 per person for dinner, but the quality of the food is inconsistent. It has 75 seats and a private room for 150 and offers its customers a beautiful view overlooking the Grand River. Jan was offered the Mill when it was in receivership in 1990. When we looked at the figures, we found that rent, including the parking lot, was running at $10,000 per month. We would have needed annual sales of $1.5 million just to survive.

> Twelve years ago Graystones was the best and the only classy restaurant in Cambridge. However, it didn't move with the times and now has a reputation for being old fashioned, stuffy, and expensive. It has about 50 seats but no banquet facilities. Although it has brought its prices down to about the same level as ours, it can't seem to shake its reputation. Graystones is located at the far end of the main street through the Preston section of Cambridge, some five kilometres northwest of here near the Speed River, not far south of the 401.

> Another nearby competitor is Café 13, but it is in the casual dining segment. It has great atmosphere and fair prices. An average dinner cheque is about $20 per person. Its owner is a very good businessman who promotes his business heavily. It is the only restaurant in town with some class to which you can go just to have a drink. Although I don't think its food is very good, it is edible — there are no surprises. I think it is Cambridge's most successful restaurant.

THE PROPOSAL

Recently, Jan had felt less motivated to continue Blackshop Bistro's current operations. He also wanted higher profits to prepare for an early retirement. Because of these factors and the high demand for Blackshop Bistro's service, Jan hoped to expand the company's operations. The current lease agreement was due to expire in October 1993. The landlord would not agree to Blackshop Bistro's expanding the current facility; consequently, Jan began looking for other opportunities.

In November 1991, John Lammer, a developer from the neighbouring city of Guelph, approached Jan. John was erecting a 1,100-square-metre, two-floor building on Hobson Street at the corner of Park Hill Road. John Lammer's design called for an elegant natural stone building in a style similar to the historic 150-

year-old buildings common in the area. He wanted a prosperous restaurant in the building and strongly believed that Jan would be a success. The project was due for completion in April 1992, just five months away.

The location was about 400 m across the Grand River (via the Park Hill Road bridge) from Blackshop Bistro. It was on the edge of a residential area about a 15-minute walk from the centre of Cambridge's main business district. Although the building would abut the Grand River, views of the river and the dam at that site would be restricted to the building's upper floors. Hobson Street was scheduled to become a main thoroughfare connecting Cambridge with Kitchener-Waterloo.

The new restaurant could occupy up to 315 square metres, which would accommodate a lounge with 20 seats, a bar with 10 stools, a dining room with 65 seats, and a banquet room with 80 to 100 seats. The new lease would cost $162 per square metre annually. In Jan's opinion, the leasehold improvements, shown in Exhibit 4, would be generous. The restaurant would also have the first right of refusal on the entire second floor until December 1992. Property and business taxes would be about $25,000 per year, a significant increase from the current level of about $1,500. Alec estimated that the annual costs of the proposed expansion would include food and beverages, 33 percent of sales; labour, 30 percent to 35 percent; interest, $13,500; depreciation on new equipment, $23,300; all other operating costs (except rent, property taxes, and advertising), $55,000.

The building would have 40 parking spots that Blackshop Bistro could use. In addition, customers would have access to a free, city-owned, 120-parking-spot lot just across Hobson Street. The building would allow the Bistro to broaden its service offerings. It could have a banquet room suitable for Christmas parties, wedding receptions, and other group functions. The front lounge and bar could have a fireplace and serve as a pleasant area for customers waiting for a table in the dining room. The lounge would also allow Blackshop Bistro to offer a menu with lighter meals for customers who did not want a full-course meal.

Because of the option offered, the building also allowed ample potential growth. Alec believed that expanding to the second floor could offer advantages such as a river view and an opportunity to add a conference room and a banquet room should demand exist.

Shafiq Rao, one of Blackshop Restaurants waiters, on the other hand, believed such a location would prove to be troublesome:

> My experience working at the Cambridge Mill has opened my eyes to second-floor locations. Turnover of tables is slower, as people spend more time watching the river, especially if it is flowing slowly or if people are fishing or something. The river sets the pace of the whole meal!

THE DECISION   Alec didn't have much time to decide what to do and to report to his father. Because Blackshop Bistro's reputation and its strong base of loyal customers were valuable, he did not want to damage either of these elements. Alec also wanted to preserve the company's family-oriented service concept and worried about the implications of trying to implement it on a larger scale. He expressed his views:

I am concerned about a lot of things. I am not sure that our current market niche is large enough for this possible expansion. The ethnic groups in this community traditionally don't eat out often. We might have to go after another target in the future. I wonder if there is one. We should be helped out by local trends. Lots of restaurants are leaving downtown Kitchener. Their move north to Waterloo makes Cambridge more attractive to people coming from the south end of Kitchener or off Highway 401.

At Western I took a course in service management. The professor described service concepts as the core of what service is all about — the answer to the question, What business are we in? He elaborated by saying that you had to think carefully about the marketing mix — product, place, price, and promotion — and, particularly for services, how the process would work, what characteristics the servers and customers should have, and what the place would look like. He believed that a good concept was one that had a consistent marketing mix and was aimed at meeting the needs of an identified target market. It makes sense. Now I have to figure out what our concept should be.

If we did go after another group, what changes would be necessary to our current concept so it would appeal to a larger market? And what effect would those changes have on our current clients?

If I decide to support the proposal, I will need a thorough plan of action. What operational, staffing, and marketing concerns will I have to consider? I guess we should start by looking at our name. Should it remain Blackshop Bistro? Or should it go back to a restaurant? Perhaps we should change the Blackshop name too.

If a chain opened a restaurant of the calibre we are thinking about, it would probably spend $350,000 on start-up costs. I think if we did a lot of the work ourselves, we could probably cut that figure in half. But that is still a lot of money. Where and how can the family get access to such a sum? My father could probably invest up to $10,000 personally, but no one in the family could come up with much more.

If we were to offer banquet room services, what factors would we have to consider? It seems to me that anyone could make money from banquet facilities in peak periods such as Christmas. The secret is to do well in the slack periods too. What would be required to make it fly?

I also think about the second floor. It would offer a nice view. The ground floor has no view at all. On the other hand, as Shafiq says, a view could screw up our process. If we don't take the second floor and want it later, there is no way it will be available. If we take both floors, we will have a lot of tables to sell and I am not sure we could afford it. And the second floor is only one timing issue. Our current lease doesn't run out until October 1993. What should we do about that?

The last thing I want to do is to ruin a good thing and destroy the business my father and the rest of us have worked so hard to establish. We have a nice "family" atmosphere here that certainly includes all our staff and extends to our regular customers as well. I am not sure it will be easy to maintain that if we grow. Growth might reduce quality too, although if we had two chefs instead of one we would be able to extend our hours. What do I have to do to ensure the success of the potential venture? I am involved in the restaurant now and I don't want to work on Bay Street, but I am not sure I or my brother, John, wants to make a career out of being a restaurateur. I could usually do a decent job on the cases we analyzed at university, but now the dollars are real and the stakes are personally high. I wonder what I should do.

Alec had two weeks to assess the opportunities that the developer was offering his family's business and to determine Blackshop's, and his own, future.

Notes

1. E.J. Graham, ed., *Canadian Markets* (Toronto: Financial Post Publications, 1991).
2. *Canada's Postal Markets 1990: A Source of Business and Consumer Demographics and Buying by FSA* (Toronto: Compusearch Market and Social Research Ltd. and Financial Post Information Service, 1990).
3. The Canadian Restaurant and Food Association and Crest Canada, 1990.

Exhibit 1
Maps of a
Portion of
Southern
Ontario

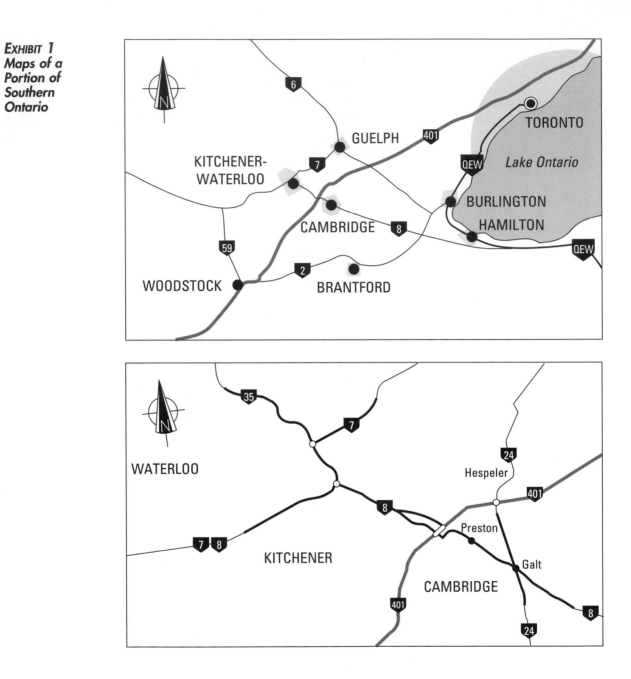

Exhibit 2

	Income Statements for the Years Ended January 31			
	1990		**1991**	
Sales	$262,814	100%	$265,674	100%
Cost of sales				
Purchases	96,902	36,9	99,434	37.4
Wages and benefits	96,758	36,8	101,354	38.2
TOTAL	$ 193,660	73.7	$200,788	75.6
Gross margin				
Operating expenses				
Rent	12,242	4,7	14,624	5.5
Advertising and promotion	3,188	1.2	2.957	1.1
Bank charges and interest	7,324	2.8	6,411	2.4
Depreciation and amortization	6,740	2.6	5,029	1.9
Utilities	4,710	1.8	5,487	2.1
Other expenses	24,174	9.2	26,641	10.0
Total[1]	$ 58,378	22.2	$ 61,149	23.0
New income before tax	10,776	4.1	3,737	1.4
Income taxes (recoverable)	851	0.3	(577)	(0.2)
Net income	$ 9,925	3.8	$ 4,314	1.6
Deficit (beginning)	$ 31,577		$ 21,652	
Deficit (ending)	$ 21,652		$ 17,338	

Exhibit 2 (cont.)

	Balance Sheet as of January 31	
	1990	1991
ASSETS		
Current assets:		
Cash	$ 0	$ 2,292
Inventories	10.000	11,000
Income taxes recoverable	0	577
Prepaid expenses	1,717	1,0334
Total[1]	$11,717	$14,903
Fixed assets:		
Equipment	30,075	30,525
Leasehold improvements	25,251	25,251
Vehicle	16,000	16,000
Total	$ 71326	$71,776
Less: accumulated depreciation and amortization	51,164	56,193
Total	$20,162	$15,583
Total Assets	$31,879	$30,486
LIABILITIES		
Current		
Bank overdraft	$ 981	$ 0
Bank loan	2,000	0
Accounts payable	11,186	16,857
Income taxes payable	851	0
Current portion of long-term debt	14,125	15,724
Total	$29,143	$32,581
Noncurrent portion of long-term debt	11,151	12,726
Due to shareholders	13,227	2,507
Shareholders' deficit		
State capital[2]	10	10
Deficit	21,652	17,338
Total	$21,642	$17,328
TOTAL LIABILITIES AND SHAREHOLDERS' DEFICIT	$31,879	$30,486

1. Some totals may not add exactly due to rounding.
2. Authorized and issued: 100 common shares without par value.

Source: Company files.

**EXHIBIT 3
Map of
Downtown
Cambridge
(GALT)**

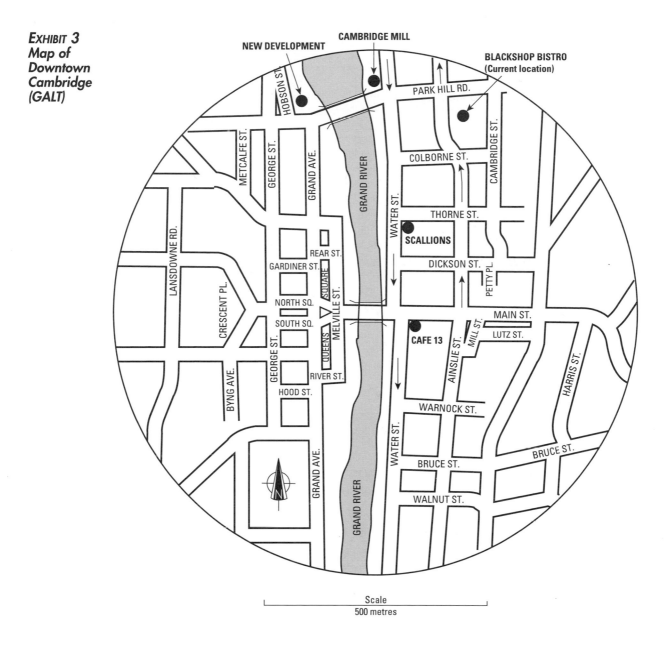

Exhibit **4**

Summary of Leasing Proposal for 20 Hobson Street
Commercial Complex Ground Floor Restaurant Space

SPACE INFORMATION:

- total leased area is 315 square metres
- rent is $162 per square metre net-net[1] or $4,250 per month
- taxes are anticipated to be approximately $32 per square metre
- all common area expenses are included

LEASEHOLD IMPROVEMENTS INCLUDED:

- complete heating and air-conditioning system
- kitchen exhaust fan and make-up air system
- all ceramic flooring in kitchen and bathrooms
- complete bar with refrigeration
- complete gas-burning fireplace
- all electrical rough-ins and basic wiring
- an electrical service sufficient to accommodate the kitchen equipment and fixtures
- plumbing for all washrooms, including fixtures
- all engineering and architectural fees related to the interior design, seating and lighting plan, and kitchen layout
- all partition walls, doors, hardware, and locks
- fluorescent lighting for kitchen and bathrooms
- prime-coat-finished drywall walls and ceilings

LEASEHOLD COSTS:

- all light fixtures except as above
- walk-in cooler
- stainless steel hood and CO_2 system
- tables and chairs, including booths and flower planters
- carpet for dining areas and flooring for all storage, office, and staff rooms
- the balance of the decorating and interior improvements

---

1. Net-net means that all common area costs, such as snow removal and outside work, are included in the rent.

Source: Company files.

CASE 7.2   THE BODY SHOP CANADA

By John Haywood-Farmer and B. Seligman

"You're not the kind of fanchise applicant we usually get," said Harry Robertson, company lawyer for the Body Shop Canada, as he opened his meeting with potential franchisee Richard Paul. "I suppose we'll find out whether that's an advantage or disadvantage," replied Mr. Paul. Mr. Robertson's comment had taken Mr. Paul by surprise, and though he was pleased with his response, the comment had produced a sinking feeling in the pit of his stomach.

RICHARD PAUL

Mr. Paul, age 36, was about to graduate from the M.B.A. program at the University of Western Ontario. His employment background included a stint as a high-school business education teacher and seven years of retail management. He had managed independent stores and also had managed for one of Canada's national department store chains.

He had investigated a number of job possibilities, but he had received no offers and was still unclear about the direction he wished to follow. His strengths appeared to lie in the marketing and human resources area. He had little interest in joining a major retail company: "I've been on that treadmill before," he said. He felt that whatever his eventual career choice would be, he wanted to do "something that will make some difference to me and to others." The idea of working for himself was appealing: "At least I'd be sweating to put money in my own pocket."

While perusing the job advertisements in *The Globe and Mail*, Canada's "national newspaper," he came across one placed by the Body Shop Canada. The notice stated that the company had a number of operating stores available for franchise, including locations in City A and City B. Mr. Paul was aware of the company's enormous international success and was surprised to discover that franchises might be available. Furthermore, he had never known the Body Shop Canada to advertise for franchisees.

THE BODY SHOP

The Body Shop was the brain-child of Anita Roddick, a forward-thinking Briton with a strong commitment to an ideal.[1] The company offered conventional consumer products with a twist: it sold only naturally based products and disdained

---

its competitors' exaggerated product claims. In fact, it did no advertising at all. The company positioned itself as a champion of social responsibility and activism. It promoted holistic health, environmental responsibility, charitable acts, Third World development, women's issues, and other causes. It generated considerable publicity for itself by these means.

In the 14 years since its founding, one little store had grown into a chain of over 450 stores located in 37 countries worldwide. In Canada there were 72 shops — 56 franchised and 16 corporate owned.

The Body Shop Canada stores, averaging about 100 square metres, were in prime retail locations, either on main shopping arteries or in malls. Stores sold only proprietary products, always at "list prices." There were no sales and there was no discounting. The line consisted of nearly 400 items that could be purchased at every store or ordered from stores through the mail. All stores were of similar appearance: they were decorated in identical colour schemes, with displays, fixtures, and even window displays standardized from store to store across the country. Customers tended to be loyal, even fanatical, in their support of the company. Once someone became a customer, he or she would probably not purchase a competitor's product again.

THE INITIAL CONTACT

Mr. Paul was well aware of the success record of franchise operations, and of this one in particular. In fact, he had just attended a conference where a major national retailer had spoken of the Body Shop Canada in glowing terms! However, he had never given serious consideration to purchasing a franchise. He thought that for someone with imagination and good business sense, a franchise would be far too restrictive. However, with a "what have I got to lose?" mentality, he wrote to the address listed in the advertisement and asked for more information. Within a week he received a reply, on recycled paper.

FRANCHISE INFORMATION

The package that arrived in the mail contained 35 pages of information about the company and its operations. The presentation seemed almost amateur, with much of the material obviously photocopied. Nonetheless, Mr. Paul took a night off from analyzing cases to study the documents. The material consisted of:

- Company background   8 pages
- Environmental issues   15 pages
- Information on the franchise agreement   3 pages
- Financial data   6 pages
- List of current franchisees   3 pages

The synopsis of the franchise agreement outlined the standard elements of a franchise agreement and included the following additional facts:

- The Body Shop Canada would lease the premise and sublet it to the franchisee;
- The franchisee must operate the business and be in the store at least 40 hours per week;

- The franchisee must purchase the complete product line;
- The franchisee must retain effective ownership and control;
- Any sale of the franchise to a new franchisee must be approved by the franchisor;
- The franchisor may terminate the franchise if the franchisee fails to operate within the law or fails to carry on business as prescribed by the franchise agreement; and
- No royalty fees would be paid except a monthly administration fee of $200, and a promotion and publicity fee of 2 percent of gross sales.

Costs to start a new franchise were estimated as:	
Franchise fee	$ 15,000
Fixtures	100,000–120,000
Design fee	5,000
Opening inventory	90,000–110,000
Legal fees	5,000
First and last month's rent	5,000–6,000
Training accommodation costs*	0–5,000
Site selection	6,000
Public relations**	0–3,000
Management aptitude tests***	900
Total	$226,900–$257,900

* Potential franchisees must attend a seven-week training program in Toronto at their own expense. At the end of the course they must pass an exam before being awarded a franchise.

** This fee would depend on whether the Body Shop had an existing store in the market.

*** The Body Shop Canada was phasing out its management aptitude test. At the time of this case the test was used only to choose between two applicants who were otherwise tied.

Mr. Paul estimated that he could come up with about $125,000 himself. He would have to finance the inventory and part of the fixtures through a bank loan. Given the excellent track record of the Body Shop Canada and his experience and qualifications, Mr. Paul believed he would have no trouble borrowing the necessary capital from a bank. Using the company's sales and operating projections, he created pro forma financial statements for the first two years. Exhibit 1 shows the statements.[2] Mr. Paul thought that the numbers looked promising and that it was worth devoting additional time, even at the expense of preparing cases, to find out more about the Body Shop Canada.

MR. PAUL'S PLAN

If buying a franchise for the Body Shop Canada made sense, then why not try to buy two? Mr. Paul's education and personality combined to make him ambitious.

He had examined the list of franchisees and realized that 13 of them had multiple stores. One couple owned five!

Mr. Paul reasoned that there would be economies of scale for a multi-store operation because some of the start-up costs and operating expenses would be no higher than for a single store operation. Would he have enough capital? Would he be able to secure competent management to operate on a broader scale? Both problems seemed resolved after discussions with two close friends.

His two friends, both women, were tremendously enthusiastic about the possibility of becoming involved with the Body Shop Canada. Both said they would quit their current jobs at a moment's notice and would want to purchase a minority equity position, probably 10 to 15 percent of the store they managed. Mr. Paul was certain the two women would be ideal managers and business partners. Their equity holdings would provide him with additional capital and them with a strong incentive to work hard. If worse came to worst, he would be in a strong position to buy them out in the future.

Mr. Paul thought that the best organizational structure would be to create a holding company with him as a sole owner, and for the company to enter into separate partnership agreements with each of the women. Each partnership would hold one store. He revised his pro forma statements (see Exhibit 2).

Mr. Paul was thrilled with the projected results. He believed that he had used a conservative set of assumptions and that even under these conditions he could expect to eliminate all debt within three years. Even if there were zero sales growth after the second year he could expect after-tax earnings in the area of $150,000. That night he completed the formal application for a franchise and began to dream....

THE OPTION OF BUYING EXISTING FRANCHISES

In the course of his investigations, Mr. Paul had been able to discover more about the two existing locations available for franchise. The store located in City A was already a franchise operation. The current owner had been experiencing personal problems and was keen to sell the business. The store was small, only 40 square metres, but was favourably located in the best mall in the city. Many people described the location as the only good retail location in the city. A friend who lived in City A expressed some small concern that the store had not always been well managed, sometimes appearing to be poorly staffed and inadequately stocked.

The City B store was corporately owned and was being offered as part of a plan by the parent company to divest itself of all corporate stores (except for some in Vancouver and Toronto). It was one of three outlets in City B and was located in one of the newest malls in an area surrounded by upscale housing and extensive development. A major university was less than five km away, and plans were under way to expand the mall by some 70 stores within two years. The Body Shop Canada had recently been moved to a better location within the mall and almost doubled in size to about 80 square metres.

Mr. Paul felt certain that sales in these stores would be well above the levels projected for start-up operations, but he had no way to determine by how much. The locations really interested him. He owned a house in City B and he would be happy to stay. One of his two potential partners also lived there, and the other had recently moved to City A, near the United States border. The Body Shop's Canadian operation had the right to expand into the virgin territory of several United States border states, including the one nearest to City A. Growth prospects seemed unlimited! It appeared to be a perfect fit. The only question was how much of a premium the ongoing operations would command.

About 10 days after completing the franchise application, Mr. Paul received a phone call from the Body Shop Canada inviting him to go to Toronto for a meeting with Harry Robertson. Mr. Paul felt he had already passed a major hurdle because the franchise application had required extensive personal and financial information. If the company wanted to meet him, he must be an acceptable candidate. On a beautiful spring day he pulled into the parking lot of the Body Shop Canada head office, full of excitement at the prospect of what was about to unfold.

THE MEETING

Mr. Robertson described the typical Body Shop Canada franchisee: "female 35 to 45, married with school age/adolescent children, limited formal education, and crazy about the Body Shop. Anyway, none of our franchisees have M.B.A. degrees!" Mr. Paul realized he had a fight on his hands. "It seems to me you have a view of what M.B.A.s are like, that they're all fanatical, hard-nosed, money-hungry tyrants," said Mr. Paul. "I don't think that's fair, any more than it would be fair to say that all lawyers are alike."

This comment seemed to break some of the ice. But if the relationship between the two men had begun to thaw, the discussion that ensued and the information that surfaced over the next hour did nothing to cheer Mr. Paul. His plan had obviously been a pipe-dream.

Mr. Robertson was adamant on a number of points. The Body Shop Canada would not grant multiple franchises to a new franchisee; the company first wanted franchisees to demonstrate their potential to handle more than one outlet. The franchisee must personally work in the store full time. Although many Body Shop Canada franchises were held by partnerships, the company was cautious; it was particularly wary of nonoperating financial partners. If the company did acquiesce, it would want absolute discretion over the content of the agreement. "We want operators, not investors."

Mr. Paul pressed for information about the City A and City B stores. The news on these fronts was no better. Goodwill charges would be about $125,000 for City A and $250,000 for City B! Expected sales for the two stores for 1990 were $600,000 and $750,000, respectively. Apparently, volume at the City B had increased 66 percent since its relocation. City A sales were up 33 percent over the previous year.

The meeting ended on an amicable note, with Mr. Paul promising to let Mr. Robertson know within two weeks whether he was interested in proceeding. If the answer was yes, Mr. Robertson would consider whether to place Mr. Paul on a shortlist of candidates. The shortlist would be subjected to a 12-hour battery of interviews and then placed in a store for a week. After the trial, both parties would decide whether to commence training. The Body Shop Canada would not award the franchise until after training had been completed. However, even at this advanced stage, the franchisor could still reject the potential franchisee and leave him or her without recourse.

THE DECISION

When Mr. Paul returned home from Toronto his immediate instinct was to rush to his computer to create new pro forma statements, but before doing so he thought it would be helpful to note down his options and his concerns. See Exhibit 3 for his notes.

Mr. Paul knew he had a tough problem on his hands. He decided to produce pro forma statements along the lines of his first projections. He had fairly accurate percentage cost data that Mr. Roberston had provided for the existing stores. He wanted to compare performance for each of the existing operations to a start-up, assuming each was operated as a single entity by a sole proprietor. Exhibit 4 contains the statements.

Mr. Paul had some important questions to consider beyond the financial analysis. Could he see himself inside an 80-square-metre store for the next 10 years? Could Mr. Robertson be persuaded to compromise? After all, how many people could fit his ideal profile of someone with the right balance of spiritual devotion to the Body Shop Canada's philosophy, business acumen, and access to the required capital of around $250,000? Was there anything Mr. Paul had missed in his analysis? Somehow this was going to be a lot more difficult than doing a case. This was his life!

Notes

1. For a recent history of the Body Shop, see Ms Roddick's book *Body and Soul* (London: Ebury Press, 1991).
2. The company made no provision for profit sharing among nonmanagement level employees. Mr. Paul's decision to allocate 10 percent of store gross profit for this purpose was consistent with his business philosophy

Exhibit 1

Pro Forma for a Single Franchise					
Capital Costs	**Minimim**	**Maximum**		**Year 1**	**Year 2**
Franchise fee	$ 15,000	$ 15,000	Sales	$475,000	$617,500
Fixtures	100,000	120,000	Cost of goods sold	247,000	321,100
Design fee	5,000	5,000	GROSS PROFIT	$228,000	$296,400
Legal documentation	5,000	5,000			
Site selection	6,000	6,000	Rent	42,000	49,400
Management test[1]	900	900	Salaries	65,000	68,250
TOTAL	$131,900	$151,900	Common area	9,600	10,080
			Publicity and advertising	9,500	9,975
ONE-TIME COSTS			Insurance	1,200	1,260
			Business taxes	1,200	1,260
Public relations fee	0	3,000	Telephone	900	945
Last month's rent	2,500	3,500	Travel	1,500	1,575
Training costs	2,500	5,000	Service charge	2,400	2,520
Opening inventory[2]	60,000	60,000			
Legal and incorporation	2,000	2,000	OPERATING PROFIT	$ 94,700	$151,135
TOTAL	$ 67,000	$ 73,500			
			Profit share	9,470	15,114
CAPITAL REQUIRED	$198,900	$225,400	Debt charge	13,073	13,073
			Depreciation	22,000	17,600
EQUITY (Mr. Paul)	$125,000	$125,000			
			INCOME BEFORE TAX	$ 50,157	$105,348
LOAN	$ 73,900	$100,400	One-time costs	10,250	0
			Income tax	19,156	50,568
			NET PROFIT	$ 20,751	$ 54,780
			CASH FLOW	$ 42,751	$ 72,380

Assumptions:
Loan @ 15%
Income tax @ 48%
Inflation @ 5%
Sales growth @ 30%
Operator/Manager's base salary $24,000
No debt repayment

---

1. The Body Shop Canada was phasing out its management aptitude test. At the time of this case the test was used only to choose between two applicants who where otherwise tied.
2. $60,000 of the opening inventory had to be paid for COD; the balance and future shipments were Net 30.

Exhibit 2

			Pro Forma for Two Stores		
Capital Costs	**Minimim**	**Maximum**		**Year 1**	**Year 2**
Franchise fee	$ 30,000	$ 30,000	Sales	$950,000	$1,235,000
Fixtures	200,000	240,000	Cost of goods sold	494,000	642,200
Design fee	10,000	10,000	GROSS PROFIT	$456,000	$ 592,800
Legal documentation	5,000	5,000			
Site selection	12,000	12,000	Rent	84,000	98,800
Management test[1]	900	900	Salaries	130,000	136,500
TOTAL	$257,900	$297,900	Common area	19,200	20,160
			Publicity and advertising	19,000	19,950
ONE-TIME COSTS			Insurance	2,400	2,520
			Business taxes	2,400	2,520
Public relations fee	3,000	6,000	Telephone	1,800	1,890
Last month's rent	5,000	7,500	Travel	1,500	1,575
Training costs	5,000	10,000	Service charge	4,800	5,040
Opening inventory[2]	120,000	120,000			
Legal and incorporation	2,000	2,000	OPERATING PROFIT	$190,900	$ 303,845
TOTAL	$135,000	$145,000			
			Profit share	19,090	30,385
CAPITAL REQUIRED	$392,900	$442,900	Debt charge	37,935	0
			Depreciation	44,000	35,200
EQUITY (Mr. Paul)	$125,000	$125,000			
			INCOME BEFORE TAX	$ 89,875	$ 238,260
EQUITY (Partners)	$ 40,000	$ 40,000	One-time costs	20,000	0
			Income tax	33,540	114,365
LOAN	$227,900	$277,900	NET PROFIT	$ 36,335	$ 123,895
			CASH FLOW	$ 80,335	$ 159,095

Assumptions:
Loan @ 15%
Income tax @ 48%
Inflation @ 5%
Sales growth @ 30%
Operator/Manager's base salary $24,000
No debt repayment

1. The Body Shop Canada was phasing out its management aptitude test. At the time of this case the test was used only to choose between two applicants who where otherwise tied.
2. $60,000 of the opening inventory had to be paid for COD; the balance and future shipments were Net 30.

Exhibit 3

Options

1. Forget the whole thing.
2. Try to get a new franchise.
3. Buy City A.
4. Buy City B.
5. Try to find a way to buy both stores.

Concerns

1. Are either of the operating stores worth the asking price?
2. How hard would it be to get a bank loan to finance goodwill?
3. If I proceed, should I try a partnership or go it alone?
4. Roberston says when corporate stores become franchised sales increase at least 30 percent overnight. Is that realistic?
5. Robertson says City A should be moved within the mall if a bigger site becomes available. That would mean more sales but another $125,000 for new fixtures. Could I afford that?
6. If the Body Shop Canada proceeds with its plan to open four stores in the United States near City A this year, how will City A's sales be affected?
7. Do I need to consider the Canada–United States Free Trade Agreement in my projections?
8. If City B is up 66 percent so far this year, is it reasonable to expect that growth to continue over the whole year?
9. Would construction at City B hurt sales?

Exhibit 4

Pro Forma Statement for Existing Operations					
Capital Costs	**City A**	**City B**		**City A[1] Year 1**	**City B[1] Year 1**
Franchise fee	$ 15,000	$ 15,000	Sales	$600,000	$750,000
Fixtures	60,000	120,000	Cost of goods sold	312,000	390,000
Goodwill	125,000	250,000	GROSS PROFIT	$288,000	$360,000
Legal documentation	3,000	3,000			
Management test[2]	900	900	Rent	48,000	60,000
TOTAL	$203,900	$388,900	Salaries	90,000	112,500
			Publicity and advertising	12,000	15,000
ONE-TIME COSTS			Insurance	1,200	1,200
			Business taxes	1,200	1,200
Inventory[3]	90,000	90,000	Telephone	2,000	1,800
Last month's rent	4,067	5,083	Travel	1,800	1,500
Training costs	3,750	3,750	Service charge	2,400	2,400
Legal and incorporation	2,000	2,000			
TOTAL	$ 99,817	$100,833	OPERATING PROFIT	$129,400	$164,400
CAPITAL REQUIRED	$303,717	$489,733	Profit share	12,940	16,440
			Debt charge	26,807	54,710
AVAILABLE	$125,000	$125,000	Depreciation	12,000	24,000
LOAN	$178,717	$364,733	INCOME BEFORE TAX	$ 77,653	$ 69,250
			One-time costs	9,817	10,833
			Income tax	32,561	28,040
			NET PROFIT	$ 35,275	$ 30,377
			CASH FLOW	$ 47,275	$ 54,377

Assumptions:
Loan @ 15%
Income tax @ 48%
Inflation @ 5%
Sales growth @ 30%
Operator/Manager's base salary $24,000
No debt repayment

1. Based on current sales.
2. The Body Shop Canada was phasing out its management aptitude test. At the time of this case the test was used only to choose between two applicants who were otherwise tied.
3. The entire store inventory must be paid for up front.

EXHIBIT **4** (cont.)

	City A Year 2	City B Year 2	City A Year 2	City B Year 2	City A Year 2	City B Year 2
	Pessimistic	Pessimistic	Expected	Expected	Optimistic	Optimistic
Sales	600,000	750,000	690,000	862,500	798,000	997,500
C.O.G.S.	312,000	390,000	358,800	448,500	414,960	518,700
Gross profit	288,000	360,000	331,200	414,000	383,040	478,800
Rent	48,000	60,000	55,200	69,000	63,840	79,800
Salaries	90,000	112,500	90,000	112,500	90,000	112,500
Pub. and adv.	12,000	15,000	13,800	17,250	15,960	19,950
Insurance	1,200	1,200	1,200	1,200	1,200	1,200
Business taxes	1,200	1,200	1,200	1,200	1,200	1,200
Telephone	2,000	1,800	2,000	1,800	2,000	1,800
Travel	1,800	1,500	1,800	1,500	1,800	1,500
Service Charge	2,400	2,400	2,400	2,400	2,400	2,400
OP. PROFIT	129,400	164,400	163,600	207,150	204,640	258,450
Profit share	12,940	16,440	16,360	20,715	20,464	25,845
Debt charge	26,807	54,710	26,807	54,710	26,807	54,710
Depreciation	8,160	19,200	8,160	19,200	8,160	19,200
INC. BEF. TAX	81,493	74,050	112,273	112,525	149,209	158,695
One-time costs	0	0	0	0	0	0
Income tax	39,116	35,544	53,891	54,012	71,620	76,174
NET PROFIT	42,377	38,506	58,382	58,513	77,589	85,521
CASH FLOW	50,537	57,706	66,542	77,713	85,749	101,721

C A S E 7.3   BRADDOCK MANUFACTURING MAQUILADORA

By Paul W. Beamish and Joyce Miller

In August 1990, Douglas Procter, director of corporate purchasing for Braddock Manufacturing, had to make a recommendation about moving production to Mexico. Procter's boss, Michael Lane, had asked him to submit a report evaluating how and where to operate in Mexico. A consultant had already identified several labour intensive processes in Braddock's ground transportation business as good candidates for transfer. Procter knew that both Lane and Braddock's president had been looking for an opportunity to do something in Mexico, but the question was, Would the maquiladora option offer Braddock the kind of ongoing cost savings it needed to make more competitive contract bids?

COMPANY BACKGROUND

Braddock Manufacturing was part of the materials technology division of a holding company based in the northeastern United States with interests in chemicals, aluminum, packaging, and aerospace. Headquartered in Austin, Texas, Braddock employed over 1,300 people in three defence-related businesses, which generated annual revenues of about $234 million. Braddock prided itself on its state-of-the-art manufacturing and product engineering capabilities. It had pioneered the use of aluminum hybrids, ceramics, and composite metals to enhance the durability of military equipment. These materials met the tough performance requirements regarding weight, strength, and durability that were critical for defence applications. Only two of Braddock's competitors had similar design, materials, and production capabilities. These firms had manufacturing facilities only in the United States.

Braddock's three businesses operated in an extremely compartmentalized manner with little information shared between the units. This conservatism was as much a reflection of the company culture as a prerequisite for involvement in the defence business.

The U.S. defence industry constituted $300 billion of the $1.2 trillion annual U.S. budget. Since 1987, Congress had held the budget deficit at around $150 billion per year. With the Gramm-Rudman law calling for that figure to be lowered to $64 billion by 1991, there was pressure to reduce spending in all aspects of government. This force was felt especially in the area of defence, which resulted in a move away from the use of sole vendors to more competitive bidding for contracts to supply military parts. In fact, price was becoming the major selection criterion. While U.S.-based firms were the major suppliers, some foreign-produced goods were purchased by the U.S. military.

THE GROUND TRANSPORTATION BUSINESS

With increasing pressure on defence contractors, Braddock's management was looking critically at its ground transportation unit for ways to lower costs. The innovative use of composite metals, while meeting the military's need for high performance equipment, was expensive. The unit owned plants near Los Angeles and Phoenix and had recently acquired a 300-person company in Oregon with operations similar to the steering column component manufacturing in its California site.

The production of steering column components (SCCs) for military vehicles generated annual revenues of about $75 million. As a replacement item, there was continual demand for SCCs, in addition to orders generated by the annual procurement wave. The manufacture of SCCs required a heavy capital investment, although there were some labour intensive activities — mostly deburring (filing) — within the production process. By adhesively bonding thin, composite metal strips and filing and "sandwiching" the layers to fit a specific profile, the finished assembly combined strength and lightness with the capacity to withstand rugged, all-terrain travel. Manual filing did a better job than any machine technology currently available, and this process was critical to producing high quality components. Manual filing required great patience and precision and was done mostly by females. These workers earned an average of $10.05/hour and were entitled to 20 holiday/vacation days annually. They received about 25 hours of training, and even after a three-month probationary period, some of them had not mastered the task. The rejection rate averaged 10 percent monthly. Aside from the exacting performance standards, working with metals made this an unattractive job, and turnover had always been relatively high — up to 12 percent monthly. Michael Lane observed: "Such labour intensive tasks are excellent candidates for us to test the waters of offshore production, if we're serious about getting more competitive."

To stay competitive, many U.S. firms had transferred the labour intensive and assembly portions of their manufacturing to developing countries. In undertaking "production sharing," U.S. companies initially favoured the developing nations of East Asia, particularly Hong Kong, Singapore, South Korea, and Taiwan. Wages there were quite low, and for historical, cultural, and political reasons, the work ethic was relatively strong.

After evaluating the manufacturing sites in the ground transportation unit, a consultant had identified several labour intensive activities in the large California SCC manufacturing plant as appropriate to transfer. These deburring, shearing, and assembly tasks were one-off processes and involved 46 direct labourers. It was possible that some operations associated with the recent Oregon acquisition would also be suitable to move offshore.

Lane had done some regional analysis on the Pacific Rim and Caribbean Basin but was anxious to explore the Mexican option. Ever since Braddock's president, Ed Mason, had encouraged him to attend a June 1989 conference on manufacturing in Mexico, he had been looking for an opportunity to do something in this area. Lane had sent Procter to this year's conference in the hope that he would gain some insight into the maquiladora program. Upon his return, Lane had asked him to make a recommendation about moving production offshore. Procter commented:

> This assignment was quite a surprise. Coming from a purchasing background, I didn't have much experience with manufacturing. I knew our president was really interested in Mexico, and in fact, my boss had been sending me articles about the maquiladora industry for months, but I had no context for making sense of the stuff. Even though my fiancée is Mexican, I didn't know anything about doing business in Mexico. What stood out the most was the high labour turnover. We already had a turnover problem in the ground transportation business, and I really didn't see the benefit for Braddock to be in Mexico. The Asian countries, on the other hand, have a reputation for their production know-how and diligent workers.

THE PACIFIC RIM

Beginning in the late 1960s, electronics and apparel goods were increasingly being assembled in East Asian countries to take advantage of the average pay levels of less than $1/hour.[1] Western companies established subsidiaries, entered joint ventures, and subcontracted production to local firms. Technology was quickly absorbed and adapted. Local firms were soon supplying most of the components used in the plants. These assembly operations were well integrated into the national economy, and there were no restrictions limiting the sale of output into the home market. It did not take long for Taiwanese, South Korean, Hong Kong, and Singaporean firms to manufacture many of these products from start to finish. Thus, assembly activities were an important springboard for the industrialization of the "four tigers." By the mid-1980s, they were looked on as formidable global competitors. Fully fringed wage levels in low skill assembly operations averaged $2.44 to $2.72/hour (see Exhibit 1). On their own, assembly operations contributed less than 1 percent to foreign exchange earnings.

While the four tigers had seen production costs and general living standards increase, Thailand, Malaysia, Indonesia, and the Philippines still offered competitive labour rates for companies considering offshore production. In recent years, a considerable amount of investment had been made in electronic assembly facilities in Malaysia and Thailand. Such operations were typically managed by expatriates and staffed indigenously. The annual cost for an expatriate manager ran upwards of $300,000, which covered salary, rent, car, club memberships, home leave, sending any children to U.S. schools, and so forth.

The savings would be on the plant floor. Fully fringed wages for low skill jobs averaged $0.80 to $1.00/hour in these countries. Labour was plentiful. However, Procter was concerned about the general lack of proprietary protection for both product and process. He had heard several stories about how adept some local entrepreneurs were at copying technology, actually beating the original product to the market.

THE CARIBBEAN BASIN

The Caribbean Basin offered a source of cheap labour close to the U.S. market. Minimum wages ranged from approximately $3.00 a day in El Salvador, Guatemala, Haiti, Honduras, and Jamaica, up to 10 times that for more skilled workers in Bahamas and Barbados.

Owing to the efforts of investment promotion organizations, there was growing interest in establishing production-sharing activities throughout the Caribbean region. The proximity enabled U.S. companies to easily troubleshoot operations. Furthermore, favourable entry into the United States was provided under Item 9802.00.80 HTS of the U.S. Tariff Schedules. For articles assembled abroad from U.S.-made components that were imported into the United States, the duty was assessed based on the full value less the cost of the U.S.-fabricated components.

To qualify for exemption of duties under the generalized system of preferences program (GSP), 35 percent of the value of an article, in materials, the direct cost of processing, or both, had to be attributable to the beneficiary developing country. Direct costs of processing were those costs that were either directly incurred in, or could be reasonably allocated to, the growth, production, manufacture, or assembly of the specific merchandise under consideration. Direct costs of processing did not include administrative salaries, general expenses, brokerage charges, legal expenses, finance charges, janitorial service and office supplies, rent on the building space used for administrative offices, and shipping costs involved in moving the finished articles to the border.

The GSP program permitted duty-free entry of over 3,100 products into the United States from 140 beneficiary developing nations — including Mexico. The theory was that developing countries, because of their limited resources and infrastructure, often had difficulty competing in the U.S. market with similar products from developed countries. The intention was to encourage economic growth by stimulating their export sectors. However, certain categories of merchandise, such as textiles, footwear, and import sensitive electronic articles and glass products, were denied favourable GSP entry.

MEXICO

With the May 1990 announcement of informal free trade talks between Mexico and the United States, there was renewed interest in the nation as a strategic location for production. Mexico, officially the United Mexican States, was the world's

13th-largest country in area and shared a 3,200 km border with the United States, bordering on California, Arizona, New Mexico, and Texas. With an annual growth rate of about 2.5 percent, the population was almost 90 million in 1990. Unemployment ranged from 12 to 20 percent depending on the region. Mexico comprised 31 states and the Federal District of Mexico City, which, with 17 million inhabitants, was the nation's capital and a centre for commerce, government, and culture. Although Spanish was the official language, English was often used for international business.

The collapse of oil prices in the early 1980s had sent the Mexican economy reeling into recession. Since coming to power in 1988 for a six-year term, President Carlos Salinas de Gortari had abandoned the traditional development strategy of state ownership and import substitution in an effort to open up the Mexican economy. Educated at Harvard University, Salinas was a leader in the broader Latin American movement toward privatization, liberalized investment laws, tariff reductions, and export promotion. A renewed program of wage and price controls had brought soaring inflation down from 160 percent in 1987 to 20 percent in 1989, while slashing the buying power of Mexican citizens by 40 percent. The massive devaluation of the peso saw its value drop from about $0.04 to less than $0.004 by the end of the decade. As a result, Mexican wages fell from among the highest in the Third World to among the lowest in dollar terms. U.S. manufacturers flocked to the border to set up production-sharing facilities and take advantage of the maquiladora program. By 1990, over 1,800 maquiladora plants employing 500,000 people contributed $3 billion worth of added value to products destined for export. This represented 1 percent of the Mexican labour force, 2 percent of wages, and 10 percent of foreign exchange. The maquiladora industry was the economy's most dynamic sector and generated a level of foreign exchange second only to petroleum's $9 billion.

THE MAQUILADORA PROGRAM

The term *maquiladora* traces its origin to colonial Mexico. When the miller ground someone else's grain, the portion of the finished product he retained in return for his services was known as the *maquila*. The current use of the term maquiladora refers to a Mexican company that assembles, processes, manufactures, and/or repairs materials imported temporarily by others for eventual re-exportation.

The maquiladora program was initiated in 1965. After the 1964 termination of the U.S.–Mexican Bracero Program, which had brought workers to the southern United States to harvest crops, some means of dealing with the substantial increase in unemployment along Mexico's northern border were required. In addition to creating jobs, the Mexican government sought to attract investment, industry, and technology and to develop the northern frontier while not displacing other industrial activities.

Thus, the maquiladora industry was born of a new policy that allowed machinery, equipment, materials, and component parts to be imported duty free on an "in-bond" basis. The posting of a bond with the Mexican Customs Bureau guaranteed that products, once assembled or manufactured, were exported back to their country of origin or to a third country. Some U.S. firms established "twin plants," one on each side of the border, under one management. The U.S. plant handled the capital intensive operations and shipping and receiving, while the Mexican side performed the labour intensive processes. By 1990, 19 percent of maquiladora plants operated in nonborder locations.

Maquiladora manufacturing was a magnet to companies opening new markets or going to Mexico for the first time. Through the late 1980s, increasing numbers of companies had set up maquiladora operations in the face of competition from Asian-produced goods. Companies ranged from the very small to the Fortune 500. Although the maquiladora industry was dominated by U.S. firms, there was growing representation from companies based in Japan, South Korea, Taiwan, Hong Kong, Sweden, France, and Canada. The location placed these firms next door to their largest market. Moreover, they could exploit the favourable U.S. tariff provisions (Item 9802.00.80 HTS) and gain the advantages of Mexico's abundant labour force and low cost power. The costs of electricity and potable water were 40 to 50 percent cheaper than in the United States. Upon entry into Mexico, no duty was paid on U.S.-made components shipped in-bond that were assembled or manufactured in maquiladora operations and subsequently sent back to the United States for final assembly, processing, or distribution. When these products entered the United States, the duty paid was based on the value added in Mexico (labour, overhead, and profit) and was generally on the order of 5 percent or less. Because the Mexican government treated foreign-owned maquiladoras as cost centres, the parent company determined the profit margin and could easily repatriate profits from Mexico, provided certain minimum tax levels were met.

Maquiladoras handled a variety of tasks, ranging from producing toys and sporting goods, to sorting retail coupons, to assembling sophisticated medical equipment. Electric/electronic goods represented the most important activity. Typically, a maquiladora plant imported virtually all of its materials, machinery, and components from the United States, and the United States was nearly always the final market destination for the finished maquila product. The value added in maquiladoras was low, averaging 25 percent of the total production costs. All but a fraction of production costs consisted of wages and overhead. Only 2 percent of raw materials were sourced in Mexico because of the difficulty in finding local suppliers able to meet international prices, quality standards, and delivery schedules. As a result, assembly operations were not well integrated into the national economy, and the industry remained an essentially foreign enclave with more ties to the United States than to the Mexican interior. In fact, some Mexican capitalists saw maquiladoras as demeaning, a "taking in of foreigners' dirty laundry." They found it more profitable to produce for the highly protected domestic market, or alternatively, to devote their efforts to the development of high value-added exportable products.

With a fully fringed labour rate of $1.20 to $1.40/hour, Mexico was edging out traditional offshore manufacturing countries such as South Korea and Taiwan. Procter knew that one of Braddock's other business units already operated a large maquiladora in Acuna in the state of Coahuila. After a visit, he concluded that its electronic assembly activities were far different from a metals operation and more information would have to be obtained from an outside source. As a result, Procter retained a consultant, John Shackley, to evaluate a move to Mexico.

THE CONSULTANT'S REPORT

As a maquiladora consultant, Shackley conducted feasibility studies for operating in Mexico, researched location and site selection, and appraised Mexican subcontractors and shelter operators. He submitted his report in early August based on transferring the deburring, shearing, and assembly activities identified in the ground transportation business. The 46 direct labourers this move affected would be absorbed into other Braddock operations or terminated with a severance package. Shackley determined that a 1,800-square-metre facility would be adequate and still accommodate an increase of at least 50 percent in future head count. Several benches, wood or steel tables, and some holding fixtures were all the equipment that would be required. He commented:

> These activities were labour intensive, had documented descriptions of the method, sequence, and dimensions, and would qualify for favorable 9802 treatment. The California site had a significant problem with turnover in this area because working with metals was a dirty job. With proper training, young Mexican women would likely perform these tasks better than their American counterparts as they have more patience. Even by taking a conservative number like $1.50 as the fully fringed hourly pay, the direct labour savings would be considerable.

After investigating numerous sites, Shackley concluded that Piedras Negras/Eagle Pass was the best border site and Monterrey was the best in the interior. Exhibit 2 indicates that these cities were in more or less easy reach of Braddock's headquarters in Austin, Texas. Exhibit 3 profiles the two locations. Border locations minimized transportation costs, facilitated troubleshooting by managers and engineers based in U.S. headquarters, and permitted factory managers to live in the United States and work across the border in Mexican plants. However, the influx of maquiladora operations had strained the infrastructure of many border cities. The most significant problem was the housing shortage created by workers from the interior seeking maquila jobs. Shackley commented:

> People are lured from the interior by the promise of a job. They move in with relatives or friends then quit when they can't find permanent accommodation. The Mexican government doesn't have the resources to fund construction of sufficient low cost housing, and I don't think the situation will improve for several years.

The housing shortage resulted in a significant labour problem for maquiladora operators along the border. Turnover ranged from 8 to 15 percent per month (lower in the interior), although some sources claimed that turnover could be much higher, and would worsen in the future. While transportation costs were higher and the interior offered a lower quality of life for foreign managers, this was offset by the slightly lower wage scale and lower cost of Mexican materials. However, the roads, housing, utilities, and especially communications in the interior would have to be carefully evaluated.

In his report, Shackley also discussed the three options for operating as a maquiladora: subcontracting, establishing a wholly owned subsidiary, or using a shelter operator.

SUB-CONTRACTING

The easiest way to operate in a maquiladora involved subcontracting the manufacturing services of a Mexican company. The subcontractor obtained all raw materials and import/export permits and produced according to the client's specifications. The foreign firm rarely supplied a plant manager. This arrangement made sense for well-documented operations requiring a small number of employees. The Mexican subcontractor was generally paid on a piece basis that ranged upward depending on how much equipment was used and the risks incurred owing to swings in the production schedule. Shackley estimated that a Mexican firm could be subcontracted at a rate of about $5.00 per direct labour hour.

DIRECT OWNERSHIP

Establishing a wholly owned subsidiary offered potentially the lowest operating cost, provided overheads were strictly controlled. Such an operation was often the best alternative when significant engineering and/or product development support was required. This approach was the most complex of the three options. The foreign firm would have to establish relationships at several government levels and understand and manage the details of doing business in Mexico, which could be particularly burdensome in the area of hiring, compensating, and terminating labour.

After incorporating in Mexico, the company had to register as a maquiladora with SECOFI, the Ministry of Commerce and Industrial Promotion, and provide information about the product, production process, and any imported equipment. The application form had to be completed in Spanish, with all values denoted in pesos. Registration was subject to renewal every 24 months. Under this arrangement, the Mexican corporation built or leased a plant, obtained all permits, handled customs matters, and hired, trained, and directed the labour force in all manufacturing and assembly activities. The foreign parent retained control over day-to-day operations, patents, and technology. Some typical costs for operating a subsidiary in Mexico (as of June 1990) were:

Consultant's feasibility study	$15,000+
Legal incorporation, Mexican legal fees	$5,000–8,000

Construction: for shell building including land	$1.30–1.40/m^2
with improvements	$1.75–2.05/ m^2
Annual leasing: minimum	$.28/m^2
with improvements	$.50/ m^2
Unskilled labour rate (including fringes)	$1.20–1.40/hour
Plant manager (including fringes)	$72,500/year

SHELTER PLAN

A shelter was an intermediary option that allowed foreign firms to operate in Mexico without actually owning a maquiladora or incorporating as a wholly owned subsidiary. There were two types of shelter operators. The first was an industrial park developer/shelter operator, who functioned foremost as a developer and offered a shelter program to encourage companies to lease or buy buildings in the industrial park. The second was a "pure" shelter operator, who provided services in buildings and industrial parks in which he did not have a financial interest. Terminating a shelter contract was easier with a developer/shelter operator than with a pure operator.

Under a shelter plan, the foreign company controlled the production process and provided equipment, raw materials, components, and a plant manager. For a charge of about $3.75 per direct labour hour, a shelter operator would handle the legal incorporation and accounting requirements, provide customs services (prepare import/export documentation, handle clearance), supply the direct labour force and Mexican supervision and execute labour policies, as well as other negotiated activities.

Shackley noted that there were also non-maquila alternatives for operating in Mexico. Joint ventures could be formed to export or sell into the domestic market. Duty, of course, was paid on any raw materials or production equipment brought into Mexico. The joint venture was subject to all Mexican laws and taxes. The corporate income tax rate was about the same as in the United States. In practice, few foreign companies were involved in joint ventures, aside from the large automobile manufacturers.

Alternatively, a company could choose to operate under the Temporary Import Pitex Program. Authorization from SECOFI and the Ministry of Finance and Public Credit was given for a three-year renewable term. Applicants had to have at least $1 million worth of export sales annually to obtain the import permits for raw materials and packaging. Under this arrangement, an entity could be wholly foreign owned and sell up to 30 percent of its output in the Mexican market, provided that at least 10 percent of sales were made in the border area.

LABOUR CONSIDERATIONS

Almost all maquiladora workers along the northeastern border were organized, while the area to the west bordering California was essentially free of unions. Collective contracts usually secured wage levels only slightly higher than the legally required minimum but often contained improvements in fringe benefits.

Workers along the eastern end of the border generally put in a 40-hour week, while those further west and in the interior worked 48 hours for the same pay. Vacation periods, retirement benefits, and indemnities for discharge without good cause were all legally enshrined.

Under Mexican law, companies also paid an amount equal to 5 percent of total wages to the Federal Workers Housing Fund to fund the construction of low cost employee housing. In addition, maquiladoras provided individual year-end bonuses worth about 15 days' salary. Increasingly, companies also offered additional benefits in the form of savings funds, punctuality, attendance and productivity bonuses, cafeteria and transportation subsidies, and food coupons. Shackley estimated that miscellaneous costs would amount to $31,250 annually and that the company could expect to pay $10,000 in Mexican corporate taxes. The one-time cost of the Braddock startup in Mexico would be about $75,000, which included training of a manager, visits from the California staff, a facility upgrade, and learning curve costs.

TRANSPORTATION ISSUES

Air service was generally used only to transport foreign management on visits to maquiladora sites. The rule of thumb was that the closer the foreign parent was to a large U.S. city, the better the quality of air transportation to the maquiladora. Most maquiladora machinery, raw materials, and products entered and left Mexico by truck. By law, the transportation industry was reserved for Mexican nationals. A few Mexican border communities gave entry to U.S. trucks, but U.S. carriers were completely denied access beyond the frontier zone. In practice, most maquiladora shipments in Mexico were made by Mexican tractors pulling U.S.-owned trailers.

The consultant commented that although extortion attempts were not uncommon in the maquiladoras, bribes were rarely paid. Border crossing delays presented the major problem and arose primarily out of the time required to clear U.S. Customs. Trucks were usually able to get through most border locations within a day. The average round trip rate from a maquiladora in Piedras Negras was $140. Similar costs to locations in the interior ranged from $700 to 900, depending on the site. U.S. and Mexican broker fees accounted for an additional $500 per round trip shipment. Shackley estimated that shipments of four pallets from the California plant would be required every three weeks at a shipping cost of $1,150 to provide the maquiladora operation with a sufficient inventory of semifinished SCCs.

At the close of his report, Shackley concluded that fulfilling the financial, legal, and logistical requirements would merely enable a maquiladora to operate. Managing the human relations aspect would determine its success or failure. He remarked:

> Managing a maquiladora is not at all the same as managing a plant in the United States. You'll only have success by paying attention to what consti-

tutes good management practice in Mexico. The maquiladora's management has to become acquainted with the cultural values and customs of its workers, and this understanding has to carry over to home office. Just because a facility is only five minutes south of the border doesn't make it any less Mexican to its workers. The plant will be staffed by people oriented to traditional Mexican values.

PROCTER'S RECOMMENDATION

After reading Shackley's report, Procter concluded that a decision to go to Mexico would have to be implemented carefully if Braddock were to get the advantages of low cost offshore production. It would take a very special team to successfully launch and manage a maquiladora operation. The plant manager could not be just oriented to production or manufacturing, relying on head office for major support. Setting up a maquiladora would mean learning to operate in an environment with a set of values and social considerations completely different from those in the United States.

Procter knew that management was anxious to get on with the "Mexico experiment." Although the manufacturing in Mexico conference chairman contended that there was no difference in the productivity of a properly trained Mexican against an American worker, Procter was concerned about the high turnover that was endemic to the maquiladora industry. It was already mid-August, and Lane was counting on a recommendation about where and how to operate in Mexico by the end of the month. Once these decisions were made, the company could apply for licensing from the State Department and the Department of Defense to move the manufacturing documentation across the border. The application process took up to six months.

NOTE

1. All figures are given in U.S. dollars.

Exhibit **1**

Country Selection Factors 1988				
Factor	United States	Mexico	Singapore, Hong Kong, Taiwan, South Korea	China
Fully fringed hourly wages	$13.92	$1.10–1.30	$2.44–2.72	$0.35–0.50
Material costs	Base case	U.S. cost + freight	Lower than U.S.	Lower than U.S.
Duty costs	None	None if 35% local content, (GSP), 9802	Lost GSP in 1989; most favoured nation rate	None if 35% local content, 9802 applies[1]
Finished goods transit (time to market)	Base case	U.S. plus 2–3 days	U.S. plus 5–6 weeks	U.S. plus 6–8 weeks
Work ethic	Base case	Generally okay	Better than U.S.	Varies but generally okay
Ease of expatriate management control	Base case	Same as U.S.	Requires expat managers	Requires managers
Patent protection	Superb	Good	Poor	Poor
Political risk	Base case	Slight	Singapore: small South Korea and Taiwan: some Hong Kong: more	High

1. Goods imported from countries with most favoured nation status are charged duties averaging 5 to 10 percent, depending on the product classification.

Source: Maquiladora Consultant.

EXHIBIT 2

The Maquiladora Industry, June 1990			
City	No. of Maquilas	City	No. of Maquilas
Agua Prieta	28	Monterrey/NL	75
Cd. Acuna	36	Nogales	65
Cd. Juarez	309	Nuevo Laredo	67
Cd. Obregon/Navojoa	3	Piedras Negras	39
Chihuahua	61	Reynosa	57
Ensenada	33	Saltillo	5
Guadalajara	14	San Luis Rio Colorado	12
Guaymas	3	Tecate	86
Hermosillo	16	Tijuana	530
La Paz	16	Torreon/Gomez Palacios	29
Matamoros	89	Naco	6
Merida	28	Other cities	30
Mexicali	148	**TOTAL**	**1785**

MAP OF MEXICO

Exhibit 3

Location Profiles

---

1. Border Site: Piedras Negras/Eagle Pass

Piedras Negras, State of Coahuila, Mexico

- Population of 200,000 with about 10,000 maquila workers. This percentage is one of the lowest along the entire border.

- Monthly turnover averages 8 to 9 percent.

- Unions represent 70 percent of maquila workers; basically, all maquilas with over 25 employees can expect to be organized. Union militancy not strong in this area.

- Thirty-nine maquilodoras are involved in ceramics, electronics, sewing, and metal products, among other activities. Two large operations each employ about 1,500 workers.

- Amistad is the only shelter operator and manages one of the area's four industrial parks, which are all located near worker housing. Only a few available buildings were observed. Monthly lease costs range from $2.80 to $4.05 per square metre.

- Water, electricity, and propane are available. Telephone lines can be obtained within two to three months in the industrial parks. Microwave transmission can be accommodated, but it is expensive. No data lines are available.

- The housing situation is better than in many other border locations. Most employees live close to the maquilas and either walk or take public buses to work.

- Some Mexican management, technical, and clerical workers are available, but recruiting in Monterrey and other industrialized cities will be necessary. Offering slightly higher salaries will induce professionals and semiprofessionals to relocate here.

- There are three technical schools in the area.

- Mexican machining subcontractors available in Monclova, three hours south on a good road.

- Some American truckers are allowed to take cargo in and out of this location; Mexican trucking costs to the border range from $130 to 150 for a return trip.

- A border crossing delay of 15 to 20 minutes to return to the United States is typical.

- In the consultant's opinion, local maquilas would not feel threatened by additional operations since the market for labour is not as tight as at some other border locations.

Exhibit 3 (cont.)

Location Profiles

Eagle Pass, Texas

- City population is 28,000. Maverick County population is 40,000.

- Unemployment rate averages 25 percent.

- Maverick County is disproportionately Hispanic (90 percent) with the balance being Anglo and American Indian.

- Limited choice of housing, although there are a few houses in the $175,000 to 225,000 range.

- Only one motel offers reasonable quality facilities.

- There is one large shopping mall and few good restaurants.

- There are 10,400 students enrolled in 10 elementary schools, two middle schools, and one high school. Two private schools account for an additional 500 students. Many wealthy Mexicans in Piedras Negras send their children to private schools here.

- There are no commercial air flights into Eagle Pass.

- Eight American trucking companies serve Eagle Pass, which is 200 km, over a good road, from Austin. Laredo is 195 km southeast, and Monterrey is 435 km south.

2.   Interior Site: Monterrey, State of Nuevo Leon, Mexico

- The metropolitan area consists of nine counties with a population of 2,970,000. 75 maquiladoras employ 15,000 workers, primarily females.

- Monterrey is a very industrialized city with numerous Mexican and American companies producing for the domestic market. Many of these non-maquila companies are classified as heavy industries, and about 80 percent of their employees are male.

- Labour turnover is in the range of 4 to 6 percent monthly. Most maquilas have Mexican plant managers.

- Virtually all industrial employees are organized by the two national unions or FNSI, an independent labour movement. FNSI is not affiliated with any Mexican political party and represents 60 percent of Monterrey workers. Historically, labour militancy is low.

Exhibit **3** *(cont.)*

Location Profiles

- Monterrey has three competent shelter operators. American Industries acts as a general contractor and shelter operator in its own 37-hectare industrial park but will offer shelter services in other parks. Amistad offers shelter services in a 88-hectare park near the airport. Prodensa, a "pure" shelter operator, offers its services without any affiliation to a particular industrial park. Prodensa would likely bid on a shelter contract only where the Mexican payroll is over 50.

- Four major universities are represented, as well as the prestigious Monterrey Institute of Technology. There are 76 vocational and trade schools in the area.

- There is excellent availability of Mexican management, technical, supervisory, clerical, and production workers. As well, Monterrey has numerous machining subcontractors.

- Many Monterrey residents are second and third generation industrial workers and show a strong entrepreneurial spirit. As is common in Mexico, about six powerful organizations, or grupos, control significant parts of the local economy.

- The roundtrip trucking cost from the U.S. border is about $800. It is a 2.5 hour drive, one way, over a good road.

- American Airlines has three daily flights from Austin to Monterrey via Dallas/Fort Worth. By car, Laredo is 352 km from Austin and Monterrey is a further 228 km.

- In the consultant's opinion, the community would be receptive to new maquiladora operations, as this is a relatively minor factor in the local employment situation.

Exhibit **4**

Mexican Hourly Minimum Wage, January 1998		
	Minimum Wage (Pesos)	**Minimum Wage ($US)**
1. Regional minimum daily salary	7,765	$ 3.52
2. Annual salary (365 days)	2,834,225	1,285.95
3. Christmas bonus (15 days) and vacations	128,122	58.13
4. Employer's payroll taxes, social security, and nursery, educational, housing, and state tax	311,046	141.13
	243,111	$ 110.30
Total annual costs	**3,516,506**	**$1,595.51**

365 days in a year less: Sundays (52), legal holidays (8), vacations (6) = 299 total working days x 8 hours per day = 2,392 hours worked annually

Total cost per hour	**1,470**	**0.67**
Average fringe benefits	925,091	419.73
Total annual cost	**4,441,597**	**2,015.24**
Fully fringed hourly cost	**1,856**	**0.84**

Note: The consultant estimated that in June 1990, the daily minimum wage was 10,480 pesos. At this time, 2,880 pesos = US $1.00.

Source: Ministry of Commerce and Industrial Promotion (SECOFI).

C A S E 7.4   ENGLISH CENTER FOR NEWCOMERS

By Elizabeth Grasby and Ewa Borzecka

"One more exam and I'm done! I can hardly wait to start setting up my business," Dona Ronaldson, an English major at Baruch College, New York, exclaimed. In order to enhance her skills, she had enrolled also in a business course, and on graduation she was planning to turn her knowledge of English and business into a profitable operation.

Ronaldson had done extensive market research in preparation for opening her own school of English in New York City. She wanted to at least break even in the first year and achieve a small profit of $10,000 to $20,000 in the second year. However, she wondered whether her project was feasible and her goals realistic. If she decided to go ahead, she had to act quickly in order to have her English Center for Newcomers ready for September 1998.

THE STUDENTS

Ronaldson had identified four major student group markets: immigrants to the United States, refugees, foreign visa students, and local youth.

Immigrants

The first student group was immigrants. To improve their current employment situation, they took English as a second language (ESL) courses at different levels of difficulty, depending on their English language proficiency. Immigrants with good writing skills but limited ability to speak English took courses focusing on spoken English, while others who could speak English well but had trouble with writing sought written English courses. However, most immigrants, particularly those at the beginner and intermediate levels, needed both the spoken and written English skills that were taught in a typical ESL course. Immigrants close to and at advanced levels were occasionally interested in specialized ESL courses related to their professions. Most immigrants took ESL courses to increase their chances of employment, to improve their current employment situation, or just to "get started" in a new country. They relied on recommendations from others and shopped around, looking for bargains and a class schedule outside of work hours. They appreciated getting advice (for example, on legal matters) and help with translating their documents.

Refugees

There was also a segment of refugees (people forced to flee their homeland, usually owing to political persecution). Their language needs were similar to those of immigrants; however, their education was usually paid for by the U.S. government once they had been granted refugee status.

Foreign Visa Students

Foreign visa students came to the United States on student visas arranged from their home country or applied for a student visa after arriving in the United States. To attract these students, some schools offered help with obtaining a student visa. Depending on their proficiency, foreign visa students took different ESL courses as well as English courses, such as American literature, history, and culture. Sometimes, taking classes at an English school was their first step before attending a U.S. college or university.

Local Youth

The fourth student group was made up of local youth who needed remedial ESL and/or English courses in order to get accepted to a college or university or for advancement.

Since the immigrant segment was the largest and, therefore, most attractive of the four groups, Ronaldson further researched this segment and its related issues.

THE U.S. IMMIGRATION POLICY

In general, there were two groups of immigrants: legal and illegal. The former encompassed the newcomers to the country, whose status as immigrants was sanctioned by a legal process before or after their arrival in the United States and who, therefore, had the right to remain in the country.[1] Between 1981 and 1993, most immigrants came from countries in northern Central America (many from Mexico and the Caribbean), and a smaller number came from Asia. However, the statistics were reversed in the mid-1990s when Asia (headed by the Philippines, Vietnam, China, and India) contributed 37 percent of the total legal immigration to the United States, followed by northern Central America (32 percent), Europe (18 percent), South America (6 percent), and Africa (less than 6 percent).[2]

Illegal immigrants were people who remained in the country illegally according to the U.S. laws. This category included those who stayed beyond the visiting dates on their visas or who crossed the U.S. border illegally. In 1997, it was estimated that there were five million undocumented immigrants living in the United States.[3]

Over the past decade, the Congress of the United States had sharply reduced its federal aid to immigrants, pushing the costs of supporting legal immigrants more and more onto the individual states. In 1996, the U.S. government increased the number of guards on the U.S. borders, tightened asylum rules, and made it tougher for illegal immigrants to become legal. At the same time, the numbers of immigrants had risen to their highest levels yet.[4] The foreign-born population of the United States had been steadily rising, reaching 24.5 million in 1996. In 1997, 9.5 percent of all U.S. inhabitants were born outside the United States. Two states had the highest immigrant population: 25 percent of Californians were born outside the United States (in Los Angeles, this figure was close to 40 percent), while 16 percent of the New York state population was foreign born (33 percent in New York City).[5]

In the mid-1990s, public polls indicated rising hostility by Americans towards immigrants in the United States. The earlier consensus that immigrants provided a source of hard-working, cheap labour had eroded, and many Americans believed that even legal immigration should be reduced.

THE NEW YORK CITY MARKET

New York City, known as "the Big Apple," was one of the most robust U.S. cities. It was made up of five distinct divisions known as boroughs, only one of which — the Bronx — was situated on the North American continent. The island of Manhattan was the central borough, whereas Brooklyn (largest in population) and Queens (largest in area) were located in the western part of Long Island (which itself stretched miles into the Atlantic). These four boroughs were well connected by the local transit system of subway and bus lines. The fifth borough was Staten Island, situated near the state of New Jersey. Every year, New York City attracted thousands of tourists, as well as immigrants, from all over the world. Most visitors to New York were struck by its extremes of wealth, and poverty.

Nearly 15 percent of the U.S. immigration influx in both the 1980s and early 1990s was to New York City. During 1990 to 1994, 563,000 legal immigrants settled in the city, representing an annual average of 112,600 immigrants (compared with some 86,000 per year in the 1980s). The majority of immigrants were from the Caribbean, followed by the former Soviet Union and then China. Thirty-five percent of all immigrants to New York City in the 1990 to 1994 period settled in Brooklyn, with another 30 percent settling in Queens, 20 percent in Manhattan, 14 percent in the Bronx, and 2 percent in Staten Island. The greatest increase in immigration during this period was observed in Washington Heights and Chinatown and vicinity in Manhattan, and Gravesend-Homecrest in Brooklyn.[6] (See Exhibit 1.) Recent immigrants to New York were much younger than the general population, the median age being 27 years, compared with 34 years for the general population.

THE ENGLISH CENTER MARKET

Ronaldson decided to concentrate on three boroughs: Brooklyn, Manhattan, and Queens (Exhibit 2). She considered the Bronx dangerous and, although the Bronx represented over 16 percent of New York's total population in 1990, its foreign-born population made up only 13 percent of New York's foreign-born inhabitants.[7] She deemed Staten Island's socioeconomic and demographic data unsuitable.

Although the number of vehicles per household had increased over the years, Ronaldson knew there were still many families with no car, especially in Manhattan, where there was an excellent transit system. She realized that accessibility to a good transit system would be one of the factors affecting her choice of the location for the centre.

THE COMPETITION/ OTHER ENGLISH CENTERS

English centres were numerous in the three boroughs. Although some centers exited the market from time to time, the overall number of centers had been growing, and no single center dominated the market.

The English Language Institute Inc.

The English Language Institute, Inc., located in Manhattan, was the least typical of the schools because of its unique strategy. It targeted immigrants, refugees, students, businesspeople, and visitors. The school had operated since the early 1960s, offering training in both ESL and American culture and literature, in an informal and relaxed setting. Participation in classes depended on two kinds of memberships: a six-month basic membership, which cost $125, and a 12-month membership for $150.[8] The basic membership entitled students to attend any of the 42 English group classes taught by a volunteer instructor, under the supervision of an ESL teacher (Exhibit 3). Although classes were taught at three different levels of difficulty (high beginner, intermediate, and advanced), most group classes were open to all members on a walk-in basis. The group size was limited to the number of seats in the classroom. The 12-month membership entitled students to purchase additional one-to-one programs: a 16-hour conversation partnership (one hour per week for 16 weeks) cost $80, 32 hours of grammar lessons cost $160, and a 12-hour mentoring program was $80; the cost of materials was included in the fee. Student-members had access to a library, listening lab, and a lounge, as well as to a resource centre providing information and referrals for jobs, housing, and college application. The English Language Institute, Inc., organized workshops (topics included job-search techniques, computer skills development, and immigration issues), social and cultural events (holiday celebrations and international festivals featuring food, dance, and music from around the world), forum discussions, trips and tours, and more.

International Schools

The International Schools in New York was located in Manhattan close to the United Nations building. The International Schools in New York offered 10 levels of ESL, from basic to the most advanced levels, as well as some advanced specialized courses. The school did not offer additional activities for students and had strict requirements and policies (Exhibit 4). Students had to pay a $50 nonrefundable registration fee and could choose from either day or evening classes. One hundred class hours taken during the day cost $595. Evening classes were taught three days a week (three class hours per evening) for eight weeks at a cost of $425. The daytime ESL courses were also offered during the summer. In its promotion, the school emphasized its authorization under the federal law to enroll nonimmigrant foreign students. The school was also certified by the New York State Department of Education.

The English Language School

The English Language School, a smaller school with which Ronaldson expected to compete, was located in Greenpoint, Brooklyn. Ronaldson believed that the school's location was one of the major factors contributing to its success. It was located close to the subway, in an area densely populated by immigrants, who were the primary students of the school. Since no Green Card or passport was required during the registration process, the school attracted both legal and illegal immigrants. Like International Schools in New York, the English Language School in Greenpoint did not organize any after-school events for students. The school offered eight levels of ESL from beginners to advanced. Students could choose from daily evening courses running for four months from 8 p.m. to 9:30 p.m. Monday through Friday (at $260), daily intensive courses running for one month between 9:30 a.m. and 1:30 p.m. Monday through Friday ($365), Saturday morning and Saturday afternoon courses, as well as Sunday morning and Sunday afternoon courses. Combined Saturday-Sunday afternoon courses were also available. Weekend courses were most popular among students because many of the students worked during the week. The maximum number of students per group was 15. Every course ended with an exam.

Other Schools

Ronaldson counted over 20 schools of English listed in the Queens Yellow Pages alone and worried that English courses were becoming a commodity. An increasing number of schools offered their students free access to computers and free computer classes in order to stay competitive.

CENTER OPERATIONS

Staffing

Ronaldson considered hiring either one full-time or two part-time teachers initially. Since there were numerous qualified candidates, she did not think she would need to pay more than $30,000 annually, including benefits, for one full-time position. She wondered what qualities she should look for when selecting the teaching staff. As an English major herself, Ronaldson was planning to teach some classes, in addition to handling administrative responsibilities. Although she expected to work long hours, Ronaldson decided to draw a minimal salary of $25,000 a year until the center was financially stable.

Location

One of the most important decisions Ronaldson had to make was the choice of location. Commercial real estate in Manhattan was the most expensive of all three boroughs. She could lease 110 square metres in the Washington Heights neighbourhood of Manhattan for $2,200 per month (other Manhattan areas were more expensive). Her real estate agent had also told her about an 1,100-square-metre space at $2.20 per square metre a month in the Bensonhurst area of Brooklyn, located close to the subway. Since the Brooklyn location was in a "hot" market, Ronaldson had to make her decision quickly.

Other costs and conditions were similar for the two leases. Both Manhattan and Brooklyn locations could be converted to three classrooms and required about $5,000 worth of leasehold improvements in order to make the spaces suitable for classrooms and an office. A one-time fee equal to one month's rent had to be paid to the agent. A lessee was usually expected to sign at least a five-year lease; however, favourable agreements as to the breaking of the lease could occasionally be negotiated with the landlord. When comparing the two sites, Ronaldson recalled, however, that Washington Heights already had one well-established English school. She also wondered if she should not try to find a location in Queens, where one square metre of commercial space cost on average from $1.90 to $2.00.

Equipment

Ronaldson identified a few school furniture and equipment providers (Exhibit 5). She planned to have up to 15 students per class, sitting at their own desks. She also considered buying used furniture and equipment, which she estimated would save her from 10 to 20 percent.

Promotion

Since Ronaldson could not afford an experienced marketing manager, she had to develop the centre's marketing strategy. Smaller players, like the English Language School in Greenpoint, advertised in some of the local ethnic daily newspapers. Rates differed depending on the newspaper; for example, placing a small print ad in the *Polish Daily News* cost $10 per day if the ad appeared in the Monday, Tuesday, or Wednesday issue, $12 on Thursday or Friday, and $14 on the weekend; the weekly rate was $50, while a four-week placement cost $185. Another newspaper, the *Daily News*, however, charged about $100 per day for a small print ad. Ronaldson wondered in how many ethnic newspapers she should advertise and with what frequency. Should she advertise in more upscale newspapers, like the *New York Times*, or on the radio or TV? She also had to decide what these advertisements would say and look like.

Other marketing costs Ronaldson considered were related to the use of the telephone and advertising in the Yellow Pages. For a 1-800 number, Bell Atlantic (a telephone company) charged a one-time service fee of $56, rental fee of $10 per month, and $12 per hour of use. A regular business phone cost $19.73 per month per line, plus the cost of local and long-distance calls. Although Ronaldson was not sure whether she should go ahead with the 1-800 number, she knew that placing the information about her school in the Yellow Pages was crucial. The closing date to submit an ad differed within each borough; to have a business listed in the Queens Borough Yellow Pages, the ad had to be in by the end of July; in the case of Brooklyn Yellow Pages, it was June; and for the Manhattan Yellow Pages, February. Should she place her ad in all three boroughs' Yellow Pages? (See Exhibit 6 for Yellow Pages advertisement costs.)

Finance

In addition to the costs mentioned previously, Ronaldson estimated that another $4,000 to $5,000 would be needed for office and classroom supplies (chalk, sponges, paper, etc.), utilities, licensing fees, registration of the business, and miscellaneous costs. She could invest only $20,000 from her savings; however, her boyfriend offered to lend her $15,000 at no interest, repayable at her convenience. She also believed that she could secure some financing from her bank with a solid business plan.

DECISION

Ronaldson looked back at all the research she had done and wondered how many levels of ESL and what kind of policies should be implemented in order to ensure full enrollment; how to schedule classes to satisfy students' demand and maximize the center's capacity at the same time; and how many students she needed in order to break even on all the costs. Ronaldson wondered how she could differentiate her school from the rest. If she decided to open the center, she wanted to have the right strategy in place and have developed a solid business plan.

NOTES

1. The premise for the legalization of their stay could have been an application for a political asylum, marriage to a U.S. resident or citizen, sponsoring by family or work, etc.
2. "Statistical Abstract of the U.S., 1997," *The National Data Book,* 117th ed. (Washington, D.C.: U.S. Department of Commerce, Economics and Statistics Administration Bureau of the Census, 1997), 11.
3. L. Wirpsa, "Immigrants Uncertain as Deadline Nears," *National Catholic Reporter,* 17 October 1997.
4. Almost 10 million immigrants arrived in the United States in the 1980s.
5. Sources: "Turn of the Tide? Immigration," *The Economist,* 27 September 1997, and *The Newest New Yorker 1990–1994: An Analysis of Immigration to NYC in the Early 1990s,* New York City Department of City Planning, 1997.
6. *The Newest New Yorker 1990–1994,* xi, xiii.
7. Information based on Richard L. Schaffer, Director, *Socioeconomic Profiles: A Portrait of New York City's Community Districts from the 1980 and 1990 Censuses of Population and Housing,* Department of City Planning, March 1993, 8, 14.
8. All dollar values given in the case, including the exhibits, are given in U.S. currency unless otherwise stated.

Exhibit 1
New York City
Neighbourhoods

Source: *The Newest New Yorker 1990–1994: An Analysis of Immigration to NYC in the Early 1990s,*
New York City Department of City Planning, 1997, 55.

EXHIBIT 2

New York City Population						
NEW YORK CITY	**1980**		**1990**		**Change 1980–1990**	
(All five boroughs)	**Number**	**%**	**Number**	**%**	**Number**	**%**
Total Population	7,071,639	100.0	7,322,564	100.0	250,925	3.5
Nativity						
Foreign born	1,670,199	100.0	2,082,931	100.0	412,732	24.7
As a percent of total population	23.6		28.4			
Year of entry						
1980 to March 1990	N/A	–	953,449	45.8	–	–
1970 to 1979	669,892	40.1	502,850	24.1	(167,042)	(24.9)
1965 to 1969	268,963	16.1	199,778	9.6	(69,185)	(25.7)
1960 to 1964	147,970	8.9	116,381	5.6	(31,589)	(21.3)
Prior to 1960	583,374	34.9	310,473	14.9	(272,901)	(46.8)
Language Spoken at Home[1]						
Persons five years of age and over	6,606,223	100.0	6,820,456	100.0	214,233	3.2
Speaks a language other than English at home	2,342,299	35.5	2,793,773	41.0	451,474	19.3
Does not speak English "very well"	1,195,598	18.1	1,361,746	20.0	166,148	13.9
Per Capita Income (1989 constant $)	$12,190		$16,281		$4,091	33.6
BROOKLYN						
Total Population	2,230,936	100.0	2,300,664	100.0	69,728	3.1
Nativity						
Foreign born	530,973	100.0	672,569	100.0	141,596	26.7
As a percent of total population	23.8		29.2			
Year of entry						
1980 to March 1990	N/A	–	313,692	46.6	–	–
1970 to 1979	227,995	42.9	171,844	25.6	(56,151)	(24.6)
1965 to 1969	85,385	16.1	61,993	9.2	(23,392)	(27.4)
1960 to 1964	41,445	7.8	32,919	4.9	(8,526)	(20.6)
Prior to 1960	176,148	33.2	92,121	13.7	(84,027)	(47.7)
Language Spoken at Home[1]						
Persons five years of age and over	2,056,856	100.0	2,124,614	100.0	67,758	3.3
Speaks a language other than English at home	723,436	35.2	844,374	39.7	120,938	16.7
Does not speak English "very well"	367,314	17.9	410,338	19.3	43,024	11.7
Per Capita Income (1989 constant $)	$9,642		$12,388		$2,246	28.5

Exhibit 2 (cont.)

			New York City Population				
MANHATTAN	**1980** **Number**	**1990** **%**	**Number**	**%**	**Change** **1980–1990** **Number**	**%**	
Total Population	1,428,285	100.0	1,487,536	100.0	59,251	4.1	
Nativity							
Foreign born	348,581	100.0	383,866	100.0	35,285	10.1	
As a percent of total population	24.4		25.8				
Year of entry							
1980 to March 1990	N/A	–	164,801	42.9	–	–	
1970 to 1979	145,868	41.8	91,339	23.8	(54,529)	(37.4)	
1965 to 1969	55,003	15.8	38,552	10.0	(16,451)	(29.9)	
1960 to 1964	32,763	9.4	25,609	6.7	(7,154)	(21.8)	
Prior to 1960	114,947	33.0	63,565	16.6	(51,382)	(44.7)	
Language Spoken at Home[1]							
Persons five years of age and over	1,359,838	100.0	1,409,243	100.0	49,405	3.6	
Speaks a language other than English at home	496,277	36.5	549,149	39.0	52,872	10.7	
Does not speak English "very well"	265,972	19.6	271,394	19.3	5,422	2.0	
Per Capita Income	$18,074		$27,862		$9,788	54.2	
(1989 constant $)							
QUEENS							
Total Population	1,891,325	100.0	1,951,598	100.0	60,273	3.2	
Nativity							
Foreign born	540,818	100.0	707,153	100.0	166,335	30.8	
As a percent of total population	28.6		36.2				
Year of entry							
1980 to March 1990	N/A	–	323,653	45.8	–	–	
1970 to 1979	212,837	39.4	170,729	24.1	(42,108)	(19.8)	
1965 to 1969	91,646	16.9	71,045	10.0	(20,601)	(22.5)	
1960 to 1964	53,033	9.8	40,869	5.8	(12,164)	(22.9)	
Prior to 1960	183,302	33.9	100,857	14.3	(82,445)	(45.0)	
Language Spoken at Home[1]							
Persons five years of age and over	1,781,488	100.0	1,833,315	100.0	51,827	2.9	
Speaks a language other than English at home	616,285	34.6	805,411	43.9	189,126	30.7	
Does not speak English "very well"	309,238	17.4	404,669	22.1	95,431	30.9	
Per Capita Income	$12,652		$15,348		$2,696	21.3	
(1989 constant $)							

1. English-speaking proficiency of those persons who spoke a foreign language at home was measured in terms of those who spoke English "very well," "well," "not well," or "not at all." The category shown in the table is the sum of the last three items

Source: Prepared by Ronaldson on the basis of the information compiled from Richard L. Schaffer, Director, Socioeconomic Profiles: A Portrait of New York City's Community Districts from the 1980 and 1990 Censuses of Population and Housing, Department of City Planning, March 1993, 9–37.

EXHIBIT **3**

English Group Classes by Subject				
Pronunciation				
Pronunciation	Mon.	4:00–4:55	Rm. 3	Beg.*
Sounds Great	Mon.	6:30–7:45	Rm. 1	Int.*
Pronunciation	Tues.	2:30–3:25	Rm. 1	Beg.
Funny Thing about English	Wed.	1:00–2:00	Rm. 2	Int.
Pronunciation and Then Some	Thurs.	3:00–3:55	Rm. 2	Beg.
Vocabulary/Idioms				
Basic Idioms	Tues.	11:30–1:00	Rm. 2	Int.
Contact in U.S.A.	Tues.	4:00–5:00	Rm. 2	Beg.
Word Power	Thurs.	10:30–11:30	Rm. 1	Int.
Idioms and Vocabulary	Thurs.	4:30–5:30	Rm. 3	Adv.*
Idioms	Fri.	1:00–3:00	Rm. 2	Int.
Vocabulary through Slides	Fri.	3:00–4:25	Rm. 2	Beg.
Conversation/Discussion				
Problems in Conversational English	Mon.	11:00–1:00	Rm. 1	Int.
Speak Out	Mon.	3:00–4:00	Rm. 2	Adv.
Conversation	Tues.	3:00–4:00	Rm. 2	Int.
What's Buzzing?	Tues.	5:00–6:00	Rm. 2	Int.
Talking Pictures	Wed.	10:30–12:00	Rm. 2	Int.
Conversation	Wed.	2:00–3:30	Rm. 1	Int.
Interactive Conversation	Wed.	6:30–7:50	Rm. 2	Int.
Conversation	Thurs.	11:00–12:55	Rm. 2	Int.
Drop In	Fri.	2:30–3:45	Rm. 3	Beg.
Plain English	Fri.	5:00–6:00	Rm. 1	Beg.
Words, Words, Words	Sat.	10:00–11:55	Rm. 3	Int.
TOEFL				
TOEFL	Wed.	2:00–2:55	Rm. 2	Adv.
TOEFL	Wed.	3:00–3:55	Rm. 2	Adv.
TOEFL Practice	Thurs.	10:30–12:25	Rm. 3	Adv.
TOEFL	Sat.	3:00–4:25	Rm. 4	Adv.
Grammar				
Intermediate English Grammar	Wed.	10:30–11:25	Rm.3	Int.
Everyday Grammar	Wed.	4:45–6:00	Rm. 3	Int.
Troublespots in Grammar	Thurs.	3:30–4:30	Rm. 3	Adv.

*Beg.   Beginning
 Int.   Intermediate
 Adv. Advance

Exhibit 3 (cont.)

English Group Classes by Subject				
Writing				
Practical Writing	Wed.	10:00–12:00	Rm. 1	Int.
Literature				
Literature	Mon.	5:30–7:55	Rm. 3	Int.
American Short Stories	Fri.	3:30–5:00	Rm. 1	Int.
Literature	Sat.	12:0–2:55	Rm. 4	Adv.
Specific Subjects				
How to Use the Classifieds	Mon.	2:00–4:00	Rm. 1	Int.
Reading the *NY Times*	Tues.	11:00–11:55	Rm. 3	Int.
Media Chat	Tues.	12:00–1:30	Rm. 3	Adv.
The World of Jazz	Tues.	5:00–5:55	Rm. 3	Int.
Food, Kitchens, Cooking	Thurs.	12:00–1:55	Rm. 1	Int.
Television	Tues.	1:00–2:00	Rm. 2	Int.
Great Decisions	Thurs.	6:00–7:25	Rm. 1	Int.
U.S. History, Government, and Laws	Fri.	5:30–6:45	Rm. 4	Adv.
New York City History	Sat.	10:00–11:55	Rm. 4	Int.

NOTES: Open English Group Classes are not structured classes.

Levels indicated are guidelines only — members may attend any group.

Registration is not required for these classes.

If a leader is absent, a sign will be posted on the classroom door.

PLEASE COME TO THE CLASS AS CLOSE TO THE STARTING POINT AS POSSIBLE!

Exhibit 4

International Schools in New York

We offer 10 levels of English, from the very basic to the most advanced levels. A one-hour placement test is given at the time of registration to determine the student's entry level.

An Introductory Level (0)

This level emphasizes the basic elements of the language for students who have little or no previous exposure to English.

Beginning Levels (I, II)

The beginning classes emphasize the simple tenses through spoken English and listening comprehension. Reading comprehension and writing skills are also introduced at these levels.

Intermediate Levels (III, IV, V, VI)

The intermediate levels involve the difficult but necessary perfect tenses, modals, passive voice and subjunctive mood. Spoken English with idiom practice, listening comprehension, reading comprehension, wrting skills, and vocabulary building are all emphasized.

Advanced Levels (VII, VIII, IX)

The advanced levels take the student to increased proficiency in both spoken and written English. Vocabulary building is continued through reading and listening comprehension.

Advanced Specialized Courses

Courses are also available in TOEFL, conversation, reading and vocabulary building, writing, fluency development, and explorations in American culture. For further information, please contact the school.

Entrance Requirements

The following items must be presented to the school at the time of registration:

All students
1.   One recent passport-sized photograph
2.   Passport or Green Card

and for Student Visa (I-20) students
3.   One Xerox copy of your high school or college transcript or diploma
4.   One Xerox copy of your affidavit of support, and/or bank statement

and for Student Visa (I-20) requested for students coming from abroad
5. $95 deposit + $5 handling charge

All students issued an I-20 from International Schools in New York must attend day classes.

Exhibit 4 (cont.)

International Schools in New York

Day Schedule	**Evening Schedule**
Monday–Friday	Monday, Tuesday, and Thursday

Each level:	Each level:
4 class hours per day	3 class hours per evening
5 weeks	8 weeks
100 class hours	72 class hours

Morning classes: LEVELS V–IX	All levels
9:00 a.m. to 1:00 p.m.	6:15 p.m. to 9:00 p.m.

Afternoon classes: LEVELS 0–V
1:30 p.m. to 5:30 p.m.

Fees: All fees payable in advance

Registration	$50	Registration	$50
Tuition (1 level–5 weeks)	$595	Tuition (1 level–8 weeks)	$425

Mastercard and Visa accepted

Refund Policy:

1. The registration fee is not refundable.

2. If the student cancels this agreement 24 hours before instruction begins, the school will refund all tuition fees paid.

3. If the student withdraws or is discontinued after instruction has begun, the student will receive as a refund no less than

   a. 100 percent of tuition paid if termination is during the first 2 days of the course
   b. 75 percent of tuition if termination is after completion of the first 2 days, but during the first 20 percent of the course
   c. 50 percent of tuition if termination is during the second 20 percent of the course
   d. 25 percent of tuition if termination is during the third 20 percent of the course
   e. 0 percent of tuition if termination is after completion of 60 percent of the course

Any monies paid to the school in excess of the sum due to the school by the student who cancels, withdraws, or is discontinued will be refunded within thirty (30) days of such action.

EXHIBIT 5

Comparison of Prices Charged by School Equipment Providers		
	School Furniture & Equipment, Inc.	Office Products
Student's table	n/a	$40–$45
Student's chair	n/a	$20–$25
Teacher's desk	n/a	$225
Chalkboard	4'x 4' $160 4'x 6' $180	4'x 6' lowest priced model: $120 best steel frame model, with a life-long guarantee: $225
Corkboard	4'x 4' $125	4'x 4' $85
Display case	2'x 3' • 3-week lead time • will customize to suit customer's needs	2'x 3' $185–$200 • delivery costs included

EXHIBIT 6

Yellow Pages Pricing[1]			
	Queens	**Brooklyn**	**Manhattan**
Regular listing: small print business name, address, and phone number	$4.25/month	$4.25/month	$4.25/month
Regular listing: bold business name and phone number; small print address	$27/month	$29.75/month	$31.75/month
Display: 1/16 page (2"x 2.5") yellow background and black ink	$311/month *(Ronaldson's estimate)*	$351/month	$375/month *(Ronaldson's estimate)*
Display: 1/8 page yellow background and black ink	$603/month	$702/month	$754/month

1. Exhibit compiled by Ronaldson presents prices charged by Bell Atlantic for Yellow Pages listings. Ronaldson learned also that when requesting a display ad, a business owner received help from Bell Atlantic. A sales representative discussed the design and needs of the business and worked with the business owner on the design.

CASE 7.5   THE GREEK COSMOBOB

By Frank A. Mastrandrea and Richard H. Mimick

In early February 1999, Mr. Cosmo Panetta, owner of Cosmo's Restaurants Ltd. in Niagara Falls, Ontario, felt that some important decisions had to be made about the future of the family business. Panetta realized the benefits of opening a third drive-in/take-out restaurant, but his current thoughts revolved around the restaurant's best-selling product — the Cosmobob. Originally an in-house product, in September 1998 Cosmo's Restaurants began producing the Cosmobob for other restaurants. The results of that decision had been very encouraging, and by February 1999 the demand for the product had outgrown the restaurant's production facilities. Mr. Panetta knew that it was time to determine a future strategy for the family business, but with only $25,000 available before having to turn to a bank, he was also concerned about the financial requirements of any future plans.

THE FOOD INDUSTRY

In 1996, the average Canadian household spent 28 percent of its total weekly food expenditures away from home. Both general merchandise and food service entities have benefited from changing economic and demographic factors. During 1998, there were hundreds of food processors vying for a share of the $37.8 billion Canadian food market. These food processors were marketing their products either to the food service market or to the home consumer via retail grocery outlets.

The Food Service Market

The food service market covered all foods eaten away from home. This broad spectrum included schools, hospitals, prisons, and nursing homes, as well as hotels, motels, and restaurants of all types. In 1995, Canadians ate 36 percent of their meals away from home. This figure rose to 38 percent in 1996. In the away-from-home market, 92 percent of the meals were eaten in institutions, where the consumer had little choice of where or what to eat. Hotels and restaurants served at least 960 million meals, representing the remaining 8 percent of the total market for meals away from home. Fast-food service accounted for 80 percent of the hotel and restaurant dollar volume.

IVEY Frank A. Mastrandrea prepared this case under the supervision of Richard H. Mimick solely to provide material for class discussion. The authors do not intend to illustrate either effective or ineffective handling of a managerial situation. The authors may have disguised certain names and other identifying information to protect confidentiality. Ivey Management Services prohibits any form of reproduction, storage or transmittal without its written permission. This material is not covered under authorization from CanCopy or any reproduction rights organization. Copyright © 1999, Ivey Management Services.

In the food service market, whether the operation was an institution, a hotel, or a restaurant, the major cost, in both food and labour, of any meal was the entrée. As the entrée was the main part of the meal, the quality was of primary importance to the customer. There were four basic food service systems for delivering an entrée. First, there was the conventional food system, where food of all types was purchased raw and was totally processed on the premises shortly before serving. The semi-conventional food system eliminated some food preparation by purchasing pre-proportioned meat cuts, frozen vegetables, and desserts, and some prepared salads. The "ready" foods system produced precooked frozen entrées on the premises for use later on.

Finally, there was the total convenience system, which purchased 90 to 95 percent of all food items in the convenience form, including entrées, from outside commercial suppliers. Since food production was eliminated, direct food production personnel were replaced by less-skilled people, who prepared the meal simply by heating the product. The benefits derived from total convenience foods were uniformity in quality and cost of the product; a reduction in initial capital costs because less floor space and less equipment were needed; and a reduction in the need to find qualified help as fewer positions needed to be filled. By 1990, a quarter of all hotels and restaurants used solely full convenience foods, and the other three-quarters had doubled their usage of convenience foods. Because 80 percent of the sales volume in most restaurants took place during only 20 percent of the day, the use of convenience foods contributed to efficient service during peak periods, permitting faster customer turnover and, hence, increased sales volume.

All food services products were distributed either through food wholesalers or directly by the food manufacturer. Food wholesalers such as Serca Foods, Signet Foods, Chef Foods, Loeb, and National Grocers had large warehouses located throughout Canada and distributed thousands of manufacturers' products. Small restaurants and hotels usually opted for the simplicity of dealing with only one food wholesaler. Large institutional accounts were visited weekly by a sales representative from each food wholesaler. The institution would submit a quote sheet outlining the products required for the following week. When the quotes were completed by the wholesaler, the institution would choose the food wholesalers with the best price and the best brand for each product. Institutional buyers required unscheduled delivery to satisfy their requirements, while the smaller buyers were on a regular delivery pattern. The food wholesalers offered both groups 2 percent/10 net 30 purchase terms.

Food manufacturers that did not use wholesalers were either under contract for product supply, such as most dairy companies were, or they had a truck-driver/salesperson who made regular calls for their narrow product line. For the smaller restaurant accounts, seven-day purchase terms were usually established. However, institutional buyers demanded more liberal purchase terms, which often strained the working capital needs of the food manufacturer.

*The Grocery
Retailing Market*

The retail grocery business in Canada was characterized by strong competition. Exhibit 1 shows a market profile of the larger supermarket chains. Many of the changes in retailing during the past few years had resulted from the efforts of retailers to tailor their product selection, prices, services, and other store characteristics to meet the needs of consumers within their marketing area better than their nearest competitor.

Economic changes contributed most to the evolution of grocery retailing. The food industry responded to these changes by creating vast arrays of refrigerated and frozen foods, convenience items, and improved housekeeping aids, in addition to existing staple goods. Consumers readily adapted to supermarket concepts while supporting the local neighborhood convenience store to satisfy interim shopping needs.

Food processors, the food industry, and the retail grocers took advantage of trends in consumer tastes and preferences. The market for delicatessen and fast-food products, such as prepared and cured meats, sandwiches, entrées, salads, and specialty cheeses, was strong and likely to continue growing. Successful retailers became attuned to the need for different types of outlets, different product mixes, and different merchandising approaches to serve the needs of the widely varying market segments. Typical supermarkets offered approximately 15,000 items.

As a result of their vast distribution network and customer acceptance, grocery retailers had developed a powerful base for dealing with food processors and food manufacturers. New product introduction was definitely an area where retailers held the upper hand. Creative promotion was the key to getting retailer cooperation with the manufacturer. A $20,000 placement fee per product per supermarket chain, plus standard industry price discounts, samples, free food allowances, and cooperative advertising were all needed to develop retail chain acceptance of a new product. Trade promotion could run as high as 15 percent of the manufacturer's selling price. Once those costs were incurred, the manufacturer would need to develop promotional techniques that would generate consumer acceptance of the product. Consumer promotion for an established food product ranged between $80,000 and $500,000 per year, with the launch year somewhat higher.

**THE PANETTA
FAMILY**

Cosmo Panetta was 74 years of age. Mr. Panetta, his wife, Josephine, and their eldest son, Joe, immigrated to Niagara Falls from Greece in 1958. For two years Panetta worked in northern Ontario mines as a labourer, before returning home to his family for a job with the City of Niagara Falls in 1960. In 1968, Mr. Panetta used personal savings and a small loan from his brother-in-law to purchase a small variety store. It had always been Panetta's dream to establish a family business, and the variety store seemed to be a good place to start. Panetta worked at the store 18 hours per day, with his son Joe assisting him as a stockboy. Josephine Panetta spent her time at home, caring for their younger sons, Frank and Andy.

In 1970, the variety store was demolished and a new variety store, with a four-room motel, was erected on the same site. By 1975, both Joe and Frank were helping their father in the store. Neither of the boys was academically inclined, and both sons indicated the desire to make the family business their livelihood.

In 1975, a convenience store chain purchased the variety store from Panetta for $150,000. With the proceeds from the sale and a small bank loan, Panetta purchased an existing drive-in restaurant, which he renovated and renamed Cosmo's Drive-In. Panetta purchased a second drive-in/take-out restaurant in 1979. The restaurants were operated by Cosmo and Joe, with Joe's wife, Cindy, Frank, and the youngest son, Andy, helping out with miscellaneous kitchen work. Both restaurants were open 15 hours per day, seven days a week and used mostly part-time help. Mr. Panetta maintained that a good location, high product quality, and a fair price were the necessary ingredients for a successful restaurant business. The business was incorporated in 1979. A small bookkeeping firm was retained to handle the company's books and accounting needs.

COSMO'S RESTAURANTS

The Concept

Cosmo's Drive-In was really a combination drive-in and take-out establishment. The restaurant prepared and sold wrapped meals of specific foods for consumption away from the premises or in a seating area. Cosmo's concentrated on a limited menu of fast-food items, such as hamburgers, hot dogs, chicken, fish, french fries, onion rings, and beverages. Cost-conscious consumers were continually attracted to Cosmo's because of the good food and the perceived value for their money, resulting from the efficient and standardized operations.

Cosmo's Restaurants resembled the Harvey's drive-in restaurant concept. The buildings and equipment had been structured for specific purposes, and production systems were developed for an efficient product flow. When a customer arrived at the inside counter, he or she placed an order and paid the cashier. The cook made and assembled the order, while the cashier prepared and placed the drinks. The whole process took approximately two minutes.

Although, to some extent, the concept of limited selection had been retained to preserve efficiency, some highly successful new products had been developed and introduced to give drive-in/take-out restaurants a competitive edge. One of the most widespread methods of diversifying menus was for companies that had previously served mainly hamburgers to introduce various specialty sandwiches. The more popular specialty sandwiches included chicken, steak, roast beef, fish, ham, and cheese. A few chains were also trying pork and veal preparations. Cosmo's, for example, created and developed the pork-based Cosmobob. The introduction of salad bars in some fast-food restaurants had probably been the most important factor in improving the industry's nutrition image. A few fast-food establishments also produced light gourmet food, such as quiches, soups, and fruit-based desserts. A significant new product in the fast-food industry was alcoholic beverages. Licensing fast-food establishments to serve alcohol was continually occurring in the industry. Other than introducing the Cosmobob, however, Cosmo's had not undertaken menu diversification.

The Niagara Falls Market

The city of Niagara Falls had a population exceeding 79,000 and was located in southern Ontario, 100 kilometres south of Toronto, at the United States border. Each year, over 13.4 million visitors were attracted to the famous natural wonder of the world. Most of the tourism occurred from June to August.

Niagara Falls boasted a strong hotel, motel, and restaurant industry to handle the annual influx of visitors. Most of the tourist accommodation was located on Lundy's Lane and in the Clifton Hill area. Exhibit 2 provides information on Niagara Falls. Famous international restaurants and hotels in Niagara Falls included the Sheraton Brock Hotel, the Casa D'oro Restaurant, the Capri Restaurant, and the Hungarian Tavern. The city also had a significant number of franchised hotel establishments, such as Howard Johnson's and Best Western Hotels. The franchised restaurants were mostly of the fast-food variety: McDonald's, Burger King, Wendy's, Harvey's, Arthur Treachers, etc. These outlets were very busy in the summer and moderately busy during the rest of the year.

Cosmo's Restaurants Operations

Cosmo's Restaurants had two locations in Niagara Falls. The first location was opened on Lundy's Lane, 6.5 km from the Falls and the Clifton Hill area. That section of Lundy's Lane was known by local residents as "the fast-food strip" since most fast-food chains were located in that area. The second restaurant was located on Thorold Stone Road, a main industrial thoroughfare. Cosmo Panetta managed the Thorold Stone Road outlet, and Joe Panetta the Lundy's Lane restaurant.

There were two to six employees on duty at each outlet at any one time. The size of the staff could be expanded or contracted to meet demand. The units expected 50 percent of their business between 12:00 noon and 2:00 p.m. Another 30 percent occurred between 5:00 and 7:00 p.m. The remainder was evenly distributed throughout the day. It was estimated that the level of business on Sunday was only half of what might be expected on the other days of the week. An average bill for a customer would be $6.88.

Cosmo's Restaurant had grown to $480,000 in assets in 1998 and almost $1,117,000 in sales. Exhibits 3 and 4 show income statements and balance sheets for Cosmo's Restaurants operations. Exhibit 5 outlines selected ratios for Cosmo's Restaurants and other fast-food establishments.

Cosmo's Restaurants were popular with visitors to Niagara Falls and with local residents. The restaurants were most celebrated for the Cosmobob. The widespread popularity of the Cosmobob was attributed to the product's consistent quality, which was widely broadcasted by in-restaurant promotions, over the local radio, and through newspaper advertising. In 1998, the Cosmobob accounted for 35 percent of the Thorold Stone Road restaurant's sales and 30 percent of the Lundy's Lane outlet's sales.

THE COSMOBOB   In 1979, Mr. Panetta began developing the Cosmobob, and by 1998 the Cosmobob was a product he felt had potential for mass-market introduction and development. The Cosmobob was a portion-controlled food product that consisted of small cubes of pork that were seasoned and mounted on a bamboo skewer. Exhibit 6 shows the Cosmobob ready to be served. Souvlaki was the generic name of the Greek Cosmobob. Some people referred to the product as shishkabob. However, since some restaurants did not produce good quality souvlaki, the generic product's image was inconsistent. For this reason, Panetta chose the unique Cosmobob name for the fairly well-known Greek souvlaki.

Mr. Panetta believed that the major attributes of the Cosmobob were its consistent size and quality and the food preparation savings resulting from volume production. These features would guarantee higher, more stable gross margins for the product, as well as developing a consistent superior quality souvlaki for the consumer. Prior to serving, the Cosmobob was cooked, rolled in warm pita bread, where the skewer was removed, and then garnished with the Cosmobob sauce, onions, tomato, and pickle. The Cosmobob was also served with rice and vegetable. Exhibit 7 outlines the presentation and preparation of the Cosmobob.

In September 1998 Panetta decided to try to manufacture the Cosmobob on a large scale and sell it to area restaurants and institutions. A 14-square-metre area in the backroom of the Thorold Stone Road restaurant was used for production. The room was concrete block and not insulated, thereby providing the necessary cool production facility. Minor facility upgrading was completed for the room to pass local health inspection. The restaurant had limited freezing facilities, so arrangements were made to store the finished product at a Niagara Falls icehouse. The icehouse charged $400 per month for its unused area.

Three people were initially hired on a part-time basis. One worker cut the pork in cubes, seasoned the pork with dry spice, and let it set for two days. The other two workers would skewer the seasoned pork in 50-gram portions, vacuum-pack 10 portions per package, box six packages per case, and ship the cases to the icehouse. Labour was paid $9.00 per hour. Exhibit 8 provides data on labour productivity for producing the Cosmobob at the end of December.

Mr. Panetta and his son Frank introduced and attempted to sell the product to restaurants and institutions in the 100-kilometre corridor from Fort Erie to Hamilton, Ontario. Sales visits included preparation and serving demonstrations of the Cosmobob. Panetta felt that it was necessary to create demand before any of the 18 Ontario food wholesalers would consider carrying the product. The Cosmobob sold for $48.96 per case. Initial acceptance was strong, and Panetta sensed some lucrative extra revenue from his fairly modest investment. Fast-food restaurants that purchased the Cosmobob would serve it on pita bread with Cosmobob sauce and garnish and sell the product for $2.50. Restaurants that served the Cosmobob on rice or noodles sold the dinner entrée for as much as $12.95. Sales of the Cosmobob went from 100 cases in each of September and October to 400 cases in November and close to 600 cases in December. In

December, production staff was increased to six people and, by February, the backroom facilities had reached their capacity for both in-house and external orders and could not handle an increased level of demand. Exhibit 9 outlines operating results associated with the Cosmobob until the end of December. The variable cost per case was $31.20 at that time.

FUTURE OPPORTUNITIES

In February 1999 Panetta was approached by a commercial developer who was seeking a fast-food operation to locate in a new Victoria Avenue mall (see Exhibit 2). The mall, which was scheduled to open in June 1999, was located on Victoria Avenue between the Clifton Hill tourist area and Queen Street, the Niagara Falls business district. The list of mall tenants included a convenience milk store, a hair styling salon, a flower shop, and a dry cleaner. The developer felt that approximately 500 cars would visit the mall on an average day.

Rent at the mall was set at $1,600 per month. Panetta was expected to sign a 20-year lease, calling for annual rent increases of inflation plus 1 percent. The lease could be broken any time after five years by paying the penalty clause of full rent for one-half the remaining years on the contract. Panetta thought that the location had good potential and that although sales would initially be about 60 percent of the Thorold Stone Road sales, that outlet's sales could be matched in two years. He further estimated that $10,000 in leasehold improvements would be necessary, as well as $50,000 in equipment, but that a check with vendors would provide more accurate figures.

Panetta's thoughts were also with the Cosmobob. Delighted with the product's early success, Panetta realized that it was time to define the Cosmobob's role in the family business. The backroom production facilities were cramped for space, and the icehouse freezing arrangement caused problems with shipping. Any strategy that would cause sales to increase would require new production facilities to produce the Cosmobob. In February, Panetta was aware of two potential sites.

One site was an old mushroom factory in Grimsby, Ontario. Grimsby was located between Toronto and Niagara Falls. Rental charges for the factory were $2,000 per month for the first-year lease. The rent would be raised by 15 percent in each subsequent year. The lease also gave the tenant a $300,000 purchase option along with the first right of refusal to any change in ownership.[1] Facilities improvements for the mushroom factory, in order to meet provincial health standards, would cost $100,000 to $120,000. This amount would cover the cost of refrigerating the work area and of building a walk-in cooler. All food processed for sale in Ontario was required to adhere to provincial health standards.

The second option was an old dairy plant in Niagara Falls. The dairy had a refrigerated work area and prefabricated freezer units. To meet provincial health standards, miscellaneous leasehold improvements that would cost $30,000 were needed. The tenant was expected to sign a three-year lease, with rent at $2,000 per month for the first six months, $2,400 per month for the next six months, $3,000 in year two, and $3,400 in year three. The building was appraised at $450,000, and the lease would include the first right of refusal with a $400,000 purchase option. Panetta preferred the Niagara Falls location if the Cosmobob was introduced on a large scale, because lower capital costs would get the plant operational, and a Niagara Falls location would permit him to use existing labour.

Panetta figured that it would cost $30,000 to $40,000 extra for either of the buildings to pass federal government inspection. These changes would include paving the parking lots, installing stainless steel racks, sealing all wall and floor cracks, and using various other techniques to control bacteria. Federal inspection was necessary for products to be sold in more than one province. Equipping a plant with weigh scales, trays, knives, packaging equipment, etc., would cost approximately $80,000, although operations could start up with one-half that amount. Labour needs would also have to be determined but would likely depend on product demand.

Panetta felt that a decision to pursue the Cosmobob would require a clear marketing plan. The company could attempt to establish a customer base in the food services market either on a provincial or national scale. This would require the company to either establish its own sales force to visit the various restaurants and institutions or to arrange for food wholesalers to distribute the Cosmobob to those outlets. A salesperson would have to be paid at least $30,000 per year and would incur $10,000 in expenses. Serca Foods, a food wholesaler with distribution in both the Ontario and national markets, had already approached Panetta about obtaining the right to distribute the Cosmobob. Serca Foods requested a 20 percent margin on their purchase price. If a food wholesaler were selected, Panetta wondered if the Cosmobob could be sold as a single product. In the Niagara Falls area, it was the Cosmobob concept, with pita bread and Cosmobob sauce, that was sold to local establishments. Since either pita bread or the sauce was not available in all Ontario markets, a decision on whether or not to carry those products would have to be made. Cosmobob sauce was made once a month, and the pita bread was purchased from a local bakery and repackaged. The bookkeeper indicated that additional working capital would be required to cover approximately 22 days of receivables and four weeks of inventory. Payments on most accounts payable would have to be made in seven days.

A second marketing approach was the possibility of distributing the Cosmobob to the home user through supermarket chains. This market was larger than the food services market, and there was no existing "ready to serve" souvlaki available to the home user. Panetta realized that although the market was large, federal inspection would be required if the Cosmobob were introduced nationally, and a great deal of promotion would be necessary. Supermarket chains would expect 25 percent margin on retail selling price, good promotion support, and guaranteed delivery.

CONCLUSION　　As Panetta sat back to review his possible courses of action, he knew that whatever strategy was chosen would have to be in the best interests of his wife and sons. He realized that marketing and production changes involved in any decision would have to be operational, but the most difficult task would be to estimate the financial requirements and feasibility of the chosen strategy.

NOTE

1. First right of refusal gives Cosmo Panetta priority over any third-party offer to purchase the building by paying the $300,000 purchase option price.

EXHIBIT 1

Market Profile of Selected Canadian Supermarket Chains (1999)

Retail Food Chain	Canadian Market Share	Ontario Outlets	Ontario Market Share
Loblaws Companies	19.5%	69	31%
Provigo	9.3	n/a	n/a
Safeway	8.4%	n/a	n/a
A&P	5.7%	111	13%
Loeb	unknown	28	9%
Other	57.1%	–	47%

Source: *Market Share Reporter*, Gale Researcher, Inc., 1998

EXHIBIT 2
Partial Map of
Niagara Falls

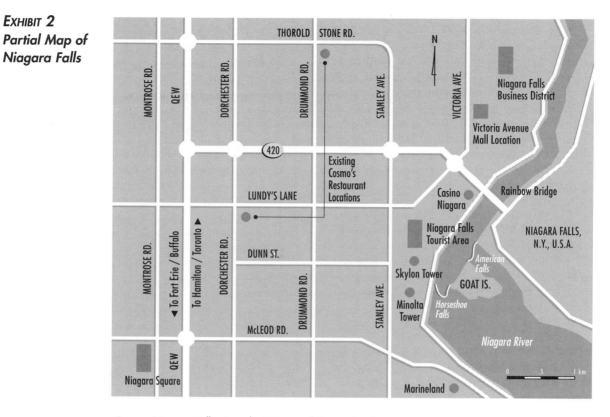

Source: Niagara Falls, Canada, Visitor and Convention Bureau.

EXHIBIT **3**

	Cosmo's Restaurants Ltd.			
	Income Statements for the Years Ending December 31, 1997, 1998			
	Thorold Stone Road Outlet		Lundy's Lane	
	1997	**1998**	**1997**	**1998**
Sales	$502,354	$537,506	$563,626	$624,862
Cost of Goods Sold:				
Food costs	177,842	194,578	201,214	224,950
Paper costs	29,638	32,250	32,690	36,866
Wages and salaries	164,772	177,376	185,996	207,454
Other production costs	16,076	17,738	16,346	18,746
Total cost of goods sold	388,328	421,942	436,246	488,016
Gross profit	114,026	115,564	127,380	136,846
Operating expenses:				
Advertising and promotion	25,070	16,126	16,908	19,370
Maintenance and repairs	6,028	6,450	6,764	7,498
Utilities	26,122	27,950	27,054	29,368
Administratrive expenses	6,400	7,400	7,200	8,200
Depreciation expense	10,795	11,150	12,173	13,090
Other expenses (including interest)	15,070	16,126	15,782	18,122
Total operating expenses	79,485	85,202	85,881	95,648
Net profit before tax	34,541	30,362	41,499	41,198
Tax (40 percent)	13,816	12,145	16,600	16,479
Net income	$ 20,725	$ 18,217	$ 24,899	$ 24,719

Exhibit **4**

		1997	1998
Cosmo's Restaurants Ltd. **Balance Sheet** **as at December 31, 1997, 1998**			

	1997	1998
ASSETS		
Current Assets		
Cash	$ 9,258	$ 13,146
Accounts receivable	24,576	29,060
Inventories	23,818	27,804
Prepaid expenses	4,284	4,712
Total current assets	61,936	74,722
Fixed assets		
Land	170,000	170,000
Buildings (cost)	280,000	292,246
Less: accumulated depreciation buildings[1]	78,400	89,600
Net buildings	201,600	202,646
Equipment	130,400	137,000
Less: accumulated depreciation equipment[2]	91,280	104,320
Net equipment	39,120	32,680
Total fixed assets	410,720	405,326
TOTAL ASSETS	472,656	480,048
LIABILITIES AND EQUITY		
Current liabilities		
Notes payable to bank	20,000	10,000
Accounts payable	75,574	90,996
Accrued expenses payable	3,926	2,052
Current portion long-term debt	2,000	2,000
Total current liabilities	101,500	105,048
Long-term debt (net of current portion)	40,000	30,000
Total liabilities	141,500	135,048
Shareholders' equity		
Common stock, Cosmo and Josephine Panetta	200,000	200,000
Retained earnings	131,156	145,000
Total shareholders' equity	331,156	345,000
TOTAL LIABILITIES AND SHAREHOLDERS' EQUITY	472,656	480,048

1. Buildings were depreciated "straight line" over 20 years.
2. Equipment and leashold improvements were depreciated "straight line" over 10 years.

Exhibit 5

	Financial Ratios					
	Thorold Stone Road		Lundy's Lane		Wendy's	McDonald's[1]
	1997	1998	1997	1998	1998	1998
PROFITABILITY						
Sales	100%	100%	100%	100%	100%	100%
Cost of goods sold:						
Food	35.4	36.2	35.7	36.0		
Paper	5.9	6.0	5.8	5.9		
Wages and salaries	32.8	33.0	33.0	33.2		
Other	3.2	3.3	2.9	3.0		
Cost of goods sold	77.3	78.5	77.4	78.1		
Gross profit	22.7	21.5	22.6	21.9		
Operating expenses						
Advertising and promotion	3.0	3.0	3.0	3.1		
Maintenance and repairs	1.2	1.2	1.2	1.2		
Utilities	5.2	5.2	4.8	4.7		
Administrative	1.3	1.4	1.3	1.3		
Depreciation	2.1	2.1	2.2	2.1		
Other expenses	3.0	3.0	2.8	2.9		
Rent	n/a	n/a	n/a	n/a		
Total operating expenses	15.8	15.9	15.3	15.3		
Net profit before tax	6.9	5.6	7.3	6.6	11.29	22.24
LIQUDITY						
Current ratio	.61:1	.71:1				
Acid test	.33/1	.40/1				
EFFICIENCY						
Age of accounts receivable	8.4 days	9.1 days				
Age of inventory	10.5 days	11.2 days				
Age of payables	33.5 days	36.5 days				
STABILITY						
Net worth/total assets	70%	71.9%			n/a	63%
GROWTH			**1997–98**			
Sales			8.3%			
Net profit			–6.3%			
Assets			1.5%			
Equity			4.0%			

1. Source: *Moody's Industry Review*, Vol. 17, No. 41 (April 30, 1999).

EXHIBIT 6
The Cosmobob

Exhibit **7**

The Cosmobob's Preparation and Presentation

- The Cosmobob can be cooked on griddle, broiler, charcoal pit, barbecue, or in microwave.
- When cooking on griddle or in microwave, Cosmobobs must be covered with a lid at all times.
- When cooking, flatten Cosmobobs with palm of hand to increase cooking surface and heat conductivity and to speed up cooking.
- To sear meat, place on cooking surface for one or two minutes each side to lock in juices and keep meat from drying out.
- Once Cosmobobs have been seared, they can be wrapped in foil (shiny side in) to be cooked to serve as required. Holding time of precooked Cosmobobs is approximately 24 hours, if refrigerated after cooling at room temperature.
- The Cosmobob is seasoned with herbs and spices but no salt. Good for no-sodium diets, ideal for hospitals or institutions where this is important.
- We do suggest using lemon and salt on Cosmobobs after cooking to bring out flavour — tastes great!
- To make Cosmobob-Schnitzels, flatten meat with meat hammer (rough side), roll in all-purpose flour, dip in whole beaten egg (do not add milk or water to eggs as they may add sour flavour), roll in coarse unseasoned bread crumbs. Fry in corn oil for better flavour and no greasy taste. Set temperature at 375°F and place breaded Cosmobobs in hot oil; when juices rise on top, turn over and finish cooking, approx. 6 to 7 minutes. Do not deep fry.
- The Cosmobob is a very versatile food product and can be served in many ways, on rice or noodles with a sauce and wedge of lemon, as a lunch or dinner item, or alone as a bar or finger food item, plain or schnitzeled. Great with fries or baked potatoes. Good on pita bread with Cosmobob Sauce and garnish. Any way you like it, simply delicious!
- Being high quality and portion controlled is by far the most important advantage. Food cost is controlled and consumer affordability is maintained.

Exhibit 8

Labour Productivity Data	
Job and Function	**Cases per Employee per day**
Cutter: trim, debone, and cube pork; season cubes	50 cases
Skewer: weigh pork, insert cubes onto bamboo skewers	10 cases
Packer: pack, seal, flash, freeze, and box Cosmobobs	100 cases

Exhibit 9

Unaudited Operating Results for the Cosmobob (1998)				
	September	**October**	**November**	**December**
Volume	100 cases	100 cases	400 cases	600 cases
Sales	$ 4,896	$ 4,896	$19,584	$29,376
Cost of goods sold:				
Meat and packaging	1,860	1,860	7,440	11,160
Labour	1,280	1,080	3,744	5,616
Other production costs	324	324	1,296	1,944
Total cost of goods sold	3,464	3,264	12,480	18,720
Gross profit	1,432	1,632	7,104	10,656
Operating expense:				
Administrative expenses[1]	500	650	1,000	1,640
Selling expenses[2]	1,700	2,410	4,050	4,740
Other operating expenses[3]	1,000	2,000	250	140
Total operating expenses	3,200	5,060	5,300	6,520
Operating profit	−1,768	−3,428	1,804	4,136

1. Panetta expected $20,000 per year administrative expenses if the Cosmobob was produced on a large scale.

2. These expenses were incurred by Cosmo and Frank while selling the Cosmobob. A fulltime salesperson would have to be paid at least $30,000 per year and would incur $10,000 per year in expenses.

3. Other expenses referred to miscellaneous start-up costs. Panetta felt that these costs would not exceed $10,000 if the Cosmobob was produced on a large scale.

C A S E 7.6   INN AT THE FALLS

By Elizabeth Grasby and Niels Billou

"Jan, I don't know if it's the right thing to do or if it's the right time to do it," Peter Rickard commented to his wife, Jan, while sitting in the Inn's dining room overlooking the thawing Muskoka River. It was March 1997 and Peter and Jan Rickard, owners of Inn at the Falls, Bracebridge, Ontario, were discussing the future direction of their business. The inn's sales and profits had levelled off after nine consecutive years of growth, and the Rickards were considering expansion plans in order to rekindle growth. Since the busy season was only a few months away, decisions needed to be made quickly if changes were to be implemented for the upcoming summer season.

TOURISM IN THE MUSKOKA REGION

With hundreds of lakes, countless islands, and miles of spectacular scenery, the Muskoka region of Ontario attracted millions of travellers each year (see Exhibit 1). The travel and tourism industry had recently rebounded from several poor years in the recessionary times of the early 1990s. Tourism was expected to grow at a higher rate than the 4.2 percent forecast for Ontario's domestic economy in 1997. An estimated $300 million was spent in the region in the summer of 1996.[1]

Of total tourism expenditures in 1994, it was estimated that 11 percent was spent on accommodation and 23 percent was spent on food and beverages.[2]

ACCOMMODATION

Accommodation preferences were further segmented according to type and frequency of use (see Exhibit 2).

Private Cottages

Tourists who either used their own, a friend's, or a relative's cottage treasured the convenience of relaxing on the shores of their own private patch of beach. Many viewed this serenity as a fair trade-off against the high initial investment (some cottages cost more than the price of a home in an urban centre) and the high yearly maintenance bills.

Hotels

Most of the full-service hotels were located in the centre of towns and cities, since hotels generally catered to the business traveller rather than the vacationer. Prices ranged from $70 per night for a room at a nonprime property to more than $400 for executive suites at an upscale property.

Camping

Camping facilities were readily available in provincial parks and commercial facilities throughout the region for those tourists looking for a more adventurous holiday experience. Campground facilities costs averaged $10 per person plus usage fees (i.e., electrical connection).

Motels

Motels in this region were most often located close to a major highway. The majority of the motels offered rooms only and no other services for $35 to $60 per night. Motels primarily served as stopovers for tourists travelling through the region.

Resorts

Resorts offered recreational and entertainment facilities. The majority of these resorts were open solely during the summer months. These facilities usually included a stay for a minimum period of time and offered accommodation and meal plan packages. Depending on the multitude of activities offered and the type of accommodation provided, the cost to stay at a resort could range from $600 to $2,000 per person per week.

Commercial Cottages

Commercial cottages provided the privacy and convenience of a cottage without the high investment. These facilities usually offered housekeeping services and recreation equipment such as canoes, boats, and jetskis for an additional fee. They generally operated in the summer only and, depending on the type and location of the cottage, cost from $350 to $1,800 per week per cottage.

Country Inns

Country inns were owner operated and set in historic buildings. Many of these inns were small, often in one building with a dozen or fewer rooms with a small dining facility; however, others had several buildings and offered the full services of a hotel in a quainter atmosphere. Overnight stays ranged in price from $80 to $150 per person for a standard room.

THE INN AT THE FALLS

The Inn at the Falls was built in 1862, in Bracebridge, Ontario, as a private residence for the first federally appointed judge to Muskoka and was located on a quiet cul-de-sac overlooking the Muskoka River. In 1942, the home was converted into a small hotel with six rooms and remained that way until the early 1960s, when a free-standing addition, adding another 10 rooms, was built. The addition also included a small banquet room and a bar, making the hotel the town's social centre until the late 1970s.

In the late 1970s, the hotel began to decline. The property's poor condition drove away guests to newer establishments. During this time, the hotel changed hands twice. In 1983, the owners started a major renovation campaign, but by 1987 they had been unable to improve the business sufficiently to avoid bankruptcy, and the property was sold by auction at a "fire sale"[3] price. The new owners spent little time at the hotel, and, while some capital improvements were made, the hotel continued to operate at a loss.

In 1988, Peter and Jan Rickard purchased the property for $600,000, investing $150,000 of their own capital and assuming a $450,000 mortgage through the Royal Bank of Canada. The Rickards further invested $100,000 on renovations that included upgrading all aspects of the inn, from the rooms to the buildings' exteriors.

Over the next nine years, the remaining five properties on the cul-de-sac were purchased by the Rickards and converted to accommodations and a small conference centre, creating a village-like atmosphere (see Exhibit 3). In 1996, the Rickards purchased the last building on the street as their private residence.

THE RICKARDS

Prior to purchasing the inn, the Rickards had spent 28 years in the hotel industry managing first-class hotels in Bermuda, Bahamas, Jamaica, Barbados, Malaysia, Canada, and the United States. Peter commented on the decision to buy the inn and move to Bracebridge:

> After spending close to 30 years moving from one country to the next, Jan and I decided it was time to settle down in one place and provide a stable upbringing for our two children. As well, we wanted to be able to establish our own lifestyle with the ultimate goal of providing retirement income from the sale of the business.

The Rickards planned to retire from the business within five years. Since neither of their children had expressed any interest in taking over the business, the Rickards were considering selling the business, but they had no idea what price to ask for the inn.

FACILITIES AT THE INN

In 1997, the inn offered 37 rooms for accommodation, including eight suites (see Exhibit 4 for layout of the inn and Exhibit 5 for views of the pool and patio). Each suite was individually decorated in a Victorian theme. The dining room, decorated with elegant Victorian furniture, offered both traditional and international cuisine (see Exhibit 6), as well as a picturesque view of the Muskoka River and Bracebridge Falls. The dining room was open for breakfast and dinner but closed for lunch, except for functions, and could accommodate up to 110 people.

The inn also had a pub and a large outdoor patio with a pool. The pub could seat 95 people and the patio 120 people. Both were open for lunch and dinner; however, this area did not stay open very late, and it was closed most evenings before midnight. Patrons of both the pub and the dining room were primarily "cottagers" in the summer months.

In addition to dining and accommodation, the inn offered conference facilities. It had a small conference centre with two meeting rooms with a combined capacity of 80 people, a small meeting room in the main building seating 24 people, as well as a small lounge in the main building that could accommodate up to 15 people.

Total revenues for the inn in 1996 were $1,700,000 (see Exhibit 7 for financial statements). Average occupancy was 55 percent, with an average daily room rate of approximately $100 (see Exhibit 8 for daily room rates and sales data within the area).

THE CONSUMERS

The inn was open year-round, offering a full range of services for the leisure and corporate traveller (see Exhibit 9 for sales by consumer segment), as well as for weddings and other social events. Peter estimated that 82 percent of the inn's business was repeat and referral, with the rest of the business generated by various forms of advertising (see Exhibit 9 for more details). The inn spent 2 percent of sales on advertising, mostly on guides — i.e., Resorts Ontario Guide, local advertising for the pub and dining room — and a small amount on newspaper advertising in southwestern Ontario.

During the peak summer season of June, July, and August, the inn targeted married, dual-income professionals and blue-collar skilled labourers with children under 10 years of age. These travellers looked for unique accommodation, with good food and beverage facilities, yet they did not require extensive recreational facilities. Most leisure travellers visited the inn from Toronto and the southwestern Ontario region. (See Exhibit 9 for geographic residence of guests).

Weddings were generally booked from May to August, with the inn catering in a season 20 to 30 weddings of up to 110 people. Most wedding bookings were generated by summer cottagers, and in nearly all cases these bookings would fill all of the rooms. These consumers looked for a unique, "country" atmosphere, for which they were willing to pay above-average prices.

In the fall and spring "shoulder seasons,"[4] young couples and retirees, looking for a quiet interlude in scenic surroundings, visited the inn.

The corporate traveller frequented the inn mainly during the shoulder seasons. This traveller looked for a full-service convention facility with a more intimate atmosphere. Most of the inn's corporate business was generated by large, U.S.-based multinationals that conducted business in the area and municipal and provincial governments that held conferences and meetings in the region.

OPERATIONS

Peter and Jan oversaw the inn's operations with the assistance of a hotel manager. Jan spent her time managing the wedding and dining business (including designing wedding cakes), while Peter looked after financing, maintenance, and capital projects. At the same time, both the Rickards were not averse to "rolling up their sleeves" and helping out wherever they were needed — from cleaning dishes to making beds.

The inn employed approximately 24 permanent staff and an additional 12 summer season staff of mostly students (see Exhibit 10 for an organizational chart). The work atmosphere was friendly and informal: there were no job descriptions, and staff from different departments cross-performed duties. In general, employee morale was high, and turnover was low among permanent staff. Turnover was higher among summer staff, and good employees were hard to find in the summer because there was not enough good local labour and the inn was unable to offer accommodations for labour from outside the area. New employees were trained on the job, and all employees were given performance reviews by their department supervisors every six months. Peter commented:

> We look for people with a positive attitude and a willingness to learn rather than the necessary skills. Our guests come back as a result of the service they receive and we need the right people to deliver high quality service.

THE COMPETITION

Competition in the Muskoka region was intense. With a short operating season, all cottages, campgrounds, motels, resorts, and inns competed heavily for the consumers' vacation dollars. In the Bracebridge area, there were several inns, motels, and lodges (see Exhibit 11). Of these, only one property, the Riverside Inn, had comparable facilities to the inn.

The Riverside Inn, located on the Muskoka River in downtown Bracebridge, was a full-service inn. It had 55 rooms, a dining room with a seating capacity of 100, a coffee shop seating 30 to 40 people, and a large ballroom that could accommodate 250 to 300 people. The Riverside Inn also had a bowling alley and a playroom for children. The Riverside Inn had previously been poorly run, with well-worn facilities, poor service, and poor food. During the last two years, management had taken steps to improve the property and the service.

Despite the competition, Peter believed that his inn had a distinct competitive advantage:

> We have a unique property, a prime location with exciting views of the falls and the river, and excellent dining facilities. On top of that, we have people who are committed to providing outstanding hospitality. All of this combines to give the inn a country character and we feel that is hard to replicate.

THE EXPANSION PROPOSAL

Over the past nine years, the inn had increased its room accommodations by nearly 120 percent. This growth not only significantly improved the overall profitability of the business, but it also created an awareness and interest in the community, which the owners felt were an important part of the inn's success. Peter explained:

> In a small town such as Bracebridge, people take a keen interest in the achievements in the community and word-of-mouth travels quickly. So, whenever we expand or upgrade our facilities, we are seen as a successful business that is making a positive contribution to the community.

The current expansion proposal the Rickards were considering entailed building a two-storey extension onto the front of the building, which overlooked the Bracebridge Bay (see Exhibit 12). This addition would create a new dining room/function room, allowing the present dining room to be used as a reception room/lounge. The lower floor of the extension would be turned into a meeting/function room, and the conference centre would be converted into additional room accommodations. Peter estimated that the expansion would take approximately six weeks to complete and would cost $325,000, of which they would need to borrow $250,000.[5]

Financially, Peter felt that the expansion would provide the inn with four new and improved sources of income:

1. The new function room on the lower level would eliminate the need for the Conference Centre building. This Conference Centre building could then be converted into three unique rooms. The Rickards estimated that they had turned away business on approximately 100 to 120 nights last year owing to the inn being full. Peter estimated that the three new rooms would provide additional revenue ranging from $30,000 to $43,000 per year, assuming a daily room rate of $100 to $120.

2. The new function room, located in the main building of the Inn, would attract more small conferences, increasing the inn's occupancy in the off-season. Peter estimated this new function room would add $6,000 in rental revenue alone.

3. A larger dining room would be able to accommodate larger wedding receptions in the 120- to 150-person range. At an average revenue of $70 to $80 per person per wedding and 20 to 30 weddings per year, the dining room could generate $40,000 to $50,000 in additional revenue.

4. Currently, any wedding business forced closure of the dining room for non-wedding guests. With the new function room on the lower level it would be possible during the height of the summer season to use the newly expanded dining room on the upper level as a reception area prior to dinner and then hold the wedding meal in the function area. This would enable the dining room to be reset for use by the inn's other guests, adding $16,000 to $18,000 revenue in the months of July and August alone.

Servicing the new dining room extension would require no additional management and only minimal additional kitchen staff during the peak of the summer season. Additional dining room staff would be required to service the larger functions. Similarly, no additional housekeeping staff would be required for the increase in room inventory.

With a larger increase in revenues than in variable costs, Peter believed the total gross profit for the inn would be improved.

In addition to the additional revenues, Peter felt the expansion would offer other benefits:

- It would position the inn as a more upscale property, attracting guests who would help increase the average room rate and food and beverage revenue.
- It would allow the inn to more aggressively promote to small conferences in the off-season.
- It would strengthen the loyalty of guests through a constantly growing and improving facility.

Despite these benefits, Peter still had some reservations:

> We've brought the business to the point that we are comfortable, not to mention profitable, providing a unique hospitality service to the upper-middle income market. It comes down to the age-old question: Do we continue as we are with what is working — though hitting a ceiling — or do we take on extra debt to expand in a notoriously questionable area — food and beverage? In addition, it puts extra strain on the management of the property. During the busy season we are working flat out, and Jan and I would like to retire from the day-to-day operations of the hotel in the next two to five years by either selling the business or employing competent management. With this in mind, will this expansion increase the final price to efficiently cover the expense?

The Rickards knew that they had to make a decision quickly if they wanted to be ready for the upcoming summer season.

Notes

1. Muskoka Tourism.
2. Ontario Travel Monitor Survey 1994, Ontario Ministry of Tourism and Economic Development.
3. Fire sale: sale at a cost significantly less than its actual worth.
4. September to November and March to May were considered the shoulder seasons.
5. Interest on the loan for the expansion would be charged at prime plus 1 percent. At the time, prime was 5 percent per year.

EXHIBIT 1
Location of Huntsville and Bracebridge in the Muskoka Region of Ontario

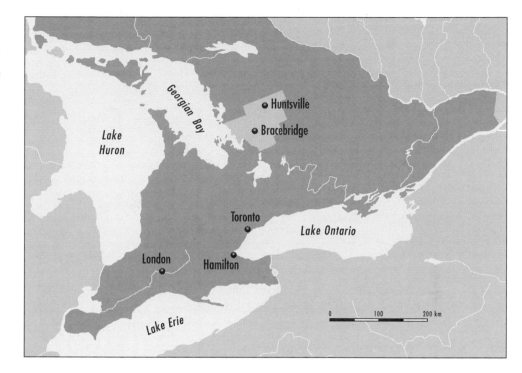

EXHIBIT 2

Tourist Accommodation Usage	
Accommodation Type	Percentage of Tourists Using This Accommodation
Private Cottages	67
Hotels	12.2
Camping	7.6
Motels	6.0
Resorts	1.4
Commercial Cottages	1.1
Other[1]	4.7

1. Includes inns, bed and breakfasts, and hostels.

Source: *Ontario Travel Monitor Survey 1994*, Ontario Ministry of Tourism and Economic Development.

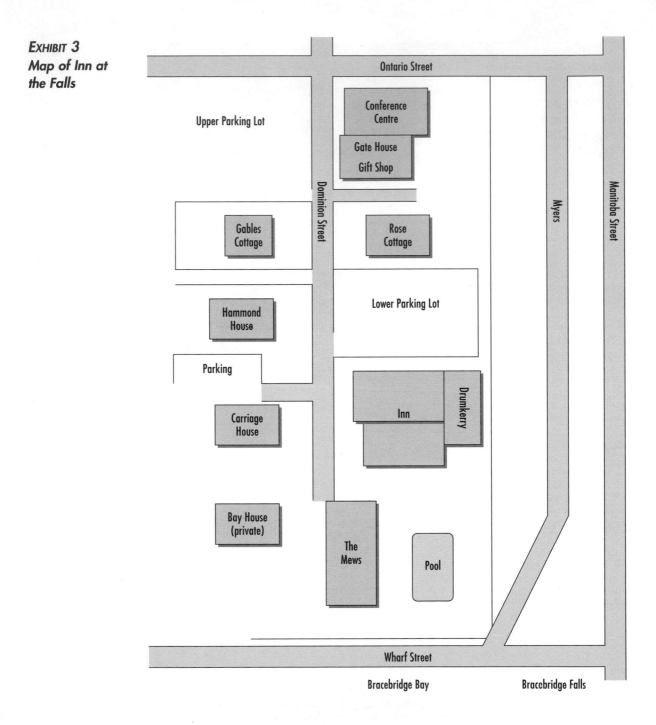

EXHIBIT 3
Map of Inn at the Falls

EXHIBIT 4
The Inn's
Grounds

Exhibit 5

Inn at the Falls
Accommodation
1997
(All rates include a Continental breakfast buffet.)

Cancellation Policy 48 hours
Extra person - add $16.00

Check in 3:00 p.m. Check out 12:00

			Rate	
			Single	Double
THE INN (1876) Some Antiques. One flight stairs. (7 suits)				
101	Mahaffy Suite		140	195
	Two storey premier suite. Queen. Gas fireplace. Wet bar. Jacuzzi. Full bath. View-Bay.			
102	The Alexander Bailey		98	125
	Large bright corner room. King. Full bath. View-Bay, grounds. A/C			
103	The Samuel Armstrong Suite		110	138
	Two room suite. Queen. Full Bath. View-Bay A/C			
104	The Thomas McMurray		82	98
	Small, cozy room. Double. Shower only. Facing parking lot. A/C			
105	the William Mullock		98	125
	Large room, bay window. Raised King. Full bath. Facing front of hotel			
106	the John Beal		90	110
	L-shaped room. Double. Full bath. Facing front of hotel A/C			
107	The Charles Lount		79	88
	Small sunny corner room. Double. Shower only. View -Bay, front of hotel.			
THE MEWS – Adjacent to Inn, overlooking grounds, pool and bay. (10 units)				
"Street Level" – All rooms same size. Large picture windows. Skylights. Full baths.				
Balcony. View–grounds/bay/pool.				
115	Two double beds.		95	115
116	Queen bed.		95	115
117	Queen bed. Gas fireplace.		98	125
118	Two double beds. Gas fireplace.		98	125
119	King Bed or Two Twins. Gas fireplace. End unit. Private balcony. Spectacular view.		110	145
Stairs to "Pool Level" – All rooms same size. Large picture windows. Full baths. Verandas overlooking pool.				
121	Two double beds.		90	105
122	Two double beds		90	105
123	Two double beds. Gas fireplace.		95	115
124	Two double beds. Gas fireplace.		95	115
125	Two double beds. End unit. Private balcony. Great view. Gas fireplace.		98	135
Carriage House – Across from the Inn (4 units) A/C				
131	Large room facing Inn. Queen. Shower only. Ground floor.		90	105
132	Two room units. Queen. Wet bar. Log fireplace. Full bath. Ground floor. Private patio.		110	148
133	Two room suite. Queen. Wet bar. full bath. View. Second floor.		110	148
134	Two room suite. Queen. Wet bar. Full bath. View. Second floor.		110	148
Hammond House – Adjacent to Carriage House. (6 units) A/C				
140	Large room. Two doubles. Basement level. Sliding doors to Patio. Full bath (Jacuzzi).		98	125
141	Two room suite. Two double beds. Full bath. Verandah. Ground floor.		98	148
142	Two room suite. King bed. Full Bath. Verandah. Ground floor. View - garden		98	148
143	Large room. Two double beds. Shower only. Second floor.		79	98
144	Smaller room. One double bed. Full bath. View-garden. Second floor.		79	89
145	Two room suite. King bed. Sitting room facing garden. Second floor.		98	148
Gables Cottage – Adjacent to Hammond House. Own grounds. (1 unit)				
130	Two bedrooms (Queen/Double), large sitting area, log fire, wet bar, full bath. A/C		140	185
Gate House – Adjacent to Rose Cottage. (1 unit)				
129	Top floor suite. Double bed. Sitting room. Full bath		98	125
Rose Cottage – Adjacent to Inn. (4 units)				
160	Large room. King or Two Twins. Gas fireplace. Full bath. Jacuzzi, sep. shower. Street level		110	138
161	Large room. King or Two Twins. Bay window. Full bath (raised Jacuzzi), sep. shower. Private deck. Street level.		110	148
162	Large room. King or Two Twins. Full bath. Second floor.		98	125
163	Large room. Two double beds. Full bath. Second floor.		110	138
Drumkerry Wing – Located at back of Inn. Smaller rooms (3 units)				
126	Double. Full bath.		79	85
127	Double. Full bath. Connects with 128.		79	85
128	Double. Full bath. View (Patio/Bay)		79	95

P.O. Box 1139 BRACEBRIDGE, Ont., P1L 1V3.
Tel: 705-645-2245 Fax: 705-645-5093

Exhibit 6

Sample of Menu Items
Dinner Menu

Entrecote Steak
Charbroiled, seasoned New York Steak with Mushroom Caps
8 oz. $15.95 10 oz. $17.95
With Madagascar Green Peppercorn Sauce Add $3.00

Filet Mignon
8 oz. Beef Tenderloin topped with Mushrooms and
Sauce Béarnaise
$20.95

Tournedos of Beef Tenderloin Chanterelle
Medallions of Beef topped with Chanterelle Mushroom Sauce
$19.95

Prime Rib au Jus with Yorkshire Pudding
8 oz. $16.95 10 oz. $18.95

Rack of new Zealand Lamb Pommeray
$19.95

Pork Tenderloin Bleu
Medallions of Pork with a Bleu Cheese Sauce
$16.95

"Peaches and Cream"
Boneless Breast of Chicken in a Peach Schnapps Sauce
$16.95

Blackened Chicken with Tomato Concassée
$16.95

Supreme of Chicken
Boneless Breast of Chicken filled with Almonds, Hazelnuts, and Ginger
Sautéed in Cointreau and garnished with Raisins, Oranges, and Grapes
$18.95

Loin of Local Venison
Sautéed in a Cranberry and Raspberry Red Wine Sauce
$20.95

EXHIBIT 7A

Statement of Income and Retained Earnings
(Unaudited)
for the Year Ending December 31

	1996	1995	1994
Sales	$1,617,212	$1,522,295	$1,506,249
Cost of sales	798,961	806,988	769,914
Gross profit	$ 818,251	$ 715,307	$ 736,335
Expenses			
Advertising and promotion	$ 35,199	$ 27,298	$ 31,504
Depreciation	84,158	74,631	61,561
Bad debts expense	0	662	0
Bank charges and interest	29,408	29,155	27,119
Consulting fees	0	0	10,727
Dues, fees, and licences	2,480	2,937	3,233
Equipment lease	12,009	23,282	16,474
Entertainment	10,335	11,740	9,524
General and office	14,372	13,051	15,353
Insurance	20,220	17,458	15,453
Interest on long-term debt	61,772	68,909	42,742
Management salaries	139,425	107,787	94,650
Office salaries and benefits	21,000	20,020	18,779
Professional fees	6,027	8,079	7,665
Rent	32,596	30,856	32,904
Repairs and maintenance, equipment	31,728	43,632	53,965
Repairs and maintenance, grounds and buildings	64,271	43,802	23,429
Taxes	27,650	26,349	25,730
Telephone	17,370	15,698	17,580
Travel and automotive	16,301	10,419	8,560
Utilities	50,257	48,264	48,551
Total expenses	$ 676,578	$ 624,029	$ 565,503
Income from operations	$ 141,673	$ 91,278	$ 170,832
Other income (expense)			
Interest income	$ 5,728	$ 2,817	$ 2,010
Miscellaneous	16,934	16,380	13,086
Gain (loss) on short-term investments	0	0	(1,569)
	$ 22,662	$ 19,197	$ 13,527
Income before provisions for income taxes	$ 164,335	$ 110,475	$ 184,359
Provision for income taxes, current	38,482	26,404	42,117
Net income for the year	$ 125,853	$ 84,071	$ 142,242
Retained earnings, beginning of year	$ 516,592	$ 432,521	$ 290,279
Retained earnings, end of year	$ 642,445	$ 516,592	$ 432,521

Exhibit 7b

	Balance Sheet (Unaudited) as at December 31		
	1996	**1995**	**1994**
ASSETS			
Current assets:			
Cash	$ 78,624	$ 74,585	$ 108,800
Short-term investments	0	23,507	23,507
Accounts receivable	26,470	32,635	19,974
Inventories	24,167	13,260	15,464
Prepaid expenses	7,251	19,514	7,408
Total current assets	$ 136,512	$ 163,501	$ 175,153
Fixed assets:			
Land	$ 236,587	$ 236,587	$ 170,833
Buildings	1,360,151	1,209,053	957,941
Less: accumulated depreciation	278,054	224,314	179,094
Equipment	291,723	260,399	243,460
Less: accumulated depreciation	180,510	156,622	132,795
Pool	14,028	14,028	14,028
Less: accumulated depreciation	12,058	11,566	10,950
Parking lot and grounds	59,329	59,329	30,697
Less: accumulated depreciation	13,872	9,918	6,867
Computers	15,915	13,314	10,966
Less: accumulated depreciation	9,752	7,668	5,751
Total fixed assets	1,483,487	1,382,622	1,092.468
TOTAL ASSETS	$1,619,999	$1,546,123	$1,267,621
LIABILITIES			
Current Liabilities:			
Accounts payable	$ 69,844	$ 73,480	$ 63,219
Customer deposits	1,000	11,000	0
Income taxes payable	18,982	6,404	8,724
Current portion of long-term debt	76,992	59,847	38,793
Total current liabilities	$ 166,818	$ 150,731	$ 110,736
Long-term liabilities	810,636	878,700	724,264
Total liabilities	$ 977,454	$1,029,431	$ 835,000
SHAREHOLDERS' EQUITY			
Share capital	$ 100	$ 100	$ 100
Retained earnings	642,445	516,592	432,521
Total shareholders' equity	$ 642,545	$ 516,692	$ 432,621
TOTAL LIABILITIES AND SHAREHOLDERS' EQUITY	$1,619,999	$1,546,123	$1,267,621

EXHIBIT 8

Month	Number of Rooms Sold by Month						
Room Sales Data							
	1990	*1991*	*1992*	*1993*	*1994*	*1995*	*1996*
January	149	205	221	294	306	344	308
February	161	226	230	262	325	270	444
March	158	171	282	279	335	280	739
April	212	236	213	228	288	318	256
May	242	319	293	314	424	468	444
June	308	312	373	356	548	413	550
July	395	409	502	529	736	804	745
August	424	414	472	534	740	805	914
September	339	472	407	536	617	673	688
October	413	288	357	453	584	477	624
November	323	238	308	453	354	255	276
December	304	220	228	359	252	283	338
	3,428	3,450	3,886	4,597	5,509	5,390	6,326
Average occupancy rate	55%	55%	61%	68%	66%	58%	55%
Number of rooms available for the year (i.e., number of rooms x 365 days)	6,171	6,171	6,412	6,760	8,300	9,250	11,600
Average room rate/night	$82.00	$85.91	$88.00	$90.96	$93.43	$100.45	$100.23

Exhibit 9

Inn at the Falls Information
Sales by Consumer Segment

Leisure 47%[1]   Corporate 53%

Geographic Residence of Guests
(%)

Toronto	46.0
United States	12.0
North Ontario	9.0
Kingston/Ottawa	9.0
London/Guelph/Kitchener	6.5
Barrie/Orillia	6.0
Hamilton/Burlington	4.5
Other provinces	3.0
Europe	2.5
St. Catharines/Windsor	1.5
	100.0

Source of Business
(%)

Repeat/referral/friends	82.0
Resorts Ontario	6.9
Ontario ministry	2.0
Newspaper ads	1.5
Guidebooks	1.4
Government directory	1.4
Brochure	1.4
Muskoka Tourism	0.5
Other	2.9

1. Of this figure, 5.5 percent were walk-in customers (i.e., people who walk in with no reservation).

Source: Company records, 1996.

EXHIBIT **10**
Organizational
Chart

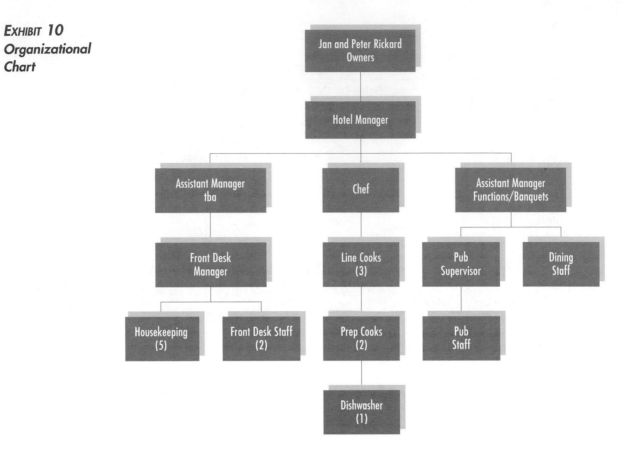

Exhibit 11

Tourist Facilities Available in the Bracebridge Area			
Name	**R-Rooms C-Cottages**	**Nightly Rates**	**Convention Facilities and Capacity**
Bellwood Motel	16R	$64–74	n/a
Cedar Lane Motel	10R	$70–83	n/a
High Falls Chalet Inn	6R	$91–102	50-80
Inn At The Falls	37R	$79–195	80-100
Islander Inn	37R	69–79	n/a
Muskoka Riverside Inn	54R	79–100	n/a
Patterson-Kaye Lodge	5R 12C	$99–135	50–130

Exhibit 12
Floor Plan of Inn

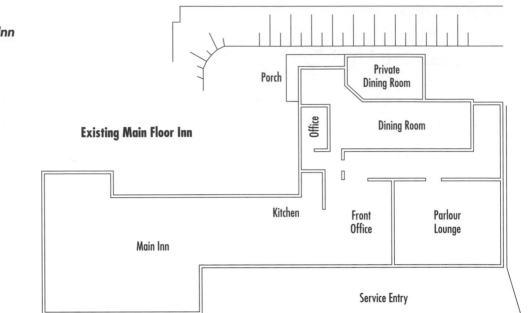

Existing Main Floor Inn

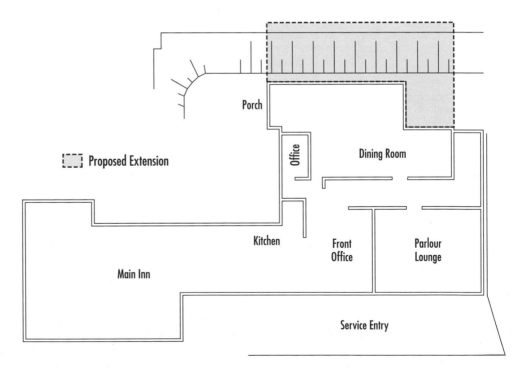

🔲 Proposed Extension

Exhibit 13

	Ratio Analysis		
	1996	**1995**	**1994**
PROFITABILITY			
1) Vertical Analysis			
Sales	100%	100%	100%
Cost of sales	49% 48	53%	51%
Gross profit	51%	47%	49%
Operating expenses	42%	41%	38%
Other income	1%	1%	1%
Net income before tax	10%	7%	12%
Income tax (as a % of NI)	23%	24%	23%
Net income after tax	8%	6%	9%
2) Return on Investment	22	18	39
LIQUIDITY			
Current ratio	.82:1	1.08:1	1.58:1
Acid test	.63:1	.87:1	1.38:1
EFFICIENCY			
Age of accounts receivable	6 days	7.8 days	4.8 days
Age of inventory	11 days	6 days	7.3 days
Age of payables[1]	70.9 days	73.9 days	66.6 days
STABILITY			
Net worth/total assets	40%	33%	34%

GROWTH	**1995–96**	**1994–95**
Sales	6%	1%
Net income	50%	(41%)
Assets	5%	22%
Equity	24%	19%

1. Assumes purchases are 45 percent of cost of goods sold.

C A S E 7.7   MAIL-ORDER IN CANADA

By John Graham and L.L. McInychyn

On April 10, 1991, Linda King, an Honours Business Administration student at the University of Western Ontario put the finishing touches on a 50-page business plan that she had prepared for a course entitled New Enterprise Management. Her report proposed the opening of a retail lingerie and leisure wear store in London, Ontario, modelled after the highly successful Victoria's Secret in the United States. To increase awareness of the products and company name, she proposed introducing the venture with a mail-order catalogue. It was this area about which Linda was most enthusiastic, and she was now wondering how she could go about breaking into the Canadian mail-order and lingerie market.

THE LINGERIE AND LEISURE WEAR MARKET

Lingerie can be defined as "women's underwear and nightclothes made of lace, silk, nylon, etc." This broad category includes underwear, brassieres, undershirts, teddies, nighties, and pyjamas. Leisure wear includes all other casual night clothes and lounge wear, night shirts, long johns, flannel pyjamas, bathrobes, and slippers. Lingerie and leisure wear products can be categorized by briefs, sleep wear, and lounge wear.

Lingerie and leisure wear can be found in retail boutiques, in department stores, and through mail-order catalogues. Currently, the latter make up an insignificant part of the Canadian market. Although the retail industry has suffered over the last few years, there have been some positive signs for specialty stores, which include specialty lingerie stores. Over the last five years, sales at women's stores have grown significantly. Between 1986 and 1990, sales in the category of "intimate apparel" have grown consistently. Between 1989 and 1990, sales growth was 14.7 percent.

The industry is expected to grow at an average of 6 percent for the next 5 to 10 years. Underwear is the most popular women's wear item. Imports of women's underwear in 1990 totalled 13 million pairs, and the total Canadian production is estimated at about 13.5 to 15 million pairs per year.

THE LINGERIE CONSUMER

Lingerie consumers are considered to be women aged 16 and over. Within Canada there are approximately 5.2 million such women who purchase two to

---

three items of bras and underwear every year. These women purchase items for personal consumption or to be given as a gift. Lingerie is purchased all year, with seasonal fluctuations over the holiday season in December and the summer months. Most women who purchase the more adventurous items prefer to shop in malls where they can blend into traffic inconspicuously.

THE LONDON MARKET

London, Ontario, is located about 160 km southwest of Toronto, easily accessed by the MacDonald-Cartier Freeway (Highway 401). With a metropolitan population in excess of 300,000, London is nationally known as "the Forest City" for its tree-lined streets. Many of the small towns surrounding the city (Exeter, Ilderton, Lucan, Grand Bend, Ailsa Craig, Parkhill, Thorndale, and St. Thomas) utilize London's many services and conveniences. Residents from as far away as Sarnia, Goderich, and Stratford (a 70-km radius) frequently make the journey to London for shopping and other amenities.

The economy of the city could be characterized as stable, white collar, and mainly service based. Unemployment was lower than the national average, while individual personal income was 9 percent above the national average. With a higher personal disposable income than most Canadian cities, London boasted more retail shopping space per capita than any other city in North America.[1]

COMPETITION

Janet Alexander currently operates two stores in the London area. These stores carry brand name items such as Voguebra, Warners, and Lejaby. The product line includes lingerie and sleep wear.

Lingerie Elisse is another local competitor targeting the quality conscious consumer. The products it offers are similar to those of Janet Alexander and are supplied by Canadian manufacturers. Its London location has been open since 1989, but they have a more established store in Markham, Ontario.

La Vie En Rose is the only national competitor. With 19 stores across Canada, it is the second-largest Canadian lingerie retailer in five provinces. Its stores are located in both malls and street-front boutiques. The image of quality is achieved through its elegant store atmosphere. No difference in product quality was observed between this store and the previously mentioned ones.

Frederick's of Hollywood is a major U.S. lingerie retailer. Frederick's began as a mail-order company and added the retail units once the name was established. As of 1988, mail-order made up 40 percent of Frederick's sales and 60 percent of the company's profits. Frederick's stores have had trouble establishing themselves in the market because consumers have tended to purchase their items as jokes or novelties. This chain has had extreme difficulty shaking this image and has yet to break into the everyday underwear market.

Victoria's Secret offers a wide variety of lingerie and leisure wear products that are perceived to be superior in quality and value to anything currently offered in Canada. It is owned by a larger U.S. retailer, The Limited. Victoria's Secret also operates a very extensive mail-order business.

**THE CLOTHING
MAIL-ORDER
INDUSTRY**

The mail-order industry is a division of a marketing technique called direct marketing. Direct marketing involves selling products directly to the consumer via mail advertisements, catalogues, phone solicitation, or TV sales (i.e., the home shopping network). Mail-order is the most popular of these options. Mail-order involves having a catalogue delivered to the residence of a consumer. The catalogue describes product features, shows pictures of the products being sold, and details their prices, availability, and order process. Typical products sold through the mail include books, appliances, clothing, shoes, audio items, and camping gear. The order process can take several forms. The most popular one is an agent marketing system, which has successfully been employed by Avon Cosmetics. This system provides back-up sales people who make house calls to deliver the catalogue and then follow-up calls to collect the customers' orders. Another common method of ordering from a catalogue requires customers to place their orders over the phone direct to the company via a 1-800 phone number.

Offering products through a mail-order catalogue presents the potential for national awareness. It also provides the advantage of achieving quantity discounts from manufacturers sooner than would be available using a solely retail operation. A mail-order business can be started with a smaller capital investment than is required to open a retail store. This kind of customer service can create lifetime customers. Mail-order also offers some challenges. First, Canada has the largest number of malls and department stores per capita in North America. This offers the consumer many alternative places to shop. Second, Canadians tend to be more conservative than their neighbours south of the border. Third, the climate and changing seasons mean a constantly changing product line, which requires a fast turnover of merchandise.

**THE
MAIL-ORDER
CONSUMER**

Although the majority of mail-order is unsolicited, it is carefully targeted toward those whom the company considers to be potential customers. Clothing mail-order consumers are considered to be individuals aged 18 to 30. The market can be segmented based on past mail-order purchase history. Someone who has shopped mail-order would already have a good understanding of how the system works, would have different shopping habits, and would also be less averse to risk. The individual who has never shopped mail-order should not be ignored, however, since this segment makes up the majority of the Canadian market.

**Have Bought
Through
Mail-Order**

Those who have bought clothing through mail-order before and have been satisfied with the outcome will not have to be convinced of its merits. These consumers have likely shopped through some of the more established mail-order companies and will be used to prompt delivery and excellent service. These individuals likely have a relative who lives in the United States or live themselves within 200 km of the U.S. border. Many of the mail-order items bought in Canada are a result of catalogues filtering across from the United States. These consumers tend to be adventurous and willing to "take a chance" on a product. These individuals do not have a lot of time on their hands to browse through conventional malls to look for a certain product. Furthermore, they tend to have a higher discretionary income to spend on indulgent items for themselves. Consumers that are sold on this method of shopping usually cite its convenience and flexibility as well as the variety of available products as its main advantages. Flexibility refers to the time of day in which they can shop. It is not unusual to have 24 hour per day service. Customers are not constrained by the usual 10 a.m. to 6 p.m. store hours.

Have Never Shopped Mail-Order

This segment consists of those who have never been given the opportunity, and those who have never taken the chance. The most common excuses for resistance to mail-order are that you can't touch the material to feel its quality, you can't try items on, and you experience a hassle in returning a product that doesn't fit. These consumers tend to be more risk-averse than someone who is willing to try mail-order and would sooner go without the product than risk unnecessary disappointment.

THE NEW VENTURE PROPOSAL

The original report proposed opening a retail store that would offer an alternative to the traditional marketing of lingerie. The concept intended to create an elegant atmosphere that would draw the consumer into the store on impulse, rather than out of necessity. This atmosphere would be achieved by placing emphasis on the store front, layout, fixtures, and lighting to create a real "shopping experience." The sales at the retail store would be supplemented by a mail-order catalogue. The products to be sold included ladies' sleep wear, hosiery, underwear, bras, robes, toiletries, accessories, and men's wear.

After considerable thought, Linda thought it might be best to start the business with just the mail-order division. This would help to promote awareness of the products and store name, while keeping costs low.

Mail-Order Distribution

The process would begin by mailing the catalogue to the target consumer.

The production of the catalogue would be contracted out to a printing company called Charterhouse Printing Services (CPS). CPS estimated a cost of $4,650 for 2,000 catalogues. The catalogues would be 8 1/2″ x 11″ in size, with 28 pages including the cover. Photography would be supplied free of charge from a friend who was studying at the Ontario College of Art. Depending on the target consumer group, there would be two possible methods of catalogue distribution. Canada Post admail delivery service would be used for national distribution, and an independent agency called Star Mail-Ibax would be used for any deliveries within London (Exhibits 1 and 2).

A successful mail-order depends on the consumer group targeted. In order to reach the "has shopped mail-order" segment, Linda could call a list broker and purchase a list of all women aged 18 to 30 who have subscribed to mail-order catalogues in the past. Lists cost $100 for every 1,000 names. The list is then sent in the form of address labels, which can be placed directly on the catalogue. Using a list broker allows national distribution, since names from across Canada are included.

Since there would be no list available for the "never shopped mail-order" segment, a cold-call strategy would have to be used. Because this method would require a lot more effort, Linda decided to use London as a test market. Linda discovered that Statistics Canada published demographic data on the households in London. Combined with a postal code map of the city, this information would help to pinpoint an area of the city that would be most responsive to a mail-order lingerie catalogue (Exhibits 3A and 3B).

Once the customers received the catalogue, they would be free to browse at their leisure. When they decided upon the products they would like to purchase, they could place their orders via a 1-800 phone number. To provide 24 hour per day service, an answering machine would have to be purchased. The information gained over the phone would include the item number, colour, size, customer address, and method of payment (only Visa or Mastercard would be accepted).

Upon receipt of the order all the relevant customer information would be input into a database. The supplier would then be called and the merchandise ordered. In order to maintain good service for the customers, a one-week lead time from the suppliers between placement and receipt of the order would be necessary. This way the customers would receive their orders within 10 days. The average order size per week from the supplier was expected to be 5 kg. When the products were received, they would be mailed out to the customer. Canada Post's Priority Courier would be employed for delivery. Each delivery per household was not expected to exceed 1 kg. The Priority Courier costs are $1.40 for delivery of up to 5 kg within London and $4.70 for 1 kg within Canada. These costs would be paid by the customer.

Supplier Sourcing

Production of the products would be contracted out to lingerie manufacturers. Two manufacturers were currently being considered, one in Canada and one in Hong Kong. The candidate would be chosen based on the ability to meet design and delivery requirements at the lowest cost.

When importing goods from Hong Kong, the production process becomes slightly more complicated and time consuming, but the potential cost savings can justify the effort. One of the biggest costs involved in dealing with overseas manufacturers is the trip to Hong Kong to see the quality of their work before placing the initial order. Ordering from Hong Kong requires a longer lead time, as it is necessary to account for the delivery. The time involved from the point of order to receipt of the product runs between four and six months. Linda wondered what effect this would have on the mail-order process. All payment to these manufacturers must be made with a letter of credit, which involves a banking fee and interest cost.

Of several Hong Kong manufacturers, Linda had narrowed her choice down to Oodways International Limited. They had been the most helpful in replying to requests for product lists and cost data information. Oodways' terms of delivery were 75 days after receipt of the letter of credit. They also specified minimum orders of 300 items. Average manufacturer's selling price was expected to be $10 for briefs, $25 for sleep wear, and $40 for lounge wear.

The Canadian manufacturer, Delicate Lingerie, was based in Montreal. They required credit terms of 30 days and had a returns policy for accepting returns due to an error in shipment or defective merchandise. All claims for returns must be made within five days of receipt of goods. The delivery terms were quite different from Oodways. Fall delivery took place from June 1 through October 25; winter delivery was from October 15 through November 15. Average manufacturer's selling price was expected to be $12 for briefs, $21 for sleep wear items, and $31 for lounge wear.

Mail-Order Costs

The mail-order business would be run out of the basement of a friend's house in London and would not require a lot of time commitment after the initial start-up. The same product lines would be sold through the mail-order, and the "atmosphere" could be achieved through quality photography and layout of the catalogue.

Most of the costs for the mail-order operation would be fixed. These included rent at $400 per month for the use of the basement office in London; an answering machine for $217.35; catalogue production; catalogue distribution; the 1-800 number at $1,880 for 55 hours of calls plus an additional $32 per hour for an additional 50 hours; $1,500 for a computer and database program advertising; and promotion; and, finally, the salaries for the personnel who would operate the division. The operation would require one full-time employee to answer phone orders and another part-time employee to provide support for order processing. The full-time employee would earn a salary of $18,000 per year, while the part-time employee would earn $7 per hour. Other miscellaneous expenses were expected to total $3,000 in the first year. The charges for accepting Visa and Mastercard would be 4 percent of sales, which would be treated as a variable cost.

Retail Store

The retail store would require a large investment of both time and money in the start-up months. Masonville Mall was chosen as a potential location for the retail store. It is estimated that 60 percent of mall traffic consists of women aged 25 to 40 with above-average disposable income levels. A research survey conducted in 1989 indicated that in 1991, $24 million would be spent on women's wear. Mall management projected that its primary market would grow an average of 7 percent over the next 10 years, and with the recent mall expansion, they expected to capture more consumer spending.

The same supplier chosen for the mail-order division would be secured for the retail store.

Rent would be $4,375 per month, and capital costs covering store fixtures and decor were expected to be $25,000. An advertising budget of $15,000 was set for the first year. Salaries and wages would be $2,900 per month, covering the salary of one full-time manager and three part-time workers. Other miscellaneous expenses should total $6,000.

Combined Strategy

The final strategy would be to open the retail store and mail-order business simultaneously. The mail-order division would start off selling merchandise identical to that which was sold in the store. The mail-order business might be nation wide or restricted to London, depending on which target market is chosen.

It was expected that briefs would account for approximately 60 percent of all sales, sleep wear 25 percent of sales, with the remainder of sales coming from lounge wear. Total sales for the retail store in the first full year of operation were expected to reach $150,000. Sales for the mail-order division were expected to reach $50,000. Margin on cost of 42 percent was projected for all briefs, 50 percent for sleep wear, and 48 percent for lounge wear.

Advertising and Promotion

Linda was not sure how much she would have to spend on advertising and promotion. She maintained that an effective distribution of the catalogue for the mail-order concept should serve as good advertising. "But what about everyone who's not on your mailing list?" a friend questioned. "An ad in a newspaper or magazine could include information on how to get a catalogue mailed to you, if you are not in the London area." Linda wondered if this was a valid point.

Several advertising options were available to solve this problem. A newspaper ad could be taken out in the mail-order section of either *The Globe and Mail,* the *Toronto Star*, or the *London Free Press* (see Exhibit 4). Linda liked this idea and remembered reading that Tilley Endurables started out with an ad in a newspaper, and had since turned out to be quite a success story. The average cost of a magazine ad in Canadian homemaker magazines runs at $2,000 for a full-page ad.

Other Considerations

Linda was confident that she could secure bank financing of $65,000 for the first year of operations. She could afford to put in only $10,000 from personal savings; two classmates had offered to match this amount in exchange for partnerships in the company.

In August, Linda was going to start a full-time job with a management consultant firm in Toronto, so she would not have a lot of time available to spend on the venture.

Linda was hoping eventually to reach the goal of $500,000 in sales. This was a milestone she had set for herself and she wondered how long it would take to reach it. She also wanted to achieve a return on investment of 15 percent over five years.

FINAL CONSIDERATIONS

Can the Canadian market support a lingerie mail-order catalogue and retail store? This was the question Linda was pondering. She was relatively risk-averse and did not want to get in over her head.

Linda understood that establishing a retail and/or mail-order company in Canada would pose a great many challenges in the start-up months. It still had to be decided whether or not to open the retail store, develop a mail-order business, or do both at the same time. In addition to that, she had to decide which consumer segment to target for the mail-order division, how to attract customers, and where to source the product (domestic or abroad). All this and she had yet to decide upon a name for the company!

NOTES

1. *Canadian Markets 1993*, 67th ed. (Toronto: The Financial Post Data Group, 1993, and Statistics Canada, 1993). Excerpted from *The Ugly Dog Pizza Company*, April 1995.

EXHIBIT 1

Canada Post Admail Rates				
Single Mailing Volume Rates (Residential Delivery Only)[1]				
Customers mailing large volume Single Mailings of Printed Matter may qualify for volume discount rates as outlined below.				
Volume per Mailing	*Premium Rates (Standard Items)*		*Economy Rates (Nonstandard Items)*	
	0–50 g	*over 50 g*	*0–50 g*	*over 50 g*
5,000	7.1¢	4.8¢ + 46¢/kg	6.6¢	4.5¢ + 42¢/kg
10,000	7.0	4.8 + 44	6.5	4.4 + 42
20,000	6.9	4.7 + 44	6.4	4.3 + 42
30,000	6.8	4.6 + 44	6.2	4.2 + 40
40,000	6.7	4.5 + 44	6.1	4.1 + 40
50,000	6.6	4.5 + 42	5.9	4.0 + 38
100,000	6.5	4.4 + 42	5.8	4.0 + 36

All volume rates apply to items deposited at the office of delivery. Customers wishing to have Canada Post forward items to any other delivery office(s) may do so for an additional transportation fee of $4 per 1,000 items ($0.004 per piece).

1. Compliments of Canada Post.

Exhibit **2**

Cost of Catalogue Distribution

Star Mail-Ibax — Independent Admail Delivery Service

	2,500 units — 9,999 units (minimum order: 2,500 units) $40 for every 1,000
or	4.0 cents per unit (1 catalogue)
	10,000 units — 19,999 units $34 for every 1,000
or	3.4 cents per unit
	20,000 units — 99,999 units $31 for every 1,000
or	3.1 cents per unit

EXHIBIT 3A

Demographic and Income Data for Postal Code Areas, 1988[1]

Area	All Taxfilers % by Age					Taxfilers Reporting Total Income % with Income Greater Than						
London, Canada	Number	<25	25–44	45–64	>64	Number	$15,000	$25,000	$35,000	$50,000	$75,000	$100,000
N5V – 1	14,175	20	48	27	6	14,125	57	34	16	3	0	X
N5W – 1	16,675	167	43	27	14	16,600	55	29	13	3	0	X
N5X – 1	10,125	17	45	29	9	10,100	67	48	33	17	5	3
N5Y – 1	20,500	20	46	22	13	20,400	53	29	14	4	1	0
N5Z – 1	14,775	17	48	23	11	14,700	54	28	12	3	0	X
N6A – 1	7,825	17	40	22	21	7,800	61	40	26	14	6	4
N6A4B5–RR	200	14	43	29	14	200	63	38	25	X	X	X
N6A4B6–RR	275	17	33	33	17	275	64	45	27	18	9	X
N6A4B7–RR	225	11	44	33	X	225	56	44	22	11	X	X
N6A4B8–RR	375	20	33	33	13	375	60	33	20	X	X	X
N6A4B9–RR	325	17	33	33	27	325	69	46	31	15	X	X
N6A4C1–RR	200	13	38	38	13	200	50	38	13	X	X	X
N6A4C2–Rr	300	18	45	27	9	300	58	33	17	X	X	X
N6A4C3–RR	450	17	44	28	11	450	61	39	22	6	X	X
N6C – 1	21,725	16	49	22	14	21,675	63	39	21	8	2	1
N6E – 1	16,850	19	59	17	4	16,800	60	36	19	4	0	0
N6G – 1	14,025	17	52	23	8	13,975	61	43	28	13	5	3
N6H – 1	16,775	15	35	25	25	16,750	62	39	23	11	3	2
N6J – 1	17,350	17	44	26	13	17,300	60	36	20	8	2	1
N6K – 1	14,825	16	45	26	13	14,800	65	46	31	16	5	3
OTHER	2,950	13	32	18	37	2,959	55	36	22	13	6	3

1. Statistics Canada Catalogue No. 17–202, Issue 1990, pp. 170–73, Table #1.

Reproduced with permission of the Minister of Supply and Services Canada, 1992.

Exhibit **3B**
City of London

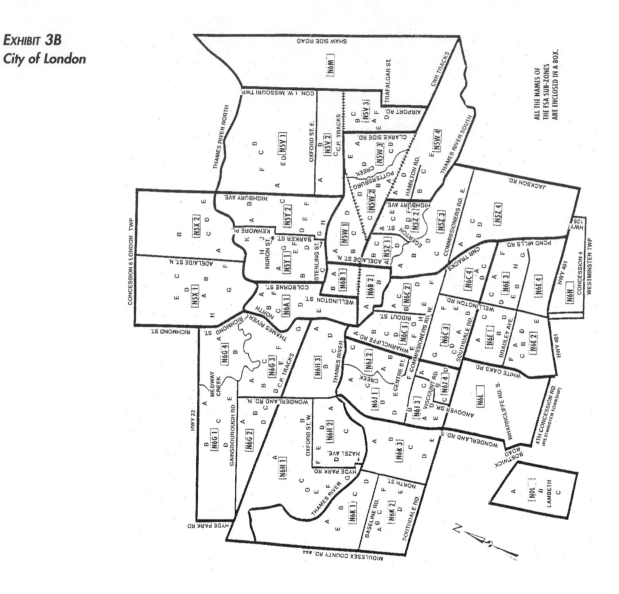

Sheldon's Retail Directory by the United States and Canada, 1991. Reproduced with permission from Phelon, Sheldon & Marsar, Inc.

Exhibit 4

Advertising Cost Data

Toronto Star
Costs listed are for approximately 1/8 of a page (2 1/16 inches by 4 inches).

	Circulation	Cost	Readership
Mon–Fri	550,000	$ 874/day	1.6–1.8 million/day
Saturday	850,000	$1,076/day	2.6 million/day
Sunday	540,000	$ 687/day	1.3 million/day

The Globe and Mail
Costs listed for 2 1/16 by 3 3/8 inch, the smallest size of ad available. For a larger ad, double both dimension and price.

	Circulation	Cost	Readership
Mon–Sat	330,000	$1,554/6 days + GST	1 million/day

London Free Press
Costs listed for an 1/8 of a page.

	Circulation	Cost	Readership
Mon–Thurs and Sat	125,610	$967/day	N/A
Friday	136,633	$967/day	N/A

CASE 7.8   MONDETTA EVERYWEAR

By John F. Graham and Leena Malik

In June 1992, the office of Mondetta Clothing Company in Winnipeg, was alive with activity as Mondetta's four owners and their support staff were busy at work. In the company's meeting room, samples were being examined for the upcoming fall fashion line, while in the back warehouse, new clothing shipments were being sorted. After several years of rapid growth in the Canadian casual wear industry, Mondetta's managers were committed to making their company a success through further market penetration. They wondered whether they should continue to solidify clothing sales in Canada or proceed with their desire to expand into the U.S. and, eventually, European markets. In order to make a reasonable decision, each expansion alternative would require careful examination of market and industry data, as well as the company's ability to handle another phase of increased growth.

COMPANY BACKGROUND

Mondetta Clothing Company was founded as a partnership in Winnipeg by brothers Ash and Prashant Modha and Raj and Amit Bahl. The brothers were close friends who started by operating a small business selling cards and stationery while studying at university. In 1987, they decided to offer local casual wear buyers unique fashions by designing and manufacturing a line of beachwear and casual pants. Working out of their families' basement, they managed product designs, production, marketing, and distribution and were rewarded with $10,000 in sales in that year.

During the following two summers, the company's casual cotton pants, shorts and tops were sold outside the city from a booth at Winnipeg's popular Grand Beach. With a population of approximately 650,000, Winnipeg was the largest distribution centre between Vancouver and Toronto and offered a direct connection to the United States.

As the Mondetta name proceeded to gain exposure in the Winnipeg market, the brothers were awarded the Small Business Achiever Award by Winnipeg's *Uptown Magazine*, as well as other distinguished industry and media honours. In

1988, their sales grew to $25,000 and reached $125,000 by 1989. In May 1990, after most of the brothers had completed their undergraduate studies, they incorporated the business and started full-time company operations. Soon Mondetta expanded from a few local retail stores to more than 350 outlets across Canada, with sales beyond $2.4 million. The company's financial statements are presented in Exhibits 1 and 2, and a ratio sheet is shown in Exhibit 3.

MONDETTA EVERYWEAR

The name Mondetta was based on French word-play for "small world" and the focus of the collection was the high quality appliqué and embroidery on cotton clothing. Mondetta catered to a market that generally desired clothing that offered something different from what was available in most regular stores. Their most popular items were their "flagshirts," sweatshirts adorned with the flags of world countries, and their styles were targeted to the socially or politically concerned man, woman, or young adult who enjoyed superior quality casual or street wear.

Consumers over 30 years old generally looked for a product made of high quality materials with superior graphic designs, while younger customers looked mainly for quality through an established brand name. Although the younger 13- to 30-year-old segment was highly influenced by fashion trends, the price of the apparel remained an important consideration in their buying process. Word-of-mouth and the visual appearance of the clothing also influenced both consumer groups, who approached trendy wear stores to find the hottest new clothing available.

THE TRADE ENVIRONMENT

Innovative clothing companies like Mondetta often started their businesses by selling clothing to trend-setting independent stores in the hope that their products would create a new fashion craze. Once a trend had been created, product visibility and sales were increased through movement into the mainstream clothing stores.

Independent Stores

Independent store owners usually managed one or, at most, two local stores in a city or town. Some independents were considered to be local trend setters, while others were followers who copied the trend makers after product exposure had been created. Purchases were performed from one location, usually the store itself, using fashion trend information. Since independent stores generally did not have the ability to purchase in large quantities, volume and early payment discounts were not granted. Payment terms to producers were 30 to 60 days, with a 50 percent mark-up to retail customers.

Many independents were considered to be poor credit risks owing to their limited financial resources, unstable management, and variable clientele. The most successful independents distinguished themselves through their management style and the establishment of their own reputation, visibility, and local market niche. Even though placement in an independent store appeared risky, it was an important channel for brand name and trend creation.

The Chain Stores

The chain store network was divided into regional chains that serviced either western or eastern Canada, and national chains. Chain stores were more stable and creditworthy than independent stores and had more purchasing power than the department stores. Chain stores expected a 55 percent product mark-up, as well as a 2 percent warehousing discount. Early payment terms were 3 percent in 10 days net 60 days.

Most chain stores offered relatively little product advertising and relied on in-store displays and word-of-mouth to attract customers. The need to approach only one or two buying offices for each chain offered the provision of wide geographic distribution with less selling effort than required for the independent stores.

The Department Stores

Canadian department stores such as the Bay and Sears were generally less flexible and entrepreneurial than other retail outlets and relied on more tightly controlled planning of operations. Department stores purchased clothing (based on product type) from central or regional buying offices through designated buyers. Some department stores also specifically allocated budgets for the exploration of goods from local companies to match merchandise with local demand. In order to get placement in a department store, clothing company representatives had to approach the appropriate buying officer. For casual and street wear, this officer was more likely to be the men's wear or women's wear buyer.

Department store demands were usually very high. Most expected signed contracts specifying desired prices, mark-ups, volume discounts, and early payment discounts. Mark-ups on cost for casual wear were close to 50 percent, while volume and early payment discounts ranged between 3 to 5 percent each. Although product distribution was usually allocated per store location by the clothing firm, products had to be sent to the department store's central warehouse before being shipped to designated store outlets. This system resulted in an additional 2 percent warehousing discount. Some department stores also demanded a 1 to 2 percent advertising discount. The resulting 9 to 14 percent worth of discounts allowed Canadian department stores to sell products at a lower price than other retailers, thereby creating the perception that department stores sold discount low quality clothing.

U.S. Stores

With expansion into the United States a serious consideration, the brothers recognized that U.S. trade dynamics differed from Canadian dynamics in several important ways. First, the discount image of Canadian department stores made independent and chain stores hesitant to take on products originally featured in a department store. However, in the United States, department stores such as Bloomingdales, Macy's, and Nordstroms were perceived as leaders in the fashion industry. Therefore, initial placement in these stores created a fashion trend that the independent and chain stores were willing to endorse. Second, the U.S. market was dominated by numerous strong retail stores and apparel companies that were more aggressive and demanding than their conservative Canadian counterparts. Third, highly diverse consumer tastes and the desire for more bold and flashy items resulted in an intensely competitive retail environment.

The U.S. apparel industry was also undergoing a period of change and restructuring. By 1989, discount stores and mail order firms had gained market share at the expense of specialty department and chain stores. In fact, discounters replaced department stores as the largest retail segment. Another trend in the U.S. apparel industry was the formation of close, interdependent relationships between retailer and supplier based on a joint commitment to mutual profitability through in-store boutiques. In addition, in order to improve efficiency and lower costs, retailers were making efforts to narrow their supplier structure with larger commitments and bigger orders.

THE COMPETITION

Competitors in the casual wear industry sold similar products (jeans, sweatshirts, and T-shirts) adorned with their brand names in retail chain, department, and independent stores throughout Canada and the United States. In Winnipeg, an independent company called Passport International had recently opened a retail outlet next to Eaton's downtown store. Passport's designs were identical to Mondetta's, with the exception of the logo, and the clothing was also sold at a lower price. For example, Mondetta's highly successful flagshirt, which retailed for $79.95, was sold for $64.99 in Passport. Passport also offered customized flags of any country compared with Mondetta's 45 flags. Although Passport was made of lower quality materials, customers wanting a Mondetta but not able to afford one generally turned to Passport for their designs. Passport International was rumoured to be opening a new location in Toronto's Fairview Mall by fall 1992.

Nationally, Mondetta clothing was placed side by side with other established brand name products such as Guess Jeans, Request, and Pepe Jeans. However, the companies selling these labels had wider retail distribution networks in both Canada and the United States. Top industry names such as Guess Jeans, Buffalo Jeans, and B.U.M. Equipment were all associated with large U.S. and European firms, and the success of these companies was due to the creation of a highly visible media hype focused on brand name and product promotion. Because competing products were normally placed side-by-side in the store, sales depended more on brand name and reputation than on product differentiation.

Guess and B.U.M. were also beginning to license themselves in the European market. Through licensing, a European manufacturer had the right to produce and sell approved designs using a clothing's brand name and logo. In the European and U.S. high fashion markets, country of origin was less important than factors such as quality, style, and price, particularly in the medium to higher price ranges. Exhibit 4 presents an overview of major international apparel markets and producers, as well as their main strengths and weaknesses.

THE ENVIRONMENT

Increased opportunities for Canadian apparel firms to enter the large U.S. market were becoming available because of the gradual reduction of trade tariffs under the recent Canada–U.S. Free Trade Agreement. However, Canadian companies wishing to export to the United States faced many established competitors. In addition, their flexibility was reduced because of a requirement to place 50 percent Canadian content in their goods. As a general rule, apparel made from third-country fabrics was not eligible for duty-free treatment under the agreement. Freer trade with the United States also prompted several large U.S. retailers to expand into Canada, thereby increasing competition for the Canadian consumer. By June 1992, North American free trade talks with Mexico were well underway, and an agreement was expected to be reached before the end of 1992.

Currency fluctuations appeared to have little impact on export competitiveness with the United States. On the other hand, the devaluation of the Canadian dollar relative to European currencies over the past two years had sparked renewed interest by Canadian manufacturers in the European market. However, in Europe the duty-free movement of goods among European community countries, strong competition from European designer labels, and the aggressive marketing of private-label manufacturers, hindered Canada's apparel trade in this market.

MONDETTA'S CURRENT STRATEGY

Mondetta's strategy focused on product exclusivity rather than market saturation. This focus was achieved through careful selection of industry sales agents and retailers for clothing promotion. In 1989 and early 1990, Mondetta clothing was sold throughout western Canada in high quality regional and national chain stores and local independent stores. Since heavy price discounting by department stores compromised Mondetta's high quality exclusive image, department store sales were restricted to Eaton's in Winnipeg. In late 1991, after the establishment of western Canadian sales, Mondetta expanded into Ontario, Quebec, and the Maritimes. Management's sales goal for the 1992 fiscal year was $5 million to $6 million, which they hoped to achieve through increased national and international market penetration.

Finance

Although monthly cash flow forecasts based on prebooked orders were prepared, the frequent opening of new accounts resulted in completely different cash requirements than those projected. This situation was beginning to strain Mondetta's $250,000 line of credit for inventory financing. While government incentives to support small business were available to companies that promoted local employment, poor economic conditions in 1992 and the company's young age made government agencies hesitant to provide funds. Banks were also afraid to lend funds to what they labelled as "here today, gone tomorrow" businesses.

This feeling was created by the recent bankruptcy of several highly successful Winnipeg clothing companies that were owned and operated by young managers.

In order to deal with a difficult cash situation, Mondetta operated by customer order. This system enabled the company to match receivables with payables while carefully managing supply relationships to ensure timely payments. Management hoped that a new computerized system for accounting, purchase orders, production, marketing, and receivables would assist with the development of strict cash management plans.

Marketing

Mondetta's managers tried to foster a mystique cult following and to avoid market saturation by restricting their products to a limited number of superior quality stores. To create visibility for its flagshirts, the company employed industry agents who targeted trendy name-setting stores in each location before distributing to the high quality chain stores. Agents received a 10 percent commission on the Mondetta selling price (industry commissions ranged from 8 to 12 percent). Marketing communications consisted mainly of press exposure, word-of-mouth and the graphics appeal of the clothing. In Winnipeg, Mondetta clothing was also displayed on transit shelters.

The brothers participated in two semiannual trade shows hosted by Salon International. Trade shows created product visibility and were attended by numerous retail sales agents and buyers. The spring/summer show was held during February in Montreal, while the fall/winter show was held during August in Toronto. A trade show booth cost approximately $20,000, with a space cost of $5,000. Travelling and on-site expenses resulted in a total cost of $30,000 per show.

Mondetta's major customers were Bootlegger (nationwide), Below the Belt and Off the Wall (western regional chains), and Eaton's in Winnipeg. Approximately 40 percent of the company's sales volume resulted from these accounts. In terms of overall sales, western Canadian sales made up 80 percent of the company's business, with 18 percent in Ontario and only 2 percent in Quebec and the Maritimes. In contrast, Canadian retail apparel sales in 1991 were around 37 percent in Ontario, 34 percent in Quebec and the Maritimes, and 29 percent in western Canada.

Mondetta's most popular logos, "Mondetta Everywear" and "The Spirit of Unification," were company trademarks. Traditionally, the two fashion lines (spring and fall) focused on the theme of international awareness and globalization. In 1993, the company hoped to sell four fashion lines (one per season) that placed more emphasis on the Mondetta name than on the flags.

Operations

The apparel design led to either rapid product acceptance or rejection, thus making it the first and most crucial step in the production process. Other major steps in apparel manufacture were material sourcing, pattern making, fabric cutting, sewing, and finishing.

During the first two years of operations, Mondetta clothing was produced in Winnipeg by eight to 10 medium-sized clothing manufacturers. However, when the product's quick success raised producer demands, unit labour and material costs escalated, forcing management to search for offshore manufacturers in order to reduce production costs and increase production capacity. An agent was subsequently secured for Hong Kong through some well-established industry contacts. Although offshore production created periodic quality control problems, the cost of wasted production was much less than the cost of local production, and a 20 percent savings was realized on every T-shirt produced abroad.

By 1992, approximately 40 percent of Mondetta's product line was produced in Hong Kong. While both local and offshore manufacturers had the capacity to produce approximately 10,000 T-shirts per month, shipment time for overseas production took an additional month. To avoid sales forecast misjudgments, Mondetta relied on prebooked orders to trigger production, with an additional 20 to 25 percent buffer inventory built into each order.

Imports from Hong Kong were highly dependent on a quota system, whereby the Canadian government allowed a maximum number of goods to be imported annually from Hong Kong based on product type and category. After the appropriate quota had been determined, the Hong Kong government divided it among manufacturers who produced goods for Canadian companies. This system placed the burden on the manufacturer to find adequate quota to supply the desired amount requested by the Canadian importer. If quota was unavailable, the manufacturer had to purchase the desired amount from a quota market before beginning production.

Human Resources

Mondetta Clothing Company was managed by Ash, Prashant, Raj, and Amit. The company also employed a customer service representative and a support staff of four people. Ash Modha, Mondetta's president and chief executive officer, was 23 years old and had just completed a bachelor of arts in economics from the University of Manitoba. His brother, Prashant, aged 25, had completed a bachelor of science in chemistry in 1988 and received a master of business administration degree from the University of Manitoba in June 1991. Raj Bahl, also 25 years of age, had a bachelor of arts degree in applied economics from the University of Manitoba. His brother, Amit, had attended the University of Winnipeg but chose to work instead.

The company had no structured hierarchy, and the brothers operated in an informal team-oriented atmosphere. Internal communications and reporting structures were also not formally specified. Traditionally, day-to-day operations were completed by the most experienced and available person. Major operating decisions were given deliberate individual consideration before a consensus was reached. During crisis situations, decisions were made quickly after careful consideration of available alternatives.

Although responsibilities were not formally segmented, increased growth had started to create a more divisionalized approach to management. Ash and Raj were primarily responsible for the company's fashion designs. Ash also managed the company's production requirements, while Raj was responsible for marketing and sales force management. Prashant monitored the company's financial operations, and Amit organized distribution, shipping, and receiving.

FUTURE STRATEGY

The four brothers were committed to the company's growth and were considering several growth opportunities such as further penetration into eastern Canada, expansion into the United States, and licensing in western Europe.

Continue Penetration into Eastern Canada

Consumer acceptance of Mondetta clothing in eastern Canada, particularly in Quebec, appeared slower than in western Canada. Mondetta's managers believed that slow sales in Quebec were due to poor product visibility created by inexperienced sales agents. In addition, retail sales in Quebec were controlled by large, powerful buying groups. Established relationships with the buyers of these groups would be essential to product acceptance.

Although the company was experiencing healthy growth in Ontario, the Mondetta name was still relatively unknown in a large potential market. Management's biggest concern was Passport International's expansion to Toronto's Fairview Mall, where Mondetta was also sold. If necessary, mall advertising and billboards would cost approximately $6,800 for six months.

Other marketing communications could also be used to speed up product exposure in both Ontario and Quebec. Economical advertisements, such as point of purchase ads, would cost approximately $25,000 per year. A Mondetta fashion catalogue could also be printed and distributed at an annual cost of $10,000 to $15,000. Advertising in the French version of Elle fashion magazine in Quebec would cost $7,000 per issue. Management wondered which forms of advertising should be purchased in eastern Canada and what sales level would be required to break even.

Expand to the United States

The nature of the apparel industry demanded that management approach their U.S. entry with caution in order to avoid unmanageable rapid product acceptance or damaging product rejection. First, management had to consider which areas of the country to target. Exhibit 5 outlines U.S. apparel consumption by region. Largely populated areas with the highest apparel consumption were the eastern states, while the northwestern states more closely resembled the Canadian market. In addition, the appropriate distribution channels and distribution strategy for market penetration and trend creation had to be determined.

The brothers also needed to determine suitable product selection and market penetration strategies. Since production in Manitoba would be insufficient for demand, apparel would have to be shipped directly from Hong Kong to the United States, requiring quota negotiations similar to those for Canada. Sales agent commissions would be approximately 10 percent of Mondetta's selling price, and U.S. retailers would likely demand a 50 to 60 percent product mark-up on cost. Some chains would also try to negotiate buy-back options or replacement of nonselling styles and volume discounts. Annual travelling and other expenses were estimated at CDN$5,000 to $10,000, while annual trade show expenses would be $25,000 for the summer Magic Show in Las Vegas. The Magic Show was one the largest trade shows in the United States, attracting 52,000 agents, buyers, and retailers.

U.S. sales growth could not expand beyond CDN$500,000 in the first year owing to Mondetta's limited ability to handle rapid international growth. Profit margins would be similar to those earned in Canada, since losses on export duties would likely be recovered with the currency exchange.

Pursue Licensing in Europe

Successful name licensing could create new product demand and expand brand name exposure in both the United States and western Europe. Many well-known names such as Guess Jeans and Buffalo Jeans were already licensed. Guess Jeans already had 22 licences across the world, while Buffalo was licensed in major European centres.

Through licensing, another company would be granted exclusive rights to manufacture, promote, distribute, and sell products using the Mondetta name with Mondetta designs or approved designs. The major advantage of licensing was widespread market penetration with minimal capital and financing requirements. There were also several risks. First, finding appropriate licensees could be difficult owing to the required product specifications, quality, and commitment. Second, licensees could demand that Mondetta handle the majority of product advertising. Third, a licensee could copy Mondetta's sample designs and sell clothing under a new brand name. The brothers hoped that careful selection of licensees would reduce the risks, and they were planning to attract licensees for kids' wear, shoes, and women's wear, while continuing their main fashion designs and product lines.

The average licence agreement was usually three years. During the three-year term, the licensee would be required to pay a nonrefundable initial licence fee, as well as an annual licence fee. Initial and annual fees could range from $10,000 to $1,000,000, depending on the size and reputation of the licensee. Management hoped major licensees would generate $2 million to $3 million in sales during their first year of operations. In every calendar year throughout the term, licensees would have to spend an average of 6 percent of sales to advertise and promote the apparel. In addition, a royalty of 8 to 10 percent of sales would be owed to Mondetta. Mondetta would also incur lawyers' fees and trademark costs for different geographic areas. For example, Canadian trademarks for "Mondetta Everywear" and "The Spirit of Unification" each cost approximately $1,500.

DECISIONS

Clearly, the task of determining where to take Mondetta Clothing Company was not an easy one. While the company's rapid market acceptance appeared to promise greater success in the future, further market penetration demanded careful consideration of alternatives before making the appropriate strategic decisions.

Exhibit **1**

	Statement of Operations (for the Year Ended April 30)		
	1990[1]	**1991**	**1992**
Total revenue	$104,896	$247,970	$2,436,644
Cost of goods sold	75,506	178,543	1,863,427
Gross profit	$ 29,390	$ 69,427	$ 573,217
Operating expenses:			
Accounting and legal	2,649	2,699	7,732
Advertising and promo	1,224	8,964	29,135
Bank charges and interest	3,198	8,762	14,726
Bad debts	3,702	4,031	21,735
Depreciation and amortization	0	2,504	9,038
Factoring commissions	0	920	52,006
Insurance	0	593	810
Leases and equipment	265	1,398	8,498
Management bonus	0	0	110,400
Miscellaneous	307	1,531	1,328
Printing and stationery	695	1,167	9,055
Parking	0	207	46
Property and business tax	0	822	1,276
Rent	1,288	9,246	12,696
Repairs and maintenance	0	182	528
Salaries and benefits	1,437	29,005	75,339
Telephone	1,136	6,516	12,091
Travel and entertainment	1,693	7,974	14,731
Utilities	0	477	970
Total operating expenses	$ 17,594	$ 86,998	$ 382,140
Earning (loss) before tax	11,796	(17,571)	191,077
Income taxes	0	0	43,517
Income tax reduction resulting from loss carry forward	0	0	3,864
Net earnings (loss)	$ 11,796	$ (17,571)	$ 151,424

1. For the period covered by this date the organization was a partnership. The firm was incorporated 1 May 1990.

Exhibit 2

	Balance Sheet (as of April 30)		
	4-Month Period		
	1990	**1991**	**1992**
ASSETS			
Current assets:			
Accounts receivable	$ 76,473	$ 72,789	$ 875,641
Inventories	38,780	54,961	433,653
Prepaid expenses	1,472	1,794	3,752
Total current assets	$116,725	$129,544	$1,313,046
Fixed assets:			
Equipment and leasehold improvements	$ 0	$ 13,583	$ 53,895
Accumulated depreciation	0	2,306	10,982
Fixed assets (net)	$ 0	$ 11,277	$ 42,913
Other assets	0	3,588	6,593
TOTAL ASSETS	$116,725	$144,409	$1,362,552
LIABILITIES AND SHAREHOLDERS' EQUITY			
Liabilities			
Current liabilities:			
Bank overdraft	$ 1,539	$ 14,041	$ 57,936
Bank loan	41,400	58,880	185,840
Accounts payable	27,585	62,676	790,847
Bonus payable	0	0	110,400
Income taxes payable	0	0	39,653
Total current liabilities	$ 70,524	$135,597	$1,184,676
Long-term liabilities:			
Note payable	$ 34,049	$ 7,820	$ 0
Payable to shareholders	0	18,379	22,218
Total long-term liabilities	$ 34,049	$ 26,199	$ 22,218
Shareholder's equity			
Share capital	$ n/a	$ 184	$ 21,804
Retained earnings	12,152	(17,571)	133,854
Total equity	$ 12,152	$ (17,387)	$ 155,658
TOTAL LIABILITIES AND SHAREHOLDERS' EQUITY	$116,725	$144,409	$1,362,552

Exhibit 3

Ratio Sheet			
	1990	**1991**	**1992**
Profitability			
Total revenue	100.0%	100.0%	100.0%
Cost of sales	72.0%	72.0%	76.5%
Gross margin	28.0%	28.0%	23.5%
Operating expenses:			
Accounting and legal	2.5%	1.1%	0.3%
Advertising and promotion	1.2%	3.6%	1.2%
Bank charges and interest	3.0%	3.5%	0.6%
Bad debts	3.5%	1.6%	0.9%
Depreciation and amortization	0.0%	1.0%	0.4%
Factoring commissions	0.0%	0.4%	2.1%
Insurance	0.0%	0.2%	0.0%
Leases and equipment	0.3%	0.6%	0.3%
Management bonus	0.0%	0.0%	4.5%
Miscellaneous	0.3%	0.6%	0.1%
Printing and stationery	0.7%	0.5%	0.4%
Parking	0.0%	0.1%	0.0%
Property and business tax	0.0%	0.3%	0.1%
Rent	1.2%	3.7%	0.5%
Repairs and maintenance	0.0%	0.1%	0.0%
Salaries and benefits	1.4%	11.7%	3.1%
Telephone	1.1%	2.6%	0.5%
Travel and entertainment	1.6%	3.2%	0.6%
Utilities	0.0%	0.2%	0.0%
Total operating expenses	16.8%	35.1%	15.7%
Earning (loss) before tax	11.2%	–7.1%	7.8%
Income tax	0.0%	0.0%	1.6%
Net earnings (loss)	11.2%	–7.1%	6.2%
Liquidity			
Current ratio	1.66	0.96	1.11
Acid test	1.11	0.55	0.74
Working capital	$46,201	$(6,053)	$128,370
Efficiency			
Age of accounts receivable	266	107	131
Age of inventory	187	0	0
Age of payables	133	117	129
Stability			
Net worth/total assets	10.0%	(12.0%)	11.0%
Interest coverage	4.7%	(1.0%)	14.5%

Growth	**1990–91**	**1991–92**
Sales	136.4%	882.6%
Net income	(249.0%)	0.0%
Assets	23.7%	843.5%

EXHIBIT 4
The International
Apparel Market

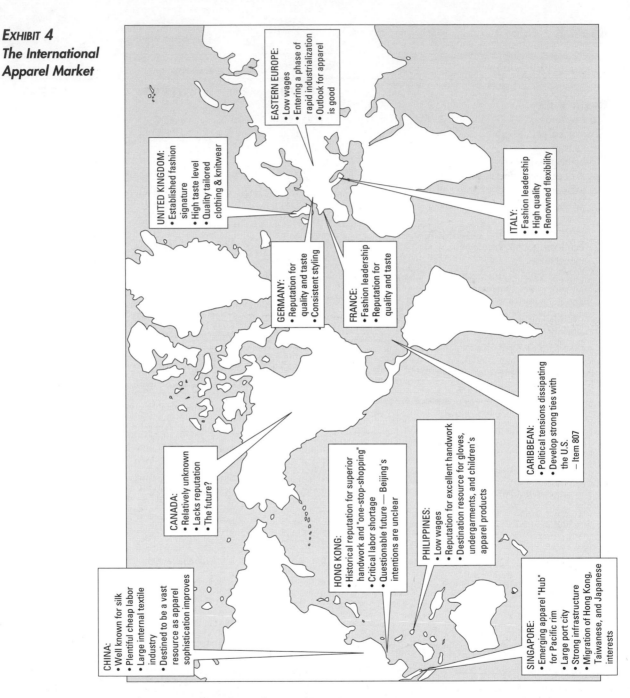

Source: Apparel Retailing in the United States.

EXHIBIT 5
U.S. Apparel
Consumption
by Region

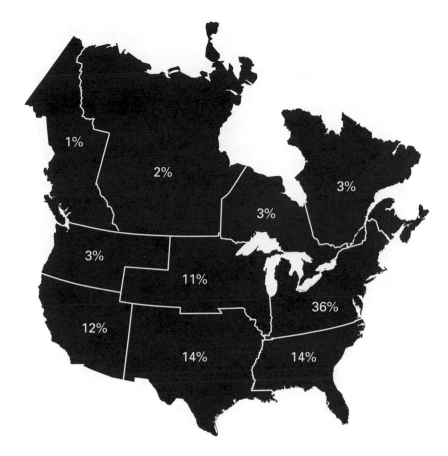

Source: U.S. and Canadian governments.

CASE 7.9   RAMPAC DISTRIBUTORS

By Michael Wexler, Lisa Luinenburg, and Michael R. Pearce

It was late March 1999 when Michael Wexler found himself contemplating the future of his business distributing household paper products and cleaning supplies in Montreal. Several decisions had to be made that could drastically alter the operations of his summer company. These decisions included three ways to expand (enlarge the sales force, target a new market, and pursue a franchise program) and three ways to change the nature of the venture (launch an environmental line, distribute nonperishable foods, and reduce delivery quantities). Underlying all of these choices was the possibility of selling the business and pursuing an opportunity with a multinational corporation.

BACKGROUND

RAMPAC Distributors was registered in 1995 as a partnership between Robert Bard and Michael Wexler, two college students in Montreal, a city of 3.3 million people. The name of the company was an acronym that stood for Robert and Michael's Paper Company. The two youths had no significant business experience or financial assets but had a desire to run their own business. After they examined the assets available to them (Michael's mother's station wagon and extra warehouse space from Rob's father), they decided on a distribution or delivery business. The partners proposed to deliver paper products to households and companies. They hoped that corporate business could be won with superior prices, given their lack of overhead. Similarly, they thought that retail business could be achieved by offering a delivery service that stores did not offer, and by selling bulk quantities (i.e., sufficient for a household for six months to one year).

THE INITIAL MONTHS

There were two key tasks in starting the business: finding suppliers and generating sales. Every paper goods company in the Yellow Pages was contacted and asked for a quotation to supply RAMPAC. The first quotations were at prices higher than retail, as suppliers sensed the inexperience of the owners, who did not know the jargon of the industry (i.e., sizes, formats, brands, qualities, terms, and volumes). Initial quotations were as high as $31.08 per bulk case. After gaining familiarity with the business and being less than truthful about the age of

IVEY Michael Wexler and Lisa Luinenburg prepared this case under the supervision of Professor Michael R. Pearce solely to provide material for class discussion. The authors do not intend to illustrate either effective or ineffective handling of a managerial situation. The authors may have disguised certain names and other identifying information to protect confidentiality. Ivey Management Services prohibits any form of reproduction, storage or transmittal without its written permission. This material is not covered under authorization from CanCopy or any reproduction rights organization. Copyright © 1999, Ivey Management Services.

the business and expected volumes, first purchases were negotiated at $17.76 per bulk case. Over the next four years, as volumes grew and management developed buying skills, prices were haggled down as low as $6.66 per bulk case.

During the first three months, business was very slow. Commercial accounts took much longer to acquire than expected. When the summer came, Bard wanted to travel for two months. Since the venture had already strained their friendship, and it would have been unfair to build a partnership alone, Wexler purchased Bard's half of the business for $222. Operating alone, Wexler spent the majority of his time soliciting households, selling door-to-door for 16 weeks straight. He would present a customer (usually the lady of the house) with a listing of his products and prices and explain the business concept (see Exhibit 1). If an order was not received, he would follow up at the door again within three days and possibly phone after one week. The business grew steadily as a customer base of over 300 customers was developed.

The commercial side of the business, which received only minor attention, floundered for two reasons, in Wexler's opinion. First, cleaning supplies seemed to be of minor concern to most businesses; hence, cold callers were quickly dismissed. Second, making contacts and bypassing red tape took months. Wexler was going away to university in the fall and believed he did not have enough time to secure and service commercial accounts during the school year.

THE SECOND YEAR: A FOCUS ON SERVICE

In selling door-to-door, Wexler noticed that the customers who ordered were not price sensitive. This was surprising to him, since price was the traditional competitive dimension in paper products in the grocery business. Apparently, customers liked the idea of not having to continually replenish these paper supplies and carry bulk goods from the store. He decided to "price what the market will bear," so prices were increased substantially, such that many items were more expensive than in local supermarkets. RAMPAC's new emphasis was quality, convenience, and service.

A typical order began with a salesperson offering to meet with the customer at any time and place (i.e., lunch break at work or evening at home). While details could easily be discussed over the phone, this measure helped to develop loyalty to the business and demonstrated concern for the customer's needs. The salespeople were extremely well trained with regard to product knowledge (i.e., detergent effectiveness for various fabrics, microwavability of different brands of plastic wrap, and other queries product labels didn't usually cover).

Wexler stressed that every order was special, hence no special requests were refused. This included finding nonstandard bag sizes for discontinued garbage pails, importing a stain remover not sold in Canada, delivering dog food, seeking product information from manufacturers, and taking returns of items not sold by RAMPAC.

Delivery was available whenever the customer wanted, including immediately after placing the order, on the weekend, or at 7 a.m. before going to work. The previous summer, RAMPAC had limited its inventory needs by ordering from suppliers only after accumulating several customer orders. Delivery time from RAMPAC to the customer had averaged four days. The second summer saw increased inventory levels.

When an order was delivered, the delivery person insisted on carrying all boxes to a basement or storage area. He or she then unpacked items, explained features, and ensured satisfaction. All products were of the highest quality (e.g., the softest tissues, strongest garbage bags, stickiest plastic wrap, etc.). If a customer was for any reason dissatisfied (for reasons legitimate or not, in Wexler's opinion), a full refund was given apologetically without asking for return of the goods.

EXPANSION OF PRODUCTS, PROFITS, AND CUSTOMERS

Over time, the profits of the business expanded for three reasons, according to Wexler: increased profit per case, greater volume per customer, and more customers. These ends were pursued in different ways.

1. Profit per Case

Initially, the contribution margin averaged 26 percent of selling price, whereas the average grocery store achieved a gross margin less than 21 percent (see Exhibit 2). With a new focus on service, margins were increased from 26 to 42 percent of selling price, without negatively affecting sales. The increased margins allowed RAMPAC to be very generous with customers in the return policy and satisfaction effort.

2. Volume per Customer

The first flyer listed only paper products, about eight items and 13 SKUs (stockkeeping units — i.e., unique items by brand and size). This range was expanded to include cleaning products, 17 items with 50 SKUs (see Exhibit 3). These products were as well received by customers as the paper products, effectively doubling sales per customer. Also, as customers reordered (there was a 85 to 90 percent repeat rate over a year), they increased the number of products purchased as their appreciation for the concept grew and their confidence in the quality and service swelled. The average order size grew from $44.40 in 1995 to $77.70 in 1996 and $148.00 in 1997.

In the summer of 1997, the product line was further extended to include soft drinks and mineral water, also bulky items that consumers stock. This addition was very successful, as the quantity of these items consumed by a family over one year is tremendous. As a final means to increase sales from the established customer base, small volume customers (three cases or less) were lured with a "10 percent off" strategy. After receiving an order for X number of cases, and ensuring that the customer wanted nothing else, the salesperson would inform the customer that there was an "opportunity for additional savings, because any cases in addition to X are 10 percent off." As well, any customer who ordered fewer items than had been purchased the previous year was enticed to order more by offering 10 percent off any growth in order size. These techniques almost always worked; the nature of the product range was such that there were inevitably other goods offered that the customer could use but had not ordered because they didn't consume sufficient quantities to pursue in bulk or wanted to limit the order size. Presented with the discount proposal, they usually seized the opportunity. While extra cases added to an order had 25 percent lower contribution, they were seen as incremental sales that would not have been otherwise achieved.

3.   Number of Customers

Sales force. To expand the customer base, several salespeople were recruited to target areas of the city that had not yet been solicited. They were lured by basic job posting at the Canada Summer Employment Centre and the summer employment offices of McGill and Concordia universities. Also, a notice was posted at two CEGEPs, the Quebec equivalent to Ontario grades 12 and the former 13 or OAC (see Exhibit 4). Successful applicants were hired exclusively on commission. They were trained by Mr. Wexler about the business concept, the products offered, and the selling techniques that were most effective. Their commission was a flat $6 per case to avoid complexity. This remuneration was very meaningful, as the average salesperson could sell four cases per hour when going door-to-door. Delivery time (the person who sold the goods delivered them as well) was then unpaid. While this initiative increased the customer base by approximately 20 percent, the results were seen as disappointing. Few people applied, apparently because of a stigma associated with door-to-door sales and a reluctance to work exclusively on commission. Many who tried the job disliked having to work evenings, the key selling time when people are home. Others could not tolerate the volatility of sales, earning $185 one evening and nothing the next two. Finally, some salespeople who were initially very successful selling to family, friends, and neighbours became discouraged when sales to the general public did not keep pace. Incentive schemes, including RAMPAC T-shirts, RAMPAC logo watches, business cards, and sales level bonus payments, were ineffective since the problem with the program was not a lack of tangible reward. Of 20 salespeople who were hired and trained over three summers, only three were considered successful in management's estimation.

Advertising. The first advertising campaign began in 1996. Flyers were distributed through Canada Post to several thousand households. This was complemented by local newspaper advertising (see Exhibit 5) in four weekly community papers that had circulation of about 4,000 homes each. The response to these programs was difficult to measure, and they were deemed unsuccessful. The direct response rate was less than two calls per thousand people reached. The indirect benefit of the increased name awareness when potential customers were approached at the door was not accurately determined. Despite the newspaper's claim that the ads had to be run several times to achieve any results, the program was discontinued.

COMPETITION   When the business started, there was a void in the paper products delivery business because the largest supplier had ceased to serve households, targeting the commercial market exclusively. When approached by RAMPAC, those former household customers were eager to try bulk delivery and were familiar with the process.

Many new companies entered the industry to compete directly with RAMPAC. Usually, these companies were started by students, attracted by both the opportunity to sell their time and the lack of start-up capital required. Most used a flyer listing similar products but sometimes undercutting RAMPAC on price (see Exhibit 6). The flyers varied: some were handwritten, some were professionally produced, and some were just letters to introduce the business. Most of these ventures did not exist two years after starting for a variety of reasons: owners found other summer jobs, the new business was unsuccessful as a result of poor management decisions (e.g., selling poor quality goods), and the company had difficulty penetrating upscale areas of the city where RAMPAC was firmly established.

This competition affected RAMPAC in several ways. A competitor that satisfied customers with good quality products and service but was not in business one year later served to create a household favourable to bulk delivery, and RAMPAC was often the beneficiary of this sentiment. Alternatively, a company that delivered poor quality products and service served to negatively taint customers' opinion of the bulk delivery concept for a long time. Few RAMPAC customers were actually lost to competitors, because satisfaction levels were strong, price was not the basis of competition, and the market was big enough to support several companies without crossing paths.

There were two forms of indirect competition: grocery stores and warehouse stores such as Club Price. The fundamental difference between the product offered by these outlets and that provided by RAMPAC was delivery, a critical part of the package of benefits surrounding the purchase.

The problem encountered in competing against grocery stores was their famous loss leader sales.[1] Cleaning products were often used to build store traffic; the most commonly promoted loss leader was paper towels, which would be sold as low as $0.59 (the regular price was $1.19). If a customer cited this low price to a salesperson, his or her response would be something like this: "Loss leader items usually have a quantity limit of three. The rest of the year, purchases are made at the full price. RAMPAC sells a bulk quantity at a better than normal price, resulting in savings over the full year and preventing you from running out. While it would be conceivable to get all your groceries at loss leader prices, it is not practical to run around to hundreds of different stores with each discounting different goods. The grocer offers these prices to get you into the store to buy other items at full price." However, as a result of this competition, RAMPAC offered customers one item at a loss leader price, on a minimum order of five items.

Grocery stores also tried to provide delivery convenience. Some stores offered to deliver a customer's order for a flat fee of $3.70. Wexler felt that this did not catch on for several reasons: the customer still had to come to the store and select items; time of delivery was unspecific; the delivery fee, which was not built into the price, was a deterrent; and the delivery offer was never publicized.

The grand opening of Club Price in Montreal was of greater concern to Wexler. Like RAMPAC, Club Price offered consistently discounted prices and bulk quantities. However, the Club Price shopping experience included many unpleasant aspects that RAMPAC eliminated. These included searching for a parking spot, walking a significant distance from the car to the store, pushing around jumbo carriages or flatbed carts, struggling within huge crowds on weekends, waiting in line for up to two hours (Saturday afternoon), pushing a heavily loaded carriage all the way back to the car, loading the goods into the car, and then unloading and carrying them again at home. Wexler was worried that Club Price would change its concept and offer delivery. This anxiety was substantiated by a customer survey that he encountered in the store, seeking opinion on delivery features. (He often browsed the store and was kicked out swiftly for writing down prices.)

Club Price sold many categories of products, such as food, cleaning products, clothing, and automotive supplies, such that RAMPAC could not offer itself as a complete alternative. By using RAMPAC, however, a customer could reduce the volume of goods purchased in each outing and the frequency of visits. As well, RAMPAC offered personalized service, greater variety in cleaning products, depth within a specific product category, and better quality products.

The growing popularity of Club Price did have a negative impact on sales, although the magnitude was uncertain because RAMPAC itself was growing so quickly. In Wexler's estimation, this loss of business was not because RAMPAC's selling proposition was relatively inferior. Constantly in contact with customers, he was of the opinion that less than 10 percent valued the additional cost savings above the superior variety and convenience he felt RAMPAC offered. However, it was evidently easier for customers to include cleaning products in the Club Price purchase than to remember to call RAMPAC. In order to combat this phenomenon, he stamped all RAMPAC boxes with a phone number to call when supplies were almost finished, and he was about to distribute fridge magnets.

THE FUTURE

Over several years, RAMPAC built up a significant customer base (350 regulars). The quality of products and service offered seemed to ensure the future stream of sales and a phenomenally high repeat rate. Mailing list software had been purchased and was being used to allow personalized contact with all customers (see Exhibit 7), a list of whom was carefully guarded. Upon graduation from the H.B.A. program at the University of Western Ontario, Mr. Wexler was considering several options for the future of the business.

1.   Expansion under Current Format

Three possibilities were considered to expand the business under the current format:

a. *Hire more salespeople* to achieve greater penetration in the areas of the city already served. While 350 customers was sizable, it was insufficient to justify operating the business all year and was certainly only a fraction of the potential customers that could be converted to the RAMPAC concept. With 2 percent of all anglophones in Montreal considered affluent, Wexler thought there were many more sales opportunities.

b. *Target a new market* to boost sales. Francophone Montrealers made up 85 percent of the city's population but had not been targeted due to uncertainties about cultural differences that might affect their propensity to embrace the concept.

c. *Set up a franchise program.* Experiments with this had been moderately successful in the past. Two of Wexler's friends had tried the concept in Brampton and Cambridge, Ontario. Both had earned good returns for the time and money invested. Wexler had initiated contact with Student Supplies, a paper products franchise business that operated throughout Canada but not in Montreal. After discussion with the owner, Wexler was offered the opportunity to run the entire Canadian organization for the upcoming summer.

2.   Modify the Current Format

Three possibilities were considered to change the nature of the business:

a. *Launch an environmentally friendly line of products.* A company run by students had already introduced such a line but was not aggressively advertising it. Initial contacts with the manufacturer indicated that there were environmentally friendly substitutes available for RAMPAC's entire product line, at prices less than the original products. However, their quality was inferior, if not outright poor. Wexler was unsure whether a "green line" would have to be targeted toward a different customer group, whether it was hypocritical to sell both lines of goods, and how people would react to an environmental marketing approach.

b. *Sell nonperishable food products,* including canned, boxed, and powdered foods.

c. *Deliver smaller quantities of goods* more frequently and offer credit terms.

3.   Sell the Business

With exciting job offers from several companies, Wexler wondered if it was time to sell the business and embrace corporate life. He was unsure of the value of the business and how he might go about selling it.

NOTE

1.   A loss leader is a product priced at or below cost in order to attract customers to the store. The item is usually heavily advertised and placed at a prominent end-of-aisle position. While some shoppers come to the store only to purchase that item, most also buy several other products, which, for the retailer, justifies the discounted merchandise.

Exhibit 1

Rampac Distributors Products List

LES DISTRIBUTEURS
RAMPAC
DISTRIBUTORS

A STUDENT ENTERPRISE

GARBAGE BAGS (250 bags)	
Regular	$23.09
Heavy Duty	$24.49
Garden Bags (Super strong, 100 giant bags)	$24.49
KITCHEN CATCHERS (500 bags)	
White Bags	$24.27
CLING WRAP (Borden)	
11″ x 2,500″	$26.94
ALUMINUM FOIL (Alcan Plus or Reynolds Industrial)	
300 cm x 200 m	$25.53
45 cm x 100 m	$25.53
TOILET PAPER (48 Rolls)	
2 ply: Facelle Royale (320 sheets)	$25.83
1 ply: White Swan (1,000 sheets)	$25.83
PAPER TOWELS (Facelle Royal 2 ply)	
Jumbo size (24 rolls x 100 sheets)	$25.60
FACIAL TISSUE (Facelle Royale)	
36 boxes 100 sheets 2 ply	$23.90
NAPKINS	
Lunch: Scott 180 x 9 packages	$23.83
Dinner: Duni 3 ply (500)	$28.93

Quality—Convenience—Service

For more information or to place an order, please call
Michael Wexler at 486-2055
Pour plus d'information ou pour commander, telephoner
Michael Wexler à 486-2055
Rampac will beat the price of any competitor.

Exhibit **2**

Financial Results of a Typical Canadian Supermarket 1997	
	%
Income Statement	
Sales	100.00
Cost of goods sold	80.80
Gross margin	19.20
Interest expense	0.01
Other operating expenses	16.42
Total operating expenses	16.43
Operating income	2.77
Other income	0.02
Profit before tax	2.79
Income taxes	0.29
Net profit after tax	2.50

Source: The Canadian Small Business Financial Performance Survey: 1997 Edition. Canadian Cataloguing in Publication Data, 1997.

EXHIBIT 3

Rampac Distributors Cleaning Products Extension[1]

Cleaning Products

Please note: "H" is the price for one-half the listed quantity.

Fabric softeners:	Bounce	(600)	47.29	H:29.38	Sheets
	Downy	(600)	44.25	H:28.42	Sheets
	Downy	(4x4L)	31.15	H:21.61	Liquid
	Sunggle	(2x8L)	28.27	H:20.42	Liquid
Laundry detergent:	All	(15kg)	36.26		Powder
	Arctic Power	(20kg)	43.88	H:28.49	Powder
	Family Tree	(18kg)	25.97		Powder
	Tide	(20kg)	48.77	H:29.38	Powder
	Tide	(4x4L)	42.11	H:27.31	Liquid
	Wisk	(2x8L)	39.29	H:25.75	Liquid
Dishwasher detergent:	Cascade	(6x3.5kg)	36.04	H:23.90	Powder
	Electrasol	(4x4.5kg)	36.04	H:23.90	Powder
Dishwashing soap:	Palmolive	(4x4L)	36.56	H:24.49	Liquid
Bleach:	Javex	(6x3.6L)	21.98	H:16.43	Liquid
	Javex for UnB	(20L)	31.89	H:21.61	Powder
	Javex 2	(6x3.6L)	34.11	H:23.46	Liquid
Cleaning products:	Windex	(4x5L)	32.12	H: 21.98	Refill
	Fantastic	(4x5L)	37.89	H:24.86	Refill
	Spray N' Wash	(4x5L)	42.33	H:27.08	Refill
	Pledge	(6x500g)	29.23	H:20.05	Cans
	Vim	(6x1L)	28.56		
	Mr. Clean	(4x4L)	38.33	H:25.09	
	Spic N' Span	(4x4L)	42.33	H:19.98	
	Pinesol	(4x4L)	41.22	H:26.71	
	Comet	(24x600g)	29.01	H:20.57	
	Ajax	(48x400g)	33.15	H:22.94	
	Lysol	8x450g)	32.04	H:22.05	
	Ivory Liquid	(2x4L)	29..45	H:20.94	Refill
	J-Cloths	(200)	30.34	H:20.72	
Ziploc food bags:	Freezer	(1201g ÷ 75md)	23.38		
	Sandwich	(1200)	28.64	H:20.57	
Soft drinks	72 cans	(3 types max.)	28.56		(÷dep) most brands
	Evian	(72 small)	33.23	29.45	(24 large)
	Perrier	(72 small)	41.37	29.45	(24 large)
Also Available:	Any brand or household product not listed, Styrofoam cups, plastic and paper plates, and baking chocolate!				

---

1. Reduced from actual flyer size.

Exhibit 4

Rampac Distributors' Posting to Recruit Salespeople

Opportunity for employment with

RAMPACK DISTRIBUTING
613 Victoria Ave.
Westmount, Quebec
Tel. # 486-2055

INFORMATION ON BEING A SALESPERSON FOR RAMPAC DISTRIBUTING

What We Sell: Household paper products and cleaning supplies, including garbage bags, Kitchen Catchers, Saran Wrap, aluminum foil, toilet paper, paper towels, facial tissue, napkins, fabric softeners, laundry and dish detergents, and most cleaning products. As well, we sell soft drinks, mineral water, and Ziploc bags. All products are sold in bulk quantities (i.e., larger than can be purchased in stores) to save the consumer time and money.

Who We Sell To: Mostly individual households, with some businesses as well.

How We Sell: Sales are initiated through door-to-door canvassing, and contacts through parents, relatives, friends, etc.

Individual Investment Required: None

Potential Earnings: Unlimited. Salary will be based fully on generous commission on each item sold. Salespeople will earn $6 on each "case" (standard bulk quantity of a good) sold. The average salesperson consistently sells approximately four cases per hour, earning $24 per hour. A full explanation of the commission system is available from any RAMPAC representative.

Your Obligation to Rampac After Hiring: Once hired, RAMPAC asks that you maintain a minimum level of selling each week, usually around 20 cases.

What Rampac Will Do For You: Rampac manages invoicing, purchasing, inventory, and running the business. It will deliver for you as well, for a portion of the commission. If you have access to a car, then you can choose to deliver yourself. In that case, all you need to do is pick up the products you sell from the RAMPAC outlet conveniently located in Westmount.

Advantages to Consider: As a salesperson, you can choose when to work and when not to. You control your own hours and have no boss watching over you. The average salesperson will work about half as many hours as his or her friends, but earn nearly twice as much!

If you are interested in selling or seek more information, please do not hesitate to call Michael Wexler at 486-2055.

Salespeople will be interviewed and hired starting May 5.

Exhibit 5
Rampac Distributors' Newspaper Advertisement

TIRED OF RUNNING OUT?

RAMPAC DISTRIBUTORS

Provides convenient FREE DELIVERY of household paper products and cleaning supplies

- Garbage Bags
- Paper Towels
- Food Wrap
- Toilet Paper
- Detergents
- and much more

SAVE TIME AND MONEY

by ordering

QUALITY name brand products in bulk

Call 486-2055 Michael Wexler

A Student Enterprise

Exhibit 6

Competitor's Flyer, "Student Kitchen Supply Sales"[1]

STUDENT KITCHEN SUPPLY SALES

ARI: 484-6699   To Place An Order
BILL: 738-4078   Or For Any Information

	$ PRICES $	
	Grocery Store (tax included)	Ours
Garbage Bags (Industrial)		
26" x 36" standard size (250 bags)	35.87	28.00
35" x 50" "giant size" (200 bags)	114.54	30.00
20" x 22" kitchen size (500 bags) wht.	59.66	25.00
Aluminum Foil		
Alcan or Reynolds 12" x 650 ft.		
18" x 328 ft.	24.10	20.00
Plastic Wrap		
Borden's (2,000 ft.)	41.29	22.00
Facial tissue (36 boxes/case)		
Facelle (100 TISSUES/BOX @ 66¢ each) 2 ply	20.19	19.00
Bathroom Tissue (48 rolls/case)		
Cottonelle (400 sheets/roll)	25.64	22.00
Perkins Decor (320 sheets/roll) 2 ply	19.45	16.00
Kitchen Towles		
Scott Towels (24 rolls x 90 sheets) 2 ply	27.20	22.00
Scott Dinner Napkins (600)	18.94	16.00
Ziploc Bags: (300 bags)		
Small	11.10	
Medium	14.43	
Large	15.54	

Free Delivery! Tax Included!

---

1. Reduced from actual flyer size.

EXHIBIT 7
Rampac
Distributors'
Personal Letters
to Customers

August 7, 1996

Dear ———,

I am writing to inform you, as a valued customer of RAMPAC DISTRIBUTORS, that I will be returning to the University of Western Ontario on September 1.

I would like to suggest that you place an order now to stock up for the winter season. I have enclosed a RAMPAC flyer for your convenience. For those customers who ordered in May or June, you will notice a substantial increase in the range of products available.

Thank you for your support. I look forward to serving you again next summer.

Sincerely,

Michael Wexler

———————————————

May 1, 1997

Dear ———,

I am writing to inform you, as a valued customer, that RAMPAC DISTRIBUTORS has returned to full operation for the months of May and June. I am most anxious to supply you with a wide range of paper and household products. Most prices are lower than last year, delivery is free, and accommodating service is provided with a smile. Please read the enclosed RAMPAC flyer and call me to place an order. I look forward to hearing from you.

Sincerely,

Michael Wexler

C A S E 7.10   SILK ROUTE ORIENTAL RUGS LTD.

By Paul Beamish, Joyce Miller, and Pamela Jeffery

In March 1991, eight months after their seven-year-old company, Silk Route Oriental Rugs Ltd., had gone bankrupt, Michael and Sam Hejazi were assessing if (and how) they should reenter the London, Ontario, oriental carpet retail market. Although their accountant and others were advising against trying to reestablish, the brothers' inclination was to find a means of staying in the business. If a new operation was to be started, at issue were questions of product focus, scale, location, and timing.

BRIEF HISTORY OF ORIENTAL RUGS

An oriental rug was a hand-knotted or hand-woven rug that originated from an area known as the rug belt. The rug belt was bordered by eastern Europe in the west, China on the east, and the southern republics of the ex–Soviet Union to the north, and it extended south to include most of India. It was difficult to determine when the first rugs were produced, but the oldest surviving rug, the Pazyryk, was over 2,000 years old.

Rugs were first made to satisfy household needs. As well as cushioning against the cold ground, rugs were used for curtains, canopies, tomb covers, tribute money, gifts, and currency. The rug belt dwellers also exported rugs in exchange for goods that were scarce in their area. The supply of cheap labour and fibre (wool) made it possible for these nations to later start oriental rug industries. Nations to the north of the rug belt had climates that did not support the production of wool (i.e., the raising of sheep), while nations to the south had warmer climates where the need for rugs to provide warmth did not exist.

Trade in oriental rugs began over 500 years ago. Because of Turkey's proximity to Europe, Turkish carpets were being exported to Europe by the 15th century. With the opening of more trade routes in the 16th and 17th centuries, Turkish carpets soon graced the homes of the European elite.

The features that determined a rug's value in the 15th century still determined prices in the 1990s. The quality of the wool or silk used for the pile and the

IVEY This case was prepared by Professor Paul Beamish with assistance from Joyce Miller and Pamela Jeffery. It was prepared solely to provide material for class discussion. The case is not intended to illustrate either effective or ineffective handling of a managerial situation. Certain names and other identifying information may have been disguised to protect confidentiality. Ivey Management Services prohibits any form of reproduction, storage or transmittal without its written permission. This material is not covered under authorization from CanCopy or any reproduction rights organization. Copyright © 1992, Ivey Management Services.

quality of the dye were of primary importance. Natural vegetable dyes provided a lustre that increased with age, whereas synthetic dyes destroyed the natural oil in wool, making it wear out faster. The number of knots per square inch was another criterion for judging an oriental rug, together with the quality of work-manship. Knots varied from 35 to 800 per square inch. Tighter knotting gave a rug more density and durability. Generally, a good carpet would have at least 200 knots per square inch. Design and colour were also critical in assessing a rug's value. Rugs that were mass produced using the same designs and colours cost less than those that were more unique. Finally, a rug's value depended on its area of origin and the particular weaving centre within that country. Persian (i.e., Iranian) rugs, for example, because of their history of exceptional quality tended to command a higher price than rugs from other countries. However, with the increased popularity of oriental rugs, traditional designs were no longer made exclusively in the region of origin. The ability to evaluate a rug's quality and origin required great expertise, usually built up over a lifetime.

ORIENTAL RUGS IN THE CANADIAN MARKETPLACE

With annual retail sales of over $100 million, Canada was the world's 13th-largest market for oriental rugs in 1989. Since World War II, oriental rugs had enjoyed tremendous popularity. In 1950, oriental rug imports into Canada totalled only $1.33 million (at wholesale). This low level was attributed to weak distribution channels, a lack of trade promotion to build consumer awareness, and the popu-larity of wall-to-wall carpeting in both homes and apartments. The 1960s her-alded a strong growth in demand for several reasons. First, increased production and export of rugs provided a wider selection for Canadian consumers. Tied to this was a greater responsiveness on the part of manufacturers to change the design and colours to suit North American preferences. Second, a number of Canadian importers and retailers specializing in oriental rugs went into business during this period, enhancing the profile and availability of oriental rugs. Consumer awareness increased as distribution channels improved. Third, a rise in per capita income and expenditure among high income groups increased the demand for good quality, hand-knotted oriental rugs. The main buying reasons included:

- *Tradition.* Most Canadian buyers of oriental carpets preferred genuine hand-knotted carpets as floor coverings.
- *Durability.* Oriental carpets lasted longer than machine-made carpets; area rugs could be taken up easily and moved and were popular with apartment dwellers (home owners preferred wall-to-wall carpeting).
- *Colours and designs.* Plain wall-to-wall carpeting needed additional decoration to create a warmer atmosphere.
- *Status symbol.* Oriental rugs conveyed a sense of culture and sophistication.
- *Investment.* A fine-quality hand-knotted rug would retain or sometimes increase in value over time.

The strong growth in rug imports came to a halt in the late 1970s as a result of unprecedented price hikes; by 1980, prices had risen 417 percent over 1970 levels. Both supply and demand factors came into play. Soaring prices were caused by fears about the future of the industry, given the establishment of the Islamic Republic of Iran. With village life disrupted and the chain of tradition and apprenticeship broken, it was possible that the strong weaving areas would deteriorate. As a result, Western markets placed increasing demand on all rug-producing nations. This demand coincided with a general belief on the part of the producing nations that prices had been too low and revenues could be easily increased through higher prices.

The recession in the early 1980s prolonged the slow growth of oriental rug imports. However, Canadian demand began to strengthen in 1983, and the next few years saw a significant rise in per capita consumption. From 1986 to 1989, the wholesale value of oriental rugs imported into Canada rose from $30 million to $47 million. Since some importers were known to understate their costs (in order to reduce duties payable) while still maintaining retail margins of twice their actual landed costs, an import level of $47 million translated into a $100 million retail business.

A number of factors explained the increased popularity of oriental rugs. First, the market began to correct itself after the price hikes of the late 1970s. Unfavourable consumer reaction to the sharp price rises had resulted in more exports of lower quality rugs and rugs from countries where labour was cheaper, thus increasing competition and forcing prices down. Not only were the traditional rug-producing nations exporting more rugs, but other nations such as Egypt and Romania were entering the market. Second, as Canadians became more affluent, they developed more sophisticated tastes in home decor and were spending more money on home furnishings. Third, with the increasing frequency of home moves, there was greater reluctance to purchase wall-to-wall broadloom; area rugs were a financially attractive alternative. Finally, it was rumoured that several countries had dumped carpets into foreign markets as a means of generating foreign exchange. The local government would do this by buying carpets in the local currency and then discounting them in any foreign market for the hard currency.

In 1989, Indian rugs held the largest share of the oriental rug market in Canada at 35.6 percent. Indian rug imports had been on the decline since the early 1970s owing, in part, to the Indian government's policy of allowing rugs of any quality to be exported. Canadian consumers began to think that all Indian rugs were of low quality. India subsequently improved its competitive position through active government involvement in production and export promotion. Indian rugs became increasingly better quality at an affordable price. The country's competitive advantage rested on the use of cheap labour and indigenous wool. India had also become a leader in the "programming" of oriental rugs, wherein Western importers provided specifications related to design, colours, and knot density, which the manufacturers then followed in order to produce a series of rugs.

Chinese rugs held the second-largest share of Canada's oriental rug market at 20.7 percent. Imports of Chinese rugs had risen dramatically through the 1980s because of China's use of programming. As well, the need for foreign exchange had led the Chinese government to press for higher production levels in its state-owned factories in the country's weaving centres. Chinese rugs were more expensive than Indian rugs (which had remained the least expensive type of oriental rug) but were also generally of a higher quality. Since Chinese rugs were not always as elaborate in design as rugs from other producing nations, they appealed to Canadian consumers whose tastes ran to area rugs with fewer colours and simpler designs.

With 16.9 percent, Iran held the third-largest share of the Canadian oriental rug market. Traditionally the world's largest source of hand-knotted carpets, Iran's competitiveness declined through the 1980s. Iranian labour was more expensive relative to labour in other rug-producing nations, and Iran had not adopted programming as a means to satisfy Western markets. As well, the government, preoccupied with a long war against Iraq, had not played an active role in the production and export of rugs. Although buyers realized that rug production in Iran was continuing under Ayatollah Khomeini, the 1979 takeover of the American embassy in Tehran had created strong anti-Iranian sentiment. At the same time, Pakistan and India began to produce and export rugs with Persian designs, flooding the market and forcing down the price of authentic Persian rugs.

Pakistani rugs were in fourth position in the Canadian market, with 15.2 percent share. The Pakistani country category also included carpets produced by Afghan refugees just inside Pakistan's border. Afghan rugs were never programmed and tended to be red in colour, geometric in design, and lower priced. One oriental rug expert asserted that Canadian consumers were becoming more sophisticated purchasers and were not buying Pakistani (and Turkish) rugs because they were not as good value as rugs from competing nations. According to the president of a major American oriental rug importing firm:

> The rug manufacturers in Pakistan tend to be merchants first and rug people second. They produce beautiful rugs but they don't understand colour and design. The weavers and dye houses are much more independent in Pakistan (than in India) so you don't get uniformity of product. You have to be able to order ... and have it come through in the design, colour, and quality you want. It will probably happen in Pakistan, but I don't see it yet. It took three generations for it to happen in India. I don't see the same evolutionary pattern in Pakistan that I observed in India.

Turkish rugs, with a Canadian market share of 1.9 percent, had been struggling to maintain a presence in the market despite a global market share that made Turkey the world's fourth-largest exporter of oriental rugs. In general,

Canadians had not been attracted to the rugs because of their perceived poor value. There was speculation, however, that the quality of Turkish rugs would improve in the future because of the government's effort to act as an agent, organizing the production and acquisition of rugs from across the country for export. Like the Chinese government, the Turkish government had been encouraging higher exports as a means to obtain foreign exchange.

THE LONDON MARKET

With a population of 300,000, London was the commercial, industrial, financial, and cultural centre in the southwestern part of the province. While the primary trade area for specialty stores consisted of the city of London, the secondary trade area was made up of eight counties with a total population of over half a million people.

The London market was characterized by higher incomes, education, and retail spending levels than the national average. This translated into a personal disposable income level, which was 12 percent more than the Canadian average. Although 11th in terms of population, London ranked 5th in Canada in per capita retail sales. As well, as Exhibit 1 indicates, a disproportionate number of Londoners were among one or more of the target lifestyle groups.

In 1989, the oriental rug market in London was estimated to be about $5 million at the retail level. Purchases were made in specialty oriental rug stores, specialty carpet stores, department stores, antique stores, and at special events and auctions. A history of the competitive situation for oriental carpets in the London area is shown in Exhibit 2.

SILK ROUTE ORIENTAL RUGS LIMITED

Background on Michael and Sam Hejazi

Michael (32) and Sam (30) Hejazi were born in Canada and attended high school in Windsor. While there, they worked with their father, who had emigrated from Lebanon in 1956 and sold high-end new and antique Persian rugs by referral in the Windsor/Detroit area. Their involvement in the family business included searching for old rugs at antique stores, shows, estate sales, and auctions, including those at major auction houses such as Sotheby's and Phillips. They were also involved to a small degree with overseas buying and purchasing from New York dealers. On a few occasions, they were involved with selling, but that was basically left to their father. As they said: "We had absolutely no experience in retailing, marketing, or finance. We were just knowledgeable about rugs as art!"

In 1982, the brothers came alone to London to continue their education. Natural rug dealer instincts had them out searching for old rugs in London and the surrounding area. Most of the old rugs they found were profitably sold to New York or European dealers who would retail them. Perceiving that there was no real competition, they decided to open a small showroom to test the London market.

In April 1984, they rented a small 30-square-metre store. After doing some extensive advertising and promoting, they concluded that the London market lacked the knowledge to appreciate antique rugs. At the end of that year, they were trying to decide whether to close or readjust their business focus.

They decided to readjust. They marketed high quality new Persian, Turkish, and Afghani rugs, not wanting to deal with low-end commercial quality rugs such as those of Chinese, Pakistani, or Indian origin. Because their present location was too small and not easily accessible to retail traffic, an 75-square-metre store was leased at a more central location with available nearby parking. Suppliers were willing to extend a little credit and to provide a limited quantity of rugs on consignment.

The brothers approached a number of financial institutions at this time for financing, but the banks rejected Silk Route without serious consideration. Oriental rugs were too alien to financial people to understand and the industry, on the whole, had a "horse trader" reputation.

Immediately after opening their new location, there was a dramatic increase in sales. The company went on an extensive campaign of educating their customers. The brothers conducted informative print advertising and held regular (free) lectures in the showroom. A hand-washing service was offered (the only one in the area), and a master weaver was brought to Canada to do repair work for the company. Heavy emphasis was placed on providing maximum service to customers.

The showroom was set up like stores in a traditional rug bazaar, with rugs piled shoulder high. While authentic in appearance, it posed problems. Rugs were difficult to show to more than one customer at a time, and often customers were unable to view the whole selection. Some customers felt they would be obliged to purchase after generating so much work for company staff, so they would not bother looking. The only solution for this problem would be more space.

The Hejazis also regularly noticed that customers would visit the showroom and acknowledge the beauty of the rugs but say they were unsuitable for their decor. They would be looking for more decorative types of colours. (During this period, soft pastel shades were in vogue.) The Silk Route's current suppliers did not handle this type of merchandise. The only place they could find decorative colours was in the United States. American wholesalers would set up looms in countries such as India and have weavers produce rugs in the latest fashion colours. The inability to satisfy certain customers' needs prompted another major decision: Should they enter the decorative rug market? They decided to dabble a bit in order to see what kind of response they would get. The response was very good for the limited selection they had.

SOURCING

While decorative rugs were being sourced through larger U.S.-based wholesalers, most of the other rugs were obtained through European or Mediterranean-based wholesalers (in the United Kingdom, Germany, Lebanon, Syria, or Turkey) or North American wholesalers from Toronto or New York. On occasion, a European wholesaler would go so far as to send a retailer in North America a plane ticket so that they could visit. While the least expensive source of carpets was through direct import (see Exhibit 3 for sample calculation), this method required a great deal of time for travel as well as the financial resources to purchase and ship enough carpets to gain the necessary economies. Therefore, most independent retailers, including Silk Route, purchased through an importer/wholesaler. The cost structures for the importing alternatives varied enormously and could sometimes result in customer prices as high as those noted in column 2 in Exhibit 3.

Some wholesalers were willing to provide carpets on consignment to retailers. The decision to extend credit or provide carpets on consignment was based on trust, reputation, and instinct, rather than on such things as formal education. As one retailer noted:

> This is not like some businesses where having an M.B.A. carries some weight. In fact, you'll have less chance of getting credit if you are an M.B.A. None of the suppliers would ever ask you to fill out a credit application. They either trust you, or not.

FURTHER GROWTH

In 1987, they were approached by a customer who was interested in investing in the company. His conditions were that he would receive a "handsome" return on investment, would have first opportunity to purchase (for personal use only) rugs at cost price, and would be able to "hang around." With their past cash flow problems, it was exactly what the company needed. Capital would enable the establishment of new contacts in the United States, while an experienced, credible businessperson could provide guidance to the company and establish it in the community.

At the same time, competition increased. Postians had just reopened, Registan had opened, Kashikgians had expanded their cleaning operation into a full-fledged retail operation, and there were rumours that a major retailer from Toronto was planning to open in London. All these retailers handled low quality, decorative rugs with, to various degrees, high-end decorative rugs. Also, Alexanians, the Bay, and Eatons were handling the same type of goods.

The Hejazis felt that they had to do something about capturing some of the decorative rug market. They felt strongly that the consumer, properly informed, would pay a bit more for higher quality. A complete line of decorative rugs was added to their traditional goods. With the use of the capital from the investor, the latest fashion colours in the best qualities available were brought in. The response was better than expected. Instead of spending one or two weeks with a customer to sell one or two traditional rugs, customers were coming in with a colour swatch and making a decision to purchase almost immediately. As well, traditional rug sales were not neglected. The brothers worked on building both markets.

Sales escalated dramatically (see Exhibit 4). However, it became very difficult to work from the small showroom. The Hejazis felt that it was becoming a handicap and that it was time to find a larger location.

In 1988, they leased a 325-square-metre showroom in a plaza with three large furniture stores. They also leased a warehouse behind the showroom for the cleaning services. Locating among three furniture stores was ideal for exposing their inventory to consumers who were in the market for home furnishings.

In the summer of 1988, they readied themselves for their move to the new location. They were taking possession of their new location on September 1. They ran a moving sale, which was not a great success. An event struck in August 1988 that they believed eventually led to their bankruptcy.

Our friendly investor turned on us and demanded all his loans due or he would take over our business. Within five days, we raised the funds to repay the loans, but at a devastating cost. Most of our prime inventory had to be listed at or below wholesale. What was worse was the fact that the company was left with no financial backing at a crucial moment in its history. Our closest suppliers backed us up to the best of their ability. But the crucial suppliers of decorative rugs were unable to assist us. These suppliers were located in the United States. Consignment was not practical because of customs duties, and offering credit to a Canadian company with a short history was unrealistic. Without the proper inventory that we had planned for our new store, things became a big struggle. The name of the game now was just surviving. Our sales were still increasing, but we had to do so much more advertising to get these sales.

As the Hejazis sold off inventory, replacing it became more difficult. Suppliers who handled the decorative rugs required major orders, something that they were unable to place. Their financial situation was now starting to deteriorate. Bills were not quickly paid. They tried to counter by advertising more heavily. Sales did increase, but at a heavy price. At the same time, they were seeing the consumer become more hesitant to buy. Especially after the dual budgets of the federal and provincial governments in 1989, traffic slowed to a trickle. They did even more advertising to get people in and slashed prices even further. Sales during the summer of 1990 dwindled to approximately $10,000 per month. This was when they decided that the only choice was to close.

Several days prior to the closing of the London retail store, Michael Hejazi contacted all of their suppliers to explain that they would be filing for bankruptcy. Those suppliers who had goods on consignment were encouraged to take back their unsold carpets. If the consigned carpets had already been sold, the suppliers were told that there was not any cash to pay them. The suppliers were surprised and disappointed at the closing of Silk Route. One supplier lost goods with a value of $200,000, with others variously losing $50,000, $30,000, and $12,000 worth of goods. Since supplier margins ranged from as low as 20 percent on low quality carpets to 100 percent on the finer pieces, the losses to the suppliers were real. However, some of the suppliers seemed to understand the situation and hoped the Hejazis would be back in business at some point.

Subsequent to the closing of the retail store, the Hejazis were left with a large inventory of unsold oriental carpets plus a small warehouse that they rented in another part of the city. This warehouse served as headquarters for a related carpet wholesale company that they had established years earlier. This wholesale operation was known as Silk Route, Inc. (versus Ltd.). It had supplied the Silk Route retail store in London with some of its carpets (using a 20 percent markup to cover overhead and international travel), a franchise affiliate Silk Route store in Windsor (which had been managed by an ex-London store employee and had also now gone out of business), and a small circle of antique dealers and decorators.

With no other source of income, from October 1990 to February 1991 the Hejazis operated a retail operation out of the industrial park warehouse. They felt compelled to conduct a going-out-of-business sale because the oriental carpet industry was rationalizing. Many of the 80 carpet stores in the Toronto area were closing or offering deep discounts. Sales during the five months were roughly equal to what they had been in all of 1989. With lower overhead and limited advertising, this was a profitable period.

While most of the purchasers were repeat customers, the Hejazis were able to add 150 new customers to their mailing list. This list contained 2,200 names, 90 percent of whom had purchased a carpet(s) or had carpets cleaned through Silk Route.

By March 1991, most of the remaining inventory had been either sold on a piece-by-piece basis to individual customers or in larger lots to other wholesalers. At issue now was whether to enter a new line of work or to somehow reestablish some type of oriental carpet business.

	Lifestyle Ratings in London, Ontario	
Type	**Number of Households**	
Affluent	3,723	
Upscale	11,220	
Middle class	27,215	
Young couples	10,118	
Empty nesters	21,480	

Exhibit 1

Exhibit 2

History of Local Competition

1. Postians

Original company opened in 1927 but went bankrupt in 1981. Son Paul reopened in 1982. A fire a little later forced him to close this location, and he moved downtown in 1986. Stocked mainly Indian Aubussons and Chinese rugs, with a limited selection of Indo-Persian, Persian, and Afghan rugs. Owner refused to carry Turkish rugs because he was of Armenian descent. Planned to move to a larger (185 square metre) suburban location in late 1991.

2. Cyrus Gallery

Operated from 1979 to 1982 in London. Located in 1,250 square feet, next door to where Silk Route operated from 1984 to 1987. Greatest portion of inventory was Persians, with some Afghan. Forced out of business following a major theft for which there was insufficient insurance.

3. Kashikgians

Located in 1,200 square feet in an industrial park. Established in 1952 as a carpet cleaner but expanded into retail in 1987. Stocked mainly Indian Aubusson rugs, with a limited selection of Indo-Persians and Persians.

4. Registan Rugs

Established in 1987 with 700 square feet of space. Planned to move to 2,000-square-foot location in early 1991. Greatest portion of inventory was Indian Aubussons with a limited selection of Indo-Persians. Since Silk Route closed, Registan had moved into higher quality decorative and Persian rugs.

5. Indo-Persian

A Toronto-based company with three large stores in the Toronto area. London store was established in 1990 with 7,000 square feet of space in the London Home and Design Centre. Stocked basically Indian Aubusson rugs with a decent selection of Indo-Persians and a very limited selection of Persians. Known for their heavy advertising.

6. Alexanians

Two locations and a third planned. Basically a broadloom rug store that placed a reasonable emphasis on oriental rugs. The oriental rugs were mainly Indian Aubussons, with a limited selection of Indo-Persians and Pakistani Bokharas. Part of a 22-store chain.

7. Department Stores

The Bay, Eatons, and Kingsmills all had very small oriental rug departments. Carried mainly low-end orientals and machine made rugs.

Exhibit 2 (cont.)

History of Local Competition

8. Antique Auctions

Auctions presented another opportunity to purchase oriental rugs. London's leading auction house held separate oriental rug auctions, as well as general auctions that included rugs. Purchasing rugs through this channel put the onus on the customer to be sufficiently knowledgeable to avoid paying more than the market price.

9. Hotel Auctions

Eight to 12 times a year, oriental rug sales were held in London hotels and halls. Run by companies that imported and sold oriental rugs at similar events across Canada, these sales had a bad reputation within the trade. Often, the rugs were not good quality, and the prices were not significantly lower than those offered by the city's retailers. Usually, the rugs offered had been rejected by Canadian wholesalers and retailers. Ads often led the consumer to believe that rugs were seized by a bank or Canada customs. Some auctions were stacked with shills (people posing as customers), and rugs were falsely described. Many of these auctions had been investigated by Consumer and Corporate Affairs, who had laid some charges. Local firms found it difficult to clean these rugs because the dyes would run. Irate customers would blame the local businesses and not the firms from which they had initially purchased the rugs. In spite of the problems, these sales were very popular and attracted unsuspecting customers with little knowledge of oriental rugs.

Exhibit **3**

Breakdown of Importing Costs for an Average Carpet		
	Direct Importing	**Purchasing through Importer**
Importer's price (varied according to volume and expertise)	$ 950.00	$ 870.00
+ Agent (15 percent of price)	142.50	130.50
= Importer's net price	1,092.50	1,000.50
+ Shipping (overland, ocean freight, and bunker charges)	75.20	75.20
+ Insurance	8.00	8.00
= Landed cost	1,175.70	1,083.70
+ Canadian federal goods and services tax	82.30	75.80
+ Customs broker	10.00	10.00
= Importer's cost	1,268.00	1,169.56
+ Importer's margin (100 percent on cost)	50.00	1,169.56
= Retailer's cost	1,318.00	2,339.12
+ Retailer's margin (75 percent on cost)	988.50	1,754.34
= Retail price	$2,306.50	$4,093.46

Assumptions

1. A single 12-metre container that measured 60 cubic metres held 75 carpets of 3 metres x 4 metres valued at $1,000 per piece for duty purposes.
2. Shipping costs (including overland costs from Teheran and bunker charges) for a nonconference line 12-metre container totalled US$4,800. CDN$1 = US$0.85
3. Insurance cost approximately $.80 per $100 value of cargo.
4. A customs broker charged approximately 1 percent of the value of cargo.
5. The 13.5 percent federal sales tax was replaced by a national 7 percent goods and services tax effective January 1, 1991.
6. The importer's margin covered travel expenses, carrying costs, and the importer's profit. Assume $15,000 travel expenses would be incurred to import 300 carpets (i.e., $50/each).
7. Normal duties of 10 percent were reduced to zero for rug imports to Canada from India, Pakistan, China, Iran, Afghanistan, and Turkey with the presentation of a completed Form (A). This form confirmed the country of origin.

Exhibit 4

	Silk Route Oriental Rugs Limited **Statement of Income** **for the Year Ended December 31**				
	1989	**1988**	**1987**	**1986**	**1985**
Sales	$631,686	$518,632	$367,950	$299,278	$127,337
Cost of sales	369,747	302,608	233,388	162,371	69,118
Gross profit	261,939	216,024	134,562	136,907	58,219
Expenses					
Advertising	116,345	71,362	28,134	35,400	15,004
Bank charges	4,899	3,062	2,013	1,252	655
Business and capital tax	2,774	1,049	737	874	462
Depreciation	2,614	6,081	3,689	775	591
Insurance	5,366	6,355	3,777	3,176	2,382
Interest on long-term debt	1,152	9,592	4,106	–	–
Legal and accounting	3,314	4,568	2,300	1,400	2,200
Miscellaneous	3,320	344	289	406	2,867
Office	8,548	14,546	15,640	6,846	8,372
Rent	38,634	24,050	12,166	8,470	6,195
Repairs and maintenance	5,388	3,296	4,793	11,630	3,795
Telephone	7,364	12,224	5,781	4,469	3,128
Travel	6,015	5,488	5,829	3,248	5,939
Vehicle	20,172	11,205	4,641	9,763	11,032
Wages and employee benefits	83,964	54,351	39,511	32,387	15,867
	309,869	227,573	133,406	120,096	78,507
Net income for the year	$(47,930)	$(11,549)	$ 1,156	$ 16,811	($20,290)

Notes:
Almost 10 percent of sales were from carpet cleaning.
Inventory turned on average once per year.

CASE 7.11   SWO SERVICE

By John Graham and C.G.J. Albison

Dave Airey and George Albinson left their second annual retreat wondering in what direction to take their Mississauga-based company. It was August 1991, and the recession did not seem to be improving. However, they had sealed two major sales that would contribute $88,000 in cash over the next six months. A decision, whether to sell or expand the business, would be required soon.

BACKGROUND SUMMARY

SWO was a small software firm formed as a 50/50 partnership by Dave Airey and George Albinson in 1984. The firm specialized in accounting and inventory software packages for distribution firms in the Toronto area. It used exclusively a programming language called PICK, which was well known for its ability to manipulate large amounts of data.

Dave had extensive programming experience, had worked for several software firms in the past, and wanted to work for himself. George worked in a refinery in Sarnia, had saved a substantial amount of money, and wanted to open a business. In 1984, they agreed to start a software business, where Dave would invest his know-how and George his money to start the firm.

The first six years were extremely volatile. They started with a base of two customers and built up a software package. The strategy was to sell the first few installations cheaply and then sell the rest for a higher price after the "bugs were out."

They had been fairly successful with the strategy. The company developed a software package that was highly praised by its customers. Hardware suppliers felt initially that it was one of the best PICK systems on the market.

However, the firm found itself pulled in different directions by its customers. Its program was constantly being upgraded and changed with each new customer. The customers still demanded a low cost product and many product alterations. This led to the majority of sales in software service, but occasionally a big hardware and software sale would occur. It also led to wide fluctuations in profitability. The company made large profits when it sold software packages, but it lost money on their ongoing service.

SWO had an extremely difficult year in 1991. These difficulties arose primarily from the poor shape of the economy. There were also unrelated internal problems.

THE SOFTWARE INDUSTRY FOR DISTRIBUTORS

The distributor market was divided into three categories based primarily on the size of the customer. Needs of the different segments varied greatly. Needs also differed from customer to customer, especially for the larger distributors.

Small Distributors

There were thousands of these operations all over Toronto. They sold everything from lamps to rice and had less than $2 million in sales each. The companies were most often owner operated, and the owners were eager to talk about software. The primary need of these consumers was an accounting package to handle their payables and receivables. They could not afford the service costs of adapting their software, although they often wanted alterations. The majority of these businesses bought off-the-shelf software like ACCPAC. Their knowledge of packages was limited to word-of-mouth reputation and in-store promotions.

Mid-sized Distributors

These firms were mainly owner operated; however, they also had professional management staff. They often had greater needs for their software, so off-the-shelf packages were not sophisticated enough. Their primary need was for a good inventory control system that was tied into their accounting package.

These firms demanded sophisticated service for their package. They often wanted design modifications and immediate service for day-to-day problems. They had a better knowledge of software and had often had at least one bad experience with a cheap package. As a result, they did not like paying for service but would do so.

There were a wide variety of businesses in this segment. Their sales ranged from $2 million to $20 million. At this size, they knew their competition. They often saw their computer system as their competitive advantage and did not want their competitors to obtain a similar package. They expected their software firm to know their business and their needs. The packages were purchased by both experienced and inexperienced staff. The majority of product information came from word-of-mouth and testimonials from satisfied customers. There were approximately one thousand distributors of this size in the Toronto area.

Large Distributors

These distributors had sales over $20 million and demanded much of their software suppliers. They expected and were willing to pay for 24-hour service. The software had to be fully integrated and able to handle the diverse and specific requirements of the company. Large distributors often purchased packages specifically designed for their company. They also insisted that the package could not be used by any other company.

Distributors of this size could demand a lot of their software supplier. They expected perks such as a 1-800 number or permanent on-site programmers for service. These companies would spend a million dollars or more on a system. The system represented a key part of the business, and the supplier had to be dependable and experienced. The purchase decision was usually made by a company board on the recommendation of consultants or by company experts. The purchase decision was usually a long, involved process that could extend more than two years. There were several hundred distributors of this size in the Toronto area.

COMPETITION

Competition in the software industry was stiff. Any programmer with a basic program could set up shop in his or her house and start a business. These cottage industry programmers put pressure on prices in the industry. They also hurt the reputation of the industry. Often, these small shop software houses would sell flawed software at a cheap price. Since most distributors did not have the ability to tell the difference between good and bad software, this resulted in many small and medium-sized distributors distrusting software houses. Distributors often commented that software houses overpromised and underdelivered.

The lower end of the market for small businesses was mostly taken up by one-person shops and off-the-shelf packages. The cost of these packages was usually around $600 to $4,000, with very limited after-sale service. ACCPAC was the industry leader in this segment. It had a large portion of the North American market, and many accountants recommended this package to small distributors. ACCPAC often trained accountants and consultants on its system for free to encourage the use of the package.

The mid-range of the market was splintered. Off-the-shelf packages did not do well, due to the more sophisticated needs of the clients. There was an infinite variety of software and hardware combinations in this segment; the combination of hardware and software was the key to success. Many of the problems faced by the distributors were related to incompatibilities between software and hardware. Successful competitors developed relationships with one or two hardware manufacturers. This allowed better systems and better support.

In this segment, the range of prices for a system was $10,000 to $200,000. The product features and level of service depended on the price. The challenge to the software house was to convince the distributors that they needed to invest in order to get the software they needed. This was difficult, given the small margins in the distribution industry and the number of low-priced packages that promised to do the same things. Software firms used a combination of direct mail, hardware supplier referrals, consultant and accountant referrals, and customer testimonials to promote their products.

Competition for the large distributors was fierce, though limited to a few competitors. These competitors were usually wings of accounting firms or divisions of large hardware manufacturers. Large distributors limited their business to these suppliers due to their need for stability. The cost of a system was usually $500,000 or more. Arthur Andersen and IBM were two of the leading competitors in the segment. These firms were well financed and had extensive expertise.

TRADE IN THE COMPUTER INDUSTRY

The majority of software sales also included hardware sales. The sale could be initiated by either the hardware firm or the software house. Usually, small and medium-sized software houses developed a relationship with one or two hardware suppliers. The relationship was based on the mutual exchange of business and trust. The software house did not want hardware that made its product look bad, and the hardware firm did not want software to make its hardware look bad. As a result, these relationships took time and were limited to established software firms.

Software houses often received a 30 percent margin on the hardware they sold. However, the hardware firms did not provide good credit terms. The majority of system deals involved a leasing company. Leasing companies bought the hardware from the hardware firm and paid the software house a commission. They then leased the equipment and sometimes the software to the distributor. This changed the system cost into an annual payment instead of an upfront investment for a cash-strapped distributor.

EXTERNAL FACTORS

Several factors affected the industry. A primary factor was the economy, which had been in a recession for over two years. Although a recovery was said to be under way, the economy was sluggish. Numerous distributors had gone out of business, and those that had not were pushing their payables. There was little or no purchase of new systems.

However, computer systems were continuing to be more critical to the already competitive distribution industry. Many distributors attributed their ability to survive to their competitive advantage in their system. Distributors realized that better inventory and accounts management was the key to success.

Politically, the federal government had initiated the GST (goods and services tax) two years earlier. This complex value-added tax on business had prompted many companies to computerize in order to manage the process. The government was also keen to expand the computer industry. As a result, there were several programs that would subsidize wages and help firms cover the cost of training their employees.

INTERNAL ANALYSIS

SWO had two primary sources of income: system sales and ongoing service revenue. These sources had not, however, provided SWO with a stable base of income. In years when SWO made two or three system sales, the company made a good profit. The money was then used to develop a new facet of the product. See Exhibits 1, 2, 3, 4, and 5 for the financial statements for the past three years.

System Sales

System sales, in particular, were a "hit or miss" proposition. The two system sales that SWO had just concluded were two years in the making. Hours and hours of time were required to establish relationships with the customers. Dave had done the majority of the sales work to date; however, he did not enjoy it. He found cold calls on new customers extremely difficult, and he liked to talk only to small distributors because they were chatty.

Recently, SWO had tried to improve its sales effort. Nine months ago, the company had hired a salesman who was the brother of a marketing consultant they had used. He had not generated any sales yet, but he was good at mailings and cold calls on potential customers.

SWO tried several marketing blitzes. It targeted distributors that were similar to its current customers. The company felt that its knowledge of their business areas would help it gain new customers. However, it had limited success. Dave did not have the time to follow up on the letters, and George, who was in Sarnia, did not either. The new salesman had some success in this area; however, he did not know enough about the system to fully follow up.

Further, current customers were reluctant to help SWO sell the product to their competitors. They would recommend the product only to potential customers who were not direct threats. For example, SWO was able to use its computer parts client to get a computer parts distributor in Niagara Falls. Unfortunately, SWO was unable to service this new client quickly enough and lost the account.

The brightest spot in marketing was the new relationship with Data General. SWO had attempted several relationships with hardware firms in the past. All had failed. Either the hardware firm was too undependable and SWO terminated the relationship, or the hardware firm was not interested in SWO. This was the first respectable hardware firm that had indicated a desire to develop a relationship with SWO. Data General sales reps had already given SWO some good sales leads and had helped to close its latest sale. SWO, in turn, was promoting Data General equipment to its customers, who seemed to find it reliable and affordable.

Ongoing Service Revenue

This area of the company had suffered greatly in recent times. The company charged firms by the hour for service; however, it charged below market rates. Dave believed that SWO had to charge less because its customers could not afford regular rates. George felt that the company was currently charging less than the cost of its people.

SWO had two technicians who did the majority of its service work. Dave also did some of this work on a part-time basis. SWO had another technician whom the customers liked because she explained things well. However, she was let go when revenues declined in 1990. She was not as technically strong as the other two, although she got better reviews from customers.

George often wondered if the existing staff knew how to make customers happy. He often heard that customers became very happy when small screen displays were changed and did not appreciate when complex programming tasks were completed. The firm currently did no proactive customer development. The overwhelming amount of customer service work was done at the customer's request.

SWO's Current Customer Base

The SWO customer base included a business forms distributor, a computer parts distributor, and 10 small distributors. Their two new medium-sized customers were an electrical parts distributor and a popcorn distributor. Currently, the business forms distributor was almost bankrupt, and the computer parts distributor was unhappy with SWO's service. The small distributors provided steady income, but also caused numerous receivable problems. Also, some major companies used SWO programmers for assistance but did not have SWO software.

FINANCES AT SWO

SWO was currently fully funded by investments made by the shareholders. George had invested over $100,000 over the years, $20,000 just recently. Dave had invested $40,000 plus receiving a salary far below what he could have received as a corporate programmer. The two men debated the amounts that they invested at the retreat but then decided it really didn't matter.

The banks would not loan SWO any money because it had no assets to speak of, and software firms were not good risks. George had to use personal lines of credit to get the firm money. However, he now wanted to get this money out to pay the bank back.

George calculated that the monthly expenses of the company were $16,000 and that the monthly service revenue was $10,000. The shortfall was covered by George's cash injections. Cash flow remained a major concern for the company.

These financial difficulties were compounded by a complex financial management system. SWO was in the process of moving its books off ACCPAC on George's computer in Sarnia, onto its own system in Mississauga. However, Dave did not fully understand how the system was to work for SWO and lacked time to do the entries. George preferred to have the financials on his computer, but he agreed to put it in Mississauga so that Dave could better understand the company's finances.

A lack of consistent data entry also meant that SWO was poor at collecting its receivables. Receivables often were not entered into the computer until weeks after a job was done. They were then billed weeks later, and finally chased after by George if they were more than three months past due. However, George's full-time job in Sarnia made it difficult for him to put much time into this process.

FUTURE OPPORTUNITIES

The two recent sales had pumped new hope into the company. Both George and Dave wanted the company to do well and grow. However, neither one of them was willing to put much more money into it. The cash from these sales would be the last chance for SWO to break the cycle of boom and bust. The only other option was sell the business and get out as much money as they could.

Expanding the Business

Dave and George were uncertain of how to proceed on this course. They knew that several key areas of the company needed help. The expansion of the business would require a detailed and well-executed marketing plan.

They felt that with the right marketing assistance SWO could hope for $400,000 worth of systems sales with a 75 percent margin. This sales figure would be on top of regular service sales. Sales could go as high as $800,000 or as low as

$250,000 depending on the success of the marketing effort. This success would depend greatly on the people SWO hired.

Dave felt that the company's greatest need was for a system analyst. This would be particularly important with the two new installations of the SWO system coming up in the fall. He knew that he would be too busy managing the company and looking after current customers to do this work. The cost of a system analyst would be approximately $45,000. Dave had chosen a dependable analyst for this position who could start right away.

On the other hand, George felt that the company needed a general manager most. This person would run day-to-day operations and coordinate the sales effort. The majority of people qualified to do a good job in this area would want a stake in the company. George figured that the company would have to provide a $36,000 salary and offer 30 percent of the company. George felt that if the person did the job well, after a three-month trial run, he or she could then be offered a third of the company.

Dave thought that they needed only a sales manager. He felt that he could run the company in time. He was still having difficulty understanding the finance side but was sure he would learn as he went along. George also had difficulty with the idea of giving up control of the company, but he had decided that they did not have a choice. He had been interviewing several candidates and thought he had found one who would fit the bill.

They agreed that they also needed a full-time receptionist. SWO needed to have someone in the office to take calls and to input the receivables to the computer; this employee would cost $27,000. They also felt that they should invest some money in training their current staff, who had not had any formal training in almost a year.

Exhibit 6 presents a preliminary revised organization chart to accommodate their expansion plans for SWO.

Selling the Business

This option was not one that Dave and George were excited about; however, it needed to be investigated. They realized that the only real tangible assets of the company were the customer base and the software.

As there were not many software houses currently using a PICK system for distributors, the customer base would be valued differently by different software houses. There would likely be a bid on a multiple of the service earnings for the customer base. The software would not likely be worth much more than this. In addition, the receivables from the two new sales could not be collected until the systems were installed.

Exhibit 1

	INCOME STATEMENT for the Years Ending April 30 ($000s		
	1991	**1990**	**1989**
Income	$354	$248	$437
Cost of goods sold	81	48	141
Gross profit	273	200	296
Expenses:			
Advertising and promotion	2	0	0
Bad debt	28	21	15
Consulting	14	7	0
Depreciation	5	5	6
Loan interest	14	12	4
Maintenance and repair	3	8	4
Miscellaneous	12	12	20
Office and computer supplies	8	6	11
Rent	15	13	4
Software expense — research	0	5	8
Telephone	11	12	12
Travel	3	6	5
Wages	158	162	183
Vehicle lease	9	7	8
	282	276	280
Net income (loss) (note 4)	($ 98)	($ 76)	$ 13

Exhibit **2**

STATEMENT OF RETAINED EARNINGS for the Years Ending April 30 ($000s)			
	1991	**1990**	**1989**
Accumulated earnings (deficit) — Beginning of year	($64)	$12	($ 1)
Net income (loss)	(8)	(76)	13
Accumulated (deficit) — End of year	($72)	($64)	$12

Exhibit **3**

	Balance Sheet[1] as at April 30 ($000s)		
	1991	**1990**	**1989**
ASSETS			
Current assets:			
Bank	$ 23	$ 25	$ 0
Accounts receivable (net of allowance of $14,200; $6,000 in 1990)	55	57	111
Inventory (note 1 and 5)	53	45	6
	$131	$126	$118
Fixed assets: (note 1)	18	18	18
Computers	18	18	16
Office equipment	19	8	18
Software	$ 54	$ 53	$ 51
	(40)	(36)	31
Less accumulated depreciation	$ 14	$ 17	$ 21
Other assets:			
Incorporation costs			1
TOTAL ASSETS	$145	$144	$140
LIABILITIES AND SHAREHOLDERS' EQUITY			
Current liabilities:			
Bank overdraft (note 2)	$ 0	$ 0	$ 5
Accounts payable and accruals	36	15	14
Taxes payable	0	0	4
Deferred revenue (note 5)	36	36	0
	$ 72	$ 51	$ 23
Long-term liabilities:			
Lease payable	1	2	4
Other loans (note 3)	144	54	101
	$217	$208	$104
Shareholders' equity:			
Retained earnings (deficit)	(72)	(64)	12
TOTAL LIABILITIES AND SHAREHOLDERS' EQUITY	$145	$144	$140

1. Totals may vary to rounding of figures.

EXHIBIT 4

**Notes to Financial Statements
as at April 30
($000s)**

---

1. ACCOUNTING POLICIES:
The accounting policies of the Company are in accordance with generally accepted accounting principles.
Inventory: The Inventory is recorded at the lower of cost and net realizable value (note 5).
Depreciation: Depreciation is calculated using the following methods and rates:

Office equipment	20 percent declining balance
Software	100 percent straight line
Hardware	30 percent declining balance

Income Taxes: The Company follows the tax allocation basis of accounting for income taxes, whereby tax provisions are based on accounting income, and taxes relating to timing differences between accounting and taxable income are deferred.

2. BANK OVERDRAFT:
The bank overdraft results from cheques that were written but not cashed.

3. OTHER LOANS:
The other loans are due to a shareholder and other related people. Interest on these loans consists of a reimbursement to the shareholder for interest paid on a personal bank loan whose proceeds were reloaned to the Company at interest of various rates approximating 10 percent.

	1991	1990	1989
Shareholder	$105	$ 98	$83
Shareholder	33	38	0
Shareholder's mother	7	8	8
Shareholder's brother	0	10	10
	$144	$154	$101

4. LOSS CARRY FORWARD:
The company has a loss carry forward of $73 ($70 in 1990), which may be used to reduce taxable income in future years. This loss carry forward expires as follows:

1997	$70
1998	3
	$ 73

In addition, the company has written off more depreciation that it has claimed for tax purposes in the amount of $10 ($6 in 1990). This amount can also be used to reduce taxable income in future years.

5. REVISION TO EARLIER STATEMENTS:
Subsequent to the publication of the statements, management discovered that certain prices of inventory that had previously been recorded as cost of sales had, in fact, never been transferred to the customer despite the fact that payment had been received. As a result of ongoing discussions with the customer management has determined that the inventory may not be accepted by the customer. As a result, these statements have been revised to reflect deferred revenue of $36 and decreased cost of sales of $36. The effect of this revision on the income and retained earnings of the company is nil.

Exhibit 5

	Ratio Analysis for the Years Ending April 30 ($000s)		
	1991	**1990**	**1989**
PROFITABILITY			
Sales	100%	100%	100%
Cost of goods sold	22.9%	19.3%	32.3%
Gross profit	77.1%	80.7%	67.7%
EXPENSES			
Advertising and promotion	0.4%	0.1%	0.1%
Bad debt	7.8%	8.4%	3.4%
Consulting	4.0%	2.6%	0.0%
Depreciation	1.3%	2.1%	1.4%
Loan interest	3.9%	4.7%	0.9%
Maintenance	0.9%	3.3%	0.8%
Miscellaneous	3.5%	4.7%	4.5%
Office and computer supplies	2.2%	2.4%	2.6%
Rent	4.3%	5.1%	2.8%
Software expenses R&D	0.0%	2.2%	1.8%
Telephone	3.0%	4.9%	2.8%
Travel	0.8%	2.6%	1.2%
Wages	44.6%	65.4%	41.8%
Vehicle lease	2.5%	2.8%	1.8%
Net income (Loss)	−2.2%	−30.7%	2.8%
LIQUIDITY			
Current ratio	1.8:1	2.5:1	5.1:1
Acid test	1.1:1	1.6:1	4.8:1
EFFICIENCY			
Age of accounts receivable	56.9	83.7	92.7
Age of inventory	240.1	339.6	16.6
Age of payables	160.7	113.5	36.2
STABILITY			
Net worth/total assets	0%	0%	8.0%

GROWTH	**1991–90**	**1990–89**
Sales	48%	−76.3%
Net profit	880%	−603%
Assets	1%	3%
Equity	−12%	−543%

EXHIBIT 6
SWO
Organizational
Chart

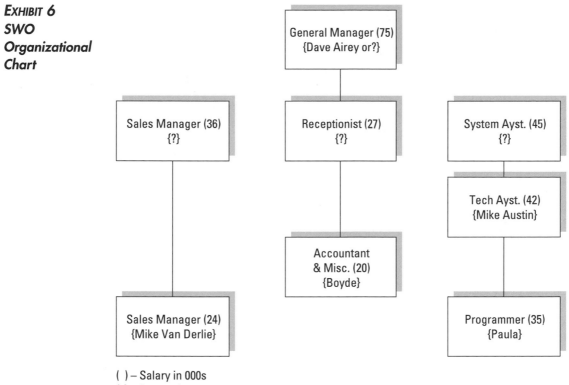

( ) – Salary in 000s
{ } – Person for spot

To the owner of this book

We hope that you have enjoyed *Business Decision Making* by Grasby et al. (ISBN 0-17-616737-4), and we would like to know as much about your experiences with this text as you would care to offer. Only through your comments and those of others can we learn how to make this a better text for future readers.

School _____ Your instructor's name _____

Course _____ Was the text required? _____ Recommended? _____

1. What did you like the most about *Business Decision Making?*

_____

_____

_____

2. How useful was this text for your course?

_____

_____

_____

3. Do you have any recommendations for ways to improve the next edition of this text?

_____

_____

_____

4. In the space below or in a separate letter, please write any other comments you have about the book. (For example, please feel free to comment on reading level, writing style, terminology, design features, and learning aids.)

_____

_____

_____

_____

Optional

Your name _____ Date _____

May Nelson Thomson Learning quote you, either in promotion for *Business Decision Making,* or in future publishing ventures?

Yes _____ No _____

Thanks!

You can also send your comments to us via e-mail at **college@nelson.com**

PLEASE TAPE SHUT. DO NOT STAPLE.

FOLD HERE

Nelson
Thomson Learning™

MAIL POSTE
Canada Post Corporation
Société canadienne des postes
Postage paid   Port payé
if mailed in Canada si posté au Canada
Business Reply   **Réponse d'affaires**
0066102399   **01**

0066102399-M1K5G4-BR01

NELSON THOMSON LEARNING
HIGHER EDUCATION
PO BOX 60225 STN BRM B
TORONTO ON M7Y 2H1